Irene C. Fountas **&** Gay Su Pinnell

The Reading Minilessons Book

Your Every Day Guide for Literacy Teaching

GRADE 3

HEINEMANN
Portsmouth, NH

Heinemann
361 Hanover Street
Portsmouth, NH 03801–3912
www.heinemann.com

Offices and agents throughout the world

©2019 by Irene C. Fountas and Gay Su Pinnell

The author and publisher wish to thank those who have generously given permission to reprint borrowed material: Please see the Credits section at the back of the book, starting on page 567.

Library of Congress Cataloging-in-Publication Data is on file at the Library of Congress.
ISBN: 978-0-325-09864-7

Editor: Sue Paro
Production: Cindy Strowman
Cover and interior designs: Ellery Harvey
Illustrator: Will Sweeney
Typesetter: Sharon Burkhardt
Manufacturing: Deanna Richardson

Printed in the United States of America on acid-free paper

22 21 20 19 18   LSC   1 2 3 4 5 6

CONTENTS

2 Literary Analysis

Fiction and Nonfiction

General

Genre

Messages and Themes

Organization

Topic

Illustration/Graphics

Book and Print Features

Fiction

Genre

Illustrations

3   Strategies and Skills

4 Writing About Reading

Chapter 1 The Role of Reading Minilessons in Literacy Learning

THE GOAL OF ALL READING is the joyful, independent, and meaningful processing of a written text. As a competent reader, you become immersed in a fiction or nonfiction text; you read for a purpose; you become highly engaged with the plot, the characters, or the content. Focused on the experience of reading the text, you are largely unconscious of the thousands of actions happening in your brain that support the construction of meaning from the print that represents language. And, this is true whether the print is on a piece of paper or an electronic device. Your purpose may be to have vicarious experiences via works of fiction that take you to places far distant in time and space—even to worlds that do not and cannot exist! Or, your purpose may be to gather fuel for thinking (by using fiction or nonfiction) or it may simply be to enjoy the sounds of human language via literature and poetry. Most of us engage in the reading of multiple texts every day—some for work, some for pleasure, and some for practical guidance—but what we all have in common as readers is the ability to independently and simultaneously apply in-the-head systems of strategic actions that enable us to act on written texts.

Young readers are on a journey toward efficient processing of any texts they might like to attempt, and it is important every step of the way that they have successful experiences in reading independently those texts that are available at each point in time. In a literacy-rich classroom with a multitext approach, readers have the opportunity to hear written texts read aloud through interactive read-aloud, and so they build a rich treasure chest of known stories and nonfiction books that they can share as a classroom community. They understand and talk about these shared texts in ways that extend comprehension, vocabulary, and knowledge of the ways written texts are presented and organized. They participate with their classmates in the shared reading of a common text so that they understand more and know how to act on written language. They experience tailored instruction in small guided reading groups using leveled texts precisely matched to their current abilities and needs for challenge. They stretch their thinking as they discuss a variety of complex texts in book clubs. They process fiction and nonfiction books with expert teacher support—always moving in the direction of more complex texts that will lift their reading abilities. *But it is in independent reading that they apply everything they have learned across all of those instructional contexts.* So the goal of all the reading instruction is to enable the young reader to engage in effective, efficient, and joyful independent and meaningful processing of written text *every day* in the classroom. This is what it means to grow up literate in our schools.

Independent reading involves choice based on interests and tastes. Competent, independent readers are eager to talk and write about the books they have read for themselves. They are gaining awareness of themselves as readers with favorite authors, illustrators, genres, and topics; their capacity for self-regulation is growing. The key to this kind of independent reading is making an explicit connection between all other instructional contexts— interactive read-aloud, shared reading, guided reading, and book clubs—and the reader's own independent work. Making these explicit links is the goal of minilessons. All teaching, support, and confirmation lead to the individual's successful, independent reading.

Making Learning Visible Through Minilessons

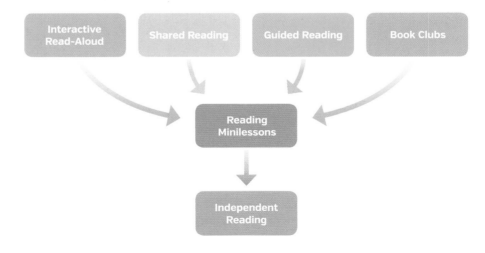

Figure 1-1: Various reading experiences supported by explicit instruction in reading minilessons lead to independent reading.

What Is a Reading Minilesson?

A reading minilesson is a concise and focused lesson on any aspect of effective reading or classroom reading work that is important for students to explicitly understand at a particular point in time. It is an opportunity to build on all of the students' literacy experiences, make one important understanding visible, and hold the students accountable for applying it consistently in reading. Minilessons place a strong instructional frame around independent reading.

A minilesson takes only a few minutes and usually involves the whole class. It builds on shared literary experiences the students in your class have experienced prior to the lesson. You can quickly bring these shared texts to mind as powerful examples. Usually, you will teach only one focused lesson each day, but minilessons will be logically organized and build on each other. Each minilesson engages your students in an inquiry process that leads to the discovery and understanding of a general principle. Most of the time interactive read-aloud books and shared reading texts that students have already heard serve as mentor texts, from which they generalize the understanding. The reading minilesson provides the link between students' previous experience to their own independent reading (see Figure 1-1). The reading minilesson plays a key role in systematic, coherent teaching, all of which is directed toward each reader's developing competencies.

To help students connect ideas and develop deep knowledge and broad application of principles, related reading minilessons are grouped under "umbrella" concepts (see Chapter 3). An umbrella is the broad category within which several lessons are linked to each other and all of which contribute to the understanding of the umbrella concept. Within each umbrella, the lessons build on each other (see Figure 1-2). In each lesson, you create an "anchor chart" with the students. This visual representation of the principle will be a useful reference tool as students learn new routines, encounter new texts, and draw and write about their reading in a reader's notebook.

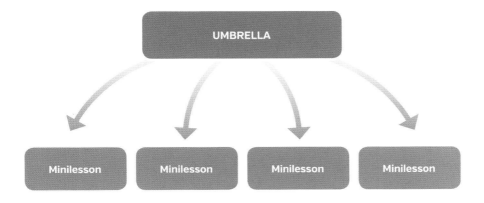

Figure 1-2: Each minilesson focuses on a different aspect of the larger umbrella concept.

Four Types of Reading Minilessons

In this book, you will find 200 minilessons that are organized into four types:

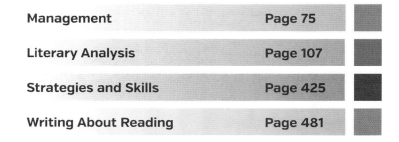

Management	Page 75	
Literary Analysis	Page 107	
Strategies and Skills	Page 425	
Writing About Reading	Page 481	

Figure 1-3: The minilessons in this book are organized into four sections.

Management Minilessons. These lessons include routines that are essential to the smooth functioning of the classroom and student-centered, independent literacy learning. The management minilessons are designed to support students' development of independence and self-regulatory behavior. They also provide opportunities for students to learn the structures and routines for choosing books from the classroom library and getting started with independent reading. Most of your minilessons at the beginning of the school year will focus on management. You will want to repeat any of the lessons as needed across the year. A guiding principle: teach a minilesson on anything that prevents the classroom from running smoothly.

Literary Analysis Minilessons. These lessons build students' awareness of the characteristics of various genres and of the elements of fiction and nonfiction texts. The books that you read during interactive read-aloud and shared reading serve as mentor texts when applying the principles of literary analysis. Through these lessons, students learn how to apply new thinking to their independent reading; they also learn how to share their thinking with others.

Strategies and Skills Minilessons. Readers need to develop a robust body of in-the-head strategic actions for the efficient processing of texts. For example, they need to monitor their reading for accuracy and understanding, solve words (simple and complex), read fluently with phrasing, and constantly construct meaning. Teaching related to processing texts will best take place in guided reading and shared reading. The general lessons included in this volume reinforce broad principles that every reader in your class may need to be reminded of from time to time.

Writing About Reading Minilessons. Throughout the third-grade year, students will have opportunities to use a reader's notebook to respond to what they read in the forms of drawing and writing. These lessons introduce *Reader's Notebook: Intermediate* (Fountas and Pinnell 2011) and help students use this important tool for independent literacy learning. Third graders will use a reader's notebook to keep track of their reading and writing, keep a record of the principles taught in minilessons, write a weekly letter, and have many opportunities to write about the thinking they do while reading.

The goal of all minilessons is to help students to think and act like readers and to build effective processing strategies while reading continuous text independently. Whether you are teaching management lessons, literary analysis lessons, strategies and skills lessons, or writing about reading lessons, the characteristics of effective minilessons, listed in Figure 1-4, apply.

Characteristics of Effective Minilessons

Effective Minilessons . . .

- have a **clear rationale and a goal** to focus meaningful teaching
- are **relevant to the specific needs of readers** so that your teaching connects with the learners
- are **brief, concise, and to the point** for immediate application
- use **clear and specific language** to avoid talk that clutters learning
- stay **focused on a single idea** so students can apply the learning and build on it day after day
- **build one understanding on another** across several days instead of single isolated lessons
- use an **inquiry approach** whenever possible to support constructive learning
- often include **shared, high-quality mentor texts** that can be used as examples
- are **well paced** to engage and hold students' interest
- are **grouped into umbrellas** to foster depth in thinking and coherence across lessons
- provide time for students to **"try out" the new concept** before independent application
- engage students in **summarizing the new learning** and thinking about its application to their own work
- build **academic vocabulary** appropriate to the grade level
- help students become **better readers and writers**
- **foster community** through the development of shared language
- **can be assessed** as you observe students in authentic literacy activities to provide feedback on your teaching
- help **students understand what they are learning** how to do and how it helps them as readers

Figure 1-4: Characteristics of effective minilessons

Constructing Anchor Charts
for Effective Minilessons

Anchor charts are an essential part of each minilesson in this book (see Figure 1-5). They provide a way for you to capture the students' thinking during the lesson and reflect on the learning at the end. When you think about a chart, it helps you think through the big, important ideas and the language you will use in the minilesson. It helps you think about the sequence and your efficiency in getting down what is important.

Each minilesson in this book provides guidance for adding information to the chart. Read through lessons carefully to know whether any parts of the chart should be prepared ahead or whether the chart is constructed during the lesson or left until the end. After the lesson, the charts become a resource for your students to use as a reference throughout the day. They provide a visual resource for students who need to not only hear but also see the information. They can revisit these charts as they apply the principle in reading, talking, and writing about books, or as they try out new routines in the classroom. You can refer to them during interactive read-aloud, shared reading, reading conferences, guided reading, and book clubs.

Though your charts will be unique because they are built from the ideas your students share, you will want to consider some of the common characteristics among the charts we have included in this book. We have created one example in each lesson, but vary it as you see fit. When you create charts with students, consider the following:

▸ **Make your charts simple, clear, and organized.** The charts you create with your students should be clearly organized. It is important in third grade to keep them simple without a lot of dense text. Provide white space and print neatly in dark, easy-to-read colors. You will notice that some of the sample charts are more conceptual. The idea is conveyed through a few words and a visual representation. Others use a grid to show how the principle is applied specifically across several texts.

▸ **Make your charts visually appealing and useful.** Many of the minilesson charts for third grade contain visual support, and this is especially helpful to English language learners. For example, you will see book covers, symbols, and drawings. Even in third grade, some students will benefit from the visuals to help them in reading the words on the chart and in understanding the concept. The drawings are intentionally simple to give you a quick model to draw yourself. English language learners might need to rely heavily on a graphic representation of the principle ideas. You might find it helpful to prepare these drawings on separate pieces of paper or sticky notes ahead of the lesson and tape or glue them on the chart as the students construct their understandings. This time-saving tip can also make the charts look more interesting and colorful, because certain parts stand out for the students.

When you teach English language learners, you must adjust your teaching—not more teaching, but different teaching—to teach effectively. Look for this symbol to see ways to support English language learners.

ELL CONNECTION

▶ **Make your charts colorful.** Though the sample minilesson charts are colorful for the purpose of engagement or organization, be careful about the amount and types of color that you use. You may want to use color for a purpose. Color can help you point out particular parts of the chart. For example, "Look at the purple word on the chart." Color can support English language learners by providing a visual link to certain words or ideas. However, color can also be distracting if overused. Be thoughtful about when you choose to use colors to highlight an idea or a word on a chart so that students are supported in reading continuous text. Text that is broken up by a lot of different colors can be very distracting for readers who are still becoming accustomed to using the visual information in print. You will notice that the minilesson principle is usually written in black or a dark color across the top of the chart so that it stands out and is easily recognized as the focus of the lesson.

Anchor charts support language growth in all students, and especially in English language learners. Conversation about the minilesson develops oral language and then connects that oral language to print when you write words on the chart and provide picture support. By constructing an anchor chart with your students, you provide print that is immediately accessible to them because they helped create it and have ownership of the language. After a chart is finished, revisit it as often as needed to reinforce not only the ideas but also the printed words.

Figure 1-5: Constructing anchor charts with your students provides verbal and visual support for all learners.

The author of a biography gives an important message.

Title	Message
Magic Trash	Ordinary people can do extraordinary things.
ODD BOY OUT	Everyone is different, and that's what makes us special.
Tree Lady	Significant things people accomplish can live on long after they're gone.
WANGARI MAATHAI	One person can do something to make the world and other people's lives better.
	Dreams can come true through hard work and dedication.

Using Reading Minilessons with Third-Grade Students

A minilesson brings to students' conscious attention a focused principle that will assist them in developing an effective, independent literacy processing system. It provides an opportunity for students to do the following:

- Respond to and act on a variety texts
- Become aware of and be able to articulate understandings about texts
- Engage in further inquiry to investigate the characteristics of texts
- Search for and learn to recognize patterns and characteristics of written texts
- Build new ideas on known ideas
- Learn how to think about effective actions as they process texts
- Learn to manage their own reading lives
- Learn how to work together well in the classroom
- Learn to talk to others about their thinking about books
- Learn how to use and care for books and materials

Reading minilessons help readers build in-the-head processing systems. In the following chapters, you will explore how minilessons support students in using integrated systems of strategic actions for thinking *within*, *beyond*, and *about* many different kinds of texts and also how to use minilessons to build a community of readers who demonstrate a sense of agency and responsibility. You will also look in more depth at how minilessons fit within a design for literacy learning and within a multitext approach.

We conclude this chapter with some key terms we will use as we describe minilessons in the next chapters (see Figure 1-6). Keep these in mind so we can develop a common language to talk about the minilessons you teach.

Figure 1-6: Important terms used in *The Reading Minilessons Book*

Key Terms When Talking About Reading Minilessons

Umbrella	A group of minilessons, all of which are directed at different aspects of the same larger understanding.
Principle	A concise statement of the understanding students will need to learn and apply.
Mentor Text	A fiction or nonfiction text that offers a clear example of the principle toward which the minilesson is directed. Students will have previously heard and discussed the text.
Text Set	A group of fiction or nonfiction or a combination of fiction and nonfiction texts that, taken together, support a theme or exemplify a genre. Students will have previously heard all the texts referenced in a minilesson and had opportunities to make connections between them.
Anchor Chart	A visual representation of the lesson concept, using a combination of words and images. It is constructed by the teacher and students to summarize the learning and is used as a reference tool by the students.

Chapter 2

Using *The Literacy Continuum* to Guide the Teaching of Reading Minilessons

WE BELIEVE SCHOOLS SHOULD BE places where students read, think, talk, and write every day about relevant content that engages their hearts and minds. Learning deepens when students engage in thinking, talking, reading, and writing about texts across many different instructional contexts and in whole-group, small-group, and individual instruction. Students who live a literate life in their classrooms have access to multiple experiences with texts throughout a day. As they participate in interactive read-aloud, shared reading, guided reading, book clubs, and independent reading, they engage in the real work of reading and writing. They build a network of systems of strategic actions that allow them to think deeply within, beyond, and about text.

The networks of in-the-head strategic actions are inferred from observations of proficient readers, writers, and speakers. We have described these networks in *The Fountas & Pinnell Literacy Continuum: A Tool for Assessment, Planning, and Teaching* (Fountas and Pinnell 2017c). This volume presents detailed text characteristics and behaviors and understandings to notice, teach for, and support for prekindergarten through middle school, across eight instructional reading, writing, and language contexts. In sum, *The Literacy Continuum* describes proficiency in reading, writing, and language as it changes over grades and over levels.

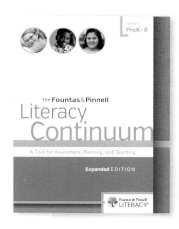

Figure 2-1: Minilesson principles are drawn from the observable behaviors of proficient students as listed in *The Literacy Continuum*.

	INSTRUCTIONAL CONTEXT	BRIEF DEFINITION	DESCRIPTION OF THE CONTINUUM
1	Interactive Read-Aloud and Literature Discussion	Students engage in discussion with one another about a text that they have heard read aloud or one they have read independently.	• Year by year, grades PreK–8 • Genres appropriate to grades PreK–8 • Specific behaviors and understandings that are evidence of thinking within, beyond, and about the text
2	Shared and Performance Reading	Students read together or take roles in reading a shared text. They reflect the meaning of the text with their voices.	• Year by year, grades PreK–8 • Genres appropriate to grades PreK–8 • Specific behaviors and understandings that are evidence of thinking within, beyond, and about the text
3	Writing About Reading	Students extend their understanding of a text through a variety of writing genres and sometimes with illustrations.	• Year by year, grades PreK–8 • Genres/forms for writing about reading appropriate to grades PreK–8 • Specific evidence in the writing that reflects thinking within, beyond, and about the text
4	Writing	Students compose and write their own examples of a variety of genres, written for varying purposes and audiences.	• Year by year, grades PreK–8 • Genres/forms for writing appropriate to grades PreK–8 • Aspects of craft, conventions, and process that are evident in students' writing, grades PreK–8
5	Oral and Visual Communication	Students present their ideas through oral discussion and presentation.	• Year by year, grades PreK–8 • Specific behaviors and understandings related to listening and speaking, presentation
6	Technological Communication	Students learn effective ways of communicating and searching for information through technology; they learn to think critically about information and sources.	• Year by year, grades PreK–8 • Specific behaviors and understandings related to effective and ethical uses of technology
7	Phonics, Spelling, and Word Study	Students learn about the relationships of letters to sounds as well as the structure and meaning of words to help them in reading and spelling.	• Year by year, grades PreK–8 • Specific behaviors and understandings related to nine areas of understanding related to letters, sounds, and words, and how they work in reading and spelling
8	Guided Reading	Students read a teacher-selected text in a small group; the teacher provides explicit teaching and support for reading increasingly challenging texts.	• Level by level, A to Z • Genres appropriate to grades PreK–8 • Specific behaviors and understandings that are evidence of thinking within, beyond, and about the text • Specific suggestions for word work [drawn from the phonics and word analysis continuum]

Figure 2-2: From *The Literacy Continuum* (Fountas and Pinnell 2017c, 3)

Systems of Strategic Actions

The systems of strategic actions are represented in the wheel diagram shown in Figure 2-3 and on the inside back cover of this book. This model helps us think about the thousands of in-the-head processes that take place simultaneously and largely unconsciously when a competent reader processes a text. When the reader engages the neural network, he builds a literacy processing system over time that becomes increasingly sophisticated. Teaching in each instructional context is directed toward helping every reader expand these in-the-head networks across increasingly complex texts.

Four sections of *The Literacy Continuum* (Fountas and Pinnell 2017c)—Interactive Read-Aloud and Literature Discussion, Shared and Performance Reading, Guided Reading, and Writing About Reading—describe the specific competencies or goals of readers, writers, and language users:

Within the Text   (literal understanding achieved through searching for and using information, monitoring and self-correcting, solving words, maintaining fluency, adjusting, and summarizing) The reader gathers the important information from the fiction or nonfiction text.

Beyond the Text   (predicting, making connections with personal experience, content knowledge and other texts, synthesizing new information, and inferring what is implied but not stated) The reader brings understanding to the processing of a text, reaching for ideas or concepts that are implied but not explicitly stated.

About the Text   (analyzing or critiquing the text) The reader looks at a text to appreciate or evaluate its construction, logic, or literary elements.

The Literacy Continuum is the foundation for all the minilessons. The minilesson principles come largely from the behaviors and understandings in the interactive read-aloud continuum, but some are selected from the shared reading, oral and visual communication, and writing about reading continua. In addition, we have included minilessons related to working together in a classroom community to assure that effective literacy instruction can take place. In most lessons, you will see a direct link to the goals from *The Literacy Continuum* called Continuum Connection.

As you ground your teaching in support of each reader's development of the systems of strategic actions, it is important to remember that these actions are never applied one at a time. A reader who comprehends a text engages these actions rapidly and simultaneously and largely without conscious attention. Your intentional talk and conversations in the various instructional contexts should support students in engaging and building their processing systems while they respond authentically as readers and enjoy the text.

Figure 2-3: All of your teaching will be grounded in support of each reader's development of the systems of strategic actions (see the inside back cover for a larger version of the Systems of Strategic Actions wheel).

Relationship of Intentional Talk to Reading Minilessons

Intentional talk refers to the language you use that is consciously directed toward the goal of instruction. We have used the term *facilitative talk* to refer to the language that supports student learning in specific ways. When you plan for intentional talk in your interactive read-aloud and shared reading experiences, think about the meaning of the text and what your students will need to think about to fully understand and enjoy the story. You might select certain pages where you want to stop and have students turn and talk about their reading so they can engage in sharing their thinking with each other. The interactive read-aloud and shared reading sections of *The Literacy Continuum* can help plan what to talk about. For example, when you read a book like *Enemy Pie,* you would likely invite talk about the character's traits and motivations, make predictions about the ending, and notice and discuss the details in the illustrations. When you read a text set of biographies, you might invite students to comment on why the author wrote a book about the subject, how the author gives information, and what they think is the author's message.

As you talk about texts together, embed brief and specific teaching in your read-aloud and shared reading lessons while maintaining a focus on enjoyment and support for your students in gaining the meaning of the whole text. In preparation, mark a few places with sticky notes and a comment or question to invite thinking. Later, when you teach explicit minilessons about concepts such as character feelings, illustrations, and text organization, your students will already have background knowledge to bring to the minilesson and will be ready to explore how the principle works across multiple texts.

In reading minilessons, you explicitly teach the principles you have already embedded in the students' previous experiences with text in these different instructional contexts. Intentional talk within each context prepares a foundation for this explicit focus. Through each interactive read-aloud and shared reading experience, you build a large body of background knowledge, academic vocabulary, and a library of shared texts to draw on as you explore specific literary principles. You will read more about this multitext approach in Chapter 9.

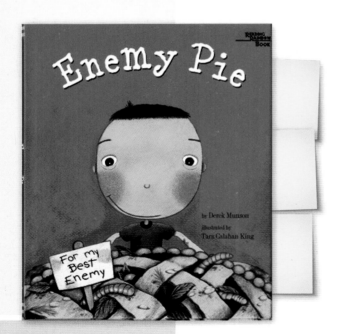

Figure 2-4: Mark a few pages to invite students to think about in the reading minilesson.

Chapter 3   Understanding the Umbrellas and Minilessons

MINILESSONS IN THIS BOOK ARE organized into conceptual groups called "umbrellas," in which a group of principles are explored in sequence, working toward larger concepts. Within each section (Management, Literary Analysis, etc.), the umbrellas are numbered in sequence and are often referred to by *U* plus the number; for example, U1 for the first umbrella. A suggested sequence of umbrellas is presented in Figure 8-2 to assist you in planning across the year, but the needs of your students always take priority.

Umbrella Front Page

Each umbrella has an introductory page on which the minilessons in the umbrella are listed and directions are provided to help you prepare to present the minilessons within the umbrella (see Figure 3-1). The introductory page is designed to provide an overview of how the umbrella is organized and the texts from *Fountas & Pinnell Classroom*™ (FPC) *Collections* that are suggested for the lessons. In addition, we provide types of texts you might select if you are not using the *FPC Collections* referenced in the lessons. Understanding how the umbrella is designed and how the minilessons fit together will help you keep your lessons focused, concise, and brief. Using familiar mentor texts that you have previously read and enjoyed with your students will help you streamline the lessons in the umbrella. You will not need to spend a lot of time rereading large sections of the text because the students already know the texts so well.

When you teach lessons in an umbrella, you help students make connections between concepts and texts and help them develop deeper understandings. A rich context such as this one is particularly helpful for English language learners. Grouping lessons into umbrellas supports English language learners in developing shared vocabulary and language around a single and important area of knowledge.

Following the umbrella front page, you will see a series of two-page lesson spreads that include several parts.

A list of minilessons is organized under the umbrella.

Prepare to present the minilessons in this umbrella with these suggestions.

Use these suggested mentor texts as examples in the minilessons in this umbrella or use books that have similar characteristics.

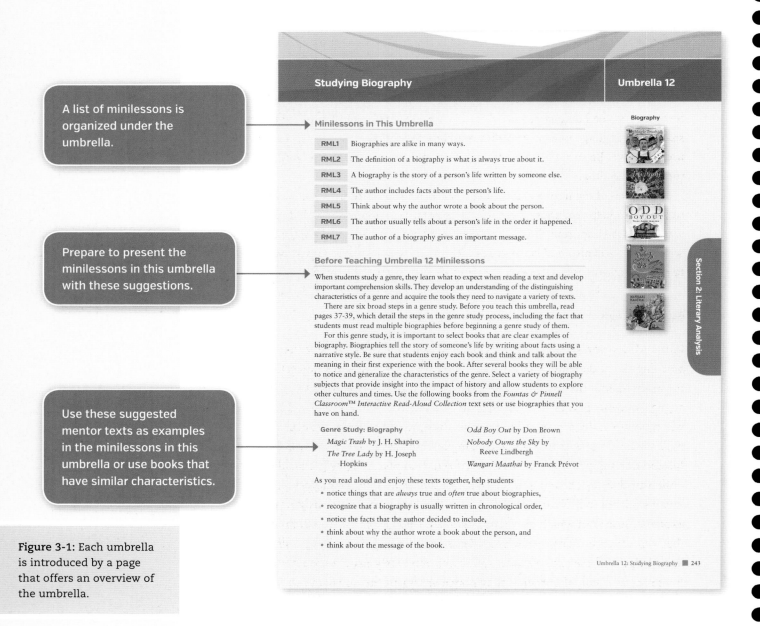

Studying Biography   **Umbrella 12**

Minilessons in This Umbrella

RML1 Biographies are alike in many ways.

RML2 The definition of a biography is what is always true about it.

RML3 A biography is the story of a person's life written by someone else.

RML4 The author includes facts about the person's life.

RML5 Think about why the author wrote a book about the person.

RML6 The author usually tells about a person's life in the order it happened.

RML7 The author of a biography gives an important message.

Before Teaching Umbrella 12 Minilessons

When students study a genre, they learn what to expect when reading a text and develop important comprehension skills. They develop an understanding of the distinguishing characteristics of a genre and acquire the tools they need to navigate a variety of texts.

There are six broad steps in a genre study. Before you teach this umbrella, read pages 37-39, which detail the steps in the genre study process, including the fact that students must read multiple biographies before beginning a genre study of them.

For this genre study, it is important to select books that are clear examples of biography. Biographies tell the story of someone's life by writing about facts using a narrative style. Be sure that students enjoy each book and think and talk about the meaning in their first experience with the book. After several books they will be able to notice and generalize the characteristics of the genre. Select a variety of biography subjects that provide insight into the impact of history and allow students to explore other cultures and times. Use the following books from the *Fountas & Pinnell Classroom™ Interactive Read-Aloud Collection* text sets or use biographies that you have on hand.

Genre Study: Biography

Magic Trash by J. H. Shapiro

The Tree Lady by H. Joseph Hopkins

Odd Boy Out by Don Brown

Nobody Owns the Sky by Reeve Lindbergh

Wangari Maathai by Franck Prévot

As you read aloud and enjoy these texts together, help students

• notice things that are *always* true and *often* true about biographies,

• recognize that a biography is usually written in chronological order,

• notice the facts that the author decided to include,

• think about why the author wrote a book about the person, and

• think about the message of the book.

Umbrella 12: Studying Biography ■ 243

Figure 3-1: Each umbrella is introduced by a page that offers an overview of the umbrella.

Two-Page Minilesson Spread

Each minilesson includes a two-page spread that consists of several parts. The section (for example, Literary Analysis), umbrella number (for example, U1), and minilesson number (for example, RML1) are listed at the top to help you locate the lesson you are looking for. For example, the code LA.U1.RML1 identifies the first minilesson in the first umbrella of the Literary Analysis section.

Principle, Goal, Rationale

The **principle** describes the understanding the students will need to learn and apply. The idea of the principle is based on *The Literacy Continuum* (Fountas and Pinnell 2017c), but the language of the principle has been carefully crafted to be precise, focused on a single idea, and accessible to students. We have placed the principle at the top of the lesson on the left-hand page so you have a clear idea of the understanding you will help students construct through the example texts used in the lesson. Although we have crafted the language to make it appropriate for the age group, you may shape the language in a slightly different way to reflect the way your students use language. Be sure that the principle is stated simply and clearly and check for understanding.

The **goal** of the minilesson is stated in the top section of the lesson, as is the **rationale,** to help you understand what this particular minilesson will do and why it may be important for the students in your classroom. In this beginning section, you will also find suggestions for specific behaviors and understandings to observe as you assess students' learning during or after the minilesson.

Minilesson

In the Minilesson section of the lesson, you will find an example lesson for teaching the understanding, or principle. The example includes suggestions for teaching and the use of precise language and open-ended questions to engage students in a brief, focused inquiry. Effective minilessons include, when possible, the process of inquiry so students can actively construct their understanding from concrete examples, because telling is not teaching. Instead of simply being told what they need to know, students get inside the understanding by engaging in the thinking themselves. In the inquiry process, invite students to look at a group of texts that were read previously (for example, stories in which characters change). Choose the books carefully so they represent the characteristics students are learning about. They will have knowledge of these texts because they have previously experienced them. Invite them to talk about what they notice across all the books. As students explore the text examples using your questions and supportive comments

A Closer Look at a Reading Minilesson

The **Goal** of the minilesson is clearly identified, as is the **Rationale**, to support your understanding of what this particular minilesson is and why it may be important for the students in your classroom.

The **Reading Minilesson Principle**—a brief statement that describes the understanding students will need to learn and apply.

This code identifies this minilesson as the seventh reading minilesson (RML7) in the twelfth umbrella (U12) in the Literary Analysis (LA) section.

Specific behaviors and understandings to observe as you assess students' learning after presenting the minilesson.

Academic Language and **Important Vocabulary** that students will need to understand in order to access the learning in the minilesson.

Suggested language to use when teaching the minilesson principle.

RML7
LA.U12.RML7

Studying Biography

You Will Need

- a variety of biographies, such as these in Text Set: Biography:
  - *Magic Trash* by J. H. Shapiro
  - *Odd Boy Out* by Don Brown
  - *The Tree Lady* by H. Joseph Hopkins
  - *Wangari Maathai* by Franck Prévot
  - *Nobody Owns the Sky* by Reeve Lindbergh
- chart paper and markers
- basket of biographies

Academic Language / Important Vocabulary

- author
- biography
- message

Reading Minilesson Principle
The author of a biography gives an important message.

Goal

Infer the larger idea or author's message in a biography.

Rationale

When students think about the author's message in a biography, they begin to think about the overarching reason why an author chooses to write about a person's life and apply messages from the book to their own lives.

Assess Learning

Observe students when they think and talk about the messages authors give in biographies. Notice if there is evidence of new learning based on the goal of this minilesson.

- Are students able to infer the messages that authors give in biographies?
- Are they beginning to think about how to apply messages from reading about the lives of others to their own lives?
- Do they use vocabulary such as *author*, *biography*, and *message*?

Minilesson

To help students think about the minilesson principle, provide an interactive lesson to help them think about the messages authors give in biographies. Here is an example.

- Display the cover of *Magic Trash*.
  - Think about this biography that J. H. Shapiro wrote about the life of Tyree Guyton. Listen as I reread a page from the beginning and a few pages from the end of the book to refresh your thinking.

- Reread the first page and the last two pages.
  - Turn and talk about the message that J. H. Shapiro gives you in this book.

- After time for discussion, have students share ideas. As needed, guide the conversation, depending on how much experience your students have had with identifying an author's message.
  - How could I write the message in one sentence on a chart?

- Using student ideas, create a chart with the title and the message of the book.
  - Think about the message in several other biographies you know.

- Display the covers of the remaining books in the text set.
  - Turn and talk about one or more of these biographies. What message does the author want you to have after reading?

Figure 3-2: All the parts of a single minilesson are contained on a two-page spread.

RML7
LA.U12.RML7

▶ Allow time for discussion.

What biographies did you talk about? What was the author's message?

▶ Ask volunteers to share ideas. Add each title and message to a new row on the chart.

Have a Try

Invite the students to talk the messages authors give in biographies.

Think about the messages in these biographies. Turn and talk about how these messages might help you in your own life. In what ways can messages that you learn when reading about other people help you make life choices?

Summarize and Apply

Summarize the learning and remind students to think about the messages authors give in biographies.

Today you talked about the messages authors give in biographies and how those messages might help you in your own lives.

▶ Add the principle to chart.

Today when you read, choose a biography and think about the messages in the book. Bring the book when we meet so you can share.

Share

Following independent reading time, gather the students in small groups.

In groups, talk about the messages that the author gave in the biography you read. Have a conversation about how one or more of those messages might apply to your own lives.

Extend the Lesson (Optional)

After assessing students' understanding, you might decide to extend the learning.

▶ As students write their own biographies, use the student-written biographies to repeat this minilesson and think about the messages. You can also use a shared writing biography to think about the messages and how they might apply to students' own lives.

The author of a biography gives an important message.	
Title	Message
	Ordinary people can do extraordinary things.
ODD BOY OUT	Everyone is different, and that's what makes us special.
	Significant things people accomplish can live on long after they're gone.
	One person can do something to make the world and other people's lives better.
	Dreams can come true through hard work and dedication.

as a guide, co-construct the anchor chart, creating an organized and visual representation of the students' noticings and understandings. (See the section on Anchor Charts in Chapter 1 for more information on chart creation.) From this exploration and the discussion surrounding it, students derive the principle, which is then written at the top of the chart.

Throughout this book, you will find models and examples of the anchor charts you will co-construct with students. Of course, the charts you create with the students will be unique because they reflect your students' thinking. Learning is more powerful and enjoyable for students when they actively search for the meaning, find patterns, and talk about their understandings. Students need to form networks of understanding around the concepts related to literacy and to be constantly looking for connections for themselves.

ELL CONNECTION

Creating a need to produce language is an important principle in building language, and reading minilessons provide many opportunities for students to express their thoughts in language and to communicate with others. The inquiry approach found in these lessons invites more student talk than teacher talk, and that can be both a challenge and an opportunity for English language learners. In our previous texts, we have written that Marie Clay (1991) urges us to be "strong minded" about holding meaningful conversations even when they are difficult. In *Becoming Literate*, she warns us that it is "misplaced sympathy" to do the talking for those who are developing and learning language. Instead, she recommends "concentrating more sharply, smiling more rewardingly and spending more time in genuine conversation." Building talk routines, such as turn and talk, into your reading minilessons can be very helpful in providing these opportunities for English language learners in a safe and supportive way.

When you ask students to think about the minilesson principle across several texts that they have previously listened to and discussed, they are more engaged and able to participate because they know these texts and can shift their attention to a new way of thinking about them. Using familiar texts is particularly important for English language learners. When you select examples for a reading minilesson, choose texts that you know were particularly engaging for the English language learners in your classroom. Besides choosing accessible, familiar texts, it is important to provide plenty of wait and think time. For example, you might say, "Let's think about that for a minute" before calling for responses.

When working with English language learners, value partially correct responses. Look for what the child knows about the concept instead of focusing on faulty grammar or language errors. Model appropriate language use in your responses, but do not correct a child who is attempting to use language to learn it. You might also provide an oral sentence frame to get the students' response started. Accept variety in pronunciation and intonation, remembering that the more students speak, read, and write, the more they will take on the understanding of grammatical patterns and the complex intonation patterns that reflect meaning in English.

Have a Try

Because students will be asked to apply the new thinking independently during independent literacy work, it is important to give students a chance to apply it with a partner or a small group while still in the whole-group setting. Have a Try is designed to be brief, but it offers you an opportunity to gather information on how well students understand the minilesson principle. In many minilessons, students are asked to apply the new thinking to another concrete example from a familiar book. In management lessons, students quickly practice the new routine that they will be asked to do independently. You will often add further thinking to the chart after the students have had the chance to try out their new learning. On occasion, you will find lessons that do not include Have a Try because students will practice the routine or concept as part of the application. However, in most cases, Have a Try is an important step in reinforcing the principle and moving the students toward independence.

The Have a Try portion of the reading minilesson is particularly important for English language learners. Besides providing repetition and allowing for the gradual release of responsibility, it gives English language learners a safe place to try out the new idea before sharing it with the whole group. These are a few suggestions for how you might support students during the Have a Try portion of the lesson:

ELL CONNECTION

▶ Pair students with specific partners in a way that will allow for a balance of talk between the two.

▶ Spend time teaching students how to turn and talk. (You will find a minilesson in Section Two: Literary Analysis, Umbrella 1: Thinking and Talking About Books, that helps students develop this routine.) Teach students how to provide wait time for one another, invite the other partner into the conversation, and take turns.

▶ Provide concrete examples to discuss so that students are clear about what they need to talk about and are able to stay grounded in the text. English language learners will feel more confident if they are able to talk about a text that they know really well.

▶ Observe partnerships involving English language learners and provide support as needed.

▶ When necessary, you might find it helpful to provide the oral language structure or language stem for how you want your students to share. For example, ask them to start with the phrase "I think the character feels . . ." and to rehearse the language structure a few times before turning and talking.

Summarize and Apply

This part of the lesson consists of two parts: summarizing the learning and applying the learning to independent reading.

The **summary** is a brief but essential part of the lesson. It provides a time to bring together all of the learning that has taken place through the inquiry and to help students think about its application and relevance to their own learning. It is best to involve the students in constructing the minilesson principle with you. Ask them to reflect on the chart you have created together and talk about what they have learned that day. In simple, clear language, shape the suggestions. Other times, you may decide to help summarize the new learning to keep the lesson short and allow enough time for the students to apply it independently. Whether you state the principle or co-construct it with your students, summarize the learning in a way that makes the principle generative and applicable to future texts the students will read.

After the summary, the students **apply** their new understandings to their independent reading. Before students begin their independent reading, let them know what you expect them to discuss or bring for the group sharing session so they can think about it as they read. They know they are accountable for trying out the new thinking in their own books or reflect on their participation because they are expected to share upon their return.

Students engaged in independent reading will choose books from the classroom library. Some teachers choose to have students shop for books in the library at specific times and have them keep selected books in their personal literacy boxes. When you designate certain times for browsing, you maximize students' time spent on reading and are able to carve out time to assist with book selection. Individual book bags will contain mostly books the students select from the classroom library, but there may also be books you have chosen for them based on your observation of individual reading behaviors and interests. When needed, plan to supply independent reading books that will provide opportunities to apply the principle. For example, if you teach the umbrella on studying biographies, make sure students have access to biographies. You will notice that in some of the lessons, students are invited to read from a certain basket of books in the classroom library to ensure that there are opportunities to apply their new learning.

We know that when students first take on new learning, they often overgeneralize or overapply the new learning at the exclusion of some of the other things they have learned. The best goal when students are reading any book is to enjoy it, process it effectively, and gain its full meaning. Always encourage meaningful and authentic engagement with text. You don't want students so focused and determined to apply the minilesson principle that they make superficial connections to text that actually distract from their understanding of the book. You will likely find the opportunity in many reading conferences, guided reading lessons, or book club meetings to reinforce the minilesson understanding.

In our professional book, *Teaching for Comprehending and Fluency* (Fountas and Pinnell 2006), we write, "Whenever we instruct readers, we mediate (or change) the meaning they derive from their reading. Yet we must offer instruction that helps readers expand their abilities. There is value in drawing readers' attention to important aspects of the text that will enrich their understanding, but we need to understand that using effective reading strategies is not like exercising one muscle. The system must always work together as an integrated whole." The invitation to apply the new learning must be clear enough to have students try out new ways of thinking, but "light" enough to allow room for readers to expand and express their own thinking. The application of the minilesson principle should not be thought of as an exercise or task that needs to completed but instead as an invitation to deeper, more meaningful response to the events or ideas in a text.

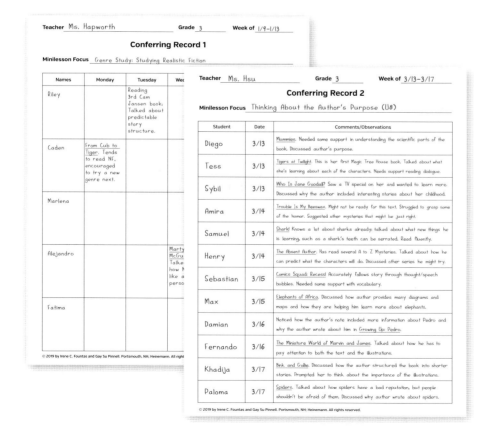

Figure 3-3: Choose one of these downloadable forms to record your observations of students' behaviors and understandings during reading conferences. Visit **resources.fountasandpinnell.com** to download this and all other online resources.

While students are reading independently, you may be meeting with small groups for guided reading or book clubs, rotating to observe students working independently, or conferring with individuals. If you have a reading conference, you can take the opportunity to reinforce the minilesson principle. We have provided two conferring record sheets (choose whichever form suits your purpose) for you to download from the online resources (see Figure 3-3) so that you can make notes about your individual conferences with students. You can use your notes to plan the content of future minilessons.

Share

At the end of the independent work time, students come together and have the opportunity to share their learning with the entire group. Group share provides an opportunity for you to revisit, expand, and deepen understanding of the minilesson principle as well as to assess learning. In Figure 3-2, you will notice that in the Share section we provide suggestions for how to have students share their new learning. Often, students are asked to bring a book to share and to explain how they applied the minilesson principle in their independent reading. Sometimes we suggest sharing with the whole group, but other times we suggest that sharing take place among pairs, triads, or quads. As you observe and talk to students engaged in independent reading, shared reading, guided reading, or book clubs, you can assess whether they are easily able to apply the minilesson principle. Use this information to inform how you plan to share. If only a few students were able to apply the minilesson to their reading, you might ask only a few students to share. Whereas if you observe most of the class applying the principle, you might have them share in pairs or small groups.

As a general guideline, in addition to revisiting the reading minilesson principle at the end of independent reading time, you might also ask students to share what they thought or wrote about their reading that day. For example, a student might share part of a letter he wrote about his reading. Another student might share a memorable line from a book or celebrate reaching the goal of trying a book in a different genre. The Share is a wonderful way to bring the community of readers and writers back together to expand their understandings and celebrate their learning at the end of the workshop time.

ELL CONNECTION

There are some particular accommodations you might want to consider to support English language learners during the Share:

▶ Ask English language learners to share in pairs before sharing with the whole group.

- Use individual conferences and guided reading to help students rehearse the language structure they might use to share their application of the minilesson principle to the text they have read.

- Teach the entire class respectful ways to listen to peers and model how to give their peers time to express their thoughts. Many of the minilessons in the Management section will be useful for developing a safe and supportive community of readers and writers.

Extending the Lesson

At the end of each lesson we offer suggestions for extending the learning of the principle. Sometimes extending the learning involves repeating the lesson over time with different examples. Third graders might need to experience some of the concepts more than once before they are able to transfer actions to their independent reading. Using the questions in the Assessment section will help you to determine if you need to repeat the lesson, move on, or revisit the lesson (perhaps in a slightly different way) in the future. Other suggestions for extending the lesson include applying the minilesson concept within other contexts, performing readers' theater, or writing and drawing in response to reading. In several cases, the suggestions will reference a reader's notebook (see Chapter 7 for more information about writing about reading and Section Four: Writing About Reading for minilessons that teach ways to use a reader's notebook).

Umbrella Back Page

Assessment and Link to Writing

Following the minilessons in each umbrella, you will see the final umbrella page that includes **Assessment** and **Link to Writing**. The last page of each umbrella, as shown in Figure 3-4, provides suggestions for assessing the learning that has taken place through the minilessons in the entire umbrella. The information you gain from observing what the students can already do, almost do, and not yet do will help inform the selection of the next umbrella you teach. (See Chapter 8 for more information about assessment and the selection of umbrellas.) For many umbrellas, this last page also provides a Link to Writing. In some cases, this section provides further suggestions for writing/drawing about reading in a reader's notebook. However, in most cases, the Link to Writing provides ideas for how students might try out some of the new learning in their own writing. For example, after learning about text features in nonfiction, you might want to teach students how to include one or more of the features, such as a table of contents or sidebar, in their own nonfiction writing.

> Gain important information by **assessing** students' understandings as they apply and share their learning of a minilesson principle. Observe and then follow up with individuals or address the principle during guided reading.

Umbrella 12	Studying Biography

Assessment

After you have taught the minilessons in this umbrella, observe students as they talk and write about their reading across instructional contexts: interactive read-aloud, independent reading and literacy work, guided reading, shared reading, and book club. Use *The Literacy Continuum* (Fountas and Pinnell 2017) to observe students' reading and writing behaviors across instructional contexts.

▸ What evidence do you have of new understandings related to biographies?
  • Are students aware that a biography is the story of someone's life written by another person?
  • Are they aware of the author's purpose in writing a book about someone's life?
  • Do they notice that a biography is written in the same order that events occurred in someone's life?
  • Can they talk about the message of a biography?
  • Do they use vocabulary, such as *facts, time order, biography,* and *events,* to discuss biographies?
▸ In what other ways, beyond the scope of this umbrella, are students talking about nonfiction?
  • Are students talking about other kinds of nonfiction books?

Use your observations to determine the next umbrella you will teach. You may also consult Minilessons Across the Year (pp. 55-57) for guidance.

Read and Revise

> Wrap up the umbrella by engaging students in an activity that uses their expanded understanding of the umbrella concept.

After completing the steps in the genre study process, help students read and revise their definition of the genre based on their new understandings.

▸ **Before:** A biography is the story of all or part of a real person's life, written by someone else.
▸ **After:** A biography is the story of all or part of a real person's life, written by someone else, and gives an important message.

Reader's Notebook

When this umbrella is complete, provide a copy of the minilesson principles (see resources.fountasandpinnell.com) for students to glue in the reader's notebook (in the Minilessons section if using *Reader's Notebook: Intermediate* [Fountas and Pinnell 2011]), so they can refer to the information as needed.

Figure 3-4: The final page of each umbrella offers suggestions for assessing the learning and, in many umbrellas, a Link to Writing.

Online Resources for Planning

We have provided examples in this book of how to engage your third-grade students in developing the behaviors and understandings of competent readers, as described in *The Literacy Continuum* (Fountas and Pinnell 2017c). However, you can modify the suggested lesson to fit your students and construct new lessons using the goals of the continuum as needed for your particular students. The form shown in Figure 3-5 will help you plan each part of a new minilesson. For example, you can design a minilesson that uses a different set of example texts from the ones suggested in this book or you can teach a concept in a way that fits the current needs of your students. The form shown in Figure 3-6 will help you plan which minilessons to teach over a period of time so as to address the goals that are important for your students. You can find both forms at **resources.fountasandpinnell.com.**

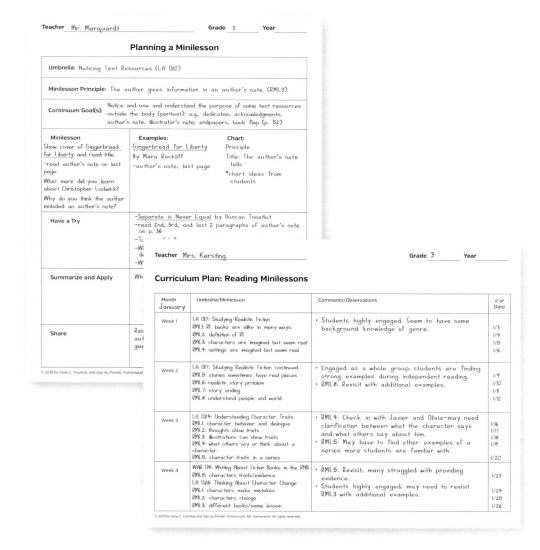

Figure 3-5: Use this downloadable form to plan your own minilessons.

Figure 3-6: Use this downloadable form to make notes about specific minilessons for future planning.

Chapter 4

Management Minilessons: Building a Literacy Community

MANAGEMENT MINILESSONS FOCUS ON ROUTINES for thinking and talking about reading and working together in the classroom. Good management allows you to teach effectively and efficiently; use these lessons to create an orderly, busy classroom in which students know what is expected as well as how to behave responsibly and respectfully in a community of learners. They learn how the classroom library is organized, how to choose books and return them, how to use their voices in the classroom, and how to engage in independent reading. You can use these minilessons to teach your students the routines for independent reading, how to use and return materials, and how to problem solve independently. Classroom management is important in implementing a multitext approach to literacy learning. You want your students to grow in the ability to regulate their own behavior and to sustain reading and writing for increasing periods of time.

Altogether, there are twelve management minilessons for your use. Teach the management minilessons in the order that fits your class, or consult the suggested sequence in Figure 8-2. You may need to reteach some management minilessons across the year, especially as students encounter more complex situations and routines. Sometimes when there is a schedule change or other disruption in classroom operations, a refresher management minilesson will be needed. Any problem in your classroom should be addressed through a management minilesson.

The Physical Space

Before students enter your classroom, prepare the physical space in a way that provides maximum support for learning. Remember that this relatively small room must support the productive work of some 20 to 30 people, 6 or 7 hours a day, 180+ days a year. Each management umbrella will help your students become acquainted with different parts of the classroom, which will make them feel secure and at home. Make sure that the classroom is:

▶ **Welcoming and Inviting.** Pleasing colors and a variety of furniture will help. There is no need for commercially published posters or slogans, except for standard references such as the Consonant Cluster Linking Chart or colorful poetry posters. The room can be filled with the work that students have produced beginning on day one. They see signs of their learning everywhere—shared writing, charts, drawings of various kinds, and their names. Be sure that students' names are at various places in the room—on desks or tables, the helper's charts, and on some of the charts that you will be making in minilessons. The classroom library should be as inviting as a bookstore or a library. Place books in baskets and tubs on shelves to make the front covers of books visible and accessible for easy browsing. Clear out old, dated, or tattered books that students never choose. Clearly label (or, even better, have students label) the tub or basket with the topic, author, series, genre or illustrator (see Figure 4-1). Add new books to the library all year and retire books that are no longer of interest.

▶ **Organized for Easy Use.** The first thing you might want to do is to take out everything you do not need. Clutter increases stress and noise. Using scattered and hard to find materials increases student dependence on the teacher. Consider keeping supplies for reading, writing, and word study in designated areas. For example, some teachers designate a writing area where they keep paper, highlighters, staplers, etc. Every work area should be clearly organized with necessary, labeled materials and nothing else. The work that takes place in each area should be visible at a glance; all materials needed for the particular activity are available. See Figure 4-2 for a list of some suggested materials to keep accessible in the different areas in your classroom.

▶ **Designed for Whole-Group, Small-Group, and Individual Instruction.** Minilessons are generally provided as whole-class instruction and typically take place at an easel in a meeting space that is comfortable and large enough to accommodate all students in a group or circle. It will be helpful to have a colorful rug with some way of helping students find an individual space to sit where they do not touch others. Often, the meeting space is adjacent to the classroom library so books are handy. The

Figure 4-1: Whenever possible, involve the students in making the classroom their own.

teacher usually has a larger chair or seat next to an easel or two so that he can display the mentor texts, make anchor charts, do shared writing, or place big books for shared reading. This space is available for all whole-group instruction; for example, the students come back to it for group share. In addition to the group meeting space, there should be designated tables and spaces in the classroom for small-group reading instruction. The guided reading table is best located in a quiet corner of the room that keeps the group focused on reading, talking, and listening and at the same time allows you to scan the room to identify students who may need help staying on task independently. The table (round or horseshoe) should be positioned so the students in the group are turned away from the activity in the classroom. You might also designate a place to meet with book clubs. Provide a space that allows everyone to comfortably see one another and engage in conversation (ideally a circle of chairs). Students also need tables and spaces throughout the classroom where they can work independently and where you can easily set a chair next to a child for a brief, individual conference.

▶ **Respectful of personal space.** Third-grade students do not necessarily need an individual desk, but they do need a place to keep a personal box, including items such as their book of choice (or several that they plan to read) and a reader's notebook. These containers can be placed on a shelf labeled for each student. A writer's notebook, writing folder, and word study folder may be stored in the same place or in groups by themselves to be retrieved easily. If students have personal poetry books (growing out of the shared reading of poetry and colorfully decorated by them), they can be placed face out on a rack for easy retrieval. Artifacts like these add considerably to the aesthetic quality of the classroom.

Figure 4-2: Adapted from *Guided Reading: Responsive Teaching Across the Grades* (Fountas and Pinnell 2017d)

Classroom Areas	Materials
Classroom Library	Organize books by topic, author, illustrator, genre, and series. Spaces for students to read comfortably and independently.
Writing Materials	Pencils, different types of paper for first and final drafts, markers, stapler, scissors, glue, sticky notes, colored pencils, and highlighters.
Word Work Materials	Blank word cards; magnetic letters; games; consonant cluster linking chart; folders for Look, Cover, Write, Check; word study principles; place for students' individualized lists.
Listening Area	Player (e.g., iPod™, iPhone™, tablet), clear set of directions with picture clues, multiple copies of books organized in boxes or plastic bags.

A Peaceable Atmosphere for a Community of Readers and Writers

The minilessons in this book will help you establish a classroom environment where students can become confident, self-determined, and kind members of the community. They are designed to contribute to an ambiance of peaceful activity and shared responsibility in the third-grade classroom. Through the management minilessons they will learn how to modulate the voice to suit various purposes (silent to outdoor). There are also lessons on keeping supplies in order, finding help when the teacher is busy, listening to and looking at others, and choosing appropriate books. The overall tone of every classroom activity is respectful. Third-grade students who enter your classroom for the first time will benefit from learning your expectations and being reminded of how to work with twenty to thirty others in a small room day after day. These minilessons are designed to help you establish the atmosphere you want. Everything in the classroom reflects the students who work there; it is their home for the year.

Getting Started with Independent Reading: A Readers' Workshop Structure

Many of the minilessons in the Management section will be the ones that you address early in the year to establish routines that students will use to work at their best with one another and independently. In the last umbrella in this section, Umbrella 3: Getting Started with Independent Reading, you will teach students the routines and structure for independent reading. We recommend a readers' workshop structure for grade 3 in which students move from a whole-class meeting, to individual reading and small-group work, and back to a whole-class meeting (see Figure 4-3). The minilessons in this book are designed with this structure in mind, providing a strong instructional frame around independent reading and regular opportunities for students to share their thinking with each other. Your use of time will depend on the amount of time you have for the entire class period. As we

Figure 4-3: A readers' workshop structure as shown in *Guided Reading: Responsive Teaching Across the Grades* (Fountas and Pinnell 2017d, 565)

Structure of Readers' Workshop		
Book Talks and Minilessons		5–10 minutes
Students: • Independent Reading • Writing in a Reader's Notebook	Teacher: • Guided Reading Groups (about 20–25 minutes each • Book Clubs (about 20 minutes each) • Individual Conferences (3–5 minutes each)	50–60 minutes
Group Share		5 minutes

explain in Chapter 23 of *Guided Reading: Responsive Teaching Across the Grades*, ideally you will have seventy-five to ninety minutes, though many teachers have only sixty minutes. You will need to adjust accordingly. The minilessons in this umbrella are focused on promoting independence and supporting students in making good book choices for independent reading, including knowing when to abandon a book. Students also learn how to keep their materials for independent reading organized and ready to use. It is possible that you will spend several days reviewing the minilessons in this umbrella until you feel students are able to choose books and read independently for a sustained period of time. At the beginning of the year, make independent reading relatively short and circulate around the room to help students select books, draw and write about their reading, and stay engaged. As students become more self-directed, you can increase independent reading time, and this should happen quickly with third graders. When you determine that students can sustain productive independent behavior, you can begin to meet with guided reading groups.

Book Talks and Minilessons

The minilessons in management Umbrella 1: Working Together in the Classroom will help you establish routines for your students that they will use throughout the year. In addition to these lessons, you will want to teach the students to sit in a specific place during book talks and reading minilessons. They might sit on a carpet or in chairs. Be sure everyone can see the chart and hear you and each other. Teachers with larger classes sometimes find it helpful to have a smaller circle sitting on the carpet and the remaining students sitting behind them in chairs. Everyone should have enough space so as not to distract others. Most importantly, make it a comfortable place to listen, view, and talk.

Figure 4-4: Readers' workshop begins with a minilesson and, often, a book talk.

Teachers often start readers' workshop with a few short book talks. Book talks are an effective way to engage students' interest in books, and that enriches independent reading. Consider giving two or three very short book talks before your reading minilesson a few times a week. Students can write titles in their notebooks for later reference (see writing about reading minilessons). Book talks are an important part of creating a community of readers and writers who talk about and share books. Once you have set the routines for book talks, you can turn this responsibility over to the students. The literary analysis Umbrella 3: Giving a Book Talk is designed to teach students how to craft an interesting book talk.

Whether you are engaging your students in a reading minilesson, a book talk, or other whole-group instruction, you will need to teach them how to listen and talk when the entire class is meeting. Management minilessons lay the foundation for this whole-group work.

Independent Reading, Individual Conferences, and Small-Group Work

After the reading minilesson, work with students individually and in small groups (e.g., in guided reading and book clubs) while other students are engaged in independent reading and writing in the reader's notebook. To establish this as productive independent time, spend time on the minilessons in management Umbrella 2: Exploring the Classroom Library and Umbrella 3: Getting Started with Independent Reading. Independent reading and the reader's notebook, while highly beneficial in themselves, also act as your management system. Students are engaged in reading and writing for a sustained period of time, freeing you to have individual conferences and to meet with small groups. You will find minilessons in Section Four: Writing About Reading to help you introduce and use the reader's notebook.

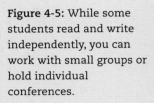

Figure 4-5: While some students read and write independently, you can work with small groups or hold individual conferences.

During this independent reading time, you will want students to maintain a "0" voice level. Students will have plenty of time during the share and small-group work to express their thinking about books. During independent reading, there should be limited opportunity for distraction. The only voices heard should be your individual conferences with students and your work with small groups. You may have to repeat the minilesson on voice level more than once for students to remember which voice level is appropriate for a particular activity.

Consider the space in your classroom and position yourself during small-group work in a way that you can scan the room frequently. This thoughtful positioning will allow you to identify problems that arise and make notes to use in individual conferences. However, if you spend the time setting and practicing these routines and expectations, students will learn to self-regulate and change inappropriate behavior with little intervention. When they are taught to make good book choices, they look forward to this quiet time of the day to read books of their own choosing.

When you first start readers' workshop, you will spend all or most of your time engaging in individual conferences to get to know your students. Conferences allow you time to evaluate whether they are making good book choices and help them become self-managed. Students who have persistent difficulty in selecting books might benefit from working with a limited selection of just-right books, which you can assemble in a temporary basket for this purpose.

In third grade, you may have some or even many students who are just beginning to sustain attention to texts and have little experience managing themselves independently. If this is the case, structure the independent work period so that it includes three independent tasks so that you have enough time to meet with individuals and small groups. Here are suggestions for the three tasks:

▸ Reading books of their choice

▸ Writing in the reader's notebook

▸ Completing a carefully designed word study/phonics activity with a partner (linked to the phonics and word study minilesson you teach at another part of the day)

This kind of transition will not be needed long because students will build stamina for reading as well as writing about their reading. The more time you invest in teaching the management minilessons to establish the foundation for a strong and independent learning environment, the quicker you will be able to make this transition.

Sharing Time

The readers' workshop ends with the community of readers and writers coming together for a short time to share discoveries made during independent reading time. Whatever is taught in the minilesson (management routines, literary analysis, strategies and skills, or writing about reading) guides the independent work time and is revisited during group share. The same routines and expectations you teach in Umbrella 1: Working Together in the Classroom (Section One: Management) apply to the sharing time in your classroom. Besides using sharing time to revisit the minilesson principle, you can use this time for your students to self-evaluate how the whole class is working together. The charts you create together during management minilessons can be a source for self-evaluation. Direct students to review the chart and evaluate the class' behavior based on the chart criteria.

In addition to evaluating independent work time, you might also ask students to evaluate the quality of their sharing time. Is everyone is able to see and hear each other? Does everyone transition well from turning and talking with a partner back to the whole group? Is everyone using an appropriate voice level? Do enough students have an opportunity to share their thinking?

In *Guided Reading: Responsive Teaching Across the Grades* (Fountas and Pinnell 2017d), we wrote the following: "The readers' workshop brings together both individual interests and the shared experiences of a literate community. Students read at a sharper edge when they know they will be sharing their thoughts with peers in their classroom. They are personally motivated because they have choice. In addition to providing an excellent management system, the workshop engages students in massive amounts of daily reading and in writing about reading" (p. 571). The management minilessons in this book are designed to set a management system in motion in which choice and independence are guiding principles. Students develop into a community of readers and writers that respect and look forward to listening to and responding to each other's ideas.

Chapter 5

Literary Analysis Minilessons: Thinking and Talking About Books

LITERARY ANALYSIS MINILESSONS SUPPORT STUDENTS in a growing awareness of the elements of literature and the writer's and illustrator's craft. Use these lessons to help students learn how to think analytically about texts and identify the characteristics of fiction and nonfiction genres. Invite them to notice characters and how they change, identify problems and solutions in stories, and notice how nonfiction writers present and organize information as well as their use of graphics and other nonfiction features. Prior to each literary analysis minilesson, students will have listened to texts read aloud or have experienced them through shared reading. You will have taught specific lessons based on the text that encourage students to discuss and explore concepts and to respond in writing, art, or drama. This prior knowledge will be accessed as they participate in the minilesson and will enable them to make the understanding explicit. They then can apply the concepts to their own reading and share what they have learned with others.

Organization of Literary Analysis Umbrellas and the Link to *The Literacy Continuum*

There are 132 literary analysis minilessons in this book. These minilessons are divided into categories according to *The Literacy Continuum* (Fountas and Pinnell 2017c), and the order of presentation in this book follows that of *The Literacy Continuum*. The categories of fiction and nonfiction are listed below.

▶ Fiction and Nonfiction

- General
- Genre
- Messages and Themes
- Style and Language

▶ Nonfiction

- Genre
- Organization
- Topic
- Illustration/Graphics
- Book and Print Features

▶ Fiction

- Genre
- Setting
- Plot
- Character
- Illustrations

As you can tell from the suggested sequence in Minilessons Across the Year (Figure 8-2), you will want to use simpler concepts (such as character traits) before more sophisticated concepts (such as good characters can be flawed or make mistakes).

Echoes of the literary analysis minilessons reverberate across all the instruction for the year in instructional contexts for reading (interactive read-aloud, shared reading, guided reading, book clubs, and independent reading) as well as for writing. The students continue to develop their understanding of the characteristics of fiction and nonfiction texts.

Genre Study

Within the Literary Analysis section, you will find six umbrellas that bring students through a process of inquiry-based study of the characteristics of a particular genre. Genre study gives students the tools they need to navigate a variety of texts with deep understanding. When readers understand the characteristics of a genre, they know what to expect when they begin to read a text. They use their knowledge of the predictable elements within a genre as a road map to anticipate structures and elements of the text. They make connections between books within the same genre and begin to develop a shared language for talking about genre. In our professional book, *Genre Study: Teaching with Fiction and Nonfiction Books* (Fountas and Pinnell 2012d), we designed a six-step approach for learning about a variety of genres. The six broad steps are described in Figure 5-1. For this book, we have designed specific minilessons based on our *Genre Study* book to help you engage your students in the powerful process of becoming knowledgeable about a range of genres.

The first two steps of the genre study process take place before and during interactive read-aloud. Steps 3–5 are accomplished through reading minilessons. Step 6 is addressed on the last page of each genre study umbrella. In third grade, we suggest six genre studies to help students develop a broader understanding of genre. Figure 5-3 is an overview of how we categorize various fiction and nonfiction genres. As students progress through the grades, they will revisit some genres to gain a deeper understanding and be introduced to new genres. In grade 3, we feature genre studies about realistic fiction, informational books (expository text), biographies, folktales, fables, and poetry. Though poetry is a form of writing, not a genre, we think it is important for students to become deeply familiar with its characteristics. The

Figure 5-1: Adapted from *Genre Study* (Fountas and Pinnell 2012d)

Steps in the Genre Study Process

1	**Collect** books in a text set that represent good examples of the genre you are studying.
2	**Immerse.** Read aloud each book using the lesson guidelines. The primary goal should be enjoyment and understanding of the book.
3	**Study.** After you have read these mentor texts, have students analyze characteristics or "noticings" that are common to the texts, and list the characteristics on chart paper.
4	**Define.** Use the list of characteristics to create a short working definition of the genre.
5	**Teach** specific minilessons on the important characteristics of the genre.
6	**Read and Revise.** Expand students' understanding by encouraging them to talk about the genre in appropriate instructional contexts (book club, independent reading conferences, guided reading lessons, and shared reading lessons) and revise the definition.

Biography

Noticings:

Always	Often
• The author tells the story of another person's life, or part of it.	• The author tells about the person's life in the order it happened.
• The author includes facts about the person's life.	• The author includes made-up dialogue, based on fact.
• The author tells about the important things a person did.	• The author includes quotes by the person.
• The author gives an important message.	• There is additional information at the end of the book (timelines).
	• The author includes photographs or illustrations.

Figure 5-2: On this anchor chart, the teacher has recorded what the students noticed was always or often true about several biographies that they had read.

steps in the genre study process allow students to discover these characteristics through inquiry.

The first step in the genre study process, **Collect,** involves collecting a set of texts. The genre study minilessons in this book draw on texts sets from the *Fountas & Pinnell Classroom™ Interactive Read-Aloud Collection.* Use these texts if you have them, but we encourage you to collect additional texts within each genre to immerse your students in as many texts as possible. Students will enjoy additional examples of the genre placed in a bin in the classroom library. You can use the texts listed in the Before Teaching section of each umbrella as a guide to making your own genre text set if you do not have access to the *Interactive Read-Aloud Collection.*

As you engage students in step 2, **Immerse,** of the genre study process, be sure that the students think and talk about the meaning of each text during the interactive read-aloud. The goal is for students to enjoy a wonderful book, so it is important for them to first enjoy and respond to the full meaning of the text before focusing their attention on the specific characteristics of the genre.

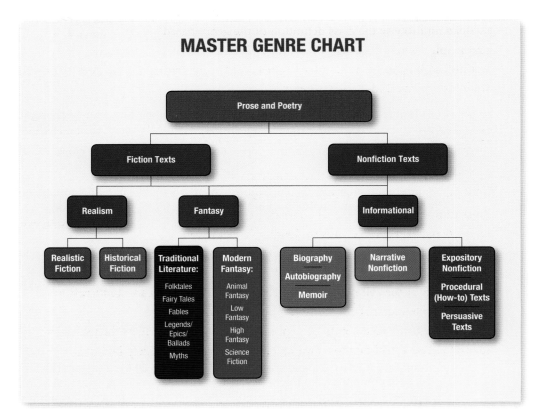

Figure 5-3: Master Genre Chart from *Genre Study: Teaching with Fiction and Nonfiction Books* (Fountas and Pinnell 2012d)

After immersing students in the books through interactive read-aloud, it is time to teach minilessons in the appropriate genre study umbrella. The first minilesson in each genre study umbrella addresses step 3 in the process, **Study.** During this initial minilesson, help students notice what is common across all of the texts. As students discuss and revisit books in the genre, list their noticings on chart paper. Distinguish between what is always true about the genre and what is often true about the genre.

The second minilesson in each genre study umbrella addresses step 4, **Define,** in the process. Use shared writing to co-construct a working definition of the genre based on the students' previous noticings. Help students understand that you will revisit and revise this definition as they learn more about the genre over the next few days.

Next, as part of step 5, **Teach,** provide specific minilessons related to each of your students' noticings about the genre. In each genre study umbrella, we offer minilessons that we think would develop out of most third graders' noticings. Pick and choose the lessons that match your own students' noticings or use these lessons as a model to develop your own minilessons. In the minilessons and throughout a genre study, support your teaching with prompts for thinking, talking, and writing about reading. Prompts and definitions for each genre are included in *Fountas & Pinnell Genre Prompting Guide for Fiction* (2012b) and *Fountas & Pinnell Genre Prompting Guide for Nonfiction, Poetry, and Test Taking* (2012c).

At the end of the umbrella, work with the students to **Read and Revise** the class definition of the genre based on the minilessons that have been taught. Using shared writing, make changes to the definition so it reflects your students' understanding of the genre.

Author and Illustrator Studies

Section Two: Literary Analysis also includes an umbrella of minilessons for conducting inquiry-based author and illustrator studies. Author and illustrator studies allow students to make connections to the people behind the books they love. They learn about the craft decisions an author or illustrator makes. For an author or illustrator study, be sure that the students think and talk about the full meaning of each text in interactive read-aloud before identifying characteristics specific to the author or illustrator.

Students will need plenty of opportunity to explore the texts during read-aloud time and on their own or in groups or pairs. As they become

Patricia Polacco

Noticings:

Always	Often
• She includes details about her own life, family, family history, and culture in her stories.	• She includes sound words in capital letters.
• The colors of her illustrations connect to the mood of the story.	• Her stories take place in the past.
• Her illustrations include patterns.	• Her stories are retellings of folktales.
• Her books have humor.	• Her illustrations are done in both color and black and white.
	• Her books include information about why the characters and events are important to her.

Figure 5-4: This chart shows what students noticed about the work of author and illustrator Patricia Polacco.

more familiar with the steps in an author or illustrator study, they learn how to notice characteristics common to a particular author's or illustrator's work. The steps in an author/illustrator study are described in Figure 5-5.

In the first minilesson in Umbrella 2: Studying Authors and Illustrators, you provide a demonstration of step 3 by working with your students to create a chart of "noticings" about an author or illustrator. In this lesson, we model a study of Patricia Polacco from the *Fountas & Pinnell Classroom™ Interactive Read-Aloud Collection*. For this author study, we have chosen to study an author who is also the illustrator of her books. You might choose to study authors and illustrators you and your students are familiar with and love. The other minilessons in this umbrella address how some writers use their own lives as inspiration for their books and how authors have unique styles that help us recognize their books. We recommend teaching the lessons in this umbrella across the year, as you conduct author or illustrator studies, instead of consecutively (see Minilessons Across the Year, Figure 8-2). Simply collect books by a particular author or illustrator and follow the steps listed in Figure 5-5. Use the same language and process modeled in the minilessons in this umbrella but substitute the authors and illustrators of your choice.

Figure 5-5: Minilessons address step 3 of an author/illustrator study.

Steps in an Author/Illustrator Study

1	Gather a set of books and read them aloud to the class over several days. The goal is for students to enjoy the books and discuss the full meaning.
2	Take students on a quick tour of all the books in the set. As you reexamine each book, you might want to have students do a brief turn and talk with a partner about what they notice.
3	Have students analyze the characteristics of the author's or illustrator's work, and record their noticings on chart paper.
4	You may choose to read a few more books by the author and compare them to the books in this set, adding to the noticings as needed.

Chapter 6

Strategies and Skills Minilessons: Teaching for Effective Processing

FOR THE STRATEGIES AND SKILLS lessons, you will usually use enlarged texts that have been created for shared reading because students can see the print and the illustrations easily. These minilessons will help them continue to strengthen their ability to process print by searching for and using information from the text, self-monitoring their reading, and self-correcting their errors. You'll notice the students engaging in these behaviors in your interactive read-aloud, shared reading, and guided reading lessons.

The large print is ideal for problem solving with a common example. Shared reading leads the way for students to apply strategic actions in guided reading lessons. Strategies and skills are taught in every instructional context for reading, but guided reading is the most powerful one. The text is just right to support the learning of all the readers in the group, enabling them to learn how to solve words and engage in the act of problem solving across a whole text.

The strategies and skills minilessons in this book are some lessons that may serve as reminders and be helpful to the whole class. They can be taught any time you see a need. For example, as students engage in independent reading, they may need to realize that a reader

▶ reads a sentence again and thinks what would make sense, sound right, and look right, and

▶ breaks apart a new word to read it.

The minilessons in Section Three: Strategies and Skills are designed to bring a few important strategies to temporary, conscious attention so that students are reminded to think in these ways as they problem solve in independent reading. By the time students participate in these minilessons, they should have engaged these strategic actions successfully in shared or guided reading. In the minilessons, they will recognize the strategic actions; bring them to brief, focused attention; and think about applying them consistently in independent reading.

Through the reading of continuous text, students develop an internal sense of actions, for example monitoring and checking, searching for and using information, and using multiple sources of information to solve words. They have a sense of how to put words together in phrases and use intonation to convey meaning. They are learning to think about how a character would speak the dialogue. And, they are learning to check their comprehension by telling the most important parts of a fiction or nonfiction text. The minilesson, the application, and the share help them better understand what they do and internalize effective and efficient reading behaviors.

Figure 6-1: Students are able to see and follow print and punctuation when you use an enlarged text, such as a big book, a poetry chart, or a projected text.

Chapter 7

Writing About Reading Minilessons: The Reading-Writing Connection

Through drawing/writing about reading, students reflect on their understanding of a text. For example, a story might have a captivating character or characters or a humorous sequence of events. A nonfiction text might have interesting information or call for an opinion. There are two kinds of writing about reading that are highly effective with third-grade students.

> **Shared Writing.** In shared writing you offer the highest level of support to the students. You act as scribe while the students participate fully in the composition of the text. You help shape the text, but the students supply the language and context.

Figure 7-1: In shared writing, the teacher acts as scribe.

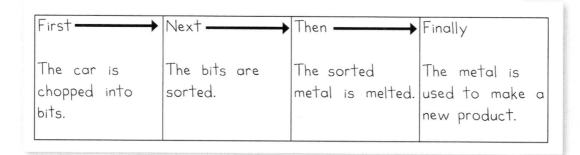

First ⟶	Next ⟶	Then ⟶	Finally
The car is chopped into bits.	The bits are sorted.	The sorted metal is melted.	The metal is used to make a new product.

▶ **Independent Writing.** For third graders, the first independent writing responses might involve just a simple paragraph, but these responses increase in complexity over time with students eventually writing multiple paragraphs about their reading. After you have introduced and modeled different forms of writing about reading, third graders begin trying these different ways independently. Occasionally, it may be helpful to provide a graphic organizer to bring structure to students' writing about both fiction and nonfiction books. Third graders also enjoy writing independently about their reading in a weekly letter to you (see Figure 7-6). Keep good examples of different writing on hand (possibly in a scrapbook) for students to use as models.

Figure 7-2: The independent writing that students do related to reading minilessons will reflect their thinking about their reading.

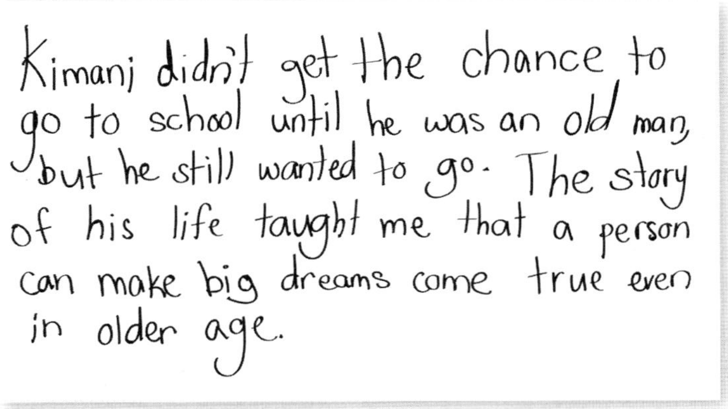

Kimani didn't get the chance to go to school until he was an old man, but he still wanted to go. The story of his life taught me that a person can make big dreams come true even in older age.

In most literary analysis lessons, you will find a suggestion for extending the learning using shared or independent writing. One other way of writing about reading is dictated writing, in which you read aloud a short piece of writing for students to write in a reader's notebook. Students will then have a model recorded in their own handwriting in their notebooks. In whatever way students write, they are exposed to different ways of thinking about their reading. Of course, the independent writing of your students will not be entirely standard spelling. They are continuing to develop systems for writing words through approximation, and their risk-taking attempts are critical to their success. You can expect third graders to accurately spell a significant number of high-frequency words as well as words with patterns that you have introduced in phonics and word study lessons; however, they will try many others using their growing knowledge of how to say words slowly and listen for the sounds and connect them with letters. You will notice that in Umbrella 3: Writing Letters About Reading, we have provided lessons that teach students how to review their writing for accurate spelling and grammar.

The students' independent writing about reading will be in a reader's notebook. The writing about reading umbrellas, Umbrella 4: Writing About Fiction Books in a Reader's Notebook and Umbrella 5: Writing About Nonfiction Books in a Reader's Notebook, both provide inquiry-based lessons to help students learn different ways to respond to their reading in independent writing. Like management minilessons, the lessons in these umbrellas might not be taught consecutively within the umbrella, but instead paired with the literary analysis lessons that support the concept students are being asked to write about. For example, after you have taught a lesson on how and why a character changes from the beginning to the end of a story, you might first extend the lesson by providing a shared writing lesson in which you write with your students' participation about how a character changes from the beginning to the end of a story. Once you feel they are ready, you might introduce them to writing in a reader's notebook about character change (see Umbrella 4: Writing About Fiction Books in a Reader's Notebook, found in Section Four: Writing About Reading). Through this gradual release of responsibility, students learn how to transition to writing about their reading independently as they learn how to use each section of the notebook. A reader's notebook is an important tool to support student independence and response to books. It becomes a rich collection of thinking across the years.

For English language learners, a reader's notebook is a safe place to practice a new language. It eventually becomes a record of their progress not only in content and literary knowledge but in acquiring a new language. However, they may do more drawing than writing as they are learning the language. Drawing is key because it provides a way to rehearse ideas. Use this opportunity to ask students to talk about what they have drawn, and then help them compose labels for their artwork so they begin to attach meaning to the English words. In some cases, you might choose to pull together small groups of students and engage them in interactive writing, in which the teacher and students share the pen. This might be particularly helpful with English language learners who might still be learning English letter and sound correlations. Students who struggle with spelling and phonics can also benefit from interactive writing in small groups.

ELL CONNECTION

Figure 7-3: Occasionally ask students to reflect on their understanding of a text by writing independently about their reading.

Eventually, the students will do more writing, but you can support the writing by providing a chance for them to rehearse their sentences before writing them and encouraging students to borrow language from the texts they are writing about. The writing in a reader's notebook is a product they can read because they have written it. It is theirs. They can read and reread it to themselves and to others, thereby developing their confidence in the language.

Using a Reader's Notebook in Third Grade

A reader's notebook is a place where students can collect their thinking about books. They draw and write to tell about themselves and respond to books and to keep a record of their reading lives. A reader's notebook includes

▶ a section for students to list the title, author, and genre of the books they have read and whether the books were easy, just right, or challenging,

▶ a section for helping students choose and recommend books, including a place to list books to read in the future,

▶ a section to glue in reading minilesson principles to refer to as needed (see Figure 7-5), and

▶ a section for students to respond to books they have read or listened to.

With places for students to make a record of their reading and respond to books in a variety of ways using different kinds of writing (including charts, webs, short writes, and letters), a reader's notebook thus represents a rich

Figure 7-4: Students write to share their thinking about reading in a reader's notebook.

record of progress. To the child, the notebook represents a year's work to reflect on with pride and share with family. Students keep their notebooks in their personal boxes, along with their bags of book choices for independent reading time. We provide a series of minilessons in Section Four: Writing About Reading for teaching students how to use a reader's notebook. As we described previously, reading minilessons in the Writing About Reading section focus on writing in response to reading.

If you do not have access to the preprinted *Reader's Notebook: Intermediate* (Fountas and Pinnell 2011), simply give each student a plain notebook (bound if possible). Glue in sections and insert tabs yourself to make a neat, professional notebook that can be cherished.

Section Two: Literary Analysis
Umbrella 24 Reading Minilesson Principles [RML1–RML5]

Understanding Character Traits

The character's behavior and dialogue show her traits.

The character's thoughts show his traits.

Sometimes an illustrator includes details in the pictures to show a character's traits.

Authors show a character's traits by telling what other characters say or think about him.

A character's traits are usually the same in each book in a series.

Figure 7-5: At the end of each umbrella, download the umbrella's principles, like the sample shown here. Students can glue the principles in the reader's notebook to refer to as needed. Encourage students to make notes or sketches to help remember the principles. To download the principles, go to **resources.fountasand pinnell.com**.

Writing Letters About Reading: Moving from Talk to Writing

In third grade, we continue the routine of having students write a weekly letter about their reading in the past week. In most cases, they address these letters to you, the teacher, although occasionally, they may write to other readers in the classroom or school. Letter writing is an authentic way to transition from oral conversation to written conversation about books. Students have had rich experiences talking about books during interactive read-aloud, guided reading, book clubs, and reading conferences. Writing letters in a reader's notebook allows them to continue this dialogue in writing and provides an opportunity to increase the depth of reader response.

By using the Writing About Reading section of *The Literacy Continuum* (Fountas and Pinnell 2017c) and carefully analyzing students' letters, you can systematically assess students' responses to the texts they are reading independently. The *Fountas & Pinnell Prompting Guide, Part 2, for Comprehension: Thinking, Talking, and Writing* (2016) is a useful resource for choosing the language to prompt the thinking you want to see in a student's response. A weekly letter from you offers the opportunity to respond in a timely way to address students individually, differentiating instruction by asking specific questions or making comments targeted at the strengths and needs of each student's individual processing system.

Figure 7-6: Weekly letters about reading allow you and your students to participate in a written dialogue to share thinking about the books the class has read together or books the students have read on their own.

Letters about reading also provide you with the opportunity to model your own thinking about reading. This reader-to-reader dialogue helps students learn more about what readers do when they actively respond to a text. The depth of their oral discussions will increase as students experience writing letters over time. Just as the discussions in your classroom set the stage for readers to begin writing letters, the writing of letters about reading will in turn enrich the discussions in your classroom.

Umbrella 3: Writing Letters About Reading, in the Writing About Reading section of this book, provides minilessons for getting dialogue letters started in your classroom. Through inquiry-based lessons, students learn the format of a letter, the routines involved in writing a weekly letter, and the qualities of a strong response. They learn to identify the different types of thinking they might include in a letter and how to integrate evidence to support their thinking.

We recommend that you teach these minilessons over two or three weeks. For example, you might teach the first minilesson in this umbrella in the first week to introduce the format and content of a letter. You might then ask students to apply these new understandings to writing their first letter. The second week you might use RML2 to introduce the routine for writing weekly letters. As students work on their second letter, you might choose to teach RML3, which helps them learn how to provide evidence for their thinking in a letter. Lastly, you may decide to wait until the third week as students embark on the third letter to teach them how to reread the letters for meaning, grammar, and spelling. When you teach these minilessons over time, you give students the opportunity to gain experience writing letters about their reading before introducing another new principle.

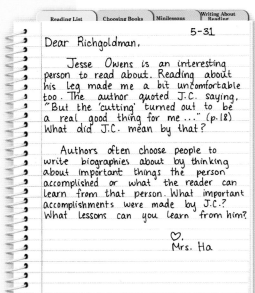

Managing Letters About Reading

Before introducing dialogue letters, think about how you will manage to read and respond to your students in a timely way. Some teachers assign groups of students to submit their letters on particular days of the week as shown in Figure 7-7. Many teachers find it more manageable to respond to five or six letters a day versus responding to the whole class at once. As the students write letters about reading, collect samples of quality letters that you might be able to share as examples in subsequent years to launch the writing of letters in your classroom.

We recommend that students work on their weekly letters during independent reading time. They can write their letters all at one time or over the course of two or three days. Monitor how long students are spending on writing versus reading to make sure they are dedicating enough time to both. However you choose to organize and manage this system, you will want to make sure it is feasible for both you and your students. It is critical that you are able to respond to the letters in a timely manner because students will quickly move on to new books and ask new questions about their reading.

You will find several other suggestions for helping students write thoughtful letters in Chapter 27 of our professional book, *Teaching for Comprehending and Fluency* (Fountas and Pinnell 2006).

Figure 7-7: To make reading and responding to students' letters manageable, set up a schedule so that only a few letters are due each day.

Letters Due

Monday	Tuesday	Wednesday	Thursday
Alonzo	Zimmie	Antonio	Ava
Jacob B.	Olivia S.	Cora	Carlos
Sofia	Liam	Owen	Elijah
Noah	Michael	Harper	Darius
Kiara	Anh	David	Jacob L.
Aiden	Lily	Olivia P.	Emma

Name Richgoldman _____ Date _____

Assessment of Letters in Reader's Notebook

Does the student share his personal response to the book?
—Expresses his opinion about information learned. Example: Shared a part of the book that made him uncomfortable and that he thinks Jessie Owens had a difficult early life
—Provide support for him to apply what he is learning to his own life

Does the student incorporate new ways of thinking about books from reading minilessons that have been taught?
UIZ Studying Biography
—thinking about the facts that the author decided to include; needs a little support in articulating why he thinks the author included them
—points out the subject's actions; needs support in articulating what that shows about the person's character
—has a beginning understanding of the author's message but does not explicitly state it

Does the student use standard writing conventions expected at this time in third grade [e.g., title and author's name spelled correctly, capitals, punctuation, spelling, legible handwriting]?
—Demonstrates mostly consistent capitalization and punctuation (needs support with commas)
—Spelling is mostly conventional (include "beginning" on his personal word study list)
—Needs support with possessives

Does the student use the format of a friendly letter for the response (date, greeting, body, closing, signature)?
—Consistently uses format of letter
—Need to teach him where to place commas in the greeting and closing
—Need to show him how to include multiple paragraphs, perhaps one answering questions from previous letter and one with new thinking

Figure 7-8: Use questions such as these to evaluate students' letters about their reading. To download the questions, visit **resources.fountasandpinnell.com**.

Chapter 8 | Putting Minilessons into Action: Assessing and Planning

As NOTED IN CHAPTER 2, the minilessons in this book are examples of teaching that address the specific bullets that list the behaviors and understandings to notice, teach for, and support in *The Literacy Continuum* (Fountas and Pinnell 2017c) for third grade. We have drawn from the sections on Interactive Read-Aloud, Shared Reading, Guided Reading, Writing About Reading, and Oral and Visual Communication to provide a comprehensive vision of what students need to become aware of, understand, and apply to their own literacy and learning. With such a range of important goals, how do you decide what to teach and when?

Deciding Which Reading Minilessons to Teach

To decide which reading minilessons to teach, first look at the students in front of you. Teach within what Vygotsky (1979) called the students' "zone of proximal development"—the zone between what the students can do independently and what they can do with the support of a more expert other. Teach on the cutting edge of students' competencies. Select topics for minilessons that address the needs of the majority of students in your class.

Think about what will be helpful to most readers based on your observations of their reading and writing behaviors. Here are some suggestions and tools to help you think about the students in your classroom:

▶ **Use *The Literacy Continuum*** (Fountas and Pinnell 2017c) to assess your students and observe how they are thinking, talking, and writing/drawing about books. Think about what they can already do, almost do, and not yet do to select the emphasis for your teaching. Look at the Selecting Goals pages in each section to guide your observations.

▶ **Use the Interactive Read-Aloud and Literature Discussion section.** Scan the Selecting Goals in this section and think about the ways you have noticed students thinking and talking about books.

▶ **Use the Writing About Reading section** to analyze how students are responding to texts in their drawing and writing. This analysis will help you determine possible next steps. Talking and writing about reading provides concrete evidence of students' thinking.

▶ **Use the Oral Language Continuum** to help you think about some of the routines your students might need for better communication between peers. You will find essential listening and speaking competencies to observe and teach.

▶ **Look for patterns in your anecdotal records.** Review the anecdotal notes you take during reading conferences, shared reading, guided reading, and book clubs to notice trends in students' responses and thinking. Use *The Literacy Continuum* to help you analyze the records and determine strengths and areas for growth across the classroom. Your observations will reveal what students know and what they need to learn next as they build knowledge over time. Each goal becomes a possible topic for a minilesson.

▶ **Consult district and state standards as a resource.** Analyze the suggested skills and areas of knowledge specified in your local and state standards. Align these standards with the minilessons suggested in this text to determine which might be applicable within your frameworks (see **fountasandpinnell.com/resourcelibrary** for an alignment of *The Literacy Continuum* with Common Core Standards).

▶ **Use the Assessment section after each umbrella.** Take time to assess student learning after the completion of each umbrella. Use the guiding questions on the last page of each umbrella to determine strengths and next steps for your students. This analysis can help you determine what minilessons to reteach if needed and what umbrella to teach next.

A Suggested Sequence

The suggested sequence of umbrellas, Minilessons Across the Year shown in Figure 8-2 (also downloadable from the online resources for record keeping), is intended to establish good classroom management early and work toward more sophisticated concepts across the year. Learning in minilessons is applied in many different situations and so is reinforced daily across the curriculum. Minilessons in this sequence are timed so they occur after students have had sufficient opportunities to build some explicit understandings as well as a great deal of implicit knowledge of aspects of written texts through interactive read-aloud and shared reading texts. In the community of readers, they have acted on texts through talk, writing, and extension through writing and art. These experiences have prepared them to fully engage in the reading minilesson and move from this shared experience to the application of the concepts in their independent reading.

The sequence of umbrellas in Minilessons Across the Year follows the suggested sequence of text sets in *Fountas & Pinnell Classroom™ Interactive Read-Aloud Collection*. If you are using this collection, you are invited to follow this sequence of texts. If you are not using it, the first page of each umbrella describes the types of books students will need to have read before you teach the minilessons. The text sets are grouped together by theme, topic, author, and genre, not by skill or concept. Thus, in many minilessons, you will use books from several different text sets, and you will see the same books used in more than one umbrella.

We have selected the most concrete and instructive examples from the recommended books. The umbrellas draw examples from text sets that have been read and enjoyed previously. In most cases, the minilessons draw on text sets that are introduced within the same month or at least in close proximity to the umbrella. However, in some cases, minilessons taught later, for example in month 8, might draw on texts introduced earlier in the year. Most of the time, students will have no problem recalling the events of these early books because you have read and discussed them thoroughly as a class. However, in some cases, you might want to quickly reread a book or a portion of it before teaching the umbrella so it is fresh in the students' minds.

If you are new to these minilessons, you may want to follow the suggested sequence, but remember to use the lessons flexibly to meet the needs of the students you teach:

▶ Omit lessons that you think are not necessary for your students (based on assessment and your experiences with them in interactive read-aloud).

▶ Repeat some lessons that you think need more time and instructional attention (based on observation of students across reading contexts).

▶ Repeat some lessons using different examples for a particularly rich experience.

▶ Move lessons around to be consistent with the curriculum that is adopted in your school or district.

The minilessons are here for your selection according to the instructional needs of your class, so do not be concerned if you do not use them all within the year. Record or check the minilessons you have taught so that you can reflect on the work of the semester and year. You can do this simply by downloading the minilessons record form (Figure 8-1) from online resources (resources.fountasandpinnell.com).

Figure 8-1: Download this record-keeping form to record the minilessons that you have taught and to make notes for future reference.

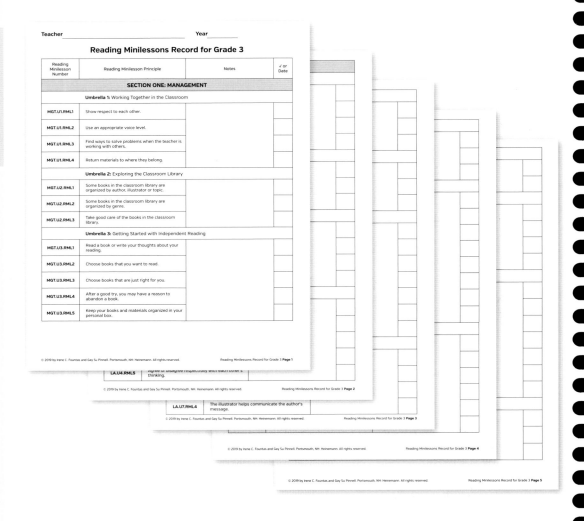

MINILESSONS ACROSS THE YEAR

Month	Recommended Umbrellas	Approximate Time
Month 1	**MGT U1:** Working Together in the Classroom	1 week
	MGT U2: Exploring the Classroom Library	0.5 week
	MGT U3: Getting Started with Independent Reading	1.5 weeks
	LA U1: Thinking and Talking About Books	1 week
	WAR U1: Introducing a Reader's Notebook	1 week
	LA U2: Studying Authors and Illustrators (RML1–RML2)	0.5 week
	Note: We recommend teaching these minilessons as part of an author study. The first lesson can be repeated each time an author/illustrator is studied. Teach the second lesson when applicable and the third lesson in the umbrella after students have experienced several author studies. If you are using the Fountas & Pinnell Classroom™ Interactive Read-Aloud Collection, *the first author study is Patricia Polacco.*	
Month 2	**LA U5:** Understanding Fiction and Nonfiction Genres (RML1–RML2)	0.5 week
	LA U3: Giving a Book Talk	1 week
	WAR U2: Using a Reader's Notebook	1 week
	LA U23: Understanding Character Feelings, Motivations, and Intentions	1 week
	LA U4: Getting Started with Book Clubs	2 weeks
Month 3	**WAR U3:** Writing Letters About Reading	2–3 weeks
	Note: We recommend teaching these lessons over two or three weeks. You may choose to introduce two or three new minilessons from the umbrella each time students begin a new weekly letter so they apply the new understandings over time to multiple letters. They do not have to be taught consecutively.	
	SAS U1: Monitoring, Searching, and Self-Correcting	0.5 week
	LA U11: Studying Informational Books	1 week
	LA U14: Thinking About the Topic in Nonfiction Books	1.5 weeks

K E Y

MGT	**Section One**	Management Minilessons
LA	**Section Two**	Literary Analysis Minilessons
SAS	**Section Three**	Strategies and Skills Minilessons
WAR	**Section Four**	Writing About Reading Minilessons

Figure 8-2: Use this chart as a guideline for planning your year with minilessons.

Month	Recommended Umbrellas	Approximate Time
Month 4	**WAR U5:** Writing About Nonfiction Books in a Reader's Notebook (RML1–RML3)	**1 week**
	LA U2: Studying Authors and Illustrators (RML1–RML2)	**1–2 days**
	Note: We recommend that you repeat the process described in RML1 each time you study a new author. If you are using the Fountas & Pinnell Classroom™ Interactive Read-Aloud Collection, *you might choose to study Janell Cannon.*	
	LA U22: Understanding Plot	**2 weeks**
	LA U21: Thinking About the Setting in Fiction Books	**1 week**
	WAR U4: Writing About Fiction Books in a Reader's Notebook (RML1–RML3)	**1 week**
Month 5	**LA U17:** Studying Realistic Fiction	**2 weeks**
	SAS U2: Solving Words	**1–2 weeks**
	Note: The minilessons in this umbrella can be taught consecutively or over time. Some teachers choose to coordinate the minilessons in this umbrella with their word study lessons. Others divide the umbrella in half and teach RML1–RML6 at one time and RML7–RML11 at another time. Choose the lessons and timing that will be most meaningful to your students based on their experiences with word study.	
	LA U24: Understanding Character Traits	**1 week**
	WAR U4: Writing About Fiction Books in a Reader's Notebook (RML5)	**1 day**
	LA U25: Thinking About Character Change	**0.5 week**
	WAR U4: Writing About Fiction Books in a Reader's Notebook (RML6)	**1 day**
Month 6	**LA U26:** Studying Illustrations in Fiction Books	**1.5 weeks**
	LA U12: Studying Biography	**1.5 weeks**
	WAR U5: Writing About Nonfiction Books in a Reader's Notebook (RML4)	**1 day**
	LA U2: Studying Authors and Illustrators (RML1–RML2)	
	Note: We recommend that you repeat the process described in RML1 each time you study a new author. If you are using the Fountas & Pinnell Classroom™ Interactive Read-Aloud Collection, *you might choose to study the work of Dianna Hutts Aston and Sylvia Long.*	**1–2 days**
	LA U9: Analyzing the Writer's Craft (RML1–RML4)	**1 week**

Month	Recommended Umbrellas	Approximate Time
Month 7	**SAS U3:** Maintaining Fluency	1.5 weeks
	LA U16: Using Text Features to Gain Information	1.5 weeks
	LA U13: Noticing How Authors Choose to Organize Nonfiction	0.5 week
	LA U15: Learning Information from Illustrations/Graphics	1 week
	WAR U5: Writing About Nonfiction Books in a Reader's Notebook (RML5–RML6)	2 days
Month 8	**LA U7:** Thinking About the Author's Message	1 week
	LA U8: Thinking About the Author's Purpose	0.5 weeks
	SAS U4: Summarizing	1 week
	Note: Teach this as an entire umbrella or teach the minilessons after corresponding literary analysis minilessons.	
	WAR U4: Writing About Fiction Books in a Reader's Notebook (RML4)	1 day
	WAR U5: Writing About Nonfiction Books in a Reader's Notebook (RML7)	1 day
	LA U18: Studying Fables	1 week
Month 9	**LA U19:** Studying Folktales	1.5 weeks
	WAR U4: Writing About Fiction Books in a Reader's Notebook (RML7)	1 week
	LA U10: Noticing Text Resources	1.5 weeks
	LA U20: Understanding Fantasy	1 week
Month 10	**LA U6:** Studying Poetry	1 week
	LA U9: Analyzing the Writer's Craft (RML5–RML8)	1 week
	LA U5: Understanding Fiction and Nonfiction Genres (RML3)	1 day
	LA U2: Studying Authors and Illustrators (RML1, RML3)	2 days

Chapter 9

Reading Minilessons Within a Multitext Approach to Literacy Learning

THIS COLLECTION OF 200 LESSONS for third grade is embedded within an integrated set of instructional approaches that build an awareness of classroom routines, literary characteristics, strategies and skills, and ways of writing about written texts. In Figure 9-8, this comprehensive, multitext approach is represented, along with the central role of minilessons. Note that students' processing systems are built across instructional contexts so that students can read increasingly complex texts independently. Our book *The Literacy Quick Guide: A Reference Tool for Responsive Literacy Teaching* (Fountas and Pinnell 2018) provides concise descriptions of these instructional contexts. In this chapter, we will look at how the reading minilessons fit within this multitext approach and provide a balance between implicit and explicit teaching that allows for authentic response and promotes the enjoyment of books.

Throughout this chapter we describe how to build the shared literary knowledge of your classroom community, embedding implicit and explicit teaching with your use of intentional conversation and specific points of instructional value to set a foundation for explicit teaching in reading minilessons. All of the teaching in minilessons is reinforced in shared reading, guided reading, and book clubs, with all pathways leading to the goal of effective independent reading.

Let's look at the range of research-based instructional contexts that comprise an effective literacy design.

Interactive Read-Aloud

Interactive read-aloud provides the highest level of teacher support for students as they experience a complex, grade-appropriate text. Carefully select sets of high-quality students' literature, fiction and nonfiction, and read them aloud to students. We use the word *interactive* because talk is a salient characteristic of this instructional context. You do the reading but pause to invite student discussion in pairs, in triads, or as a whole group at selected points. After the reading, students engage in a lively discussion. Finally, you invite students to revisit specific points in the text for deeper learning and may provide further opportunities for responding to the text through writing, drama, movement, or art.

We recommend that you read aloud from high-quality, organized text sets, which you use across the year. A text set contains several titles that are related in some conceptual way, for example:

▶ Author   ▶ Topic

▶ Illustrator   ▶ Theme or big idea

▶ Genre   ▶ Format (such as graphic texts)

When you use books organized in text sets, you can support students in making connections across a related group of texts and in engaging them in deeper thinking about texts. All students benefit from the use of preselected

ELL CONNECTION

Figure 9-1: Interactive read-aloud in a third-grade class

sets, but these connected texts are particularly supportive for English language learners. Text sets allow students to develop vocabulary around a particular theme, genre, or topic. This shared collection of familiar texts and the shared vocabulary developed through the talk provides essential background knowledge that all students will be able to apply during subsequent reading minilessons.

The key to success with reading minilessons is providing the intentional instruction in interactive read-aloud that will, first, enable the students to enjoy and come to love books and, second, build a foundation of shared understandings about texts within a community of readers and writers.

If you are using *Fountas & Pinnell Classroom™*, you will notice that we have used examples from *Interactive Read-Aloud Collection* as the mentor texts in the minilessons. If you do not have the texts from *Fountas & Pinnell Classroom™*, select read-aloud texts with the same characteristics (described at the beginning of each umbrella) to read well ahead of the minilessons and use the lessons as organized and presented in this book. Simply substitute the particular texts you selected. You can draw on any texts you have already read and discussed with your students as long as the genre is appropriate for the set of minilessons and the ideas can be connected. For example, if you are going to teach a set of minilessons about characters, pull examples from fiction stories rather than nonfiction books and include engaging characters. If you are reading rich literature in various genres to your students, the chances are high that many of the types of reading behaviors or understandings you are teaching for in reading minilessons can be applied to those texts.

At the beginning of each umbrella (set of related minilessons), you will find a section titled "Before Teaching Minilessons," which offers guidance

Figure 9-2: Examples of preselected text sets from *Fountas & Pinnell Classroom™ Interactive Read-Aloud Collection*

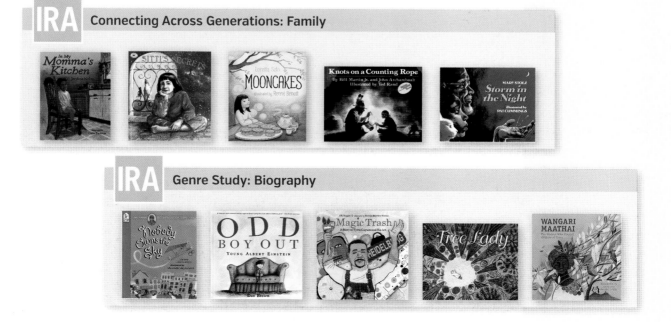

Books We've Shared

Last Day Blues by Julie Danneburg

Sophie's Masterpiece by Eileen Spinelli

The Can Man by Laura E. Williams

Mooncakes by Loretta Seto

Storm in the Night by Mary Stolz

I Love Guinea Pigs by Dick King-Smith

The Keeping Quilt by Patricia Polacco

The Bee Tree by Patricia Polacco

Tornados by Gail Gibbons

Knights in Shining Armor by Gail Gibbons

Bats! Strange and Wonderful by Laurence Pringle

Stellaluna by Janell Cannon

Figure 9-3: Keep a list of books that you have shared with your students as a record of shared literary knowledge.

in the use of interactive read-aloud as a prelude to teaching the explicit minilessons in the umbrella. It is important to note that the texts in a text set can be used for several different umbrellas. In general, text sets are connected with each other in particular ways so students can think about concepts across texts and notice literary characteristics during read-aloud lessons. But the texts have multiple uses. When you complete reading the books in a set, you will have provided students with a rich, connected set of literacy experiences that include both explicitly taught and implicitly understood concepts. Then, you have a rich resource from which you can select examples to use as mentor texts in minilessons. We have selected examples across sets. Rich, literary texts can be used for multiple types of lessons, so you will see many of the same, familiar texts referenced throughout the reading minilessons. Each time a text is used for a different focus, students have a chance to view it with new eyes and see it differently. Usually, texts are not reread in entirety during a minilesson. They are already known because of the rich and deep experiences in your classroom. The result is shared literary knowledge for the class. In minilessons, they are revisited briefly with a particular focus. It is most powerful to select examples from texts that students have heard in their *recent* experience. But, you can always revisit favorites that you read at the very beginning of the year. When texts have been enjoyed and loved in interactive read-aloud, students know them deeply and can remember them over time. It is helpful to keep an ongoing list of books read during interactive read-aloud so you and your students can reference them throughout the year (see Figure 9-3). Here are some steps to follow for incorporating your own texts into the minilessons:

1. Identify a group of read-aloud texts that will be valuable resources for use in the particular minilesson. (These texts may be from the same text set, but usually they are drawn from several different sets. The key is their value in teaching routines, engaging in literary analysis, building particular strategies and skills, or writing about reading.)

2. The mentor texts you select will usually be some that you have already read to and discussed with the students; but if not, read and discuss them with the goal of enjoyment and understanding. The emphasis in interactive

read-aloud is not on the minilesson principle but on enjoying and deeply understanding the text, appreciating the illustrations and design, and constructing an understanding of the deeper messages of the text.

3. Teach the reading minilesson as designed, substituting the texts you have chosen and read to the students.

Interactive read-aloud will greatly benefit your English language learners. In *Fountas & Pinnell Classroom™*, we have selected the texts with English language learners in mind and recommend that you do the same if you are selecting texts from your existing resources. In addition to expanding both listening and speaking vocabularies, interactive read-aloud provides constant exposure to English language syntax. Stories read aloud provide "ear print" for the students. Hearing grammatical structures of English over and over helps English language learners form an implicit knowledge of the rules. Here are some other considerations for your English language learners:

▶ Increase the frequency of your interactive read-alouds.

▶ Choose books that have familiar themes and concepts and take into account the cultural backgrounds of all the students in your classroom.

▶ Reread texts that your English language learners enjoy. Rereading texts that students especially enjoy will help them acquire and make use of language that goes beyond their current understanding.

▶ Choose texts that are simple and have high picture support. This will allow you to later revisit concrete examples from these texts during reading minilessons.

▶ Seat English language learners in places where they can easily see, hear, and participate in the text.

▶ Preview the text with English language learners by holding a small-group discussion before reading the book to the entire class. As they hear it the second time, they will understand more and will have had the experience of talking. This will encourage the students to participate more actively during the discussion.

When you provide a rich and supportive experience through interactive read-aloud, you prepare English language learners for a successful experience in reading minilessons. They will bring the vocabulary and background knowledge developed in interactive read-aloud to the exploration of the reading minilesson principle. These multiple layers of support will pave the road to successful independent reading.

Shared Reading

In shared reading, use an enlarged text, either fiction or nonfiction. Read the text to the students and then invite them to read a part of the text or the whole text in unison. Have students reread the text several times until they know it well, and then you have the option of revisiting it for different purposes (for example, to locate content words, practice fluency, or connect words with similar word parts or punctuation) and to extend the meaning through writing, art, or drama.

Like the texts in interactive read-aloud, shared reading texts offer students the opportunity to understand and discuss characters, events, concepts, and ideas. In addition, an enlarged text offers the advantage of making print, layout, and punctuation available to the readers because all can see them clearly.

You will find that some minilessons in this book refer to shared reading examples from *Fountas & Pinnell Classroom*™. If you do not have access to these resources, you can easily use the lessons in this book by collecting your own set of shared reading books and/or using a document camera to show pages of an appropriate book. Simply substitute the texts you select.

At the beginning of each umbrella, you will find a short section titled "Before Teaching Minilessons," which will have suggestions for the teaching needed prior to your use of the umbrella. Here are some steps to follow for incorporating your own shared reading texts into the minilessons:

1. Prior to implementing a lesson, select a group of books that are appropriate for teaching the principle. Use the examples in the lesson as a guide. The books may be some that you have previously read and built lessons around.

2. Engage students in a shared reading of each book that is not familiar to them. Shared reading books are designed for repeated readings, so plan to reread each several times. (Use your own judgment. Sometimes two or three readings are sufficient.) Remember, the focus is on understanding and enjoying the enlarged text, not on a specific principle.

3. Revisit the book to do some specific teaching toward any of the systems of strategic actions listed in *The Literacy Continuum* (Fountas and Pinnell 2017c). As an option, give students opportunities to respond to the text through writing, art, or drama.

4. Implement the reading minilesson as designed using the texts you have used in teaching.

In lessons using shared reading texts, students have had opportunities to notice print and how it works and to practice fluent reading. They have located individual words and noticed the use of bold and sound words.

They have learned how to use the meaning, language, and print together to process the text fluently. In addition, here, too, they noticed characteristics of the genre, the characters, and the message anchors.

Shared reading can also be important in reinforcing students' ability to apply understandings from the minilesson. You can revisit the texts to remind students of the minilesson principle and invite them to notice text characteristics or engage strategic actions to process them. When you work across texts, you help students apply understandings in many contexts.

Shared reading provides a supportive environment for English language learners to both hear and produce English language structures and patterns. Familiar shared reading texts often have repeated or rhythmic text, which is easy to learn. Using shared reading texts to teach strategies and skills minilessons can be particularly supportive for English language learners because they have had the opportunity to develop familiarity with the meaning, the vocabulary, and the language structures of the text. They can focus on exploring the minilesson principle because they are not working so hard to read and understand the text. Shared reading gives them the background and familiarity with text that makes it possible for them to easily learn the minilesson principle.

Shared reading is a context that is particularly supportive to English language learners because of the enjoyable repetition and opportunity to "practice" English syntax with the support of the group. Following are some suggestions you can use to support English language learners:

▶ Select enlarged texts with simple illustrations.

▶ Select enlarged texts with easy-to-say refrains, often involving rhyme and repeating patterns.

▶ Reread the book as much as needed to help students become confident in joining in.

ELL CONNECTION

Figure 9-4: Shared reading in a third-grade class

- Use some texts that lend themselves to inserting students' names or adding repetitive verses.
- Meet in a small group so learners can get "hands-on" experience pointing to words and pictures.

Guided Reading

Guided reading is small-group instruction using an appropriately selected leveled text that is at students' instructional level. This means that the text is more complex than the students can process independently, so it offers appropriate challenge.

Supportive and precise instruction with the text enables the students to read it with proficiency, and in the process they develop in-the-head strategic actions that they can apply to the reading of other texts. Guided reading involves several steps:

1. Assess students' strengths through the analysis of oral reading behaviors as well as the assessment of comprehension—thinking within, beyond, and about the text. This knowledge enables you to determine an appropriate reading level for instruction.

2. Bring together a small group of students who are approximately at the same level, so it makes sense to teach them together. (Ongoing assessment takes place in the form of running records or reading records so that the information can guide the emphasis in lessons and so that groups may be changed and reformed as needed.)

3. Based on assessment, select a text that is at students' instructional level and offers opportunities for new learning.

4. Introduce the text to the students in a way that will support reading and engage them with the text.

Figure 9-5: Guided reading in a third-grade class

5. Students read the text individually. (In third grade, this usually means reading silently without pointing to the words. You may choose to hear several students read softly to you so you can check on their processing.) Support reading through quick interactions that use precise language to support effective processing.

6. Invite students to engage in an open-ended discussion of the text and use some guiding questions or prompts to help them extend their thinking.

7. Based on previous assessment and observation during reading, select a teaching point.

8. Engage students in quick word work that helps them flexibly apply principles for solving words that that have been selected based on information gained from the analysis of oral reading behaviors and reinforcement of principles explored in phonics minilessons (see *The Fountas & Pinnell Comprehensive Phonics, Spelling, and Word Study Guide* [2017b] and *Fountas & Pinnell Word Study System, Grade 3* [2019]).

9. As an option, you may have students engage in writing about the book to extend their understanding, but it is not necessary—or desirable—to write about every book.

Guided reading texts are not usually used as examples in minilessons because they are not texts that are shared by the entire class. You can, however, take the opportunity to reinforce the minilesson principle across the guided reading lesson at one or more points:

▶ In the introduction to the text, refer to a reading minilesson principle as one of the ways that you support readers before reading a new text.

▶ In your interactions with students during the reading of the text, remind them of the principle from the reading minilesson.

▶ In the discussion after the text, reinforce the minilesson principle when appropriate.

▶ In the teaching point, reinforce a minilesson principle.

In small-group guided reading lessons, students explore aspects of written texts that are similar to the understandings they discuss in interactive read-aloud and shared reading. They notice characters and character change, talk about where the story takes place, talk about the problem in the story and the ending, and discuss the lesson or message of the story. They talk about information they learned and questions they have, they notice genre characteristics, and they develop phonics knowledge and word-solving strategies. So, guided reading also gives readers the opportunity to apply what they have learned in reading minilessons.

When you support readers in applying the minilesson principle within a guided reading lesson, you give them another opportunity to talk about text with this new thinking in mind. It is particularly helpful to English language learners to have the opportunity to try out this new thinking in a small, safe setting. Guided reading can provide the opportunity to talk about the minilesson principle before the class comes back together to share. Often, students feel more confident about sharing their new thinking with the whole group because they have had this opportunity to practice talking about their book in the small-group setting.

Book Clubs

For a book club meeting, bring together a small group of students who have chosen the same book to read and discuss with their classmates. The book can be one that you have read to the group or one that the students can either read independently or listen to and understand from an audio recording.

The implementation of book clubs follows these steps:

1. Preselect about four books that offer opportunities for deep discussion. These books may be related in some way (for example, they might be by the same author or feature stories around a theme). Or, they might just be a group of titles that will give students good choices.

2. Give a book talk about each of the books to introduce them to students. A book talk is a short "commercial" for the book.

3. Students read and prepare for the book club discussion. If the student cannot read the book, prepare an audio version that can be used during independent reading time. Each reader marks a place or places that he wants to discuss with a sticky note.

4. Convene the group and facilitate the discussion.

5. The students self-evaluate the discussion.

Figure 9-6: Book club in a third-grade class

Even third-grade students have much to learn about participating in a book discussion group. Book clubs provide the opportunity for deep, enjoyable talk with their classmates about books. In this book, one entire umbrella is devoted to teaching the routines of book clubs (see Umbrella 4: Getting Started with Book Clubs in Section Two: Literary Analysis).

A discussion among four or five diverse third-grade students can go in many directions, and you want to hear all of their ideas! *Prompting Guide, Part 2, for Comprehension: Thinking, Talking, and Writing* (Fountas and Pinnell 2016) is a helpful tool. The section on book discussions contains precise teacher language for getting a discussion started, asking for thinking, affirming thinking, agreeing and disagreeing, changing thinking, clarifying thinking, extending thinking, focusing on the big ideas, making connections, paraphrasing, questioning and hypothesizing, redirecting, seeking evidence, sharing thinking, and summarizing.

To help the students learn how to hold book club discussions, consider using the fishbowl technique. Before you teach the minilesson, prepare one group of students to model the minilesson concept. During the minilesson, seat those students in the center and the rest of the students in a ring around them so that they can see and hear what is going on.

 **ELL CONNECTION**

Book clubs offer English language learners the unique opportunity of entering into conversations about books with other students. If they have listened to an audio recording many times, they are gaining more and more exposure to language. The language and content of the book lifts the conversation and gives them something to talk about. They learn the conventions of discourse, which become familiar because they do it many times. They can hear others talk and respond with social language, such as "I agree with _____."

Independent Reading

In independent reading, students have the opportunity to apply all they have learned in minilessons. To support independent reading, assemble a well-organized classroom library with a range of engaging fiction and nonfiction books. Although you will take into account the levels students can read independently to assure a range of options, we do *not* suggest that you arrange the books by level. It is not productive and can be destructive for the students to choose books by "level." Instead, create tubs or baskets by author, topic, genre, and so forth. There are minilessons in Section One: Management to help you teach third graders how to choose books for their own reading (see Umbrella 2: Exploring the Classroom Library).

Students choose books from the classroom library to keep in their individual book bags. Consider the following as you develop these resources.

▶ **Personal Boxes.** A personal box is where students keep their materials (e.g., reader's notebook, writer's notebook, writing folder, books to read) all together and organized. A magazine or cereal box works well. Students can label the boxes with their names and decorate them. Management minilesson RML5 (see Umbrella 3: Getting Started with Independent Reading) provides guidance on setting up the box and keeping it organized. Keep these boxes in a central place so that students can retrieve them during independent reading time.

▶ **Classroom Library.** The classroom library is filled with baskets or tubs of books that third-grade students will love. Books are organized by topic, theme, genre, series, or author. Have students help you organize the books so that they share some ownership of the library. Shared reading books, too, are good resources in the classroom library. In some minilessons, there is a direction to guide students to read from a particular basket in the classroom library so they have the opportunity to apply the reading minilesson to books that include the characteristics addressed in the minilesson. For example, you might have them read from a particular genre or author set.

In some cases, you may find it helpful to compile browsing boxes for some students as an alternative source for independent reading. This might be particularly important for students who find it difficult to choose just-right books from the classroom library. A browsing box can include previously read guided reading books, small versions of shared reading books, or books at lower levels. The box or basket can be identified by a color or other means. During independent reading, students select books from a browsing box that has books to suit their needs. The book choices should change along with students' progress.

Figure 9-7: The goal of all literacy teaching is effective independent reading.

Becoming independent as a reader is an essential life skill for all students. English language learners need daily opportunities to use their systems of strategic actions on text that is accessible, meaningful, and interesting to them. Here are some suggestions for helping English language learners during independent reading:

▶ Make sure your classroom library has a good selection of books at a range of levels. If possible, provide books in the first language of your students as well as books with familiar settings and themes.

▶ During individual conferences, help students prepare—and sometimes rehearse—something that they can share with others about the text during group share. When possible, ask them to think about the minilesson principle.

▶ Provide opportunities for English language learners to share with partners before being asked to share with the whole group.

Combining Implicit and Explicit Teaching for Independent Reading

You are about to embark on a highly productive year of literacy lessons. We have prepared these lessons as tools for your use as you help students engage with texts, making daily shifts in learning. When students participate in a classroom that provides a multitext approach to literacy learning, they are exposed to textual elements in a variety of instructional contexts. As described in Figure 9-8, all of these instructional contexts involve embedding literary and print concepts into authentic and meaningful experiences with text. A powerful combination of many concepts are implicitly understood as students engage with books, but the explicit teaching brings them to conscious awareness and supports students' ability to articulate the concepts using academic language.

In interactive read-aloud, students are invited to respond to text as they turn and talk and participate in lively discussions after a text is read. In interactive read-aloud, you support your students to think within, beyond, and about the text because you will have used *The Literacy Continuum* to identify when you will pause and invite these conversations and how you will ask questions and model comments to support the behaviors you have selected. They experience and articulate deeper thinking about texts.

Figure 9-8: Text experiences are supported and developed by implicit and explicit teaching in all instructional contexts, including interactive read-aloud, shared reading, guided reading, book clubs, and independent reading conferences. Reading minilessons provide explicit teaching that makes learning visible and is reinforced in the other contexts.

In shared reading, students learn from both implicit and explicit teaching. They first read and discuss the text several times, enjoying the book and discussing aspects of the text that support their thinking within, beyond, and about the text. Teachers often revisit the text with an explicit focus that supports thinking within the text (e.g., gathering information from diagrams or infographics, rereading dialogue with expression). The embedded, implicit teaching, as well as some of the more explicit teaching that students experience in shared reading, lays the groundwork for the explicit teaching that takes place in reading minilessons. Reading minilessons become the bridge from these shared and interactive whole-group reading experiences to independent reading.

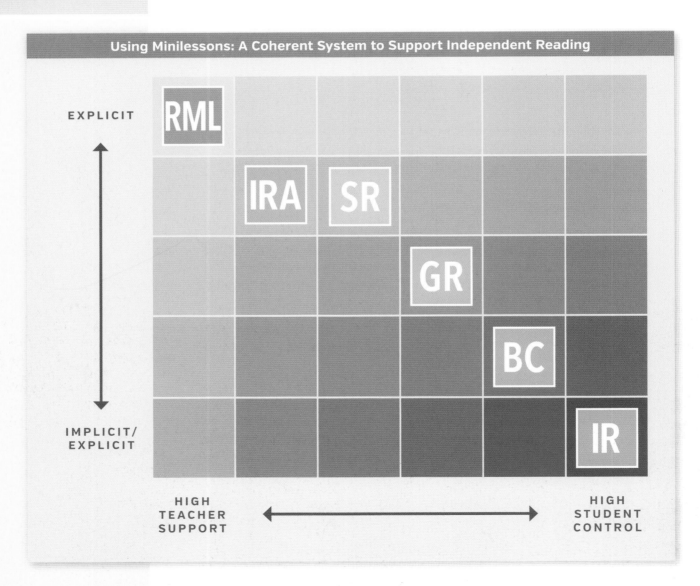

Guided reading and book clubs scaffold the reading process through a combination of implicit and explicit teaching that helps students apply the reading minilesson principles across a variety of instructional-level texts. The group share reinforces the whole process. Reading minilessons do not function in the absence of these other instructional contexts; rather, they all work in concert to build processing systems for students to grow in their ability to independently read increasingly complex texts over time.

The minilessons in this book serve as a guide to a meaningful, systematic approach to joyful, literacy learning across multiple reading contexts. Students acquire a complex range of understandings. Whole-class minilessons form the "glue" that connects all of this learning, makes it explicit, and turns it over to the students to apply it to their own independent reading and writing. You will find that the talk and learning in those shared experiences will bring your class together as a community with a shared knowledge base. We know that you and your students will enjoy the rich experiences as you engage together in thinking, talking, and responding to a treasure chest of beautiful books. Students deserve these rich opportunities—every child, every day.

Figure 9-9: A rich array of books provides the basis of shared literary knowledge for the community of readers in your classroom.

Works Cited

Clay, Marie. 2015 [1991]. *Becoming Literate: The Construction of Inner Control*. Auckland, NZ: Global Education Systems.

Fountas, Irene C., and Gay Su Pinnell. 2006. *Teaching for Comprehending and Fluency*. Portsmouth, NH: Heinemann.

———. 2011. *Reader's Notebook: Intermediate*. Portsmouth, NH: Heinemann.

———. 2012a. *Fountas & Pinnell Prompting Guide, Part 1, for Oral Reading and Early Writing*. Portsmouth, NH: Heinemann.

———. 2012b. *Fountas & Pinnell Prompting Guide for Fiction*. Portsmouth, NH: Heinemann.

———. 2012c. *Fountas & Pinnell Prompting Guide for Nonfiction, Poetry, and Test Taking*. Portsmouth, NH: Heinemann.

———. 2012d. *Genre Study: Teaching with Fiction and Nonfiction Books*. Portsmouth, NH: Heinemann.

———. 2016. *Fountas & Pinnell Prompting Guide, Part 2, for Comprehension: Thinking, Talking, and Writing*. Portsmouth, NH: Heinemann.

———. 2017a. *Fountas & Pinnell Classroom™*. Portsmouth, NH: Heinemann.

———. 2017b. *The Fountas & Pinnell Comprehensive Phonics, Spelling, and Word Study Guide*. Portsmouth, NH: Heinemann.

———. 2017c. *The Fountas & Pinnell Literacy Continuum: A Tool for Assessment, Planning, and Teaching*. Portsmouth, NH: Heinemann.

———. 2017d. *Guided Reading: Responsive Teaching Across the Grades*. Portsmouth, NH: Heinemann.

———. 2018. *The Literacy Quick Guide: A Reference Tool for Responsive Literacy Teaching*. Portsmouth, NH: Heinemann.

———. 2019. *Fountas and Pinnell Word Study System, Grade 3*. Portsmouth, NH: Heinemann.

Munson, Derek. 2000. *Enemy Pie*. San Francisco, CA: Chronicle Books.

Vygotsky, Lev. 1979. *Mind in Society: The Development of Higher Psychological Processes*. Cambridge, MA: Harvard University Press.

Section 1 | Management

Management minilessons focus on routines for thinking and talking about reading and working together in the classroom. These lessons allow you to teach effectively and efficiently. They are directed toward the creation of an orderly, busy classroom in which students know what is expected as well as how to behave responsibly and respectfully within a community of learners. Most of the minilessons at the beginning of the school year will focus on management.

1 | Management

Minilessons in This Umbrella

RML1   Show respect to each other.

RML2   Use an appropriate voice level.

RML3   Find ways to solve problems when the teacher is working with others.

RML4   Return materials to where they belong.

Before Teaching Umbrella 1 Minilessons

The purpose of this umbrella is to help you maintain a respectful, efficient, and organized classroom community. The establishment of rituals and routines supports students' ability to function as responsible members of the classroom. While teaching these routines explicitly, it is important also to incorporate opportunities to read aloud and talk about books. Read books from your library or use books from the *Fountas & Pinnell Classroom™ Interactive Read-Aloud Collection* about friendship and family to discuss what it means to be part of a caring and considerate community. Create a warm and inviting student-centered classroom in which students can take ownership of their space and materials.

▶ Designate a whole-group meeting area where the class gathers to think and learn together.

▶ Post a daily schedule so students know what to expect each day.

▶ Find appropriate places throughout the classroom to house materials and supplies.

▶ Organize and label the containers or shelves where materials are stored.

▶ Allow many opportunities for students to browse for and choose books.

▶ Set up a regular time each day for students to read books they choose from an organized, inviting classroom library.

Section 1: Management

Reading Minilesson Principle
Show respect to each other.

Working Together in the Classroom

You Will Need

- chart paper and markers

Academic Language / Important Vocabulary

- respect

Goal

Explore and define what it means to show respect to each other.

Rationale

When you engage students in discussing ways to show respect to each other, they become conscious of their behavior and ways to improve it. When they are active participants in creating a list of guidelines for being respectful, they take ownership of the guidelines and are more likely to follow them.

Assess Learning

Observe students when they interact with each other. Notice if there is evidence of new learning based on the goal of this minilesson.

- Do students behave respectfully toward each other?
- Can they talk about ways to show respect to each other?
- Do they understand the word *respect* and use it correctly?

Minilesson

To help students think about the minilesson principle, engage them in discussing and making a list of ways to show respect. Here is an example.

- Write the word *respect* in large letters on chart paper. Say the word aloud.

  Raise your hand if you've seen or heard this word before.

  What do you think it means?

- Invite several students to share their ideas.

  When you show respect for someone, you treat them in a way that shows you care about them and their feelings. What are some ways you can show respect for your classmates?

- Make a list of students' responses on the chart paper. If students have trouble generating ideas, prompt them with questions such as the following:

  - *How should you act when one of your classmates is speaking?*

  - *What words should you use if someone does something nice for you? What words should you use if you want someone to help you or do something for you?*

  - *What can you do to make sure that other people's feelings do not get hurt?*

  - *What should you do if several of you want to read the same book or use something, but there's only one of that thing?*

  - *How should you act when it's time to read a book alone or work on an activity alone? How can you help your classmates do their best work?*

Have a Try

Invite the students to talk with a partner about respect.

> Can you think of other ways you can show respect for each other? Turn and talk to your partner about anything else you think we should add to our list.

▶ Ask a few pairs to share their thinking, and add new suggestions to the list.

Summarize and Apply

Summarize the learning and remind students to show respect for each other.

▶ Reread and review the list.

> Why is it important to show respect to your classmates?

> When you show respect, you help everyone do their best work.

> After you read a book today, you're going to talk about the book with a few of your classmates. Think about ways you can show respect when you are talking in a group about the book you read.

Share

Following independent reading time, gather students together in groups of three or four to talk about their reading.

▶ Have students share a little bit about their books in small groups. Then bring the groups together.

> How did you show respect to the others in your group when you talked about the books you read? Can you give an example?

Extend the Lesson (Optional)

After assessing students' understanding, you might decide to extend the learning.

▶ Display the list of respectful behaviors, and regularly review and add to it. Positively reinforce behavior when they act respectfully, and remind them of the list when they do not.

▶ Read aloud and discuss books that focus on respect. Help students identify examples of behaviors that show respect in books they read. Discuss how the lessons in the books can be applied to students' lives.

RESPECT

- Be nice to each other.
- Say "please" and "thank you."
- Help each other.
- Share.
- Take turns.
- Listen carefully when someone else is speaking.
- Be silent during independent reading and other quiet activities. (0 voice)
- Stay focused on your work.

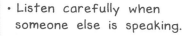
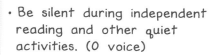

please

thank you

Section 1: Management

Reading Minilesson Principle
Use an appropriate voice level.

Working Together in the Classroom

You Will Need

- a familiar book from your classroom library
- chart paper and markers

Academic Language / Important Vocabulary

- voice level
- volume
- appropriate

Continuum Connection

- Speak at an appropriate volume (p. 335)

Goal

Learn to manage voice levels.

Rationale

When you teach students appropriate voice levels for different settings, they learn to independently determine which voice level to use and modulate their voices accordingly.

Assess Learning

Observe students when they use their voices in different settings. Notice if there is evidence of new learning based on the goal of this minilesson.

- Can students explain which voice level is appropriate for a particular situation?
- Do they adjust their voice levels according to the situation?
- Do they understand the terms *voice level*, *volume*, and *appropriate*?

Minilesson

To help students think about the minilesson principle, engage them in discussing voice levels and creating a reference chart. Here is an example.

- Demonstrate reading a book silently for a few moments.

    What did you notice about my voice while I read?

    My voice was silent while I read. When your voice is silent, your voice level is 0.

- Write *0 silent* and *reading alone* on chart paper.

    Reading alone is a time when you need to use voice level 0. What are other times when you should use voice level 0?

- Record students' responses on the chart.

- Invite a student (who may have been prepared beforehand) to sit with you and quietly talk about the book you were reading.

    What did you notice about our voice level? What type of voice did we use when we talked about the book?

    When you are talking with me privately, you should use a soft voice, which is voice level 1.

- Write *1 quiet voice* and *talking with the teacher* on the chart paper. Ask students for other examples of times when they should use a soft voice, and add to the chart.

    What kind of voice should you use when we're talking together as a class? What do you notice about my voice right now?

▶ Add 2 *strong voice* and *whole class* to the chart. Elicit other examples from students.

Have a Try

Invite the students to talk with a partner about using an outside voice.

▶ Write *3 outside voice* on the chart.

> When is it appropriate to use a loud or outside voice at school? Turn and talk about that.

▶ Ask a few pairs to share their thinking. Add students' suggestions, if appropriate, to the chart.

Summarize and Apply

Summarize the learning and remind students to use a voice level appropriate for their activities.

▶ Reread and review the chart.

> When you use an appropriate voice level, others will not be distracted and will be able to do their best work.

▶ Write the minilesson principle at the top of the chart.

> When you read today, what voice level will you use? After you read, bring your book to share. You can show the book in a small group and use an appropriate voice level.

Share

Following independent reading time, gather students together in the meeting area to talk about their reading in groups of three. After small groups, have a whole-class discussion.

> What voice level did you use when you were reading?

> What voice level did you use when you were talking in a small group?

Extend the Lesson (Optional)

After assessing students' understanding, you might decide to extend the learning.

▶ Display the voice level chart in the classroom. Review it regularly, or as needed.

Use an appropriate voice level.

0	1	2	3
Silent	Quiet Voice	Strong Voice	Outside Voice
• Reading alone • Working alone • Listening when someone else is talking • Taking a test	• Talking with the teacher • Working with a partner • Talking in a small group	• Whole class • Class meetings	• Playground

RML 3
MGT.U1.RML3

Reading Minilesson Principle
Find ways to solve problems when the teacher is working with others.

Working Together in the Classroom

You Will Need

▸ chart paper and markers

Academic Language / Important Vocabulary

▸ problem
▸ solve
▸ emergency

Goal

Learn how to problem solve independently.

Rationale

When you teach students different ways to problem solve on their own, they become more independent and confident, allowing you more time to work with small groups or with individual students.

Assess Learning

Observe students as they work independently and problem solve. Notice if there is evidence of new learning based on the goal of this minilesson.

▸ Can students explain ways to solve different kinds of problems?

▸ Do they attempt to solve most everyday problems on their own?

▸ Do they understand the words *problem*, *solve*, and *emergency*?

Minilesson

To help students think about the minilesson principle, engage them in a discussion about how to problem solve independently, so you can work with a small group without interruption. Here is an example.

> Sometimes I need to work with a small group, and it's important that the group is not interrupted. You might have a problem when you are working. Sometimes you might need to ask an adult for help, but other times you can solve your problems on your own.

> What are some problems you might have in our classroom?

▸ As students suggest ideas, ask other students how each problem might be solved. If students have trouble generating ideas, prompt them with questions such as the following:

- *What can you do if you don't know what activity to do next?*
- *What can you do if you don't know where to find the materials you need?*
- *What can you do if you don't understand something you're reading?*

▸ Record the problems and solutions students suggest on chart paper.

> Although there are many problems you can solve on your own, sometimes there are emergencies. When there is an emergency, you need to come to another adult or me right away, no matter what we're doing. What types of problems are emergencies?

▸ Ensure students understand they need to speak to an adult right away in an emergency, such as illness or injury.

Have a Try

Invite the students to discuss a problem with a partner.

▶ Propose a problem you haven't discussed, and ask students to talk with a partner about possible solutions. Here is an example.

> What do you think you should do if you finish your work early and don't know what to do next? Turn and talk to your partner about how you could solve this problem.

▶ After students turn and talk, ask a few pairs to share their thinking. Record suggested solutions on the chart.

Summarize and Apply

Summarize the learning and remind students to try to solve problems on their own.

> What did you learn about working in our classroom?

> You made a list of different problems you might have yourself and ways you might solve them.

▶ Write the minilesson principle at the top of the chart.

> Why is it important to try to solve problems instead of asking me for help when you have a problem?

> Whenever you have a problem, try to solve it yourself before you ask for help—unless it's an emergency. You can look at the chart for ideas about how to solve it.

Share

Following independent reading time, gather students together in the meeting area to discuss their problem solving.

> Who had a problem today and solved it?

> What was your problem? How did you solve it?

Extend the Lesson (Optional)

After assessing students' understanding, you might decide to extend the learning.

▶ Display the chart and remind students to refer to it when they have a problem. Positively reinforce students' behavior when they solve a problem.

▶ Review the chart occasionally and ask students if they have thought of new problems and solutions they would like to add.

Find ways to solve problems when the teacher is working with others.

Problem	Solution
• You don't understand what you're supposed to be doing.	• Reread the directions. • Ask a friend to help you.
• You don't understand something you're reading.	• Reread the words.
• You don't know where to find something.	• Look for a basket with the right label on it. **Animals**
• You have a problem with another student.	• Talk to the person about how you feel and try to find a solution together.
• You finish your work early.	• Review your work and then read, write, or draw at your table silently.

Reading Minilesson Principle
Return materials to where they belong.

Working Together in the Classroom

You Will Need

▶ a student who has been prepared beforehand to demonstrate

▶ various materials such as paper, pencils, markers, scissors, and a glue stick

▶ chart paper and markers

Academic Language / Important Vocabulary

▶ return

▶ materials

Goal

Learn to return supplies and materials independently.

Rationale

When you teach students to return materials to where they belong, they learn to be more independent and also to consider needs of others. The organization and care of materials foster a positive learning environment for everyone.

Assess Learning

Observe students when they use and return materials. Notice if there is evidence of new learning based on the goal of this minilesson.

▶ Do students return materials to where they belong?

▶ Can they explain why it is important to return materials to where they belong?

▶ Do they use the terms *return* and *materials* correctly?

Minilesson

To help students think about the minilesson principle, engage them in a demonstration and discussion of how to return materials to where they belong. Here is an example.

▶ Before class, prepare one student to act as a model for this minilesson. Set the student up at a table with various materials, such as paper, pencils, markers, scissors, and a glue stick.

    _____ has been hard at work writing and drawing, but now she is finished with this work. Watch what she does now.

▶ Have the student demonstrate returning each item to its proper place in the classroom. Before class, make sure the student knows where each item belongs.

    What did you notice _____ did when she finished?

    _____ returned the materials she was using to where they belong.

    Where did she return the paper?

    Where did she return the scissors?

▶ Ensure students understand where frequently used materials belong in your classroom. Also make sure that students know how to treat the materials with care.

Have a Try

Invite the students to discuss with a partner the importance of taking good care of materials and returning them to where they belong.

> Why is it important to return materials to where they belong when you're finished with them? Turn and talk to your partner about why this is important.

▶ After students turn and talk, ask several pairs to share ideas with the class. Make a list of responses on chart paper.

Summarize and Apply

Summarize the learning and remind students to return materials to where they belong.

> What did you learn about using materials?

> When you return materials to where they belong, everyone can find the materials they need and do their best work.

▶ Write the minilesson principle at the top the list.

> If you use materials for an activity today, remember where you found the items and make sure to return them to where they belong when you're done with them.

Share

Following independent reading time, gather students together in the meeting area to discuss returning materials.

> Raise your hand if you used materials today and returned them to where they belong.

> What materials did you use?

> Where did you return them?

Extend the Lesson (Optional)

After assessing students' understanding, you might decide to extend the learning.

▶ Make sure the materials in your classroom are organized, labeled, and easy to find and return. Many materials can be kept in labeled baskets or bins. Invite students to assist in organizing materials and creating labels.

Return materials to where they belong.

- So other students can use the materials

- So you will be able to find the materials next time you need them

- So your table is not cluttered and messy

- So the classroom is clean and nice to be in

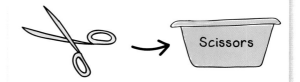

Section 1: Management

Assessment

After you have taught the minilessons in this umbrella, observe students as they work in the classroom.

▶ What evidence do you have that they understand how to work together in the classroom?

- Do students behave considerately and respectfully toward each other?

- Do they use an appropriate voice level?

- How well do they attempt to problem solve independently before asking for your help?

- Do they return materials to where they belong?

- Can they use terms such as *respect*, *voice level*, *volume*, *appropriate*, *problem*, *solve*, and *emergency*?

▶ What other minilessons might you teach to maintain and grow independent reading habits?

- Do students know where to find books they want to read in the classroom library?

- Are they able to choose books that are just right for them?

Use your observations to determine the next umbrella you will teach. You may also consult Minilessons Across the Year (pp. 55-57) for guidance.

Reader's Notebook

When this umbrella is complete, provide a copy of the minilesson principles (see resources.fountasandpinnell.com) for students to glue in the reader's notebook (in the Minilessons section if using *Reader's Notebook: Intermediate* [Fountas and Pinnell 2011]), so they can refer to the information as needed.

Minilessons in This Umbrella

RML1 Some books in the classroom library are organized by author, illustrator, or topic.

RML2 Some books in the classroom library are organized by genre.

RML3 Take good care of the books in the classroom library.

Before Teaching Umbrella 2 Minilessons

The minilessons in this umbrella allow students to explore the books in their classroom library to discover how they are organized. Before teaching this umbrella, provide students with several opportunities to choose and read books from the classroom library. These are some suggestions for making your classroom library an inviting and organized space for students:

▶ Organize books into baskets in a way that allows students to see the front covers and provides easy access for browsing.

▶ In each basket, display high-quality and interesting books that offer a range of difficulty levels.

▶ Label (or have students label) baskets with the topic, author, illustrator, series, genre, or theme.

▶ Take the students on a tour of the classroom library, so they know it is a valued and special space in their classroom.

Section 1: Management

Reading Minilesson Principle
Some books in the classroom library are organized by author, illustrator, or topic.

Exploring the Classroom Library

You Will Need

- three labeled baskets of books from your classroom library: one basket should contain books by the same author, one should contain books by the same illustrator, and one should contain nonfiction books about the same topic (e.g., animals, sports, or transportation)
- sticky notes
- chart paper (with a blank three-column chart)
- markers

Academic Language / Important Vocabulary

- classroom library
- organized
- author
- illustrator
- topic

Goal

Understand the classroom library is organized by illustrator, author, and topic to make finding books easier.

Rationale

When you teach students how the classroom library is organized, they are better able to find and select books they will enjoy reading.

Assess Learning

Observe students when they explore and select books from the classroom library. Notice if there is evidence of new learning based on the goal of this minilesson.

- Can students explain how and why the classroom library is organized?
- Do they use their understanding of the organization of the classroom library to choose books to read?
- Do they use terms such as *classroom library*, *organized*, *author*, *illustrator*, and *topic*?

Minilesson

To help students think about the minilesson principle, engage them in discussing the organization of books in the classroom library. Here is an example.

- Have students gather in the classroom library. Show them a basket of books by the same author, but cover up the label with a sticky note. Take four or five books out of the basket and display side by side.

  What do you notice about these books? Why are they together?

- Uncover the label on the basket and invite a volunteer to read it aloud.

  Every basket in our classroom library has a label. The label tells you what kind of books you will find in the basket. How are these books organized?

- Write *Author* at the top of the first column of the chart. Then write the name of the author whose books you shared.

- Show a basket of books by the same illustrator. Keep the label covered. Display four or five of the books and read the titles, authors, and illustrators.

  What do you notice about these books? What do they have in common?

- Help students realize the books have the same illustrator. Uncover the label.

  When you see this basket, you'll know all the books are illustrated by the same person. How are these books organized?

- Add *Illustrator* and the example illustrator to the chart.

Have a Try

Invite the students to discuss the books in the third basket with a partner.

▶ Repeat the process with a third basket. This time, all the books in the basket should have the same topic. Read the titles, authors, and illustrators.

　　Turn and talk about what you notice about the books in this basket.

▶ After turn and talk, ask a few students to share what they noticed. When someone identifies that the books are about the same topic, uncover the label and add to the chart.

Summarize and Apply

Summarize the learning and remind students to think about how the classroom library is organized.

　　What did you notice about these baskets of books in our classroom library?

▶ Write the minilesson principle at the top of the chart.

　　When you choose a book to read today, think about if you want to read a book by a certain author or illustrator or about a topic that interests you.

Share

Following independent reading time, gather students together in the meeting area to talk about the books they chose for independent reading.

　　Turn and talk about the book you chose today and what basket you found it in.

Extend the Lesson (Optional)

After assessing students' understanding, you might decide to extend the learning.

▶ Teach students that there are other ways to organize books in the library. For example, series books could be grouped together in a basket.

▶ Regularly rotate the books and categories of books in the classroom library. Involve students in categorizing the new books.

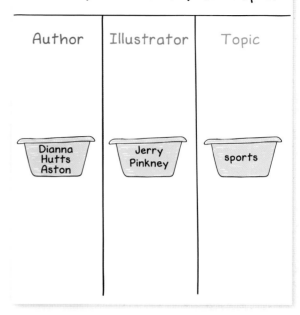

Some books in the classroom library are organized by author, illustrator, or topic.

Author	Illustrator	Topic
Dianna Hutts Aston	Jerry Pinkney	sports

Reading Minilesson Principle
Some books in the classroom library are organized by genre.

Exploring the Classroom Library

You Will Need

- a labeled basket of realistic fiction books (set aside one familiar book)
- a labeled basket of fantasy books (set aside one book)
- a labeled basket of informational books (set aside one book)
- a labeled basket of biographies (set aside one book)
- chart paper and markers

Academic Language / Important Vocabulary

- genre
- realistic fiction
- fantasy
- informational
- biography

Goal

Understand some books in the classroom library are organized by genre.

Rationale

When you teach students that some of the books in their classroom library are organized by genre, they are better able to select books they will enjoy. They also gain a better understanding of genre characteristics. When they are involved in the organization of the classroom library, they develop a sense of ownership and responsibility for maintaining the library. They learn some books could go in more than one basket. You might want to either use this minilesson as a preview or teach it after Umbrella 5: Understanding Fiction and Nonfiction Genres in Section Two: Literary Analysis.

Assess Learning

Observe students when they explore and select books from the classroom library. Notice if there is evidence of new learning based on the goal of this minilesson.

- Can students explain how and why the classroom library is organized?
- Can they use academic language, such as *genre, realistic fiction, fantasy, informational*, and *biography*?

Minilesson

To help students think about the minilesson principle, engage them in discussing the organization of books by genre in your classroom library. Introduce only genres that you think your students will understand. Here is an example.

- Display the four prepared baskets of books. Ask a volunteer to read the labels.

  How are these baskets of books organized?

  The books in these baskets are organized by genre. Remember the genre of a book is what kind of book it is. I have more books I would like to organize by genre, but I need your help.

- Hold up the familiar, realistic fiction book you set aside. Read the title.

  In which basket should I put this book?

  What makes you think that?

- When students correctly identify the book as realistic fiction, place it in the realistic fiction basket.

- Start a two-column chart on chart paper. Write *Fiction* and *Nonfiction* as the headings. Under *Fiction*, write *Realistic fiction*.

- Repeat the process above with the fantasy book and the informational book you set aside.

Have a Try

Invite the students to discuss the genre of another book with a partner.

▶ Hold up the biography you set aside. Read the title.

   Turn and talk to your partner about the basket this book goes in. Be sure to explain the reasons for your choice.

▶ After students turn and talk, ask a few pairs to share their thinking. Place the book in the biography basket and add *Biography* to the chart.

Summarize and Apply

Summarize the learning and remind students to think about how the classroom library is organized when they select books for independent reading.

   Today you thought about how some of the books in our classroom library are organized. What did you notice about the baskets of books you looked at today?

▶ Write the minilesson principle at the top of the chart.

   When you choose a book to read, think about what kind of book you would like to read. Look for the basket with the label of the genre you'd like to read.

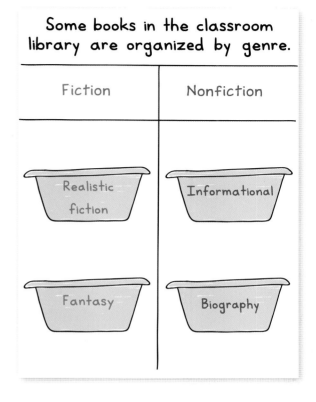

Share

Following independent reading time, gather students together in the meeting area to discuss their book choices.

   Raise your hand if you chose a book today from one of the genre baskets in our classroom library. What book did you choose and which basket was it in?

Extend the Lesson (Optional)

After assessing students' understanding, you might decide to extend the learning.

▶ Repeat this lesson with other genres (e.g., historical fiction, folktale, narrative nonfiction) or special types of fiction and nonfiction (e.g., series, mysteries, adventure stories, animal stories, diaries).

▶ Have students sort books into genre categories and make labels for them. You might even have students give a tour of the new categories for the rest of the class.

Exploring the Classroom Library

You Will Need

- chart paper and markers

Academic Language / Important Vocabulary

- classroom library

Goal

Take care of the books in the classroom library.

Rationale

When you teach students to handle their materials with care, they develop independence and a sense of responsibility in the classroom community. They also learn to consider the needs of their classmates and develop empathy.

Assess Learning

Observe students when they handle books. Notice if there is evidence of new learning based on the goal of this minilesson.

- ❯ Do students handle books carefully and return them to the right place?
- ❯ Can they explain why it is important to handle books properly?
- ❯ Do they use the term *classroom library*?

Minilesson

To help students think about the minilesson principle, talk with them about how to care for books. Here is an example.

> Our classroom library is a wonderful place for you to use and enjoy books, and we want it to stay that way for the school year. What are some ways you can help keep our library a wonderful place?

- ❯ Record students' responses on chart paper. If necessary, prompt them with questions, such as the following:
  - *How can you help make sure your classmates will be able to find the books they want?*
  - *Where should you put your books when you are finished with them?*
  - *What should you do if you don't know where to return a certain book? (You may want to have a basket designated for this purpose and show students how to use it.)*
  - *How should you place a book back in the basket?*
  - *How can you make sure the books in our library don't get dirty or torn?*

Have a Try

Invite the students to talk with a partner about taking care of the books in the classroom library.

> Is there anything else you think should be added to the list? Turn and talk to your partner about what else you can do to take good care of our books.

▶ After students turn and talk, ask for volunteers to share their thinking. Add new ideas to the list.

Summarize and Apply

Summarize the learning and remind students to take good care of the books in the classroom library.

> What does the chart tell you?

> The list shows ways to take good care of the books in the classroom library.

▶ Write the minilesson principle at the top of the chart.

> Why is it important to take good care of our books?

> When you take good care of the books in our classroom library, your classmates can read and enjoy the books.

> When you read today, remember to take good care of the books.

Share

Following independent reading time, gather students together in the meeting area to talk about how they took care of their books.

> How did you take good care of the books today?

Extend the Lesson (Optional)

After assessing students' understanding, you might decide to extend the learning.

▶ Have students work in small groups to create a poster about how to take good care of books. Display the posters in the classroom or school library.

Take good care of the books in the classroom library.

- Be gentle with them and turn the pages carefully.

- Put them in the same basket where you found them.

- Put them in the basket right side up and with the cover facing forward.

Assessment

After you have taught the minilessons in this umbrella, observe students as they explore and select books from the classroom library.

⫸ What evidence do you have of new understandings relating to using the classroom library?

- Can students explain how the classroom library is organized?
- Do they use the organization of the classroom library to help them find and select books?
- How well do they take care of the books in the classroom library?
- Do they use terms such as *library*, *organized*, *author*, *illustrator*, *topic*, and *genre* when they talk about using the classroom library?

⫸ What other minilessons might you teach to maintain and grow independent reading habits?

- Are students able to choose books that are just right for them?

Use your observations to determine the next umbrella you will teach. You may also consult Minilessons Across the Year (pp. 55-57) for guidance.

Reader's Notebook

When this umbrella is complete, provide a copy of the minilesson principles (see resources.fountasandpinnell.com) for students to glue in the reader's notebook (in the Minilessons section if using *Reader's Notebook: Intermediate* [Fountas and Pinnell 2011]), so they can refer to the information as needed.

Minilessons in This Umbrella

RML1   Read a book or write your thoughts about your reading.

RML2   Choose books that you want to read.

RML3   Choose books that are just right for you.

RML4   After a good try, you may have a reason to abandon a book.

RML5   Keep your books and materials organized in your personal box.

Before Teaching Umbrella 3 Minilessons

The minilessons in this umbrella introduce how to use the classroom library for independent reading. It includes a lesson explaining that independent reading is a time for reading books and writing in a reader's notebook. For more information on introducing and establishing a reader's notebook, see Umbrella 1: Introducing a Reader's Notebook in Section Four: Writing About Reading. Another lesson addresses the materials each student keeps in a personal box. Ideally, each student has a personal box for his books and materials and a designated place to keep the box. As an alternative to individual boxes, you could use crates with hanging file folders. For example, you could have a crate that has all the students' writing materials (e.g., writing folder, writer's notebook) and another with reading materials (e.g., reader's notebook, book the student is reading now, one extra book).

Before teaching this umbrella, provide students with numerous opportunities to select and read books from the classroom library. It would also be a good idea to teach the previous umbrella in this section, Umbrella 2: Exploring the Classroom Library, to acquaint students with the organization of the classroom library.

Section 1: Management

Reading Minilesson Principle
Read a book or write your thoughts about your reading.

You Will Need

- chart paper and markers

Academic Language / Important Vocabulary

- independent reading
- classroom library
- reader's notebook

Goal

Read silently and write about reading during independent reading.

Rationale

When students have opportunities to read independently and write about reading, they develop stronger reading and writing skills. Having full control over which books they read makes it more likely they will enjoy reading and become lifelong readers.

Assess Learning

Observe students during independent reading. Notice if there is evidence of new learning based on the goal of this minilesson.

- ▸ Do students read silently or write their thoughts about their reading during independent reading?
- ▸ Can they explain why it is important to read silently during independent reading?
- ▸ Do they work well independently?
- ▸ Do they use the terms *independent reading, classroom library,* and *reader's notebook?*

Minilesson

To help students think about the minilesson principle, engage them in a discussion about how to work during independent reading time. Here is an example.

> Reading is thinking. Whenever you're reading, you're thinking about what you're reading. What does it have to be like in the classroom for you to do your best thinking while you read?

> You can do your best thinking when it is quiet. When it is independent reading time, you need to read silently so you and your classmates can do your best thinking. When I am talking to a reader during independent reading, we will whisper to each other, so we will be sure not to interrupt anyone's thinking.

> Most of the time, you will spend your time reading silently during independent reading. Sometimes you will be asked to write your thinking about your reading in different ways. One way is to write a letter to me every week. Sometimes you might find it helpful to jot down notes about your thinking about your reading or put a sticky note in your book so that you will have ideas about what to share in your letter. What kinds of things might you write about?

Have a Try

Invite the students to talk with a partner about what they will do during independent reading.

> Turn and talk to your partner about what you will do when it's independent reading time.

▶ After students turn and talk, ask a few pairs to share their thinking.

> When it's independent reading time, you will read a book or write your thoughts about your reading.

Summarize and Apply

Summarize the learning and remind students to read silently or write their thoughts about their reading during independent reading.

▶ Work with students to make a chart about what to do during independent reading time.

> What are two things you can do during independent reading?

▶ Record responses on the chart and then write the principle at the top.

> When you read today, choose a book from the classroom library and read it silently. Then write your thoughts about your reading in your reader's notebook. The chart can remind you of some things you can write.

Share

Following independent reading time, gather students together in the meeting area to talk about their experience during independent reading.

> What worked well for you today during independent reading? What will you do differently next time?

Extend the Lesson (Optional)

After assessing students' understanding, you might decide to extend the learning.

▶ **Writing About Reading** Teach minilessons, as appropriate, in Section Four: Writing About Reading to familiarize students with different ways of writing about reading.

Read a book or write your thoughts about your reading.

Read a book silently so you and your classmates can do your best thinking.

Write your thoughts about your reading.

- What you think about the book

- What you think about the characters

- What you learned from the book

Reading Minilesson Principle
Choose books that you want to read.

Getting Started with Independent Reading

You Will Need

- chart paper and markers
- four or five books from your classroom library

Academic Language / Important Vocabulary

- classroom library
- independent reading

Goal

Choose a book for independent reading.

Rationale

When you teach students to be aware of the ways they choose books, they become more independent and develop their interests and identities as readers.

Assess Learning

Observe students when they choose books for independent reading. Notice if there is evidence of new learning based on the goal of this minilesson.

- ▶ Do students choose books they want to read for independent reading?
- ▶ Can they explain what interests them about a particular book?
- ▶ Can they discuss the different ways they choose books?
- ▶ Do they use the terms *classroom library* and *independent reading*?

Minilesson

To help students think about the minilesson principle, engage them in a discussion about how to choose books. Here is an example.

- ▶ Gather the students in the classroom library area.

    You have so many wonderful books to choose from in our classroom library. With so many choices, sometimes it can be hard to pick just one book to read. There are many different ways to choose books. For example, I love fantasy stories, so I often look for that type of book. What are some of the ways you choose a book to read?

- ▶ Record students' responses on chart paper.
- ▶ If students need more guidance, ask them to think about the last book they read and tell why they chose it.
- ▶ Remind students that the books in the library are organized to help them make good choices.

Have a Try

Invite the students to talk with a partner about how they choose books.

▶ Display a diverse selection of four or five books from your classroom library.

> Turn and talk to your partner about which of these books you would choose to read and why.

▶ After students turn and talk, ask a few students to share how they made their choices. Record responses on the chart.

Summarize and Apply

Summarize the learning and remind students to choose books they want to read during independent reading.

> Review the chart.

> Why do you think it's important to choose books that you want to read during independent reading?

> Today when you read, think about the ways you can choose books, and choose a book you want to read. Be ready to share why you chose your book when we come back together.

Share

Following independent reading time, gather students together in the meeting area to talk about the books they chose.

> Turn and talk to your partner about what book you chose today and why you chose it.

Extend the Lesson (Optional)

After assessing students' understanding, you might decide to extend the learning.

▶ Teach students how to give book talks about books they have read and enjoyed (see Umbrella 3: Giving a Book Talk in Section Two: Literary Analysis for more information).

▶ **Writing About Reading** Create a section devoted to peer recommendations in your classroom library. Have students write recommendations for books on index cards, and display with the books. Rotate the recommended books regularly.

Ways to Choose Books

- Interesting title →
- Front cover illustration
- Have read the book before
- Interested in the topic
- Like the author or illustrator
- Book recommendations
- Part of a series
- Like the genre
- Saw the movie version of the book
- Read the first page and liked it

BIG *BAD* BUBBLE

Section 1: Management

RML3
MGT.U3.RML3

Reading Minilesson Principle
Choose books that are just right for you.

Getting Started with Independent Reading

You Will Need

▸ chart paper and markers

Academic Language / Important Vocabulary

▸ just right
▸ easy
▸ difficult

Goal

Learn to consider whether a book is easy, just right, or too hard for them at this time.

Rationale

When you teach students how to determine if a book is just right for them, they get more from their reading. However, students should understand a book that is too difficult might eventually become just right or even easy as they learn more about reading. Occasionally students may choose books that are difficult or enjoy an easy read and that is fine. Your goal, however, is to help them learn how to make choices they can enjoy.

Assess Learning

Observe students when they choose and read books during independent reading. Notice if there is evidence of new learning based on the goal of this minilesson.

▸ Can students explain what makes books easy, difficult, or just right?

▸ Can they explain why a particular book is easy, difficult, or just right for them?

▸ Do they understand the terms *just right, easy,* and *difficult?*

Minilesson

To help students think about the minilesson principle, engage them in a discussion about just-right books. Here is an example.

> When you choose a book you want to read for independent reading, it's important to think about whether the book is just right for you. Just-right books are books that are not too easy and not too difficult for you to read. What does it feel like when you're reading a book that is just right for you?

▸ Start a three-column chart on chart paper. Label the middle column *Just Right* and record students' responses.

> Raise your hand if you've ever started reading a book and found it was too difficult for you.

> If it's way too hard, it's just not fun. What makes a book too difficult to read?

▸ Label the third column *Difficult* and record students' responses.

> Sometimes you might start a book and find it is easy for you. Easy books are good books to read when you want to relax. What makes a book easy to read?

▸ Label the first column *Easy* and record students' responses.

Have a Try

Invite students to talk with a partner about a book they have read recently.

> Turn and talk about a book you have read recently. Was it easy, just right, or difficult? What made it so?

Summarize and Apply

Summarize the learning and remind students to try to choose books that are just right.

> You thought about what makes a book just right, difficult, or easy for you. Which type of book do you think you should choose most of the time? What makes you think that?

> Once in a while, you might choose a book that is easy or a little difficult, but most of the time you should choose books that are just right. Sometimes a book that is difficult might become just right in a short time.

▶ Write the minilesson principle at the top the chart.

> When you read today, think about whether the book is easy, just right, or difficult for you. Be ready to share when we come back together.

Share

Following independent reading time, gather students together in the meeting area to discuss book choices.

> Who read a book that was just right for you?

> How did you know it was just right?

▶ Repeat questioning for easy and difficult books.

Extend the Lesson [Optional]

After assessing students' understanding, you might decide to extend the learning.

▶ If a student consistently has a hard time choosing books, make a basket of books that are just right for the student at that time.

▶ **Writing About Reading** Have students keep a log in a reader's notebook of books they have read and note whether each book was easy, just right, or difficult (see Umbrella 1: Introducing a Reader's Notebook in Section Four: Writing About Reading). There is also a Books to Read list in *Reader's Notebook: Intermediate* (Fountas and Pinnell 2011).

Choose books that are just right for you.

Easy	Just Right 👍	Difficult
• You know all the words.	• You read the book smoothly.	• You have trouble reading many of the words.
• You read it very quickly.	• You can read most of the words.	
• You may have read the book before.	• You only have to slow down a few times.	• You don't understand most of the book.
	• You understand the book.	• You get frustrated.

Reading Minilesson Principle
After a good try, you may have a reason to abandon a book.

Getting Started with Independent Reading

You Will Need

▶ chart paper and markers

Academic Language / Important Vocabulary

▶ abandon

Goal

Learn people sometimes abandon books after giving them a good try.

Rationale

When students understand it is okay to abandon a book after giving it a good try, they spend more time reading books they enjoy. They are therefore more likely to enjoy the process of reading and to become lifelong readers.

Assess Learning

Observe students when they talk about books. Notice if there is evidence of new learning based on the goal of this minilesson.

- ▶ Do students choose books they enjoy most of the time?
- ▶ Are they willing to give books a chance even if they do not initially like them?
- ▶ Can they offer a reason for abandoning a book?
- ▶ Do they understand and use the word *abandon*?

Minilesson

To help students think about the minilesson principle, discuss the reasons people sometimes abandon books. Here is an example.

> Raise your hand if you have ever started reading a book, decided you didn't like it very much, and stopped reading it before you got to the end.

> When a reader stops reading a book before the end, it's called abandoning a book.

> What are some of the reasons a reader might abandon a book?

- ▶ Use the students' responses to create a list of the reasons readers abandon books.

> Sometimes you might not like a book very much at first, but you might find that it gets better as you read more. You should always give a book a good try before you abandon it. Once you've given it a good try, there's nothing wrong with abandoning a book if you still don't enjoy it.

Summarize and Apply

Summarize the learning and remind students to always give a book a good try before abandoning it.

>   What does the chart show you?
>
>   It shows reasons readers might abandon a book.

▶ Write the minilesson principle at the top of the chart.

>   When you choose a book to read today, try to choose a book you think you'll like. However, if you don't like it right away, be sure to give it a good try before abandoning it. If you do decide to abandon the book, try to find another book you will like more.

Share

Following independent reading time, gather students together in the meeting area to talk about their reading.

>   Raise your hand if you enjoyed the book you read today.
>
>   Did anyone decide to abandon a book today?
>
>   Why did you abandon it?

Extend the Lesson (Optional)

After assessing students' understanding, you might decide to extend the learning.

▶ Explain to students that even if they have a good reason to abandon a book now, they may come back to it and enjoy it later. Encourage students to give a second chance to books they abandoned in the past.

▶ **Writing About Reading** Teach students how to record an *A* for *Abandoned* in their reading log next to books they have abandoned.

After a good try, you may have a reason to abandon a book.

Why Readers Abandon Books

- Boring, not interesting

- Not enough action

- Don't like the genre

- Too difficult or too easy

- Don't like the characters

- Too sad or scary

- Too confusing

- Different from author's other books

RML 5

Reading Minilesson Principle

Keep your books and materials organized in your personal box.

Getting Started with Independent Reading

You Will Need

- a personal box prepared with materials for each student and yourself (materials, such as reader's notebook, writer's notebook, writing folder, two books, in no particular order (see p. 70))
- chart paper and markers

Academic Language / Important Vocabulary

- personal box
- organized
- reader's notebook
- writer's notebook
- writing folder
- word study folder

Goal

Keep books and materials organized for use during independent reading time.

Rationale

When you teach students to keep their materials organized, they spend less time trying to find materials and more time reading, writing, and learning. A magazine box or cereal box with each student's name works well for a personal box. You might consider also numbering each student's box and the folders so each student has a consistent number on all items.

Assess Learning

Observe students when they handle their personal boxes. Notice if there is evidence of new learning based on the goal of this minilesson.

- ▶ Can students easily find materials in their personal boxes?
- ▶ Can they explain why it is important to keep their books and materials organized in their personal boxes?
- ▶ Do they return the box to the right place?
- ▶ Do they use terms such as *personal box, organized, reader's notebook, writer's notebook, writing folder,* and *word study folder*?

Minilesson

To help students think about the minilesson principle, provide a short demonstration of how to organize materials in a personal book box. Here is an example.

- ▶ Show students a personal book box. Hold up each item and briefly explain what it is for (e.g., "This is the book that I'm reading right now").
- ▶ Shuffle through the box, as if trying to find something.

  I want to take out my reader's notebook, but I can't find it.

  How can I make it easier to find things in my personal box?

  If I put my materials in the same order in the box every day, I will always be able to find what I need.

- ▶ Remove all of the items from the box.

  What do you think I should put in my box first?

- ▶ With students' input, model putting the materials in the box in a particular order with the front covers, or spines, facing forward. Write the order on chart paper.

  What did you notice about how I placed each item in my box?

Have a Try

Invite the students to organize their personal boxes.

▸ Invite a few students at a time to get their personal boxes and return to their desks or tables. Once all students have their boxes, direct them to remove the materials and place them in a neat pile beside the box.

> Put your books and materials back in your box in the right order. If you forget the order, look at the chart.

Summarize and Apply

Summarize the learning and remind students to keep their personal boxes organized.

> Why is it important to keep your box organized?

> Keeping your materials organized will make it easier for you to find the things you need. Always put your box back in its place.

▸ Write the minilesson principle at the top of the chart.

> During independent reading today, read the book or books in your personal box. If you need another book, you can go shopping in the classroom library. After you read, write your thoughts about your reading in a reader's notebook. Remember to put everything back in your box in the right order.

Share

Following independent reading time, gather students together in the meeting area to talk about their personal boxes.

> What do you think of the way you organized materials in your personal boxes today? Is there anything you could do differently?

Extend the Lesson (Optional)

After assessing students' understanding, you might decide to extend the learning.

▸ You might have students add items to their personal boxes during the school year. As you introduce a new item, discuss where in the box it should go and remind students to keep their boxes organized.

Keep your books and materials organized in your personal box.

1. The book you are reading now

2. One extra book

3. Reader's notebook

4. Writer's notebook

5. Writing folder

6. Word study folder

Section 1: Management

Assessment

After you have taught the minilessons in this umbrella, observe students during independent reading.

▶ What evidence do you have that students understand how to use the classroom library for independent reading?

- During independent reading, do they read silently or write in a reader's notebook?

- Do they usually choose books they enjoy and that are an appropriate reading level?

- Are they willing to give books a good try before abandoning them?

- Do they keep their books and materials organized in their personal boxes? And do they return the box to the designated place?

- Can they use terms such as *easy, just right, abandon, reader's notebook, writer's notebook, personal box, word study folder,* and *difficult*?

▶ What other minilessons might you teach to maintain and grow independent reading habits?

- Do students know where to find books they want to read in the classroom library?

- Are they able to choose books that are just right for them?

Use your observations to determine the next umbrella you will teach. You may also consult Minilessons Across the Year (pp. 55-57) for guidance.

Reader's Notebook

When this umbrella is complete, provide a copy of the minilesson principles (see resources.fountasandpinnell.com) for students to glue in the reader's notebook (in the Minilessons section if using *Reader's Notebook: Intermediate* [Fountas and Pinnell 2011]), so they can refer to the information as needed.

Section 2 | Literary Analysis

Literary analysis minilessons support student's growing awareness of the elements of literature and the writer's and illustrator's craft. The minilessons help students learn how to think analytically about texts and to identify the characteristics of fiction and nonfiction genres. The books that you read during interactive read-aloud and shared reading can serve as mentor texts when applying the principles of literary analysis.

2 Literary Analysis

Minilessons in This Umbrella

RML1 Think about the books you read and share your thinking with others.

RML2 Turn and talk to share your thinking.

RML3 When you read, mark places you want to talk about.

RML4 Share your opinion and support it with evidence.

Before Teaching Umbrella 1 Minilessons

Many third graders have a rich background of knowledge about stories and nonfiction books. They have had experience talking about books and sharing their opinions with others. If that is the case for your entire group, you may not need to use the minilessons in this umbrella. However, for many third graders who have not yet had enough experience reading and discussing books, this umbrella will be helpful. Others may need a quick review to learn how things are done in a new classroom.

To prepare for this umbrella, read and discuss a variety of high-quality fiction and nonfiction picture books that cover a wide range of grade-appropriate themes and topics. Use the following text sets from the *Fountas & Pinnell Classroom™ Interactive Read-Aloud Collection* or choose familiar books from your classroom library.

The Importance of Kindness

Last Day Blues by Julie Danneburg

Under the Lemon Moon by Edith Hope Fine

Sophie's Masterpiece by Eileen Spinelli

The Can Man by Laura E. Williams

Connecting Across Generations: Family

Mooncakes by Loretta Seto

Storm in the Night by Mary Stolz

Sharing Our World: Animals

I Love Guinea Pigs by Dick King-Smith

As you read aloud and enjoy these texts together, help students

> ▶ think and talk about books in a variety of ways,

> ▶ share their thinking with others, and

> ▶ articulate opinions and support them with evidence.

Kindness

Family

Animals

Section 2: Literary Analysis

RML1
LA.U1.RML1

Reading Minilesson Principle
Think about the books you read and share your thinking with others.

You Will Need

- two or three books you have read and discussed recently with your students such as the following:
  - *Last Day Blues* by Julie Danneburg, from Text Set: Kindness
  - *Mooncakes* by Loretta Seto, from Text Set: Family
  - *I Love Guinea Pigs* by Dick King-Smith, from Text Set: Animals
- chart paper and markers

Academic Language / Important Vocabulary

- character
- illustration
- author

Continuum Connection

- Use evidence from the text to support statements about the text (p. 50)

Goal

Identify ways to think and talk about books.

Rationale

When you encourage students to share their thinking about books, they develop identities as readers and deepen their understanding and appreciation of texts. They also strengthen their interpersonal and communication skills.

Assess Learning

Observe students when they talk about books. Notice if there is evidence of new learning based on the goal of this minilesson.

- ▶ Do students think about books in a variety of ways?
- ▶ Do they share their thinking about their reading?
- ▶ Do they use academic language, such as *character*, *illustration*, and *author*?

Minilesson

To help students think about the minilesson principle, engage them in a discussion about different ways to talk about books. Here is an example.

> This year, you're going to read and talk about many wonderful books together. Think about the books you read and share your thinking with each other.

▶ Show the cover of a book you recently read to your students, such as *Last Day Blues*.

> Do you remember when we read this book together? After we read it, you shared your thinking about it. What were some of the things we talked about when we read this book?

▶ Generalize students' responses to create a list of ways to think and talk about books.

▶ Show another book that you recently read together, such as *Mooncakes*, and ask students to recall ways they talked about it. Add new ideas to the list.

Have a Try

Invite the students to continue the discussion of talking about books with a partner.

▶ Show the cover of a third book you read and discussed recently, such as *I Love Guinea Pigs*.

What kinds of things did we talk about when we talked about this book? Turn and talk to your partner about that.

▶ After students turn and talk, ask a few to share. Add new ideas to the list.

Summarize and Apply

Summarize the learning and remind students to think about the books they read and to share their thinking with others.

What does this chart help you remember?

It shows ways to think and talk about books.

Why is it a good idea to share your thinking with others?

Today with a partner select a book you both would like to read and talk about. It can be a new book or one you both have read before. As you read together, take turns sharing your thinking about the book. Review the list that we made together to help you. Be ready to share what you talked about.

Share

Following independent reading time, gather students together in the meeting area to talk about their reading.

What book did you read with a partner?

What did you talk about?

Extend the Lesson (Optional)

After assessing students' understanding, you might decide to extend the learning.

▶ Regularly provide students with opportunities to share their thinking about their reading in various contexts—as a whole class, in small groups, with a partner, or with you.

▶ **Writing About Reading** Teach students how to write letters to you to share their thinking about their reading (see Umbrella 3: Writing Letters About Reading in Section Four: Writing About Reading).

Ways to Think and Talk About Books

We can think and talk about . . .

- what the characters are like

- what the characters are feeling or thinking

- the illustrations

- whether the story could happen in real life

- parts of the book that are funny, interesting, or sad

- the way the author writes

- what we learned from the book

Section 2: Literary Analysis

Reading Minilesson Principle
Turn and talk to share your thinking.

Thinking and Talking About Books

You Will Need

- two books you have read aloud recently such as the following:
  - *Under the Lemon Moon* by Edith Hope Fine, from Text Set: Kindness
  - *Storm in the Night* by Mary Stolz, from Text Set: Family
- a student prepared to model the turn and talk routine
- chart paper and markers

Academic Language / Important Vocabulary

- turn and talk
- guidelines
- agree
- disagree

Continuum Connection

- Engage actively in conversational routines: e.g., turn and talk (p. 335)

Goal

Engage in the turn and talk routine to share thinking about books.

Rationale

Turn and talk is a routine that provides students an opportunity to express their thinking and engage in conversation with just one other person in a nonthreatening way. It is an oral rehearsal before speaking to a larger group. Establishing clear guidelines for the routine will help keep the minilesson running smoothly and provide a model for appropriate student behaviors.

Assess Learning

Observe students when they turn and talk. Notice if there is evidence of new learning based on the goal of this minilesson.

- Do students follow the guidelines for turn and talk?
- Can they explain why following the guidelines is important?
- Do they listen actively?
- Do they agree or disagree with partners or add on to their partners' thinking?
- Do they understand the terms *turn and talk*, *guidelines*, *agree*, and *disagree*?

Minilesson

To help students think about the minilesson principle, use familiar texts to model the turn and talk routine. Here is an example.

- Display the cover of a book you have recently shared with your students, such as *Under the Lemon Moon*.

  Do you remember when we read this book together? _____ is my partner today. We are going to turn and talk to share our thinking about this book. Notice what we do.

- Turn and talk with the student you prepared. Share an opinion about the book and ask the student if she agrees or disagrees and why.

  What did you notice about how we turned and talked?

  What did we do with our bodies? What did we do with our eyes?

  What voice level did we use?

  What did we do when the other person was speaking?

  How did we share our thinking?

- Use students' responses to create a list of guidelines for turn and talk on chart paper.

Have a Try

Invite the students to turn and talk about a book with a partner.

▶ Display the cover of another book you have read recently together, such as *Storm in the Night*. Review some pages briefly to remind students of the story.

> Remember this story? Turn and talk to your partner about what you think about this story. Remember to follow the guidelines we made together.

Summarize and Apply

Summarize the learning and remind students to follow the guidelines for turn and talk.

> What does the chart help you remember?

> When you turn and talk with a partner, remember to follow these guidelines. Why do you think it's important to follow the guidelines for turn and talk?

> After independent reading today, you will turn and talk with a partner about the book you read. Be ready to share your thinking when we come back together.

Share

Following independent reading time, gather students together in the meeting area to talk about their reading.

> Turn and talk with your partner about what you thought about the book you read today. Remember to give reasons for your thinking.

> Now turn and talk about what you just did together. What do you like about turn and talk? Is there anything you think we should add to our guidelines?

▶ Ask a few pairs to share their ideas and add relevant new guidelines to the chart.

Extend the Lesson (Optional)

After assessing students' understanding, you might decide to extend the learning.

▶ Use turn and talk regularly in various instructional contexts.

▶ Review the guidelines for turn and talk from time to time and ask students if they would like to add any new guidelines.

Turn and Talk

- Turn your body toward your partner.

- Look at your partner.

- Use a soft indoor voice.

- Take turns telling your thinking.

- Be silent and listen carefully while your partner speaks.

- Say whether you agree or disagree with your partner or add on to what he said.

- Give reasons for your thinking.

Section 2: Literary Analysis

RML3
LA.U1.RML3

Thinking and Talking About Books

You Will Need

- a familiar book such as *The Can Man* by Laura E. Williams, from Text Set: Kindness
- chart paper and markers
- sticky notes

Academic Language / Important Vocabulary

- sticky note
- mark

Continuum Connection

- Use evidence from the text to support statements about the text (p. 50)

Goal

Identify places in a book to talk about with others.

Rationale

When students mark pages while they read, they are more thoughtful about their reading. They are better able to organize their thoughts and prepare for meaningful conversations about books.

Assess Learning

Observe students when they talk about books. Notice if there is evidence of new learning based on the goal of this minilesson.

- Do students mark pages they would like to talk about?
- Can they explain why they chose to mark particular pages?
- Do they refer to those pages when talking with a partner?

Minilesson

To help students think about the minilesson principle, model the process of marking pages in a book. Here is an example.

- Show and read pages 15–16 of *The Can Man*.

    The author wrote, "Tim nodded uneasily," which makes me wonder what Tim is thinking and feeling here. I want to think more about that.

- Add a sticky note to page 15.
- Turn to page 26, where Mr. Peters asks Tim's name.

    It's interesting that the two characters have known each other, but The Can Man didn't know Tim's name. Why did the author write this?

- Add a sticky note to page 19.

    What did you notice I was doing while I was reading?

    I marked some of the pages in the book with sticky notes, so I will remember which pages I want to talk about when I share my thinking with others.

    What are some reasons you might want to talk about a page in a book?

- Record students' responses on chart paper.

Have a Try

Invite the students to turn and talk about a book with a partner.

▶ Share again the pages you marked in *The Can Man*.

> Turn and talk about what you are thinking about one of the pages I marked.

▶ After students turn and talk, ask a few to share their thinking.

Summarize and Apply

Summarize the learning and remind students to mark pages they want to talk about as they read.

> Today you learned you can mark pages with sticky notes while you read. Why would you mark a page with a sticky note?

> You can use sticky notes to help you remember which pages you want to talk about with a partner or with your group. This will get you ready to share your thinking.

▶ Write the minilesson principle at the top of the chart.

> When you read today, use sticky notes to mark two pages that you would like to talk about with a partner. Bring your book when we come back together.

▶ Provide each student with two sticky notes.

Share

Following independent reading time, gather students together in the meeting area to talk about the pages they marked.

> Turn and talk about how you decided which pages to mark with sticky notes.

Extend the Lesson (Optional)

After assessing students' understanding, you might decide to extend the learning.

▶ Give students a stack of sticky notes to keep in their personal boxes so they have easy access to the notes while reading. Be sure to teach them how to use sticky notes sparingly.

▶ **Writing About Reading** After you have taught students how to write about books in a reader's notebook, have them mark with sticky notes pages they want to write about (see Section Four: Writing About Reading for specific minilessons on using a reader's notebook).

When you read, mark places you want to talk about.

Reasons to mark a page:

- You like the way the author has written something.

- You notice something interesting or funny.

- You really like one of the illustrations.

- You don't know what a word means.

- You learn a new word and want to remember it.

- You learn something interesting.

- You wonder what a character is feeling or thinking.

- You wonder why a character does, says, or thinks something.

- You have a question or don't understand something.

Section 2: Literary Analysis

RML4
LA.U1.RML4

Reading Minilesson Principle
Share your opinion and support it with evidence.

Thinking and Talking About Books

You Will Need

▸ a familiar book such as *Sophie's Masterpiece* by Eileen Spinelli, from Text Set: Kindness

▸ chart paper and markers

Academic Language / Important Vocabulary

▸ opinion

▸ support

▸ evidence

Continuum Connection

▸ Give reasons (either text-based or from personal experience) to support thinking (p. 50)

▸ Form and express opinions about a text and support with rationale and evidence (p. 50)

Goal

Express an opinion about a text and support with evidence from the text and/or personal experience.

Rationale

When you teach students to express an opinion about a text and support the opinion with evidence, they think more deeply about the book. They develop their identities as readers and thinkers and become more comfortable expressing ideas.

Assess Learning

Observe students when they share opinions about books. Notice if there is evidence of new learning based on the goal of this minilesson.

▸ Do students share and support their opinions with evidence from the text and/or from personal experience?

▸ Do they use terms such as *opinion*, *support*, and *evidence*?

Minilesson

To help students think about the minilesson principle, use a familiar text to model expressing an opinion. Here is an example.

▸ Show the cover of *Sophie's Masterpiece*.

> This is one of my favorite books. Sophie is very kind. The reason I think so is that in the story she works hard to knit a blanket for a baby who needs one, even though she is old and tired. The author gives beautiful descriptions like "strands of moonlight" and "wisps of night."

> That is my opinion about the book. What did you notice about what I said?

> I gave evidence, or examples, from the book to explain my opinion. You need to support your opinions with evidence so people understand why you think the way you do. You can give evidence from the book's words or illustrations, your life, or things you know.

▸ Create a chart to capture students' opinions with supporting evidence.

> When I shared my opinion that *Sophie's Masterpiece* is a story about being kind, what evidence did I give?

> Was my evidence from the book, my knowledge, or my experience?

▸ Fill in the columns with your opinion and the evidence.

> What evidence did I give for my opinion that I like the way the author writes?

> Was the evidence from the book or from my life?

▸ Add to the chart.

Have a Try

Invite the students to share their opinion about a book with a partner.

> Turn and talk to your partner about what you think about *Sophie's Masterpiece*. Remember to support your opinion with evidence from the book or from your life.

▶ After students turn and talk, ask a few students to share with the class. Record their opinions and evidence on the chart.

Summarize and Apply

Summarize the learning and remind students to support their opinions about books with evidence.

> Today you shared your opinion about the book *Sophie's Masterpiece* and supported it with evidence. What is evidence?
>
> Why is it important to support your opinions with evidence?

▶ Write the minilesson principle at the top of the chart.

> When you read today, think about your opinion about the book you're reading. Be ready to share your opinion and support it with evidence when we come back together.

Share

Following independent reading time, gather students together in the meeting area to talk about their reading.

> Turn and talk to your partner about the book you read today. Share your opinion of the book and support it with evidence.

Extend the Lesson (Optional)

After assessing students' understanding, you might decide to extend the learning.

▶ Ensure students have a clear understanding of the difference between facts and opinions. Explain that facts can be used as evidence to support opinions.

▶ **Writing About Reading** Visit resources.fountasandpinnell.com to download a graphic organizer (General: Thinking and Evidence [Personal Knowledge and the Text]) that students can use to write about their reading in a way similar to the chart.

Share your opinion and support it with evidence.

Title: <u>Sophie's Masterpiece</u>
Author: Eileen Spinelli

Thinking	Evidence from Book	Evidence from My Knowledge or Experience
Sophie is a kind character.	Sophie works very, very hard to knit a blanket for the baby.	
The author writes beautiful descriptions.	She includes beautiful phrases like "strands of moonlight" and "wisps of night."	
The illustrations make the story interesting.	They have interesting details and lots of nice colors.	
Stories about spiders make me scared.		I have been bitten by a spider before.

Assessment

After you have taught the minilessons in this umbrella, observe students as they talk about their reading across instructional contexts: interactive read-aloud, independent reading and literacy work, guided reading, shared reading, and book club. Use *The Literacy Continuum* (Fountas and Pinnell 2017) to observe students' reading behaviors across instructional contexts.

▶ What evidence do you have of new understandings related to thinking and talking about books?

  • Do students think and talk about books in a variety of ways?

  • Are they following the routines for turn and talk?

  • Do they mark pages in books they want to talk about?

  • Are they able to express an opinion and support it with evidence?

  • Do they use terms such as *character*, *opinion*, *support*, and *evidence*?

▶ In what other ways, beyond the scope of this umbrella, are they thinking and talking about books?

  • Are students expressing opinions about specific genres or authors?

  • Are they ready to give book talks?

Use your observations to determine the next umbrella you will teach. You may also consult Minilessons Across the Year (pp. 55-57) for guidance.

Link to Writing

After teaching the minilessons in this umbrella, help students link the new learning to their writing:

▶ Teach your students how to write about their reading in a variety of ways in a reader's notebook. Students can write opinion pieces, book recommendations, letters to you, and other forms of writing. See Section Four: Writing About Reading for guidance on how to introduce and use a reader's notebook.

Reader's Notebook

When this umbrella is complete, provide a copy of the minilesson principles (see resources.fountasandpinnell.com) for students to glue in the reader's notebook (in the Minilessons section if using *Reader's Notebook: Intermediate* [Fountas and Pinnell 2011]), so they can refer to the information as needed.

Minilessons in This Umbrella

RML1   Learn about authors or illustrators by reading many of their books.

RML2   Sometimes authors get ideas for their books from their own lives.

RML3   You can recognize some books by the author or illustrator.

Before Teaching Umbrella 2 Minilessons

During an author or illustrator study, students learn how to notice the decisions made by the authors and illustrators when they created a text. Students gain an understanding of the distinguishing characteristics of an author's or illustrator's work and develop the tools they need to find connections and make predictions. Author study also supports them in noticing and appreciating elements of an author's or illustrator's craft—a foundation for thinking analytically and critically about other texts and for creating texts of their own (see pages 39-40 for more on author/illustrator studies). Teach one or more of these minilessons throughout the year whenever you and your students conduct an author or illustrator study.

The first step in any author study is to collect a set of mentor texts. Use the following books from the *Fountas & Pinnell Classroom™ Interactive Read-Aloud Collection* text sets or choose texts by an author or illustrator that will engage your class.

Author/Illustrator Study: Patricia Polacco

Meteor!

Some Birthday

The Keeping Quilt

Thunder Cake

Author/Illustrator Study: Janell Cannon

Stellaluna

Crickwing

Verdi

Exploring Memory Stories

My Rotten Red-Headed Older Brother by Patricia Polacco

As you read aloud and enjoy these texts together, help students

- make connections among texts by a single author or illustrator, and

- begin to recognize what makes an author's or illustrator's work distinctive.

Patricia Polacco

Janell Cannon

Memory Stories

Section 2: Literary Analysis

Reading Minilesson Principle
Learn about authors or illustrators by reading many of their books.

Studying Authors and Illustrators

You Will Need

- three or four familiar books by the same author and/or illustrator, such as those listed below from Text Set: Patricia Polacco
  - *Meteor!*
  - *Some Birthday*
  - *The Keeping Quilt*
  - *Thunder Cake*
- a basket of additional books by Patricia Polacco
- chart paper and markers

Academic Language / Important Vocabulary

- author
- illustrator
- craft

Continuum Connection

- Make connections (similarities and differences) among texts that have the same author/illustrator, setting, characters, or theme (p.50)
- Connect text by a range of categories: e.g., author, character, topic, genre, illustrator (p. 50)
- Recognize some authors by the style of their illustrations, their topics, characters they use, or typical plots (p. 51)

Goal

Understand that an author or illustrator usually writes several books and that there are often recognizable characteristics across the books.

Rationale

When students recognize the characteristics of an author's or illustrator's work, they begin to appreciate that writing and illustrating books is a process of decision making and that artistry is involved. Students become aware of the writer's or illustrator's craft and how it contributes to the full meaning of the book. Note that this lesson format can be used for an author, illustrator, or author/illustrator study.

Assess Learning

Observe students when they talk about authors and illustrators. Notice if there is evidence of new learning based on the goal of this minilesson.

- Do students recognize similar characteristics among books by the same authors and/or illustrators?
- Can they share opinions about their own author and/or illustrator preferences?
- Do they use the words *author, illustrator,* and *craft*?

Minilesson

To help students think about the minilesson principle, provide an inquiry-based lesson about an author, illustrator, or author/illustrator. Here is an example.

- Show the covers of several books by Patricia Polacco.

  You have read many books by Patricia Polacco. What do you notice about her writing and illustrations?

- On chart paper, write Patricia Polacco's name at the top, and *Noticings* under it. Create separate sections for *Always* and *Often*. As students suggest noticings, help them distinguish between the frequency of characteristics.

  Think about more things you notice in Patricia Polacco's writing and drawing as I read a few pages from *Meteor!*

- Read the first eight pages and show the illustrations.

  What are some other things you notice?

- As needed, prompt the conversation. Continue reading a few more pages in this way. Add students' ideas to the chart, encouraging them to talk about whether to add ideas to the *Always* or *Often* category.

  If you aren't sure about whether these things happen *always* or *often* in Patricia Polacco's books, how could you find out?

▶ Continue the activity for *Some Birthday* and *The Keeping Quilt*, recording noticings on the chart.

> What are some other things you notice?

Have a Try

Invite partners to look at another book by the same author.

▶ Show the cover of *Thunder Cake* and read a few pages, showing the illustrations.

> Turn and talk about what you notice about Patricia Polacco's words and illustrations after thinking about *Thunder Cake*.

▶ Add ideas to the chart.

Summarize and Apply

Summarize the learning and remind students to notice the author's or illustrator's style as they read.

> Today you learned that if you read many books by the same author or illustrator you begin to notice the decisions she makes to write or illustrate her books. When an author or illustrator chooses what to say or how to draw, it is called craft.

> Today, you can choose to read a book by Patricia Polacco if you like. Look for the things we talked about and see if you notice anything new. Bring the book when we meet so you can share.

Share

Following independent reading time, gather students together in the meeting area to talk about their reading.

> Did anyone read a book by Patricia Polacco? Tell what you noticed about her writing or illustrations.

▶ Add any new ideas to the chart.

Extend the Lesson (Optional)

After assessing students' understanding, you might decide to extend the learning.

▶ Repeat the lesson, using books by an author who is not the illustrator, or by an illustrator who is not the author.

▶ Provide opportunities for students to view author and illustrator websites with you to learn more about the author's or illustrator's life and craft.

Patricia Polacco
Noticings:

Always	Often
• She includes details about her own life, family, family history, and culture in her stories.	• She includes sound words in capital letters.
• The colors of her illustrations connect to the mood of the story.	• Her stories take place in the past.
• Her illustrations include patterns.	• Her stories are retellings of folktales.
• Her books have humor.	• Her illustrations are done in both color and black and white.
	• Her books include information about why the characters and events are important to her.

Section 2: Literary Analysis

Reading Minilesson Principle
Sometimes authors get ideas for their books from their own lives.

Studying Authors and Illustrators

You Will Need

- several familiar fiction books that use ideas from the authors' own lives, such as the following:
  - *The Keeping Quilt* by Patricia Polacco, from Text Set: Patricia Polacco
  - *My Rotten Red-Headed Older Brother* by Patricia Polacco, from Text Set: Memory Stories
  - *Meteor!* by Patricia Polacco, from Text Set: Patricia Polacco
- a basket of books with stories based on the authors' lives
- chart paper and markers

Academic Language / Important Vocabulary

- characters
- author
- life
- lives

Continuum Connection

- Use evidence from the text to support statements about the text (p. 50)

Goal

Understand that authors sometimes get writing ideas from their own life experiences.

Rationale

When you teach students to use parts of a book—such as the dedication or author's note—to determine whether or not a story is based upon the author's life, it helps them to make a strong connection to the author and to better understand the author's story.

Assess Learning

Observe students when they talk about where authors get ideas for books. Notice if there is evidence of new learning based on the goal of this minilesson.

- ▶ Do students recognize that sometimes authors get ideas from their own lives?
- ▶ Are they able to talk about details from a book that show that the author used some ideas from his own life?
- ▶ Do they use vocabulary such as *characters, author, life,* and *lives*?

Minilesson

To help students think about the minilesson principle, provide an inquiry-based lesson to show where authors sometimes get ideas for their books. Here is an example.

- ▶ Show the cover and title page of *The Keeping Quilt* and then read the back cover.

  What do you notice about what Patricia Polacco wrote?

  She wrote about a special quilt that has been in her family for many generations. This book was based upon her family experiences.

- ▶ Hold up *My Rotten Red-Headed Older Brother* and read the title.

  I'm going to read the dedication at the front of the book and show you the last two pages of the book.

- ▶ Read the dedication and show the photographs of Polacco's brother.

  What information did you get from the dedication and the photos?

  Do you think the boy in this story, Richard, is based on Patricia Polacco's real brother?

- ▶ Hold up *Meteor!* and read the dedication, the last paragraph of the book, and the first book review on the back cover.

  What information did you get from the parts I read?

  What do we know about Patricia Polacco?

  She gets ideas for her stories from her own life. We know that from reading the dedication, the book reviews, and the author's note at the end of the book.

▶ Write *Places to Look to Find Out Where the Author Got Ideas for a Book* at the top of the chart paper.

> Where can you look to find out if an author got ideas for a story from her own life?

▶ Record responses on the chart.

Have a Try

Invite the students to talk with a partner about where authors get ideas for their books.

> Turn and talk to your partner about why an author might write a book about something from his own life.

▶ After time for discussion, ask students to share ideas.

Summarize and Apply

Help students summarize the learning and remind them to think about where authors get ideas for their books.

> What did you learn about where authors get their ideas for their books?

> When you read a book in independent reading today, look in these places to find out where the author got ideas for the book.

Share

Following independent reading time, gather students together in the meeting area to talk about their reading.

> Where do you think the author got ideas for the book you read today?

> Why do you think that?

Extend the Lesson (Optional)

After assessing students' understanding, you might decide to extend the learning.

▶ Use shared writing to compose a letter to an author with students' questions.

▶ Some children's authors and illustrators are themselves the subject of a book. Loo... a biography or autobiography of a favorite author or illustrator to share with the ...

▶ **Writing About Reading** Encourage students to use experiences from their own l... when they write stories.

Places to Look to Find Out Where the Author Got Ideas for a Book

In the Book	Online
Dedication page	Book reviews
Author's note	Book summaries
Back cover	Author interviews
	Author website

Umbr

Reading Minilesson Principle
You can recognize some books by the author or illustrator.

Studying Authors and Illustrators

You Will Need

- books from authors or illustrators with different, recognizable styles; gather multiple examples from each author/illustrator, including several the students are familiar with, and one you have not read together yet, such as the following:
  - *Stellaluna, Crickwing,* and *Verdi* by Janell Cannon, from Text Set: Janell Cannon
  - *Thunder Cake, The Bee Tree,* and *Meteor!* by Patricia Polacco, from Text Set: Patricia Polacco
- chart paper and markers
- sticky notes

Academic Language / Important Vocabulary

- author
- illustrator
- style

Continuum Connection

- Make connections (similarities, differences) among texts that have the same author/illustrator, setting, characters, or theme (p. 50)
- Recognize some authors by the style of their illustrations, their topics, characters they use, or typical plots (p. 51)

Goal

Recognize and compare different authors' writing and illustrating styles.

Rationale

When students recognize books by the same author or illustrator they can anticipate characteristics of those books, such as theme, illustrations, content, or craft. Students can then make connections between an author's or illustrator's work, and compare that work to other authors or illustrators.

Assess Learning

Observe students when they talk about authors and illustrators. Notice if there is evidence of new learning based on the goal of this minilesson.

- Do students recognize one or more books by the same author's or illustrator?
- Can they talk about similarities in the writing/illustrations of certain authors/illustrators?
- Do they use the words *author, illustrator,* and *style* to talk about books?

Minilesson

To help students think about the minilesson principle, provide an inquiry-based lesson using multiple books by the same author or illustrator. Here is an example:

- Gather three books by Janell Cannon. Cover her name with sticky notes on the front covers of the books. Hold up *Stellaluna*, and read the first couple of pages.

  Who do you think wrote this book? How do you know?

- Record noticings on the chart paper and reveal to students who the author is.
- Repeat the process for the other two books. Continue to record noticings on the chart.

  These are some of the things that you might recognize about Janell Cannon's style from her books. This helps you to know what to expect when you read more books by Janell Cannon.

- Gather three books written by Patricia Polacco and repeat the process.

  Turn and talk to your partner. Who do you think wrote these books? Why do you think that?

- Add noticings to the chart.

Have a Try

Invite the students to work with a partner to try to recognize an author's or illustrator's work.

▶ Choose one or two books from each author or illustrator discussed that students have not experienced. Repeat the process for each book, one at a time.

> Turn and talk to your partner about the person you think wrote this book. Say why you think that.

▶ Provide time for partners to discuss. Encourage them to use the chart. Ask a couple of students to share.

Summarize and Apply

Help students summarize the learning and remind them to say what makes an author's work recognizable.

> What did you learn today about authors and illustrators?

▶ Review the chart and write the principle at the top.

> When you read a book today, notice whether the author or the illustrator has a style of writing or drawing that you recognize from other books by the same person. Be prepared to share what you noticed.

Share

Following independent reading time, gather students together in the meeting area to talk about their reading.

> Who would like to share something you noticed about the author or illustrator of the book you read today? Did you recognize the author or illustrator by the style of her writing or the illustrations?

Extend the Lesson (Optional)

After assessing students' understanding, you might decide to extend the learning.

▶ Make a similar chart for two other authors or illustrators.

▶ Explore author and illustrator websites with students to learn more about the decisions authors and illustrators make when creating books.

You can recognize some books by the author or illustrator.		
	Janell Cannon	Patricia Polacco
Illustrations	Some black and white, some color	Colors connect to the mood of the story
Topics	Animals who are often feared by humans and/or misunderstood	Family stories from her childhood
Characters	Animals such as cockroaches, bats, and snakes	Family members and friends
Plot	Fictional animals are turned away by their friends at first, but then are accepted	Humorous memories from her childhood

Section 2: Literary Analysis

Assessment

After you have taught the minilessons in this umbrella, observe students as they talk and write about their reading across instructional contexts: interactive read-aloud, independent reading and literacy work, guided reading, shared reading, and book club. Use *The Literacy Continuum* (Fountas and Pinnell 2017) to observe students' reading and writing behaviors across instructional contexts.

▶ What evidence do you have of new understanding related to authors and illustrators?

- Do students understand that they can learn about an author or illustrator by reading many of his books?

- Do they understand that authors get ideas for their stories from their own lives?

- Can they recognize some books by their author or illustrator?

- Can they use vocabulary such as *author, illustrator, style,* and *craft* when they study an author's or illustrator's work?

▶ In what other ways, beyond the scope of this umbrella, are students talking about authors and illustrators?

- Are students aware that authors sometimes write several books with the same characters in them?

Use your observations to determine the next umbrella you will teach. You may also consult Minilessons Across the Year (pp. 55-57) for guidance.

Link to Writing

After teaching the minilessons in this umbrella, help students link the new learning to their own writing or drawing:

▶ Students might enjoy creating books using the writing or illustrating style of one of the authors or illustrators they studied. For example, they could use the combination of full color and black and white to illustrate in the style of Janell Cannon, or they could write a story with themselves as a character like Patricia Polacco. Encourage them to share their books with others.

Reader's Notebook

When this umbrella is complete, provide a copy of the minilesson principles (see resources.fountasandpinnell.com) for students to glue in the reader's notebook (in the Minilessons section if using *Reader's Notebook: Intermediate* [Fountas and Pinnell 2011]), so they can refer to the information as needed.

Independent Reading Collection

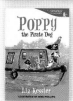

Minilessons in This Umbrella

RML1   A book talk is a short talk about a book (or series of books) you want to recommend.

RML2   Start with a good lead and end in a way that hooks your classmates.

RML3   Write a few notes and page numbers on sticky notes to prepare for your book talk.

RML4   Learn how to give a good book talk.

Before Teaching Umbrella 3 Minilessons

Prior to teaching this series of minilessons, model book talks regularly so students have a good deal of exposure before they begin learning how to give a book talk themselves. (If you are using *Reader's Notebook: Intermediate* [Fountas and Pinnell 2011], see the back of the orange tab for How to Give a Book Talk.) Students should know routines for listening to classmates and talking about books. Books used should be organized into categories, such as genre, author, and topic, and should include the range of independent reading levels of your students. For this umbrella, suggested books are from the *Fountas & Pinnell Classroom™ Independent Reading Collection*.

Independent Reading Collection

The Brave Servant: A Tale from China by Suzanne Barchers

Blast Off to Space Camp by Hillary Wolfe

Cam Jansen: The Ghostly Mystery by David A. Adler

Cam Jansen: The Mystery of Flight 54 by David A. Adler

Beavers by Gail Gibbons

The Absent Author by Ron Roy

Inspector Flytrap by Tom Angleberger

Poppy the Pirate Dog by Liz Kessler

As you model book talks using these books, make sure to

- organize thoughts before giving a book talk,
- keep them short,
- include the title, author, and just a little information about the book,
- use an exciting lead and ending that captures students' interest, and
- use eye contact, a confident voice, and engaging body language.

Section 2: Literary Analysis

Reading Minilesson Principle
A book talk is a short talk about a book (or series of books) you want to recommend.

Giving a Book Talk

You Will Need

- one fiction book, one nonfiction book, and several books in a series that students are unfamiliar with, such as the following from *Independent Reading Collection*:
  - *The Brave Servant: A Tale from China* by Suzanne Barchers
  - *Blast Off to Space Camp* by Hillary Wolfe
  - *Cam Jansen: The Ghostly Mystery* by David A. Adler
  - *Cam Jansen: The Mystery of Flight 54* by David A. Adler
- chart paper and markers

Academic Language / Important Vocabulary

- book talk
- title
- author
- series

Continuum Connection

- Use some academic language to talk about book and print features: e.g., front cover, back cover, title, author, illustrator, page, text, illustration, photograph (p. 52)
- Express opinions and support with evidence (p. 335)
- Speak about a topic with enthusiasm (p. 335)

Goal

Learn that a book talk is a short talk about a book (or series of books) and its purpose is to get others interested in reading it.

Rationale

When you teach students to talk about books in order to get others excited to read them, you encourage them to think about what makes a book interesting and help them learn more about the books in the classroom library.

Assess Learning

Observe students when they discuss giving a book talk. Notice if there is evidence of new learning based on the goal of this minilesson.

- Do students understand the purpose of a book talk?
- Do they talk about what to include in a book talk?
- Do they use the terms *book talk*, *title*, *author*, and *series*?

Minilesson

To help students think about the minilesson principle, provide a demonstration of a book talk. Here is an example.

- Show the cover of *The Brave Servant: A Tale from China*.

  Folktales that use magic are fun to read. In *The Brave Servant: A Tale from China* by Suzanne Barchers, a servant named Jun uses magic to try to save his ruler from danger. Do you want to know if Jun is able to save Lord Luchow from a large invading army? Read the book to find out!

- Show a few illustrations and then close the book.

  Why do you think I told you about this book?

  I wanted to recommend this book to you because I think that you will enjoy reading it. What information did I include? Turn and talk about that.

- After time for discussion, ask students to share their thinking. Write their statements on chart paper.

  Listen to this book talk. Notice if there is anything else about the book talk that can be added to the list.

- Give a book talk for a nonfiction book, such as *Blast Off to Space Camp*.

  What did you notice about the way I gave my book talk? Think about how my voice sounded and the information I gave.

- Add noticings to the chart.

You can also give a book talk for a book series that you enjoyed reading. One that I enjoyed is the Cam Jansen series. Listen as I give a book talk for a series and notice anything that can be added to the chart.

▶ Show a few books from the Cam Jansen series and give a book talk. Then, ask students to share their noticings and add to the chart.

Have a Try

Invite the students to have a conversation about giving a book talk.

> What things will you remember to do when you give a book talk? Turn and talk about that.

▶ After time for discussion, ask volunteers to share their thinking and add new ideas to the chart.

Summarize and Apply

Help students summarize the learning and remind them to think about giving a book talk as they read.

> What is a book talk?

> What will you remember to do when you give a good book talk? Use the chart to help you remember.

> Think of a book you really like. Reread it today. Bring the book when we meet so you can practice giving a book talk with a partner.

Share

Following independent reading time, gather students together in the meeting area to practice giving book talks in pairs.

> Practice giving your book talk to a partner, and then have your partner practice giving a book talk to you. Look back at the chart we made to help you remember what to include.

Extend the Lesson (Optional)

After assessing students' understanding, you might decide to extend the learning.

▶ Encourage students to give book talks on an author, illustrator, or genre that interests them.

▶ If students gave a book talk on a fiction book, encourage them to give one on a nonfiction book and vice versa.

Book Talks

Give a book talk about a book you have read and liked.

Read the book to find out!

Include the title.

Include the author.

Keep it short.

Tell just a little about the book.

Don't tell too much.

Talk about why others should read it.

Sound excited.

Section 2: Literary Analysis

Reading Minilesson Principle

Start with a good lead and end in a way that hooks your classmates.

Giving a Book Talk

You Will Need

- one fiction book and one nonfiction book that students are unfamiliar with, such as the following from *Independent Reading Collection*:
  - *Inspector Flytrap* by Tom Angleberger
  - *Beavers* by Gail Gibbons
- chart paper and markers

Academic Language / Important Vocabulary

- book talk
- lead
- closing
- hook
- interest

Continuum Connection

- Speak about a topic with enthusiasm (p. 335)
- Have an audience in mind before starting to speak (p. 335)

Goal

Learn how to interest other readers by crafting an interesting beginning and ending to the book talk.

Rationale

When you teach students to use different ways to begin and end a book talk, they think about the audience for the book talk and begin to understand the importance of capturing the attention of the audience.

Assess Learning

Observe students when they discuss how to give good book talks. Notice if there is evidence of new learning based on the goal of this minilesson.

- ▶ Are students becoming aware that there are techniques that can be used to make a book talk better?
- ▶ Can they use a good lead and ending in a book talk to capture the attention of the audience?
- ▶ Do they use vocabulary such as *book talk, lead, closing, hook,* and *interest*?

Minilesson

To help students think about the minilesson principle, provide an inquiry-based lesson to help them think about the lead and closing of a book talk. Here is an example.

- ▶ Show the cover of *Inspector Flytrap*.

  Can you imagine that a Venus Flytrap plant could be a big-time detective? If you read this book, *Inspector Flytrap* by Tom Angleberger, you will see how this can really happen, at least in this story! He even has an assistant named Nina the Goat who eats everything. If you enjoy hilarious stories with a little bit of mystery, this book is for you.

- ▶ Show one illustration from the story and close the book.

  What did you notice about this book talk?

  The first sentence is called the lead and the last sentence is called the closing. Turn and talk about how I started and ended this book talk.

- ▶ After time for discussion, ask volunteers to talk about how you hooked the audience with the lead and closing. On chart paper, begin a list of interesting ways to begin and end a book talk.

  I am going to give another book talk. Notice the lead and closing that I use to try to hook your attention.

▶ Give a book talk for *Beavers*, using a different lead and closing, such as starting with an interesting fact or closing with a few hints about the book.

> What did you notice about the lead and closing that I used?

▶ Add to the list. Repeat the activity with several more lead and closing styles using these same books.

Have a Try

Invite the students to talk with a partner about making book talks better by using a good lead and a good closing.

> Turn and talk about the ways you can begin or end a book talk to hook your classmates and encourage them to read the book.

▶ After time for discussion, ask students to share their thinking. Add any new ideas to the list.

Summarize and Apply

Help students summarize the learning and remind them to use a good lead and closing to hook the audience in a book talk.

> How can you make a book talk interesting?

▶ Write the principle on the chart.

> When you read today, choose a book that you want to recommend to classmates. Think about a good lead and a way to end your book talk to hook your classmates. Bring the book when we meet after independent reading time so you can share your ideas.

Share

Following independent reading time, gather the students together in the meeting area in pairs to share book talk ideas.

> Talk about the book you want to recommend and the lead and closing you could use in your book talk about the book.

Extend the Lesson (Optional)

After assessing students' understanding, you might decide to extend the learning.

▶ Repeat this minilesson with additional lead and closing ideas as needed.

▶ Encourage students to brainstorm with others to think of good lead and closing ideas for book talks.

Start with a good lead and end in a way that hooks your classmates.

Ways to Start: The Lead	Ways to End: The Closing
Ask a question.	Tell why others should read the book.
Say an interesting fact.	Give a few hints about the book.
Tell an exciting part.	Use a cliffhanger.
Surprise the audience.	Read a short quote.

Reading Minilesson Principle
Write a few notes and page numbers on sticky notes to prepare for your book talk.

Giving a Book Talk

You Will Need

- a book with which students are familiar and that is at an independent reading level, such as *The Absent Author* by Ron Roy, from *Independent Reading Collection*
- yellow rectangles of paper
- tape or glue
- sticky notes
- chart paper and markers

Academic Language / Important Vocabulary

- book talk
- notes
- page numbers
- sticky notes

Continuum Connection

- Have a plan or notes to support the presentation [p. 335]

Goal

Compose notes to remember important information about a book.

Rationale

When students learn techniques for preparing for a book talk, such as writing on sticky notes, they have to think about what is interesting in the book they have chosen. Preparation techniques will be useful for any presentation students give to an audience.

Assess Learning

Observe students while they prepare to give a book talk. Notice if there is evidence of new learning based on the goal of this minilesson.

▶ Do students understand that it is important to think about why a book is interesting before giving a book talk?

▶ Can they use sticky notes thoughtfully to prepare for a book talk?

Minilesson

To help students think about the minilesson principle, provide a demonstration of how to use a few sticky notes to prepare for a book talk. Here is an example.

> What can you do to help you remember to say something important about the book when you give a book talk?

▶ Guide students to understand that they can use two or three sticky notes to remember page numbers and important parts to include in a book talk.

▶ Show the cover of *The Absent Author*.

> What is an important part from *The Absent Author* that you would want to include in a book talk?

> What could you write on a sticky note about that?

> After you write on the sticky note, place it carefully on the page with a little bit sticking out so you can find the part you want to talk about when you give your book talk.

▶ As a volunteer suggests an idea, write it on one of the yellow pieces of paper and affix it to the chart paper. Then, begin the book talk, modeling how you use sticky notes to remember important details.

> Have you ever wanted to meet a favorite author? That's what Dink and his friends wanted to do when they heard that Wallis Wallace, a famous author, was coming to town. But the author has gone missing! Here is a mystery story about how the kids try to track Wallis down, called *The Absent Author* by Ron Roy.

▶ Show the picture of the letter from Wallis Wallace at the beginning of the book. This page shows the letter from Wallis Wallace.

> What could I write on a sticky note to help me remember this when I give the book talk?

▶ Write a response on the other yellow piece of paper and attach it to the chart. Finish the book talk.

Have a Try

Invite the students to talk with a partner about using sticky notes to prepare for a book talk.

> Turn and talk about some of the kinds of things you might write on a sticky note to help you prepare for a book talk.

Summarize and Apply

Summarize the learning and remind students to use sticky notes to prepare for a book talk.

> You learned that one way you can prepare for a book talk is to write on sticky notes.

▶ Write the principle at the top of the chart.

> Today, choose a book you want to recommend to classmates. Use two or three sticky notes to write words or page numbers from the book to prepare for your book talk. Bring the book and sticky notes when we meet so you can share.

Share

Following independent reading time, gather the students together in pairs to share their sticky notes and book.

> Share the book you want to recommend and your sticky notes with a partner. Does your partner think the parts you marked are interesting?

Extend the Lesson (Optional)

After assessing students' understanding, you might decide to extend the learning.

▶ **Writing About Reading** Students can first write notes about the important parts of a book in the Writing About Reading section of a reader's notebook. These notes can be used to get ideas for pages in the book to mark with sticky notes.

Write a few notes and page numbers on sticky notes to prepare for your book talk.

> The Absent Author
> Ron Roy
>
> Dink and friends try to solve a mystery.

> Page 9
> Letter from Wallis Wallace.
> The author who disappears.

RML4

LA.U3.RML4

Reading Minilesson Principle
Learn how to give a good book talk.

Giving a Book Talk

You Will Need

- a book that lends itself to a good book talk, such *Poppy the Pirate Dog* by Liz Kessler, from *Independent Reading Collection*
- prepared sticky notes for a book talk on *Poppy the Pirate Dog*
- chart paper and markers

Academic Language / Important Vocabulary

- book talk
- prepare
- present
- eye contact
- voice
- enthusiastic

Continuum Connection

- Speak about a topic with enthusiasm (p. 335)
- Have an audience in mind before starting to speak (p. 335)
- Look at the audience (or other person) while talking (p. 335)
- Speak at an appropriate rate to be understood (p. 335)

Goal

Prepare and present the book confidently, clearly, and enthusiastically.

Rationale

When students learn how to give a good book talk by planning, preparing, practicing, and using appropriate voice and body language, they develop presentation skills and learn to express opinions about books in a way that gets others interested in reading.

Assess Learning

Observe students when they prepare and practice book talks. Notice if there is evidence of new learning based on the goal of this minilesson.

- Are students thinking and talking about ways to give good book talks?
- Do students try using different techniques to improve book talks?
- Do they understand the terms *book talk*, *prepare*, *present*, *eye contact*, *voice*, and *enthusiastic*?

Minilesson

To help students think about the minilesson principle, provide an interactive lesson to help them think about the techniques that can be used to give a good book talk. Here is an example.

- Ahead of time, prepare a few sticky notes for a book talk on *Poppy the Pirate Dog*. Display the cover.

  As I give a book talk today for *Poppy the Pirate Dog*, notice all of the things I do to help get you interested in the book.

- Give a book talk, modeling successful techniques. Emphasize your use of prepared sticky notes and other behaviors so students can observe what a good book talk looks and sounds like.

  A dog that is also a pirate—how is that possible? Well, in this story by Liz Kessler called *Poppy the Pirate Dog*, you will learn just how this might happen.

- Show the page where Poppy finds the pirate scarf at the beach.

  Here is Poppy at the beach when she finds a scarf with skulls and decides to become a pirate dog! But every pirate needs a ship, and you will love the funny things that happen as Poppy searches for her pirate ship. If you like funny stories about dog adventures, you will love *Poppy the Pirate Dog*.

- Close the book.

  What did you notice that I did to get you interested in reading *Poppy the*

Pirate Dog? What do you think I did to prepare for the book talk? Turn and talk about your ideas.

▶ After time for discussion, ask students to share ideas. On chart paper, make a list of ways to give a good book talk.

Have a Try

Invite students to talk with a partner about how to give a good book talk.

> Turn and talk about the book you will use to give a book talk. Talk about which ideas you will use from the chart.

▶ After discussion, ask a few volunteers to share their thinking.

Summarize and Apply

Summarize the learning and remind students to use the ideas on the chart when preparing for a book talk.

> What are some ways to give a good book talk? Use the chart to remember.

> During independent reading time, prepare for and practice your book talk. Bring your book when we meet so you can practice with a partner.

Share

Following independent reading time, gather the students together in pairs.

> With a partner, take turns practicing your book talk. After each person is finished, look back at the chart and talk about which things were included and which things can be added to make each book talk even better.

Extend the Lesson (Optional)

After assessing students' understanding, you might decide to extend the learning.

▶ Refer students to the How to Give a Good Book Talk in *Reader's Notebook: Intermediate* (Fountas and Pinnell 2011) for additional support.

▶ Provide regular opportunities for students to enjoy giving and listening to book talks.

Ways to Give a Good Book Talk

1. Use a good lead and closing.

2. Use sticky notes to write important ideas or to mark a place in the book.

3. Think about what will make others excited to read it.

4. Practice standing straight and holding the book so everyone can see it.

5. Look at your audience.

6. Speak clearly.

7. Use a good voice volume.

8. Use an enthusiastic voice.

Section 2: Literary Analysis

Assessment

After you have taught the minilessons in this umbrella, observe students as they talk and write about their reading across instructional contexts: interactive read-aloud, independent reading and literacy work, guided reading, shared reading, and book club. Use *The Literacy Continuum* (Fountas and Pinnell 2017) to observe students' reading and writing behaviors across instructional contexts.

▶ What evidence do you have of new understandings related to giving a book talk?

- Do students understand that a book talk is short and is about a book they want to recommend to others?
- Can they talk about effective leads and closings?
- Are they able to prepare for and give a book talk independently?
- Do they use eye contact, body language, and voice control when giving a book talk?
- Do they use academic vocabulary, such as *title*, *author*, *series*, *lead*, and *closing* when talking about book talks?

▶ In what other ways, beyond the scope of this umbrella, are students demonstrating an ability to give a book talk?

- Do students record the titles of books in a reader's notebook that they want to read after listening to a book talk?

Use your observations to determine the next umbrella you will teach. You may also consult Minilessons Across the Year (pp. 55-57) for guidance.

Link to Writing

After teaching the minilessons in this umbrella, help students link the new learning to their own writing:

▶ Record students giving book talks. Have them write about what they did well and what they would like to improve upon for next time.

▶ Students can use what they have learned about giving a book talk in writing a book recommendation.

Reader's Notebook

When this umbrella is complete, provide a copy of the minilesson principles (see resources.fountasandpinnell.com) for students to glue in the reader's notebook (in the Minilessons section if using *Reader's Notebook: Intermediate* [Fountas and Pinnell 2011]), so they can refer to the information as needed.

Minilessons in This Umbrella

RML1 Choose a book you would like to read and talk about.

RML2 Mark the pages you want to talk about.

RML3 Talk with each other about your thinking in book club.

RML4 Show respect to each other in a book club discussion.

RML5 Agree or disagree respectfully with each other's thinking.

RML6 Ask questions to understand each other's thinking.

RML7 Add to an idea before you talk about a different idea.

RML8 Talk about what went well and what you want to work on to get better.

Before Teaching Umbrella 4 Minilessons

The minilessons in this umbrella are designed to help you introduce and teach procedures and routines to establish book clubs in your classroom. Book clubs are meetings facilitated by the teacher with about four to six students of varying reading abilities who come together to discuss a common text. The goal is for the students to share their thinking with each other and build a richer meaning than one reader could gain alone. In a small book club, it will be easier for students to get to know each other's point of view and for everyone to have more opportunities to talk (see pages 68-69 for more information on book clubs). You can also observe the students' thinking to guide your instruction.

The minilessons in this umbrella use books from the *Fountas & Pinnell Classroom™ Book Club Collection* and the *Interactive Read-Aloud Collection* (see also the Book Club Conferring Cards for more book talk suggestions).

Book Club Collection

Family

Amber Brown Is Feeling Blue by Paula Danziger

Butterfly Boy by Virginia Kroll

Friend or Fiend? with the Pain & the Great One by Judy Blume

Julian, Dream Doctor by Ann Cameron

Interactive Read-Aloud Collection

Connecting Across Generations: Family

Mooncakes by Loretta Seto

**Book Club
Family**

**Interactive Read-Aloud
Collection
Family**

Section 2: Literary Analysis

Reading Minilesson Principle
Choose a book you would like to read and talk about.

Getting Started with Book Clubs

You Will Need

▸ prepare book talks for four books students have not read or heard, such as the following from the *Book Club Collection* text set: Family:

- *Amber Brown Is Feeling Blue* by Paula Danziger
- *Butterfly Boy* by Virgina Kroll
- *Friend or Fiend? with the Pain & the Great One* by Judy Blume
- *Julian, Dream Doctor* by Ann Cameron

▸ for each student, a list of the book titles

Academic Language / Important Vocabulary

▸ book club
▸ title
▸ author
▸ illustrator

Continuum Connection

▸ Form and express opinions about a text and support with rationale and evidence (p. 50)

Goal

Learn how to make a good book choice for book club meetings.

Rationale

When students have a choice in what they read for book clubs, they are more motivated to read and engaged with the book. This contributes to a positive book club experience.

Assess Learning

Observe students when they choose books for book club meetings and notice if there is evidence of new learning based on the goal of this minilesson.

▸ Are students able to identify information that will help them select a book they want to read?

▸ Do they use the terms *book club, title, author,* and *illustrator*?

Minilesson

To help students think about the minilesson principle, demonstrate the process of choosing a book for a book club. Here is an example.

> I am going to tell you a little about four books. As I do, think about which of these books you would like to read and then talk about with your classmates.

▸ Show the cover of *Amber Brown Is Feeling Blue*.

> Poor Amber! Before the arrival of Kelly Green, Amber had the only colorful name in the class. Now she is no longer special. Worse, her parents are divorced and they have both invited her to spend Thanksgiving with them—on opposite sides of the country. What will Amber do?

> Do you think you would like to read about Amber Brown? Why?

▸ Turn through a few pages.

▸ Continue giving a short book talk for the other three books (see Book Club cards for Suggested talks).

> You have now listened to a book talk about four different books. Think about which ones you would enjoy reading.

▸ Write the title choices on chart paper to show students how to fill in the prepared paper with a list of the book titles.

> I will give you a list of the four books. Write *1* for the book that is your first choice to read, *2* for your second choice, *3* for your third choice, and *4* for your fourth choice.

Have a Try

Invite the students to talk about choosing books with a partner.

> What are some things to think about when choosing one of the books to read? Turn and talk about that.

▶ After time for discussion, ask students to share their thinking.

Summarize and Apply

Summarize the learning and remind students to think about what books they might want to read.

> What are some ways you can choose a book to read and talk about in book club?

▶ Write students' ideas on the chart and add the principle to the chart. Distribute the prepared papers.

> During independent reading time today, fill out the sheet of paper to show your preferences for the book to read for book club. Bring your numbered list when we meet together to share.

Share

Following independent reading time, gather the students together in groups of three.

> Share your book choice list with your group. Talk about the reasons you numbered your list the way you did.

Extend the Lesson (Optional)

After assessing students' understanding, you might decide to extend the learning.

▶ Organize book club groups according to students' choices as much as possible. Explain that not everyone will get his first choice this time.

▶ Keep the chart posted to remind students of what to think about when they self-select books. Revisit the list from time to time and ask students for additional ideas to add.

Choose a book you would like to read and talk about.

- It sounds interesting.

- It is about a topic you like.

- It is by an author you like.

- It sounds like it will be exciting.

- I would like to talk about the book.

Reading Minilesson Principle
Mark the pages you want to talk about.

Getting Started with Book Clubs

You Will Need

- a familiar book, such as the following:
  - *Mooncakes* by Loretta Seto, from the *Interactive Read-Aloud Collection* text set: Family
- sticky notes prepared with page numbers and a few words, as if for book club, and placed on pages in *Mooncakes*
- chart paper and markers
- sticky notes
- sets of book club books

Academic Language / Important Vocabulary

- book club
- sticky notes
- remember
- discuss

Continuum Connection

- Form and express opinions about a text and support with rationale and evidence (p. 50)

Goal

Identify the important information to discuss in preparation of book clubs.

Rationale

When students learn to mark parts of the book that they want to discuss, they think critically about the book and develop a process for preparing for discussion. Use a familiar book to model marking pages so all students can follow the lesson and apply it to their own book club selection. Students can mark pages after reading the book.

Assess Learning

Observe students when they prepare for a book club meeting and notice if there is evidence of new learning based on the goal of this minilesson.

- ▶ Do students understand the purpose of marking pages in a book?
- ▶ Are they able to identify and mark relevant pages in a book to prepare for a book club meeting?
- ▶ Do they use the terms *book club, sticky notes, remember,* and *discuss?*

Minilesson

To help students think about the minilesson principle, use a familiar book to model how to mark pages with sticky notes for a book club. Here is an example.

- ▶ Hold up *Mooncakes* with the sticky notes showing.

  Here is a book you know, *Mooncakes*. Imagine this is my choice for book club. I have done some things to prepare for the book club meeting.

- ▶ Show page 2 with the first sticky note.

  On this page, there is a sticky note that says *p. 2 Girl is happy.* I want to remember to talk about how happy the girl looks and the evidence that makes me think that.

- ▶ Place the sticky note on the left side of the chart paper.

  Now let's look at another sticky note.

- ▶ Show page 4 with the second sticky note.

  On this page, I added a sticky note that says *p. 4 Cakes are circles.* I wanted to remember to talk about how the cakes were shaped like circles just like the moon.

- ▶ Continue with the rest of the sticky notes (see the chart), explaining your thinking for each.

  What are some of the things you notice I marked on these sticky notes?

▶ Using students' ideas, write the reason for the sticky note content on the right side of the chart paper. Help with word choice so that the reason could apply to any book.

Have a Try

Invite the students to talk with a partner about using sticky notes to prepare for a book club meeting.

> Turn and talk about other types of information a sticky note could help you remember about your book.

▶ After time for discussion, ask students to share their thinking. Add new ideas to the chart.

Summarize and Apply

Summarize the learning and remind students to use sticky notes to prepare for book club meetings.

> What did you learn about using sticky notes?

▶ Add the principle to the chart.

> When you read today, use sticky notes to mark a few pages to prepare for your book club meeting. You may want to read the whole book first and then go back to mark a few places you want to talk about. Remember to add the page number in case the sticky note falls out. Write just a few words on the note. Bring the book when we meet so you can share.

Share

Following independent reading time, gather the students in groups of three.

> Share the pages that you added a sticky note to and read what you wrote. Tell your group why you want to remember each page.

Extend the Lesson (Optional)

After assessing students' understanding, you might decide to extend the learning.

▶ Once students know how to mark pages to prepare for book clubs, you may want to introduce Thinkmarks. Thinkmarks are bookmarks that provide space to record the page number and some thoughts (see resources.fountasandpinnell.com).

▶ Students can use Genre Thinkmarks to think more specifically about a particular genre (see resources.fountasandpinnell.com).

Mark the pages you want to talk about.

p. 2 Girl is happy.	• Character feelings
p. 4 Cakes are circles.	• Interesting parts
p. 10 Hou-Yi is mean.	• Problems
p. 18 Teapot design matches story.	• Details in illustrations
p. 23 Why doesn't lantern burn?	• Questions

Section 2: Literary Analysis

RML3
LA.U4.RML3

Reading Minilesson Principle
Talk with each other about your thinking in book club.

Getting Started with Book Clubs

You Will Need

- four students prepared in advance to model how to share their thinking in a book club
- students' book club books
- chart paper and markers

Academic Language / Important Vocabulary

- author
- illustrator
- book club
- discussion

Continuum Connection

- Use evidence from the text to support statements about the text (p. 50)
- Form and express opinions about a text and support with rationale and evidence (p. 50)
- Form and state the basis for opinions about authors and illustrators (p. 50)
- Express opinions and support with evidence (p. 335)

Goal

Learn how to identify different ways of talking about books during book club.

Rationale

When students learn to share ideas in a book club, it creates enthusiasm for talking about books, contributes to a rich conversation, and expands comprehension. A fishbowl technique, where a prepared group of students sits in a small circle to model a book club discussion and the remaining students sit in a large circle around the group to observe, is a useful way to demonstrate the idea. The demonstration should not be long: no more than five minutes.

Assess Learning

Observe students in a book club meeting and notice if there is evidence of new learning based on the goal of this minilesson.

- ▶ Are students able to express opinions about books?
- ▶ Do they use the terms *author, illustrator, book club,* and *discussion*?

Minilesson

To help students think about the minilesson principle, provide a fishbowl demonstration, and then engage students in an inquiry about their observations. Here is an example.

- ▶ Ahead of time, prepare a book club group to demonstrate a book club meeting. Assist students with marking pages in the book they selected for book club and deciding what to talk about. Select a few areas from the chart to focus on as you prepare the group.

- ▶ Have the prepared book club members sit in an inner circle with their books while the remaining students sit in an outside circle to observe.

  Today, this group is going to talk about the book they chose for book club. Observe what they say and do and then we will talk about it after they finish.

- ▶ Leading the conversation as needed, have the book club members talk about their thinking for a few minutes. Encourage them to show marked pages and talk about why they marked those pages.

  Think about what you noticed these book club members doing. Turn and talk about that.

- ▶ Have students move their seats so everyone can see an easel with chart paper.

  What are some things you noticed that they did and talked about?

▶ Make a list of students' noticings on chart paper. Assist them in rephrasing statements so that they can apply to other books, not just the specific book they observed students talking about.

Have a Try

Invite the students to talk with a partner about their own book club discussion ideas.

> Think about the book you are reading for book club. Turn and talk about some things you might want to talk about in a book club.

▶ After time for discussion, have students share ideas. Add to the list on the chart.

Summarize and Apply

Summarize the learning and remind students to think about different ways to talk about books in book club meetings.

> Today you noticed different ways to talk about books in book club meetings.

▶ Write the principle at the top of the chart.

> Reread your book club today and see if there is anything more you want to add to your notes for your discussion. Look at the chart for more ideas. I will be meeting with one book club today, and those students will share about their book club when we have a class meeting.

Share

Following independent reading time, gather the students together. Have the book club you met with share the things they discussed in their book club.

> Is there anything that could be added to the chart based on what these book club members shared with you?

Extend the Lesson (Optional)

After assessing students' understanding, you might decide to extend the learning.

▶ Keep the chart posted and add new ideas for sharing thinking about books.

Talk with each other about your thinking in book club.

In book club, you can talk about . . .

- the title
- the author
- the illustrator
- the characters
- the setting
- the problem
- an illustration
- an interesting fact
- a part that is interesting, funny, confusing, exciting, or surprising
- how the book ends
- the genre
- words or phrases that you like

A part that surprised me was when . . .

Section 2: Literary Analysis

RML4
LA.U4.RML4

Reading Minilesson Principle
Show respect to each other in a book club discussion.

Getting Started with Book Clubs

You Will Need

- four students prepared to show respectful book club routines using their book club choice
- students' book club books
- chart paper and markers

Academic Language / Important Vocabulary

- book club
- discussion
- behavior
- respect

Continuum Connection

- Demonstrate respectful listening behaviors (p. 335)
- Use turn-taking with courtesy in small-group discussion (p. 335)
- Look at the audience (or other person) while talking (p. 335)

Goal

Identify the routines of a book club and how to show respect during discussion.

Rationale

When students are able to follow book club routines such as ensuring everyone is on the same page and showing respect during book discussions, it helps establish positive oral communication skills and respect toward others.

Assess Learning

Observe students in book club meetings and notice if there is evidence of new learning based on the goal of this minilesson.

- Do students follow book club routines, showing respect for others in the group?
- Are they able to understand the reasons for being respectful to book club members?
- Do they use the terms *book club, discussion, behavior,* and *respect*?

Minilesson

To help students think about the minilesson principle, provide a fishbowl demonstration, and then engage students in an inquiry about their observations. Here is an example.

- Ahead of time, prepare a group of book club members to demonstrate respectful behaviors. See chart for areas to focus on as you prepare the group.
- Have the prepared book club members sit in an inner circle with their books while the remaining students sit in an outside circle to observe.

  Today, this group is going to talk about the book the club members chose for book club. Observe what they say and do and we will talk about it after they finish.

- Leading the conversation as needed, have the book club members talk about their thinking about the book for a few minutes. Focus on respectful behaviors, such as taking turns, giving everyone a chance to speak, inviting others into the conversation, looking at the speaker, listening, and making sure everyone is on the same page.

- Have students move their seats so everyone can see an easel with chart paper.

  Think about what you noticed about the way the book club members treated each other. What did you notice?

- As students share, record responses about respectful book club behaviors.

Have a Try

Invite the students to talk with a partner about ways to show respect during book club.

> These ideas all are ways to show respect toward each other. Turn and talk about other ideas you have about ways to show respect during book club.

▶ After time for discussion, have students share ideas. Record any new ideas on the chart.

Summarize and Apply

Summarize the learning and remind students to use respectful behaviors during book club meetings.

> You learned about some respectful ways to treat each other during book club meetings.

▶ Write the principle at the top of the chart.

> The next time you meet with your book club, think about how to show respect to each other in a book club discussion.

▶ Meet with a book club as the other students are engaged in independent literacy work.

Share

Following independent reading time, gather the students together. Ask the group that met in book club to share.

> What are some examples of what your group did to have a good book club today?

Extend the Lesson (Optional)

After assessing students' understanding, you might decide to extend the learning.

▶ Keep the book club chart posted so students can refer to it during book club meetings. As new issues arise during book club meetings, talk about them as a class and add to the list.

Show respect to each other in a book club discussion.

Take turns.

Be sure everyone gets time to talk.

Invite others into the discussion.

Look at the speaker.

Listen.

Make sure everyone is on the same page.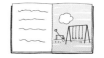

Use an appropriate voice.

Section 2: Literary Analysis

Reading Minilesson Principle
Agree or disagree respectfully with each other's thinking.

Getting Started with Book Clubs

You Will Need

- four students prepared to demonstrate agreeing and disagreeing politely while discussing their book club choice
- students' book club books
- chart paper and markers

Academic Language / Important Vocabulary

- book club
- discussion
- agree
- disagree

Continuum Connection

- Use evidence from the text to support statements about the text (p. 50)
- Use conventions of respectful conversation. Use appropriate conventions in small-group discussion (e.g., "I agree with _____ because . . ."; "I'd like to change the subject . . .") (p. 335)

Goal

Learn how to agree and disagree respectfully and to provide evidence for thinking.

Rationale

When students learn to listen and respond respectfully during book club by agreeing, disagreeing, adding on, and explaining their reasoning, they build important oral communication skills, enhance their book club discussions, and gain a deeper understanding of the book.

Assess Learning

Observe students during book club meetings and notice if there is evidence of new learning based on the goal of this minilesson.

- Are students able to agree and disagree respectfully?
- Do they provide text evidence to support thinking?
- Do they use the terms *book club, discussion, agree,* and *disagree*?

Minilesson

To help students think about the minilesson principle, provide a fishbowl demonstration, and then engage students in an inquiry about their observations. Here is an example.

- Ahead of time, prepare a group of book club members to model ways to agree or disagree respectfully in a book club meeting (see prompt examples on the next page). Include ways for them to use text evidence to support their opinions.
- Have the prepared book club members sit in an inner circle with their books while the remaining students sit in an outside circle to observe.

  Today, this group is going to talk about the book the members chose for book club. Observe how they agree and disagree with one another.

- Leading the conversation as needed, have the book club members talk about their thinking about the book for a few minutes. Focus on language they use for agreeing or disagreeing, as well as making sure they provide text evidence for their opinions.

  What did you notice about the way they agreed or disagreed with each other?

- Have students move their seats so everyone can see an easel with chart paper.

  What did you notice? What are some examples of things they said?

- Make a list on chart paper based on students' suggestions. Emphasize that the goals are to respectfully agree or disagree and to use examples from the book to support thinking.

Have a Try

Invite the students to talk with a partner about agreeing or disagreeing respectfully during book clubs.

> Turn and talk about the ways you can be respectful when you agree or disagree during book club. Tell your partner how you can use the book to support your opinion.

▶ After time for discussion, have students share ideas. Record new ideas on the chart.

Summarize and Apply

Summarize the learning and remind students to think about book clubs.

> What did you learn today about the way to talk to each other during book club meetings?

▶ Write the principle at the top of the chart.

> When you meet with your book club, look back at the chart and remember the way to talk to each other.

▶ Meet with a book club while other students are engaged in independent literacy work.

Share

Following independent reading time, gather the students together. Ask the group that met in book club to share.

> What are some examples of what your group did to have a good book club today?

Extend the Lesson (Optional)

After assessing students' understanding, you might decide to extend the learning.

▶ Keep the chart posted and refer back to it during book club meetings as needed. Add new ideas to the chart as they arise.

▶ If you have *Fountas & Pinnell Prompting Guide, Part 2, for Comprehension: Thinking, Talking, and Writing* (Fountas and Pinnell 2012), refer to the prompts for agreeing and disagreeing in Section IV: Prompts for Book Discussions.

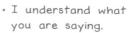

Agree or disagree respectfully with each other's thinking.

- I agree with what you are saying because _____.

- I disagree because _____.

- I thought about that in a different way.

- I understand what you are saying.

- That is interesting. I didn't think of that.

- That makes sense, but _____.

- Now I'm thinking _____.

"On the other hand . . ."

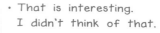

RML 6
LA.U4.RML6

Reading Minilesson Principle
Ask questions to understand each other's thinking.

Getting Started with Book Clubs

You Will Need

- four students whom you have prepared to model asking questions about their classmates' thinking
- students' book club books
- chart paper and markers

Academic Language / Important Vocabulary

- book club
- questions

Continuum Connection

- Ask questions for clarification or to gain information (p. 335)

Goal

Learn how to ask genuine questions to learn more about one another's thinking.

Rationale

Students listen to others model real questions they have about books they have read. Unlike other minilessons in this umbrella, a fishbowl technique is not used in order that students can hear a greater variety of questions.

Assess Learning

Observe students during book club meetings and notice if there is evidence of new learning based on the goal of this minilesson.

- ▸ Are students asking relevant, thoughtful questions during book club meetings?
- ▸ Do they understand why questions are an important part of book club discussions?
- ▸ Do they use the terms *book club* and *questions*?

Minilesson

To help students think about the minilesson principle, engage them in a discussion about asking questions to clarify their understanding of what their classmates are thinking. Here is an example.

- ▸ Ahead of time, prepare a group of book club members to model asking questions during book club meetings. Use the questions on the chart to guide the preparation.
- ▸ Gather students in the meeting area. Place an easel with chart paper where all can see it.

  Today, several book club members are going to have a book club discussion. Listen as they talk with each other and ask questions.

- ▸ Have the book club members read their questions aloud one at a time, placing their sticky notes on the chart paper as they read.

  Are there some questions that are similar? Let's group those together.

  How can you phrase the questions so that you can ask them about any book?

- ▸ Remove the sticky notes as the category of question is addressed. Help students rephrase the ideas in ways that can be applied to other books.

Have a Try

Invite the students to talk with a partner about questions they could ask in a book club meeting.

> Turn and talk about how you can make your voice and your questions sound respectful when you ask questions of a member of your book club.

▶ After time for discussion, have students share ideas.

Summarize and Apply

Summarize the learning and remind students to think about questions they want to ask during book club meetings.

> Today you learned some questions you could ask during a book club meeting to make sure you understand what your classmates are thinking.

▶ Write the principle at the top of the chart.

> When you prepare for a book club, think about the questions you can ask. When you meet with your book club, look at the chart and think about questions you can ask.

▶ Meet with a book club while the other students are engaged in independent literacy work.

Share

Following independent reading time, gather the students together a circle. Ask the group that met in book club to share.

> What kinds of questions did you ask in book club?

> How did the questions help make the book club better?

Extend the Lesson (Optional)

After assessing students' understanding, you might decide to extend the learning.

▶ Introduce higher-level questions as students become more proficient with asking questions during book club. If you have *Fountas & Pinnell Prompting Guide, Part 2, for Comprehension: Thinking, Talking, and Writing* (Fountas and Pinnell 2012), refer to Section IV: Prompts for Book Discussions.

Ask questions to understand each other's thinking.

I didn't understand _____.

Can you talk more about that?

I don't understand what you mean by _____.

What do you think _____?

Why do you think _____?

What surprised you?

What was interesting to you about _____?

Reading Minilesson Principle
Add to an idea before you talk about a different idea.

Getting Started with Book Clubs

You Will Need

- four students prepared to show how to build on the ideas of others and respectfully change the discussion during a book club
- students' book club books
- chart paper and markers

Academic Language / Important Vocabulary

- discussion
- idea
- change the subject
- agree
- disagree

Continuum Connection

- Follow a topic and add to a discussion with comments on the same topic (p. 335)
- Listen, respond, and build on the statements of others (p. 335)
- Use appropriate conventions in small-group discussion (e.g., "I agree with _____ because . . ."; "I'd like to change the subject . . ." (p. 335)

Goal

Learn how to build on one another's ideas before changing the topic or idea.

Rationale

When students learn ways to build on one another's ideas, they become better listeners and are better able to contribute to book discussions. To help students understand that agreeing and disagreeing is sometimes part of building on an idea, it is best to teach RML5 (pp. 146-147) prior to teaching this lesson.

Assess Learning

Observe students during book club meetings and notice if there is evidence of new learning based on the goal of this minilesson.

- Are students able to build on the idea of another student in a book club discussion?
- Are they able to change the subject in an appropriate way?
- Do they use the terms *discussion, idea, change the subject, agree,* and *disagree*?

Minilesson

To help students think about the minilesson principle, provide a fishbowl demonstration and then engage students in an inquiry about their observations. Here is an example.

- Have the prepared book club members sit in an inner circle with their books while the remaining students sit in an outside circle to observe.

  Today, this group is going to talk about the book they chose for book club. Observe how they add more to an idea before they change the topic and talk about a new idea.

- Leading the conversation as needed, have the book club members model using hand signals as well as language that respectfully builds on the ideas of others. Hand signals are a temporary technique for helping students show during a discussion that they want to change the subject or stay with an idea. Two fingers signal a connected idea; a thumb indicates a plan to change the topic.

  Think about what you noticed about the way that book club members added more to the ideas of others in the group.

- As students share, record their noticings on chart paper.

  You noticed that the group members called on people holding up two fingers first so they could build on an idea before changing the topic.

  What did the group members say to add on to someone's idea?

▶ As students respond, record responses on the chart. When students suggest details that are specific to the book choice, help them rephrase the idea in a way that can be applied to other books.

Have a Try

Invite the students to talk with a partner about how to change the subject in a book club meeting.

> Turn and talk about what you could say to change to a different idea.

▶ After time for discussion, have students share ideas. Record new ideas on the chart.

Summarize and Apply

Summarize the learning and remind students to think about ways to build on ideas and change the subject during book club meetings.

> What did you learn about conversations in a book club meeting?

▶ Write the principle at the top of the chart. Review the chart.

> Use the chart when you meet with your book club. The book club that meets with me today will share about their book club later.

▶ Meet with a book club while the other students are engaged during independent reading time.

Share

Following independent reading time, gather the students together. Ask the group that met in book club to share with the whole group.

> What did you do to have a good discussion?

> How did you build on the ideas of others?

> Did anyone change the topic or idea? How did that go?

Extend the Lesson (Optional)

After assessing students' understanding, you might decide to extend the learning.

▶ Introduce higher-level questions as students become more proficient with building on ideas and changing the subject during book clubs. If you have *Fountas & Pinnell Prompting Guide, Part 2, for Comprehension: Thinking, Talking, and Writing* (Fountas and Pinnell 2012), refer to Section IV: Prompts for Book Discussions.

Add to an idea before you talk about a different idea.

Adding to an Idea	Changing the Topic
I also think _____.	I have another idea.
To add on, _____.	Can we change the topic?
When I read this, I also felt _____.	Now, let's talk about _____.
I agree because _____.	I really want to talk about _____.
I disagree because _____.	
This part might help explain your idea.	
Now I'm thinking _____.	

Section 2: Literary Analysis

Reading Minilesson Principle

Talk about what went well and what you want to work on to get better.

You Will Need

- charts from the previous minilessons in this umbrella
- chart paper and markers
- book club checklists for Summarize and Apply

Academic Language / Important Vocabulary

- book club
- reflect
- improve
- checklist
- check mark

Continuum Connection

- Speak at an appropriate volume (p. 335)
- Use conventions of respectful conversation (p. 335)
- Use turn-taking with courtesy in small-group discussion (p. 335)
- Listen and respond to a partner by agreeing, disagreeing, or adding on and explaining reasons (p. 335)

Goal

Develop guidelines to self-assess book club meetings.

Rationale

When students reflect on an activity, they improve self-assessment skills and increase ownership and engagement over their work.

Assess Learning

Observe students when they talk about book club meetings and notice if there is evidence of new learning based on the goal of this minilesson.

- ▶ Are students able to reflect on their own book club meetings to identify what went well and what can be improved upon?
- ▶ Do they use the terms *book club, reflect, improve, checklist,* and *check mark* to evaluate a book club meeting?

Minilesson

To help students think about the minilesson principle, engage them in reflecting on book club meetings. Here is an example.

- ▶ Before teaching this minilesson, make sure that all students have participated in at least one book club meeting. Post the charts from the previous minilessons in this umbrella.

  Here are the charts we made about ways to have a good book club.

- ▶ Ask volunteers to help you review the charts by reading them.

  After you have a book club meeting, you can use a checklist to help you think about things that went well and which things you can work on.

  One question you could ask yourself is if you used sticky notes to prepare for the book club meeting.

- ▶ On chart paper, add a line where a check mark could be placed and then add a statement about using sticky notes.

  Raise your hand if you used a sticky note to prepare for a book club meeting.

- ▶ If students raised hands, add a check mark to the statement.

  Look at the charts. What else could you reflect on after a book club meeting?

- ▶ Ask students to share their thinking and add ideas to the chart. Prompt the conversation as needed to create a list for student reflection.

  After each book club meeting, you and the other book club members can use the list to reflect on the meeting. You can talk about what you want to do better next time.

Have a Try

Invite the students to talk with a partner about reflecting on book clubs.

> Turn and talk about other ideas you have about what could be added to the checklist. Look back at the charts to help you with ideas.

▸ After time for discussion, have students share ideas. Record new ideas on the chart.

Summarize and Apply

Summarize the learning and remind students to reflect after book club meetings.

> Today you helped create a list to help you think about your book club meetings.

> Think about the things on the list in your next book club and decide on areas your group wants to work on to get better.

Share

Following independent reading time, gather the students together in the meeting area. Ask the students who met in book club to share.

> Talk about the checklist that you filled out after meeting with your book club.

> How did the checklist help you think about what went well and what things you can improve upon?

Extend the Lesson (Optional)

After assessing students' understanding, you might decide to extend the learning.

▸ Have students write a sentence or two in a reader's notebook about what they want to work on to make their book club meetings better.

✓ **Our Book Club Meeting**

_____ We used sticky notes.

_____ We used good voices.

_____ We asked questions.

_____ Everyone had a turn.

_____ We listened to the speaker.

_____ We used hand signals to join the conversation.

_____ We added to ideas before changing the topic.

_____ We agreed and disagreed respectfully.

Section 2: Literary Analysis

Assessment

After you have taught the minilessons in this umbrella, observe students as they talk and write about their reading across instructional contexts: interactive read-aloud, independent reading and literacy work, guided reading, shared reading, and book club. Use *The Literacy Continuum* (Fountas and Pinnell 2017) to observe students' reading and writing behaviors across instructional contexts.

▶ What evidence do you have of new understandings related to the way students engage with book clubs?

- Are students able to choose a book for book club and talk about the choice?
- Do they mark the pages they want to talk about?
- Are they able to talk about their thinking in a respectful way?
- Are they able to build on the ideas of others before changing the topic?
- Do they reflect on book club activities in a meaningful way?
- Do they use the terms *book club, title, author, illustrator, behavior, respectful, questions, discussion, agree*, and *disagree*?

▶ In what other ways, beyond the scope of this umbrella, are students talking about books?

- Are students showing increased confidence in sharing their opinions about books they read, such as during a book talk?

Use your observations to determine the next umbrella you will teach. You may also consult Minilessons Across the Year (pp. 55-57) for guidance.

Link to Writing

After teaching the minilessons in this umbrella, help students link the new learning to their own writing:

▶ Encourage students to write book reviews for their book club selections and store them near the book sets to help others choose what to read next.

Reader's Notebook

When this umbrella is complete, provide a copy of the minilesson principles (see resources.fountasandpinnell.com) for students to glue in the reader's notebook (in the Minilessons section if using *Reader's Notebook: Intermediate* [Fountas and Pinnell 2011]), so they can refer to the information as needed.

Minilessons in This Umbrella

RML1   There are different kinds of fiction books.

RML2   There are different kinds of nonfiction books.

RML3   Hybrid books have fiction and nonfiction parts.

Before Teaching Umbrella 5 Minilessons

Before teaching Umbrella 5, read and discuss fiction and nonfiction books from a range of genre types. Make a Books We've Shared chart (see p. 62) and add to it as you read books together.

The minilessons in this umbrella support students in discussing specific characteristics of fiction and nonfiction texts. You may decide to teach this umbrella early in the year to provide students with a framework for thinking about fiction and nonfiction texts or later in the year when students have a deeper understanding of genre. (RML3, which introduces hybrid texts, requires a more sophisticated understanding of the characteristics of fiction and nonfiction texts. Confirm readiness before teaching this minilesson.) Likewise, as you consider when to teach these minilessons, think about the kinds of fiction and nonfiction your students are ready to explore in more depth (see Master Genre Chart on p. 38).

Use the following suggested books from the *Fountas & Pinnell Classroom™ Interactive Read-Aloud Collection* to enliven the discussion of genres or choose a variety of fiction and nonfiction books from your classroom library.

Author/Illustrator Study: Janelle Cannon

Stellaluna by Janell Cannon

The Importance of Kindness

The Can Man by Laura E. Williams

Genre Study: Folktales

Ming Lo Moves the Mountain by Arnold Lobel

Genre Study: Expository Nonfiction

Bats! Strange and Wonderful by Laurence Pringle

Genre Study: Biography

Nobody Owns the Sky by Reeve Lindbergh

Sharing Our World: Animals

Ape by Martin Jenkins

Hybrid Texts: Fiction and Nonfiction

Flight of the Honey Bee by Raymond Huber

Yucky Worms by Vivian French

As you read aloud and enjoy these texts together, help students notice defining characteristics of each: realistic fiction, fantasy, folktales, informational (expository) texts, biographies, narrative nonfiction, and hybrid texts.

Janelle Cannon

Kindness

Folktales

Expository Nonfiction

Biography

Animals

Hybrid Texts

Section 2: Literary Analysis

Understanding Fiction and Nonfiction Genres

You Will Need

- four or five familiar books that demonstrate the characteristics of fiction texts (e.g., realistic fiction, historical fiction, folktales, fables, fantasy), such as:
  - *Stellaluna* by Janell Cannon, from Text Set: Janelle Cannon
  - *The Can Man* by Laura E. Williams, from Text Set: Kindness
  - *Ming Lo Moves the Mountain* by Arnold Lobel, from Text Set: Folktales
- chart paper divided into three columns
- markers

Academic Language / Important Vocabulary

- fiction
- realistic fiction
- folktales
- fantasy

Continuum Connection

- Notice and understand the characteristics of some specific fiction genres: e.g., realistic fiction, historical fiction, folktale, fairy tale, fable, fantasy, hybrid text (p. 50)

Goal

Understand that there are different types of fiction texts (e.g., realistic fiction, historical fiction, folktales, fables, fantasy) and that they have different characteristics.

Rationale

Studying the characteristics of specific fiction genres—fantasy, realistic fiction, folktale, and historical fiction—helps students know what to expect when reading, and increases comprehension.

Assess Learning

Observe students when they talk about fiction books. Notice if there is evidence of new learning based on the goal of this minilesson.

- Can students distinguish between realistic fiction, folktales, and fantasy?
- Do they use that knowledge to support their understanding of the text?
- Do they use academic language, such as *realistic fiction*, *folktales*, and *fantasy*?

Minilesson

To help students think about the minilesson principle, engage students in a discussion of different kinds of fiction. Here is an example.

> How do you know that a book is fiction?

- Show the cover of *Stellaluna*. Write the title and *fantasy* on the chart.

  > This book is a special kind of fiction called fantasy. Listen as I reread a few pages and think about what makes this book a fantasy story.

- Reread a few pages.

  > What makes this a fantasy story?

- Record responses on the chart.

  > This book is fantasy because the characters are animals that can talk, and there is a problem and/or a solution that couldn't happen in real life.

- Repeat the process with the realistic fiction book *The Can Man*.

  > Books that have characters, a problem, a solution, and actions that are made-up but could happen in real life are called realistic fiction.

- Repeat the process with the folktale *Ming Lo Moves the Mountain*.

  > Folktales have events that could not happen in the real world and some have characters that could not be real. Sometimes characters play tricks on other characters.

Have a Try

Invite the students work in small groups to categorize books they have read.

> Turn and talk with your group. Name a fiction book you have read recently. Does it fit on this chart? Where? Why?

Summarize and Apply

Summarize the learning and remind students to think about what kind of fiction book they are reading.

> What does the chart show about fiction books?

▶ Review the chart and write the principle at the top.

> When you understand the kind of fiction book you read, it helps you understand the book.

> Today during independent reading time, think about what kind of fiction book you are reading. Bring the book when we come back together so you can share your thinking.

There are different kinds of fiction books.

Book	Kind of Fiction	Characteristic
Stellaluna	Fantasy	• Animals talk. • Animals act like people.
The CAN Man	Realistic fiction	• The characters, the setting, and the problems could happen in real life.
MING LO MOVES THE MOUNTAIN	Folktale	• A pretend story that cannot happen in the real world. • There is repetition. • Sometimes characters trick each other.

Share

Following independent reading time, gather students together in the meeting area to talk about their reading with the group.

> What kind of fiction book did you read today? Why did you think that?

Extend the Lesson (Optional)

After assessing students' understanding, you might decide to extend the learning.

▶ As you read and discuss other fiction texts, talk about the characteristics of those texts. Introduce the terms *historical fiction* and *fables* when you encounter those books together and add them to the chart.

▶ As students read more fiction books, teach them how to record the genre code on their reading list in a reader's notebook. Refer to Section Four: Writing About Reading, Umbrella 1: Introducing a Reader's Notebook, for more about genre coding.

▶ Add specific genre codes to the Books We've Shared chart (see p. 62).

RML2
LA.U5.RML2

Reading Minilesson Principle
There are different kinds of nonfiction books.

Understanding Fiction and Nonfiction Genres

You Will Need

- three or four familiar books that demonstrate the characteristics of nonfiction texts (e.g., informational, biography, and narrative nonfiction), such as:
  - *Bats! Strange and Wonderful* by Laurence Pringle, from Text Set: Expository Nonfiction
  - *Nobody Owns the Sky* by Reeve Lindbergh, from Text Set: Biography
  - *Ape* by Martin Jenkins, from Text Set: Animals
- chart paper, with the principle written at the top prior to the lesson
- markers
- sticky notes
- a basket of different kinds of nonfiction books (informational, biography, and narrative nonfiction)

Academic Language / Important Vocabulary

- informational
- biography
- narrative nonfiction

Continuum Connection

- Notice and understand the characteristics of some specific nonfiction genres: e.g., informational book, procedural and persuasive texts, biography, autobiography, memoir, hybrid text (p. 53)

Goal

Understand that there are different types of nonfiction texts (e.g., biography, informational, and narrative nonfiction) and that they have different characteristics.

Rationale

When students understand there are different types of nonfiction texts, and the characteristics and organization of each, they are better prepared to read and gather information from the texts.

Assess Learning

Observe students when they talk about nonfiction books. Notice if there is evidence of new learning based on the goal of this minilesson.

- How familiar are students with the characteristics of biography, informational, and narrative nonfiction texts?
- Do they use academic language, such as *informational*, *biography*, and *narrative nonfiction*?

Minilesson

To help students think about the minilesson principle, engage students in a discussion of different kinds of nonfiction. Here is an example.

- Hold up the book *Bats! Strange and Wonderful* and read a page.

  What kind of book is this? How do you know?

- Record responses on the chart. If students respond with specific information about bats, reframe their answers to be more general, such as "The book gives true information about the topic."

  Nonfiction books that give information about a certain topic, like bats, are called informational books.

- Write the word *informational* on the chart. Repeat the process with *Nobody Owns the Sky*. Read the introductory page, *Brave Bessie*.

  What is this book about?

  Nonfiction books that tell about the life of a person are called biographies.

- Write the word *biography* on the chart. Repeat the process with *Ape*, and read the section about orangutans.

  What do you notice about *how* the author tells us about orangutans? What order does the author use?

- Record responses on the chart.

  Informational books that are like a story are called narrative nonfiction.

Have a Try

Invite the students to talk about kinds of nonfiction in groups of four or five. Provide each group with a few familiar nonfiction books.

> Look at each nonfiction book with your group. What kind of nonfiction is each book? Look at the chart to remind you of the three kinds. Label each book with a sticky note and jot down why you think that.

▶ Invite each group to share with the larger group. Add responses to the chart.

Summarize and Apply

Summarize the learning and remind students to think about what kind of nonfiction book they are reading.

> What did you learn about nonfiction books?

▶ Review the chart and write the principle at the top.

> If you read a nonfiction book today during independent reading time, think about what kind of nonfiction book it is. Bring the book when we come back together so you can share.

Share

Following independent reading time, gather students together in the meeting area to talk about their reading in groups of two or three.

> If you read a nonfiction book today, talk to your partner(s) about what kind of nonfiction it is. Why do you think that?

▶ After they turn and talk, ask a few students to share with the class.

Extend the Lesson (Optional)

After assessing students' understanding, you might decide to extend the learning.

▶ As you read and discuss other nonfiction texts, talk about the characteristics of the texts and determine the type of nonfiction. Add the titles to the chart.

▶ As students read more nonfiction books, teach them how to record the genre code on a reading list in a reader's notebook (see Section Four: Writing About Reading, Umbrella 1: Introducing a Reader's Notebook).

▶ Add specific genre codes to the Books We've Shared chart (see p. 62).

There are different kinds of nonfiction books.

Book	Kind of Fiction	Characteristics
BATS! STRANGE AND WONDERFUL	Informational	Gives true information about a topic (bats)
Nobody Owns the Sky	Biography	Gives true information about a person's life
Ape	Narrative nonfiction	Gives true information about a topic told like a story

Section 2: Literary Analysis

RML 3
LA.U5.RML3

Reading Minilesson Principle
Hybrid texts have fiction and nonfiction parts.

Understanding Fiction and Nonfiction Genres

You Will Need

- two or three books that demonstrate the characteristics of hybrid texts, such as the following from Text Set: Hybrid Texts:
  - *Flight of the Honey Bee* by Raymond Huber
  - *Yucky Worms* by Vivian French
- chart paper and markers
- basket of nonfiction and hybrid books
- sticky notes

Academic Language / Important Vocabulary

- fiction
- nonfiction
- hybrid

Continuum Connection

- Recognize hybrid texts and distinguish which sections are fiction and nonfiction (pp. 50, 53)

Goal

Notice and understand the characteristics of hybrid texts.

Rationale

Authors layer genres into hybrid texts to engage students in a topic, and often use using a narrative structure, to help readers consider a topic from different points of view. Assess your students' understanding of genre characteristics before teaching this minilesson, which should be introduced only when students have a deep understanding of both fiction and nonfiction genres.

Assess Learning

Observe students when they talk about hybrid texts. Notice if there is evidence of new learning based on the goal of this minilesson.

- Can students describe what a hybrid text is?
- Do they use that knowledge to support their understanding of the text?
- Do they use academic language, such as *fiction, nonfiction,* and *hybrid*?

Minilesson

To help students think about the minilesson principle, provide an inquiry-based lesson about hybrid text. Here is an example.

- Hold up the book *Flight of the Honey Bee.*

    Think about what the author is sharing, and how he is sharing it.

- Begin reading on the page before the title page.

    What did the author share on this page? Is that fiction or nonfiction? Why do you think that?

- Make two columns on the chart paper. Label one *Fiction* and one *Nonfiction.* Record response in the nonfiction column. Then read the first two pages with text after the title page, reading only the larger print.

    What did the author share in the larger print on these pages? Is that fiction or nonfiction? How do you know?

- Record response on the chart in the fiction column. Now read the smaller print from the same pages.

    What did the author share in the smaller print on these pages? Is that fiction or nonfiction?

    How do you know?

- Record response on the chart in the nonfiction column. Repeat the process with the page that begins "A flash of feathers."

Have a Try

Invite the students to talk about *Yucky Worms* in groups of four or five.

▶ Hold up *Yucky Worms*. Read the first four pages.

> What do you notice about the ways the author shares information in this book?

▶ Invite groups to share with the class. As necessary, prompt the students with "Is that fiction or nonfiction?" Add responses to the chart.

Summarize and Apply

Summarize the learning and remind students to notice that some books have fictional and nonfictional parts.

> Look at the chart. What do you notice all of these books include?

▶ Write the principle at the top of the chart.

> Some books have a fiction part and a nonfiction part. These books are called hybrid books. In a hybrid book, the author includes a story with characters and action alongside true information about a topic.

▶ Provide a basket of nonfiction and hybrid texts for the students to choose from during independent reading.

> Today for independent reading, you may choose a book from this basket. As you read, notice if your book is a hybrid and think about what makes it so. Mark the book with a sticky note so that you can share what makes it a hybrid.

Share

Following independent reading time, gather students together in the meeting area to talk about their reading with the group.

> If you read a hybrid book, share what makes it a hybrid.

Extend the Lesson (Optional)

After assessing students' understanding, you might decide to extend the learning.

▶ Read and discuss other hybrid texts, and discuss the fictional and nonfictional aspects of the texts. Add the titles to the chart.

▶ **Writing About Reading** Have students write in a reader's notebook about a hybrid text they have read.

Hybrid texts have fiction and nonfiction parts.

Book	Fiction	Nonfiction
Flight of the Honey Bee	• Scout, a bee, leaves the hive. • A blackbird tries to eat Scout, but she escapes.	• Bees are very important. • There are more female bees than male bees in a hive. • Many creatures eat honey bees.
	• A boy is in the garden with his grandmother. • He sees a worm and thinks it should be thrown away. • Grandma teaches the boy.	• There are about 15 worms in every square yard of soil. • Worms have 5 pairs of hearts.

Section 2: Literary Analysis

Assessment

After you have taught the minilessons in this umbrella, observe students as they talk and write about their reading across instructional contexts: interactive read-aloud, independent reading and literacy work, guided reading, shared reading, and book club. Use *The Literacy Continuum* (Fountas and Pinnell 2017) to observe students' reading and writing behaviors across instructional contexts.

▶ What evidence do you have of new understandings related to the genres of fiction and nonfiction?

- Are students able to describe the characteristics of realistic fiction, fantasy, and folktales?

- Can students describe the characteristics of informational (expository), biographical, and narrative nonfiction texts?

- Do they understand that hybrid texts have both fiction and nonfiction parts?

- Do they use academic language, such as *fiction*, *nonfiction*, *folktales*, and *informational*?

▶ In what other ways, beyond the scope of this umbrella, are students talking about fiction and nonfiction genres?

- Are students familiar with characteristics of fables and fairy tales?

- Are they able to discuss the theme, message, or moral of a fiction text?

- Can they discuss the topic of informational texts?

Use your observations to determine the next umbrella you will teach. You may also consult Minilessons Across the Year (pp. 55-57) for guidance.

Link to Writing

After teaching the minilessons in this umbrella, help students link the new learning to their own writing:

▶ When students write fiction or nonfiction pieces during writers' workshop, encourage them to incorporate the characteristics of a particular genre as they write their own pieces.

▶ Use shared writing to demonstrate and try out characteristics of the different genres as students begin to write in that genre.

Reader's Notebook

When this umbrella is complete, provide a copy of the minilesson principles (see resources.fountasandpinnell.com) for students to glue in the reader's notebook (in the Minilessons section if using *Reader's Notebook: Intermediate* [Fountas and Pinnell 2011]), so they can refer to the information as needed.

Minilessons in This Umbrella

Poetry

RML1	Poems are alike in many ways.
RML2	The definition of poetry is what is always true about it.
RML3	Poetry can be fiction or nonfiction.
RML4	Poets use line breaks and white space to show how to read the poem.
RML5	Poets choose words to help you see, smell, hear, and feel things.
RML6	Sometimes poets place their words in a shape to show what the poem is about.
RML7	There are different kinds of poetry.

Before Teaching Umbrella 6 Minilessons

Poetry is not a genre, but a "broad, overarching category of language of writing that can appear in any genre. . . . Poetry is compact writing characterized by imagination and artistry and imbued with intense meaning" (Fountas and Pinnell 2012a, 19). Studying poetry using the lens of genre study, even though poetry is not a single genre, allows students to understand the role poetry plays in their lives as readers. The study of poetry allows students to think about characteristics that most poems demonstrate and prepares them to understand the range of emotions that poetry can make one feel.

In a genre study (see pp. 37-39), students learn what to expect when beginning to read a text and will comprehend it more deeply. Students must hear, read, and enjoy many different poems before beginning this study. Read poems that are fiction and nonfiction and are different types of poems (lyrical, free verse, haiku, limerick). Choose some poems that allow discussion of a poet's intentional use of line breaks and white space; have rhythm, rhyme, and descriptive or figurative language; and are in a shape. Use the following books from the *Fountas & Pinnell Classroom™ Interactive Read-Aloud Collection* text set listed below, or choose poetry texts from your own library to support students in studying poetry.

Genre Study: Poetry

Old Elm Speaks by Kristine O'Connell George

Button Up! by Alice Schertle

Flicker Flash by Joan Bransfield Graham

Splish Splash by Joan Bransfield Graham

Confetti: Poems for Children by Pat Mora

As you read aloud and enjoy poems together, help students:

- think and talk about the meaning of each poem, and

- notice and generalize the characteristics of poetry.

Section 2: Literary Analysis

Reading Minilesson Principle
Poems are alike in many ways.

You Will Need

- for each group of four students, three or four familiar poetry texts, such as those from Text Set: Poetry, that demonstrate the characteristics of poetry, or individual poems typed out for students to study in small groups
- chart paper and markers
- a basket of poetry texts
- sticky notes

Academic Language / Important Vocabulary

- poetry
- poem
- poet
- rhythm
- rhyme
- repetition

Continuum Connection

- Notice and understand some elements of poetry: e.g., figurative language, rhyme, repetition, onomatopoeia, layout/line breaks (shape), imagery, alliteration, assonance (p. 50)

Goal

Notice and understand the elements of poetry.

Rationale

When you teach students the characteristics of poetry, it prepares them to see the images that poets describe, learn the information poets share, and feel the range of emotions poetry evokes. They learn how to write poems of their own by studying other poets.

Assess Learning

Observe students when they talk about poetry. Notice if there is evidence of new learning based on the goal of this minilesson.

- Can students talk about the characteristics of poetry?
- Do they understand that some characteristics always occur, and some characteristics often or sometimes occur in poetry?
- Are they using the words *poetry, poem, poet, rhyme, rhythm,* and *repetition*?

Minilesson

To help students think about the minilesson principle, provide an inquiry-based lesson using familiar poems. Here is an example.

- Seat students in groups of four. Provide each group with a few poems they have previously read and discussed.

  Turn and talk about how these poems are alike.

- As students talk, help them decide whether the characteristic is always, often, or sometimes a characteristic of poetry.

- After time in small groups, select several poems to revisit in more detail as a whole group. Display the poems to the class by showing the poem on a chart. Help students decide whether the characteristic is always, often, or sometimes a characteristic of poetry. Record responses in three parts on the chart. Use these prompts as needed:

  - *What do you notice about the way the author wrote the poem? What is the writer describing?*
  - *Is the poem fiction or nonfiction?*
  - *What does the poem help you see, hear, or feel?*
  - *What do you notice about the words the author chose to use? What do you notice about the way the poem sounds?*
  - *What do you notice about where the author ends each line of the poem?*

Have a Try

Invite the partners to study a poem together.

> Choose one thing from the *Always* list on the chart. How do you see it in the poem? Turn and talk to your partner about that.

▶ Ask a few students to share. Record responses on the chart.

Summarize and Apply

Summarize the learning and remind students to notice the things that are always, often, or sometimes true about poems.

> Today you noticed that poems have special characteristics that are alike in many ways.

▶ Review the chart.

> If you choose to read a poetry book from this basket, look for the *Always, Often, or Sometimes* things on the chart. Mark pages with a sticky note so you can share when we come back together.

Share

Following independent reading time, gather students together in the meeting area to talk about their reading with a partner.

> If you read a poem today, share what you noticed. How was it like other poems we have read?

▶ Choose a few students to share with the class.

Extend the Lesson (Optional)

After assessing students' understanding, you might decide to extend the learning.

▶ As students continue reading poems, discuss whether to add new noticings to the *Always, Often,* or *Sometimes* part of the chart.

▶ Invite students to write their own poems, including some of the elements of poetry they noticed.

▶ **Writing About Reading** Through shared writing or in a reader's notebook, encourage students to write what they noticed about a poem they have read.

Poems

Noticings:

Always	Often
• It can be fiction or nonfiction.	• The poet's words make you see, smell, hear, and feel things.
• The poet uses fewer words to tell about an idea or to express a feeling.	
• Poets use rhythm.	**Sometimes**
• The poet places words to help you know how to read it.	• The poem has print in a shape that tells you about the meaning.
• The line breaks make it look different from other writing.	• The poet uses rhyme.

RML2
LA.U6.RML2

Reading Minilesson Principle
The definition of poetry is what is always true about it.

Studying Poetry

You Will Need

- a familiar poem, such as "Cloud Dragons" from *Confetti: Poems for Children* by Pat Mora from Text Set: Poetry
- chart from RML1
- chart paper and markers
- a basket of poetry texts

Academic Language / Important Vocabulary

- poetry
- definition
- describe

Continuum Connection

- Notice and understand some elements of poetry: e.g., figurative language, rhyme, repetition, onomatopoeia, layout/line breaks (shape), imagery, alliteration, assonance (p. 50)

Goal

Create a working definition for poetry.

Rationale

When students craft a definition of poetry, they determine the most important characteristics of poetry that apply to all poems. The definition is based on their experience to this point. As they become more familiar with poetry, they will revise their definition.

Assess Learning

Observe students when they talk about poetry. Notice if there is evidence of new learning based on the goal of this minilesson.

- Can students define *poetry*?
- Do they understand that the definition of poetry tells what is special about this form of writing?
- Are they using the words *poetry, definition,* and *describe*?

Minilesson

To help students think about the minilesson principle, engage them in crafting a definition of poetry. Here is an example.

- Display the poetry noticings chart from RML1.

  You noticed things that are always, often, or sometimes true of poems. Let's think about what you noticed so we can write a definition. Our definition of poetry will tell what is always true about poetry and what makes it a special kind of writing.

- Review the noticings chart and then write and read the word *Poetry* on a new piece of chart paper.

  Turn and talk about poetry. What is something you can say about poetry? Use the noticings chart to help you.

- After time for discussion, ask a few students to share. Combine their ideas to create a definition as a whole class. Write the definition on the chart paper.

Have a Try

Invite the students to talk in pairs about the definition of poetry. Review the definition, and then read "Cloud Dragons."

> Does this poem fit our definition of poetry? What makes you think that?

▶ After time for discussion, ask a few students to share.

Summarize and Apply

Summarize the learning and remind students that a definition of poetry is what is always true about it.

▶ Read the definition as a class.

> This is a good start on a definition of poetry. You can revise it as you learn more about poetry.

> If you choose to read a poetry book from this basket today, notice if the poems in your book fit our definition of poetry. Bring the book when we meet so you can share.

Share

Following independent reading time, gather students together in the meeting area to talk about their reading with a partner.

> If you read a poem today, share what you noticed. Did it fit the definition of poetry?

▶ Choose a few students to share with the class.

Extend the Lesson (Optional)

After assessing students' understanding, you might decide to extend the learning.

▶ Revisit and revise the definition as students gain new understandings about poetry (see Read and Revise on p. 178).

▶ Provide the opportunity for students to write their own poems, thinking about the definition of poetry as they write.

▶ **Writing About Reading** Encourage students to write in a reader's notebook about a poem they have read, including how the poem fits the class definition of poetry.

Poetry

Poetry is a **kind** of writing.

The poet uses few words to describe an idea.

The poet puts words on the paper in certain ways.

RML3
LA.U6.RML3

Reading Minilesson Principle
Poetry can be fiction or nonfiction.

Studying Poetry

You Will Need

- two or three familiar poetry texts with examples of fiction and nonfiction poems, such as the following from Text Set: Poetry:
  - "Purple Snake" from *Confetti: Poems for Children* by Pat Mora
  - "Violet's Hiking Hat" from *Button Up!* by Alice Schertle
  - "Steam" from *Splish Splash* and "Days and Years" from *Flicker Flash* by Joan Bransfield Graham
- chart paper prepared with three columns and markers
- two blue sticky notes labeled *Fiction*
- two green sticky notes labeled *Nonfiction*
- copies of familiar fiction and nonfiction poems for partners/trios to discuss
- a basket of poetry texts
- sticky notes

Academic Language / Important Vocabulary

- poetry
- poem
- poet
- genre
- fiction
- nonfiction

Continuum Connection

- Notice and understand some elements of poetry: e.g., figurative language, rhyme, repetition, onomatopoeia, layout/line breaks (shape), imagery, alliteration, assonance (p. 50)

Goal

Understand that poetry can be fiction or nonfiction.

Rationale

When you teach students that poems can be fiction or nonfiction, you prepare them to read different poems while emphasizing that poetry is not a genre, but a form of writing.

Assess Learning

Observe students when they talk about poetry. Notice if there is evidence of new learning based on the goal of this minilesson.

- ▶ Can students identify if a poem is fiction or nonfiction?
- ▶ Do they continue to talk about the characteristics of poetry?
- ▶ Can they use the words *poetry, poem, poet, genre, fiction,* and *nonfiction*?

Minilesson

To help students think about the minilesson principle, provide an inquiry-based lesson using familiar poems. Here is an example.

> Poetry can be *fiction* or *nonfiction.* As I read a few poems think about what genre the poem is—fiction or nonfiction—and what makes you think that.

- ▶ Read aloud "Purple Snake" and then "Violet's Hiking Hat."

  > Do you think these poems are fiction or nonfiction?

  > What makes you think that?

- ▶ Have a student place a Fiction sticky note in the middle column of the chart paper. Add the title and the supporting reasons for students' thinking in the two other columns as shown.

  > Now listen to two more poems.

- ▶ Read aloud "Steam" and then "Days and Years."

  > Do you think these poems are fiction or nonfiction?

  > What makes you think that?

- ▶ Have a student place the other sticky notes and fill in the columns as before.

Have a Try

Invite the students to look at poems in groups of two or three. Provide groups with two or three poems, ensuring a mix of fiction and nonfiction.

> Read a poem and then turn and talk to your partner (or trio). Is the poem fiction or nonfiction?

▶ After time for discussion, ask a few students to share. Record responses as before.

Summarize and Apply

Summarize the learning and remind students that poems can be fiction or nonfiction.

> What did you notice about poems? Use the chart to remember.

▶ Add the principle to the chart.

> If you choose to read a poetry book from this basket today, notice if the poems in your book are fiction or nonfiction. Mark them with sticky notes labeled *fiction* or *nonfiction*. Bring the book when we meet so you can share.

Share

Following independent reading time, gather students together in the meeting area to talk about their reading.

> If you read a poem today, was it fiction or nonfiction?

▶ Choose a few students to share with the class.

Extend the Lesson (Optional)

After assessing students' understanding, you might decide to extend the learning.

▶ Provide the opportunity for students to write their own poems. Encourage them to think about whether they want to write a fiction or a nonfiction poem.

▶ **Writing About Reading** Encourage students to write in a reader's notebook about a poem they have read, including what they noticed about it, and whether it was fiction or nonfiction.

Poetry can be fiction or nonfiction.		
"Purple Snake"	Fiction	• He makes a snake from wood.
"Violet's Hiking Hat"	Fiction	• The hat talks and tells a story.
"Steam"	Nonfiction	• Teaches that water turns to vapor when it gets hot.
"Days and Years"	Nonfiction	• Teaches that the earth spins and moves around the sun.

Section 2: Literary Analysis

Reading Minilesson Principle
Poets use line breaks and white space to show how to read the poem.

Studying Poetry

You Will Need

▸ a familiar poem with intentional use of line breaks and white space, such as "Lullaby" from *Old Elm Speaks* by Kristine O'Connell George from Text Set: Poetry:

▸ chart paper and markers

▸ a basket of poetry texts

▸ document camera (optional)

Academic Language / Important Vocabulary

▸ line break

▸ white space

▸ pause

Continuum Connection

▸ Use understanding of the types elements of poetry to adjust reading (p. 132)

▸ Use a poem's layout and punctuation to monitor and correct while reading (p. 132)

Goal

Learn how to read the line breaks and white space of a poem.

Rationale

Poets decide how to place words on a page, plan line breaks, and use white space intentionally, which impacts meaning and sound. When you teach students to notice this, you support them in reading poetry and thinking about meaning.

Assess Learning

Observe students when they talk about poetry. Notice if there is evidence of new learning based on the goal of this minilesson.

▸ Do students demonstrate pausing at the end of a line, as appropriate?

▸ Can they talk about how poets use white space?

▸ Do they understand the terms *line break, white space,* and *pause*?

Minilesson

To help students think about the minilesson principle, choose a familiar poem to use in an inquiry-based lesson about line breaks and white space in a poem. Here is an example.

▸ Read aloud the poem "Lullaby" while students listen. Then read the first stanza, holding the book so students can see the text (or projecting it with a document camera).

> How did I know how to read this part of the poem—what words to group together, how fast to read, or when to pause?

> Poets break the lines so that the reader reads the words in a line together as a group, and they put punctuation at the end of a line to make the reader pause, or maybe even stop. The end of the line in a poem is called a line break.

▸ Now read the whole poem, holding it so students can see the text, pausing for a longer time at the white space.

> Where did I pause a little longer?

> This is called white space—the places where there are no words. The poet uses the space to keep parts of the poem together and to tell the reader to pause a little longer.

Have a Try

Invite the students to repeat the process used for the first stanza with the second stanza, reading it together as a group.

> How would the poem be different if it were written without the line breaks?

Summarize and Apply

Summarize the learning and remind students that poets use line breaks and white space to show how to read a poem.

> What did you learn today about how a poet puts the words on paper?

▶ Use students' responses to make a chart and write the principle at the top.

> If you choose to read a poetry book from this basket today, notice how the author uses line breaks and white space. Bring the book when we meet so you can share.

Share

Following independent reading time, gather students together in the meeting area to talk about their reading with a partner.

> If you read a poem today, share it with your partner. How did the poet use line breaks and white space to help you read the poem?

▶ Choose a student's poem to read aloud. Use a document camera if available.

Extend the Lesson (Optional)

After assessing students' understanding, you might decide to extend the learning.

▶ Have students continue reading poems to practice pausing at line breaks.

▶ **Writing About Reading** Encourage students to write in a reader's notebook about a poem they have read, including what they noticed about it and how the placement of the words shows how to read it.

Poets use line breaks and white space to show how to read the poem.

Line breaks

- Group words together
- Show you where to pause
- Slow your reading

White space

- Keeps lines together
- Makes you pause a little longer

"There Was an Old Man of Peru"
by Edward Lear

There was an old man of Peru
Who dreamed he was eating his shoe.
He woke in the night
In a terrible fright,
And found it was perfectly true.

Reading Minilesson Principle
Poets choose words to help you see, smell, hear, and feel things.

You Will Need

- two or three familiar poetry texts that include poems with sensory images, such as the following from Text Set: Poetry:
  - "Ice Cubes" and "Ocean" from *Splish Splash* by Joan Bransfield Graham
  - "Leaf Soup" from *Confetti: Poems for Children* by Pat Mora
- two or three familiar poems written on chart paper large enough for all student to see the poems
- chart paper and markers
- a basket of poetry texts
- sticky notes

Academic Language / Important Vocabulary

- poetry
- poem
- poet
- create
- image
- senses

Continuum Connection

- Notice and understand some elements of poetry: e.g., figurative language, rhyme, repetition, onomatopoeia, layout/line breaks (shape), imagery, alliteration, assonance (p. 50)

Goal

Notice and understand how poets create sensory images and feelings.

Rationale

Sensory images in poetry engage our imaginations and emotions. Teaching students how a poet's word choice helps them to see, smell, hear, or feel an image helps students to understand and enjoy poetry.

Assess Learning

Observe students when they talk about poetry. Notice if there is evidence of new learning based on the goal of this minilesson.

- ▶ Can students notice when a poet uses sensory imagery?
- ▶ Can they describe how a poet evokes an image, a smell, or a feeling?
- ▶ Are they using the words *poetry, poem, poet, create, image,* and *senses*?

Minilesson

To help students think about the minilesson principle, choose the texts and poems that you think will be most meaningful to them and provide an inquiry-based lesson. Here is an example.

> Poets try to create images, or make pictures, in our minds. Listen to this poem and think about what the poet did to create an image in your mind.

- ▶ Without showing the illustrations, read "Ice Cubes." If necessary, read it two times.

    > You have five senses: hearing, sight, taste, touch, and smell.

    > Which of your senses does the poet want you to use in this poem?

- ▶ Record responses on a chart.

    > Sometimes poets use sound to help you imagine a poem.

- ▶ Without showing the illustrations, read "Ocean." If necessary, read it two times.

    > What picture does this poem create in your mind? What makes you think that?

- ▶ Record responses on the chart.

    > Sometimes poets create a picture, or image, in your mind by choosing words that help you feel something—like the water splashing on your legs.

Have a Try

Invite the students to discuss with a partner the sensory images in "Leaf Soup." Read the poem aloud.

> Turn and talk to your partner. What words help you make an image in your mind? What sense does the poet want you to use?

▶ After time for discussion, ask a few students to share. Record responses.

Summarize and Apply

Summarize the learning and remind students to notice the words poets choose.

> What did you learn about the words poets choose to use? Use the chart to help you remember.

▶ Write the principle at the top of the chart.

> If you choose to read a poetry book from this basket today, notice how the poet chose words that help you see, smell, hear, or feel things that help you make a picture in your mind. Mark an example with a sticky note. Bring the book when we meet so you can share.

Share

Following independent reading time, gather students together in the meeting area to talk about their reading with a partner.

> If you read a poem today, talk about the words the author chose to help you see, hear, or feel something. How did that help you understand or appreciate the poem?

▶ Students who read fiction or nonfiction books might also have found descriptive language to share.

Extend the Lesson (Optional)

After assessing students' understanding, you might decide to extend the learning.

▶ Provide the opportunity for students to write their own poems. Encourage them to think about choosing words that help the reader see, smell, hear, or feel something.

▶ **Writing About Reading** Encourage students to write in a reader's notebook about poems they have read, including what they noticed about the words an author chose to help them see, smell, hear, or feel something.

Poets choose words to help you see, smell, hear, and feel things.		
	Poet's Words	Create an image you . . .
Ice Cubes	• clicking • clatter • clink	Hear • the sound of the ice cubes hitting each other and the side of the glass
Oceans	• waves sneak up • waves snatch toes • water splashes	Feel • waves feel like they are grabbing your toes • water hitting your legs
Leaf Soup	• leaves sail • leaves spin	See • leaves flying through the air • leaves falling into puddles

RML 6
LA.U6.RML6

Reading Minilesson Principle
Sometimes poets place their words in a shape to show what the poem is about.

Studying Poetry

You Will Need

- two or three familiar poetry texts that include poems that create shapes using the words of the poem, such as the following from Text Set: Poetry:
  - "Steam" and "Sprinkler" from *Splish Splash* by Joan Bransfield Graham
  - "Hide and Go Seek" from *Old Elm Speaks* by Kristine O'Connell George
- chart paper and markers
- document camera (optional)
- a basket of poetry texts
- sticky notes

Academic Language / Important Vocabulary

- poetry
- poem
- poet

Continuum Connection

- Notice and understand some elements of poetry: e.g., figurative language, rhyme, repetition, onomatopoeia, layout/line breaks (shape), imagery, alliteration, assonance (p. 50)

Goal

Understand how the shape of the poem reflects what the poem is about.

Rationale

When you teach students to notice the shape of a poem, they can use layout to understand what a poem is about.

Assess Learning

Observe students when they talk about poetry. Notice if there is evidence of new learning based on the goal of this minilesson.

- ▶ Do students notice when a poem has a unique shape?
- ▶ Can they discuss how the shape of the poem reflects what the poem is about?
- ▶ Do they use the words *poetry, poem,* and *poet*?

Minilesson

To help students think about the minilesson principle, provide an inquiry-based lesson using poems that create shapes. Project the poems with a document camera, if available. Here is an example.

- ▶ Show "Steam."

    As I read this poem, think about how the poet placed the words on the page.

    What shape did the poet use for this poem?

    Why do you think he chose that?

- ▶ Record responses on chart paper. Then show and read "Hide and Go Seek."

    Why did the poet choose to place the words in this shape?

- ▶ Record responses on the chart.

Have a Try

Invite the students to think about how the shape of "Sprinkler" tells what the poem is about.

▶ Show students the poem "Sprinkler" and ask them to notice how the words look on the page.

> Turn and talk to your partner. How does the shape of the poem tell you what the poem is about?

▶ After time for discussion, ask a few students to share. Record responses on the chart.

Summarize and Apply

Summarize the learning and remind students that the shape of a poem can affect the meaning.

> What does the chart show you about how poets place their words? Look at the chart to remember.

▶ Write the principle at the top of the chart.

> If you choose to read a poetry book from this basket today, notice if the poet placed the words in a certain shape and think how that helps you know what the poem is about. Mark an example with a sticky note. Bring the book when we meet so you can share.

Share

Following independent reading time, gather students together in the meeting area to talk about their reading.

> Did anyone read a shape poem today? How did the shape help you understand what the poem was about?

Extend the Lesson (Optional)

After assessing students' understanding, you might decide to extend the learning.

▶ Provide the opportunity for students to write their own poems. Encourage them to think about how creating a shape with the words could help a reader understand what the poem is about.

▶ **Writing About Reading** Encourage students to write in a reader's notebook about a poem they have read, including what they noticed about the shape and how that helped them understand the poem's meaning.

Sometimes poets place their words in a shape to show what the poem is about.

Poem Title	The shape of the poem helps you to . . .
"Steam"	• Make a picture in your mind of a pot of boiling water with steam rising up. • Know to pause at the end of each line. • Hear the rhymes.
"Hide and Go Seek"	• Picture the tree and the girl. • Hear the rhymes. • Read more slowly to think about what is happening.
"Sprinkler"	• Picture the sprinkler. • Have fun with the poem. • Know when to pause and think about the poem.

Reading Minilesson Principle
There are different kinds of poetry.

Studying Poetry

You Will Need

- a few familiar haikus, free verse, or lyrical poems such as the following from Text Set: Poetry:
  - "No Breakfast," "Poaching," and "Broken String" from *Old Elm Speaks* by Kristine O'Connell George
  - "Cloud Dragons," "Dancing Paper," "Leaf Soup," and "Words Free as Confetti" from *Confetti: Poems for Children* by Pat Mora
- document camera, if available, or write the example poems on chart paper, large enough for all students to see the poems clearly
- three sticky notes labeled *free verse, haiku,* and *lyrical poems*
- chart paper and markers

Academic Language / Important Vocabulary

- poem
- poet
- rhythm
- free verse
- lyrical poem
- haiku

Continuum Connection

- Recognize and understand some specific types of poetry: e.g., lyrical, free verse, limerick, haiku, narrative, ballad (p. 50)

Goal

Recognize and understand some specific types of poetry: e.g., lyrical, free verse, and haiku.

Rationale

When you study different types of poems with students it helps them to recognize other poems they read, know what to expect from the form, and understand poetry more deeply.

Assess Learning

Observe students when they talk about poetry. Notice if there is evidence of new learning based on the goal of this minilesson.

- When students read poetry, can they describe what type of poem they are reading (e.g., free verse, lyrical, haiku)?
- Do they understand vocabulary related to poetry?

Minilesson

To help students think about the minilesson principle, provide an inquiry-based lesson using familiar poems. Project them with a document camera or write them on chart paper. Here is an example.

- Display or project the poems "Leaf Soup" and "Words Free as Confetti" from *Confetti: Poems for Children* so students can see them.

  As I read a few poems to you, think about how these poems are similar.

- Display or project "Leaf Soup" and "Words Free as Confetti." After time for discussion, ask a few students to share. Record responses on chart paper.

  Poems that don't have specific rules and make you think or feel a certain way are called *free verse*.

- Guide a student to place the sticky note labeled *free verse* on the chart.

- Read "No Breakfast," "Poaching," and "Broken String" from *Old Elm Speaks*.

  What do you notice is similar about these poems?

  What do you notice about the topic?

  Think about the syllables used in each line. What do you notice?

  What do you think the author is trying to get you to think about?

  Poems with these characteristics are called haiku.

- Record responses on the chart and guide a student to place the sticky note labeled *haiku* on the chart.

Have a Try

Invite students to think about lyrical poems.

▶ Repeat the process using lyrical poems: "Cloud Dragons" and "Dancing Paper" from *Confetti: Poems for Children*.

How are these poems different from free verse and haikus?

What do you notice about how these poems sound?

▶ Prompt students to notice the songlike quality.

Poems with these characteristics are called *lyrical poems*.

Summarize and Apply

Summarize the learning and remind students that there are different kinds of poetry.

Today you talked about different kinds of poetry.

▶ Review the chart and write the principle at the top.

If you choose to read a poetry book from this basket today, notice if the poems in your book are similar to any of the poems we talked about today. Bring the book when we meet so you can share.

Share

Following independent reading time, gather students together in the meeting area to talk about their reading.

If you read a poem today, share what you noticed. What type of poem is it? Why do you think that?

▶ Choose a few students to share.

Extend the Lesson (Optional)

After assessing students' understanding, you might decide to extend the learning.

▶ Have students continue reading poems and add titles of poems onto the chart under the correct type of poem.

▶ Provide the opportunity for students to write their own poems, encouraging them to think about what type of poem they would like to use to convey their message.

▶ **Writing About Reading** Encourage students to write in a reader's notebook about a poem they have read, including the type of poem they think it might be.

There are different kinds of poetry.

Free Verse

• Doesn't have rules
• Describes what something tastes, smells, or feels like
• Creates a picture in your mind

Haiku

• Short
• Describes nature or the outdoors
• Syllables 5-7-5

Lyrical Poems

• Sound like a song
• Have rhythm
• Create a picture in your mind

Assessment

After you have taught the minilessons in this umbrella, observe students as they talk and write about their reading across instructional contexts: interactive read-aloud, independent reading and literacy work, guided reading, shared reading, and book club. Use *The Literacy Continuum* (Fountas and Pinnell 2017) to observe students' reading and writing behaviors across instructional contexts.

▶ What evidence do you have of new understandings related to the characteristics of poetry?

- Can students describe how poems are alike?
- Do they understand and discuss different kinds of poetry?
- Are they able to read poems as the author intended by paying attention to line breaks and white space?
- Do they notice and discuss a poem's shape supports the meaning?
- Do they notice sensory language?
- Do they use vocabulary such as *poetry, poem, rhythm,* and *rhyme*?

▶ In what other ways, beyond the scope of this umbrella, are students talking about language?

- Do students notice how authors make specific choices about the words and punctuation they use?

Use your observations to determine the next umbrella you will teach. You may also consult Minilessons Across the Year (pp. 55-57) for guidance.

Read and Revise

After completing the steps in the genre study process, help students read and revise their definition of the genre based on their new understandings.

▶ **Before:** Poetry is a kind of writing. The poet uses few words to describe an idea. The poet puts words on the paper in certain ways.

▶ **After:** Poetry is a kind of writing that can be fiction or nonfiction. There are different kinds of poems, and they can be in different shapes and have different line breaks and spaces. Poets use language that makes a picture in your mind.

Reader's Notebook

When this umbrella is complete, provide a copy of the minilesson principles (see resources.fountasandpinnell.com) for students to glue in the reader's notebook (in the Minilessons section if using *Reader's Notebook: Intermediate* [Fountas and Pinnell 2011]), so they can refer to the information as needed.

Minilessons in This Umbrella

RML1 The author gives a message in a fiction book.

RML2 The author gives a message in a nonfiction book.

RML3 More than one author can give the same message.

RML4 The illustrator helps communicate the author's message.

Before Teaching Umbrella 7 Minilessons

The minilessons in this umbrella are designed to help students think about and discuss the author's message in both fiction and nonfiction.

It is important to note the difference between message and theme. Third graders do not need to understand the fine differences, but teachers should be aware that theme is the big, universal idea, or larger aspect of human existence, explored in a literary work (e.g., courage, friendship). The message is a specific aspect of the theme. The message in a book that explores the theme of courage might be "You can conquer fears." If the theme is friendship, the message might be "Be nice to your friends." If you feel that your students are ready, you could extend the minilessons by introducing and defining the word *theme*.

To prepare for these minilessons, read and discuss a variety of engaging fiction and nonfiction picture books with clear messages. Use the following texts from the *Fountas & Pinnell Classroom™ Interactive Read-Aloud Collection* text sets or choose books that give a message from your classroom library.

Genre Study: Realistic Fiction

Tomás and the Library Lady
by Pat Mora

Facing Challenges

Ish by Peter H. Reynolds

Author's Point of View

Meadowlands by Thomas F. Yezerski

What's So Bad About Gasoline?
by Anne Rockwell

Almost Gone by Steve Jenkins

The Importance of Determination

Nothing but Trouble
by Sue Stauffacher

Ruby's Wish by Shirin Yim Bridges

Genre Study: Biography

Nobody Owns the Sky
by Reeve Lindbergh

The Tree Lady by H. Joseph Hopkins

As you read aloud and enjoy these texts together, help students

• notice and discuss the author's message(s), and

• make connections between two or more texts that have common themes or messages.

Realistic Fiction

Challenges

Point of View

Determination

Biography

Section 2: Literary Analysis

RML1

LA.U7.RML1

Reading Minilesson Principle
The author gives a message in a fiction book.

Thinking About the Author's Message

You Will Need

- two or three familiar fiction books with clear messages, such as the following:
  - *Ish* by Peter H. Reynolds, from Text Set: Challenges
  - *Tomás and the Library Lady* by Pat Mora, from Text Set: Realistic Fiction
  - *Ruby's Wish* by Shirin Yim Bridges, from Text Set: Determination
- chart paper and markers

Academic Language / Important Vocabulary

- author
- message
- fiction
- story

Continuum Connection

- Notice that a book may have more than one message or big (main) idea (p. 50)
- Infer the messages in a work of fiction (p. 50)

Goal

Infer messages in a work of fiction.

Rationale

Authors often write stories to convey a message or messages to their readers. When students think about what the author is really trying to say, they are able to think more deeply about the story's meaning and to learn from the story.

Assess Learning

Observe students when they talk about stories. Notice if there is evidence of new learning based on the goal of this minilesson.

- Can students identify an author's message(s) in a story?
- Do they understand that a story can have more than one message?
- Do they think about how the messages in stories can apply to their own lives?
- Do they use vocabulary such as *author, message, fiction,* and *story*?

Minilesson

To help students think about the minilesson principle, use familiar stories to engage students in a discussion about author's message. Here is an example.

- Show the cover of *Ish*, and then briefly show the pages to remind students of the story.

  Think about what happens in this story. Beyond the events in the story, what do you think the author wants you to learn, or understand, from reading it?

  What the author wants you to learn or understand from the book is called the author's message.

- Accept multiple responses and record all reasonable responses on chart paper. If different students suggest different messages, emphasize that a book can have more than one message.

- Show the cover of *Tomás and the Library Lady* and show some of the pages.

  What does Tomás like about reading books?

  What do you think the author, Pat Mora, wants you to learn or understand about books? What is her message?

- Again, record all reasonable responses on the chart, and emphasize that the book can have more than one message.

Have a Try

Invite the students to talk with a partner about the author's message in a third book.

▶ Show the cover and a few pages of *Ruby's Wish*.

> Turn and talk to your partner about what you think the author's message is. What does the author want you to learn or understand from reading this story?

▶ After students turn and talk, ask a few pairs to share their ideas, and record all reasonable responses on the chart.

Summarize and Apply

Summarize the learning and remind students to think about the author's message when they read.

> What did you notice about the fiction books we looked at today?

> The author's message is something that the author wants you to learn or understand from the book.

▶ Write the principle at the top of the chart.

> What do you notice about the messages on our chart? How many messages are there for each book?

> Choose a fiction book to read today. As you read, think about what the author wants you to learn. Be ready to share the author's message when we meet after independent reading time.

Share

Following independent reading time, gather students together in the meeting area to talk about their reading.

> Turn and talk to your partner about the author's message in the story you read today.

> Did you and your partner find the same or different messages in your books?

Extend the Lesson (Optional)

After assessing students' understanding, you might decide to extend the learning.

▶ **Writing About Reading** Have students write about and reflect on an author's message in a reader's notebook. Encourage them to make connections to their own lives.

The author gives a message in a fiction book.

	• Don't try to be perfect. Be creative. • Be confident, even when other people say you're not good at something.
	• Books can carry you to amazing new worlds in your imagination. • Books can change a person's life.
	• Determination and hard work can help you reach your goals.

RML2
LA.U7.RML2

Reading Minilesson Principle
The author gives a message in a nonfiction book.

Thinking About the Author's Message

You Will Need

- two or three familiar nonfiction books with a clear message, such as the following:
  - *Meadowlands* by Thomas F. Yezerski, from Text Set: Point of View
  - *Almost Gone* by Steve Jenkins, from Text Set: Point of View
  - *Nobody Owns the Sky* by Reeve Lindbergh, from Text Set: Biography
- chart paper and markers

Academic Language / Important Vocabulary

- nonfiction
- author
- message
- big idea

Continuum Connection

- Understand that there can be different interpretations of the meanings of a text (p. 54)
- Infer the larger ideas and messages in a nonfiction text (p. 54)

Goal

Infer messages in a work of nonfiction.

Rationale

When you teach students to think about the message in a nonfiction book, you help them think not only about what information the author wants the reader to learn and understand but also why that information is important.

Assess Learning

Observe students when they talk about nonfiction books. Notice if there is evidence of new learning based on the goal of this minilesson.

- ▶ Can students identify an author's message in a nonfiction book?
- ▶ Do they understand that a nonfiction book can have more than one message?
- ▶ Do they use the terms *nonfiction, author, message,* and *big idea*?

Minilesson

To help students think about the minilesson principle, use familiar nonfiction texts to engage students in a discussion of author's message. Here is an example.

- ▶ Display the cover of *Meadowlands* and read the title.

  Remember this nonfiction book? What did you learn about from this book?

  The author's message is more than just the facts in the book. Listen carefully as I reread a few pages, and think about what the author wants you to learn or understand from reading this book.

- ▶ Reread the last four pages of the book.

  What do you think is the author's message? What is the big idea that he wants you to learn or understand?

- ▶ Record all reasonable responses on chart paper. If students supply multiple messages, emphasize that a book can have more than one message and that different people may have different opinions about what the message is.

- ▶ Display the cover of *Almost Gone*, and then reread page 5.

  What is the author trying to say about animals that are almost gone? What does he want you to understand about these animals?

- ▶ Record all reasonable responses on the chart.

Have a Try

Invite the students to talk with a partner about the author's message in a third nonfiction book.

▶ Show the cover of *Nobody Owns the Sky*.

> As I reread some of this book, think about the author's message.

▶ Reread pages 1–11.

> Turn and talk to your partner about the author's message in this book. What is the big idea that he wants you to understand?

▶ Record all reasonable responses on the chart.

Summarize and Apply

Summarize the learning and remind students to think about the author's message when they read.

> What did you notice about the nonfiction books we looked at today?

> The author's message is something that the author wants you to learn or understand from reading the book. It's a big idea— not just a fact. Some nonfiction books have more than one message.

▶ Write the principle at the top of the chart.

> Choose a nonfiction book to read today. As you read, think about the author's message. Be ready to share the author's message in your book when we meet.

Share

Following independent reading time, gather students together in the meeting area to talk about their reading.

> Turn and talk to your partner about the author's message or messages in the nonfiction book you read today.

Extend the Lesson (Optional)

After assessing students' understanding, you might decide to extend the learning.

▶ **Writing About Reading** Have students write about the message of a nonfiction book in a reader's notebook. Encourage them to give their own opinion about the author's message (e.g., why it is important) and support it with details from the book, their background knowledge, and/or their personal experiences.

The author gives a message in a nonfiction book.

	• People and nature share the same environment and depend on each other. • Stop polluting the environment.
	• Human actions have endangered many animals. • By becoming aware of things that endanger animals, people can do things to help save them.
	• Follow your dreams. • Dreams can come true through hard work and dedication.

Section 2: Literary Analysis

Reading Minilesson Principle
More than one author can give the same message.

Thinking About the Author's Message

You Will Need

- two sets of two books that share a similar message, such as the following:
  - *Ruby's Wish* by Shirin Yim Bridges and *Nothing but Trouble* by Sue Stauffacher, from Text Set: Determination
  - *Nobody Owns the Sky* by Reeve Lindbergh and *The Tree Lady* by H. Joseph Hopkins, from Text Set: Biography
- chart paper and markers

Academic Language / Important Vocabulary

- message
- author

Continuum Connection

- Infer the messages in a work of fiction [p. 50]
- Think across texts to derive larger messages, themes, or ideas [p. 50]

Goal

Think across works of fiction and nonfiction to derive larger messages.

Rationale

When you teach students that sometimes different authors give the same message through their books, they build an understanding of universal ideas and the recognition that people are connected by common ideas.

Assess Learning

Observe students when they talk about author's message. Notice if there is evidence of new learning based on the goal of this minilesson.

- ▶ Can students identify the author's message in both fiction and nonfiction?
- ▶ Do they notice when two or more books have the same or a very similar message?
- ▶ Do they use the terms *message* and *author*?

Minilesson

To help students think about the minilesson principle, use familiar fiction and nonfiction texts to provide an inquiry-based lesson about author's message. Here is an example.

- ▶ Show the cover of *Ruby's Wish*.

  When we talked about *Ruby's Wish*, you noticed that the author's message in this book is "Determination and hard work can help you reach your goals."

- ▶ Write the message on chart paper.

  Let's think about the author's message in another book you know.

- ▶ Show the cover of *Nothing but Trouble* and show some of the pages to remind students of the book.

  Remember this book about Althea Gibson? What was Althea Gibson's goal?

  How did Althea Gibson become a famous tennis player?

  What do you think the author wants you to learn or understand from Althea Gibson's story? What is the author's message?

- ▶ Write the author's message on the chart.

  What do you notice about the author's message in both these books?

  Sometimes authors give the same message or very similar messages in their books.

Have a Try

Invite the students to work with a partner to identify the author's message in *The Tree Lady*.

▶ Show the cover of *Nobody Owns the Sky*.

> You noticed that one of the author's messages in this book is "Follow your dreams."

▶ Write the author's message on the chart. Then show the cover of *The Tree Lady* and show some pages.

> Turn and talk to your partner about the author's message. Share your thoughts. What big idea does the author want you to learn or understand?

▶ Write the message on the chart.

> What do you notice about the author's message in both these books?

Summarize and Apply

Summarize the learning and remind students to think about the author's message when they read.

> What did you notice about the authors' messages in the books we looked at today?

▶ Write the principle at the top of the chart.

> When you read today, think about the author's message and be ready to share it when we meet after independent reading time. We will see if the books have the same message.

Share

Following independent reading time, gather students together in the meeting area to talk about their reading.

> Who would like to share the author's message in the book you read?

> Did anyone else read a book with the same or a similar message?

Extend the Lesson (Optional)

After assessing students' understanding, you might decide to extend the learning.

▶ Ask students to help you put together a basket of books in your classroom library that have the same message.

▶ **Writing About Reading** Have students compare and contrast in a reader's notebook how two or more authors teach the same message in their books.

More than one author can give the same message.

	Determination and hard work can help you reach your goals.
	Determination and hard work can help you reach your goals.
	Follow your dreams.
	Follow your dreams.

Reading Minilesson Principle
The illustrator helps communicate the author's message.

Thinking About the Author's Message

You Will Need

- two or three familiar books with illustrations that clearly help communicate the author's message, such as the following:
  - *Tomás and the Library Lady* by Pat Mora, from Text Set: Realistic Fiction
  - *Meadowlands* by Thomas F. Yezerski, from Text Set: Point of View
  - *What's So Bad About Gasoline?* by Anne Rockwell, from Text Set: Point of View
- chart paper and markers

Academic Language / Important Vocabulary

- message
- author
- illustrator
- illustration
- communicate

Continuum Connection

- Notice how illustrations and graphics can reflect the theme in a text (p. 52)
- Notice how illustrations and graphics help to communicate the writer's message (p. 55)

Goal

Notice how illustrations and graphics help to communicate the writer's message.

Rationale

When you teach students to notice and think about how the illustrator helps communicate the author's message, they develop a deeper understanding of the message. They also begin to understand how authors and illustrators work together toward a common goal.

Assess Learning

Observe students when they talk about illustrations. Notice if there is evidence of new learning based on the goal of this minilesson.

- ▶ Can students explain how an illustrator helps communicate an author's message?
- ▶ Do they use the terms *message, author, illustrator, illustration,* and *communicate*?

Minilesson

To help students think about the minilesson principle, engage them in a discussion about how illustrations can support the author's message. Here is an example.

- ▶ Show the cover of *Tomás and the Library Lady*.

  When we talked about this book, you noticed that one message from the author is "Books can carry you to amazing new worlds in your imagination."

- ▶ Open the book to the last two pages of the story. Reread the text.

  Talk about how the illustrator shows that books can carry you to amazing new worlds.

- ▶ Record students' responses on chart paper.

  The illustrator helps communicate, or tell, the author's message by showing what is happening in Tomás' imagination when he reads a book.

- ▶ Show the cover of *Meadowlands*. Open the book to pages 8–9 and read the text.

  A message from this book is "We need to stop polluting the environment."

  How does this illustration help teach the message that we need to stop polluting the environment?

- ▶ Record responses on the chart.

  This illustration shows what happens when we pollute the environment. If we don't want our communities to look like this illustration, we need to take good care of the environment.

Have a Try

Invite the students to talk with a partner about how the illustrations in a third book support the author's message.

▶ Show the cover and some pages of *What's So Bad About Gasoline?*

> What is the author's message about gasoline in this book?

▶ Write the message on the chart. Then reread pages 3–4.

> Look at the illustration on page 4. Turn and talk to your partner about how the illustrator helps teach the message that we need to use less gasoline.

▶ After students turn and talk, ask a few pairs to share their thinking. Record their responses on the chart.

Summarize and Apply

Summarize the learning and remind students to think about how the illustrator helps communicate the author's message when they read.

> What did you notice about the illustrations in the books we looked at today?

▶ Write the principle at the top of the chart.

> Choose a book with illustrations to read today. Look for ways that the illustrator helps communicate the author's message. Be ready to share your thinking when we come back together.

Share

Following independent reading time, gather students together in the meeting area to talk about their reading.

> Who would like to share how the illustrator helped communicate the author's message in the book you read today?

Extend the Lesson (Optional)

After assessing students' understanding, you might decide to extend the learning.

▶ When students write and illustrate their own texts, encourage them to think about how they can communicate their message through their illustrations.

The illustrator helps communicate the author's message.

Book	Message	Illustrations
TOMÁS AND THE LIBRARY LADY	Books can carry you to amazing new worlds in your imagination.	The illustrator shows what is happening in Tomás' imagination when he reads a book.
MEADOWLANDS	We need to stop polluting the environment.	The illustrator shows what happens when people pollute the environment.
What's So Bad About GASOLINE?	We need to use less gasoline and figure out ways not to depend on fossil fuels.	The illustrator shows what happens in the Earth's atmosphere when people use too much gasoline.

Assessment

After you have taught the minilessons in this umbrella, observe students as they talk and write about their reading across instructional contexts: interactive read-aloud, independent reading and literacy work, guided reading, shared reading, and book club. Use *The Literacy Continuum* (Fountas and Pinnell 2017) to observe students' reading and writing behaviors across instructional contexts.

▶ What evidence do you have of new understandings related to author's message?

- Can the students identify the author's message in both fiction and nonfiction books?

- Do they understand that a book can have more than one message?

- Do they notice when two or more books have the same or a very similar message?

- Can they explain how an illustrator helps communicate an author's message?

- Do they use the terms *author, message, illustrator,* and *communicate* when they discuss the author's message?

▶ In what other ways, beyond the scope of this umbrella, are they thinking and talking about books?

- Have they noticed that authors write for different purposes?

- Are they noticing other ways that illustrations support text?

Use your observations to determine the next umbrella you will teach. You may also consult Minilessons Across the Year (pp. 55-57) for guidance.

Link to Writing

After teaching the minilessons in this umbrella, help students link the new learning to their own writing:

▶ When students write both fiction and nonfiction texts, remind them to think about what message they want to convey to their readers and how to convey it. Encourage them to think about how they can communicate their message through illustrations, photographs, or other graphics.

Reader's Notebook

When this umbrella is complete, provide a copy of the minilesson principles (see resources.fountasandpinnell.com) for students to glue in the reader's notebook (in the Minilessons section if using *Reader's Notebook: Intermediate* [Fountas and Pinnell 2011]), so they can refer to the information as needed.

Minilessons in This Umbrella

RML1   Authors write books to interest you or entertain you.

RML2   Authors write books to give information.

RML3   Authors write books to get you to think about or do something.

Before Teaching Umbrella 8 Minilessons

Read and discuss high-quality fiction and nonfiction picture books that clearly reflect a variety of author's purposes. Choose fiction books that are humorous and highly entertaining. Choose both expository and persuasive nonfiction books whose topics appeal to the students in your class. Use the following books from the *Fountas & Pinnell Classroom™ Interactive Read-Aloud Collection* text sets or choose fiction and nonfiction books from your classroom library.

Humorous Texts

> *Those Darn Squirrels!* by Adam Rubin
>
> *Big Bad Bubble* by Adam Rubin

Animal Journeys

> *North: The Amazing Story of Arctic Migration* by Nick Dowson

Genre Study: Expository Nonfiction

> *Knights in Shining Armor* by Gail Gibbons
>
> *Tornadoes!* by Gail Gibbons
>
> *Hottest, Coldest, Highest, Deepest* by Steve Jenkins

Author's Point of View

> *Meadowlands* by Thomas F. Yezerski
>
> *What's So Bad About Gasoline?* by Anne Rockwell
>
> *Energy Island* by Allan Drummond

As you read aloud and enjoy these texts together, help students

- think about why the author might have written the text,
- identify parts that they find funny, entertaining, or interesting,
- discuss what they learned from the text, and
- express and justify opinions about the text.

Humorous Texts

Animal Journeys

Expository Nonfiction

Point of View

Section 2: Literary Analysis

Reading Minilesson Principle
Authors write books to interest you or entertain you.

Thinking About the Author's Purpose

You Will Need

- two or three familiar humorous fiction books, such as the following:
  - *Those Darn Squirrels!* by Adam Rubin, from Text Set: Humorous Texts
  - *North: The Amazing Story of Arctic Migration* by Nick Dowson from Text Set: Animal Journeys
  - *Big Bad Bubble* by Adam Rubin, from Text Set: Humorous Texts
- chart paper and markers

Academic Language / Important Vocabulary

- author's purpose
- entertain/entertaining

Continuum Connection

- Understand that a writer has a purpose in writing a fiction or nonfiction text (p. 50)
- Recognize how a writer creates humor (p. 51)

Goal

Understand that sometimes the author's purpose is to entertain (e.g., use humor).

Rationale

When students understand that some authors write books to entertain readers, they are better able to recognize, discuss, and enjoy the features of these books. They are also able to use their understanding of these features to write their own entertaining texts. This minilesson focuses on humor to make the concept of author's purpose more accessible at this level, but students should be made aware that books can be entertaining in other ways.

Assess Learning

Observe students when they read and talk about books. Notice if there is evidence of new learning based on the goal of this minilesson.

- ▶ Can students identify books that were written to entertain?
- ▶ Can they identify specific features that make such a book entertaining?
- ▶ Do they use the terms *author's purpose* and *entertain*?

Minilesson

To help students think about the minilesson principle, use highly entertaining fiction texts to provide an inquiry-based lesson. Here is an example.

- ▶ Show the cover of *Those Darn Squirrels!* and briefly show some pages to remind students of the story. Prompt students to talk about the story with questions, such as the following:
  - *What did you think of this story?*
  - *What did you like about it?*
  - *What was funny about it?*
- ▶ Record students' responses on chart paper.
- ▶ Show the cover and some pages of *North: The Amazing Story of Arctic Migration*.

  What did you think of *North*?

  This book isn't funny, but did you enjoy it? What made it interesting?

- ▶ Record students' responses on the chart.

  You enjoyed reading these books. Why do you think the authors wrote them?

  The reason an author writes a book is called the author's purpose. Some authors write books to entertain you, or so you can enjoy them. *Those Darn Squirrels!* and *North* are both entertaining but in different ways. What else could make a book entertaining to read?

Have a Try

Invite the students to talk with a partner about an author's purpose.

▶ Hold up *Big Bad Bubble* and show some pages.

> Turn and talk to your partner about why you think the author wrote this book. Be sure to explain the reasons for your thinking.

▶ After students turn and talk, ask a few students to share their thinking. Record responses on the chart.

Summarize and Apply

Summarize the learning and remind students to think about the author's purpose when they read.

> What did you notice about the three books we looked at today?

> You noticed that the authors wrote these books to entertain you. These books are fun and interesting to read.

▶ Write the principle at the top of the chart.

> When you read a book today, think about the purpose the author had for writing the book. If you read a book that was written to entertain, bring your book to share when we meet after independent reading time.

Share

Following independent reading time, gather students together in the meeting area to talk about their reading.

> Raise your hand if you read a book that was written to entertain you.

> What made your book entertaining to read?

Extend the Lesson (Optional)

After assessing students' understanding, you might decide to extend the learning.

▶ Repeat this minilesson with books that are entertaining in other ways (e.g., an exciting, suspenseful adventure story; a fascinating informational book).

▶ Discuss in more detail the specific techniques that authors use to make books entertaining (e.g., humor, suspense, interesting word choices, playful language). Encourage students to use these techniques when they write their own stories.

Authors write books to interest you or entertain you.

	• It is funny and silly. • It has funny made-up words. • The squirrels dress up as birds and do other silly things.
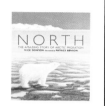	• It has interesting information. • It has fun and interesting language (big, blubbery mother walrus). • The illustrations are nice.
	• The monsters are funny looking. • It's silly that the monsters are so afraid of bubbles.

Reading Minilesson Principle
Authors write books to give information.

Thinking About the Author's Purpose

You Will Need

- two or three familiar informational books, such as the following from Text Set: Expository Nonfiction:
  - *Knights in Shining Armor* by Gail Gibbons
  - *Tornadoes!* by Gail Gibbons
  - *Hottest, Coldest, Highest, Deepest* by Steve Jenkins
- chart paper and markers

Academic Language / Important Vocabulary

- author's purpose
- information
- nonfiction
- fiction

Continuum Connection

- Understand that a writer has a purpose in writing a fiction or nonfiction text [p. 50]
- Infer a writer's purpose in writing a nonfiction text [p. 54]

Goal

Understand that sometimes the author's purpose is to inform.

Rationale

When students understand that some authors write books to give information, they are better able to recognize and discuss the features of informational books and learn from them. They are also able to use their understanding of these features to write their own informational texts.

Assess Learning

Observe students when they read and talk about informational texts. Notice if there is evidence of new learning based on the goal of this minilesson.

- Can students identify books that were written to give information?
- Can they explain what the information in such a book is about?
- Do they use the terms *author's purpose, information, nonfiction,* and *fiction*?

Minilesson

To help students think about the minilesson principle, use familiar informational texts to provide an inquiry-based lesson about author's purpose. Here is an example.

- Show the cover of *Knights in Shining Armor* and some of the pages to remind students of the book.

  Is this book fiction or nonfiction?

  How do you know?

  What did you learn about from this book?

- Record students' responses on chart paper.
- Show the cover of *Tornadoes!* and some of the pages.

  What is this book about?

  Does the author tell a story about tornadoes?

  How does she tell you about tornadoes?

- Record students' responses on the chart.

  Look at the chart. What do the two books have in common?

  Why do you think the author wrote these books?

Have a Try

Invite the students to talk with a partner about a third informational book.

▶ Show the cover of *Hottest, Coldest, Highest, Deepest* and some of the pages.

> Turn and talk to your partner about the author's purpose in writing this book.

▶ After students turn and talk, ask a few pairs to share their thinking. Record students' responses on the chart.

> Could a writer have more than one purpose?

Summarize and Apply

Summarize the learning and remind students to think about the author's purpose when they read.

> What did you notice about the three books we looked at today?

> You noticed that the authors wrote the books to give information.

▶ Write the principle at the top of the chart.

> When you read today, think about why the author might have written the book. If you read a book that the author wrote to give information, bring your book to share when we come back together.

Share

Following independent reading time, gather students together in the meeting area to talk about their reading.

> Raise your hand if you read a book that was written to give information.

> How do you know that your book was written to give information? What does it give information about?

Extend the Lesson (Optional)

After assessing students' understanding, you might decide to extend the learning.

▶ Discuss the specific ways that authors convey and organize information in informational texts (see Umbrella 13: Noticing How Authors Choose to Organize Nonfiction).

▶ **Writing About Reading** Have students write in a reader's notebook about the information the author gives in a specific informational book.

Authors write books to give information.

	The author gives information about knights.
	The author gives information about tornadoes.
	The author gives information about the hottest, coldest, highest, and deepest places on Earth.

Reading Minilesson Principle

Authors write books to get you to think about or do something.

Thinking About the Author's Purpose

You Will Need

- two or three familiar persuasive books, such as the following from Text Set: Point of View:
  - *Meadowlands* by Thomas F. Yezerski
  - *What's So Bad About Gasoline?* by Anne Rockwell
  - *Energy Island* by Allan Drummond
- chart paper and markers

Academic Language / Important Vocabulary

- author's purpose

Continuum Connection

- Understand that a writer has a purpose in writing a fiction or nonfiction text [p. 50]
- Recognize a writer's use of the techniques for persuasion in a persuasive text [p. 54]

Goal

Understand that sometimes the author's purpose is to persuade.

Rationale

Once students recognize that an author's purpose is to persuade readers to think or act differently, they can identify the point of view of the author and the evidence given to support that point of view. They become more thoughtful and critical readers, who can consider, explain, and justify their own opinions.

Assess Learning

Observe students when they read and talk about persuasive texts. Notice if there is evidence of new learning based on the goal of this minilesson.

- ▶ Can the students identify books that were written to persuade readers?
- ▶ Can they identify the point of view of the author in such a book?
- ▶ Do they understand and use the term *author's purpose*?

Minilesson

To help students think about the minilesson principle, use familiar texts to provide an inquiry-based lesson about author's purpose. Here is an example.

- ▶ Show the cover of *Meadowlands* and some of the pages.

  What did you learn about from this book?

- ▶ Reread the last four pages of the book.

  Why do you think the author tells about what Karin and other people have done to help the Meadowlands?

  What do you think he wants you to do differently after reading the book?

- ▶ Record students' responses on chart paper.

  Why do you think the author wrote this book?

  The author may have written this book to get you to think about how you can help protect the environment. For what other reasons might he have written this book?

  The author might also want to give information about the Meadowlands. An author can have more than one reason, or purpose, for writing a book.

- ▶ Show the cover of *What's So Bad About Gasoline?* Reread pages 29–31.

  Why do you think the author, Anne Rockwell, wrote this book? Why do you think that?

- ▶ Record students' responses on the chart.

Have a Try

Invite the students to talk with a partner about a different persuasive book.

▶ Show the cover of *Energy Island*. Reread the last two pages of the book, including the "Saving Energy" sidebar.

> Turn and talk to your partner about why you think the author wrote this book. What is his purpose for writing? Why do you think so?

▶ After students turn and talk, ask a few students to share their thinking. Record students' responses on the chart.

Summarize and Apply

Summarize the learning and remind students to think about the author's purpose when they read.

> What did you notice about the three books we looked at?

> You noticed that these books were written to get you to think about or do something.

▶ Write the principle at the top of the chart.

> Why is it a good idea to give information when you want to get someone to do or think about something?

> When you read today, think about why the author might have written the book. Bring your book and be ready to share your thinking when we come back together.

Share

Following independent reading time, gather students together in the meeting area to talk about their reading.

> Turn and talk to your partner about the book you read today. Why did the author write it? How do you know?

Extend the Lesson (Optional)

After assessing students' understanding, you might decide to extend the learning.

▶ Place students into small groups and give each group a selection of familiar books with different authors' purposes. Direct students to categorize their books by author's purpose.

▶ Discuss the techniques that authors use to persuade readers.

Authors write books to get you to think about or do something.

- Take care of the planet.
- Recycle more and use less.
- Conserve energy.

- Use less gasoline.
- Use fuels that are better for the planet.
- Take care of the planet.

- Save energy.
- Take a bus or train or ride a bike.

Section 2: Literary Analysis

Assessment

After you have taught the minilessons in this umbrella, observe students as they talk and write about their reading across instructional contexts: interactive read-aloud, independent reading and literacy work, guided reading, shared reading, and book club. Use *The Literacy Continuum* (Fountas and Pinnell 2017) to observe students' reading and writing behaviors across instructional contexts.

▶ What evidence do you have of new understandings related to author's purpose?

- Can students identify the author's purpose(s) in a book?
- Do they provide evidence to support their opinions about the author's purpose(s)?
- Do they understand that a book can have more than one purpose?
- Do they use vocabulary such as *entertain*, *information*, and *persuade*?

▶ In what other ways, beyond the scope of this umbrella, are they thinking and talking about books?

- Are they thinking about the message that an author wants to convey?

Use your observations to determine the next umbrella you will teach. You may also consult Minilessons Across the Year (pp. 55-57) for guidance.

Link to Writing

After teaching the minilessons in this umbrella, help students link the new learning to their own writing:

▶ When students write their own fiction and nonfiction texts, encourage them to think about their purpose for writing. Teach students how to adapt their writing for different purposes (e.g., how to make a text funny, how to clearly communicate information, how to persuade readers). You might consider having your students write about the same topic with different purposes in mind (e.g., a funny story about a dog, an informational text about dogs, and a persuasive piece about why dogs make the best pets).

Reader's Notebook

When this umbrella is complete, provide a copy of the minilesson principles (see resources.fountasandpinnell.com) for students to glue in the reader's notebook (in the Minilessons section if using *Reader's Notebook: Intermediate* [Fountas and Pinnell 2011]), so they can refer to the information as needed.

Minilessons in This Umbrella

RML1 Sometimes writers choose language to make you feel a certain way.

RML2 Sometimes writers use punctuation in interesting ways.

RML3 Sometimes writers create humor in their stories.

RML4 Writers think about where to place the words and illustrations on the page.

RML5 Sometimes writers compare one thing to another.

RML6 Writers end stories in different ways.

RML7 Sometimes writers change the characters, plot, and settings of familiar stories to make new stories.

RML8 Sometimes writers play with the way words look.

Before Teaching Umbrella 9 Minilessons

The lessons in this umbrella do not need to be taught consecutively. Use the following books from the *Fountas & Pinnell Classroom™ Interactive Read-Aloud Collection* and *Shared Reading Collection* or choose texts that will engage your class.

Interactive Read-Aloud Collection

Facing Challenges

Goal! by Mina Javaherbin

Gettin' Through Thursday by Melrose Cooper

Humorous Texts

Bedhead by Margie Palatini

The Perfect Pet by Margie Palatini

Animal Journeys

North: The Amazing Story of Arctic Migration by Nick Dowson

Series Study: Dianna Hutts Aston and Sylvia Long

An Egg Is Quiet

Fractured Fairy Tales

Kate and the Beanstalk by Mary Pope Osborne

Yours Truly, Goldilocks by Alma Flor Ada

The Frog Prince, Continued by Jon Scieszka

Exploring Pourquoi Tales

The Legend of the Lady Slipper by Lise Lunge-Larsen

The Passage of Time

The Sunsets of Miss Olivia Wiggins by Lester Laminack

Shared Reading Collection

Saving Cranes by Brenda Iasevoli

Wolf Pack by Annette Bay Pimentel

Facing Challenges

Humorous Texts

Animal Journeys

Dianna Hutts Aston

Fractured Fairy Tales

Pourquoi Tales

Passage of Time

Shared Reading Collection

Section 2: Literary Analysis

RML1
LA.U9.RML1

Reading Minilesson Principle
Sometimes writers choose language to make you feel a certain way.

Analyzing the Writer's Craft

You Will Need

- three or four familiar fiction books, such as the following from Text Set: Facing Challenges:
  - *Goal!* by Mina Javaherbin
  - *Gettin' Through Thursday* by Melrose Cooper
- chart paper prepared with sentences from *Goal!* (pp. 3 and 28) and *Gettin' Through Thursday* (p. 22)
- markers
- document camera (optional)
- sticky notes

Academic Language / Important Vocabulary

- language

Continuum Connection

- Notice language that conveys an emotional atmosphere (mood) in a text, affecting how the reader feels: e.g., tension, sadness, joy (p. 51)
- Notice how a writer uses language to convey a mood (p. 134)

Goal

Notice language that conveys an emotional atmosphere (mood) in a text, affecting how the reader feels (e.g., tension, sadness, joy).

Rationale

Writers choose words to create an emotional response and connection to the characters and plot. When you support students in noticing these language choices, you engage them in their reading and make books more enjoyable. You also help them think about how to learn from writers to support their own writing.

Assess Learning

Observe students when they talk about the writer's craft. Notice if there is evidence of new learning based on the goal of this minilesson.

- ▸ Can students identify when an author uses language to help the reader experience a feeling?
- ▸ Do they point out a writer's use of language during individual reading conferences and/or small group guided reading?
- ▸ Do they understand how the word *language* is used in this lesson?

Minilesson

To help students think about the minilesson principle, provide an inquiry-based lesson about authors' use of language. If a document camera is available, consider projecting the pages to provide visual support. Here is an example.

- ▸ From *Goal!* show and read the page ending "The streets are not always safe."

  What do these sentences tell you about where the boys live?

  How does that make you feel?

- ▸ Record ideas on the prepared chart.

  What language does the author use to create that feeling in you?

- ▸ Ask a volunteer to underline words in the sentences that give them that feeling.

- ▸ Read the page toward the end of the book that ends with "I dribble past him and—Goooooooal!"

  Think about the last sentence. Listen as I reread it.

  What feeling does the author create in you with those words? How does she do that?

- ▸ Ask a student to underline words and punctuation that create the feeling.

Have a Try

Invite the students to talk with a partner about the language writers choose.

▶ Show *Gettin' Through Thursday* and read the page beginning "I broke away and slammed the door." Reread the first sentence.

> Turn and talk to your partner. What does the sentence mean? How does it make you feel?

▶ Ask a couple of students to share. Record responses and have a volunteer underline the words that contribute to the feeling.

Summarize and Apply

Summarize the learning and remind students to notice how writers use language in the books they read.

> What did you learn about how authors choose language? Look at the chart to help you remember.

▶ Write the principle at the top of the chart.

> When you read today, think about the author's word choices. Use a sticky note to mark a page with language that makes you feel a certain way. Bring your book when we come back together so you can share.

Share

Following independent reading time, gather students together in the meeting area to talk about their reading with a partner.

> Share with your partners some of the author's language that makes you feel a certain way.

▶ Choose a few students to share with the class.

Extend the Lesson (Optional)

After assessing students' understanding, you might decide to extend the learning.

▶ Encourage students to collect in a reader's notebook words or phrases that make them feel a certain way.

▶ **Writing About Reading** As students demonstrate they can talk about a writer's use of language to create a feeling, you may suggest they begin to include examples of this language in their reading letters (see Section Four: Writing About Reading).

Sometimes writers choose language to make you feel a certain way.

Author's words . . .	Make me feel . . .
"No one runs out to play. The streets are not always safe."	• worry • suspense • fear
"I dribble past him and — Goooooooal!"	• joy • pride • the excitement of the game
"I broke away and slammed the door like Shawna and sunk down behind it."	• sad • angry • disappointed

Section 2: Literary Analysis

Reading Minilesson Principle
Sometimes writers use punctuation in interesting ways.

Analyzing the Writer's Craft

You Will Need

- three or four familiar books with interesting uses of punctuation, such as the following:
  - *Saving Cranes* by Brenda Iasevoli, from *Shared Reading Collection*
  - *Wolf Pack* by Annette Bay Pimentel, from *Shared Reading Collection*
  - *Goal!* by Mina Javaherbin, from Text Set: Facing Challenges
- document camera (optional)
- chart paper and markers
- sticky notes

Academic Language / Important Vocabulary

- punctuation
- ellipsis
- dash

Continuum Connection

- Recognize and reflect punctuation with the voice: e.g., period, questions mark, exclamation point, dash, comma, ellipses, when reading in chorus or individually (p. 133)

Goal

Notice how writers use punctuation in interesting ways to communicate meaning.

Rationale

Writers use punctuation to make their writing easy to understand and to communicate meaning. When you encourage students to notice punctuation, you help them to appreciate the writer's craft and gain a better understanding of the text (see also Umbrella 3: Maintaining Fluency, found in Section Three: Strategies and Skills). They also learn possibilities for their own writing.

Assess Learning

Observe students when they talk about the writer's craft. Notice if there is evidence of new learning based on the goal of this minilesson.

- ▶ Do students notice interesting uses of punctuation?
- ▶ Can they discuss an author's decisions about punctuation?
- ▶ Can they use the word *punctuation*, and identify and name an *ellipsis* and *dash*?

Minilesson

To help students think about the minilesson principle, use enlarged texts that they can see easily, like big books or shared reading texts. If a document camera is available, consider projecting the pages, or write the sentences on chart paper. Here is an example.

- ▶ Show page 4 in *Saving Cranes*. Read through "Until . . . *splash*. Its pointy beak snaps up a shiny fish."

  > Do you know what three periods in a row is called? These three periods are called an ellipsis. Take a look at the sentence with the ellipsis. Why do you think the author decided to use an ellipsis here?

- ▶ Briefly discuss how a reader pauses at an ellipsis and in this example it creates a bit of suspense. Record responses on chart paper.

- ▶ Show page 6 and read through "And that could mean the end of all whooping cranes—forever." Point to the dash.

  > The straight line in this sentence is called a *dash*. Why do you think the author used a dash? How does it help you get meaning?

- ▶ Show and read from page 2 of *Wolf Pack* "A wolf family, or pack, has two leaders—one male and one female."

  > How does the author use a dash?

  > An ellipsis and a dash are two types of punctuation.

- ▶ Record responses on the chart.

Have a Try

Invite the students to notice with a partner how writers use punctuation.

▶ From *Goal!*, show and read the page that includes "If he kicks the ball, the bucket will tip over and . . ."

Turn and talk to your partner about a place where the author uses punctuation in an interesting way. Why do you think she decided to do that?

▶ Ask a couple of students to share. Record responses.

Summarize and Apply

Summarize the learning and remind students to notice how writers use punctuation.

What did you learn about how writers use punctuation?

▶ Write the principle at the top of the chart.

When you read today, notice how the writer uses punctuation in your book. Put a sticky note on a page with punctuation used in an interesting way. Think about how it helps you understand what you are reading. Bring the book when we come back together so you can share.

Share

Following independent reading time, gather students together in the meeting area to talk about their reading.

Who found an interesting example of punctuation in their reading today? Why do you think the author chose that?

Extend the Lesson (Optional)

After assessing students' understanding, you might decide to extend the learning.

▶ Take time to notice and discuss an author's use of punctuation during interactive read-aloud, shared reading, and guided reading.

▶ Have students perform a readers' theater script, using the punctuation to guide how their voices reflect the author's meaning.

Sometimes writers use punctuation in interesting ways.

Ellipsis

- Adds or creates suspense
- Emphasizes a word
- Shows character's feelings

Examples:

"Until . . . splash."

"If he kicks the ball, the bucket will tip over and . . ."

Dash

- Adds more information

Examples:

"The end of all whooping cranes — forever."

"A wolf family, or pack, has two leaders—one male and one female."

Reading Minilesson Principle
Sometimes writers create humor in their stories.

Analyzing the Writer's Craft

You Will Need

▸ two or three familiar fiction books with clear examples of humor, such as the following from Text Set: Humorous texts:
  - *Bedhead* by Margie Palatini
  - *The Perfect Pet* by Margie Palatini
▸ document camera (optional)
▸ chart paper and markers
▸ sticky notes

Academic Language / Important Vocabulary

▸ humor
▸ humorous

Continuum Connection

▸ Recognize how a writer creates humor (p. 51)
▸ Notice and identify language that adds humor (p. 134)

Goal

Recognize how a writer creates humor.

Rationale

Humorous stories may feel abstract to students—it is challenging to determine what makes a story humorous because humor is personal. When you teach students to notice how writers create humor, stories become more enjoyable. They also learn to create humor in their own stories.

Assess Learning

Observe students when they talk about the writer's craft. Notice if there is evidence of new learning based on the goal of this minilesson.

▸ Can students identify places in a story that made them laugh?
▸ Can they talk about how an author made a story humorous?
▸ Do they understand the words *humor* and *humorous*?

Minilesson

To help students think about the minilesson principle, choose familiar texts that bring in an element of humor that is tangible and concrete for them and provide an inquiry-based lesson on humor. Here is an example.

▸ Show *Bedhead* and read the page beginning with, "BaaaaaaAAAddddddd! Wrong. It was that bad."

  This page is right after Oliver's parents see his hair for the first time. What is humorous here? What did the writer do to create humor, or make you laugh?

▸ Record responses on chart paper.

  The writer used the word *hairy* to describe the difficult situation. So, the problem is about Oliver's *hair,* and the situation is *hairy*. She's playing with the word *hair* to mean two different things.

▸ Now turn to the page that begins with "'Hey, kid,' said the man behind the camera."

  This is when the class is gathering for a picture, and Oliver's hair seems to be under control.

▸ Turn the page.

  What happens as the photographer takes the picture? What does the writer do to make this part of the story humorous?

▸ Record responses on the chart.

Have a Try

Invite the students to notice with a partner how writers create humor.

▶ From *The Perfect Pet*, show the page and read the sentences, "Mind you, it was a very good-looking plant as cactus plants go. And it had quite a prickly sense of humor."

> Turn and talk to your partner. What did the writer do to create humor on this page?

▶ Ask a couple of students to share. Record responses.

Summarize and Apply

Summarize the learning and remind students to notice how writers create humor.

> What did you notice today about how writers make things humorous?

▶ Write the principle at the top of the chart.

> When you read today, look for places in your book that you find funny. Put a sticky note on the page. Bring the book when we meet so you can share.

Share

Following independent reading time, gather students together in the meeting area to talk about their reading.

> Who would like to talk about a humorous story they read today? What did the writer do to create humor?

▶ Choose a few students to share with the class.

Extend the Lesson (Optional)

After assessing students' understanding, you might decide to extend the learning.

▶ Take time during interactive read-aloud to talk about where and why an author has included humor.

▶ **Writing About Reading** Students may start a page or a section in a reader's notebook to jot down ways writers make their stories funny or examples of humorous text.

▶ **Writing About Reading** Encourage students to share in their weekly letters about reading (see Umbrella 3: Writing Letters About Reading, found in Section Four: Writing About Reading) humorous parts of their reading and why they think they are humorous.

Sometimes writers create humor in their stories.		
	• The use of "hairy situation" • The illustration of Oliver sweating, and his larger than life hair • Oliver's hair becomes unruly again just as the class picture is taken.	• playing with words • funny illustrations • surprising and outrageous ending
	• The use of "prickly sense of humor" • The illustration of Elizabeth trying to hug her cactus	• playing with words • silly illustration

RML 4
LA.U9.RML4

Reading Minilesson Principle
Writers think about where to place the words and illustrations on the page.

Analyzing the Writer's Craft

Goal

Notice the placement of words on a page in relation to the illustrations.

Rationale

Authors thoughtfully arrange words and illustrations on the page to communicate meaning and enhance the text. When you help students to notice this, it improves the reading experience and lends deeper meaning to their reading. It also helps them think about possibilities for their own writing.

Assess Learning

Observe students when they talk about the writer's craft. Notice if there is evidence of new learning based on the goal of this minilesson.

▸ Do students notice how text and illustrations are arranged on a page and think about why the author made that decision?

▸ Do they discuss how text and illustrations work together to enhance the reading experience?

▸ Do they understand and use the words *illustrations, placement,* and *arranged*?

Minilesson

To help students think about the minilesson principle, provide an inquiry-based lesson using familiar texts with interesting placement of words and illustrations so they can think about the writer's decisions. If a document camera is available, consider projecting the pages to provide visual support. Here is an example.

▸ Hold up (or use a document camera to display) *North*. Read and show the last paragraph on page 12.

> What do you notice about where the author and illustrator decided to place the words on this page?

> Why do you think the words are at the bottom of the page?

▸ Add noticings to the chart paper.

▸ Read pages 14–17 and show the illustrations.

> How are the illustrations and words different on these pages?

▸ Help students notice how the illustrations are split horizontally on the page and the few words are spaced out.

> Why do you think the author and illustrator designed these pages differently? What do the words and pictures tell you about the whale's travels?

Have a Try

Invite the students to notice word and illustration placement with a partner.

▶ From *An Egg Is Quiet*, read the pages with the heading "An egg is shapely."

> Turn and talk to your partner about how the author arranged the words and illustrations on this page. What does the placement of the words and illustrations show?

▶ Ask a couple of students to share. Help students notice that the author chose to place the text next to the illustrations.

Summarize and Apply

Summarize the learning and remind students to notice word and illustration placement.

> What does the chart show you about words and illustrations?

▶ Write the principle on the chart.

> During independent reading, choose a picture book to read. Notice how the words and illustrations are placed on the page. Put a sticky note where the writer's decision about where to put the words and illustrations is meaningful. Bring the book when we meet so you can share.

Share

Following independent reading time, gather students together in the meeting area to talk about their reading.

> Did anyone notice a special way the writer placed the words or illustrations?

▶ Choose a few students to share with the class.

Extend the Lesson (Optional)

After assessing students' understanding, you might decide to extend the learning.

▶ Provide opportunities for students to discuss the interaction between text and illustrations during interactive read-aloud.

▶ As students continue noticing how authors place words and illustrations on the page, encourage them to experiment with word and picture placement when they write stories or make nonfiction books.

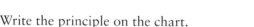

Writers think about where to place the words and illustrations on the page.

NORTH THE AMAZING STORY OF ARCTIC MIGRATION NICK DOWSON · PATRICK BENSON Past Los Angeles San Francisco, Vancouver Island	• The words leave you wondering where the whale will travel. • The words are spaced out to show that the whale travels very far. The words go with the pictures of the cities.
An Egg Is Quiet Chicken egg	• The labels are shaped like the eggs. • The words that tell about each egg are placed below the egg.

RML 5
LA.U9.RML5

Sometimes writers compare one thing to another.

Analyzing the Writer's Craft

You Will Need

- three or four familiar texts or poems with figurative language (e.g., similes, metaphors), such as the following:
  - *The Legend of the Lady Slipper* by Lise Lunge-Larsen, from Text Set: Porquoi Tales
  - *The Sunsets of Miss Olivia Wiggins* by Lester Laminack, from Text Set: Passage of Time
- chart paper and markers
- document camera (optional)
- sticky note

Academic Language / Important Vocabulary

- compare
- comparisons

Continuum Connection

- Notice and understand how the author uses literary language, including some figurative language and symbolism (p. 51)

Goal

Notice and understand how the author uses figurative language (e.g., similes, metaphors).

Rationale

Writers use figurative language, such as metaphors and similes, to make abstract ideas more concrete. Introduce these terms if your students are ready to use them (*simile* might be a simple enough term), or use the word *compare* to help them understand the writer's technique.

Assess Learning

Observe students when they talk about the writer's craft. Notice if there is evidence of new learning based on the goal of this minilesson.

- Do students notice figurative language in books they read or hear and understand what it means?
- Do they understand why a writer uses figurative language?
- Are they using the words *compare* and *comparisons*?

Minilesson

To help students think about the minilesson principle, provide an inquiry-based lesson using familiar texts with strong figurative language. If a document camera is available, consider projecting the pages to provide visual support. Here is an example.

- Hold up *The Legend of the Lady Slipper*. Read the page that begins with "He was strong as a bear."

  What does the author tell about the older brother? What does comparing him to a bear help you know?

  The author helps you understand something about the older brother by comparing him to something you know. Two words will help you know an author is making a comparison. When you read the words *like* or *as*, think about what the author is comparing.

- Record responses on the chart paper.
- Show and read the last paragraph on the page that starts with "Suddenly, the snow collapsed around her."

  What does the author compare the sister to? What does that tell you about the sister?

- Record responses on the chart.

Have a Try

Invite the students to think with a partner about how writers sometimes compare one thing to another.

▶ From *The Sunsets of Miss Olivia Wiggins*, read and show the page that starts with "She remembered a late afternoon, so very long ago."

> Turn and talk to your partner. How does the author use comparison to help you make a picture in your head?

▶ Ask a couple of students to share.

Summarize and Apply

Summarize the learning and remind students to think about how writers sometimes compare one thing to another.

> Today you noticed that writers sometimes compare one thing to another. Sometimes they use the word *like* or *as*.

▶ Have a volunteer draw a line under *like* and *as* in the examples on the chart. Then write the principle at the top.

> When you read today, notice if the author of your book uses comparison. Mark the page with a sticky note, and bring the book when we meet so you can share.

Share

Following independent reading time, gather students together in the meeting area to talk about their reading.

> Who found a comparison in your book? What did it help you to understand?

Extend the Lesson (Optional)

After assessing students' understanding, you might decide to extend the learning.

▶ As students find examples of comparisons in their reading, add them to the chart.

▶ Discuss similes and metaphors as they appear in interactive read-aloud texts and in poetry.

▶ **Writing About Reading** Encourage students to include examples of comparisons in reading letters in a reader's notebook.

Sometimes writers compare one thing to another.

Title	Comparisons	Purpose/Meaning
	• Strong as a bear • Fast as a rabbit • Smart as a fox • Smart like a fox who thinks his way around the trap	• Describes the character • The older brother is stronger, faster, and smarter than the others. • The sister is very smart.
	• The sky is full of pink ribbons for my little angel.	• It makes the writing interesting. • You can imagine the pink streaks of color in the sunset.

Section 2: Literary Analysis

Reading Minilesson Principle
Writers end stories in different ways.

Analyzing the Writer's Craft

You Will Need

- three or four familiar books with different kinds of endings, such as following:
  - *Goal!* by Mina Javaherbin, from Text Set: Facing Challenges
  - *The Perfect Pet* by Margie Palatini, from Text Set: Humorous Texts
  - *The Sunsets of Miss Olivia Wiggins* by Lester Laminack, from Text Set: Passage of Time
  - *Gettin' Through Thursday* by Melrose Cooper, from Text Set: Facing Challenges
- chart paper and markers

Academic Language / Important Vocabulary

- big idea
- message

Continuum Connection

- Recognize and discuss aspects of narrative structure: e.g., beginning, series of events, high point of the story, problem resolution, ending (p. 51)

Goal

Notice the different ways writers craft endings to their stories.

Rationale

Writers craft story endings to give readers satisfaction and a lasting impression (e.g., hope, a strong message, empowerment, surprise). Teaching this aspect of writer's craft helps students better understand texts. It also helps them think of possibilities for their own stories. Before teaching this lesson, familiarize students with Umbrella 7: Thinking About the Author's Message.

Assess Learning

Observe students when they talk about the writer's craft. Notice if there is evidence of new learning based on the goal of this minilesson.

- Can students discuss why a writer has ended a story in a particular way?
- Do they understand and use the term *big idea* or *message*?

Minilesson

To help students think about the minilesson principle, provide an inquiry-based lesson using familiar texts with a variety of endings. Here is an example.

- From *Goal!*, show and read the last page to the students.

  Turn and talk about the ending of *Goal!* What did the author write about?

- After they turn and talk, invite a few students to share.

  This ending gets to the big idea, or message, of this book—the children know when they work together and stick together, they can do anything. What do you call this type of ending?

- Endings fall into multiple categories. *Goal!* ends with a message that makes you think, which could also be considered a happy ending. Record responses on chart paper.

- Repeat this process with the last page of *The Perfect Pet*.

- Hold up *The Sunsets of Miss Olivia Wiggins*. Read the first sentence on the first page and then read the last page.

  Turn and talk about how the author chose to end the book. Why do you think he made this decision?

  This ending is called a circular ending. The ending is like the beginning; it connects the circle.

- Record on the chart.

Have a Try

Invite the students to talk with a partner about the ending of a story.

▶ Read the last page of *Gettin' Through Thursday*.

Turn and talk to your partner about how the author ends this story. Does the ending fit into one of the endings on our chart, or do we need to add another type of ending?

▶ Ask a couple of students to share. Record responses.

Summarize and Apply

Help students summarize the learning and remind them to think about how a writer ends a story.

What did you learn about how writers end stories? Use the chart to help you remember.

▶ Write the principle at the top of the chart.

When you read today, notice how the author chose to end the story. Is it like one of the ways we talked about or another way? Bring your book when we meet so you can share.

▶ If students are reading longer chapter books, consider providing a bin of familiar interactive read-aloud books for them to choose from.

Share

Following independent reading time, gather students together in the meeting area to talk about their reading.

Who would like to share how your book ended? Does it fit into one of the endings on our chart?

Extend the Lesson (Optional)

After assessing students' understanding, you might decide to extend the learning.

▶ As students read and listen to more books, add them to the chart.

▶ Explore ways in which writers end stories and add to the chart categories, such as *unexpected ending* or *call to action*.

▶ **Writing About Reading** As students become more comfortable talking about different story endings, encourage them to include their noticings in letters about their independent reading in a reader's notebook.

Writers end stories in different ways.

	The ending leaves you thinking about the BIG IDEA, or message, of the story. Hmmm...
	Happy ending
	Circular ending

Reading Minilesson Principle

Sometimes writers change the characters, plot, and settings of familiar stories to make new stories.

You Will Need

- three or four texts from Text Set: Fractured Fairy Tales, such as the following:
  - *Yours Truly, Goldilocks* by Alma Flor Ada
  - *Kate and the Beanstalk* by Mary Pope Osborne
  - *The Frog Prince, Continued* by Jon Scieszka
- chart paper and markers
- basket of fractured fairy tales

Academic Language / Important Vocabulary

- characters
- setting
- plot

Continuum Connection

- Make connections (e.g., content, theme) across fiction texts that are read aloud (p. 50)

Goal

Notice when authors change the characters, plot, and settings of traditional tales to create a new version of the tale.

Rationale

Writers may change a familiar text to make it humorous, provide a new perspective, or appeal to a broader audience. Teaching students about fractured fairy tales provides an opportunity to make a connection to another text and talk about why an author would write a new version of a familiar story. It may also motivate your students to create their own.

Assess Learning

Observe students when they talk about the writer's craft. Notice if there is evidence of new learning based on the goal of this minilesson.

- Can students talk about the similarities and differences between traditional text and an altered version?
- Do they use the terms *characters, setting,* and *plot*?

Minilesson

To help students think about the minilesson principle, choose examples of fractured fairy tales and provide an inquiry-based lesson. Here is an example.

- Hold up *Yours Truly, Goldilocks* and show the first several pages.

  What is special about the characters in this book?

  What details are different from the original stories?

- Record responses on chart paper.

  Why do you think the author made these changes?

- Record responses. Then hold up *Kate and the Beanstalk*.

  What story does this remind you of?

  The author of *Kate and the Beanstalk* wrote a different version of *Jack and the Beanstalk*. What changes did the author make to the original story to make this new story?

  Why do you think the author changed the original story?

- Record responses on the chart.

Have a Try

Invite the students to talk with a partner about a fractured fairy tale.

▶ Hold up *The Frog Prince, Continued* and show a few pages to reacquaint students with the story.

> Turn and talk to your partner about the changes the author made to the original story. Why do you think he did that?

▶ Ask a couple of students to share. Record responses on the chart.

Summarize and Apply

Help students summarize the learning and remind them to notice how authors alter traditional stories.

> How do authors get ideas for new stories?

▶ Write the principle at the top of the chart.

> You can choose a book from this basket to read today. It has stories that are called fractured fairy tales—familiar fairy tales that have been changed in some way. Think about what the author changed and why. Bring your book to share when we come back together.

Share

Following independent reading time, gather students together in the meeting area to talk about their reading.

> Who read a fractured fairy tale? Tell what is different in the new story from the original. Why do you think the author decided to do that?

Extend the Lesson (Optional)

After assessing students' understanding, you might decide to extend the learning.

▶ Invite students to think about traditional stories they know well and talk about how they might change them to be more humorous or modern or appeal to a wider or different audience.

▶ Encourage students to write their own versions of well-known stories with different characters, settings, plots, and endings.

Sometimes writers change the characters, plot, and settings of familiar stories to make new stories.

	Changes	Why Author Made the Changes
Yours Truly, Goldilocks	• Characters know each other • Takes place after all the original stories	• Gives extra information about the characters • Adds humor to the story
Kate and the Beanstalk	• Has girl as main character • More information about the characters	• Makes the story more interesting • Has a girl hero • Makes the story more like it could happen today
The Frog Prince Continued	• Takes place after the original ends • Frog Prince not living happily ever after • Has witches from other fairy tales	• More humorous • Fun to imagine what characters do after the story ends

RML 8

LA.U9.RML8

Reading Minilesson Principle
Sometimes writers play with the way words look.

You Will Need

- three or four familiar fiction books with font, size, and/or color used to convey meaning, such as following:
  - *The Sunsets of Miss Olivia Wiggins* by Lester Laminack, from Text Set: Passage of Time
  - *Kate and the Beanstalk* by Mary Pope Osborne, from Text Set: Fractured Fairy Tales
  - *Yours Truly, Goldilocks* by Alma Flor Ada, from Text Set: Fractured Fairy Tales
- document camera (optional)
- chart paper and markers
- sticky notes

Academic Language / Important Vocabulary

- font

Continuum Connection

- Notice how illustrations and graphics go together with the text in a meaningful way (p. 52)

Goal

Notice how the writer's choice of font, size, and color of print conveys meaning.

Rationale

Writers use variation in text font, color, or size to affect meaning, draw attention to or set apart a word or phrase, or signal change in speaker. Teaching students to understand writers' decisions and to notice how the print appears helps them understand the meaning more fully. They also learn possibilities for communicating meaning in their own writing.

Assess Learning

Observe students when they talk about the writer's craft. Notice if there is evidence of new learning based on the goal of this minilesson.

- Do students notice when a writer changes the font, size, or color of text?
- What can they determine about the meaning added by the altered font, color, or size?
- Do they understand the word *font*?

Minilesson

To help students think about the minilesson principle, provide an inquiry-based lesson using familiar texts in which the writer has changed the look of the text. If a document camera is available, consider projecting the pages to provide visual support. Here is an example.

- Hold up *The Sunsets of Miss Olivia Wiggins*. Read any two pages, beginning with a page in regular type followed by a page with italic.

  How do the words look on these pages?

  Why do you think the writer changed the font—the way the print looks—from page to page?

  The slanted font is called italics. Notice the writer always introduces the page in italics by saying "she began to think."

- Record responses on chart paper. Hold up *Kate and the Beanstalk*. Show pages 6 (". . . up and up and up") and 26 ("Down and down and down . . .").

  What do you notice about the words? Why do you think the writer did this?

  The words look like they are going up and then down the beanstalk, and they get smaller as the action gets farther away.

- Record responses on the chart.

  Could the writer have used the same font all the way through this book?

Have a Try

Invite the students to notice with a partner how words look.

▸ Show several letters from *Yours Truly, Goldilocks.*

> Turn and talk to your partner. What do you notice about the fonts? Why do you think the author made these choices?

▸ Ask a couple of students to share. Record responses.

Summarize and Apply

Summarize the learning and remind students to notice how words look.

> Today you noticed how writers play with the way words look.

▸ Write the principle on the chart and review the chart.

> When you read today, notice if the writer plays with the way the words look. Put a sticky note on the page. Bring the book when we come back together so you can share.

Share

Following independent reading time, gather students together in the meeting area to talk about their reading.

> Who read a book where the writer played with the way the words look? Why do you think the author decided to do that?

Extend the Lesson (Optional)

After assessing students' understanding, you might decide to extend the learning.

▸ Encourage students to play with the way words look in their writing where and when appropriate.

▸ Explore and discuss more ways writers play with the way words look, adding ideas to the chart.

▸ If students can compose stories on a computer, suggest they experiment with different fonts to emphasize or add meaning to certain words. Caution them against using too many different fonts.

Sometimes writers play with the way words look.	
She began to think *She remembered*	**What:** There are two fonts. **Why:** One font shows the story and the other shows what Miss Olivia Wiggins is thinking.
 up and up and up	**What:** Words look like they are going up or down the beanstalk. They get smaller as the character moves farther away. **Why:** The placement and size show which way the character is moving—up or down.
 *Dear Goldilocks* Dearest Goldilocks	**What:** Each character's letter has a different font. **Why:** The different fonts make the letters look like they came from different characters.

Assessment

After you have taught the minilessons in this umbrella, observe students as they talk and write about their reading across instructional contexts: interactive read-aloud, independent reading and literacy work, guided reading, shared reading, and book club. Use *The Literacy Continuum* (Fountas and Pinnell 2017) to observe students' reading and writing behaviors across instructional contexts.

▶ What evidence do you have of new understandings related to analyzing the writer's craft?

- Do students notice and discuss the decisions writers make about how they use language and punctuation, create humor, and end a story?
- Are they able to explain how the words and illustrations work together?
- Do they recognize when a writer has altered the characters, settings, or plot from a well-known story to create a new story?
- Can they discuss a writer's decision to change the way words look?
- Do they use vocabulary such as *language, punctuation, illustrations,* and *font* to talk about a writer's craft?

▶ In what other ways, beyond the scope of this umbrella, are students talking about writer's craft?

- Are students able to recognize an author's style of writing?
- Do they talk about how a writer reveals character traits?

Use your observations to determine the next umbrella you will teach. You may also consult Minilessons Across the Year (pp. 55-57) for guidance.

Link to Writing

After teaching the minilessons in this umbrella, help students link the new learning to their writing:

▶ Invite students to explore elements of writer's craft in their writing by adding figurative language, sensory details, and humor; experimenting with types of endings; or using a variety of punctuation. If they are using computers, they might include text of different fonts, sizes, and colors or play with the placement of words on a page.

Reader's Notebook

When this umbrella is complete, provide a copy of the minilesson principles (see resources.fountasandpinnell.com) for students to glue in the reader's notebook (in the Minilessons section if using *Reader's Notebook: Intermediate* [Fountas and Pinnell 2011]), so they can refer to the information as needed.

Minilessons in This Umbrella

RML1 The front flap and back cover give information about the book.

RML2 Sometimes authors write a dedication to honor or show they care about someone.

RML3 Sometimes authors give information in an author's note.

RML4 Sometimes authors write acknowledgments to thank the people who helped them with the book.

RML5 Sometimes illustrators use endpapers to show important information about the book.

RML6 An author page gives information about the person who wrote the book.

RML7 The glossary gives the definition of important words in the book.

RML8 The table of contents lists the chapters or topics of a book.

Before Teaching Umbrella 10 Minilessons

The minilessons in this umbrella help students understand text resources outside the body of the text, called peritext (it is not necessary to use this term with students). Read and discuss engaging fiction and nonfiction books that have peritext resources from the *Fountas & Pinnell Classroom™ Interactive Read-Aloud Collection*, *Independent Reading Collection*, and *Shared Reading Collection* or from your classroom library.

Interactive Read-Aloud Collection

Genre Study: Expository Nonfiction

A Day and Night in the Desert by Caroline Arnold

Tornadoes! by Gail Gibbons

The Passage of Time

The Quilt Story by Tony Johnston

Our Seasons by Grace Lin and Ranida T. McKneally

Author's Point of View

Meadowlands by Thomas F. Yezerski

What's So Bad About Gasoline? by Anne Rockwell

Energy Island by Allan Drummond

Genre Study: Fables

The Contest Between the Sun and the Wind by Heather Forest

The Grasshopper and the Ants by Jerry Pinkney

Exploring Pourquoi Tales

Cat and Rat by Ed Young

Series Study: Dianna Hutts Aston and Sylvia Long

A Butterfly Is Patient

Independent Reading Collection

Matilda by Roald Dahl

Shared Reading Collection

Tiny but Fierce by Cheri Colburn

As you read aloud and enjoy these texts together, help students notice and discuss the pictures and information on the covers and flaps, as well as peritext resources.

Expository Nonfiction

Passage of Time

Point of View

Fables

Pourquoi Tales

Dianna Hutts Aston

Independent Reading Collection

Shared Reading Collection

Section 2: Literary Analysis

Reading Minilesson Principle

The front flap and back cover give information about the book.

Noticing Text Resources

You Will Need

- two or three familiar books that have information about the book on the front flap and/or back cover, such as the following:
  - *A Day and Night in the Desert* by Caroline Arnold, from Text Set: Expository Nonfiction
  - *Meadowlands* by Thomas F. Yezerski, from Text Set: Point of View
  - *The Quilt Story* by Tony Johnston, from Text Set: Passage of Time
- chart paper and markers

Academic Language / Important Vocabulary

- front flap
- back cover
- information

Continuum Connection

- Notice and use and understand the purpose of some text resources outside the body (peritext): e.g., dedication, acknowledgments, author's note, illustrator's note, endpapers, book flap (p. 52)

Goal

Notice, use, and understand the purpose of the front flap and back cover of books.

Rationale

When students know to look for information about a book on the front flap or back cover, they are better equipped to make decisions about which books to read. They are more likely to choose books that they will enjoy and therefore more likely to become lifelong readers. This information also helps them take a stance toward the book that supports comprehension.

Assess Learning

Observe students when they select books to read. Notice if there is evidence of new learning based on the goal of this minilesson.

- Do students read the information on the front flap and/or back cover to decide whether to read a book?
- Do they use vocabulary such as *front flap*, *back cover*, and *information*?

Minilesson

To help students think about the minilesson principle, provide an inquiry-based lesson about reading the information on the front flap and/or back covers of books. Here is an example.

- Show the cover of *A Day and Night in the Desert* and read the title.

  This book looks interesting, but first I would like to know more about it. Where can I look to find more information about it?

- Show the back cover and read the blurb.

  What information about the book is on the back cover?

- Record students' responses on chart paper.
- Show the cover of *Meadowlands* and read the title.

  Where do you think I should look to find more information about this book?

- If someone suggests the back cover, show the back cover and read the review.

  What is on the back cover of this book?

  Where else might there be information about this book?

- Display the front flap of the book and read the text.

  What information is given on the front flap?

- Record responses on the chart.

Have a Try

Invite the students to talk with a partner about the front flap and/or back cover of another book.

▸ Show the cover of *The Quilt Story* and read the title.

   Turn and talk to your partner about where you can look for more information about this book.

▸ Ask for volunteers to share their thinking. Display the back cover and read the text.

   Now turn and talk about what information you learned about the book from the back cover.

▸ Ask a few pairs to share their responses, and record them on the chart.

Summarize and Apply

Summarize the learning and remind students to read the information on the front flap and/or back cover when they are selecting books.

   What did you notice about the front flaps and back covers of the books we looked at today?

▸ Write the principle at the top of the chart.

   When you are choosing a book today, read the front flap or back cover. Bring the book you choose when we meet after independent reading time.

Share

Following independent reading time, gather students together in the meeting area to talk about their reading.

   Raise your hand if you read the front flap or back cover of books when you were choosing a book to read today. How did that information help you?

Extend the Lesson (Optional)

After assessing students' understanding, you might decide to extend the learning.

▸ During interactive read-aloud, share the information from the front flaps and back covers of books. If students discover new types of information, add them to the chart.

▸ **Writing About Reading** Read aloud a book but do not share the front flap or back cover. Then have students create their own front flap or back cover for the book.

The front flap and back cover give information about the book.

- what the book is about

- names of the author and illustrator

- name of the publisher

Front Flap

- the title of the book

- the price of the book

Back Cover

- reviews of the book

- awards the book has won

Section 2: Literary Analysis

Reading Minilesson Principle

Sometimes authors write a dedication to honor or show they care about someone.

Noticing Text Resources

You Will Need

- two or three familiar books that have a dedication, such as the following:
  - *The Quilt Story* by Tony Johnston, from Text Set: Passage of Time
  - *Our Seasons* by Grace Lin and Ranida T. McKneally, from Text Set: Passage of Time
  - *What's So Bad About Gasoline?* by Anne Rockwell, from Text Set: Point of View
- chart paper and markers

Academic Language / Important Vocabulary

- dedication
- author

Continuum Connection

- Notice and use and understand the purpose of some text resources outside the body (peritext): e.g., dedication, acknowledgments, author's note, illustrator's note, endpapers, book flap (p. 52)

Goal

Notice, use, and understand the purpose of the dedication.

Rationale

When you teach students to read and think about the dedication, they learn to think of the author as a real person, who has friends and family, just like they do, and they may gain some insight into who or what inspired the author to write the book. The dedication may motivate students to write their own pieces.

Assess Learning

Observe students when they read and talk about books. Notice if there is evidence of new learning based on the goal of this minilesson.

- Do students notice and read the dedication in a book?
- Can they infer why the author dedicated the book to a particular person?
- Do they use academic language, such as *dedication* and *author*?

Minilesson

To help students think about the minilesson principle, engage them in a short discussion about the author's dedication in one or two familiar books. Here is an example.

- Show the cover of *The Quilt Story* and read the title. Open to the copyright page and point to the author's dedication. Read it aloud.

  What do you think this is? What do you notice about it?

  This part of the book is called the dedication. The author dedicates the book to someone she cares about. Why do you think Tony Johnston dedicated *The Quilt Story* to Ann Doherty Johnston? Why is this person special to her?

- Record students' responses on chart paper.
- Show the cover of *Our Seasons* and read the title and authors' names.

  Let's see if this book has a dedication.

- Turn to the copyright page and point to the dedications.

  What do you notice about this dedication page?

  Why do you think there are two dedications?

  It has two dedications because there are two authors.

- Read the dedications.

  Why do you think the authors decided to dedicate the book to these people?

- Record students' responses on the chart.

Have a Try

Invite the students to talk with a partner about the author's dedication in a third book.

- Show the cover of *What's So Bad About Gasoline?* and read the title.

  What is this book about?

  Let's see if this book has a dedication.

- Open to the dedication page and read the first dedication aloud.

  What do you think the author means by "the starting-to-drive members of my family"?

  Turn and talk to your partner about why you think the author dedicated this book to these people.

- After students turn and talk, ask a few pairs to share their thinking, and record their responses on the chart.

Sometimes authors write a dedication to honor or show they care about someone.

Dedication	The Book Is About	Dedicated To
"For . . . , who taught me the joy of quilting"	Quilting	The person who taught the author quilting
"To . . . , who has been with me through many seasons"	The seasons	People the authors have known for many seasons
"For the starting-to-drive members of my family"	Saving gas	The new drivers in the author's family so they will think about driving less

Summarize and Apply

Summarize the learning and remind students to read and think about the dedication when they read a book.

What did you learn about dedications today? What is a dedication, and what is it for?

- Write the principle at the top of the chart.

  When you read today, see if your book has a dedication. If it does, be sure to read it. Think about why the author might have decided to dedicate the book to that person.

Share

Following independent reading time, gather students together in the meeting area to talk about their reading.

Raise your hand if the book you read today has a dedication. To whom did the author dedicate the book?

Why do you think the author dedicated it to that person?

Extend the Lesson (Optional)

After assessing students' understanding, you might decide to extend the learning.

- Encourage students to include a dedication when they write their own books.

Reading Minilesson Principle
Sometimes authors give information in an author's note.

Noticing Text Resources

You Will Need

- two or three familiar books that have an author's note, such as the following:
  - *Energy Island* by Allan Drummond, from Text Set: Point of View
  - *The Contest Between the Sun and the Wind* by Heather Forest, from Text Set: Fables
  - *Cat and Rat: The Legend of the Chinese Zodiac* by Ed Young, from Text Set: Pourquoi Tales
- chart paper and markers

Academic Language / Important Vocabulary

- author
- author's note

Continuum Connection

- Notice and use and understand the purpose of some text resources outside the body (peritext): e.g., dedication, acknowledgments, author's note, illustrator's note, endpapers, book flap (p. 52)

Goal

Notice, use, and understand the purpose of the author's note.

Rationale

The author's note may reveal the author's inspiration for writing the book or offer important contextual information. When students read and think about the author's note, they gain a deeper understanding of the book and of the author's process.

Assess Learning

Observe students when they read and talk about books. Notice if there is evidence of new learning based on the goal of this minilesson.

- ▶ Do students understand the purpose of an author's note?
- ▶ Can they explain what they learned from an author's note?
- ▶ Do they use academic language, such as *author* and *author's note*?

Minilesson

To help students think about the minilesson principle, guide them to notice and understand the purpose of an author's note. Here is an example.

- ▶ Show the cover of *Energy Island* and read the title.

    Do you remember this book about the island of Samsø in Denmark? What did you learn about this island?

    The author wrote a special page at the end of the book that I'd like to share with you. This page is called the author's note.

- ▶ Turn to the author's note on the final page and read the first paragraph aloud.

    What did you learn about the book from the author's note?

- ▶ Record students' responses on chart paper.

    Let's read the author's note in another book you know.

- ▶ Show the cover of *The Contest Between the Sun and the Wind* and read the title. Turn to the author's note and read the first sentence.

    What does this author's note tell you about the book?

- ▶ Record students' responses on the chart.

Have a Try

Invite the students to talk with a partner about the author's note in another book.

▶ Show the cover of *Cat and Rat: The Legend of the Chinese Zodiac* and then read the author's note (on the first page).

> Turn and talk to your partner about the kind of information the author gives in the author's note of this book. What did you learn from this author's note?

▶ Ask a few pairs to share their responses.

> Why do you think the author tells information about the animals of the zodiac? What does this have to do with the story?

▶ Record students' responses on the chart.

Summarize and Apply

Summarize the learning and remind students to look for an author's note when they read.

> Why do some authors put author's notes in their books?

▶ Write the principle at the top of the chart.

> Sometimes the author's note is at the beginning of a book, and sometimes it is at the end. When you read today, see if your book has an author's note. If so, be sure to read it. Be ready to share what you learned from the author's note when we meet.

Share

Following independent reading time, gather students together in the meeting area to share what they learned from reading an author's note.

> Raise your hand if you read a book today that has an author's note. What kind of information was in the author's note?

Extend the Lesson (Optional)

After assessing students' understanding, you might decide to extend the learning.

▶ Continue to read and discuss author's notes as you encounter them during interactive read-aloud.

▶ Encourage students to include an author's note when they write their own books.

Sometimes authors give information in an author's note.	
Book	**The author's note tells . . .**
energy island	• where the author got the idea for the book
Sun Wind	• where the story originally came from
Cat and Rat	• information about the Chinese calendar and the animals of the zodiac (the inspiration for the story)

Section 2: Literary Analysis

Noticing Text Resources

You Will Need

▶ two or three familiar books that include acknowledgments, such as the following:

- *Meadowlands* by Thomas F. Yezerski, from Text Set: Point of View
- *What's So Bad About Gasoline?* by Anne Rockwell, from Text Set: Point of View
- *Tornadoes!* by Gail Gibbons, from Text Set: Expository Nonfiction

▶ chart paper and markers

Academic Language / Important Vocabulary

▶ acknowledgments
▶ author

Continuum Connection

▶ Notice and use and understand the purpose of some text resources outside the body (peritext): e.g., dedication, acknowledgments, author's note, illustrator's note, endpapers, book flap (p. 52)

Goal

Notice and understand the purpose of the acknowledgments in books.

Rationale

When you teach students to read and think about the acknowledgments, they begin to understand that writing and publishing a book is a complicated process that involves the work and cooperation of several people—not just the author.

Assess Learning

Observe students when they read and talk about books. Notice if there is evidence of new learning based on the goal of this minilesson.

▶ Do students notice and read the acknowledgments in a book?
▶ Can they identify whom the author is thanking and explain why?
▶ Can they explain the purpose of acknowledgments?
▶ Do they use academic language, such as *acknowledgments* and *author*?

Minilesson

To help students think about the minilesson principle, guide them to notice and understand the purpose of acknowledgments. Here is an example.

▶ Show the cover of *Meadowlands* and read the title.

Listen carefully as I read a very small, but important, part of this book.

▶ Turn to the copyright page, and then point to and read the acknowledgment.

What do you notice about this part of the book? What is the author saying here?

▶ Reread the acknowledgment if necessary, clarifying the meaning of any unfamiliar words (e.g., *review* and *assistance*).

▶ Paraphrase the acknowledgment on chart paper.

Why is the author thanking these people?

This part of the book is called the acknowledgments. *Acknowledge* means "to thank or show appreciation for someone." Some authors put an acknowledgments section in their book to thank the people who helped them make the book.

▶ Read aloud the acknowledgment in *What's So Bad About Gasoline?*

Whom is the author of this book thanking?

How do you think this person might have helped the author?

▶ Record a paraphrase of the acknowledgment on the chart.

Have a Try

Invite the students to talk with a partner about the acknowledgments in *Tornadoes!*

▶ Show the cover of *Tornadoes!* Open to the copyright page and read the acknowledgments.

> Turn and talk to your partner about the author's acknowledgments. Whom did the author thank, and why do you think she thanked these people?

▶ Ask a few pairs to share their thinking, and add the acknowledgments to the chart.

Summarize and Apply

Summarize the learning and remind students to read any acknowledgments they encounter.

> Why do some authors put acknowledgments in their books?

▶ Write the principle at the top of the chart.

> Creating a book takes a lot of work from many different people. Authors sometimes write acknowledgments to thank some of the people who helped them with their book.

> When you read today, see if your book has acknowledgments. If so, be sure to read them and think about whom the author is thanking and why. Be ready to share your example when we meet.

Share

Following independent reading time, gather students together in the meeting area to share what they learned about acknowledgments.

> Raise your hand if the book you read today has acknowledgments.

> Whom did the author of your book thank and why?

Extend the Lesson (Optional)

After assessing students' understanding, you might decide to extend the learning.

▶ Continue to read and discuss acknowledgments as you encounter them during interactive read-aloud.

▶ Encourage students to include acknowledgments when they write and illustrate their own books.

Sometimes authors write acknowledgments to thank the people who helped them with the book.

- Thanks to ... and ... for their review and assistance

- Special thanks to ... for his valuable assistance

- Special thanks to ...

Thank You!

Section 2: Literary Analysis

RML5

LA.U10.RML5

Reading Minilesson Principle
Sometimes illustrators use endpapers to show important information about the book.

Noticing Text Resources

You Will Need

- two or three familiar books with endpapers that show pictures of something important in the book, such as the following:
  - *Energy Island* by Allan Drummond, from Text Set: Point of View
  - *The Grasshopper and the Ants* by Jerry Pinkney, from Text Set: Fables
  - *A Butterfly Is Patient*, from Text Set: Dianna Hutts Aston
- chart paper and markers
- basket of books with endpapers

Academic Language / Important Vocabulary

- endpapers
- author
- illustrator

Continuum Connection

- Notice and use and understand the purpose of some text resources outside the body (peritext): e.g., dedication, acknowledgments, author's note, illustrator's note, endpapers, book flap (p. 52)

Goal

Notice and understand how the endpapers in a book are connected to the meaning of the book.

Rationale

The endpapers are part of the art of the book and add to or enhance its meaning. When you encourage students to notice the endpapers and think about how they relate to the meaning of the book, they gain a deeper understanding. They also gain an appreciation for the thought and care that went into creating every aspect of the book.

Assess Learning

Observe students when they read and talk about books. Notice if there is evidence of new learning based on the goal of this minilesson.

- ▶ Can students explain how the pictures on the endpapers relate to the rest of the book?
- ▶ Do they use academic language, such as *author*, *illustrator*, and *endpapers*?

Minilesson

To help students think about the minilesson principle, guide them to notice and discuss the endpapers in familiar books. Here is an example.

- ▶ Show the cover of *Energy Island*. Turn to the endpapers.

  These are the last pages in the book. What do you notice about them?

  What do you think is happening in the illustration?

  Why do you think Allan Drummond included this illustration at the end of his book? Why is it important?

- ▶ Record students' responses on chart paper.

  The pages in a book after the end of the words are called endpapers. They don't usually have words on them, but they often have pictures. The pictures often show something important from the book.

- ▶ Turn to the last pages with text in *The Grasshopper and the Ants*.

  What happens at the end of this story?

  Even though this is the last page with words in the story, there are a few more pages in the book.

- ▶ Turn the page.

  Why are the endpapers in this book important?

- ▶ Record students' responses on the chart.

Have a Try

Invite the students to talk with a partner about endpapers.

▶ Hold up *A Butterfly Is Patient*. Read the title and show the first pair of endpapers.

> Turn and talk to your partner about what you notice about these endpapers. Then talk about why you think the author and illustrator included these endpapers in their book. Why are they important?

▶ After students turn and talk, ask a few pairs to share their thinking with the class and record their responses on the chart.

Summarize and Apply

Summarize the learning and remind students to look at and think about the endpapers when they read.

> What did you notice about the endpapers in the books we looked at today?

> You noticed that the endpapers often show pictures of something important in the book. Sometimes they show what happens after the story ends, remind you about something you read about, or provide additional information about the book's topic.

▶ Record the principle at the top of the chart.

▶ Provide students with a basket of books that contain endpapers.

> The books in this basket all have endpapers. You may want to choose a book from this basket during independent reading today. If so, be sure to look at the endpapers and think about what they show.

Share

Following independent reading time, gather students together in the meeting area to share what they learned about endpapers.

> Raise your hand if you read a book today that has endpapers. Tell us what the endpapers show and why that is important.

Extend the Lesson (Optional)

After assessing students' understanding, you might decide to extend the learning.

▶ When students make their own books, encourage them to include endpapers that show pictures of something important in the book.

Book	What do the endpapers show?	Why are they important?
energy island (allan drummond)	The people of Samsø waving goodbye, with windmills in the background	It shows how the people of Samsø get their energy now (from windmills).
GRASSHOPPER & the ANTS	The grasshopper entering the ants' house and having tea with the queen ant	They show what happens after the words in the story end.
A Butterfly Is Patient	Illustrations of different kinds of butterflies with labels	They provide more information about what different butterflies look like and what they're called.

Sometimes illustrators use endpapers to show important information about the book.

Reading Minilesson Principle

An author page gives information about the person who wrote the book.

You Will Need

- two or three familiar books that contain information about the author, such as the following:
  - *What's So Bad About Gasoline?* by Anne Rockwell, from Text Set: Point of View
  - *Our Seasons* by Grace Lin and Ranida T. McKneally, from Text Set: Passage of Time
  - *Meadowlands* by Thomas F. Yezerski, from Text Set: Point of View
- chart paper and markers

Academic Language / Important Vocabulary

- author

Continuum Connection

- Notice and use and understand the purpose of some text resources outside the body (peritext): e.g., dedication, acknowledgments, author's note, illustrator's note, endpapers, book flap (p. 52)

Goal

Notice and understand that the author page gives information about the author.

Rationale

When students read the information about the author, they begin to think of the author as a real person and may even start envisioning themselves as a future author. In some cases, the author's biography may provide insight into the author's creative process or reasons for writing.

Assess Learning

Observe students when they read and talk about books. Notice if there is evidence of new learning based on the goal of this minilesson.

- Do students notice when a book has information about the author?
- Do they talk about what they learned about the author?
- Do they use the term *author*?

Minilesson

To help students think about the minilesson principle, guide them to notice and understand the purpose of the author page. Here is an example.

- Show the cover of *What's So Bad About Gasoline?*

  What's So Bad About Gasoline? was written by an author named Anne Rockwell. Listen carefully as I read aloud a special part of this book.

- Turn to the inside back cover and read the information about Anne Rockwell.

  What do you notice about this part of the book? What does it tell you?

  What did you learn about Anne Rockwell from this page?

- Record students' responses on chart paper.

- Show *Our Seasons* and read the title. Then turn to the back cover and read the information about Grace Lin.

  What do you notice about the information about the author in this book?

  This book has the information about the author on the back cover. What did you learn about Grace Lin?

- Record students' responses on the chart.

Have a Try

Invite the students to talk with a partner about the author page in another book.

▶ Show the cover of *Meadowlands* and read the title. Turn to the back flap and read the information about the author.

> Turn and talk to your partner about what you learned about the author.

▶ After students turn and talk, ask a few students to share their thinking, and record their responses on the chart.

Summarize and Apply

Summarize the learning and remind students to look for the author page when they read.

> What did you notice about the books we looked at today?

> You noticed that all these books have an author page. The author page gives information about the author and can be located in different parts of the book.

▶ Write the principle at the top of the chart.

> When you read today, see if there is an author page in your book. If so, read what it says and be ready to share what you learned when we come back together.

Share

Following independent reading time, gather students together in the meeting area to share what they learned about authors.

> Raise your hand if you read a book that has an author page.

> What did you learn about the author of your book?

Extend the Lesson (Optional)

After assessing students' understanding, you might decide to extend the learning.

▶ When students write their own books, encourage them to include an author page.

▶ Help students find more information about their favorite authors by visiting authors' websites.

An author page gives information about the person who wrote the book.

Book	About the Author
What's So Bad About GASOLINE?	She has written over 100 books. She lives in Connecticut.
Our Seasons	Grace Lin has written and illustrated many books for children. She lives in Massachusetts.
Meadowlands	He lived near the Meadowlands for 12 years. He wrote the book out of love for the Meadowlands. He lives in Hoboken, New Jersey.

Reading Minilesson Principle

The glossary gives the definition of important words in the book.

Noticing Text Resources

You Will Need

- two books that contain a glossary, such as the following:
  - *Our Seasons* by Grace Lin and Ranida T. McKneally, from Text Set: Passage of Time
  - *A Day and Night in the Desert* by Caroline Arnold, from Text Set: Expository Nonfiction
- chart paper and markers
- basket of books with glossaries
- projector (optional)

Academic Language / Important Vocabulary

- glossary
- definition

Continuum Connection

- Notice and use and understand the purpose of some other text resources: e.g., glossary (pp. 52, 55)

Goal

Notice, use, and understand the purpose of the glossary.

Rationale

When students know how to use a glossary, they are better equipped to determine the meaning of unfamiliar words while reading independently. As a result, they better understand what they read and learn more from their reading.

Assess Learning

Observe students when they read and talk about books. Notice if there is evidence of new learning based on the goal of this minilesson.

- Do students know how to use a glossary to determine the meaning of unknown words?
- When they come across an unfamiliar word in a book, do they look to see if the book has a glossary?
- Do they understand that the words in most glossaries are in alphabetical order?
- Do they use academic language, such as *glossary* and *definition*?

Minilesson

To help students think about the minilesson principle, provide an inquiry-based lesson around using the glossary of a familiar book. Here is an example.

- Show the cover of *Our Seasons*. Open to the last page and display the glossary. (Project the text if you are able so that students can see it better.) Read the first three or four entries, and then prompt discussion with questions such as the following:
  - *What do you notice about this page?*
  - *What kind of information does this page give?*
  - *A glossary gives the definition, or meaning, of important words in the book. When might you use this page?*
  - *When you come across a word in a book that you don't know the meaning of, you can look up the word in the glossary to find out what it means.*
- Read the list of words (not the definitions) in the glossary, pointing to each word as you read it.

  What do you notice about the order of the words on the page?

- If necessary, guide students to recognize that the words are in alphabetical order.

Have a Try

Invite the students to talk with a partner about how to use a glossary.

▸ Show the cover *of A Day and Night in the Desert*. Turn to page 5 and read the text aloud.

> Turn and talk to your partner about how we can find out what *venomous* means.

▸ Ask a few students to share their thinking. Use their instructions to find the entry for *venomous* and read the definition.

Summarize and Apply

Summarize the learning and remind students to use a glossary to understand the meaning of an unfamiliar word when they read.

> What did you notice about the glossaries we looked at today? Why are glossaries useful?

▸ Write a list of students' comments on chart paper. Then write the principle at the top.

> Not all books have a glossary, but the books in this basket do. You may want to choose a book from this basket when you read today. If so, use the glossary to find out the definitions of words you don't know.

Share

Following independent reading time, gather students together in the meeting area to share what they learned from and about glossaries.

> Raise your hand if you read a book today that has a glossary.

> How did the glossary help you while you read?

> What new words did you learn from the glossary?

Extend the Lesson (Optional)

After assessing students' understanding, you might decide to extend the learning.

▸ Teach students other ways to determine the meanings of unfamiliar words (e.g., context, a dictionary).

▸ **Writing About Reading** Using shared writing, help students create a glossary for a book that doesn't already have one.

The glossary gives the definition of important words in the book.

- A glossary lists difficult or important words in the book.
- It gives the definition, or meaning, of each word.
- The words are listed in ABC order.
- The glossary is at the end of the book.
- When you come to a word you don't know, you can look to see if it's in the glossary.
- The glossary helps you better understand the book.

> **Glossary**
>
> Climate — the weather year round
>
> desert — a place that gets very little rain

Section 2: Literary Analysis

RML8
LA.U10.RML8

Noticing Text Resources

You Will Need

- one nonfiction book and one fiction book that have a table of contents, such as the following:
  - *Tiny but Fierce* by Cheri Colburn, from *Shared Reading Collection*
  - *Matilda* by Roald Dahl, from *Independent Reading Collection*
- chart paper and markers

Academic Language / Important Vocabulary

- table of contents
- chapter
- topic
- fiction
- nonfiction

Continuum Connection

- Notice and use and understand the purpose of some organizational tools: e.g., title, table of contents, chapter title, heading, subheading (pp. 52, 55)

Goal

Notice, use, and understand the purpose of the table of contents in both fiction and nonfiction books.

Rationale

When students know how to use a table of contents, they are able to find out what topics or chapters are included in a book and where each topic or chapter is located. Using a table of contents also helps students notice and think about the organization of the book.

Assess Learning

Observe students when they read and talk about books. Notice if there is evidence of new learning based on the goal of this minilesson.

- Are students able to use the table of contents to find a specific chapter or information about a specific topic?
- Can they explain the purpose of a table of contents?
- Do they use academic language, such as *table of contents, chapter, topic, fiction,* and *nonfiction*?

Minilesson

To help students think about the minilesson principle, use a book with a table of contents to provide an inquiry-based lesson. Here is an example.

- Show the cover of *Tiny but Fierce* and read the title. Then open to the table of contents. Read the table of contents, pointing to each element as you read it.

  What do you notice about this page?

- Reread the second line and point to the number 4.

  Why is there a number 4 here? Let's see what's on page 4.

- Turn to page 4 and read the text.

  What do you notice about this page? How do the words on this page relate to what you saw on the table of contents?

- Repeat this sequence with other table of contents entries as necessary to confirm students' understanding of how the table of contents relates to the rest of the book.

Have a Try

Invite the students to talk with a partner about the table of contents in a fiction book.

▶ Show the cover of *Matilda* and read the title.

> This is a chapter book that some of you may have read before. It is a fiction story about a girl with very special powers.

▶ Turn to the table of contents and read the first few lines aloud.

> Turn and talk to your partner about what the table of contents tells you about this book. How is it the same as or different from the nonfiction book table of contents?

▶ Invite a few students to share their thinking.

Summarize and Apply

Summarize the learning and remind students to read and use tables of contents.

> What is a table of contents for? Why would you use it?

▶ Make a list of students' observations on chart paper. Then write the principle at the top.

> When you read today, notice if the book you're reading has a table of contents. If so, use it to find out the topics or chapters before you start reading.

Share

Following independent reading time, gather students together in the meeting area to share what they learned about using a table of contents.

> Raise your hand if you read a book today that has a table of contents.

> How did you use it when you read the book?

Extend the Lesson (Optional)

After assessing students' understanding, you might decide to extend the learning.

▶ Encourage students to include a table of contents when they make their own books.

▶ **Writing About Reading** Use shared writing to create a table of contents for a book that does not already have one.

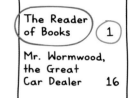

The table of contents lists the chapters or topics of a book.

The table of contents tells you . . .

- what topics you are going to read about in a nonfiction book

- what each chapter is called in a fiction book

- what page each chapter or topic begins on

Contents
The Dragonfly   2
Eyes   3

Contents
The Reader
of Books   1
Mr. Wormwood,
the Great
Car Dealer   16

Section 2: Literary Analysis

Assessment

After you have taught the minilessons in this umbrella, observe students as they talk and write about their reading across instructional contexts: interactive read-aloud, independent reading and literacy work, guided reading, shared reading, and book club. Use *The Literacy Continuum* (Fountas and Pinnell 2017) to observe students' reading and writing behaviors across instructional contexts.

▶ What evidence do you have of new understandings related to text resources?

  • Do students understand the purpose of peritext resources outside the body of the text, such as the dedication, acknowledgments, author's note, and endpapers? Do they use peritext resources?

  • Do they understand the purpose of and use other text resources, such as the glossary?

  • Do students understand and use organizational tools, such as the table of contents?

  • Do they use academic language, such as *table of contents*, *author*, *glossary*, *topic*, and *chapter*, when they talk about books?

▶ In what other ways, beyond the scope of this umbrella, are students thinking and talking about books?

  • Are students paying close attention to illustrations and graphics?

  • Are they noticing the different ways nonfiction books are organized?

Use your observations to determine the next umbrella you will teach. You may also consult Minilessons Across the Year (pp. 55-57) for guidance.

Link to Writing

After teaching the minilessons in this umbrella, help students link the new learning to their own writing:

▶ Encourage students to create text resources when they write their own books.

Reader's Notebook

When this umbrella is complete, provide a copy of the minilesson principles (see resources.fountasandpinnell.com) for students to glue in the reader's notebook (in the Minilessons section if using *Reader's Notebook: Intermediate* [Fountas and Pinnell 2011]), so they can refer to the information as needed.

Minilessons in This Umbrella

RML1 Informational books are alike in many ways.

RML2 The definition of an informational book is what is always true about it.

RML3 The author of an informational book gives facts about a topic.

RML4 The author of an informational book organizes the facts in several ways.

Before Teaching Umbrella 11 Minilessons

Genre study supports students in knowing what to expect when beginning to read a text in a genre. It helps students develop an understanding of the distinguishing characteristics of a genre and gives students the tools they need to navigate a variety of texts. There are six broad steps in a genre study, which are described on pages 37-39.

The first step in any genre study is to collect a set of mentor texts. For this genre study, collect a variety of high-quality informational (i.e., expository nonfiction) picture books. Before guiding students to look for genre characteristics, be sure that they first become immersed in the books, thinking and talking about the information in each text. Use the following books from the *Fountas & Pinnell Classroom™ Interactive Read-Aloud Collection* text sets or choose informational books with which your students are familiar.

Genre Study: Expository Nonfiction

Hottest, Coldest, Highest, Deepest by Steve Jenkins

Shell, Beak, Tusk by Bridget Heos

Knights in Shining Armor by Gail Gibbons

Bats! by Laurence Pringle

Tornadoes! by Gail Gibbons

A Day and Night in the Desert by Caroline Arnold

As you read aloud and enjoy these texts together, help students

- notice similarities between them,
- identify the topic of each text,
- discuss what they learned from each text, and
- notice how the information in each text is organized.

Expository Nonfiction

Section 2: Literary Analysis

RML1
LA.U11.RML1

Reading Minilesson Principle
Informational books are alike in many ways.

Studying Informational Books

You Will Need

▸ a collection of familiar informational books, such as the following from Text Set: Expository Nonfiction:

- *Hottest, Coldest, Highest, Deepest* by Steve Jenkins
- *Shell, Beak, Tusk* by Bridget Heos
- *Knights in Shining Armor* by Gail Gibbons
- *Bats!* by Laurence Pringle
- *Tornadoes!* by Gail Gibbons
- *A Day and Night in the Desert* by Caroline Arnold

▸ chart paper prepared with the headings *Informational Books* and *Noticings* and sections for *Always* and *Often*

▸ markers

Academic Language / Important Vocabulary

▸ informational

▸ nonfiction

▸ fact

▸ topic

▸ organize

Continuum Connection

▸ Notice and understand the characteristics of some specific nonfiction genres: e.g., informational book, procedural and persuasive texts, biography, autobiography, memoir, hybrid text (p. 53)

Goal

Notice and understand the characteristics of informational books (i.e., expository nonfiction) as a genre.

Rationale

When students study informational (i.e., expository nonfiction) books through inquiry, they gain a deeper understanding both of individual books and of the genre as a whole. When they develop an understanding of the genre they will know what to expect when they encounter books of that genre (see pages 37-39 for more about genre study).

Assess Learning

Observe students when they read and talk about informational books. Notice if there is evidence of new learning based on the goal of this minilesson.

▸ Are students able to identify and talk about the characteristics of informational books?

▸ Do they use vocabulary such as *informational, nonfiction, fact, topic*, and *organize* to talk about nonfiction books?

Minilesson

To help students think about the minilesson principle, choose informational books that you have read aloud recently and provide an inquiry-based lesson. Here is an example.

▸ Put students into small groups, and give each group several informational books that they have heard read aloud recently.

We have read and discussed all of these informational or nonfiction books together. Look through the books I gave you and talk with your group about the ways your books are alike.

What did you notice about how your informational books are alike?

▸ As the students share their noticings, prompt them, as necessary, with questions such as the following:

- *What do authors tell about in informational books?*
- *Besides the words, what else gives information in an informational book?*
- *What have you noticed about how authors decide what order to give information in?*
- *What features in informational books help you find specific information?*
- *How do you think authors decide what topic to write about?*

▶ Help students decide whether each noticing is *always* or *often* a characteristic of informational books by asking other groups if all their books have the same characteristic.

▶ Record students' noticings on chart paper.

Have a Try

Invite the students to talk with a partner about the characteristics of informational books.

> Think about the last book that you either read or heard read aloud. Was it an informational book? How do you know? Think about what we wrote on the chart.

▶ After students turn and talk, ask a few students to share their responses with the class.

Summarize and Apply

Summarize the learning and remind students to think about the characteristics of informational books when they read.

> What did you notice about the informational books you looked at today?

▶ Review the noticings chart.

> Choose a book to read during independent reading time. As you read, think about whether the book is an informational book. If it is, bring it to share when we come back together.

Share

Following independent reading time, gather students together in the meeting area to talk about their reading.

> Raise your hand if you read an informational book today.

> How did you know that your book is informational?

Extend the Lesson (Optional)

After assessing students' understanding, you might decide to extend the learning.

▶ Continue to add to the noticings chart as students read more informational books and notice more about the genre.

▶ Have students set up a display of student-recommended informational books in the classroom library.

Informational Books

Noticings:

Always	Often
• The author gives facts about a topic.	• There are sidebars, labels, diagrams, and maps.
• The author organizes the information to show it clearly.	• The book includes a table of contents, index, and glossary.
• There are photographs and illustrations that give information.	• The author shows he cares or gives a message about the topic.

Section 2: Literary Analysis

RML2
LA.U11.RML2

Reading Minilesson Principle
The definition of an informational book is what is always true about it.

Studying Informational Books

You Will Need

- a familiar informational book, such as *Hottest, Coldest, Highest, Deepest* by Steve Jenkins, from Text Set: Expository Nonfiction
- the noticings chart created during RML1
- chart paper and markers

Academic Language / Important Vocabulary

- informational
- definition
- fact
- topic
- organized
- information

Continuum Connection

- Notice and understand the characteristics of some specific nonfiction genres: e.g., informational book, procedural and persuasive texts, biography, autobiography, memoir, hybrid text (p. 53)

Goal

Create a working definition for informational (i.e., expository nonfiction) books.

Rationale

Writing a definition is part of the genre study process. When you work with students to create a definition of a genre, you help them summarize the most important characteristics of that genre. Over time, the students can revise the definition as they read more examples of that genre.

Assess Learning

Observe students when they read and talk about informational books. Notice if there is evidence of new learning based on the goal of this minilesson.

- ▶ Do students discuss what they notice about informational books?
- ▶ Can they explain whether a particular book fits the definition of informational books?
- ▶ Do students use academic language, such as *informational, fact,* and *topic*?

Minilesson

Guide students in writing a definition of informational books. Here is an example of how to do so.

- ▶ Display and review the noticings chart created during the previous minilesson.

  You have noticed how informational, or nonfiction, books are alike. Now you're going to use what you noticed to write a definition of informational books. The definition will tell in one or two sentences what is always true about informational books.

- ▶ Write the words *Informational books* on chart paper.

  Turn and talk to your partner about how you would finish this sentence to tell what informational books are. Use our noticings chart to help you.

  How would you finish this sentence?

- ▶ Use students' responses to create a whole-class definition. Write the rest of the definition on the chart paper.

Have a Try

Invite the students to talk with a partner about a familiar informational book.

▶ Show the cover of *Hottest, Coldest, Highest, Deepest*. Briefly review the book to remind students of its contents.

> Turn and talk to your partner about whether this book fits our definition of informational books. If so, how does it fit?

▶ After students turn and talk, ask a few pairs to share their thinking.

Summarize and Apply

Summarize the learning and remind students to think about the definition of informational books as they read.

▶ Review the definition.

> Today we thought even more about what informational or nonfiction books are like, and we worked together to write a definition to describe informational books. The definition tells what is always true about informational books.

> When you read today, think about whether your book fits our definition. If so, bring your book to share when we come back together.

Share

Following independent reading time, gather students together in the meeting area to talk about their reading.

> Raise your hand if you read an informational book today.

> How does your book fit our definition of informational books?

Extend the Lesson (Optional)

After assessing students' understanding, you might decide to extend the learning.

▶ During interactive read-aloud or shared reading, compare books against the definition of informational books to determine whether the book is, indeed, informational.

▶ Add titles of informational books to the chart as the class encounters them in interactive read-aloud and independent reading.

Informational Books

Informational books give facts about a topic and are organized in a way to make the information clear.

They often include special features that give more information.

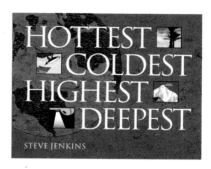

HOTTEST
COLDEST
HIGHEST
DEEPEST
STEVE JENKINS

RML3
LA.U11.RML3

Reading Minilesson Principle
The author of an informational book gives facts about a topic.

Studying Informational Books

You Will Need

- two or three familiar informational books, such as the following from Text Set: Expository Nonfiction:
  - *Bats!* by Laurence Pringle
  - *Knights in Shining Armor* by Gail Gibbons
  - *Tornadoes!* by Gail Gibbons
- chart paper and markers
- three sticky notes labeled with *Bats, Knights, Tornadoes*
- a basket of informational books

Academic Language / Important Vocabulary

- informational
- nonfiction
- fact
- topic
- author

Continuum Connection

- Understand that a writer is presenting related facts about a single topic [p. 54]

Goal

Understand that authors give facts about a single topic in informational books.

Rationale

When you teach students that authors give facts about a single topic in informational books, they begin to make connections and understand the relationship between multiple pieces of information. They are also better able to recognize and identify informational books.

Assess Learning

Observe students when they read and talk about informational books. Notice if there is evidence of new learning based on the goal of this minilesson.

- Can students identify the topic of and facts in an informational book?
- Do they recognize that all the facts are related to a single topic?
- Do they use academic language, such as *informational, nonfiction, fact, topic,* and *author*?

Minilesson

To help students think about the minilesson principle, use familiar informational books to provide an inquiry-based lesson. Here is an example.

- Show the cover of *Bats!*

  What is the topic of this book?

- Record responses on chart paper. Then reread pages 5 and 12 of *Bats!*

  What did you learn from these pages?

- Record students' responses on the chart.

  What do you notice about all these facts? What do they all have in common?

- Have a volunteer place the *Bats* sticky note on the chart. Then reread page 2 of *Knights in Shining Armor*.

  What facts did you learn from this page?

- Record students' responses on the chart. Then reread pages 6 and 10 and ask students to identify the facts they heard. Add facts to chart.

  What do you notice about the facts in this book? What are they all about?

  What is the topic of this book?

- Have a volunteer place the *Knights* sticky note on the chart.

Have a Try

Invite the students to work with a partner to identify the topic of and facts in *Tornadoes!*

▶ Read page 4 of *Tornadoes!*

Turn and talk to your partner about what facts you learned from this page.

▶ Ask a couple of students to share their responses, and then record the facts on the chart. Repeat the sequence above with pages 22–23.

What are all the facts in this book about? Turn and talk to your partner about the topic.

▶ Have a volunteer place the *Tornadoes* sticky note.

Summarize and Apply

Summarize the learning and remind students to think about the topic of and the facts in informational books.

What did you notice about what the author tells in the informational books we looked at today?

▶ Write the principle at the top of the chart.

Choose an informational book from this basket. As you read, think about the topic of the book and notice what facts the author tells about the topic. Be ready to talk about your book when we come back together.

Share

Following independent reading time, gather students together in the meeting area to talk about their reading.

Turn and talk to your partner about the informational book you read today. Tell your partner the topic of your book and some of the facts.

Extend the Lesson (Optional)

After assessing students' understanding, you might decide to extend the learning.

▶ Guide students to understand that while informational books mostly contain facts, they may also occasionally contain the author's opinions. Help them distinguish between facts and opinions in informational books.

▶ **Writing About Reading** Have students make a list in a reader's notebook of interesting facts they learned from an informational book.

The author of an informational book gives facts about a topic.

Book	Facts	Topic
BATS! STRANGE AND WONDERFUL	• Bats are mammals. • 44 Kinds of bats live in North America. • Bats use echolocation to locate objects.	Bats
GAIL GIBBONS	• Knights wore strong armor and fought on horseback. • It took many years of training to become a Knight. • A Knight carried a shield to protect himself.	Knights
TORNADOES!	• Tornadoes begin inside cumulonimbus clouds. • Most tornadoes in the U.S. happen in Tornado Alley and in Florida.	Tornadoes

Reading Minilesson Principle

The author of an informational book organizes the facts in several ways.

Studying Informational Books

You Will Need

▸ two or three familiar informational books that are organized in different ways, such as the following from Text Set: Expository Nonfiction:

  • *Bats!* by Laurence Pringle

  • *A Day and Night in the Desert* by Caroline Arnold

  • *Shell, Beak, Tusk* by Bridget Heos

▸ chart paper and markers

▸ a basket of informational books

Academic Language / Important Vocabulary

▸ information

▸ organize

▸ order

▸ facts

▸ category

Continuum Connection

▸ Identify the organization of a text: e.g., chronological sequence, temporal and established sequences, categories (p. 53)

Goal

Notice and identify the different organizational structures of informational (i.e., expository nonfiction) texts.

Rationale

When you teach students to notice different organizational structures in informational texts, they begin to think about and understand the relationships between different pieces of information. They also understand that authors must make decisions about how to organize their books.

Assess Learning

Observe students when they read and talk about informational books. Notice if there is evidence of new learning based on the goal of this minilesson.

  ▸ Can students talk about how and why the information in an informational book is organized the way it is?

  ▸ Do they use the terms *information, organize, order, facts,* and *category*?

Minilesson

To help students think about the minilesson principle, use familiar informational texts to provide an inquiry-based lesson about text organization. Here is an example.

  ▸ Show the cover of *Bats!* and read the title. Reread pages 12–13 of the book.

    What are these pages of the book about?

  ▸ Write students' responses on chart paper. Reread page 18 and then pages 20–21.

    What kind of information or facts about bats does the author give on these pages?

    What do you notice about how the author organized the information in this book? How do you think he decided what facts to put together on each page?

  ▸ Record responses.

    Each part focuses on a small topic that relates to the big topic, bats.

  ▸ Show the cover of *A Day and Night in the Desert* and read the title. Reread pages 2–3. Point to "6:00 A.M." in the upper left corner of page 2.

    What do you notice about the information at the beginning of this book?

  ▸ Record students' responses. Then reread pages 8–9 and pages 14–15.

    How did the author decide what to put in the beginning, middle, and end of her book?

  ▸ Record students' responses on the chart.

Have a Try

Invite the students to talk with a partner about the organization of an informational book.

▶ Show the cover of *Shell, Beak, Tusk* and read the title. Reread pages 8–9.

Turn and talk to your partner about what you notice about the facts on these pages. What are these pages about?

▶ Continue in a similar manner with pages 12–13 and 18–19.

▶ Ask a few students to share their thinking, and record their responses on the chart.

Summarize and Apply

Summarize the learning and remind students to notice how authors organize informational books.

What did you notice about the organization of information in the books we looked at today?

▶ Write the principle at the top of the chart.

Sometimes authors tell information in the order that it happens, and sometimes they group information together into small topics or categories.

Choose an informational book to read from this basket. As you read, think about how the author organizes the information in your book. Be ready to share your thinking when we come back together.

Share

Following independent reading time, gather students together in the meeting area to talk about their reading.

Turn and talk to your partner about how the author organized the information in the book you read today.

Extend the Lesson (Optional)

After assessing students' understanding, you might decide to extend the learning.

▶ **Writing About Reading** Teach students how to use graphic organizers to show the organization of a nonfiction book (see Umbrella 5: Writing About Nonfiction Books in a Reader's Notebook, in Section Four: Writing About Reading).

The author of an informational book organizes the facts in several ways.		
BATS! STRANGE AND WONDERFUL	• how bats use echolocation • what bats eat • where bats sleep	The author groups together information that goes together.
Day and Night in the DESERT	• 6:00 A.M. • 3:00 P.M. • midnight	The author tells information in the order that it happens.
SHELL BEAK TUSK	• shells • wings • beaks	The author puts information into smaller groups or categories.

Section 2: Literary Analysis

Assessment

After you have taught the minilessons in this umbrella, observe students as they talk about their reading across instructional contexts: interactive read-aloud, independent reading and literacy work, guided reading, shared reading, and book club. Use *The Literacy Continuum* (Fountas and Pinnell 2017) to observe students' reading behaviors across instructional contexts.

▶ What evidence do you have of new understandings related to informational books?

- Are students able to identify and describe informational books?
- Can they identify the topic of an informational book? Can they identify facts about that topic?
- Can they explain the organization of an informational book?
- Do they use vocabulary such as *informational, nonfiction, fact, topic,* and *organize* to talk about nonfiction books?

▶ In what other ways, beyond the scope of this umbrella, are they thinking and talking about nonfiction books?

- Are students noticing that there are other types of nonfiction books?
- Are they noticing graphics and text features in nonfiction?

Use your observations to determine the next umbrella you will teach. You may also consult Minilessons Across the Year (pp. 55-57) for guidance.

Read and Revise

After completing the steps in the genre study process, help students read and revise their definition of the genre based on their new understandings.

▶ **Before:** Informational books give facts about a topic and are organized in a way to make the information clear. They often include special features that give more information.

▶ **After:** Informational books give facts about a single topic and often include special features that give more information about that topic. The information can be organized in different ways (time order, by category).

Reader's Notebook

When this umbrella is complete, provide a copy of the minilesson principles (see resources.fountasandpinnell.com) for students to glue in the reader's notebook (in the Minilessons section if using *Reader's Notebook: Intermediate* [Fountas and Pinnell 2011]), so they can refer to the information as needed.

Minilessons in This Umbrella

Biography

RML1	Biographies are alike in many ways.
RML2	The definition of a biography is what is always true about it.
RML3	A biography is the story of a person's life written by someone else.
RML4	The author includes facts about the person's life.
RML5	Think about why the author wrote a book about the person.
RML6	The author usually tells about a person's life in the order it happened.
RML7	The author of a biography gives an important message.

Before Teaching Umbrella 12 Minilessons

When students study a genre, they learn what to expect when reading a text and develop important comprehension skills. They develop an understanding of the distinguishing characteristics of a genre and acquire the tools they need to navigate a variety of texts.

There are six broad steps in a genre study. Before you teach this umbrella, read pages 37-39, which detail the steps in the genre study process, including the fact that students must read multiple biographies before beginning a genre study of them.

For this genre study, it is important to select books that are clear examples of biography. Biographies tell the story of someone's life by writing about facts using a narrative style. Be sure that students enjoy each book and think and talk about the meaning in their first experience with the book. After several books they will be able to notice and generalize the characteristics of the genre. Select a variety of biography subjects that provide insight into the impact of history and allow students to explore other cultures and times. Use the following books from the *Fountas & Pinnell Classroom™ Interactive Read-Aloud Collection* text sets or use biographies that you have on hand.

Genre Study: Biography

Magic Trash by J. H. Shapiro

The Tree Lady by H. Joseph Hopkins

Odd Boy Out by Don Brown

Nobody Owns the Sky by Reeve Lindbergh

Wangari Maathai by Franck Prévot

As you read aloud and enjoy these texts together, help students

- notice things that are *always* true and *often* true about biographies,
- recognize that a biography is usually written in chronological order,
- notice the facts that the author decided to include,
- think about why the author wrote a book about the person, and
- think about the message of the book.

Reading Minilesson Principle
Biographies are alike in many ways.

Studying Biography

You Will Need

- a variety of biographies with which students are familiar
- chart paper and markers
- sticky notes
- basket of biographical books

Academic Language / Important Vocabulary

- biography
- genre
- characteristics

Continuum Connection

- Notice and understand the characteristics of some specific nonfiction genres: e.g., informational book, procedural and persuasive texts, biography, autobiography, memoir, hybrid text (p. 53)
- Understand that a biography is the story of a person's life written by someone else (p. 53)

Goal

Notice and understand the characteristics of a biography as a genre.

Rationale

When you teach students that a biography is a story written about a person's life that includes facts and important things that the person did, they will know what to expect when reading one.

Assess Learning

Observe students when they read and talk about biographies. Notice if there is evidence of new learning based on the goal of this minilesson.

- ▶ Are students able to talk about the ways that biographies are alike?
- ▶ Can they talk about the characteristics of biographies?
- ▶ Do they understand that some characteristics *always* occur and some characteristics *often* occur?
- ▶ Do they understand the terms *biography, genre,* and *characteristics*?

Minilesson

To help students think about the minilesson principle, provide an inquiry-based lesson about the characteristics of biographies. Here is an example.

- ▶ Have students sit in small groups. Show the covers of multiple biographies with which students are familiar.

  Think about these biographies and the different ways they are all alike. In your group, talk about the ways that the biographies are alike.

- ▶ After time for discussion, ask students to share noticings. As students share, record responses on chart paper. Create an *always* and an *often* section to record responses.

  As you share your ideas, think about whether each is *always* or *often* part of a biography. Tell the category for the idea on the chart.

- ▶ Select several biographies to revisit in more detail as a whole group.

  What else do you notice about these biographies?

- ▶ Continue to record responses. Consider providing one or more of the following prompts.

  - *What did you notice about the people, or subjects, of the biographies?*
  - *What did you notice about how the authors present the information?*
  - *What types of events do the authors write about?*

Have a Try

Invite the students to examine a biography with a small group.

▶ Provide each group with a biography.

Look through the pages at the words and illustrations and talk about the things on the chart. See how many you can find in the story.

Summarize and Apply

Summarize the learning and remind students to notice the characteristics of biographies.

Today you noticed the ways that biographies are alike.

▶ Add the title *Biography* to the chart and review the noticings.

When you finish reading the book you are reading now, choose a biography to read. As you read, see if you notice some of the things from the chart and add a sticky note to that page. Bring the book when we meet so you can share.

Share

Following independent reading time, gather the students in the meeting area.

Did anyone read a biography today? Share what you noticed. How many things from the chart did you find in the book?

Extend the Lesson (Optional)

After assessing students' understanding, you might decide to extend the learning.

▶ Continue to add noticings to the chart as students read and listen to other biographies.

▶ Introduce your students to Genre Thinkmarks for biography (to download the Genre Thinkmark, see resources.fountasandpinnell.com). A Genre Thinkmark is a tool that guides students to note certain elements of a genre in their reading. They can quickly note the page numbers of parts of the book where they see evidence of the characteristics of biographies and then share the information with their classmates.

▶ **Writing About Reading** Encourage students to write in a reader's notebook about a biography they have read or heard.

Biography
Noticings:

Always	Often
• The author tells the story of another person's life, or part of it.	• The author tells about the person's life in the order it happened.
• The author includes facts about the person's life.	• The author includes made-up dialogue, based on fact.
• The author tells about the important things a person did.	• The author includes quotes by the person.
• The author gives an important message.	• There is additional information at the end of the book (timelines).
	• The author includes photographs or illustrations.

Section 2: Literary Analysis

RML2
LA.U12.RML2

Reading Minilesson Principle
The definition of a biography is what is always true about it.

Studying Biography

You Will Need

- noticings chart from RML1
- chart paper and markers
- a biography with which students are familiar, such as *The Tree Lady* by H. Joseph Hopkins, from Text Set: Biography
- basket of biographies

Academic Language / Important Vocabulary

- biography
- genre
- definition

Continuum Connection

- Understand that a biography is the story of a person's life written by someone else (p. 53)

Goal

Create a working definition for a biography.

Rationale

When you teach students to construct a working definition of a biography, they are able to form their own understandings so they will know what to expect of the genre. They learn to revise their understandings as they gain additional experiences with stories written about a person's life.

Assess Learning

Observe students when they read and talk about biographies. Notice if there is evidence of new learning based on the goal of this minilesson.

- Do students participate in creating a working definition of a biography?
- Do they understand that a definition of biography is what is always true about the genre?
- Do they understand the terms *biography, genre,* and *definition*?

Minilesson

To help students think about the minilesson principle, provide an inquiry-based lesson to help them think about the definition of a biography. Here is an example.

- Show the biography noticings chart and review the characteristics.

    What did you notice about biographies?

    The definition of a biography tells what books that are in the genre of biography *always* are like.

- On chart paper, write the words *A biography is,* leaving space for constructing a working definition.

    If you want to finish this sentence with a definition that tells what a biography is, what would you write? Turn and talk about that, thinking about the noticings chart.

- After time for discussion, ask students to share ideas. Use the ideas to create a working definition for the class, and write it on chart paper. Read the definition.

Have a Try

Invite the students to talk with a partner about how *The Tree Lady* fits the definition of a biography.

▸ Review the definition.

> With a partner, talk about whether *The Tree Lady* fits the definition of a biography. What makes you think that?

Summarize and Apply

Remind students to think about the definition of a biography.

> When you read today, you can choose a biography from the basket and think about how the book fits the definition. Bring the book when we meet so you can share.

Share

Following independent reading time, gather the students in the meeting area.

> Did anyone read a biography? Share whether it fits the definition and what examples help you know that.

Extend the Lesson (Optional)

After assessing students' understanding, you might decide to extend the learning.

▸ As students encounter biographies in interactive read-aloud or independent reading, remind them to notice how a book fits the definition.

Biography

A biography is the story of all or part of a real person's life, written by someone else.

RML3

LA.U12.RML3

Reading Minilesson Principle
A biography is the story of a person's life written by someone else.

Studying Biography

You Will Need

- several biographies that students are familiar with, such as these from Text Set: Biography:
  - *Nobody Owns the Sky* by Reeve Lindbergh
  - *Magic Trash* by J. H. Shapiro
  - *Wangari Maathai* by Franck Prévot
- chart paper and markers
- basket of biographies

Academic Language / Important Vocabulary

- author
- life
- biography

Continuum Connection

- Understand that a biography is the story of a person's life written by someone else (p. 53)

Goal

Understand that a biography is the story of a person's life written by someone else.

Rationale

When students understand that an author makes a decision about whom to choose as the subject of a biography, they understand that the subject of the book is important and that authors have a choice about who to write about.

Assess Learning

Observe students when they read and talk about biographies. Notice if there is evidence of new learning based on the goal of this minilesson.

- Are students aware that a biography is a book about someone's life?
- Do they notice that a biography is written by someone about another person's life?
- Do they use the terms *author, life,* and *biography* when talking about biographies?

Minilesson

To help students think about the minilesson principle, engage students in an interactive discussion about biography. Here is an example.

- Display the cover of *Nobody Owns the Sky.*
- On chart paper, add a column for the title, the author, who the book is about, and what the book is about.
- Display and read pages 5–6.

    What types of things does the author, Veronica Chambers, tell you about?

- As needed, guide students to understand that the book is about Bessie Coleman's life. Record the information on the chart.

    Let's think about another biography, *Magic Trash.*

    Who is the author?

    Who is the book about?

- In a new row, add the information to the chart.

    What types of things does J. H. Shapiro write about in this book?

- Add to the chart, guiding students to understand that the book is about Tyree's life.

Have a Try

Invite the students to talk about a biography with a partner.

▶ Show the cover of *Wangari Maathai*.

Look at this biography, *Wangari Maathai* by Franck Prévot. Turn and talk about what you notice about who wrote the book and who the book is about.

▶ After time for discussion, ask students to share their thinking and add a row to the chart with the details of this biography.

Summarize and Apply

Summarize the learning and ask students what they notice about biographies.

What does the chart show you about biography?

▶ Add the principle to the top of the chart.

Today when you finish reading the book you are reading now, choose a biography from this basket to read. As you read, notice who wrote the book and whom the book is about. Bring the book when we meet after so you can share.

Share

Following independent reading time, gather the students in the meeting area to talk about biographies.

Did anyone read a biography? Share what you noticed about whom the book is about and who wrote the book.

Extend the Lesson (Optional)

After assessing students' understanding, you might decide to extend the learning.

▶ **Writing About Reading** Assist students with finding information from the library or online about a famous person. Then have them write a biography about that person and share their biographies with other students in the class. Add to the chart, asking students to tell you how to fill in the columns.

A biography is the story of a person's life written by someone else.

Title	Author	Who?	What?
Nobody Owns the Sky	Reeve Lindbergh	Bessie Coleman	Bessie's life
Magic Trash	J. H. Shapiro	Tyree Guyton	Tyree's life
Wangari Maathai	Franck Prévot	Wangari Maathai	Wangari's life

Section 2: Literary Analysis

Reading Minilesson Principle
The author includes facts about the person's life.

Studying Biography

You Will Need

- a biography students are familiar with, such as *Odd Boy Out* by Don Brown, from Text Set: Biography
- chart paper and markers
- basket of biographies

Academic Language / Important Vocabulary

- biography
- author
- facts

Continuum Connection

- Understand that a biography is the story of a person's life written by someone else (p. 53)

Goal

Understand that the author includes important facts about the person's life in a biography.

Rationale

When students think about the facts that authors choose to include when writing biographies, they consider the choices an author makes as well as discern which facts are important when telling someone's life story.

Assess Learning

Observe students when they think and talk about biographies. Notice if there is evidence of new learning based on the goal of this minilesson.

- Do students identify the facts included about a person's life in a biography?
- Can they talk about the reasons an author might have decided to include certain facts in a biography?
- Do they use the terms *biography, author,* and *facts* when talking about biographies?

Minilesson

To help students think about the minilesson principle, provide an interactive lesson to help them think about the facts that authors choose to include in biographies. Here is an example.

- Display page 4 of *Odd Boy Out* and read the first paragraph.

  What did the author choose to write about Albert in this part of the book?

- Guide students to talk about the facts about Albert in the text. Create a chart and list the facts as students give you suggestions.

  Turn and talk about why you think Don Brown decided to include the fact that Albert was a late talker?

- Create a new column and add students' suggestions next to the facts on the chart.

  Listen as I read another page and think about the facts that Don Brown included and why he might have decided to include those facts.

- Read page 8.

  What did you notice about the facts on this page?

  Why do you think Don Brown included these facts?

- Add ideas to the chart. Show and read pages 11–12.

What did you notice?

▶ Add new ideas to the chart about the facts and why the author might have decided to include those facts.

Have a Try

Invite students to talk about the choices an author makes about what facts to include when writing a biography.

> Don Brown had to make choices about which facts to include in this book about Albert Einstein. Turn and talk about how and why you think he made those choices.

Summarize and Apply

Summarize the learning and remind students to think about the facts that authors include when writing a biography.

> Today you noticed that authors make choices when deciding what facts to include in a biography.

▶ Add the principle to the top of the chart.

> When you read today, choose a biography from the basket. Think about the facts that the author decided to include and why you think the author made those choices. Bring the book when we meet so you can share.

Share

Following independent reading time, gather the students together in pairs.

> Turn and talk with your partner about the biography you read today. Share some facts you noticed and tell your partner why you think the author included those facts.

Extend the Lesson (Optional)

After assessing students' understanding, you might decide to extend the learning.

▶ **Writing About Reading** Have each student choose a famous person, and then gather facts about that person by reading a biography or searching online. As facts are gathered, students make a list of the facts. After research is complete, students place a star next to each fact they feel would be important to include in a biography. Then have them write biographies about the person to share with classmates, making sure to include the facts that have a star.

The author includes facts about the person's life.

Title	Fact	Why the Fact Is Important
	Albert did not talk as early as other children.	You do not need to talk early to be smart.
ODD BOY OUT	Albert wondered how a compass worked.	He has curiosity about how things work, which is important for a scientist.
	Albert did not like to play sports like the other boys.	He had other interests and was different from other kids his age.

Reading Minilesson Principle
Think about why the writer wrote a book about the person.

Studying Biography

You Will Need

▶ two biographies that students are familiar with, such as the following from Text Set: Biography:
  • *Odd Boy Out* by Don Brown
  • *Nobody Owns the Sky* by Reeve Lindbergh
▶ chart paper and markers
▶ basket of biographies

Academic Language / Important Vocabulary

▶ author's note
▶ biography
▶ accomplishment

Continuum Connection

▶ Infer the importance of a subject's accomplishments (biography) (p. 53)

Goal

Infer the importance of a subject's accomplishments.

Rationale

When you teach students to infer the importance of the subject of a biography's accomplishments, they begin to understand why the person's life was important and why someone would want to write a book about the person.

Assess Learning

Observe students when they read and talk about biographies. Notice if there is evidence of new learning based on the goal of this minilesson.

▶ Do students think about why an author wrote a biography?

▶ Do they understand the terms *author's note, biography,* and *accomplishment*?

Minilesson

To help students think about the minilesson principle, provide an interactive lesson about why writers choose the subjects of their biographies. Here is an example.

▶ Show the cover of *Odd Boy Out* and the author's note at the end.

> Think about this biography, *Odd Boy Out*. Listen to what the author, Don Brown, says about Albert Einstein in the author's note.

▶ Read the author's note.

> What do you notice about what Don Brown says?

▶ As students offer suggestions, create a chart with two columns. In the first column, write the title. In the second column, write students' ideas about why the author wrote about Albert Einstein.

> Notice what we wrote here. Why do you think Don Brown chose to write about Albert Einstein? Turn and talk about that.

▶ After time for discussion, ask students to share their ideas. Add a heading and students' responses to the chart.

> Think about another biography you know, *Nobody Owns the Sky*. Listen to what the author says about Bessie Coleman.

▶ Show the cover of *Nobody Owns the Sky*. Open to the author's note before the book begins and read it. Then, open to and read the note about the author at the end of the book.

> Why do you think Reeve Lindbergh chose to write about Bessie Coleman?

▶ Add responses to the chart.

Have a Try

Invite students to talk with a partner about how authors decide to write about a particular person.

> Turn and talk about the chart. Why do you think authors decide to write biographies about certain people?

> ▸ After time for discussion, ask students to share their thinking.

Summarize and Apply

Summarize the learning and remind students to think about the choice that authors make in deciding to write a biography.

> Today you learned that when you read a biography it is important to think about why the author wrote about that person.

> ▸ **Add the principle to the top of the chart.**

> When you read today, if you choose a biography think about why the author might have decided to write about that person. Bring the book when we meet so you can share.

Share

Following independent reading time, gather students in the meeting area to talk about biographies.

> Did anyone read a biography today? Tell why you think the author wrote a book about the person.

Extend the Lesson (Optional)

After assessing students' understanding, you might decide to extend the learning.

> ▸ **Writing About Reading** Ask the librarian to assist students with locating the biography section in the school library and learning how it is organized. Have groups work together to choose a person to read about and check out a book about that person. Then, have them work together to talk about why that person's life might be interesting to write about. Next, have them each write a short biography about the person, including a sentence at the end telling why they chose that person to write about.

Think about why the writer wrote a book about the person.

Title	Why the Author Wrote About the Person
 ODD BOY OUT — YOUNG ALBERT EINSTEIN — Don Brown	The author wanted to show that we should respect people for who they are. People thought Einstein was odd, but he was very smart.
Nobody Owns the Sky	The author thought Bessie Coleman was a very brave pilot, but hardly anyone knew about her. She wanted to tell people about Bessie's accomplishments.

Section 2: Literary Analysis

RML 6
LA.U12.RML6

Reading Minilesson Principle
The author usually tells about a person's life in the order it happened.

Studying Biography

You Will Need

- two biographies that students are familiar with, such as these from Text Set: Biography:
  - *Magic Trash* by J. H. Shapiro
  - *Odd Boy Out* by Don Brown
- chart paper and markers
- basket of biographies

Academic Language / Important Vocabulary

- author
- biography
- time order
- events

Continuum Connection

- Identify the organization of a text: e.g., chronological sequence, temporal and established sequences, categories (p. 53)
- Understand when a writer is telling information in a sequence (chronological order) (p. 53)

Goal

Understand that biographies are usually told in chronological order.

Rationale

When students understand that biographies are usually told in chronological order, they begin to notice how a person is shaped over time by life events and can apply this knowledge to their own lives.

Assess Learning

Observe students as they read and talk about biographies. Notice if there is evidence of new learning based on the goal of this minilesson.

- Do students notice time order when reading and talking about biographies?
- Can they understand that a biography is usually written in the order that events happen in a person's life?
- Do they use the terms *author, biography, time order* and *events*?

Minilesson

To help students think about the minilesson principle, provide an interactive lesson to help them understand that biographies are usually written in chronological order. Here is an example.

- Show page 1 of *Magic Trash*.

  Let's think about this biography written about the life of Tyree Guyton.

- Read page 1.

  How does the author, J. H. Shapiro, begin this book?

- On chart paper, draw a timeline graphic, along which you can place Tyree's life events.

- Turn to page 6 and read the first two paragraphs.

  What does the author tell about now?

- Add to the timeline.

- Repeat, revisiting pages 13 and 16 and adding information to the timeline.

- Show the cover of *Odd Boy Out*.

  Now, think about the way the author, Don Brown, wrote about Albert Einstein's life.

- Draw a new timeline on the chart. Then, turn to and read page 1.

  How does Don Brown begin this book about Albert Einstein?

▶ Add students' suggestions to the chart and then revisit several pages throughout the book and ask students what happened next. Add to the chart.

Have a Try

Invite the students to apply the new thinking.

▶ Invite the students to talk with a partner about the events on the chart.

> Turn and talk about what you notice about the way the author told about the events in these biographies and the reason.

▶ After time for discussion, ask students to share their thinking. Guide them as needed to notice that the events are written in the order they happened in the person's life.

Summarize and Apply

Summarize the learning and remind students to think about the order of events when they read biographies.

> Today you noticed that authors of biographies usually tell about the subject's life in time order, which means that they tell the events in the same order that they happened in the person's life.

▶ Write the principle at the top of the chart.

> Today, you might choose a biography from the basket to read. If you do, notice whether the author wrote about the person's life in the order that events happened. Bring the book when we meet so you can share.

Share

Following independent reading time, gather the students together in groups of three.

> Did anyone read a biography? In your group, talk about what you noticed about time order in the book.

Extend the Lesson (Optional)

After assessing students' understanding, you might decide to extend the learning.

▶ Talk with students about how some biographies are not written in chronological order. They might, for example, start with a later event and then go back to an earlier time in the subject's life.

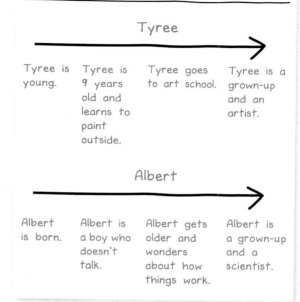

The author usually tells about a person's life in the order it happened.

Tyree

| Tyree is young. | Tyree is 9 years old and learns to paint outside. | Tyree goes to art school. | Tyree is a grown-up and an artist. |

Albert

| Albert is born. | Albert is a boy who doesn't talk. | Albert gets older and wonders about how things work. | Albert is a grown-up and a scientist. |

Section 2: Literary Analysis

RML7
LA.U12.RML7

Reading Minilesson Principle
The author of a biography gives an important message.

Studying Biography

You Will Need

- a variety of biographies, such as these in Text Set: Biography:
  - *Magic Trash* by J. H. Shapiro
  - *Odd Boy Out* by Don Brown
  - *The Tree Lady* by H. Joseph Hopkins
  - *Wangari Maathai* by Franck Prévot
  - *Nobody Owns the Sky* by Reeve Lindbergh
- chart paper and markers
- basket of biographies

Academic Language / Important Vocabulary

- author
- biography
- message

Goal

Infer the larger idea or author's message in a biography.

Rationale

When students think about the author's message in a biography, they begin to think about the overarching reason why an author chooses to write about a person's life and apply messages from the book to their own lives.

Assess Learning

Observe students when they think and talk about the messages authors give in biographies. Notice if there is evidence of new learning based on the goal of this minilesson.

- Are students able to infer the messages that authors give in biographies?
- Are they beginning to think about how to apply messages from reading about the lives of others to their own lives?
- Do they use vocabulary such as *author, biography,* and *message*?

Minilesson

To help students think about the minilesson principle, provide an interactive lesson to help them think about the messages authors give in biographies. Here is an example.

- Display the cover of *Magic Trash*.

    Think about this biography that J. H. Shapiro wrote about the life of Tyree Guyton. Listen as I reread a page from the beginning and a few pages from the end of the book to refresh your thinking.

- Reread the first page and the last two pages.

    Turn and talk about the message that J. H. Shapiro gives you in this book.

- After time for discussion, have students share ideas. As needed, guide the conversation, depending on how much experience your students have had with identifying an author's message.

    How could I write the message in one sentence on a chart?

- Using student ideas, create a chart with the title and the message of the book.

    Think about the message in several other biographies you know.

- Display the covers of the remaining books in the text set.

    Turn and talk about one or more of these biographies. What message does the author want you to have after reading?

▶ Allow time for discussion.

> What biographies did you talk about? What was the author's message?

▶ Ask volunteers to share ideas. Add each title and message to a new row on the chart.

Have a Try

Invite the students to talk the messages authors give in biographies.

> Think about the messages in these biographies. Turn and talk about how these messages might help you in your own life. In what ways can messages that you learn when reading about other people help you make life choices?

Summarize and Apply

Summarize the learning and remind students to think about the messages authors give in biographies.

> Today you talked about the messages authors give in biographies and how those messages might help you in your own lives.

▶ Add the principle to chart.

> Today when you read, choose a biography and think about the messages in the book. Bring the book when we meet so you can share.

Share

Following independent reading time, gather the students in small groups.

> In groups, talk about the messages that the author gave in the biography you read. Have a conversation about how one or more of those messages might apply to your own lives.

Extend the Lesson (Optional)

After assessing students' understanding, you might decide to extend the learning.

▶ As students write their own biographies, use the student-written biographies to repeat this minilesson and think about the messages. You can also use a shared writing biography to think about the messages and how they might apply to students' own lives.

The author of a biography gives an important message.

Title	Message
Magic Trash	Ordinary people can do extraordinary things.
ODD BOY OUT Young Albert Einstein	Everyone is different, and that's what makes us special.
Tree Lady	Significant things people accomplish can live on long after they're gone.
WANGARI MAATHAI	One person can do something to make the world and other people's lives better.
Nobody Owens the Sky	Dreams can come true through hard work and dedication.

Assessment

After you have taught the minilessons in this umbrella, observe students as they talk and write about their reading across instructional contexts: interactive read-aloud, independent reading and literacy work, guided reading, shared reading, and book club. Use *The Literacy Continuum* (Fountas and Pinnell 2017) to observe students' reading and writing behaviors across instructional contexts.

▶ What evidence do you have of new understandings related to biographies?

- Are students aware that a biography is the story of someone's life written by another person?
- Are they aware of the author's purpose in writing a book about someone's life?
- Do they notice that a biography is written in the same order that events occurred in someone's life?
- Can they talk about the message of a biography?
- Do they use vocabulary, such as *facts*, *time order*, *biography*, and *events*, to discuss biographies?

▶ In what other ways, beyond the scope of this umbrella, are students talking about nonfiction?

- Are students talking about other kinds of nonfiction books?

Use your observations to determine the next umbrella you will teach. You may also consult Minilessons Across the Year (pp. 55-57) for guidance.

Read and Revise

After completing the steps in the genre study process, help students read and revise their definition of the genre based on their new understandings.

▶ **Before:** A biography is the story of all or part of a real person's life, written by someone else.

▶ **After:** A biography is the story of all or part of a real person's life, written by someone else, and gives an important message.

Reader's Notebook

When this umbrella is complete, provide a copy of the minilesson principles (see resources.fountasandpinnell.com) for students to glue in the reader's notebook (in the Minilessons section if using *Reader's Notebook: Intermediate* [Fountas and Pinnell 2011]), so they can refer to the information as needed.

Minilessons in This Umbrella

RML1 Sometimes nonfiction authors tell information in time order like a story.

RML2 Sometimes nonfiction authors tell about something that always happens in the same order.

RML3 Sometimes nonfiction authors group information that goes together.

RML4 Sometimes nonfiction authors use questions and answers.

RML5 Sometimes nonfiction authors use bulleted or numbered lists to give information.

Before Teaching Umbrella 13 Minilessons

Read and discuss a variety of high-quality, engaging nonfiction picture books that are organized in different ways. Use the following texts from the *Fountas & Pinnell Classroom™ Interactive Read-Aloud Collection* and *Shared Reading Collection* or choose appropriate books from your classroom library.

Interactive Read-Aloud Collection

Sharing Our World: Animals

Moon Bear by Brenda Z. Guiberson

Ape by Martin Jenkins

A Friend for Lakota by Jim and Jamie Dutcher

Series Study: Dianna Hutts Aston and Sylvia Long

A Seed Is Sleepy

A Butterfly Is Patient

The Passage of Time

Our Seasons by Grace Lin and Ranida T. McKneally

Genre Study: Biography

Magic Trash by J. H. Shapiro

Odd Boy Out by Don Brown

Shared Reading Collection

From Flower to Honey by June Schwartz

From Beans to Chocolate by June Schwartz

Wolf Pack by Annette Bay Pimentel

Trapped in Tar by Hannah Cales

Exploring Underground by Louis Petrone

As you read aloud and enjoy these texts together, help students notice the different ways that authors organize information.

Animals

Dianna Hutts Aston

Passage of Time

Biography

Shared Reading

Reading Minilesson Principle
Sometimes nonfiction authors tell information in time order like a story.

Noticing How Authors Choose to Organize Nonfiction

You Will Need

- two or three familiar narrative nonfiction books (including at least one biography), such as the following:
  - *Magic Trash* by J. H. Shapiro, from Text Set: Genre Study: Biography
  - *A Friend for Lakota* by Jim and Jamie Dutcher, from Text Set: Animals
  - *Odd Boy Out* by Don Brown, from Text Set: Biography
- chart paper and markers

Academic Language / Important Vocabulary

- nonfiction
- author
- organize
- information
- narrative
- time order

Continuum Connection

- Identify the organization of a text: e.g. chronological sequence, temporal and established sequence, categories (p. 53)
- Notice a nonfiction writer's use of narrative text structure in biography and narrative nonfiction (p. 53)
- Understand that a nonfiction text can be expository or narrative in structure (p. 53)

Goal

Notice when an author uses a narrative text structure and tells information in chronological order.

Rationale

Some nonfiction authors choose to convey information in time order: biographies are a good example of this. When you teach students that some nonfiction books have a narrative text structure, they understand that, though such a book may seem like a story, it is still nonfiction. They also learn that nonfiction authors must make decisions about how best to convey information.

Assess Learning

Observe students when they read and talk about nonfiction books. Notice if there is evidence of new learning based on the goal of this minilesson.

- Can students identify the chronological sequence of events in a narrative nonfiction book?
- Do they use vocabulary such as *nonfiction*, *author*, *organize*, *information*, *narrative*, and *time order* to talk about nonfiction?

Minilesson

To help students think about the minilesson principle, use familiar nonfiction texts to provide an inquiry-based lesson about the organization of nonfiction text. Here is an example.

- Show the cover *Magic Trash* and read the title.

  Let's think about how the author of this book, J. H. Shapiro, tells information about Tyree Guyton's life.

- Reread the first two pages of the book.

  What happens at the beginning of this book?

  How old is Tyree Guyton in this part?

- Reread pages 12–13.

  What do you notice about Tyree in this part of the book? How old is he now?

- Reread the last three pages.

  What do you notice about Tyree at the end of the book?

  How do you think J. H. Shapiro decided what information to write at the beginning, middle, and end of her book? How did she organize the information?

▶ Record students' responses on chart paper. Then show the cover of *A Friend for Lakota*. Reread pages 5–12.

> What happens to the wolves in the pages I read? What happens first? What happens next?

▶ Record students' responses on the chart.

Have a Try

Invite the students to talk with a partner about a book's organization.

▶ Read pages 1–6 of *Odd Boy Out*.

> What do you notice about the order of the information in this book? Turn and talk to your partner about what you think.

▶ After students turn and talk, ask a few to share their responses. Record their responses on the chart.

Summarize and Apply

Summarize the learning and remind students to notice the organization of nonfiction books.

> When nonfiction authors tell information in time order, or in the order that it happens, the writing is called a narrative. This can make nonfiction books seem like stories, but they are not because they tell true facts and information.

▶ Write the principle at the top of the chart.

> Choose a nonfiction book today. As you read, notice how the author organized the information. Bring your book to share when we come back together.

Share

Following independent reading time, gather students together in the meeting area to talk about their reading.

> Raise your hand if your book is organized in time order. What happens at the beginning, middle, and end?

Extend the Lesson (Optional)

After assessing students' understanding, you might decide to extend the learning.

▶ **Writing About Reading** Have students make a timeline of the events in a narrative nonfiction book.

Sometimes nonfiction authors tell information in time order like a story.	
Magic Trash	• young child at beginning • then older child, teenager • adult at end
A Friend for Lakota	• Lakota and Kamots grow • three new wolves join them and find their positions in the family • wolves jump on top of Lakota at end
Odd Boy Out	• born at beginning • then grows bigger • is three when his sister is born • prepares for school at end

Section 2: Literary Analysis

Reading Minilesson Principle

Sometimes nonfiction authors tell about something that always happens in the same order.

Noticing How Authors Choose to Organize Nonfiction

You Will Need

- two or three familiar nonfiction books that describe something that always happens in the same order (life cycles, seasons, etc.), such as the following:
  - *A Seed Is Sleepy*, from Text Set: Dianna Hutts Aston
  - *Our Seasons* by Grace Lin and Ranida T. McKneally, from Text Set: Passage of Time
  - *A Butterfly Is Patient*, from Text Set: Dianna Hutts Aston
- chart paper and markers

Academic Language / Important Vocabulary

- nonfiction
- author
- organize
- order

Continuum Connection

- Identify the organization of a text: e.g., chronological sequence, temporal and established sequence, categories (p. 53)

Goal

Understand that a writer can tell about something that always happens in the same order (e.g., the seasons, life cycles, etc.).

Rationale

Some nonfiction books are about something that always happens in the same order, such as the seasons or the water cycle. This is called temporal sequence. When authors choose to write about a regularly occurring cycle, the order is determined for them. When students recognize this, they understand how the book will go.

Assess Learning

Observe students when they read and talk about nonfiction books. Notice if there is evidence of new learning based on the goal of this minilesson.

- Do students notice when a nonfiction author is describing something that always happens in the same order?
- Do they use vocabulary such as *nonfiction, author, organize,* and *order*?

Minilesson

To help students think about the minilesson principle, use familiar nonfiction texts to provide an inquiry-based lesson about the organization of nonfiction text. Here is an example.

- Show the cover of *A Seed Is Sleepy*. Read pages 21–28.

  Think about what you learned about seeds from these pages. What happens to a seed first? What happens next? What happens after that? What is the last thing that happens?

- Record students' responses on chart paper.

  What do you notice about how the author, Dianna Hutts Aston, tells information about a seed's life? In what order does she tell the information?

  The author of this book is telling about something that always happens in the same order.

- Show the cover of *Our Seasons*. Read pages 3–4, 9–10, 15–16, and 21–22.

  What do you notice about how the authors give information about the seasons in this book? In what order do they write about the seasons?

- Record students' responses on the chart.

  Why do you think they write about autumn, winter, spring, and summer in that order?

  The seasons always happen in the same order.

Have a Try

Invite the students to talk with a partner about the sequence of events in a nonfiction book.

> Show the cover of *A Butterfly Is Patient* and read the title. Read pages 1–6.

> > Turn and talk to your partner about how the author organized the information about butterflies.

> After students turn and talk, ask a few to share their thinking. Record their responses on the chart.

Summarize and Apply

Summarize the learning and remind students to think about the organization of nonfiction books.

> > What did you notice about how the authors organized the information in the nonfiction books we read today?

> Write the principle at the top of the chart.

> > Choose a nonfiction book to read today. As you read, notice how the author organized the information. Bring your book to share when we come back together.

Share

Following independent reading time, gather students together in the meeting area to talk about their reading.

> > Raise your hand if you read a book about something that always happens in the same order. What happens in your book?

Extend the Lesson (Optional)

After assessing students' understanding, you might decide to extend the learning.

> When your students study something that always happens in the same order (e.g., life cycles), have them write about the topic to show the sequence of events.

> **Writing About Reading** Have students make a timeline or life-cycle diagram of the events in a nonfiction book.

Sometimes nonfiction authors tell about something that always happens in the same order.

RML3

LA.U13.RML3

Reading Minilesson Principle
Sometimes nonfiction authors group information that goes together.

Noticing How Authors Choose to Organize Nonfiction

You Will Need

- a familiar nonfiction book that is organized by subtopic, such as *Ape* by Martin Jenkins, from Text Set: Animals
- chart paper prepared with a blank outline of a three-level organizational chart
- markers

Academic Language / Important Vocabulary

- nonfiction
- author
- organize
- fact
- information
- topic

Continuum Connection

- Identify the organization of a text: e.g. chronological sequence, temporal and established sequence, categories (p. 53)
- Understand that a nonfiction text can be expository or narrative in structure (p. 53)
- Notice that a nonfiction writer puts together information related to the same topic or subtopic (category) (p. 53)

Goal

Notice when an author puts together information in categories.

Rationale

Authors who write about topics that have many details group the details together logically, sometimes in a chapter or under a heading. When students notice this information, they are better equipped to learn about the topic. Recognizing this kind of organization will help them when they write their own nonfiction texts.

Assess Learning

Observe students when they read and talk about nonfiction books. Notice if there is evidence of new learning based on the goal of this minilesson.

- ❯ Do students notice when a nonfiction book is organized by category or subtopic and identify related details?
- ❯ Do they use vocabulary such as *nonfiction, author, organize, fact, information,* and *topic*?

Minilesson

To help students think about the minilesson principle, use familiar nonfiction texts to provide an inquiry-based lesson about the organization of nonfiction text. Here is an example.

> As I reread a few pages from this book, listen very carefully and think about what information you are learning.

- ❯ Reread pages 10–15.

  > What facts did you learn from these pages?

- ❯ Write students' responses in the bottom row of the organizational chart.

  > What do you notice about all these facts? What do they all have in common?

  > All these facts are about orangutans. The author grouped all his facts about orangutans together in one part of the book.

- ❯ Write *Orangutans* above the facts, in the second row of the chart.
- ❯ Show pages 8–9.

  > What do you notice about these pages?

  > The author wrote the heading *Orangutan* here to let you know that you're going to read about orangutans. Let's take a look at another part of the book.

- ❯ Repeat the process with facts about chimpanzees on pages 18–24.

Have a Try

Invite the students to talk with a partner about another section of the book.

▸ Reread pages 29–32.

Look at the chart. What does all this information have in common? Turn and talk to your partner about that.

▸ Ask a few pairs to share their responses and record the title (*Apes*) on the chart.

Summarize and Apply

Summarize the learning and remind students to notice the organization of nonfiction books.

The topic of this book is apes, but the author divided the facts into categories. Each section of the book is about a different kind of ape. He put together information that goes together.

▸ Write the principle at the top of the chart.

Why do you think nonfiction authors group together information that goes together?

Choose a nonfiction book to read today. As you read, notice if the author groups information that goes together. Bring your book to share when we come back together.

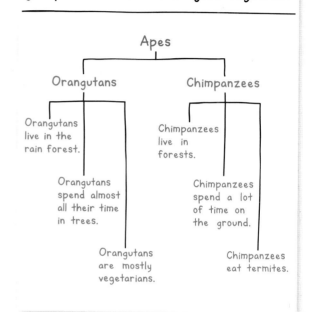

Share

Following independent reading time, gather students together in the meeting area to talk about their reading.

Who would like to share a page or a section in your book that shows how the author chose to organize the information? Tell us about the information on the page.

Extend the Lesson (Optional)

After assessing students' understanding, you might decide to extend the learning.

▸ During interactive read-aloud or guided reading, point out indicators of a book's organization, such as chapter titles and headings.

▸ **Writing About Reading** Have students use a graphic organizer to show how an author organized information about a topic into subtopics (see also Umbrella 14: Thinking About the Topic in Nonfiction Books, found in this section).

Section 2: Literary Analysis

RML4

LA.U13.RML4

Reading Minilesson Principle
Sometimes nonfiction authors use questions and answers.

Noticing How Authors Choose to Organize Nonfiction

You Will Need

- two or three familiar nonfiction books that have a question-and-answer structure, such as the following:
  - *From Flower to Honey* by June Schwartz, from *Shared Reading Collection*
  - *Moon Bear* by Brenda Z. Guiberson, from Text Set: Animals
  - *From Beans to Chocolate* by June Schwartz, from *Shared Reading Collection*
- chart paper and markers

Academic Language / Important Vocabulary

- nonfiction
- author
- organize
- question
- answer

Continuum Connection

- Notice when a writer uses a question-and-answer structure [p. 53]

Goal

Notice when an author uses a question-and-answer structure.

Rationale

Authors use a question-answer structure when they want to get their readers thinking about a topic. When students notice this structure, they know what to expect from the book and are therefore better able to comprehend the book's message and information.

Assess Learning

Observe students when they read and talk about nonfiction books. Notice if there is evidence of new learning based on the goal of this minilesson.

- ▶ Do students notice when a writer uses a question-and-answer structure?
- ▶ Do they use vocabulary such as *nonfiction*, *author*, *organize*, *question*, and *answer* when they talk about nonfiction?

Minilesson

To help students think about the minilesson principle, use familiar nonfiction texts to provide an inquiry-based lesson about the organization of nonfiction text. Here is an example.

- ▶ Show the cover of *From Flower to Honey* and read the title. Reread page 2. Point to the question at the bottom of the page.

    What do you notice about this part of the page?

    Where do you think you can find the answer to this question?

- ▶ Reread the first line on page 4 ("At the Store").

    What do you notice?

- ▶ Write the question and answer on chart paper.

- ▶ Reread the rest of page 4.

    Where is there a question on this page?

- ▶ Show the cover of *Moon Bear* and read the title. Reread the first three pages of text.

    What do you notice about how the author, Brenda Z. Guiberson, organizes information in this book?

    What questions and answers did you hear?

- ▶ Record students' responses on the chart.

Have a Try

Invite the students to talk with a partner about the organization of a nonfiction book.

▶ Show the cover of *From Beans to Chocolate*.

Listen carefully as I read and notice how the author organized the information.

▶ Reread pages 2–6.

Turn and talk to your partner about how the author chose to organize the information in this book.

▶ Ask a few students to share their thinking.

What questions and answers did you hear?

▶ Record responses on the chart.

Summarize and Apply

Summarize the learning and remind students to notice how nonfiction books are organized.

What did you notice about how the nonfiction books we looked at today were organized?

▶ Write the principle at the top of the chart.

Choose a nonfiction book to read today. As you read, notice how the writer organized the information. Bring your book to share when we come back together.

Share

Following independent reading time, gather students together in the meeting area to talk about their reading.

Raise your hand if the writer of the book you read today used questions and answers. Tell an example of a question and answer from your book.

Extend the Lesson (Optional)

After assessing students' understanding, you might decide to extend the learning.

▶ Have students write their own nonfiction books with a question-and-answer structure. They could, for example, write biographical books using this type of structure (e.g., "What is _____'s favorite color? Where was _____ born?").

▶ **Writing About Reading** Have students use a question-and-answer structure to summarize what they learned from a particular nonfiction book.

Sometimes nonfiction authors use questions and answers.

Book	Question	Answer
From Flower to HONEY	But where does Jayden get the honey?	At the store
Moon Bear	Who claws the tree trunks in the rhododendrom forest?	Cautious moon bear, marking her territory
From Beans to Chocolate	But how are the chocolates made into different shapes?	In molds

Reading Minilesson Principle
Sometimes nonfiction authors use bulleted or numbered lists to give information.

You Will Need

▶ two or three familiar nonfiction books that contain bulleted or numbered lists, such as the following from *Shared Reading Collection*:

- *Exploring Underground* by Louis Petrone
- *Trapped in Tar* by Hannah Cales
- *Wolf Pack* by Annette Bay Pimentel

▶ chart paper and markers

Academic Language / Important Vocabulary

▶ nonfiction
▶ author
▶ information
▶ bulleted
▶ numbered
▶ list

Continuum Connection

▶ Be aware when the teacher is reading bulleted or numbered lists (p. 53)

Goal

Notice when an author uses a bulleted or numbered list.

Rationale

Authors use bulleted or numbered lists to make important information stand out or to present information in a more easily understandable way. When you teach students to notice bulleted or numbered lists, they learn that the information in the lists is important to notice.

Assess Learning

Observe students when they read and talk about nonfiction books. Notice if there is evidence of new learning based on the goal of this minilesson.

▶ Do students understand why nonfiction authors sometimes use lists?

▶ Do they use vocabulary such as *nonfiction, author, information, bulleted, numbered,* and *list*?

Minilesson

To help students think about the minilesson principle, use familiar nonfiction texts to provide an inquiry-based lesson about the organization of nonfiction texts. Here is an example.

▶ Show the cover of *Exploring Underground* and read the title. Point to the list at the bottom of the page.

> What do you notice about this part of the page? How does the author, Louis Petrone, tell the information about caves here?

> This is a list. A list shows several pieces of information, each on its own line. This is a special kind of list called a bulleted list. The dots at the beginning of each line are called bullets.

> Why do you think the author used a list to tell this information instead of sentences and paragraphs?

▶ Show the cover of *Trapped in Tar* and read the title. Display page 15 and read the text aloud, pointing to each line as you read it.

> What do you notice about the facts about each animal? How does the author tell them?

> Why do you think the author used bulleted lists to tell these facts?

Have a Try

Invite the students to talk with a partner about bulleted or numbered lists in a nonfiction book.

▶ Show the cover of *Wolf Pack* and read the title. Display page 7 and read the text aloud.

> Turn and talk to your partner about the author's decision to show the information this way.

▶ Ask a few students to share their thinking.

> Numbered lists use a number instead of a bullet at the beginning of each line to show the order or importance of the information. Let's make a numbered list of what you do in the morning.

▶ Record responses on the chart.

Summarize and Apply

Summarize the learning and remind students to notice bulleted or numbered lists in nonfiction books.

> What did you notice about the nonfiction books we looked at today?

▶ Make a bulleted list of reasons authors use lists. Then write the principle at the top.

> Choose a nonfiction book to read today. Notice if there are lists, and be sure to read them. Bring your book to share when we come back together.

Share

Following independent reading time, gather students together in the meeting area to talk about their reading.

> Raise your hand if you found a bulleted or numbered list in the book you read today.

> What information was in the list or lists in your book?

Extend the Lesson (Optional)

After assessing students' understanding, you might decide to extend the learning.

▶ Teach students how to make lists in a reader's notebook (see Umbrella 2: Using a Reader's Notebook in Section Four: Writing About Reading).

▶ **Writing About Reading** Have students make a bulleted or numbered list of things they learned from a nonfiction book.

Sometimes nonfiction authors use bulleted or numbered lists to give information.

My Morning

1. Wash my face and hands.
2. Brush my teeth and hair.
3. Eat breakfast.
4. Go to school.

Why do authors use lists?

- to make it easier to read
- to make it easier to remember important information
- to tell several facts about the same topic
- to make the page look more interesting

Assessment

After you have taught the minilessons in this umbrella, observe students as they talk about their reading across instructional contexts: interactive read-aloud, independent reading and literacy work, guided reading, shared reading, and book club. Use *The Literacy Continuum* (Fountas and Pinnell 2017) to observe students' reading behaviors across instructional contexts.

▶ What evidence do you have of new understandings related to organizational structures in nonfiction?

  • Are students able to identify organizational structures of nonfiction (e.g., chronological, temporal, question and answer)?

  • Do they notice when related facts are grouped together?

  • Are they able to explain the purpose of bulleted and numbered lists?

  • Do they use vocabulary such as *nonfiction, sequence,* and *organize* when talking about how nonfiction is organized?

▶ In what other ways, beyond the scope of this umbrella, are they thinking and talking about nonfiction books?

  • Have they noticed that there are different types of nonfiction books (e.g., biography, informational)?

  • Are they noticing and talking about illustrations and graphics in nonfiction books?

  • Are they noticing text features, such as headings and tables of contents?

Use your observations to determine the next umbrella you will teach. You may also consult Minilessons Across the Year (pp. 55-57) for guidance.

Link to Writing

After teaching the minilessons in this umbrella, help students link the new learning to their own writing:

▶ Give students various opportunities to write their own nonfiction texts throughout the school year. Remind them of the different ways to organize nonfiction and discuss how to choose the most appropriate organizational structure for the topic.

Reader's Notebook

When this umbrella is complete, provide a copy of the minilesson principles (see resources.fountasandpinnell.com) for students to glue in the reader's notebook (in the Minilessons section if using *Reader's Notebook: Intermediate* [Fountas and Pinnell 2011]), so they can refer to the information as needed.

Minilessons in This Umbrella

RML1 Writers have opinions about the topics they write about.

RML2 Think about why the topic of the book is important.

RML3 Think about what you know about a topic before you read and what you learned after you read.

RML4 Sometimes authors divide a topic into smaller topics.

RML5 You can learn about the same topic from several nonfiction books.

RML6 Think about the quality and accuracy of the nonfiction books you read.

Before Teaching Umbrella 14 Minilessons

Most minilessons in this book require that students have read, enjoyed, and discussed the books used as examples. However, RML3 is an exception because it uses a book (*Our Seasons*) that students have not yet read. For all other minilessons, read and discuss engaging, high-quality nonfiction picture books that focus on a single topic. Use the following texts from the *Fountas & Pinnell Classroom™ Interactive Read-Aloud Collection* and *Shared Reading Collection* or choose appropriate nonfiction books from your classroom library.

Interactive Read-Aloud Collection

Sharing Our World: Animals

I Love Guinea Pigs by Dick King-Smith

Ape by Martin Jenkins

A Friend for Lakota by Jim and Jamie Dutcher

Genre Study: Expository Nonfiction

Bats! by Laurence Pringle

Tornadoes! by Gail Gibbons

Shell, Beak, Tusk by Bridget Heos

The Passage of Time

Our Seasons by Grace Lin and Ranida T. McKneally

Shared Reading Collection

Wolf Pack by Annette Bay Pimentel

As you read aloud and enjoy these texts together, help students

- think about why the topic of each book is important,
- infer the author's attitude toward the topic,
- discuss what they learned from the book,
- notice when a book is organized by subtopic,
- notice when two or more books are about the same topic, and
- express opinions about nonfiction books.

Animals

A Friend for Lakota by Jim and Jamie Dutcher

Expository Nonfiction

Passage of Time

Shared Reading Collection

Section 2: Literary Analysis

Reading Minilesson Principle
Writers have opinions about the topics they write about.

You Will Need

- two or three familiar nonfiction books that reveal clues about the author's opinion about the topic, such as the following:
  - *I Love Guinea Pigs* by Dick King-Smith, from Text Set: Animals
  - *Ape* by Martin Jenkins, from Text Set: Animals
  - *Bats!* by Laurence Pringle, from Text Set: Expository Nonfiction
- chart paper and markers

Academic Language / Important Vocabulary

- nonfiction
- author
- topic
- opinion

Continuum Connection

- Use evidence from the text to support statements about the text (p. 53)
- Infer the writer's attitude toward a topic (p. 54)

Goal

Infer the author's attitude toward the topic of a nonfiction book.

Rationale

When students notice or make inferences about the author's opinion about a topic, they begin to understand that the author's feelings about the topic influence how the book is written. Eventually they will come to the understanding that, although nonfiction books are based in fact, they are not completely objective.

Assess Learning

Observe students when they read and talk about nonfiction books. Notice if there is evidence of new learning based on the goal of this minilesson.

- ▶ Do students make inferences about the author's opinion about the topic?
- ▶ Do they support their inferences with evidence from the text?
- ▶ Do they use academic vocabulary such as *nonfiction*, *author*, *topic*, and *opinion*?

Minilesson

To help students think about the minilesson principle, use familiar nonfiction texts to provide an inquiry-based lesson. Here is an example.

- ▶ Show the cover of *I Love Guinea Pigs* and read the title.

    What is the topic of this book?

    As I read a couple of pages from this book, think about how the author, Dick King-Smith, feels about guinea pigs.

- ▶ Read pages 5–6.

    How does the author feel about guinea pigs? What is his opinion?

    How do you know?

- ▶ Record students' responses on chart paper.

- ▶ Show the cover of *Ape* and read the title.

    Now I'm going to read a couple of pages from this book. As I read, think about the author's opinion about the topic.

- ▶ Read pages 42–43.

    What is the topic of this book?

    How do you think the author feels about apes? What is his opinion?

    How can you tell?

- ▶ Record students' responses on the chart.

Have a Try

Invite the students to talk with a partner about how an author feels toward a topic.

▸ Show the cover of *Bats!* and then read page 4.

Turn and talk to your partner about what the author thinks about bats. Be sure to explain how you know.

▸ Ask a few students to share their thinking, and record their responses on the chart.

Summarize and Apply

Summarize the learning and remind students to think about the author's opinion when they read nonfiction.

You noticed that nonfiction authors have opinions about the topics they choose.

▸ Write the principle at the top of the chart.

Choose a nonfiction book to read today. As you read, think about the author's opinion of the book's topic. Be ready to share your thinking when we come back together.

Share

Following independent reading time, gather students in pairs in the meeting area to talk about their reading.

Turn and talk to your partner about the nonfiction book you read today. Tell what you think is the author's opinion about the topic of the book, and be sure to explain how you know.

Extend the Lesson (Optional)

After assessing students' understanding, you might decide to extend the learning.

▸ Ensure that students understand the difference between facts and opinions. Explain that a fact can be proven to be true, while an opinion cannot, although it can be supported by evidence. Teach students how to check the accuracy of facts (see RML6 in this umbrella for suggestions on how to do so).

▸ When students write their own nonfiction texts, encourage them to think about their opinion about the topic. Tell them that nonfiction texts should mostly contain facts but that it is okay to occasionally share their opinions. Explain that opinions should be supported by facts whenever possible, and teach students how to do so.

Writers have opinions about the topics they write about.

Book	Author's Opinion	How do you know?
I LOVE GUINEA PIGS	He loves guinea pigs and likes how they look.	• The title • "It's the way they look that I've always liked." • "I've had hundreds of guinea pigs."
Ape	Apes are smart. Apes are important and should be protected.	• "We're all smart, too." • "We're trying to protect them now."
BATS! STRANGE AND WONDERFUL	Bats are gentle, intelligent, fascinating, and important.	• "Bats are gentle, intelligent, and fascinating animals. Bats are among the most beneficial animals on earth."

Section 2: Literary Analysis

Reading Minilesson Principle
Think about why the topic of the book is important.

Thinking About the Topic in Nonfiction Books

You Will Need

▶ two or three familiar nonfiction books that reveal clues about why the topic of the book is important, such as the following:

- *Ape* by Martin Jenkins, from Text Set: Animals

- *Tornadoes!* by Gail Gibbons, from Text Set: Expository Nonfiction

- *Shell, Beak, Tusk* by Bridget Heos, from Text Set: Expository Nonfiction

▶ chart paper and markers

Academic Language / Important Vocabulary

▶ nonfiction
▶ topic
▶ author

Continuum Connection

▶ Give reasons (either text-based or from personal experience) to support thinking (p. 53)

▶ Infer the importance of a topic of a nonfiction text (p. 54)

Goal

Infer the importance of a topic of a nonfiction book.

Rationale

When students think about why the topic of a book is important, they understand why an author chose to write about the topic. The importance of the topic leads to an understanding of the author's message and of the significance of the content of the book for the world and/or their own lives.

Assess Learning

Observe students when they read and talk about nonfiction books. Notice if there is evidence of new learning based on the goal of this minilesson.

▶ Can students infer why the topic of a book is important?

▶ Can they support their inferences with evidence from the text?

▶ Do they use academic language, such as *nonfiction*, *topic*, and *author*?

Minilesson

To help students think about the minilesson principle, use familiar nonfiction texts to provide an inquiry-based lesson about the topic of a book. Here is an example.

▶ Show the cover of *Ape*.

  What is the topic of this book?

▶ Reread pages 42–43.

  Why do you think the author, Martin Jenkins, decided to write a book about apes? Why is this topic important?

▶ Record students' responses on chart paper. Then show the cover of *Tornadoes!*

  What is this book about?

▶ Reread pages 28–31.

  Why do you think Gail Gibbons wrote a book about tornadoes?

  Why is it important for people to learn about tornadoes?

▶ Record responses on the chart.

Have a Try

Invite the students to talk with a partner about why the topic of a book is important.

▶ Briefly review *Shell, Beak, Tusk* to remind students of its contents.

What did you learn from this book?

▶ Reread page 4.

Why are animal body parts like shells, beaks, and tusks important? What does the author want you to understand about them? Turn and talk to your partner about that.

▶ Ask a few students to share their thinking, and record their responses on the chart.

Summarize and Apply

Summarize the learning and remind students to think about why the topic of a nonfiction book is important.

When you think about why the topic of a book is important, you understand why the author chose to write about it. Authors write about topics that they think are important.

▶ Write the principle at the top of the chart.

Read a nonfiction book today and think about why the topic of the book is important. Be ready to share your thinking when we come back together.

Share

Following independent reading time, gather students in pairs in the meeting area to talk about their reading.

Turn and talk to your partner about the topic of the book you read today and why this topic is important.

Extend the Lesson (Optional)

After assessing students' understanding, you might decide to extend the learning.

▶ During interactive read-aloud, discuss the importance of a book's topic. Encourage students to connect the topic to the world and/or to their own lives.

▶ **Writing About Reading** Have students write in a reader's notebook about why the topic of a particular nonfiction book is important.

Think about why the topic of the book is important.

Book	Why is the topic important?
Ape	Because of things humans have done, there are not many apes left. It's important that we work hard to protect them.
Tornadoes	If people know about tornadoes, they will know how to stay safe if a tornado happens.
Shell Beak Tusk	Certain traits are important because they keep animals safe. Sometimes unrelated animals have similar traits, which helps explain how animals evolve.

Reading Minilesson Principle
Think about what you know about a topic before you read and what you learned after you read.

Thinking About the Topic in Nonfiction Books

You Will Need

- a nonfiction book about a familiar topic that your students have not already read, such as *Our Seasons* by Grace Lin and Ranida T. McKneally, from Text Set: Passage of Time
- chart paper and markers

Academic Language / Important Vocabulary

- nonfiction
- topic
- information

Continuum Connection

- Use background knowledge of content to understand nonfiction topics (p. 53)
- Understand and talk about both familiar topics and those that offer new and surprising information and ideas (p. 54)

Goal

Think about prior knowledge before reading nonfiction and newly acquired knowledge after reading.

Rationale

When students think about what they already know about a topic before reading, they are prepared to acquire new knowledge and make connections with their prior knowledge. When they think about what they learned after reading, they develop greater self-awareness as readers and learners and are more likely to retain their newly acquired knowledge.

Assess Learning

Observe students when they read and talk about nonfiction books. Notice if there is evidence of new learning based on the goal of this minilesson.

- Can students tell what they know about a topic before reading a nonfiction book?
- Can they talk about what they learned from a nonfiction book after reading?
- Do they use academic language, such as *nonfiction*, *topic*, and *information*?

Minilesson

To help students think about the minilesson principle, use a book that students have not yet read to provide an inquiry-based lesson about the topic of a book. Here is an example.

- Show the cover of *Our Seasons* and read the title and the authors' names.

  What do you think this book is going to be about?

  The topic of this book is the seasons. What do you know about the seasons?

- Make a list of students' responses on chart paper. If students need more guidance, prompt them with questions such as the following:

  - *How many seasons are there?*
  - *What are the seasons called?*
  - *How are the four seasons different?*
  - *Why do we have four different seasons?*

- Read aloud a short portion of the book (e.g., pages 1–8).

Have a Try

Invite the students to talk with a partner about what they learned from the book.

> Wow, this book has a lot of interesting information about the seasons! Turn and talk to your partner about what you learned about the seasons from this book.

▶ After students turn and talk, ask a few to share their thinking. Record their responses on the chart.

Summarize and Apply

Summarize the learning and remind students to think about what they know about a topic before reading and what they learned after reading.

> What is a good practice to do when you read a nonfiction book? Look at the chart for ideas.

▶ Write the principle at the top of the chart.

> Choose a nonfiction book to read today. Before you read, think about what you already know about the topic. After you read, think about what you learned. Be ready to share your thinking when we come back together.

Share

Following independent reading time, gather students in pairs in the meeting area to talk about their reading.

> Turn and talk to your partner about the nonfiction book you read today. Be sure to tell at least one thing you knew about the topic of your book before you read it and at least one thing you learned from reading the book.

Extend the Lesson (Optional)

After assessing students' understanding, you might decide to extend the learning.

▶ Encourage students to compare what they learned about a topic with what they already knew (or thought they knew) about the topic before reading. Do they know more about the topic after reading? Did they learn that something they thought was true is not true? Create a third column for listing what they are wondering about or still want to know.

▶ **Writing About Reading** In a reader's notebook, have students write questions that they have after reading a nonfiction book (see Umbrella 5: Writing About Nonfiction Books in a Reader's Notebook in Section Four: Writing About Reading).

Think about what you know about a topic before you read and what you learned after you read.

Book: Our Seasons
Topic: the seasons

Know	Learned
• 4 seasons	• The tilt of the Earth's axis toward or away from the sun causes seasons.
• winter, spring, summer, and autumn	
• winter colder than summer	• Wind is caused by a difference in air pressure.
• days get shorter	• Leaves change color when they stop making chlorophyll.
• days get longer	

Section 2: Literary Analysis

Reading Minilesson Principle
Sometimes authors divide a topic into smaller topics.

Thinking About the Topic in Nonfiction Books

You Will Need

- two or three familiar nonfiction books that are organized by subtopic, such as the following:
  - *Shell, Beak, Tusk* by Bridget Heos, from Text Set: Expository Nonfiction
  - *Ape* by Martin Jenkins, from Text Set: Animals
- chart paper prepared with two blank organizational charts
- markers

Academic Language / Important Vocabulary

- nonfiction
- author
- topic

Continuum Connection

- Understand that a writer is presenting related facts about a single topic [p. 54]
- Notice the topic of a nonfiction text and that subtopics are related to the main topic [p. 54]

Goal

Notice the main topic of a nonfiction text and subtopics.

Rationale

When students notice that nonfiction authors sometimes divide a topic into subtopics, they begin to understand that authors must make decisions about what information to present and how to present it.

Assess Learning

Observe students when they read and talk about nonfiction books. Notice if there is evidence of new learning based on the goal of this minilesson.

- Do students notice when the topic of a book is divided into subtopics?
- Can they identify the topic and subtopics in a nonfiction book?
- Do they use academic language, such as *nonfiction*, *author*, and *topic*?

Minilesson

To help students think about the minilesson principle, use familiar nonfiction texts to provide an inquiry-based lesson about subtopics. Here is an example.

- Briefly review *Shell, Beak, Tusk* to remind students of the book's content.

  What topic did you learn about from this book?

- Write *Shared Animal Traits* in the top row of the first organizational chart.

- Reread pages 6–7.

  What is this part of the book about?

  The whole book is about shared animal traits, but this part is about one specific trait—spines.

- Write the word *Spines* in the second row of the organizational chart.

- Continue in a similar manner with pages 8–9 (shells) and 10–11 (tall ears).

  The author, Bridget Heos, divided the topic of her book into smaller topics. Although the whole book is about shared animal traits, each section is about a specific trait.

Have a Try

Invite the students to talk with a partner about subtopics in a different book.

▶ Briefly review *Ape* to remind students of its content.

> Turn and talk to your partner about how the author of this book divided the topic of the book into smaller topics.

▶ After students turn and talk, ask a few students to share their thinking and use their responses in an organizational chart for *Ape*.

Summarize and Apply

Summarize the learning and remind students to notice when the topic of a nonfiction book is divided into smaller topics.

> What did you notice about how authors sometimes present information in a nonfiction book? Look at the chart to remember.

▶ Write the principle at the top of the chart.

> Choose a nonfiction book to read today. As you read, notice whether the author divides the topic of the book into smaller topics. Be ready to share your thinking when we come back together.

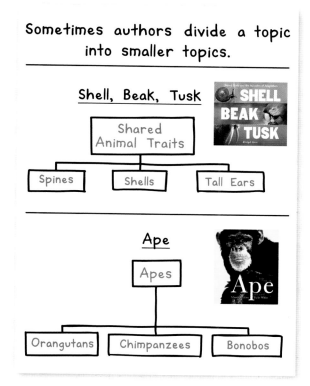

Share

Following independent reading time, gather students together in the meeting area to talk about their reading.

> Raise your hand if you read a nonfiction book that has a topic that is divided into smaller topics.

> Tell us the topic and how the author divided it into smaller topics.

Extend the Lesson (Optional)

After assessing students' understanding, you might decide to extend the learning.

▶ During interactive read-aloud, point out that some authors use headings to organize information. Often the headings show the smaller topics.

▶ **Writing About Reading** Have students use an organizational chart to show how an author divided a topic into subtopics.

RML5
LA.U14.RML5

Reading Minilesson Principle
You can learn about the same topic from several nonfiction books.

Thinking About the Topic in Nonfiction Books

You Will Need

- two familiar nonfiction books that are about the same topic, such as the following:
  - *A Friend for Lakota* by Jim and Jamie Dutcher, from Text Set: Animals
  - *Wolf Pack* by Annette Bay Pimentel, from *Shared Reading Collection*
- chart paper and markers
- a basket that contains several pairs of books about the same topic

Academic Language / Important Vocabulary

- nonfiction
- author
- topic

Continuum Connection

- Think across nonfiction texts to construct knowledge of a topic (p. 54)

Goal

Think across nonfiction texts to construct knowledge of a topic.

Rationale

When students realize that they can learn about the same topic from more than one nonfiction book, they begin to notice and think about the different ways that authors write about the same topic. They learn that authors choose which information to include and which to leave out and also how to organize the information.

Assess Learning

Observe students when they read and talk about nonfiction books. Notice if there is evidence of new learning based on the goal of this minilesson.

- Do students understand that they can learn about the same topic from more than one nonfiction book?
- Can they identify what they learned from different sources about the same topic?
- Do they use academic language, such as *nonfiction, author,* and *topic*?

Minilesson

To help students think about the minilesson principle, use familiar nonfiction texts to provide an inquiry-based lesson about learning about the same topic from multiple sources. Here is an example.

- Show the cover of *A Friend for Lakota* and briefly review the book. Reread a few pages.

  What is the topic of this book?

  What did you learn about wolves from this book?

- Make a list of students' responses on chart paper.
- Show the cover of *Wolf Pack*. Reread a few pages.

  What do you notice about this book and *A Friend for Lakota*? What is the same about them?

  Both these books are about the same topic. What did you learn about wolves from this book?

- Record students' responses in a separate list.

  You learned about the same topic from two different nonfiction books. You know a lot about wolves now!

Have a Try

Invite the students to talk with a partner about why it is important to read several books about the same topic.

> Turn and talk to your partner about why it's a good idea to read several books about the same topic. How can this help you learn about the topic?

▶ After students turn and talk, ask a few students to share their thinking with the class.

Summarize and Apply

Summarize the learning and remind students to read different nonfiction books about the same topic.

> Today you thought about why it's important to read different nonfiction books about the same topic. When you want to learn about a topic, it's a good idea to read more than one book about it so you can compare them and learn even more.

▶ Write the principle at the top of the chart.

▶ Provide students with a basket that contains several pairs of books about the same topic.

> If you want to learn about one of these topics, choose a pair of books from this basket. As you read two books about the same topic, notice when information is the same or different.

Share

Following independent reading time, gather students together in the meeting area to talk about their reading.

> Raise your hand if you read two nonfiction books about the same topic today.

> Why was it helpful to read two books about the same topic?

Extend the Lesson (Optional)

After assessing students' understanding, you might decide to extend the learning.

▶ Teach students how to check the accuracy of facts in a nonfiction book using other sources of information on the same topic (see the next minilesson in this umbrella).

▶ **Writing About Reading** Help students use a Venn diagram (have students make their own or download a copy from resources.fountasandpinnell.com) to compare and contrast the information provided in two nonfiction books on the same topic.

You can learn about the same topic from several nonfiction books.

Topic: Wolves

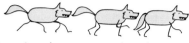

A Friend for Lakota	Wolf Pack
• Different wolves have different personalities.	• A wolf pack has two leaders.
• Wolves live in packs.	• Wolves live in many places around the world.
• Each wolf in a pack has a job to do.	• One wolf in a pack is the pupsitter.
• Wolves have friends.	• Wolf pups like to play. They also learn important things from play.
• Sometimes wolves bully other wolves.	

Section 2: Literary Analysis

Reading Minilesson Principle
Think about the quality and accuracy of the nonfiction books you read.

Thinking About the Topic in Nonfiction Books

You Will Need

- two familiar nonfiction books, such as the following:
  - *Bats!* by Laurence Pringle, from Text Set: Expository Nonfiction
  - *Tornadoes!* by Gail Gibbons, from Text Set: Expository Nonfiction
- another reliable source of information (book or website) about the topic of the first book you are using
- chart paper and markers

Academic Language / Important Vocabulary

- nonfiction
- quality
- accuracy
- opinion
- information

Continuum Connection

- Examine the quality or accuracy of the text, citing evidence for opinions (p. 54)

Goal

Examine the quality or accuracy of the text, citing evidence for opinions.

Rationale

When students learn how to examine the quality and accuracy of nonfiction texts, they begin to read with a critical eye. They understand that although nonfiction books are based in fact, they are not necessarily perfect sources of information. They therefore learn the importance of reading multiple sources of information to learn about a topic.

Assess Learning

Observe students when they read and talk about nonfiction books. Notice if there is evidence of new learning based on the goal of this minilesson.

- Do students understand that some nonfiction books may contain inaccurate information?
- Do they express their opinions about the quality of nonfiction texts and cite evidence for their opinions?
- Do they understand and use the terms *nonfiction, quality, accuracy, opinion,* and *information*?

Minilesson

To help students think about the minilesson principle, model examining the quality and accuracy of a familiar nonfiction book. Here is an example.

- Show the cover of *Bats!* and then reread page 5.

  I wonder if it's true that almost a thousand kinds of bats live on Earth and that forty-four different kinds of bats live in North America.

- Display another reliable source of information that contains information about the same topic. Explain how you know it is a good source of information.

  This website says that there are more than 1,300 species of bats and that forty-seven different kinds of bats live in the United States. That's a little different from what the book says, but pretty close. I am not sure which source is right. What did you notice about what I just did?

  When you think about the accuracy of information, you think about whether it's true or correct. You can use other books or websites to check.

  Even though I'm not sure if all the facts in this book are exactly accurate, I still think it's a high-quality book. The writing is interesting and enjoyable to read. The illustrations are very detailed and true to life.

  That is my opinion about the quality of this book. Quality is how well done something is. What did you notice about how I talked about the quality of this book?

Have a Try

Invite the students to talk with a partner about how to evaluate the accuracy and quality of a nonfiction book.

▶ Show the cover of *Tornadoes!* and some pages.

Turn and talk to your partner about how you could check the accuracy of the information in this book.

▶ Ask a few students to share. Make a list of responses on chart paper.

Now turn and talk about what you think of the quality of this book. Be sure to explain your reasons for your opinion.

▶ Ask a few students to share their thinking, and make a general list of the kinds of things they talk about.

Summarize and Apply

Summarize the learning and remind students to think about the quality and accuracy of the nonfiction books they read.

▶ Review the chart and add the principle at the top.

Choose a nonfiction book to read today. As you read, think about the quality and accuracy of the book. You can look at other books to find out if the information is accurate. Be ready to share your opinion about the quality and accuracy of your book when we come back together.

Share

Following independent reading time, gather students in pairs in the meeting area to talk about their reading.

Turn and talk to your partner about the quality and accuracy of the book you read. Explain the reasons for your opinions.

Extend the Lesson (Optional)

After assessing students' understanding, you might decide to extend the learning.

▶ Discuss how to determine if a website is a reliable source of information. Explain that web addresses that end in .edu or .gov are usually good sources of information. You may want to provide your students with a list of trustworthy websites about various topics.

▶ Explain that the date of the information is important. An author uses the latest avialble information, but later there might be new information that is more accurate.

Think about the quality and accuracy of the nonfiction books you read.

Accuracy	Quality
• Check the credentials of the writer. Check research the writer has done on the topic.	• Is the book well written?
• Find other books or websites about the topic.	• Is it interesting and enjoyable?
• Compare the information in the nonfiction book to the information in other books or on websites.	• Are the facts accurate?
	• Are the photographs or illustrations good?

Assessment

After you have taught the minilessons in this umbrella, observe students as they talk about their reading across instructional contexts: interactive read-aloud, independent reading and literacy work, guided reading, shared reading, and book club. Use *The Literacy Continuum* (Fountas and Pinnell 2017) to observe students' reading behaviors across instructional contexts.

▶ What evidence do you have of new understandings related to thinking about the topic in nonfiction books?

- Can students infer and talk about the author's opinion about the topic and why the topic is important?

- Do they think and talk about what they know about a topic before reading and what they learned after reading?

- What do they notice about the topic?

- What do they say about the quality and accuracy of the nonfiction books?

- Do they use the terms *opinion, topic, author, nonfiction, quality*, and *accuracy*?

▶ In what other ways, beyond the scope of this umbrella, are they thinking and talking about nonfiction books?

- Have they noticed that there are different types of nonfiction books?

- Are they noticing how nonfiction books are organized?

Use your observations to determine the next umbrella you will teach. You may also consult Minilessons Across the Year (pp. 55-57) for guidance.

Link to Writing

After teaching the minilessons in this umbrella, help students link the new learning to their own writing:

▶ Encourage students to think about their opinion and the importance of the topic before writing. Remind them to consider dividing the topic into subtopics. Emphasize the importance of including accurate information in nonfiction texts and help students find reliable sources of information.

Reader's Notebook

When this umbrella is complete, provide a copy of the minilesson principles (see resources.fountasandpinnell.com) for students to glue in the reader's notebook (in the Minilessons section if using *Reader's Notebook: Intermediate* [Fountas and Pinnell 2011]), so they can refer to the information as needed.

Minilessons in This Umbrella

RML1   Illustrators use art to show information about a topic.

RML2   Authors use labels and captions to tell important information about the illustrations.

RML3   Authors and illustrators use maps and legends to give information.

RML4   Authors and illustrators use diagrams and infographics to give information.

Before Teaching Umbrella 15 Minilessons

Read and discuss high-quality, engaging nonfiction picture books that have a variety of graphics, including illustrations (any art form, including photographs), maps, diagrams, and infographics. Use the following books from the *Fountas & Pinnell Classroom™ Interactive Read-Aloud Collection* text sets or choose nonfiction books from your classroom library.

Sharing Our World: Animals

Moon Bear by Brenda Z. Guiberson

Ape by Martin Jenkins

A Friend for Lakota by Jim and Jamie Dutcher

Series Study: Dianna Hutts Aston and Sylvia Long

A Seed Is Sleepy

A Butterfly Is Patient

The Passage of Time

Our Seasons by Grace Lin and Ranida T. McKneally

Author's Point of View

Almost Gone by Steve Jenkins

What's So Bad About Gasoline? by Anne Rockwell

As you read aloud and enjoy these texts together, help students

• notice and discuss illustrations,

• notice labels and captions on illustrations,

• notice maps and use them to obtain information, and

• understand information conveyed through diagrams and other infographics.

Animals

Dianna Hutts Aston

Passage of Time

Point of View

RML1
LA.U15.RML1

Reading Minilesson Principle
Illustrators use art to show information about a topic.

Learning Information from Illustrations/Graphics

You Will Need

- two or three familiar nonfiction books with illustrations or photographs, such as the following:
  - *A Seed Is Sleepy*, from Text Set: Dianna Hutts Aston
  - *A Friend for Lakota* by Jim and Jamie Dutcher, from Text Set: Animals
  - *What's So Bad About Gasoline?* by Anne Rockwell, from Text Set: Point of View
- chart paper and markers
- sticky notes

Academic Language / Important Vocabulary

- author
- illustrator
- information
- topic
- photograph
- illustration
- art
- graphics

Continuum Connection

- Understand that graphics provide important information (p. 55)

Goal

Understand that graphics provide important information.

Rationale

Graphics or art includes a variety of visuals that communicate information. Graphics include photographs or other media images. Images in nonfiction books communicate information just like the words, as they often give additional information and add to the reader's understanding of the topic.

Assess Learning

Observe students when they read and talk about nonfiction books. Notice if there is evidence of new learning based on the goal of this minilesson.

- Do students notice and talk about the illustrations in nonfiction books?
- Can they explain what they learned from the illustrations in a nonfiction book?
- Do they use vocabulary such as *author, illustrator, information, topic, photograph, art, graphics,* and *illustration*?

Minilesson

To help students think about the minilesson principle, use familiar nonfiction books to notice the images or art. Here is an example.

- Show the cover of *A Seed Is Sleepy*.

    You learned a lot about seeds and plants from this nonfiction book. Look and listen carefully as I reread a couple of pages from this book.

- Reread and display pages 11–12.

    What kind of art do you see on these pages?

- Point out that an illustrator made the drawings. Record this on a sticky note and have a student post it to the chart.

    Why are the graphics here? What do they show?

- Record students' responses on the chart. Then show some pages from *A Friend for Lakota*.

    What do you notice about the art in this book?

    This book has photographs that a person created.

- Reread and display pages 9–10.

    What do you notice about the wolves in this photograph? What does this photograph help you understand about wolves?

- Record responses as before.

Have a Try

Invite the students to talk with a partner about the art in a nonfiction book.

▶ Show the cover of *What's So Bad About Gasoline?* Then display and reread page 16.

Look carefully at the art on this page and think about what it shows. Turn and talk to your partner about what you learned from it.

▶ Ask a few students to share their thinking, and record their responses as before.

Summarize and Apply

Summarize the learning and remind students to look at and think about the art when they read nonfiction.

Why should you read the words *and* look at the art when you read a nonfiction book?

▶ Write the principle at the top of the chart.

Choose a nonfiction book to read today and remember to look carefully at the art. Be ready to talk about what you learned from the graphics when we come back together.

Share

Following independent reading time, gather students together in the meeting area to talk about their reading.

Who would like to share what she learned from the art in the nonfiction book you read today?

Extend the Lesson (Optional)

After assessing students' understanding, you might decide to extend the learning.

▶ Lead a discussion about why the author of a nonfiction book might choose to use photographs over illustrations or vice versa.

▶ When students write their own nonfiction texts, remind them to include illustrations.

▶ **Writing About Reading** Have students write in a reader's notebook about what they learned from the art in a nonfiction book.

Illustrators use art to show information about a topic.

Book	Type of Art	What the Art Shows
A Seed Is Sleepy	The illustrators made drawings.	What different plants and their seeds look like
A Friend for Lakota	The authors took photographs.	Wolves are fast runners
What's So Bad About Gasoline?	The illustrators made drawings.	How the distilling process works

Reading Minilesson Principle
Authors use labels and captions to tell important information about the illustrations.

Learning Information from Illustrations/Graphics

You Will Need

▸ two or three familiar nonfiction books with labeled or captioned illustrations or photographs, such as the following:

  • *A Butterfly Is Patient*, from Text Set: Dianna Hutts Aston

  • *Moon Bear* by Brenda Z. Guiberson, from Text Set: Animals

  • *Ape* by Martin Jenkins, from Text Set: Animals

▸ chart paper prepared with a three-column chart

▸ two sticky notes, one labeled *Caption* and one labeled *Label*

▸ markers

Academic Language / Important Vocabulary

▸ author

▸ information

▸ photograph

▸ illustration

▸ label

▸ caption

Continuum Connection

▸ Recognize and use information in a variety of graphics: e.g., photo and or drawing with label or caption, diagram, cutaway, map with legend, infographic (p. 55)

Goal

Recognize and use labels and captions to gain information from illustrations.

Rationale

Labels and captions provide important information about images, such as what is shown in the image, what the different parts of something are called, or where or by whom a photograph was taken. When students read labels and captions, they understand what is shown in the illustrations and learn more.

Assess Learning

Observe students when they read and talk about nonfiction books. Notice if there is evidence of new learning based on the goal of this minilesson.

▸ Do students notice when there are labels or captions on illustrations or photographs in nonfiction books?

▸ Do they understand the purpose of and difference between labels and captions?

▸ Do they use vocabulary such as *author, information, photograph, illustration, label,* and *caption*?

Minilesson

To help students think about the minilesson principle, use familiar nonfiction books to provide an inquiry-based lesson about captions and labels. Here is an example.

▸ Show the cover *of A Butterfly Is Patient* and pages 11–12.

  What do you see next to each butterfly or caterpillar?

▸ Point to and read aloud each label.

  How do the words help you learn more about butterflies?

▸ Record students' responses on the chart.

  These wor[...]ll you the name of each butterfly or caterpill[...]

▸ Have a studen[...] on the chart.

▸ Show the cov[...] o the author's note at the back of the book.

  What do y[...]aph?

▸ Point to and read each caption.

  What do these words tell you about the photographs?

▸ Record students' responses on the chart.

These words tell you the names of the bears and what they are doing. They are called captions. Captions are similar to labels, but they usually give more information than labels.

▸ Have a student place the sticky note for *Caption* on the chart.

Have a Try

Invite the students to talk with a partner about the labels or captions in a nonfiction book.

▸ Reread pages 29–31 of *Ape*. Point to the captions as you read them.

Turn and talk to your partner about what you learned from these words. Is this a label or a caption?

▸ After students turn and talk, ask a few to share their thinking, and record their responses on the chart.

Summarize and Apply

Summarize the learning and remind students to read the labels and captions.

▸ Review the chart and write the principle at the top.

Choose a nonfiction book to read today. Remember to read any labels or captions and think about what you are learning from them. Be ready to share what you learned when we come back together.

Share

Following independent reading time, gather students together to talk about their reading.

Raise your hand if you read a nonfiction book that has labels or captions.

What did you learn from them?

Extend the Lesson (Optional)

After assessing students' understanding, you might decide to extend the learning.

▸ When students write their own nonfiction books, encourage them to add labels and/or captions to the illustrations.

▸ **Writing About Reading** Have students write their own labels or captions for images in a book that does not have labels or captions.

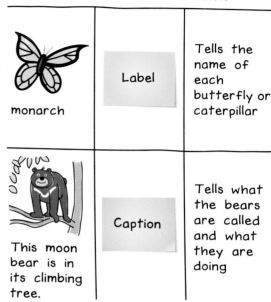

Authors use labels and captions to tell important information about the illustrations.

monarch	Label	Tells the name of each butterfly or caterpillar
This moon bear is in its climbing tree.	Caption	Tells what the bears are called and what they are doing

Reading Minilesson Principle

Authors and illustrators use maps and legends to give information.

Learning Information from Illustrations/Graphics

You Will Need

▸ two or three familiar nonfiction books that contain maps with legends, such as the following:

- *A Friend for Lakota* by Jim and Jamie Dutcher, from Text Set: Animals
- *Almost Gone* by Steve Jenkins, from Text Set: Point of View
- *Ape* by Martin Jenkins, from Text Set: Animals

▸ document camera (optional)

▸ chart paper and markers

▸ a basket of other nonfiction books that contain maps

Academic Language / Important Vocabulary

▸ map

▸ legend

Continuum Connection

▸ Recognize and use information in a variety of graphics: e.g., photo and or drawing with label or caption, diagram, cutaway, map with legend, infographic (p. 55)

Goal

Recognize and use maps and legends to gain information about a topic.

Rationale

When students know how to use maps and legends in nonfiction books, they are able to find geographic information and visualize the locations of places discussed in the text. This process helps them to better understand the content of the book.

Assess Learning

Observe students when they read and talk about nonfiction books. Notice if there is evidence of new learning based on the goal of this minilesson.

▸ Can students explain what a map is and what it is used for?

▸ Do they understand how to read maps and legends?

▸ Do they use vocabulary such as *map* and *legend*?

Minilesson

To help students think about the minilesson principle, use familiar nonfiction books to provide an inquiry-based lesson about maps and legends. Here is an example.

▸ Show the cover of *A Friend for Lakota* and the map at the end. Point to and read the label *Sawtooth Mts. (Lakota's home)*.

  What does this label tell you?

▸ Point to and read the words *Map Key* and *Area where wolves live*.

  What do you think this part of the map is for?

  A map legend helps you find information on the map. This legend says that the area where wolves live is shown in orange. Who would like to come up here and point to the orange area on the map?

▸ Show the cover of *Almost Gone* and then the map on the last two pages.

  What do you notice about the map on these pages?

  This map shows the whole world. What do you think the numbers on the map mean?

▸ Point to the first entry in the legend.

  It says the amur leopard is number one. Who would like to find the number one on the map?

▸ Repeat with a couple of other animals.

  What do the map and legend show about the animals in the book?

Have a Try

Invite the students to talk with a partner about a map and its legend.

▶ Show the cover of *Ape* and then open to the map on page 45. If possible, project the map. Read and point to all the labels and the legend.

> Turn and talk to your partner about what you notice about this map and what it teaches you.

▶ Ask a few students to share their responses.

Summarize and Apply

Summarize the learning and remind students to notice and read maps in nonfiction books.

> Why do you think authors put maps in nonfiction books?

> What is the purpose of the legends on maps? How do they help you?

▶ Record students' responses on chart paper and write the principle at the top.

▶ Provide students with a basket of nonfiction books that have maps.

> All the books in this basket have maps in them. You may want to choose a book from this basket when you read today. If so, be sure to look at, read, and think about the maps.

Share

Following independent reading time, gather students together in the meeting area to talk about their reading.

> Raise your hand if you read a nonfiction book that has maps.

> What did you learn from a map in your book?

Extend the Lesson (Optional)

After assessing students' understanding, you might decide to extend the learning.

▶ Have students create a map and legend of a familiar location.

▶ Hang a large world map on one wall of the classroom. Whenever you read aloud a book that takes place in, or is about, a specific place, mark it on the map.

Authors and illustrators use maps and legends to give information.

Maps . . .
- show where different places are.
- can show where certain animals live.
- help you understand the places in the book.
- show how far apart places are.

Legends . . .
- help you find where something is located on the map.

● Lakota's home

Section 2: Literary Analysis

RML 4
LA.U15.RML4

Reading Minilesson Principle
Authors and illustrators use diagrams and infographics to give information.

Learning Information from Illustrations/Graphics

You Will Need

- two or three familiar nonfiction books that contain diagrams or other infographics, such as the following:
  - *Our Seasons* by Grace Lin and Ranida T. McKneally, from Text Set: Passage of Time
  - *A Seed Is Sleepy*, from Text Set: Dianna Hutts Aston
  - *What's So Bad About Gasoline?* by Anne Rockwell, from Text Set: Point of View
- chart paper and markers
- two sticky notes labeled *Infographic*, one sticky note labeled *Diagram*

Academic Language / Important Vocabulary

- author
- illustrator
- information
- nonfiction
- diagram
- infographic

Continuum Connection

- Recognize and use information in a variety of graphics: e.g., photo and or drawing with label or caption, diagram, cutaway, map with legend, infographic (p. 55)

Goal

Recognize and use diagrams and infographics to gain information about a topic.

Rationale

Authors choose to use a diagram or infographic to convey information visually. These graphics enhance the information in the text. When students understand how to acquire information from diagrams and other infographics in nonfiction books, they are better able to understand the parts of something or how something works.

Assess Learning

Observe students when they read and talk about nonfiction books. Notice if there is evidence of new learning based on the goal of this minilesson.

- Can students explain what diagrams and infographics are and their purpose?
- Do they talk about what they learned from diagrams and infographics?
- Do they use academic vocabulary, such as *author, illustrator, information, nonfiction, diagram,* and *infographic*?

Minilesson

To help students think about the minilesson principle, use familiar nonfiction books to provide an inquiry-based lesson about diagrams and infographics. Here is an example.

- Show the cover of *Our Seasons* and read the title. Open the book to pages 1–2 and reread the text.

  What do you notice about the illustration on these pages?

- Point to the arrows.

  Why do you think there are arrows in this illustration?

  This is a special kind of illustration called a diagram. A diagram is a picture that shows how something works or the parts of something. What does the diagram help you understand?

- Have a student place the sticky note for *Diagram* and record students' responses on chart paper. Show the cover of *A Seed Is Sleepy*. Then display page 17. Point to and read aloud the words.

  What do you notice about this illustration?

  This is a special kind of illustration called an infographic. An infographic shows information using words and pictures. What information does this infographic show?

- Record students' responses as before.

Have a Try

Invite the students to talk with a partner about a diagram in a nonfiction book.

▶ Show the cover of *What's So Bad About Gasoline?* and then open to page 9. Point to and read each of the labels on the diagram.

Turn and talk to your partner about what you learn from this diagram.

▶ After students turn and talk, ask a few to share their thinking.

Summarize and Apply

Summarize the learning and remind students to read diagrams or infographics.

Why do some authors and illustrators put diagrams or infographics in their nonfiction books?

▶ Write the principle at the top of the chart.

Choose a nonfiction book to read today. As you read, notice if it has any diagrams or infographics. If so, be sure to read them and think about what you are learning from them.

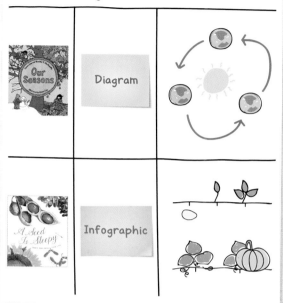

Share

Following independent reading time, gather students together in the meeting area to talk about their reading.

Raise your hand if you read a nonfiction book that has diagrams or infographics.

What did you learn from the diagrams or infographics?

Extend the Lesson (Optional)

After assessing students' understanding, you might decide to extend the learning.

▶ Have students create a diagram or infographic about a topic they are studying in school.

▶ **Writing About Reading** Read aloud part of a nonfiction book that explains how something works or what the parts of something are called. Have students make a diagram showing what they learned.

Section 2: Literary Analysis

Assessment

After you have taught the minilessons in this umbrella, observe students as they talk about their reading across instructional contexts: interactive read-aloud, independent reading and literacy work, guided reading, shared reading, and book club. Use *The Literacy Continuum* (Fountas and Pinnell 2017) to observe students' reading behaviors across instructional contexts.

▶ What evidence do you have of new understandings related to learning information from illustrations and graphics?

  • Do students talk about what they learned from illustrations and other graphics in nonfiction books?

  • Do they read and understand labels and captions?

  • Do they read and talk about maps, diagrams, and infographics?

  • Do they use academic vocabulary, such as *illustration, photograph, author, illustrator, map, diagram, label, caption,* and *infographic*?

▶ In what other ways, beyond the scope of this umbrella, are students thinking and talking about nonfiction books?

  • Are they noticing some of the different ways authors organize nonfiction books?

  • Are they noticing text features, such as headings and tables of contents, in nonfiction books?

Use your observations to determine the next umbrella you will teach. You may also consult Minilessons Across the Year (pp. 55-57) for guidance.

Link to Writing

After teaching the minilessons in this umbrella, help students link the new learning to their own writing:

▶ Give students numerous opportunities to write their own nonfiction books. Let them decide whether to include illustrations, photographs, maps, diagrams, and/or infographics, and help them find or create relevant graphics. Remind them to use images that help the reader learn more information about the topic, and encourage them to add labels and/or captions when appropriate.

Reader's Notebook

When this umbrella is complete, provide a copy of the minilesson principles (see resources.fountasandpinnell.com) for students to glue in the reader's notebook (in the Minilessons section if using *Reader's Notebook: Intermediate* [Fountas and Pinnell 2011]), so they can refer to the information as needed.

Minilessons in This Umbrella

RML1 Authors use headings to tell what the part is about.

RML2 Authors use sidebars to give information.

RML3 Authors use timelines to show when important things happen.

RML4 Authors use an index to list the topics in a nonfiction book in alphabetical order.

Before Teaching Umbrella 16 Minilessons

Before teaching this umbrella, read and discuss engaging, high-quality nonfiction books that include a variety of text and organizational features, such as headings, sidebars, timelines, and indexes. Use the following texts from the *Fountas & Pinnell Classroom™ Interactive Read-Aloud Collection* and *Shared Reading Collection* or choose appropriate books from your classroom library.

Interactive Read-Aloud Collection

The Passage of Time

Our Seasons by Grace Lin and Ranida T. McKneally

Genre Study: Expository Nonfiction

Shell, Beak, Tusk by Bridget Heos

A Day and Night in the Desert by Caroline Arnold

Author's Point of View

Energy Island by Allan Drummond

Shared Reading Collection

Exploring Underground by Louis Petrone

Tiny but Fierce by Cheri Colburn

Trapped in Tar by Hannah Cales

Saving Cranes by Brenda Iasevoli

As you read aloud and enjoy these texts together, help students

- discuss the main idea of each page or section, and

- notice and use text features and organizational tools, such as headings, timelines, indexes, and sidebars.

Passage of Time

Expository Nonfiction

Point of View

Shared Reading Collection

Reading Minilesson Principle
Authors use headings to tell what the part is about.

Using Text Features to Gain Information

You Will Need

- two or three familiar nonfiction books that have headings, such as the following:
  - *Our Seasons* by Grace Lin and Ranida T. McKneally, from Text Set: Passage of Time
  - *Shell, Beak, Tusk* by Bridget Heos, from Text Set: Expository Nonfiction
  - *Tiny but Fierce* by Cheri Colburn, from *Shared Reading Collection*
- chart paper and markers

Academic Language / Important Vocabulary

- author
- nonfiction
- heading

Continuum Connection

- Notice, use, and understand the purpose of some organizational tools: e.g., title, table of contents, chapter title, heading, subheading (p. 55)

Goal

Understand the purpose of headings as an organizational tool.

Rationale

When students understand why nonfiction authors use headings, they begin to internalize the concept of text structure, or organization. Learning about headings builds a foundation for recognizing important ideas and supporting details.

Assess Learning

Observe students when they read and talk about nonfiction books. Notice if there is evidence of new learning based on the goal of this minilesson.

- ▶ Do students understand the purpose of headings?
- ▶ Can they describe the physical differences between headings and body text (font size, color, capital letters, etc.)?
- ▶ Can they use headings to predict what a page or section will be about?
- ▶ Do they use academic language, such as *author*, *nonfiction*, and *heading*?

Minilesson

To help students think about the minilesson principle, use familiar nonfiction texts with headings to provide an inquiry-based lesson about headings. Here is an example.

- ▶ Display page 2 of *Our Seasons*. Point to the heading.

  What do you notice about how these words look? How are they different from the other words on the page?

- ▶ Read the heading aloud.

  What do you think this page will be about?

- ▶ Read the rest of the text on the page.

  The large words at the top of the page are called the heading. What did the heading tell?

- ▶ Show page 10 of *Shell, Beak, Tusk*.

  Where is the heading on this page?

  How do you know it's the heading?

- ▶ Read the heading and then the rest of the text on the page.

  What did the heading tell about this page?

Have a Try

Invite the students to talk with a partner about the headings in *Tiny but Fierce*.

▶ Show the cover of *Tiny but Fierce* and then display page 12. Point to and read the heading.

> Turn and talk to your partner about what you think this page will be about.

▶ Read the rest of the text on the page.

> What does the heading tell about this page?

Summarize and Apply

Help students summarize the learning and remind them to read headings.

> What do headings look like? How do headings help you when you read nonfiction?

▶ Record students' responses in two lists on chart paper. Write the principle at the top of the chart.

> Choose a nonfiction book to read today. If it has headings, remember to read the headings and think about what the section will be about.

Share

Following independent reading time, gather students in pairs in the meeting area to show headings to a partner.

> If you read a nonfiction book with headings today, show your partner the headings.

> How did the headings help you while you read?

Extend the Lesson (Optional)

After assessing students' understanding, you might decide to extend the learning.

▶ Encourage students to include headings when they write their own nonfiction texts.

▶ **Writing About Reading** Project or make an enlarged copy of a page from a nonfiction book that does not have headings. Work together with students to write headings, as appropriate.

Authors use headings to tell what the part is about.

What Do Headings Look Like?

- Headings are bigger than the other words on the page.
- Headings are sometimes a different color.
- Headings have capital letters.

What Are Headings For?

heading

- Headings tell what each part of the book is about.
- Headings can help you find information in a book.

Reading Minilesson Principle
Authors use sidebars to give information.

Using Text Features to Gain Information

You Will Need

- two or three familiar nonfiction books that contain sidebars, such as the following:
  - *Energy Island* by Allan Drummond, from Text Set: Point of View
  - *Tiny but Fierce* by Cheri Colburn, from *Shared Reading Collection*
  - *Exploring Underground* by Louis Petrone, from *Shared Reading Collection*
- chart paper and markers

Academic Language / Important Vocabulary

- nonfiction
- author
- illustrator
- sidebar
- topic
- information

Continuum Connection

- Gain new understandings from searching for and using information found in text body, sidebars, and graphics (p. 55)

Goal

Notice when authors include extra information to help you understand a topic.

Rationale

When students know how to look for, read, and think about the additional information provided in sidebars, they gain a deeper understanding of the topic of the book.

Assess Learning

Observe students when they read and talk about nonfiction books. Notice if there is evidence of new learning based on the goal of this minilesson.

- ▶ Do students understand the purpose of sidebars?
- ▶ Can they explain how the information in the sidebars relates to the information in the text body?
- ▶ Can they explain why authors sometimes include sidebars?
- ▶ Do they use academic language, such as *nonfiction, author, illustrator, sidebar, topic,* and *information*?

Minilesson

To help students think about the minilesson principle, use familiar nonfiction texts to provide an inquiry-based lesson about sidebars. Here is an example.

- ▶ Show the cover of *Energy Island* and read the title. Then display pages 7–8. Read aloud the text body and then the sidebar. Point to the sidebar.

  What do you notice about this part of the page?

  How does it look different from the rest of the page?

  This part of the page is called a sidebar. What do you notice about the information in the sidebar? What does it have to do with the information on the rest of the page? How is it different?

  The author uses sidebars to share scientific information that relates to the people of Samsø.

- ▶ Show the cover of *Tiny but Fierce* and read the title. Then turn to pages 2–3.

  Who can point to the sidebar on this page?

  How do you know that's a sidebar?

- ▶ Read the text body and then the sidebar.

  What do you notice about the print in the sidebar?

  Why is the author talking about sharks and lions in a book about dragonflies? What does this information have to do with the information about dragonflies? It doesn't quite fit in the main part of the book about dragonflies, but it gives you some extra, interesting information to think about.

Have a Try

Invite the students to talk with a partner about sidebars.

▶ Show the cover of *Exploring Underground* and read the title. Then read pages 2, 4, 10, and 12. Point to each "Caving Rules" sidebar as you read it.

> Turn and talk to your partner about how the author of this book uses sidebars. What information is in the sidebars, and how does it relate to the rest of the book?

▶ Ask a few students to share their thinking.

Summarize and Apply

Help students summarize the learning and remind them to read sidebars.

> Why do some nonfiction authors put sidebars in their books?

▶ Make a chart to remind students what they have learned about sidebars. Write the principle at the top of the chart.

> Choose a nonfiction book to read today, and remember to read every part of every page. If your book has sidebars, think about what you are learning from them and how they relate to the rest of the book, and bring the book when we meet.

Share

Following independent reading time, gather students together in the meeting area to talk about their reading.

> Raise your hand if you found any sidebars in the book you read today.

> What did you learn from the sidebars in your book?

Extend the Lesson (Optional)

After assessing students' understanding, you might decide to extend the learning.

▶ Encourage students to include sidebars when they write their own nonfiction books.

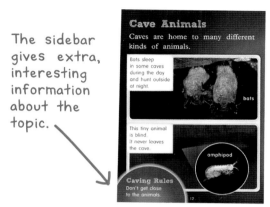

Authors use sidebars to give information.

The sidebar gives extra, interesting information about the topic.

Section 2: Literary Analysis

Reading Minilesson Principle
Authors use timelines to show when important things happen.

Using Text Features to Gain Information

You Will Need

- two familiar nonfiction books that contain timelines, such as the following from *Shared Reading Collection*:
  - *Trapped in Tar* by Hannah Cales
  - *Saving Cranes* by Brenda Iasevoli
- chart paper and markers

Academic Language / Important Vocabulary

- nonfiction
- author
- timeline

Continuum Connection

- Gain new understandings from searching for and using information found in text body, sidebars, and graphics (p. 55)
- Notice and understand the purpose of some organizational tools: e.g., title, table of contents, chapter tiles, heading, subheading (p. 55)

Goal

Notice when authors use a timeline to show important events.

Rationale

When students know how to read timelines, they are better able to understand and remember the dates of important events, as well as understand patterns and relationships between events.

Assess Learning

Observe students when they read and talk about nonfiction books. Notice if there is evidence of new learning based on the goal of this minilesson.

- ▶ Do students understand what a timeline is for and how to read one?
- ▶ Can they explain why authors use timelines?
- ▶ Do they use academic language, such as *nonfiction*, *author*, and *timeline*?

Minilesson

To help students think about the minilesson principle, use familiar nonfiction texts to provide an inquiry-based lesson about timelines. Here is an example.

- ▶ Show the cover of *Trapped in Tar* and read the title. Reread pages 2–4. Display pages 4–5.

  What do you notice about the words and pictures at the bottom of these pages?

- ▶ Read the heading "La Brea Tar Pits Timeline" and then read and point to each entry on the timeline.

  What information does this timeline give you?

- ▶ Record students' responses on chart paper.

  This timeline shows what the La Brea Tar Pits looked like 50,000 years ago, a hundred years ago, and today. It shows how it has changed over time.

Have a Try

Invite the students to talk with a partner about a timeline in another book.

▶ Show the cover of *Saving Cranes* and read the title. Then display pages 8–9.

> What do you notice at the bottom of these pages?

▶ Read the text in the timeline aloud.

> Turn and talk to your partner about what you learned from this timeline.

▶ Ask a few students to share their thinking, and record their responses on the chart.

Summarize and Apply

Summarize the learning and remind students to read and think about the information shown in timelines.

> Today you thought about the timelines in a couple of nonfiction books. Why do authors sometimes put timelines in nonfiction books?

▶ Write the principle at the top of the chart.

> Choose a nonfiction book to read today. If your book has a timeline in it, remember to read and think about the information in the timeline. Bring your book to share when we come back together.

Share

Following independent reading time, gather students together in the meeting area to talk about their reading.

> Raise your hand if you found a timeline in the book you read today.

> Show us your timeline. What does the timeline show?

Extend the Lesson (Optional)

After assessing students' understanding, you might decide to extend the learning.

▶ After reading aloud a nonfiction book, write each important event from the book on a separate sheet of paper. Mix up the papers, and then have students arrange the events in the correct chronological order to make a timeline.

▶ **Writing About Reading** Have students make a timeline in a reader's notebook showing the important events from a nonfiction book (see pp. 550-551).

> **Authors use timelines to show when important things happen.**
>
> **Trapped in Tar** The timeline shows what the tar pits looked like at different times in history.
>
> | 50,000 years ago | 100 years ago | today |
>
> **Saving Cranes** The timeline shows what happens in the life of a crane.
>
> | May Lay Eggs | June Eggs Hatch | July Chicks grow | August Chicks Fly Away |

Section 2: Literary Analysis

Reading Minilesson Principle
Authors use an index to list the topics in a nonfiction book in alphabetical order.

Using Text Features to Gain Information

Goal

Notice, use, and understand the purpose of an index in a nonfiction book.

Rationale

When students know how to use an index, they are able to find information about a specific subtopic in a nonfiction book.

Assess Learning

Observe students when they read and talk about nonfiction books. Notice if there is evidence of new learning based on the goal of this minilesson.

- Do students know how to use an index?
- Do they use indexes to find information about specific subtopics?
- Do they understand that the entries in an index are arranged in alphabetical order?
- Do they use the terms *index, topic, nonfiction*, and *alphabetical*?

Minilesson

To help students think about the minilesson principle, use familiar nonfiction texts to provide an inquiry-based lesson about indexes. Here is an example.

- Show the cover of *Shell, Beak, Tusk* and read the title. Then turn to the index on page 31. Read the *A* and the *B* entries.

  What do you notice about this page?

  What do you think is the purpose of this page?

  Why is the number 13 next to the word *bats*? What does this mean?

- Turn to page 13 and read the first paragraph.

  What do you notice?

  The index tells us that the information about bats is on page 13.

  Who can help me find the information about elephants?

- Invite a volunteer to come up and find the entry for elephants in the index. Turn to page 25 and read the information about elephants.

  What do you notice about the order of the topics in the index?

  The topics are listed in alphabetical, or ABC, order. The topics that begin with *A* are at the beginning, then *B*, then *C*, and so on.

Have a Try

Invite the students to talk with a partner about the index in another book.

▶ Show the cover of *A Day and Night in the Desert* and read the title. Turn to the index on page 24. Project it, if possible.

> Turn and talk to your partner about how you would find the information about insects in this book.

> Now turn and talk about where you would look for the information about tarantulas.

▶ After students turn and talk, ask a few to share their thinking.

Summarize and Apply

Help students summarize the learning and remind them to use indexes to find information in nonfiction books.

> Why do authors make an index for a nonfiction book?

▶ Make a chart to remind students what they learned about indexes. Write the principle at the top.

> Choose a nonfiction book to read today. Look to see if it has an index. If so, try using the index to find information about a specific topic. Bring your book to share when we come back together.

Share

Following independent reading time, gather students together in the meeting area to talk about their reading.

> Raise your hand if the book you read today has an index.

> Show how you used it to find some information.

Extend the Lesson (Optional)

After assessing students' understanding, you might decide to extend the learning.

▶ Discuss the similarities and differences between a table of contents and an index.

▶ Encourage students to include an index when they write their own nonfiction books.

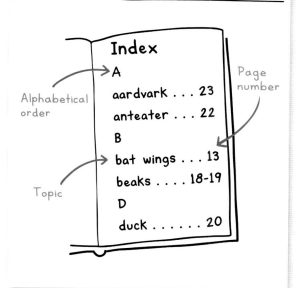

Authors use an index to list the topics in a nonfiction book in alphabetical order.

Index

Alphabetical order →
A
aardvark . . . 23
anteater . . . 22
B
bat wings . . . 13
beaks 18-19
D
duck 20

Page number

Topic

Assessment

After you have taught the minilessons in this umbrella, observe students as they talk about their reading across instructional contexts: interactive read-aloud, independent reading and literacy work, guided reading, shared reading, and book club. Use *The Literacy Continuum* (Fountas and Pinnell 2017) to observe students' reading behaviors across instructional contexts.

▶ What evidence do you have of new understandings related to using text features to gain information?

- Do students understand the purpose of headings?
- Can they explain how the headings relate to the content that follows it?
- Do they read and discuss information found in sidebars and timelines?
- Are they able to use an index to find information?
- Do students use academic language, such as *nonfiction, heading, information, sidebar, index,* and *topic*?

▶ In what other ways, beyond the scope of this umbrella, are they thinking and talking about nonfiction books?

- Have they noticed that there are different types of nonfiction books (e.g., biography, informational)?
- Are they noticing different ways nonfiction books are organized?
- Are they noticing and talking about illustrations and graphics?

Use your observations to determine the next umbrella you will teach. You may also consult Minilessons Across the Year (pp. 55-57) for guidance.

Link to Writing

After teaching the minilessons in this umbrella, help students link the new learning to their own writing:

▶ When students write their own nonfiction texts, encourage them to use headings to tell what each page or section is about. Suggest that they use sidebars and/or timelines to include extra information about the topic. Encourage them to include an index to help readers find information.

Reader's Notebook

When this umbrella is complete, provide a copy of the minilesson principles (see resources.fountasandpinnell.com) for students to glue in the reader's notebook (in the Minilessons section if using *Reader's Notebook: Intermediate* [Fountas and Pinnell 2011]), so they can refer to the information as needed.

Realistic Fiction

Minilessons in This Umbrella

RML1	Realistic fiction books are alike in many ways.
RML2	The definition of realistic fiction is what is always true about it.
RML3	The characters are always imagined but they seem real.
RML4	The story's settings are imagined but they could be real.
RML5	Sometimes the story has real places in it even though the characters and story are imagined.
RML6	The author creates a story problem that could be real.
RML7	The story ends in a way that is like real life.
RML8	The story can help you understand more about people and the world.

Kindness

Before Teaching Umbrella 17 Minilessons

Genre study supports students in knowing what to expect when beginning to read a text in a genre. It helps students develop an understanding of the distinguishing characteristics of a genre and gives students the tools they need to navigate a variety of texts. There are six broad steps in a genre study, which are described on pages 37-39.

The first step in any genre study is to collect a set of mentor texts in the genre. For this genre study, collect a variety of high-quality picture books that are easily identifiable as realistic fiction. Before guiding students to look for genre characteristics, be sure that they first become immersed in the books, thinking and talking about the meaning of each text and enjoying the stories. Use the following books from the *Fountas & Pinnell Classroom™ Interactive Read-Aloud Collection* text sets or choose realistic fiction books with which your students are familiar.

Patricia Polacco

Genre Study: Realistic Fiction

Dancing in the Wings by Debbie Allen

Tomás and the Library Lady by Pat Mora

Dumpling Soup by Jama Kim Rattigan

Owl Moon by Jane Yolen

The Importance of Kindness

The Can Man by Laura E. Williams

Author/Illustrator Study: Patricia Polacco

Meteor!

Thunder Cake

As you read aloud and enjoy these texts together, help students

- notice similarities between them,
- think about if the characters, settings, and problems seem real,
- make connections to their own lives, and
- live vicariously through the characters.

Section 2: Literary Analysis

Reading Minilesson Principle
Realistic fiction books are alike in many ways.

Studying Realistic Fiction

You Will Need

- a collection of familiar realistic fiction books
- chart paper with the headings *Realistic Fiction* and *Noticings* and sections for *Always* and *Often*
- markers

Academic Language / Important Vocabulary

- realistic fiction
- story
- character
- setting
- alike

Continuum Connection

- Notice and understand the characteristics of some specific fiction genres: e.g., realistic fiction, historical fiction, folktale, fairy tale, fable, fantasy, hybrid text (p. 50)

Goal

Notice and understand the characteristics of realistic fiction.

Rationale

When students study the realistic fiction genre through inquiry, they gain a deeper understanding both of individual stories and of the genre as a whole. When they develop an understanding of realistic fiction, they will know what to expect when they encounter books of that genre (see pages 37-39 for more information about genre study).

Assess Learning

Observe students when they read and talk about realistic fiction stories. Notice if there is evidence of new learning based on the goal of this minilesson.

- Can students identify similarities between multiple realistic fiction stories?
- Are they able to identify and talk about the characteristics of realistic fiction?
- Do they use vocabulary such as *realistic fiction, setting,* and *alike*?

Minilesson

To help students think about the minilesson principle, choose realistic fiction books that you have read aloud recently and provide an inquiry-based lesson. Here is an example.

- Divide students into small groups, and provide each group with several examples of familiar realistic fiction books.

  We have read and talked about all these realistic fiction books together. Look at the books. Then talk with your group about how they are alike.

  What did you notice about how your books are alike?

- As the students share their noticings, prompt them, as necessary, with questions such as the following:

  - *What have you noticed about the characters in realistic fiction books?*
  - *What have you noticed about the settings, or places, in realistic fiction books?*
  - *What could you say about the problems that characters in realistic fiction stories face?*
  - *What have you learned from reading realistic fiction stories?*

- Help students decide whether each noticing is *always* or *often* a characteristic of realistic fiction by asking other groups if all their books have the same characteristic.

- Record students' noticings on the prepared chart paper.

Have a Try

Invite the students to talk with a partner about the characteristics of realistic fiction.

> Turn and talk to your partner about a book you have read or heard recently. Is this book realistic fiction? How do you know? Think about what we wrote about realistic fiction on our chart.

▶ After students turn and talk, ask a few students to share their thinking with the class.

Summarize and Apply

Summarize the learning and remind students to think about the characteristics of realistic fiction when they read.

> Today you thought about the ways that realistic fiction stories are alike.

▶ Review the noticings chart.

> When you read today, think about whether the book you are reading is realistic fiction. Remember the things we talked about and wrote on our chart. If your book is realistic fiction, bring it to share when we come back together.

Share

Following independent reading time, gather students together in the meeting area to talk about their reading.

> Who read a realistic fiction book today?

> How do you know your book is realistic fiction?

Extend the Lesson (Optional)

After assessing students' understanding, you might decide to extend the learning.

▶ Continue to add to the noticings chart as students read more realistic fiction stories and notice more about the genre.

▶ Introduce your students to Genre Thinkmarks for realistic fiction. A Genre Thinkmark is a tool that guides readers to note certain elements of a genre in their reading. They can quickly note the page numbers of parts of the book where they see evidence of the characteristics of realistic fiction and share it with others (see resources.fountasandpinnell.com).

Realistic Fiction
Noticings:

Always	Often
• The story has characters that are imagined, but they could be real.	• The story helps you understand people and your world.
• The story has settings that are imagined, but they could be real.	• The story has real places in it even though the characters and story are imagined.
• The characters have imagined problems that could be real.	
• The story ends in a way that is like real life.	

Section 2: Literary Analysis

Reading Minilesson Principle
The definition of realistic fiction is what is always true about it.

Studying Realistic Fiction

You Will Need

- a familiar realistic fiction story, such as *Tomás and the Library Lady* by Pat Mora, from Text Set: Realistic Fiction
- the realistic fiction noticings chart from RML1
- chart paper and markers

Academic Language / Important Vocabulary

- realistic fiction
- story
- definition

Continuum Connection

- Notice and understand the characteristics of some specific fiction genres: e.g., realistic fiction, historical fiction, folktale, fairy tale, fable, fantasy, hybrid text (p. 50)

Goal

Create a working definition of realistic fiction.

Rationale

Writing a definition is part of the genre study process. When you work with students to create a definition of a genre, you help them summarize the most important characteristics of that genre. Over time, the students can revise the definition as they read and learn more about realistic fiction.

Assess Learning

Observe students when they read and talk about realistic fiction stories. Notice if there is evidence of new learning based on the goal of this minilesson.

- Do students discuss what they notice about realistic fiction?
- Can they explain whether a particular book fits the definition of realistic fiction?
- Do they use vocabulary such as *realistic fiction, story,* and *definition*?

Minilesson

Guide students in writing a definition of realistic fiction. Here is an example of how to do so.

- Display and review the noticings chart created during the previous minilesson.

  You noticed how realistic fiction stories are alike. Now we're going to use the noticings to write a definition of realistic fiction. The definition will tell what is true about all realistic fiction stories.

- Write the words *Realistic fiction stories are* on chart paper.

  Turn and talk to your partner about how you would finish this sentence. Use the noticings chart to give you ideas, if you need help.

  What is true about realistic fiction?

- Combine students' responses to create a whole-class definition. Write the rest of the definition on the chart paper.

Have a Try

Invite the students to talk with a partner about a familiar realistic fiction book.

▶ Show the cover of *Tomás and the Library Lady* or another familiar realistic fiction book. Show a few pages to remind students of the story.

> Turn and talk to your partner about whether this book fits our definition of realistic fiction.

> Is *Tomás and the Library Lady* realistic fiction? How do you know?

Summarize and Apply

Summarize the learning and remind students to think about the definition of realistic fiction as they read.

> What did we write today?

> We thought more about what realistic fiction is like, and we worked together to write a definition of realistic fiction.

▶ Reread the definition.

> Choose a fiction book to read today, and think about whether your book fits the definition of realistic fiction. Bring your book to share when we come back together.

Share

Following independent reading time, gather students together in the meeting area to talk about their reading.

> Turn and talk to your partner about whether the book you read today fits our definition of realistic fiction. Be sure to explain how it does or does not fit the definition.

> Did anyone notice anything else about realistic fiction that they think we should add to our definition?

Extend the Lesson (Optional)

After assessing students' understanding, you might decide to extend the learning.

▶ If students write their own realistic fiction stories, remind them to think about the definition of realistic fiction and make sure that their stories fit it.

▶ **Writing About Reading** Have students write in a reader's notebook about how a particular story does or does not fit the definition of realistic fiction.

Realistic Fiction

Realistic fiction stories are made up by the author but have characters, settings, and problems that could be real.

Realistic fiction stories often help you understand people and the world around you.

RML3
LA.U17.RML3

Reading Minilesson Principle
The characters are always imagined but they seem real.

Studying Realistic Fiction

You Will Need

- two or three familiar realistic fiction books, such as the following:
  - *Thunder Cake* by Patricia Polacco, from Text Set: Patricia Polacco
  - *Tomás and the Library Lady* by Pat Mora, from Text Set: Realistic Fiction
  - *Dumpling Soup* by Jama Kim Rattigan, from Text Set: Realistic Fiction
- chart paper and markers (prepare a three-column chart with the headings *Character, Seems Real or Not Real,* and *Why?*)
- three sticky notes labeled *Real*

Academic Language / Important Vocabulary

- realistic fiction
- character
- story

Continuum Connection

- Express opinions about whether a character seems real (p. 51)
- Notice how the writer reveals characters and makes them seem real (p. 51)

Goal

Understand that characters are always imagined but seem real in realistic fiction.

Rationale

When students recognize that the characters in realistic fiction are imagined but seem real, they are better able to understand, talk about, and make authentic personal connections with these characters.

Assess Learning

Observe students when they talk about realistic fiction stories. Notice if there is evidence of new learning based on the goal of this minilesson.

- Can students explain whether a character seems real and give reasons for their thinking?
- Do they understand that the characters in realistic fiction are not real people despite seeming like they could be?
- Do they use the terms *realistic fiction, character,* and *story*?

Minilesson

To help students think about the minilesson principle, use familiar realistic fiction texts to provide an inquiry-based lesson about the characters. Here is an example.

- Show the cover of *Thunder Cake*, and then show a few pages to remind students of the story.

  Who is the main character in this realistic fiction story?

  Does she seem like a real person to you?

  How does the author make her seem real? What does the character do or say that convinces you?

- Have a student place a sticky note on the prepared chart paper. Add students' supporting evidence.

- Show the cover of *Tomás and the Library Lady* and enough pages to refresh students' memory of the story.

  Who is the main character in *Tomás and the Library Lady*?

  Does Tomás seem like he could be a real person? Why or why not? Give an example from the book.

- Have a student place a sticky note on the chart and add students' supporting evidence.

Have a Try

Invite the students to talk with a partner about the main character in *Dumpling Soup*.

▶ Show the cover and some pages of *Dumpling Soup*.

Think about what you know about the main character in *Dumpling Soup* and whether she seems like a real person. Turn and talk to your partner about whether Marisa seems like a real person. Be sure to explain why you think so.

▶ After students turn and talk, ask a few students to share, and record their responses on the chart as before.

Summarize and Apply

Summarize the learning and remind students to think about whether the characters in stories seem real.

What did you notice about the characters in the realistic fiction books we looked at today?

The characters in realistic fiction seem like real people. Are they actually real people?

What makes you think that?

▶ Write the principle at the top of the chart.

Choose a fiction book to read today during independent reading. As you read, think about whether the characters in your book seem real. Be ready to explain why they seem real or not real when we come back together.

Share

Following independent reading time, gather students together in the meeting area to talk about their reading.

Turn and talk to your partner about whether the characters in the book you read today seemed real.

Extend the Lesson (Optional)

After assessing students' understanding, you might decide to extend the learning.

▶ Have students compare a character in a realistic fiction book to one in a fantasy book. Discuss what makes one seem real and the other not real. Make the examples clear.

▶ If the students write their own realistic fiction stories, remind them to think about how to make the characters seem real.

The characters are always imagined but they seem real.

Character	Seems Real or Not Real	Why?
The girl in Thunder Cake	Real	She is afraid of thunder. She cooks with her grandmother.
Tomás in Tomás and the Library Lady	Real	He spends time with his family, plays games, goes to the library, and reads books.
Maria in Dumpling Soup	Real	She spends time with her family, plays games, cooks food, and celebrates the new year.

Reading Minilesson Principle
The story's settings are imagined but they could be real.

You Will Need

- two or three familiar realistic fiction books set in an imagined place (not a specific city), such as the following:
  - *Dancing in the Wings* by Debbie Allen, from Text Set: Realistic Fiction
  - *Owl Moon* by Jane Yolen, from Text Set: Realistic Fiction
  - *The Can Man* by Laura E. Williams, from Text Set: Kindness
- chart paper and markers (prepare a four-column chart with the headings *Book, Settings, Seems Real or Not Real,* and *Why?*)
- three sticky notes labeled *Real*

Academic Language / Important Vocabulary

- realistic fiction
- story
- setting
- author

Continuum Connection

- Recall important details about setting after a story is read (p. 51)

Goal

Understand that realistic fiction stories are sometimes set in an imagined place that could exist in real life.

Rationale

When students recognize that realistic fiction stories are often set in an imagined place that seems real, they begin to understand that the settings and situations in realistic fiction are universal, and they are able to make authentic personal connections to these stories.

Assess Learning

Observe students when they talk about realistic fiction stories. Notice if there is evidence of new learning based on the goal of this minilesson.

- ▶ Do students discuss what they notice about a story's settings?
- ▶ Can they explain what makes a story's settings seem real or not real?
- ▶ Do they understand why the setting needs to seem real in a realistic fiction story?
- ▶ Do they use academic language, such as *realistic fiction, story, setting,* and *author*?

Minilesson

To help students think about the minilesson principle, use familiar realistic fiction books to provide an inquiry-based lesson about setting. Here is an example.

- ▶ Show the cover of *Dancing in the Wings* and then review the first twelve pages.

  What do you notice about the settings, or places, in this story? What kinds of places do you see?

  Do these seem like places that could exist in real life? What makes you think that?

- ▶ Have a student place a sticky note on the chart and add students' responses.

  Have any of you been to a place that looks like one of the places in the story?

  Where did you go, and how it was like the place in the story?

  Let's take a look at the setting in another realistic fiction book you know.

- ▶ Show the cover of *Owl Moon*, and then flip through its pages.

  Tell what you notice about the setting in *Owl Moon*. Are there places like this in the real world? How do you know?

- ▶ Have a student place a sticky note on the chart and add students' responses.

  Why is it important for the author to make the setting seem real in a realistic fiction story?

Have a Try

Invite the students to talk with a partner about the setting of *The Can Man*.

▶ Show the cover and some pages of *The Can Man*.

> Turn and talk to your partner about what you notice about the settings in this story. What do you see in the illustrations?

▶ Ask a few students to share what they noticed, and record their responses on the chart.

> Now turn and talk about whether you think the settings in this story could be real and why.

▶ Record responses on the chart as before.

Summarize and Apply

Summarize the learning and remind students to think about whether the settings in fiction books seem real.

> What did you notice about the settings in the realistic fiction books we looked at today?

▶ Write the principle at the top of the chart.

> Choose a fiction book to read during independent reading today. Be sure to notice the settings in your story and think about whether they seem real. If they do, bring your book to share when we come back together.

Share

Following independent reading time, gather students together in the meeting area to talk about their reading.

> Raise your hand if the settings in the story you read seem real.

> What makes them seem like real places?

Extend the Lesson (Optional)

After assessing students' understanding, you might decide to extend the learning.

▶ Discuss a fantasy book with realistic settings to help students understand that not all fiction books with realistic settings are realistic fiction.

▶ Have students set up a display of recommended realistic fiction books in the classroom library.

The story's settings are imagined but they could be real.

Book	Setting	Seems Real or Not Real	Why?
Dancing in the Wings	• school, dance studio, stage, buildings, car, house	Real	They look like places that I have been to before.
Owl Moon	• countryside, woods, trees, hills, lots of snow	Real	There are real places in the countryside that look like this in the winter.
The Can Man	• big city, big buildings, shops, park, bakery, apartments	Real	Real cities have big buildings, shops and bakeries, parks, and apartments.

Section 2: Literary Analysis

Reading Minilesson Principle
Sometimes the story has real places in it even though the characters and story are imagined.

Studying Realistic Fiction

You Will Need

- two or three familiar realistic fiction books that mention a specific real place, such as the following:
  - *Dumpling Soup* by Jama Kim Rattigan, from Text Set: Realistic Fiction
  - *Meteor!* by Patricia Polacco, from Text Set: Patricia Polacco
  - *Tomás and the Library Lady* by Pat Mora, from Text Set: Realistic Fiction
- chart paper and markers
- United States map

Academic Language / Important Vocabulary

- realistic fiction
- story
- setting
- character

Continuum Connection

- Notice and understand the characteristics of some specific fiction genres: e.g., realistic fiction, historical fiction, folktale, fairy tale, fable, fantasy, hybrid text (p. 50)

Goal

Understand that realistic fiction stories are sometimes set in real places even though the characters and stories are imagined.

Rationale

When you teach students that some stories are set in real places, they understand that realistic fiction authors use both their imaginations and their knowledge of the real world to make their stories seem realistic.

Assess Learning

Observe students when they talk about realistic fiction stories. Notice if there is evidence of new learning based on the goal of this minilesson.

- Can students make connections between a real place in a story and what they know about it?
- Do they understand that the characters and plot are still imagined even when the story is set in a real place?
- Do they use academic language, such as *realistic fiction, story, setting,* and *character*?

Minilesson

To help students think about the minilesson principle, use familiar realistic fiction texts to provide an inquiry-based lesson about realistic fiction stories. Here is an example.

- Show the cover of *Dumpling Soup*, and then read from the beginning of page 1 through the first paragraph of page 2.

  What did you learn from these pages about where this story takes place?

  The author mentions Oahu and Honolulu. Are these real places or places that the author made up? What makes you think that?

- If possible, point out Hawaii, Oahu, and Honolulu on a map. If any students have firsthand knowledge of Hawaii, ask them to share briefly.

- Record on chart paper that *Dumpling Soup* is set in Hawaii.

- Show the cover of *Meteor!* and several pages.

  What do you notice about the setting of this book? What kind of place is it?

- Reread the last two paragraphs of the last page of the book.

  Where does this story take place?

  Do you think Union City, Michigan, is real? What makes you think that?

- If possible, point out Union City, Michigan, on a map. Add *Meteor!* and its setting to the chart.

Have a Try

Invite the students to apply the new thinking.

▶ Reread pages 2–3 of *Tomás and the Library Lady*.

What did you learn from these pages about where Tomás lives? Turn and talk to your partner about it.

▶ Record students' responses on the chart.

Are Iowa and Texas real places? How do you know?

▶ Point out Iowa and Texas on a map, and ask students to share what they know about these states.

Summarize and Apply

Summarize the learning and remind students to notice when there are real places in realistic fiction books.

What did you notice about the settings in all the realistic fiction books we just looked at?

An author sometimes places imagined characters in real settings. This is one way the author makes the story seem real.

▶ Write the principle at the top of the chart.

Choose a fiction book to read today. As you read, notice if you see the names of any real places. If so, bring your book to share when we come back together.

Share

Following independent reading time, gather students together in the meeting area to talk about their reading.

Raise your hand if you read a realistic fiction book that has real places in it. What real places were in your story? What did you learn about those places?

Extend the Lesson (Optional)

After assessing students' understanding, you might decide to extend the learning.

▶ Continue adding real settings to the chart. Post a world map if you read books that take place around the world (e.g., West Africa: *Bintou's Braids* by Sylviane A. Diouf, from Text Set: Honoring Traditions; Brazil: *Soccer Star* by Mina Javaherbin, from Text Set: The Importance of Determination).

▶ **Writing About Reading** Help students conduct research about a real place from a realistic fiction book and write what they learned in a reader's notebook.

Sometimes the story has real places in it even though the characters and story are imagined.

Key

Dumpling Soup (Hawaii)

Meteor! (Union City, Michigan)

Tomás and the Library Lady (Iowa and Texas)

Section 2: Literary Analysis

Reading Minilesson Principle
The author creates a story problem that could be real.

Studying Realistic Fiction

You Will Need

- two or three familiar realistic fiction books with a clearly stated problem, such as the following:
  - *Dancing in the Wings* by Debbie Allen, from Text Set: Realistic Fiction
  - *Dumpling Soup* by Jama Kim Rattigan, from Text Set: Realistic Fiction
  - *The Can Man* by Laura E. Williams, from Text Set: Kindness
- chart paper and markers (prepare a four-column chart with the headings *Book, Problem, Could It Be Real?*, and *What Makes You Think So?*)
- three sticky notes labeled *Yes*

Academic Language / Important Vocabulary

- realistic fiction
- story
- problem
- character

Continuum Connection

- Give opinions about whether a problem seems real (p. 51)

Goal

Understand that authors create story problems that could be real in realistic fiction.

Rationale

When students recognize that the problems in realistic fiction stories could happen in real life, they are better able to make connections to their own lives, live vicariously through the characters, and learn from how the characters deal with their problems.

Assess Learning

Observe students when they talk about realistic fiction stories. Notice if there is evidence of new learning based on the goal of this minilesson.

- Can students express and justify an opinion about whether a problem in a story seems like it could be real?
- Can they make connections between problems in realistic fiction stories and problems they have experienced themselves or have heard about someone else experiencing?
- Do they use academic language, such as *realistic fiction, story, problem*, and *character*?

Minilesson

To help students think about the minilesson principle, use familiar realistic fiction texts to provide an inquiry-based lesson about story problems. Here is an example.

- Show the cover of *Dancing in the Wings* and then reread pages 5–8.

  What problem does Sassy have in this story?

  Do you think someone could have this problem in real life? What makes you think that?

- Have a student place a sticky note on the prepared chart and add students' responses.

  Have you ever had a problem like Sassy's? What happened?

- Show the cover of *Dumpling Soup* and then reread pages 7–10.

  What problem does Marisa have?

  Could someone in real life have this problem? How do you know?

- Have a student place a sticky note on the prepared chart and add students' responses.

  Raise your hand if you have had a problem like Marisa's.

  What was your problem?

Have a Try

Invite the students to talk with a partner about the problem in *The Can Man*.

▶ Show the cover of *The Can Man*, and then reread page 5 ("A few minutes later").

> Turn and talk to your partner about the problem that Tim has. Could this problem happen in real life? Be sure to explain the reasons for your thinking.

▶ After students turn and talk, ask a few students to share their responses. Record them on the chart as before.

Summarize and Apply

Summarize the learning and remind students to think about the problem when they read stories.

> What did you notice about the problems in the realistic fiction stories we looked at today?

> Another way the author makes a story seem real is to make the characters have a realistic problem. Seeing how the characters deal with their problems can help you deal with problems in your own life.

▶ Write the principle at the top of the chart.

> Choose a fiction book to read today. As you read, think about whether the problem in the story could really happen. Be ready to share your thinking when we come back together.

Share

Following independent reading time, gather students together in the meeting area to talk about their reading.

> What was the problem in the fiction book you read today?

> Do you think this problem could really happen? Why?

Extend the Lesson (Optional)

After assessing students' understanding, you might decide to extend the learning.

▶ If students write their own realistic fiction stories, remind them to think about how to make the problem seem real.

▶ **Writing About Reading** Have students write in a reader's notebook about what makes the problem in a story seem real or not real.

The author creates a story problem that could be real.

Book	Problem	Could It Be Real?	What Makes You Think So?
Dancing in the Wings	Sassy wants to be a dancer, but she looks different from other dancers. Other children say mean things to Sassy.	Yes	Real children can be afraid they won't be able to do what they want because of how they look. Real children sometimes say mean things to each other.
Dumpling Soup	Marisa is afraid no one will want to eat her "ugly" dumplings.	Yes	Real children sometimes make things that don't look perfect and may feel bad about it.
The Can Man	Tim wants a skateboard, but his family doesn't have enough money.	Yes	In real life, most people don't have enough money to buy everything they want.

Reading Minilesson Principle
The story ends in a way that is like real life.

Studying Realistic Fiction

You Will Need

- two or three familiar realistic fiction books, such as the following from Text Set: Realistic Fiction:
  - *Dumpling Soup* by Jama Kim Rattigan
  - *Dancing in the Wings* by Debbie Allen
  - *Owl Moon* by Jane Yolen
- chart paper and markers (prepare a four-column chart with the headings *Book, Ending, Like Real Life?*, and *Why?*)
- three sticky notes labeled *Yes*

Academic Language / Important Vocabulary

- realistic fiction
- story
- ending

Continuum Connection

- Understand when a story could happen in real life (realistic fiction) and when it could not happen in real life (traditional literature, fantasy) (p. 50)

Goal

Understand that realistic fiction stories end in a realistic way.

Rationale

When you teach students that realistic fiction stories end in a realistic way, they begin to understand that books in this genre have to be realistic all the way through.

Assess Learning

Observe students when they talk about realistic fiction stories. Notice if there is evidence of new learning based on the goal of this minilesson.

- Can students express and justify an opinion about whether a story ends in a realistic way?
- Do they understand that realistic fiction stories have to be realistic from beginning to end?
- Do they use academic vocabulary, such as *realistic fiction, story*, and *ending*?

Minilesson

To help students think about the minilesson principle, use familiar realistic fiction texts to provide an inquiry-based lesson. Here is an example.

- Show the cover of *Dumpling Soup*, and then reread the last three pages of text.

  How does this story end? What does Marisa's family do at the end of the story?

  Do you think that could happen in real life? What makes you think that?

- Have a student place a sticky note on the prepared chart and add students' responses.

  This story ends in a way that is like real life. In real life, families celebrate holidays and eat meals together.

- Show the cover of *Dancing in the Wings*, and then reread the last two pages.

  What happens at the end of *Dancing in the Wings*?

  Do you think that an ending like this could happen in real life? Why or why not?

- Have a student place a sticky note on the prepared chart and add students' responses.

Have a Try

Invite the students to talk with a partner about the ending of *Owl Moon*.

▶ Show the cover of *Owl Moon* and then reread the last two pages.

Turn and talk to your partner about how this story ends. Explain whether you think the story ends in a way that is like real life, and be sure to give reasons for your thinking.

▶ After students turn and talk, ask a few students to share their thinking. Record their responses on the chart.

Summarize and Apply

Summarize the learning and remind students to think about the endings of stories.

What did you notice about the ending of each story we looked at today?

Realistic fiction stories end in a way that is like real life. Realistic fiction stories are realistic all the way through—from the beginning to the end.

▶ Write the principle at the top of the chart.

Today during independent reading, choose a fiction book to read. Think about the ending. Could it be real? Be ready to share your thinking when we come back together.

The story ends in a way that is like real life.

Book	Ending	Like Real Life?	Why?
Dumpling Soup	Marisa's family eats the dumpling soup. Everyone likes Marisa's dumplings.	Yes	Real families celebrate holidays and eat meals together.
Dancing in the Wings	Sassy goes to the summer dance festival and dances in the concert.	Yes	Real children can dance in recitals. Real children can achieve their goals if they work hard at them.
Owl Moon	They see an owl and then they go home.	Yes	Real children can watch owls at night and go home afterward.

Share

Following independent reading time, gather students together in the meeting area to talk about their reading.

Turn and talk to your partner about whether the book you read today ended in a way that is like real life. Remember to give reasons for your thinking.

Extend the Lesson (Optional)

After assessing students' understanding, you might decide to extend the learning.

▶ If students have learned to give a book talk, have them recommend a realistic fiction book to their classmates (see Umbrella 3: Giving a Book Talk in Section Two: Literary Analysis).

▶ **Writing About Reading** Have students write in a reader's notebook about whether they think the ending of a particular story is realistic.

Reading Minilesson Principle
The story can help you understand more about people and the world.

Studying Realistic Fiction

You Will Need

- two or three familiar realistic fiction books that have a clear message, such as the following:
  - *Dancing in the Wings* by Debbie Allen, from Text Set: Realistic Fiction
  - *Dumpling Soup* by Jama Kim Rattigan, from Text Set: Realistic Fiction
  - *The Can Man* by Laura E. Williams, from Text Set: Kindness
- chart paper and markers

Academic Language / Important Vocabulary

- realistic fiction
- story
- author
- lesson

Continuum Connection

- Notice and infer the importance of ideas relevant to their world: e.g., sharing, caring for others, doing your job, helping your family, taking care of self, staying healthy, caring for the world or environment, valuing differences, expressing feelings, empathizing with others, problem solving, learning about life's challenges, social justice (p. 50)

Goal

Relate texts to their own lives and think about the author's message.

Rationale

When students recognize that a realistic fiction story can help them understand more about people and the world, they think more deeply about the author's message and how it can be applied to their own lives. They are able to learn from the characters and situations in the story.

Assess Learning

Observe students when they talk about realistic fiction stories. Notice if there is evidence of new learning based on the goal of this minilesson.

- Can students say what a character in a story learned?
- Can they infer what an author is trying to teach?
- Do they understand how the author's message can be applied to their own lives?
- Do they use vocabulary such as *realistic fiction, story, author,* and *lesson*?

Minilesson

To help students think about the minilesson principle, use familiar realistic fiction texts to provide an inquiry-based lesson. Here is an example.

- Show the cover of *Dancing in the Wings* and then reread the last four pages.

  What does Sassy learn at the end of this story?

  What do you think the author wants you to learn from reading this story? What is her message?

- Record students' responses on chart paper.
- If possible, share with students a relevant anecdote about a time when you, like Sassy, worked hard to achieve a goal or realized that it is okay to be different. Ask students to share their own relevant experiences.
- Show the cover of *Dumpling Soup* and then reread the last page.

  What does Marisa realize about her dumplings at the end of the story?

  Marisa realizes that it doesn't matter that her dumplings don't look perfect, but this lesson isn't just about dumplings. Even if you never make dumplings, how can this story help you in your own life? What do you think the author wants you to understand about life from reading this story?

- Record students' responses on the chart.

Have a Try

Invite the students to talk with a partner about the message in *The Can Man*.

▶ Show the cover of *The Can Man* and then reread the last three pages of text.

> Turn and talk to your partner about what you think the author wants you to learn from this story.

▶ After students turn and talk, ask a few students to share their ideas. Record their responses on the chart.

Summarize and Apply

Summarize the learning and remind students to think about how they can apply the lessons in realistic fiction to their own lives.

> What did you notice about the realistic fiction stories we looked at today?

> Realistic fiction stories are like real life, so you can learn from what the characters learn. A story can help you understand more about people and the world.

▶ Write the principle at the top of the chart.

> During independent reading today, choose a realistic fiction story to read. As you read, think about what the author wants you to learn from the story. Be ready to share your thinking when we come back together.

Share

Following independent reading time, gather students together in the meeting area to talk about their reading.

> Who read a realistic fiction book today that teaches an important lesson about people or the world?

> What lesson is the author trying to teach? How will it help you in your life?

Extend the Lesson (Optional)

After assessing students' understanding, you might decide to extend the learning.

▶ Expand the discussion to other media. For example, what makes a movie seem real or not real?

▶ **Writing About Reading** Have students write in a reader's notebook about how a realistic fiction story helps them understand more about people or the world.

The story can help you understand more about people and the world.	
Dancing in the Wings	It is important to believe in yourself and be willing to take risks. It is okay to be different.
Dumpling Soup	Sharing a meal together as a family is much more important than how the meal looks. It's okay if your first try at doing something is not perfect.
The Can Man	Helping others is more important than helping yourself.

Assessment

After you have taught the minilessons in this umbrella, observe students as they talk and write about their reading across instructional contexts: interactive read-aloud, independent reading and literacy work, guided reading, shared reading, and book club. Use *The Literacy Continuum* (Fountas and Pinnell 2017) to observe students' reading and writing behaviors across instructional contexts.

- Are students able to define realistic fiction?
- Can they express and justify opinions about whether particular elements (e.g., characters, setting, problem, ending) of a fiction book seem realistic?
- Can they connect realistic fiction books with their knowledge and/or experience of the real world?
- Do they discuss the author's message in realistic fiction books and understand that they can use the message in their own lives?
- Do they use academic language, such as *character, setting, problem*, and *ending*, when discussing realistic fiction?

▶ In what other ways, beyond the scope of this umbrella, are the students talking about books?

- Do the students notice that there are other types of fiction stories?

Use your observations to determine the next umbrella you will teach. You may also consult Minilessons Across the Year (pp. 55-57) for guidance.

Read and Revise

After completing the steps in the genre study process, help students refine their definition of the genre based on their new understandings.

▶ **Before:** Realistic fiction stories are made up by the author but have characters, settings, and problems that could be real. Realistic fiction stories often help you understand people and the world around you.

▶ **After:** Realistic fiction stories seem like they could be real, but the author imagines them. All parts of the story, from beginning to end, are imagined but realistic. The authors of realistic fiction stories often teach important lessons that help you understand more about people and the world.

Reader's Notebook

When this umbrella is complete, provide a copy of the minilesson principles (see resources.fountasandpinnell.com) for students to glue in the reader's notebook (in the Minilessons section if using *Reader's Notebook: Intermediate* [Fountas and Pinnell 2011]), so they can refer to the information as needed.

Fables

Minilessons in This Umbrella

RML1	Fables are alike in many ways.
RML2	The definition of a fable is what is always true about it.
RML3	Fables often have characters with the same kinds of traits.
RML4	Fables have a moral that is often stated at the end.
RML5	The characters often use cleverness or trickery to solve the problem or win something.

Before Teaching Umbrella 18 Minilessons

When students study a genre, they learn what to expect when reading a text, expand important comprehension skills, examine the distinguishing characteristics of a genre, and develop the tools they need to navigate a variety of texts. There are six broad steps in a genre study, which are described on pages 37-39.

Before beginning a genre study of fables, select a variety of clear examples of fables for students to read and enjoy. Fables are a type of traditional literature along with folktales, fairy tales, legends/epics/ballads, and myths. You might want to introduce the term *traditional literature*, which is used to classify fables in *Reader's Notebook: Intermediate* (Fountas and Pinnell 2011). Use the following books from the *Fountas & Pinnell Classroom™ Interactive Read-Aloud Collection* text sets or use fables that you have on hand.

Genre Study: Fables

The Contest Between the Sun and the Wind by Heather Forest

The Little Red Hen by Jerry Pinkney

Grasshopper and the Ants by Jerry Pinkney

The Tortoise and the Hare by Jerry Pinkney

Seven Blind Mice by Ed Young

As you read aloud and enjoy these texts together, help students

- notice how fables are alike,

- notice what is always true and often true about fables,

- talk about the characters and what they have in common,

- recognize the moral, and

- notice if cleverness or trickery is used.

Studying Fables

You Will Need

- a variety of fables with which students are familiar
- chart paper and markers
- sticky notes
- basket of fables

Academic Language / Important Vocabulary

- fable
- genre
- characteristics
- traditional literature (optional)

Continuum Connection

- Notice and understand the characteristics of some specific fiction genres: e.g., realistic fiction, historical fiction, folktale, fairy tale, fable, fantasy, hybrid text. (p. 50)

Goal

Notice and understand the characteristics of fables as a genre.

Rationale

When you teach students the ways that fables are alike, they will know what to expect when reading fables and understand the characteristics of this kind of traditional literature.

Assess Learning

Observe students when they read and talk about fables. Notice if there is evidence of new learning based on the goal of this minilesson.

- ▶ Are students able to talk about the ways that fables are alike?
- ▶ Do they understand that some characteristics always occur and some characteristics often occur in fables?
- ▶ Do they use academic language, such as *fable, genre, characteristics,* and *traditional literature?*

Minilesson

To help students think about the minilesson principle, provide an inquiry-based lesson to help them think about the characteristics of fables. Here is an example.

- ▶ Have students sit in small groups. Show the covers of multiple fables that students are familiar with.

    Think about these fables and the different ways they are all alike. In your group, talk about the ways that the fables are alike.

- ▶ After time for discussion, ask students to share noticings. As students share, record responses on chart paper. Create an *always* and an *often* section to record responses.

    As you share your ideas, think about whether each is *always* or *often* true in a fable. Let me know so I can add it to the correct place on the chart.

- ▶ Select several fables to revisit in more detail as a whole group.

    What other things do you notice about these fables?

- ▶ Continue to record responses. Consider providing one or more of the following prompts.

    - *What did you notice about the characters?*
    - *What did you notice about the ending?*
    - *How do the characters solve their problems?*

Have a Try

Invite the students to examine more fables with a small group.

▶ Provide each group with one of the fables.

> In your group, look through the book and notice the words and illustrations. Talk with each other about the things on the chart. See how many you can find in the story.

Summarize and Apply

Summarize the learning and remind students to notice the characteristics of fables.

> Today you noticed the ways that all fables are alike.

▶ Add the title *Fables* to the chart and review the noticings.

> Today you can choose a fable to read. As you read, see if you notice things from the chart and add a sticky note to that page. Bring the book when we meet so you can share.

Share

Following independent reading time, gather the students in pairs.

> Talk about the fable you read today. Tell your partner which things from the chart you found in the book. Show any pages that you marked with sticky notes and point out what you noticed on that page.

Extend the Lesson (Optional)

After assessing students' understanding, you might decide to extend the learning.

▶ Students can keep track of the number of fables they read using a reader's notebook in two ways: first, by marking *Traditional Literature* on their reading list, and second, by tallying how many fables they have read on the reading requirement page (see Umbrella 2: Using a Reader's Notebook, found in Section Four: Writing About Reading).

▶ Introduce your students to Genre Thinkmarks for fables. A Genre Thinkmark is a tool that guides readers to note certain elements of a genre in their reading. They can quickly note the page numbers of parts of the book where they see evidence of the characteristics of fables and share it with others. To download this resource, visit resources.fountasandpinnell.com.

Fables

Noticings:

Always	Often
• People have told the story for a long time.	• The characters use cleverness or trickery to solve the problem.
• The story has characters that are good, bad, wise, foolish, lazy, or clever. The characters don't change.	• The bad characters are punished and the good characters are rewarded.
• The characters are animals or things that talk and act like people.	• The moral is stated at the end.
• The story has a moral at the end.	
• The story is short.	

Reading Minilesson Principle
The definition of a fable is what is always true about it.

Studying Fables

You Will Need

- a fable with which students are familiar, such as the following:
  - *Seven Blind Mice* by Ed Young, from Text Set: Fables
- chart paper and markers
- basket of fables
- sticky notes

Academic Language / Important Vocabulary

- fable
- genre
- definition
- traditional literature (optional)

Continuum Connection

- Notice and understand the characteristics of some specific fiction genres: e.g., realistic fiction, historical fiction, folktale, fairy tale, fable, fantasy, hybrid text (p. 50)

Goal

Create a working definition for fables.

Rationale

When you teach students to construct a working definition of fables, they are able to form their own understandings so they will know what to expect of the genre, and learn to revise their understandings as they gain additional experiences with traditional literature.

Assess Learning

Observe students when they read and talk about fables. Notice if there is evidence of new learning based on the goal of this minilesson.

- Do students participate in creating a working definition of a fable?
- Do they understand that a definition of fables is what is always true about them?
- Do they use vocabulary such as *fable, genre, definition,* and *traditional literature*?

Minilesson

To help students think about the minilesson principle, provide an interactive lesson to help them think about the definition of a fable. Here is an example.

- Show the fable noticings chart and review the characteristics.

  What are some things you know about fables?

  The definition of a fable tells what is always true about fables.

- On chart paper, write the words *Fables are*, leaving space for constructing a working definition.

  What would you write to finish this sentence with a definition that tells what fables are? Turn and talk about that, thinking about the noticings chart.

- After time for discussion, ask students to share ideas. Use the ideas to create a working definition for the class, and write it on chart paper. Ask a volunteer to read the definition.

- If appropriate, you might want to introduce the term *traditional literature*.

  A fable is a story that is passed down orally from one group to another over a long time. These types of stories are called *traditional literature*. Fables are just one type of traditional literature.

Have a Try

Invite the students to talk with a partner about how *Seven Blind Mice* fits the definition of a fable.

> With a partner, talk about whether *Seven Blind Mice* fits the definition of a fable. What makes you think that?

▶ Ask a few students to share. Add to the definition as new ideas emerge from the conversation.

Summarize and Apply

Summarize the learning and remind students to think about the definition of a fable.

▶ Read the definition aloud with students and ask whether there is anything else that should be added.

> When you read, you can choose a fable from the basket and think about how the book fits the definition. Add a sticky note to any pages that make you think about the definition of a fable. Bring the book when we meet so you can share.

Share

Following independent reading time, gather the students in small groups.

> With your group, talk about the fable you read today. Share whether the story fits the definition and what examples from the fable help you know that. Show any pages with sticky notes and talk about what you noticed on those pages.

Extend the Lesson [Optional]

After assessing students' understanding, you might decide to extend the learning.

▶ Have students create a display of fables in your classroom or school library. Include book reviews or posters in the display.

▶ If students have been giving book talks, have them give one on a fable (see Umbrella 3: Giving a Book Talk in Section Two: Literary Analysis).

Fables

Fables are short tales that have animal characters and that teach a moral.

Section 2: Literary Analysis

Reading Minilesson Principle
Fables often have characters with the same kinds of traits.

Studying Fables

You Will Need

- several fables that students are familiar with, such as these from Text Set: Fables:
  - *The Tortoise and the Hare* by Jerry Pinkney
  - *The Little Red Hen* by Jerry Pinkney
  - *The Contest Between the Sun and the Wind* by Heather Forest
- chart paper and markers
- highlighters in several colors
- basket of fables

Academic Language / Important Vocabulary

- fable
- character
- traits

Continuum Connection

- Understand that the same types of characters may appear over and over again in traditional literature: e.g., sly, brave, silly, wise, greedy, clever (p. 51)

Goal

Understand that in fables the same types of characters (e.g., sly, brave, silly) appear over and over again.

Rationale

When students notice the recurring characters and their traits in fables, they will recognize clear examples of these traits in their own lives and gain a deeper understanding of traditional literature.

Assess Learning

Observe students when they read and talk about fables. Notice if there is evidence of new learning based on the goal of this minilesson.

- ▶ Are students aware that the same types of characters recur in fables?
- ▶ Do they use academic language, such as *fable, character,* and *traits*?

Minilesson

To help students think about the minilesson principle, engage them in an interactive discussion about recurring character traits in fables. Here is an example.

- ▶ Display the cover of *The Tortoise and the Hare*

  Think about the characters in this fable, *The Tortoise and the Hare*. Turn and talk about the words you would use to describe the two main characters, or tell what they are like. When you tell what they are like, you tell their traits.

- ▶ After time for discussion, create a three-column chart with headings for the title, characters, and traits. Ask students to share ideas about the characters and add student observations to the chart.

  Now think about another fable, *The Little Red Hen*. What words would you use to describe the characters' traits?

- ▶ As students share ideas, add a new row to the chart.

  Do you notice anything that is the same about the characters in these two fables?

  Who can highlight any words that are the same?

- ▶ Ask another student to come up and use a different-color highlighter to show another word that is repeated. Continue until all similar words are highlighted.

  Looking at the chart, what do you notice about the traits of the characters in these two fables?

  The characters act in some similar ways, don't they?

Do these characters change their personalities from the beginning of the fable to the end?

▶ As needed, guide the conversation so students recognize that characters in fables do not change their personalities from the beginning to the end.

Have a Try

Invite the students to talk about a fable with a partner.

▶ Show the cover of *The Contest Between the Sun and the Moon*.

> Think about *The Contest Between the Sun and the Moon* by Jerry Pinkney. Turn and talk about what Sun and Wind are like.

▶ After time for discussion, ask students to share their thinking and add a row to the chart. Ask a volunteer to highlight any words that match the characters in the other fables.

Summarize and Apply

Summarize the learning and ask students what they notice about fables.

> Look at the chart. What do you notice about the traits of these characters?

▶ Add the principle to the top of the chart.

> Today you can choose a fable to read. As you read, notice the characters. Add a sticky note to any pages that show you if the characters are like the characters we talked about today. Bring the book when we meet so you can share.

Share

Following independent reading time, gather the students in small groups to talk about fables.

> What did you notice about the traits of the characters in the fable you read today? Share with your group what you noticed. Talk about whether the characters in different books had things in common.

Extend the Lesson (Optional)

After assessing students' understanding, you might decide to extend the learning.

▶ Continue adding to the chart as students notice other traits of characters in fables.

▶ **Writing About Reading** Have students write in a reader's notebook a description of a character from a fable.

Fables often have characters with the same kinds of traits.

Book	Character	Traits
The Tortoise and the Hare	Tortoise	wise, determined, brave
	Hare	lazy, overconfident
The Little Red Hen	Little Red Hen	wise, determined, clever
	Dog, Rat, Goat, Pig	lazy
The Contest Between the Sun and the Wind	Sun	clever, wise, determined
	Wind	overconfident, aggressive

Section 2: Literary Analysis

Reading Minilesson Principle
Fables have a moral that is often stated at the end.

Studying Fables

You Will Need

- several fables students are familiar with that have clearly stated morals at the end, such as the following from Text Set: Fables:
  - *Seven Blind Mice* by Ed Young
  - *The Tortoise and the Hare* by Jerry Pinkney
- chart paper and markers
- basket of fables

Academic Language / Important Vocabulary

- fable
- moral
- lesson

Continuum Connection

- Infer the "lesson" in traditional literature (p. 50)
- Notice when a fiction writer is communicating a moral lesson (p. 50)
- Understand that the "lesson" in traditional literature can be applied to their own lives (p. 50)

Goal

Notice that fables have a moral lesson that is often stated at the end of the story.

Rationale

When students notice the moral that is often stated at the end of a fable, they begin to apply lessons learned from reading fables to their own lives. They also anticipate the characteristics of a fable as they read.

Assess Learning

Observe students when they talk about fables. Notice if there is evidence of new learning based on the goal of this minilesson.

- Do students recognize that fables provide a moral and that the moral is often stated at the end?
- Can they talk about how a moral can be applied to their own lives?
- Do they use vocabulary such as *fable, moral,* and *lesson* to talk about traditional literature?

Minilesson

To help students think about the minilesson principle, provide an interactive lesson about the morals at the end of fables. Here is an example.

- Show the cover of *Seven Blind Mice*.

  Remember this fable, *Seven Blind Mice*? Listen as I reread the last few pages.

- Reread the last five pages, including the moral at the end.

  The moral is the lesson that the characters learn in the fable. Turn and talk about what the mice learned.

- Create a three-column chart with headings for title, moral, and meaning.

  What is the moral?

- Add the title and moral to the chart.

  How can you say the moral, or the lesson, in your own words?

- Ask students to share ideas and have a conversation about the moral, and how it can best be stated in simple language.

  What are some ways that this moral could help you in your own lives?

- Ask students to share ideas.

Have a Try

Invite students to talk with a partner about the moral in *The Tortoise and the Hare.*

> Here is another fable you know, *The Tortoise and the Hare.* Think about what Jerry Pinkney wrote at the end of the book.

▸ Read the stated moral at the end of the book.

> Turn and talk about the moral of this story, and how you might use this lesson in your own lives.

▸ After time for discussion, ask students to share. Add a new row to the chart and add students' ideas.

Summarize and Apply

Summarize the learning and remind students to think about the morals at the end of fables.

> What is a moral, and where do you usually find it?

▸ Add the principle to chart.

> When you read today, choose a fable. Think about the moral of the story. Bring the book when we meet so you can share.

Share

Following independent reading time, gather the students together in the meeting area.

> Did anyone read a fable today? Tell us what the moral is and what it means.

▸ Ask a few students to share with the whole group. After a student shares a moral, ask classmates to suggest ways that the morals could be applied to their everyday lives.

Extend the Lesson (Optional)

After assessing students' understanding, you might decide to extend the learning.

▸ **Writing About Reading** Encourage students to write in a reader's notebook about the moral at the end of a favorite fable. Have them write about how the moral could be applied to their own lives.

Fables have a moral that is often stated in the end.

Title	Moral or Lesson	What It Means
Seven Blind Mice	"Knowing in part may make a fine tale, but wisdom comes from seeing the whole."	You have to know all the information before you say what something is like.
The Tortoise and the Hare	"Slow and steady wins the race."	You can do something if you keep working on it.

Section 2: Literary Analysis

RML 5
LA.U18.RML5

Reading Minilesson Principle
The characters often use cleverness or trickery to solve the problem or win something.

Studying Fables

You Will Need

▶ two fables that students are familiar with in which cleverness or trickery are evident, such as the following from Text Set: Folktales:
- *Seven Blind Mice* by Ed Young
- *The Contest Between the Sun and the Wind* by Heather Forest

▶ chart paper and markers
▶ basket of fables

Academic Language / Important Vocabulary

▶ fable
▶ cleverness
▶ trickery

Continuum Connection

▶ Notice recurring themes or motifs in traditional literature and fantasy: e.g., struggle between good and evil (p. 50)

Goal

Understand that the characters in fables often use cleverness or trickery to solve a problem and usually get rewarded in the end.

Rationale

When students think about the way characters solve their problems in fables through cleverness or trickery, they develop an understanding of the character's decisions when they interact with other characters and think about how some behaviors are rewarded, whereas others are not.

Assess Learning

Observe students when they read and talk about fables. Notice if there is evidence of new learning based on the goal of this minilesson.

▶ Do students think about how characters use cleverness or trickery to solve problems in fables?

▶ Do they use vocabulary such as *fable, cleverness,* and *trickery*?

Minilesson

To help students think about the minilesson principle, provide an interactive lesson about cleverness and trickery. Here is an example.

▶ Show the cover of *Seven Blind Mice*.

> Think about the problem that the mice had and how it was solved as I reread a few pages.

▶ Reread pages 29–34.

> What did you notice about the problem and how it was solved?

▶ Guide the conversation and introduce the word *cleverness* if needed.

> Often, characters in fables use cleverness or trickery to get what they want. How could you describe what the mouse did to solve the problem?

▶ Create a chart to record how characters in fables solve problems. Ask students to share ideas as you fill in the chart.

▶ As needed, use the following prompts to generate discussion:
- *Why was it necessary for the white mouse to be clever in order to figure out what the mice were all standing on?*
- *Why were the other mice not able to solve the problem?*
- *How was the mouse rewarded by being clever?*
- *How does it help to be clever in order to solve a problem or win something?*

Have a Try

Invite students to talk with a partner about cleverness or trickery in a different fable.

▶ Show the cover of *The Contest Between the Sun and the Wind*.

> Think about what the Sun and the Wind were trying to do in this fable. Talk to your partner about that and how the Sun accomplished his goal.

▶ After time for discussion, ask students to share ideas. If needed, introduce the word *trickery*. Add a new row to the chart and add students' ideas.

Summarize and Apply

Summarize the learning and remind students to notice cleverness or trickery in fables.

> Today you learned that characters in fables often use cleverness or trickery.

▶ Add the principle to the chart.

> When you read today, choose a fable and think about how one character is clever or uses trickery. Bring the book when we meet so you can share.

Share

Following independent reading time, gather students in the meeting area to talk about fables.

> Did anyone notice cleverness or trickery in a fable they read today? Tell us about that.

Extend the Lesson (Optional)

After assessing students' understanding, you might decide to extend the learning.

▶ **Writing About Reading** Have students write in a reader's notebook how a character in a fable solves a problem.

The characters often use cleverness or trickery to solve the problem or win something.

	The white mouse ran around the entire elephant to finally realize what it was.	Cleverness
	The sun chose a game she knew she could win. She knew the man would take his coat off when he got warm.	Cleverness and Trickery

Assessment

After you have taught the minilessons in this umbrella, observe students as they talk and write about their reading across instructional contexts: interactive read-aloud, independent reading and literacy work, guided reading, shared reading, and book club. Use *The Literacy Continuum* (Fountas and Pinnell 2017) to observe students' reading and writing behaviors across instructional contexts.

▶ What evidence do you have of new understandings related to fables?

- Do students notice the ways that fables are alike?
- Are they aware that fables are short tales that have animal characters and that teach a moral?
- Can they identify the things that characters in fables have in common?
- Can they identify how a problem is solved using cleverness or trickery?
- Do they use academic language, such as *genre, fable, character, traits,* and *moral,* when talking about traditional literature?

▶ In what other ways, beyond the scope of this umbrella, are students talking about traditional literature?

- Are students noticing how an author shows what a character is like through the character's actions and dialogue?
- Do they show an interest in reading other kinds of traditional literature?

Use your observations to determine the next umbrella you will teach. You may also consult Minilessons Across the Year (pp. 55-57) for guidance.

Read and Revise

After completing the steps in the genre study process, help students refine their definition of the genre based on their new understandings.

▶ **Before:** Fables are short tales that have animal characters and that teach a moral.

▶ **After:** Fables are short tales that have animal characters and that teach a moral. Fables often have the same types of characters. The characters often use cleverness or trickery to solve a problem.

Reader's Notebook

When this umbrella is complete, provide a copy of the minilesson principles (see resources.fountasandpinnell.com) for students to glue in the reader's notebook (in the Minilessons section if using *Reader's Notebook: Intermediate* [Fountas and Pinnell 2011]), so they can refer to the information as needed.

Folktales

Section 2: Literary Analysis

Pourquoi Tales

Minilessons in This Umbrella

RML1 Folktales are alike in many ways.

RML2 The definition of a folktale is what is always true about it.

RML3 Folktales are stories that have been retold for a long time and can be found in different cultures.

RML4 There are different kinds of folktales.

RML5 Folktales have characters with good or bad traits.

RML6 Folktales have a lesson.

RML7 The characters often use trickery or cleverness to solve the problem.

RML8 Folktales usually have repeating patterns.

Before Teaching Umbrella 19 Minilessons

When students study a genre, they learn what to expect when reading a text, expand important comprehension skills, understand the distinguishing characteristics of a genre, and develop the tools they need to navigate a variety of texts. There are six broad steps in a genre study, which are described on pages 37-39.

Because students must be familiar with multiple folktales before beginning a genre study, select books that are clear examples. Folktales are a type of traditional literature along with fables, fairy tales, legends, epics, ballads, and myths. Introduce the term *traditional literature*, which is used to classify folktales in the *Reader's Notebook: Intermediate* (Fountas and Pinnell 2011). Types of folktales include beast tales, cumulative tales, pourquoi tales, trickster tales, noodlehead tales, realistic tales, and tall tales. Use the following books from the *Fountas & Pinnell Classroom™ Interactive Read-Aloud Collection* text sets or use folktales you have on hand.

Genre Study: Folktales

The Boy of the Three-Year Nap by Dianne Snyder

Babushka Baba Yaga by Patricia Polacco

Ming Lo Moves the Mountain by Arnold Lobel

Baby Rattlesnake by Te Ata and Lynn Moroney

Conejito by Margaret Read MacDonald

Martina the Beautiful Cockroach by Carmen Agra Deedy

Exploring Pourquoi Tales

The Legend of the Lady Slipper by Lise Lunge-Larsen and Margi Preus

Why Mosquitoes Buzz in People's Ears by Verna Aardema

Dragonfly's Tale by Kristina Rodanas

As you read aloud and enjoy these texts together, help students notice what the characters are like, what the lesson is, and how cleverness or trickery is used.

Studying Folktales

You Will Need

- a variety of familiar folktales
- chart paper and markers
- basket of folktales
- sticky notes

Academic Language / Important Vocabulary

- folktale
- genre
- characteristics
- traditional literature (optional)

Continuum Connection

- Connect texts by a range of categories: e.g., author, character, topic, genre, illustrator (p. 50)
- Notice and understand the characteristics of some specific fiction genres: e.g., realistic fiction, historical fiction, folktale, fairy tale, fable, fantasy, hybrid text (p. 50)

Goal

Notice and understand the characteristics of folktales as a genre.

Rationale

When you teach students the ways folktales are alike, and how they are different from other genres, they will know what to expect when reading folktales and understand the characteristics of traditional literature.

Assess Learning

Observe students when they talk about folktales. Notice if there is evidence of new learning based on the goal of this minilesson.

- ▶ Are students able to talk about the ways folktales are alike?
- ▶ Can they talk about the characteristics of folktales?
- ▶ Do they understand that some characteristics always occur and some characteristics often occur in folktales?
- ▶ Do they use the terms *folktale, genre,* and *characteristics*?

Minilesson

To help students think about the minilesson principle, provide an inquiry-based lesson to help them think about the characteristics of folktales. Here is an example.

- ▶ Have students sit in small groups. Show the covers of multiple folktales that are familiar to students.

  Think about these folktales and the different ways they are all alike. In your group, talk about the ways they are alike.

- ▶ After time for discussion, ask students to share their noticings. As students share, record responses on the chart paper. Create an *always* and an *often* section to record responses.

  As you share your ideas, think about whether each idea is always or often part of a folktale. I will add it to the correct place on the chart.

- ▶ Select several folktales to revisit in more detail as a whole group.

  What other things do you notice about these folktales?

- ▶ Continue to record responses. Consider providing one or more of the following prompts.

  - *What did you notice about the characters?*
  - *What did you notice about where the story takes place?*
  - *How did the characters solve their problems?*
  - *What did the characters learn?*

Have a Try

Invite the students to discuss a folktale in small groups.

▶ Provide each group with a folktale.

> In your group, look through the book and notice the words and illustrations. Talk about things on the chart. See how many you can find in the story.

Summarize and Apply

Summarize the learning and remind students to notice the characteristics of folktales.

▶ Add the title *Folktales* to the chart and review noticings.

> Today you can choose a folktale to read from this basket. As you read, see if you notice if something from the chart is true of your book. Add a sticky note to the page. Bring the book when we meet so you can share.

Share

Following independent reading time, gather the students in small groups.

> Talk about the folktale you read today. Tell your group which noticings from the chart you found. Point out what you noticed on the pages you marked with a sticky note.

Extend the Lesson (Optional)

After assessing students' understanding, you might decide to extend the learning.

▶ There are two ways students can keep track of the number of folktales they read using a reader's notebook. First, they can mark *Traditional Literature* on the reading list. Second, they can tally how many folktales they have read on the reading requirement page.

▶ Introduce students to Genre Thinkmarks for Folktales. A Genre Thinkmark is a tool that guides readers to note elements of a genre. They can note the page numbers of parts of the book where they see evidence of the characteristics of folktales and share with others. Visit resources.fountasandpinnell.com to download Genre Thinkmarks.

Folktales

Noticings:

Always	Often
• The story has been told for a long time.	• The characters are animals that act like people.
• The characters do good things or bad things.	• Cleverness or trickery is used to solve a problem.
• There is a lesson in the story.	• The story has a satisfying ending.
• There are folktales from many different cultures.	• The story has repeating patterns (language, phrases, events).
• The details in the story tell you something about the place the story comes from.	• There are some good characters and some bad characters.

Reading Minilesson Principle

The definition of a folktale is what is always true about it.

Studying Folktales

You Will Need

- noticings chart from RML1
- several familiar folktales, such as the following from Text Set: Folktales
  - *Baby Rattlesnake* by Te Ata and Lynn Moroney
  - *Conejito* by Margaret Read MacDonald
- chart paper and markers
- basket of folktales
- sticky notes

Academic Language / Important Vocabulary

- folktale
- genre
- definition
- traditional literature (optional)

Continuum Connection

- Notice and understand the characteristics of some specific fiction genres: e.g., realistic fiction, historical fiction, folktale, fairy tale, fable, fantasy, hybrid text (p. 50)

Goal

Create a working definition for folktales.

Rationale

When you teach students to construct a working definition of folktales, they can form their own understandings so they will know what to expect of the genre. They will learn to revise their understandings as they gain additional experiences with traditional literature.

Assess Learning

Observe students when they talk about folktales. Notice if there is evidence of new learning based on the goal of this minilesson.

- ▶ Do students participate in creating a working definition of a folktale?
- ▶ Do they understand the definition of a folktale will tell what is always true about a folktale?
- ▶ Do they use the terms *folktale*, *genre*, and *definition*?

Minilesson

To help students think about the minilesson principle, provide an interactive lesson to help them think about the definition of a folktale. Here is an example.

- ▶ Show the folktale noticings chart and review the characteristics.

  What do you now know about folktales?

  The definition of a folktale tells what folktales always are like.

- ▶ On chart paper, write the words *Folktales are*, leaving space for constructing a working definition.

  What would you write to finish this sentence to describe what folktales are like? Think about the noticings chart we created to help you with ideas.

- ▶ As students share ideas, create a working definition with the class by writing the ideas on chart paper. Ask a volunteer to read the definition.
- ▶ Show the cover of *Baby Rattlesnake*.
- ▶ After time for discussion, ask students to share.

  Does *Baby Rattlesnake* fit the definition of a folktale?

- ▶ Go through each part of the definition and ask students to give an example from the story that shows that *Baby Rattlesnake* fits the definition of a folktale. Revise the definition as needed based on the new thinking.

Have a Try

Invite the students to talk with a partner about how a folktale fits the definition of a folktale.

> Turn and talk about whether *Conejito* fits the definition of a folktale. What makes you think that?

▶ Ask a few students to share. Revise or add to the definition as new ideas emerge from the conversation.

Summarize and Apply

Summarize the learning and remind students to think about the definition of a folktale.

> Today you wrote a definition of a folktale. When you read, you can choose a folktale from the basket and think about how the book fits the definition. Add sticky notes to any pages that make you think about the definition of a folktale. Bring the book when we meet so you can share.

Share

Following independent reading time, gather the students in small groups to talk about folktales.

> With your group, talk about the folktale you read today. Share whether the story fits the definition and show any pages with sticky notes that help you know that.

Extend the Lesson (Optional)

After assessing students' understanding, you might decide to extend the learning.

▶ Have students create a display for the folktales in your classroom or school library. Include book reviews or posters in the display.

▶ Ask a few volunteers to create a section for folktales in the classroom library. You can decide whether to include all types of folktales together or whether to group kinds of folktales.

Folktales

Folktales are made-up stories that have been told and retold in different cultures for a long time.
They teach a lesson.
The characters are good or bad.

Reading Minilesson Principle
Folktales are stories that have been retold for a long time and can be found in different cultures.

Studying Folktales

Goal

Understand that folktales are retold over time and they are found in all different cultures.

Rationale

When students recognize that folktales have been retold for many years and come from different cultures, they understand that folktales include lessons that can be applied to all people and may begin to apply the lessons to their own lives.

Assess Learning

Observe students when they talk about folktales. Notice if there is evidence of new learning based on the goal of this minilesson.

- ▶ Do students recognize that folktales have been around for many years?
- ▶ Are they aware that folktales come from many different cultures and the same folktales can be told in many cultures?
- ▶ Do they use the terms *folktale* and *culture*?

Minilesson

To help students think about the minilesson principle, provide an interactive lesson about folktales. Here is an example.

- ▶ Show the cover of *Martina the Beautiful Cockroach*.

  After the title, it says *A Cuban Folktale, Retold by Carmen Agra Deedy*. What information do those words give you?

- ▶ As students offer suggestions, create a chart and add their comments.

  The cover tells you where the folktale comes from and tells you it has been retold. *Retold* tells you the story has been around for a long time and it has been told by many people. Some folktales are told in many countries.

- ▶ Turn to the copyright page and read the paragraph at the top.

  What new information do you learn about where this folktale comes from?

- ▶ Add students' suggestions to the chart.

  The author tells you other countries have versions of this folktale, so it's likely the folktale has been told for a long time.

  Let's see if the story gives you other clues.

- ▶ Read words or sentences on several pages that indicate where the folktale is from or how long it has been around. Highlight illustrations that may provide clues. Add students' ideas to the chart.

Have a Try

Invite students to talk with a partner about a folktale.

▶ Show *Conejito*. Read the cover, the author's note at the end, and page 2.

> Turn and talk about how you know this folktale has been told for a long time and what country it comes from.

▶ After time for discussion, ask students to share ideas. Add to chart.

Summarize and Apply

Summarize the learning and remind students to think about folktales.

> Today you noticed that folktales have been around for a long time and come from different places. A folktale can be told in many countries.

▶ Add the minilesson principle to the top of the chart.

> When you read today, choose a folktale from this basket and look for clues that tell you whether it has been around for a long time and where it comes from. Place a sticky note on pages with clues. Bring the book when we meet so you can share.

Share

Following independent reading time, gather students in small groups to talk about folktales.

> Talk with your group about the folktale you read today. Show the pages you marked with sticky notes and tell how you know the folktale has been around for a long time and where it comes from.

Extend the Lesson (Optional)

After assessing students' understanding, you might decide to extend the learning.

▶ Gather different versions of the same folktale that come from a variety of cultures. Read the folktales and have students work in groups to talk about similarities and differences.

▶ When you read a folktale, provide background information for the country of origin by locating it on a map and sharing a bit of information about it.

Folktales are stories that have been retold for a long time and can be found in different cultures.		
Title	Where the Folktale Comes From	How Do You Know?
Martina the Beautiful Cockroach (A Cuban Folktale)	• Cuba • Latin America • Spain • Persia • India • Africa	• The cover says "A Cuban Folktale." • There is an author's note in the book. • There are Spanish words, like *abuela* and *senora*. • Martina lives in Havana, Cuba. • The story talks about a Cuban grandmother.
Conejito	• Panama	• The cover says "A Folktale from Panama." • There are Spanish words, like *conejito* and *gordito*.

Studying Folktales

You Will Need

- three familiar pourquoi tales, such as the following from Text Set: Pourquoi Tales:
  - *The Legend of the Lady Slipper* by Lise Lunge-Larsen and Margi Preus
  - *Why Mosquitoes Buzz in People's Ears* by Verna Aardema
  - *Dragonfly's Tale* by Kristina Rodanas
- one familiar trickster tale, such as *Conejito* by Margaret Read MacDonald, from Text Set: Folktales
- one familiar beast tale, such as *Martina the Beautiful Cockroach* by Carmen Agra Deedy, from Text Set: Folktales
- chart paper and markers

Academic Language / Important Vocabulary

- folktale
- beast tale
- trickster tale
- pourquoi tale

Continuum Connection

- Notice and understand the characteristics of some specific fiction genres: e.g., realistic fiction, historical fiction, folktales, fairy tale, fable, fantasy, hybrid text (p. 50)

Goal

Understand different kinds of folktales.

Rationale

When students know the characteristics of different kinds of folktales, they know what to expect when reading each kind and can better understand the characters and events in the story. There are several different kinds of folktales (e.g., beast tales, cumulative tales, realistic tales, trickster tales, tall tales, pourquoi tales, noodlehead tales). This lesson focuses on only a few of these kinds. As students become familiar with more folktales, you can expand the list.

Assess Learning

Observe students when they read and talk about folktales. Notice if there is evidence of new learning based on the goal of this minilesson.

- ▶ Do students name and describe different kinds of folktales?
- ▶ Do they use as the terms *folktale, beast tale, trickster tale,* and *pourquoi tale*?

Minilesson

To help students think about the minilesson principle, use familiar folktales to provide an inquiry-based lesson about different kinds of folktales. Here is an example.

- ▶ Show the covers of *Why Mosquitoes Buzz in People's Ears* and *The Legend of the Lady Slipper*.

  A pourquoi tale is a special kind of folktale. *Pourquoi* is a French word that means "why." Why do you think these stories are called pourquoi tales?

  Why Mosquitoes Buzz in People's Ears explains exactly what the title says. What does *The Legend of the Lady Slipper* explain?

- ▶ Write the definition and the examples on chart paper.
- ▶ Show the cover of *Conejito*.

  This is a type of folktale called a trickster tale. A trickster is someone who plays tricks on people. Why would we call this story a trickster tale?

- ▶ Add the definition and example to the chart.
- ▶ Show the cover of *Martina the Beautiful Cockroach*.

  What did you notice about the cockroaches in this story?

  A folktale that has animal characters that talk and act like people is called a beast, or animal, tale.

- ▶ Add the definition and example to the chart.

Have a Try

Invite the students to talk about another folktale with a partner.

▶ Show the cover of *Dragonfly's Tale*.

> Look at the chart. Where does this story fit? Turn and talk to your partner about what kind of folktale you think it is and why.

▶ Ask a few students to share their thinking. Add *Dragonfly's Tale* to the pourquoi tale section of the chart.

Summarize and Apply

Summarize the learning and remind students to notice what kind of folktale they are reading.

> You noticed that there are different kinds of folktales. We talked about three different kinds of folktales today, but there are other kinds, too.

▶ Write the principle at the top of the chart.

> Choose a folktale to read today. After you read it, think about whether it is one of the kinds of folktales we talked about today: pourquoi tales, trickster tales, and beast tales. Not all folktales are one of these. Bring your book to share when we come back together.

Share

Following independent reading time, gather students together in the meeting area to talk about their reading.

> Raise your hand if you read a pourquoi tale, trickster tale, or beast tale today.

> What folktale did you read? What kind of folktale is it? How do you know?

Extend the Lesson (Optional)

After assessing students' understanding, you might decide to extend the learning.

▶ As you read aloud additional examples of pourquoi tales, trickster tales, and beast tales, discuss what kind of folktale they are and add them to the chart.

▶ As students encounter additional kinds of folktales (e.g., cumulative tales, realistic tales, tall tales, and noodlehead tales), repeat this minilesson using examples of those kinds and add them to the chart.

There are different kinds of folktales.

Type of Folktale	Definition	Examples
Pourquoi Tale	explains why something happens	• Why Mosquitoes Buzz in People's Ears • The Legend of the Lady Slipper • Dragonfly's Tale
Trickster Tale	has a character that plays tricks on other characters	• Conejito
Beast Tale	animal characters talk and act like people	• Martina the Beautiful Cockroach

RML 5
LA.U19.RML5

Reading Minilesson Principle
Folktales have characters with good or bad traits.

Studying Folktales

You Will Need

- two or three familiar folktales, such as the following from Text Set: Folktales:
  - *Martina the Beautiful Cockroach* by Carmen Agra Deedy
  - *The Boy of the Three-Year Nap* by Dianne Snyder
  - *Ming Lo Moves the Mountain* by Arnold Lobel
- chart paper and markers
- sticky notes

Academic Language / Important Vocabulary

- folktale
- character
- trait

Continuum Connection

- Understand that the same types of characters may appear over and over again in traditional literature: e.g., sly, brave, silly, wise, greedy, clever (p. 51)

Goal

Understand that folktales often have characters with the same kinds of traits that can be classified as good or bad.

Rationale

When students notice examples of good and bad character traits in folktales, they will recognize examples of these traits in their own lives and gain a deeper understanding of traditional literature.

Assess Learning

Observe students when they read and talk about folktales. Notice if there is evidence of new learning based on the goal of this minilesson.

- Can students identify the traits of characters in folktales?
- Can they classify each trait as being "good" or "bad"?
- Do they use academic vocabulary such as *character*, *trait*, and *folktale*?

Minilesson

To help students think about the minilesson principle, engage them in a discussion about character traits in folktales. Here is an example.

- Show the cover of *Martina the Beautiful Cockroach*.

  Who are the characters in this book?

  Think about how the characters act and what they are like. If you could use one word to describe Martina's grandmother, what word would you use?

- As students share their words, ask them whether each trait is "good" or "bad." Make a two-column chart on chart paper and add each suggested trait to the appropriate column.

- Repeat with some of the other characters in *Martina the Beautiful Cockroach*.

- Continue in a similar manner with some of the characters in *The Boy of the Three-Year Nap*.

Have a Try

Invite the students to talk with a partner about another folktale.

▶ Show the cover of *Ming Lo Moves the Mountain*.

Think about the folktale *Ming Lo Moves the Mountain*. Turn and talk about the characters in this story. What words would you use to describe each character?

▶ Ask a few students to share their thinking. Ask whether each trait is good or bad. Add any new traits to the chart. If students name a trait that is already on the chart, point out that the same types of characters appear in many folktales.

Summarize and Apply

Summarize the learning and ask students what they notice about folktales.

Let's look at the chart. What did you notice today about characters in folktales?

▶ Write the principle at the top of the chart.

Choose a folktale to read today. As you read, think about what the characters are like and whether they have good or bad traits. Bring the book when we meet so you can share.

Share

Following independent reading time, gather the students in small groups to talk about what they noticed about folktale characters.

Share with your group what you noticed about the characters in the book you read. Talk about whether the characters have good or bad traits.

Extend the Lesson (Optional)

After assessing students' understanding, you might decide to extend the learning.

▶ Continue adding to the chart as students notice other traits of characters in folktales.

▶ Discuss how in folktales characters with good traits are usually rewarded and characters with bad traits are often punished.

▶ **Writing About Reading** Encourage students to write about whether the ending of a favorite folktale is satisfying and how the way the characters act leads to the way the story ends.

Folktales have characters with good or bad traits.	
Good Traits	**Bad Traits**
wise	overconfident
kind	lazy
clever	
hardworking	

Reading Minilesson Principle
Folktales have a lesson.

Studying Folktales

You Will Need

- several familiar folktales with a clear lesson, such as the following from Text Set: Folktales:
  - *Babushka Baba Yaga* by Patricia Polacco
  - *Baby Rattlesnake* by Te Ata and Lynn Moroney
- chart paper and markers
- sticky notes
- basket of folktales

Academic Language / Important Vocabulary

- folktale
- lesson

Continuum Connection

- Infer the "lesson" in traditional literature (p. 50)
- Understand that the "lesson" in traditional literature can be applied to their own lives (p. 50)

Goal

Infer the lesson in a folktale and understand that it can be applied to one's own life.

Rationale

When students notice the lesson in a folktale, they begin to apply lessons learned from reading folktales to their own lives.

Assess Learning

Observe students when they talk about lessons in folktales. Notice if there is evidence of new learning based on the goal of this minilesson.

- ▶ Do students recognize that folktales have a lesson?
- ▶ Can they talk about how a lesson can be applied to their own lives?
- ▶ Do they use the terms *folktale* and *lesson*?

Minilesson

To help students think about the minilesson principle, provide an interactive lesson about lessons learned in folktales. Here is an example.

- ▶ Show the cover of *Babushka Baba Yaga* and then reread pages 25–28.

  Think about this part of *Babushka Baba Yaga*. What is the lesson learned in this folktale?

- ▶ Create a three-column chart with a heading for *Title*, *Lesson*, and *My Life*. Add the title and fill in the lesson, using students' suggestions.

  How could you use this lesson in your own life? Turn and talk about that.

- ▶ While students are talking, listen in on two or three discussions. Write students' responses on sticky notes and add them to the chart.

  Here are some ways the lesson of the story can be applied to real life. Did anyone come up with something similar?

Have a Try

Invite students to talk with a partner about applying the lesson learned in a folktale.

▸ Reread page 30 of *Baby Rattlesnake*.

What lesson does Baby Rattlesnake learn? Turn and talk about the lesson and how you could use it in your own life.

▸ Record the responses on sticky notes, add them to the chart, and discuss as before.

Summarize and Apply

Summarize the learning and remind students to think about the lessons learned in folktales.

Today you talked about lessons learned in folktales.

▸ Add the minilesson principle to the chart.

When you read today, choose a folktale from this basket. Think about the lesson learned and how you could use the lesson in your own life. Bring the book when we meet so you can share.

Share

Following independent reading time, gather the students together in the meeting area to talk about folktales.

Who noticed the lesson in the folktale you read? Tell us about the lesson learned.

▸ Ask a few students to share with the whole group. After a student shares a lesson, ask classmates to suggest ways the lessons could be applied to their own lives.

Extend the Lesson (Optional)

After assessing students' understanding, you might decide to extend the learning.

▸ **Writing About Reading** Encourage students to write in a reader's notebook about the lesson at the end of a favorite folktale and how it could be applied to their own lives.

Folktales have a lesson.

Title	Lesson	My Life
BABUSHKA Baba Yaga	Have patience and do not rush to do things before you are ready.	Jackie: "I can stop asking my parents to buy me a phone." Tomás: "I can stop asking my parents to let me stay up late."
BABY RATTLESNAKE	Do not judge someone by what they look like on the outside.	Aditya: "I can take time to get to know people before I decide what they are like." Mei: "I will not treat kids differently just because they do not look like me."

Reading Minilesson Principle
The characters often use trickery or cleverness to solve the problem.

Studying Folktales

You Will Need

- two familiar folktales in which trickery or cleverness are evident, such as the following from Text Set: Folktales:
  - *Conejito* by Margaret Mead MacDonald
  - *Ming Lo Moves the Mountain* by Arnold Lobel
  - *Babushka Baba Yaga* by Patricia Polacco
- chart paper and markers
- basket of folktales

Academic Language / Important Vocabulary

- folktale
- reward
- cleverness
- trickery

Continuum Connection

- Notice recurring themes or motifs in traditional literature and fantasy: e.g., struggle between good and evil (p. 50)

Goal

Understand that characters in folktales often use trickery or cleverness to solve the problem and usually are rewarded.

Rationale

When students think about the way characters solve their problems in folktales through trickery or cleverness, they develop an understanding of the characters' decisions when they interact with other characters and think about how some behaviors are rewarded, whereas others are not.

Assess Learning

Observe students when they talk about folktales. Notice if there is evidence of new learning based on the goal of this minilesson.

- ▶ Are students aware that some behaviors are rewarded in folktales?
- ▶ Do they think about how characters use trickery or cleverness to solve problems in folktales?
- ▶ Do they use the terms *folktale, reward, cleverness,* and *trickery*?

Minilesson

To help students think about the minilesson principle, provide an interactive lesson about trickery or cleverness. Here is an example.

- ▶ Show the cover of *Conejito*.

    Think about the problem Conejito had and how it was solved.

- ▶ Revisit pages 17–18.

    How did Conejito and Tía Mónica solve the problem?

- ▶ Guide the conversation and introduce the words *cleverness* and *trickery* if needed.

- ▶ Revisit pages 27–28.

    How is cleverness rewarded at the end of the story?

- ▶ Create a three-column chart with headings for *Title, Cleverness/Trickery,* and *Reward*. Ask students to share ideas and to the chart.

- ▶ Show the cover of *Ming Lo Moves the Mountain* and read the title.

    Now think about the way the wise man helped Ming Lo solve his problem.

- ▶ Revisit pages 21–22.

    What could we add to the chart about how Ming Lo's problem was solved?

- Add a new row to the chart and add students' suggestions.

- Reread the last page.

  How did trickery and cleverness lead to the satisfying ending of this folktale?

Have a Try

Invite students to talk with a partner about trickery or cleverness.

- Show the cover of and the illustration on pages 7–8 of *Babushka Baba Yaga*.

  Turn and talk about how Baba Yaga solved her problem.

- After time for discussion, ask students to share how trickery and/or cleverness was used and add to the chart.

Summarize and Apply

Summarize the learning and remind students to notice cleverness or trickery in folktales.

  Today you learned that characters in folktales often use cleverness or trickery.

- Write the minilesson principle at the top of the chart.

  When you read today, choose a folktale from this basket and think about how one character is clever or tricky. Bring the book when we meet so you can share.

Share

Following independent reading time, gather students in the meeting area to talk about folktales.

  Did anyone notice cleverness or trickery in a folktale they read today? Tell us about that.

Extend the Lesson (Optional)

After assessing students' understanding, you might decide to extend the learning.

- **Writing About Reading** Have students write in a reader's notebook about how a character in a folktale uses cleverness or trickery.

The characters often use trickery or cleverness to solve the problem.

Title	Trickery / Cleverness	Reward
Conejito	Tía Mónica is clever by telling Conejito to roll down the hill in a barrel past the animals. She builds a fire, so the animals will think the mountain is on fire.	Conejito makes it home safely.
Sun & Wind	The wise man tricks Ming Lo and his wife into doing a backward dance to move away from the mountain.	Ming Lo and his wife live happily away from the mountain.
BABUSHKA Baba Yaga	Baba Yaga tricks the village people into thinking she is a Babushka.	Baba Yaga is accepted by the village people.

Section 2: Literary Analysis

Reading Minilesson Principle
Folktales usually have repeating patterns.

Studying Folktales

You Will Need

- two familiar folktales with recognizable sound and literary language patterns, such as the following from Text Set: Folktales:
  - *Martina the Beautiful Cockroach* by Carmen Agra Deedy
  - *Conejito* by Margaret Read MacDonald
- chart paper and markers
- basket of folktales
- sticky notes

Academic Language / Important Vocabulary

- folktale
- repeat
- pattern

Continuum Connection

- Notice a writer's use of playful or poetic language or sound devices: e.g., rhythm, repetition, rhymes, refrains, onomatopoeia, alliteration, assonance (p. 51)

Goal

Notice that folktales often have repeating words or phrases.

Rationale

When students think about the language decisions authors make when writing folktales, they begin to recognize literary language patterns and playful language. They understand how language choices contribute to the enjoyment and memorability of text.

Assess Learning

Observe students when they talk about folktales. Notice if there is evidence of new learning based on the goal of this minilesson.

- Do students notice language patterns in folktales?
- Can they identify repetition and talk about how an author's language decisions make the story enjoyable to read?
- Do they use the terms *folktale, repeat,* and *pattern*?

Minilesson

To help students think about the minilesson principle, provide an interactive lesson about language patterns in folktales. Here is an example.

> Think about what the characters who want to marry Martina the Cockroach say to her.

- Read the repeating sentence that begins with *Martina* on pages 10 and 14.

  > What do you notice about the author's words?

  > Why do you think the author chose those words?

- Guide the conversation so students notice the rhythm, rhyme, and repetition. Add the sentence to the chart, written in the style the author used.

  > Now think about the author's language choices in another folktale, *Conejito*. Listen carefully to the words as I read a few pages. Raise your hand when you notice something interesting.

- Read pages 5, 7, 9, and then 21, 24, 26. Emphasize the language and pause for students to notice the repeating language patterns. As they raise their hands and share what they notice, add to the chart.

Have a Try

Invite students to talk with a partner about repeating language patterns in folktales.

> Think about the decisions authors make when writing folktales. How do the author's decisions about the language help you enjoy the story more? Turn and talk about that.

▸ After time for discussion, ask students to share.

Summarize and Apply

Summarize the learning and remind students to notice language patterns in folktales.

> What kinds of language patterns did you notice often appear in folktales?

▸ Add the minilesson principle to the chart.

> When you read today, choose a folktale from this basket and notice any repeating language patterns the author uses. Put a sticky note on any pages with repeating or interesting language. Bring the book when we meet so you can share.

Share

Following independent reading time, gather students in the meeting area to talk about folktales.

> Did anyone notice repeating patterns or interesting language in a folktale? Tell us about that.

Extend the Lesson (Optional)

After assessing students' understanding, you might decide to extend the learning.

▸ Read examples of other folktales with repeating language of traditional literature. As students notice the repeating language, talk about how the language identifies the story as a folktale and how the language adds to the story.

▸ Read examples of folktales that use other kinds of literary language (e.g., *once upon a time, long ago and far away, therefore, finally, at long last, happily ever after*).

Folktales usually have repeating patterns.

Martina
  Josefina
    Catalina
      Cucaracha.
        Beautiful *muchacha.*
Won't you be my wife?

You don't want to eat me!
Look how skinny I am.
Flaquito! Flaquito! Flaquito!

The mountain's on fire!
Conejuto is, too!
Run quick, Senor Tigre-
Or you'll be barbecue!

Assessment

After you have taught the minilessons in this umbrella, observe students as they talk and write about their reading across instructional contexts: interactive read-aloud, independent reading and literacy work, guided reading, shared reading, and book club. Use *The Literacy Continuum* (Fountas and Pinnell 2017) to observe students' reading and writing behaviors across instructional contexts.

▶ What evidence do you have of new understandings related to folktales?

- Do students notice that folktales are alike, yet also understand that there are different kinds of folktales?

- Are they aware that folktales have been retold for many years and come from different cultures?

- Are they able to describe the typical features of a folktale: there is a lesson, characters often use cleverness or trickery to solve a problem, and authors often use repeating patterns of language?

- Do they use terms such as *genre, character, traits, trickery, cleverness, lesson,* and *reward* when they talk about folktales?

▶ In what other ways, beyond the scope of this umbrella, are students talking about fiction stories?

- Are students interested in reading other types of fiction, such as fables or fantasy?

Use your observations to determine the next umbrella you will teach. You may also consult Minilessons Across the Year (pp. 55-57) for guidance.

Read and Revise

After completing the steps in the genre study process, help students read and revise their definition of the genre based on their new understandings.

▶ **Before:** Folktales are made-up stories that have been told and retold in different cultures for a long time. They teach a lesson. The characters are good or bad.

▶ **After:** Folktales are made-up stories that have been told and retold in different cultures for a long time. They teach a lesson. The characters do good things or bad things and sometimes use cleverness or trickery.

Reader's Notebook

When this umbrella is complete, provide a copy of the minilesson principles (see resources.fountasandpinnell.com) for students to glue in the reader's notebook (in the Minilessons section if using *Reader's Notebook: Intermediate* [Fountas and Pinnell 2011]), so they can refer to the information as needed.

Minilessons in This Umbrella

RML1   Sometimes authors tell stories that could never happen in real life.

RML2   Fantasy stories often happen in an unusual place.

RML3   Normal objects and things can be magical in fantasy stories.

RML4   Characters in fantasy stories are often different from characters in realistic stories.

Before Teaching Umbrella 20 Minilessons

Read and discuss a variety of engaging fantasy books. Primary examples should come from modern fantasy, which includes animal fantasy, low fantasy, high fantasy, and science fiction. The other type of fantasy is traditional literature (folktales, fairy tales, fables, legends, epics, ballads, myths) and can be included if it is appropriate for your class. Use the following books from the *Fountas & Pinnell Classroom™ Interactive Read-Aloud Collection* text sets or choose realistic fiction and fantasy stories from your library. Note that several realistic fiction books are included in the list below to use as comparisons.

The Importance of Kindness

Sophie's Masterpiece by Eileen Spinelli

Under the Lemon Moon by Edith Hope Fine

Humorous Texts

Big Bad Bubble by Adam Rubin

Fractured Fairy Tales

Kate and the Beanstalk by Mary Pope Osborne

The Passage of Time

And Still the Turtle Watched by Sheila MacGill-Callahan

Our Seasons by Grace Lin and Ranida T. McKneally

Genre Study: Folktales

Babushka Baba Yaga by Patricia Polacco

Genre Study: Fables

The Contest Between the Sun and the Moon by Heather Forest

The Importance of Determination

The Patchwork Quilt by Valerie Flournoy

As you read aloud and enjoy these texts together, help students

• understand that a fantasy is a story that could not happen in real life,

• recognize that fantasy stories often happen in unusual places,

• understand that ordinary objects can be magical, and

• compare and contrast the characters in fantasy stories to those in realistic stories.

Kindness

Humorous Texts

Fractured Fairy Tales

Passage of Time

Folktales

Fables

Determination

RML1
LA.U20.RML1

Reading Minilesson Principle
Sometimes authors tell stories that could never happen in real life.

Understanding Fantasy

You Will Need

- several familiar fantasy stories such as the following:
  - *Sophie's Masterpiece* by Eileen Spinelli, from Text Set: Kindness
  - *And Still the Turtle Watched* by Sheila MacGill-Callahan, from Text Set: Passage of Time
  - *Big Bad Bubble* by Adam Rubin, from Text Set: Humorous Texts
- chart paper prepared with three columns, headings, and book titles
- markers
- three sticky notes labeled *No*
- basket of fantasy stories
- sticky notes

Academic Language / Important Vocabulary

- fantasy
- characters
- events
- real life

Continuum Connection

- Recall important details about the setting after a story is read (p. 51)
- Notice and understand the characteristics of some specific fiction genres: e.g., realistic fiction, historical fiction, folktale, fairy tale, fable, fantasy, hybrid text (p. 50)
- Understand when a story could happen in real life (realistic fiction) and when it could not happen in real life (traditional literature, fantasy) (p. 50)

Goal

Notice and understand that a defining characteristic of fantasy is that the story could never happen in the real world.

Rationale

When students understand that fantasy stories could not happen in real life, they begin to talk about the imaginative characters, settings, and events in fantasy books and to learn what to expect when they read books in this genre.

Assess Learning

Observe students when they talk about fantasy stories. Notice if there is evidence of new learning based on the goal of this minilesson.

- Do students understand that fantasy stories could not happen in real life?
- Are they able to identify which characters, settings, and events from a fantasy story could not happen in real life?
- Do they use the terms *fantasy*, *characters*, *events*, and *real life*?

Minilesson

To help students think about the minilesson principle, provide an inquiry-based lesson about what fantasy stories are. Here is an example.

- Display the prepared chart and the cover of *Sophie's Masterpiece*.

  Think about what Sophie did for the new mother and baby. Turn and talk about whether anything like this could happen in real life.

- After time for discussion, ask students to share their thinking.

  Could this happen in real life, or in the real world?

- Have a student place one of the labeled sticky notes in the middle column.

  Why couldn't this story happen in real life?

- As students offer suggestions, add their explanations to the third column.

  Let's think about another story, *And Still the Turtle Watched*. Could this story happen in real life? Why or why not?

- Have a student place another sticky note in the middle column. Add students' ideas about why the story could not happen in real life to the third column.

Have a Try

Invite the students to talk about a fantasy story with a partner.

> Think about another fantasy story, *Big Bad Bubble*. Turn and talk about whether this story could happen in real life and why or why not.

▶ After time for discussion, ask students to share their thinking. Have a student place the final sticky note and add students' responses.

Summarize and Apply

Summarize the learning and remind students to notice the reasons why fantasy stories could not happen in real life.

> What do you know about fantasy stories?

▶ Add the minilesson principle to the chart.

> You can select a fantasy book from this basket to read today. While you are reading think about how the author wrote about something that could not happen in real life. Use sticky notes to mark pages with words or illustrations that help you know that. Bring the book when we meet so you can share.

Sometimes authors tell stories that could never happen in real life.		
Title	Could This Happen in Real Life?	Why?
Sophie's Masterpiece	No	A spider could not make friends with a person or make a baby blanket.
And Still the Turtle Watched	No	A rock does not have feelings or watch people.
BIG BAD BUBBLE	No	Monsters do not exist, and there is no place called La La Land for monsters.

Share

Following independent reading time, gather the students together in groups of three.

> Who read a fantasy story today? Talk about the fantasy story you read in your group. Show the pages in the book that give clues about what could not happen in real life.

Extend the Lesson (Optional)

After assessing students' understanding, you might decide to extend the learning.

▶ Read stories from different types of modern fantasy (animal fantasy, low fantasy, high fantasy, science fiction), as well as traditional literature. Encourage students to talk about which characters, settings, and events could not happen in the real world.

RML 2

LA.U20.RML2

Reading Minilesson Principle
Fantasy stories often happen in an unusual place.

Understanding Fantasy

You Will Need

- several familiar fantasy stories with unusual settings such as the following:
  - *Kate and the Beanstalk* by Mary Pope Osborne, from Text Set: Fractured Fairy Tales
  - *Big Bad Bubble* by Adam Rubin, from Text Set: Humorous Texts
  - *Babushka Baba Yaga* by Patricia Polacco, from Text Set: Folktales
- chart paper and markers
- basket of fantasy books

Academic Language / Important Vocabulary

- fantasy
- unusual
- place
- setting

Continuum Connection

- Recognize and understand that fiction texts may have settings that reflect a wide range of diverse places, languages, and cultures, and that characters' behaviors may reflect those settings (p. 51)
- Notice and understand settings that are distant in time and place from students' own experiences (p. 51)
- Infer the importance of the setting to the plot of the story in realistic and historical fiction and fantasy (p. 51)

Goal

Notice and understand that fantasy stories are often set in places that could not exist in the real world and are often important to the plot of the story.

Rationale

When students understand that fantasy stories often have unrealistic settings, they understand that things that happen in fantasy stories could not happen in the real world. This will help them recognize stories that fit into the fantasy genre.

Assess Learning

Observe students when they talk about fantasy stories. Notice if there is evidence of new learning based on the goal of this minilesson.

- Do students notice the unusual setting in fantasy stories?
- Can they talk about the reasons why the setting is unusual?
- Do they use the terms *fantasy*, *unusual*, *place*, and *setting*?

Minilesson

To help students think about the minilesson principle, provide an inquiry-based lesson about the setting of fantasy stories. Here is an example.

- Show pages 5–8 of *Kate and the Beanstalk*.

  What do you notice about the setting, or where and when the story takes place?

- Create a chart with the title and information about the setting.

  How is this setting unusual, or different from, a setting in the real world?

- Add responses to the chart. Read a few more pages and encourage students to notice the way this setting is unusual.

  Turn and talk about whether the setting is important to the plot, or the events that happen in this story.

- Ask students to share their thinking. As needed, prompt the conversation so students can make the connection between the unusual setting and the plot.

  Next, think about the setting in *Big Bad Bubble* as I show and read a few pages.

- Show and read pages 11–12.

  What do you notice?

- Add students' comments about the unusual setting to the chart.

Have a Try

Invite the students to talk about an unusual setting in a fantasy story with a partner.

▶ Show pages 5–6 of *Babushka Baba Yaga*.

Turn and talk about the setting in *Babushka Baba Yaga*.

What is unusual about it? How do the unusual settings in fantasy books make the stories fun to read?

▶ After time for discussion, ask students to share their thinking.

Summarize and Apply

Summarize the learning and remind students to notice unusual settings when they read fantasy stories.

What did you notice about the place where fantasy stories take place?

▶ Add the minilesson principle to the chart.

When you read today, you can choose a fantasy book from the basket. Notice if the setting is unusual or if it could happen in the real world. Bring the book when we meet so you can share.

Share

Following independent reading time, gather the students in a circle.

Did you read a fantasy book today? Talk about the setting. Was it unusual, or could it be a place in the real world?

Extend the Lesson (Optional)

After assessing students' understanding, you might decide to extend the learning.

▶ Have students create a list of unusual places where a story could take place. They can then use the list to choose a setting in a fantasy story that they write.

▶ Encourage students to think about the setting in a fantasy story they have read. Guide a discussion on how the setting can affect the plot. Have them think about how the plot would be different if the story had a different setting.

Fantasy stories often happen in an unusual place.

Title	Place	Why Is the Place Unusual?
Kate and the Beanstalk	The castle at the top of the beanstalk	There are not really high beanstalks with castles at the top of them.
BIG BAD BUBBLE	La La Land	There is not a place called La La Land where monsters live.
BABUSHKA Baba Yaga	Russia, near a forest with witches and fairies	Witches and fairies like the ones in the story do not exist.

Section 2: Literary Analysis

RML3
LA.U20.RML3

Reading Minilesson Principle
Normal objects and things can be magical in fantasy stories.

Understanding Fantasy

You Will Need

- several familiar fantasy stories with magic such as the following:
  - *Kate and the Beanstalk* by Mary Pope Osborne, from Text Set: Fractured Fairy Tales
  - *Under the Lemon Moon* by Edith Hope Fine, from Text Set: Kindness
  - *And Still the Turtle Watched* by Sheila MacGill-Callahan, from Text Set: Passage of Time
- chart paper and markers
- basket of fantasy books

Academic Language / Important Vocabulary

- fantasy
- magical

Continuum Connection

- Notice recurring themes or motifs in traditional literature and fantasy (p. 50)

Goal

Understand a common motif in fantasy is that normal objects and things can be magical.

Rationale

When students understand that in fantasy stories, normal objects can be magical, they recognize stories as fantasy and know what to expect from the genre.

Assess Learning

Observe students when they talk about magic in fantasy stories. Notice if there is evidence of new learning based on the goal of this minilesson.

- Do students notice magic in fantasy stories?
- Can they talk about the characteristics of the magical object?
- Do they use the terms *fantasy* and *magical?*

Minilesson

To help students think about the minilesson principle, provide an inquiry-based lesson about magic in fantasy stories. Here is an example.

- Show pages 3–4 of *Kate and the Beanstalk*.

  Think about these pages of *Kate and the Beanstalk*. What happens after Kate's mom throws the beans out the window?

- Turn the page to show the beanstalk.

  What is unusual about these beans?

- If students do not use the term *magical*, introduce it. On chart paper, write the title, the magical object, and student comments about how the magical object is important to the story.

  Now think about another story, *Under the Lemon Moon*.

- Show page 18.

  What is unusual about this woman, La Anciana, and this branch?

- Show page 22.

  How are this woman and this branch different from an ordinary woman and an ordinary branch?

- Encourage students to use the term *magical* as they share. Add students' ideas to chart.

  What clues do authors and illustrators give you, so you know when an object or thing is magical?

▶ Have a conversation about the ways magical objects are different from ordinary objects, and why that is often important to the story.

Have a Try

Invite the students to talk with a partner about magic in another fantasy story.

▶ Show pages 7–8 of *And Still the Turtle Watched*.

> Turn and talk about the magic in *And Still the Turtle Watched*. Why is it important to the story?

▶ After time for discussion, have students share ideas. Record responses on the chart.

Summarize and Apply

Summarize the learning and remind students to notice if there is magic in the fantasy books they read.

> What did you notice about some objects in fantasy stories?

▶ Write the minilesson principle at the top of the chart.

> You can choose a fantasy book from this basket to read today. If you read a fantasy story today, notice if there is magic and, if so, how it might be important. Bring the book when we meet so you can share.

Share

Following independent reading time, gather the students together in small groups.

> Did you read a fantasy story today that had a magical object or thing? Talk about that. How was the magic important to the story?

Extend the Lesson (Optional)

After assessing students' understanding, you might decide to extend the learning.

▶ Encourage students to include a magical element if they write fantasy stories.

Normal objects and things can be magical in fantasy stories.

Title	Magical Object	Why Is Magic Important in the Story?
Kate and the Beanstalk	beans	The beans grew into a beanstalk. Kate climbed the beanstalk to find the castle.
Under the Lemon Moon	La Anciana, lemon branch	An old woman appeared and gave Rosalinda a lemon branch. The branch made a lot of lemons grow overnight.
And Still the Turtle Watched	stone turtle	The stone turtle has feelings and watches people, so the turtle knows all of the changes to the land.

Reading Minilesson Principle
Characters in fantasy stories are often different from characters in realistic stories.

Understanding Fantasy

You Will Need

- several fantasy stories and realistic fiction stories, such as the following:
  - *Babushka Baba Yaga* by Patricia Polacco, from Text Set: Folktales
  - *Sophie's Masterpiece* by Eileen Spinelli, from Text Set: Kindness
  - *The Patchwork Quilt* by Valerie Flournoy, from Text Set: Determination
  - *The Contest Between the Sun and the Moon* by Heather Forest, from Text Set: Fables
  - *Our Seasons* by Janet Stevens, from Text Set: Passage of Time
- chart paper and markers
- basket of fantasy stories
- basket of realistic fiction stories

Academic Language / Important Vocabulary

- character
- fantasy
- realistic

Continuum Connection

- Understand the difference between realistic characters and those that appear in fantasy (p. 51)

Goal

Understand the difference between realistic characters and some of those that appear in fantasy.

Rationale

As students examine the difference between realistic characters and some of those that appear in fantasy, they learn to pay close attention to characters, which helps them know more about the genre they are reading.

Assess Learning

Observe students when they compare fantasy characters with realistic characters. Notice if there is evidence of new learning based on the goal of this minilesson.

- Can students recognize that some fantasy stories have characters that couldn't exist in real life?
- Are they able to compare and contrast fantasy characters with realistic characters?
- Do they use the terms *character*, *fantasy*, and *realistic*?

Minilesson

To help students think about the minilesson principle, provide an inquiry-based lesson to compare and contrast the characters in fantasy stories with the characters in realistic stories. Here is an example.

- Show the covers of *Babushka Baba Yaga* and *The Patchwork Quilt*.

  Think about the older women in these two stories: *Babushka Baba Yaga* and *The Patchwork Quilt*. Turn and talk about how Baba Yaga and Grandma are the same and how they are different.

- After time for discussion, ask students to share their thinking.

  How do you know that Baba Yaga is a fantasy character and Grandma is a realistic character?

- As students share ideas, create a chart with a column for fantasy characters and a column for realistic characters. Add students' ideas to the chart.

- Show the cover of *Sophie's Masterpiece* alongside the cover of *The Patchwork Quilt*.

  Now compare Sophie from *Sophie's Masterpiece* to Tanya from *The Patchwork Quilt*. What do you notice?

- As students share, record responses. Encourage them to use the terms *fantasy* and *realistic* as they discuss the characters.

Have a Try

Invite the students to compare characters in fantasy and realistic stories with a partner.

▶ Show and read pages 5–6 of *The Contest Between the Sun and the Wind* and pages 4–5 of *Our Seasons*.

Turn and talk about the wind and the sun in these two books. What do you notice?

▶ After time for discussion, have students share ideas. Record responses on the chart.

Summarize and Apply

Summarize the learning and remind students to notice the differences between fantasy characters and realistic characters.

What did you learn today about the characters in fantasy and realistic stories?

▶ Write the minilesson principle at the top of the chart.

You can choose a fantasy or a realistic book from these baskets to read today. If you read a fiction story today, think about the characters and whether they could exist in real life. Bring the book when we meet so you can share.

Share

Following independent reading time, gather the students together in small groups.

Talk with your group about the book you read and compare the characters in each of your stories. Talk about whether the characters are fantasy characters or realistic characters and how you know.

Extend the Lesson (Optional)

After assessing students' understanding, you might decide to extend the learning.

▶ Guide students in a discussion of characters in fantasy stories. Have them notice how the author gives them fantastic abilities but at the same time makes the character seem perfectly logical within the story.

Characters in fantasy stories are often different from characters in realistic stories.

Fantasy Characters	Realistic Characters
Babushka Baba Yaga dresses like a real woman, but she is really a witch underneath.	Grandma looks and acts like a real grandma.
Sophie is a spider who has a lady's head and wears shoes.	Tanya looks and acts like a real girl.
Sun and Wind have faces and talk.	The wind and sun are the same as the wind and sun in real life, so they are not characters. The characters are people.

Section 2: Literary Analysis

Assessment

After you have taught the minilessons in this umbrella, observe students as they talk and write about their reading across instructional contexts: interactive read-aloud, independent reading and literacy work, guided reading, shared reading, and book club. Use *The Literacy Continuum* (Fountas and Pinnell 2017) to observe students' reading and writing behaviors across instructional contexts.

▶ What evidence do you have of new understandings related to fantasy?

- Do students understand that authors sometimes write about things that could never happen in real life?

- Can they discuss distinguishing features of fantasy stories (e.g., normal objects and things can be magical, the setting can be unusual)?

- Can they compare and contrast characters in fantasy stories with characters in realistic stories?

- Do they use the terms *character*, *events*, *setting*, *fantasy*, *magical*, and *imagination* to talk about fantasy stories?

▶ In what other ways, beyond the scope of this umbrella, are students talking about fantasy?

- Do students notice how authors and illustrators convey the traits of the characters?

- Are they making a connection between fantasy stories and folktales—neither could happen in real life?

Use your observations to determine the next umbrella you will teach. You may also consult Minilessons Across the Year (pp. 55-57) for guidance.

Link to Writing

After teaching the minilessons in this umbrella, help students link the new learning to their own writing:

▶ Encourage students to use their imaginations to make a list of ideas for characters, settings, and events that could be used to write a fantasy story.

Reader's Notebook

When this umbrella is complete, provide a copy of the minilesson principles (see resources.fountasandpinnell.com) for students to glue in the reader's notebook (in the Minilessons section if using *Reader's Notebook: Intermediate* [Fountas and Pinnell 2011]), so they can refer to the information as needed.

Minilessons in This Umbrella

RML1   The setting is the time and place of the story.

RML2   The setting can be a time in the past or a faraway place.

RML3   The setting is often important to the story.

Before Teaching Umbrella 21 Minilessons

Read and discuss realistic fiction and fantasy stories that take place in different locations and time periods. Include books with settings that are an important part of the story. Use the following books from the *Fountas & Pinnell Classroom™ Interactive Read-Aloud Collection* text sets or choose realistic fiction and fantasy stories from your library.

Humorous Texts

Those Darn Squirrels! by Adam Rubin

The Great Fuzz Frenzy by Janet Stevens

Big Bad Bubble by Adam Rubin

Author/Illustrator Study: Janell Cannon

Verdi

Author/Illustrator Study: Patricia Polacco

Meteor!

The Keeping Quilt

Genre Study: Realistic Fiction

Sky Sisters by Jan Bourdeau Waboose

Honoring Traditions

Crane Boy by Diana Cohn

Deep in the Sahara by Kelly Cunnane

The Importance of Kindness

Last Day Blues by Julie Danneberg

As you read aloud and enjoy these texts together, help students

• understand the setting is the time and place of the story,

• think about the setting details, and

• notice how the setting is important to the story.

Humorous Texts

Janell Cannon

Patricia Polacco

Realistic Fiction

Honoring Traditions

Kindness

Section 2: Literary Analysis

Thinking About the Setting in Fiction Books

You Will Need

- several familiar fiction books with a variety of easily identifiable settings such as the following:
  - *Those Darn Squirrels!* by Adam Rubin, from Text Set: Humorous Texts
  - *Verdi* by Janell Cannon, from Text Set: Janell Cannon
  - *Meteor!* by Patricia Polacco, from Text Set: Patricia Polacco
  - *Sky Sisters* by Jan Bourdeau Waboose, from Text Set: Realistic Fiction
- chart paper and markers
- sticky notes

Academic Language / Important Vocabulary

- author
- illustrator
- time
- the present
- place
- setting

Continuum Connection

- Recall important details about the setting after a story is read (p. 51)

Goal

Infer the setting from the pictures and words.

Rationale

When students understand the setting is the time and place of a story, they begin to notice setting details and learn the author made a deliberate choice in choosing where and when a story happens.

Assess Learning

Observe students when they talk about setting. Notice if there is evidence of new learning based on the goal of this minilesson.

- ▶ Can students identify the setting by thinking about the words and illustrations?
- ▶ Do they think and talk about the details of the setting as it relates to characters and/or story events?
- ▶ Do they use the terms *author, illustrator, time, the present, place,* and *setting*?

Minilesson

To help students think about the minilesson principle, provide an interactive lesson about setting. Here is an example.

▶ Display the covers of several fiction stories with easily identifiable settings, such as *Those Darn Squirrels!, Verdi, Meteor!,* and *Sky Sisters*. Include examples that show variety in both time and place.

> Think about where and when these stories happen. Let's look at a few details from each story.

▶ Show pages 4–5, and then pages 12–13 of *Those Darn Squirrels!*

> What do you notice about where and when *Those Darn Squirrels!* takes place?

> The place and time of a story are called the *setting*. Let's make a chart with details about the setting.

▶ Make a chart with the headings *Title* and *Setting*. As students share ideas, use one color to add *time* details and another color to add *place* details. As needed, share a few more pages to look for details to help students notice the time and place.

> Let's look at another fiction story, *Verdi*. Notice details about the setting.

▶ Show page 1 and read the first two sentences on page 2. Then show a few more pages.

> What do you notice about the setting?

> Add students' suggestions to the chart.

> Repeat with *Meteor!* and *Sky Sisters*.

Have a Try

Invite the students to talk about setting with a partner.

> What are some of the settings you have read about? Turn and talk with your partner.

> After time for discussion, have several volunteers share. Encourage students to use the term *setting* when they talk about the time and place of a story.

Summarize and Apply

Summarize the learning and remind students to notice the setting when they read fiction stories.

> What did you learn today about the setting?

> Add the minilesson principle to the chart.

> If you read a fiction story today, think about the setting. Use sticky notes to mark any pages with words or illustrations that help you know the setting. Bring the book when we meet so you can share.

Share

Following independent reading time, gather the students together in groups of three.

> Talk about the setting of the story you read. Show the pages in the book that give clues about where and when the story happens.

Extend the Lesson (Optional)

After assessing students' understanding, you might decide to extend the learning.

> Pause to discuss the setting as students experience a new story. Ask them to talk about how the author lets them know the details of the time and place.

> From time to time, ask students how a story would change if it took place in a different location or time period.

The setting is the time and place of the story.

Title	Setting	
	Time	Place
Those Darn Squirrels!	the present	Old Man Fookwire's house and yard
Verdi	the present	in the jungle on a tropical island
Meteor!	long ago	a farm in Michigan
Sky Sisters	the present	outside during winter in the north

Section 2: Literary Analysis

RML2
LA.U21.RML2

Reading Minilesson Principle
The setting can be a time in the past or a faraway place.

Thinking About the Setting in Fiction Books

You Will Need

- several familiar fiction stories with settings in the past or a faraway place such as the following:
  - *Deep in the Sahara* by Kelly Cunnane, from Text Set: Honoring Traditions
  - *Big Bad Bubble* by Adam Rubin, from Text Set: Humorous Texts
  - *The Keeping Quilt* by Patricia Polacco, from Text Set: Patricia Polacco
- chart paper and markers
- sticky notes
- basket of books with a variety of settings

Academic Language / Important Vocabulary

- author
- illustrator
- setting

Continuum Connection

- Notice and understand settings that are distant in time and place from students' own experiences (p. 51)

Goal

Notice settings can be distant in time and place from their own experience.

Rationale

When students notice settings take place in a variety of locations and different periods in time, they begin to think about how an author chooses a setting to write about as well as the impact a setting has on the story.

Assess Learning

Observe students when they talk about settings that differ from their own experiences. Notice if there is evidence of new learning based on the goal of this minilesson.

- ▶ Do students notice text and illustration details that show a setting is distant in time or place from their own experience?
- ▶ Are they thinking about how authors and illustrators use setting in a story?
- ▶ Do they use the terms *author*, *illustrator*, and *setting*?

Minilesson

To help students think about the minilesson principle, provide an inquiry-based lesson about settings that differ from their own experiences. Here is an example.

- ▶ Show and read pages 1–2 of *Deep in the Sahara*.

  Turn and talk about what you notice about the setting of *Deep in the Sahara*.

- ▶ Create a chart with the title and information about the setting. After time for discussion, ask students to share information and add to the chart.

  What do the author and illustrator do on these pages to help you know about the setting of the story?

- ▶ Add to the chart. Read a few more pages and encourage students to notice the way this setting is different from their own experience.

  Next, think about the setting in *Big Bad Bubble* as I show and read a few pages.

- ▶ Show and read pages 3–4. Show a few additional pages with illustrations that provide setting details.

  What do you notice?

  What details do the author and illustrator include about the setting?

- ▶ Add students' suggestions to the chart.

Let's look at *The Keeping Quilt*. Notice details about the setting.

▸ Show and read pages 1–4 and the last page.

What do you notice about the setting?

▸ Add to the chart.

Have a Try

Invite the students to talk about setting with a partner.

▸ Display the three books discussed in this lesson.

Turn and talk about the differences in the settings in these three books. What do you think about the decisions these authors and illustrators made?

▸ After time for discussion, ask students to share their thinking.

Summarize and Apply

Summarize the learning and remind students to notice the setting when they read a fiction story.

What did you learn about the setting? Use the chart to remember.

▸ Add the minilesson principle to the top of the chart.

When you read today, you can choose a book from the basket. These books have stories that take place long ago or in a faraway place. Add a sticky note to any pages that help you know more about the setting. Bring the book when we meet so you can share.

Share

Following independent reading time, gather the students in groups of three.

In your group, talk about the setting of the fiction book you read today. Show any pages with sticky notes and talk about why you marked those pages.

Extend the Lesson (Optional)

After assessing students' understanding, you might decide to extend the learning.

▸ Encourage students to examine the illustrations in a fiction book and talk about how the illustrator shows a particular time and place.

▸ As students have experiences with other books with settings that are long ago or faraway, talk about how the story would change if the setting were in a different time and place.

The setting can be a time in the past or a faraway place.		
Title	Setting	How Do You Know?
Those Darn Squirrels!	a town in the Sahara Desert	Illustrations: sand, desert, scorpions, buildings, clothes Words: "Deep in the Sahara"
BIG BAD BUBBLE	La La Land, where monsters live	Illustrations: monsters, donuts grow on trees Words: "It reappears in La La Land . . . where the monsters live."
The Keeping Quilt	different times in history New York City a farm in Michigan	Illustrations: clothes, trains, and cars look old Words: "When my Great-Gramma Anna came to America" "In New York City" "a farm in Michigan" "twenty years ago"

Section 2: Literary Analysis

Reading Minilesson Principle
The setting is often important to the story.

Thinking About the Setting in Fiction Books

You Will Need

▸ several familiar fiction books with settings that are important to the story, such as the following:

- *Crane Boy* by Diana Cohn, from Text Set: Honoring Traditions

- *The Great Fuzz Frenzy* by Janet Stevens, from Text Set: Humorous Texts

- *Last Day Blues* by Julie Danneberg, from Text Set: Kindness

▸ chart paper and markers

Academic Language / Important Vocabulary

▸ author

▸ illustrator

▸ setting

Continuum Connection

▸ Infer the importance of the setting to the plot of the story in realistic and historical fiction and fantasy (p. 51)

Goal

Infer the importance of the setting to the plot of the story.

Rationale

As students think about the importance setting has on the plot, they learn that where and when a story happens can be as integral to the story as the plot and characters. This kind of thinking contributes to an understanding of how an author uses setting, plot, and characters to build a story.

Assess Learning

Observe students when they talk about setting. Notice if there is evidence of new learning based on the goal of this minilesson.

▸ Can students identify and talk about a story's setting?

▸ Are they able to infer and explain the importance of the setting?

▸ Do they use academic language, such as *author*, *illustrator*, and *setting*?

Minilesson

To help students think about the minilesson principle, provide an inquiry-based lesson about the importance of setting. Here is an example.

▸ Show and read pages 9–10 of *Crane Boy*.

  Think about the setting of *Crane Boy*. How is it important for this story? Turn and talk about that.

▸ On chart paper, create a three-column organizer with the headings *Title*, *Setting*, and *Why the Setting Is Important*. As needed, show a few more pages of the book to prompt the conversation about why the setting is important to the plot. After time for discussion, ask students to share ideas.

  Now think about the setting of another fiction story, *The Great Fuzz Frenzy*, and how the setting is important to the story.

▸ Show pages 1–2 and 33–34.

  What do you notice?

▸ As needed, highlight that the dog is a pet and the wild animals are prairie dogs and an eagle, so the setting has to be a place where the animals could all live. Record responses.

Have a Try

Invite the students to talk about the importance of setting with a partner.

▷ Show page 1 of *Last Day Blues*.

Turn and talk about where and when this story takes place. How is the setting important to the story?

▷ After time for discussion, have students share ideas. Record responses on the chart.

Summarize and Apply

Summarize the learning and remind students to notice the importance of the setting in a fiction story.

What did you learn today about the setting of a fiction story?

▷ Write the minilesson principle at the top of the chart.

If you read a fiction story today, think about the setting and how it might be important. Bring the book when we meet so you can share.

Share

Following independent reading time, gather the students together in small groups.

Talk to your group about the setting in your book. Show any pages that helped you understand why the setting was important for the story to make sense.

Extend the Lesson (Optional)

After assessing students' understanding, you might decide to extend the learning.

▷ As you read additional stories with settings that clearly impact the characters or events, pause to have students talk about that.

▷ **Writing About Reading** Have students make a list in a reader's notebook of words and phrases that describe settings. The list could be useful when students write their own stories.

The setting is often important to the story.

Title	Setting	Why the Setting Is Important
CRANE BOY	Bhutan, South Asia October	The story is about the cranes, and the time of year they come to visit this area. Festivals are important in Bhutan.
THE GREAT FUZZ FRENZY	A place in North America where prairie dogs and eagles live. Humans also live there because a pet dog is there.	All of these animals have to be in the same place for the story to happen as written.
Last Day Blues	School	The book is about the last day of school, so it has to take place at school.

Section 2: Literary Analysis

Assessment

After you have taught the minilessons in this umbrella, observe students as they talk and write about their reading across instructional contexts: interactive read-aloud, independent reading and literacy work, guided reading, shared reading, and book club. Use *The Literacy Continuum* (Fountas and Pinnell 2017) to observe students' reading and writing behaviors across instructional contexts.

> ▸ What evidence do you have of new understandings related to setting?
>> • Can students identify and talk about where and when a story takes place?
>> • Can they infer and explain the importance of a story's setting?
>> • Do they use academic language, such as *author, illustrator*, and *setting*?
> ▸ In what other ways, beyond the scope of this umbrella, are students talking about fiction stories?
>> • What other elements of fiction stories (e.g., characters, plot) do students notice and talk about?
>> • Are they talking about how details in the illustrations convey information?

Use your observations to determine the next umbrella you will teach. You may also consult Minilessons Across the Year (pp. 55-57) for guidance.

Link to Writing

After teaching the minilessons in this umbrella, help students link the new learning to their own writing:

> ▸ Before students write a story, have them make sketches of the setting so they can more clearly imagine the details they will write about. The more detailed they make the sketches, the more detailed their written descriptions will be.

Reader's Notebook

When this umbrella is complete, provide a copy of the minilesson principles (see resources.fountasandpinnell.com) for students to glue in the reader's notebook (in the Minilessons section if using *Reader's Notebook: Intermediate* [Fountas and Pinnell 2011]), so they can refer to the information as needed.

Minilessons in This Umbrella

RML1 Stories have a problem that gets solved.

RML2 Sometimes stories have more than one problem.

RML3 The high point of a story is the exciting part.

RML4 Stories have a beginning, a series of events, a high point, and an ending.

Before Teaching Umbrella 22 Minilessons

Read and discuss a variety high-quality fiction picture books with events that readers can easily follow, a clearly identified problem, a high point, and a solution. The minilessons in this umbrella use the following books from the *Fountas & Pinnell Classroom™ Interactive Read-Aloud Collection* text sets; however, you can use books based on the experiences and interests of the students in your class that have the characteristics listed above.

Humorous Texts

Those Darn Squirrels by Adam Rubin

Honoring Traditions

Bintou's Braids by Sylviane A. Diouf

Crouching Tiger by Ying Chang Compenstine

The Importance of Kindness

Enemy Pie by Derek Munson

Author/Illustrator Study: Janell Cannon

Stellaluna

Verdi

Author/Illustrator Study: Patricia Polacco

Some Birthday!

As you read aloud and enjoy these texts together, help students

- think about the problem, or problems, in the story,
- notice the structure of the story, including the series of events and high point that lead to the problem being solved, and
- summarize the story, including the problem, events, high point, and solution.

Humorous Texts

Honoring Traditions

Kindness

Janell Cannon

Patricia Polacco

Section 2: Literary Analysis

Reading Minilesson Principle
Stories have a problem that gets solved.

Understanding Plot

You Will Need

- several familiar fiction books with a clearly identified problem and solution, such as the following:
  - *Those Darn Squirrels* by Adam Rubin, from Text Set: Humorous Texts
  - *Bintou's Braids*, by Sylviane A. Diouf, from Text Set: Honoring Traditions
  - *Enemy Pie* by Derek Munson, from Text Set: Kindness
- chart paper and markers
- sticky notes

Academic Language / Important Vocabulary

- problem
- solution

Continuum Connection

- Notice and understand when a problem is solved (p. 51)

Goal

Notice and understand a simple plot with problem and solution.

Rationale

When students learn to identify the problem and solution in a fiction book, they can follow the events in a story, think about cause and effect, and understand how each part of a story relates to the other parts.

Assess Learning

Observe students when they talk about fiction stories and notice if there is evidence of new learning based on the goal of this minilesson.

- ▶ Are students able to identify the problem and solution?
- ▶ Are they able to talk about how the problem and solution are interrelated?
- ▶ Do they use academic language, such as *problem* and *solution*?

Minilesson

To help students think about the minilesson principle, provide an interactive lesson that supports identifying problem and solution. Here is an example.

> Think about *Those Darn Squirrels* and the problem that Old Man Fookwire has in the story.

▶ Show and read page 10.

> Turn and talk about Old Man Fookwire's problem.

▶ After a moment for discussion, ask a volunteer to share. Create a chart and add the title and problem.

> Now think about how Old Man Fookwire's problem was solved.

▶ Show and read pages 28–30.

> What is the solution to Old Man Fookwire's problem?

▶ Add the solution to the chart. Include an arrow linking the problem and solution.

> Think about the problem and solution in another book you know, *Bintou's Braids*. Listen and think as I reread a few pages.

▶ Show and read pages 4–6. Then, show and read pages 27–28.

> What was Bintou's problem and what was the solution to her problem?

▶ Add the title, problem, and solution to the chart.

Did you notice that I selected pages from the beginning of the book that showed the problem and pages from the end of the book that showed the solution? Why do you think I did that?

Have a Try

Invite the students to talk about a problem and solution.

> Remember *Enemy Pie*? Think about the problem and solution as I read a few pages.

▸ Read the first paragraph on page 4. Then read the last two paragraphs of the book.

> Turn and talk about the problem and solution.

▸ Ask students to share. Add to chart.

Summarize and Apply

Summarize the learning and remind students to think about the problem and solution in a fiction story.

> Look at the chart. What does it make you notice about stories?

▸ Write the principle at the top of the chart.

> If you read a fiction story today, think about the problem and how it gets solved. Place sticky notes on the pages that show the problem and solution. Bring the book when we meet so you can share.

Share

Following independent reading time, gather the students together in groups of three.

> If you read a fiction story today, talk about the problem and solution in the story. Show the pages with the problem and solution.

Extend the Lesson (Optional)

After assessing students' understanding, you might decide to extend the learning.

▸ **Writing About Reading** Encourage students to use a reader's notebook to write about the problem and solution in a fiction story.

Stories have a problem that gets solved.

Title	Problem	Solution
Those Darn Squirrels!	The squirrels kept taking all the birdfood. That made Old Man Fookwire mad.	The squirrels did nice things, to make Old Man Fookwire like them.
	Bintou wants braids, but she is too young.	Grandma styles Bintou's hair with beautiful bird bows.
Enemy Pie	Mean Jeremy Ross moved into the neighborhood, so the boy feels like his summer is ruined.	The boy makes friends with Jeremy.

RML2
LA.U22.RML2

Reading Minilesson Principle
Sometimes stories have more than one problem.

Understanding Plot

You Will Need

- several familiar fiction stories that have more than one problem, such as the following from Text Set: Janell Cannon
  - *Stellaluna* by Janell Cannon
  - *Verdi* by Janell Cannon
- chart paper and markers
- sticky notes

Academic Language / Important Vocabulary

- problem

Continuum Connection

- Follow a text with a complex plot and multiple problems (longer stories) (p. 51)

Goal

Understand that stories can have more than one problem.

Rationale

When students understand that some stories have more than one problem, it enables them to follow the plot in longer fiction books and understand how each problem contributes to the overall story and its conclusion.

Assess Learning

Observe students when they read and talk about plots with multiple problems and notice if there is evidence of new learning based on the goal of this minilesson.

- ▶ Are students able to recognize when a story has multiple problems?
- ▶ Do they use the term *problem*?

Minilesson

To help students think about the minilesson principle, provide an interactive lesson about stories that have more than one problem. Here is an example.

> Think about Stellaluna and the different problems she faced.

- ▶ Show page 4.

> What happened to Stellaluna when the owl attacked her mom?

- ▶ As students share, make a list of Stellaluna's problems on chart paper.

> Think about what problem Stellaluna has next when she lands in the bird nest.

- ▶ Read the first two paragraphs on page 9.

> What is Stellaluna concerned about, or what is her problem?

- ▶ Show page 20.

> What is difficult for Stellaluna when she tries to fly like the birds? What is her problem now?

> Can you think of any other problems that Stellaluna has?

Have a Try

Invite the students to talk with a partner about the problems in *Verdi*.

> Think about another story, *Verdi*. Turn and talk about the different problems Verdi faces in the story.

▶ After time for discussion, ask students to share their thinking. As needed, revisit a few illustrations and sentences. Add to the list.

Summarize and Apply

Summarize the learning and remind students to notice when there is more than one problem in a fiction story.

> What did you learn about stories and problems? Look at the chart to help you.

▶ Write the principle at the top of the chart.

> If you read a fiction story today, notice if the characters have just one problem or more than one problem. Place a sticky note on any pages that show a problem. Bring the book when we meet so you can share.

Share

Following independent reading time, gather the students in groups of three.

> If you read a fiction story today, did the characters have one problem or more than one problem? Talk about that with your group and show any pages that you marked in the book.

Extend the Lesson (Optional)

After assessing students' understanding, you might decide to extend the learning.

▶ **Writing About Reading** Encourage students to use a reader's notebook to write about a story in which the main character has more than one problem.

Sometimes stories have more than one problem.

Title	Problem
Stellaluna	• Stellaluna got separated from her mom. • Stellaluna was very hungry. • Stellaluna couldn't do the same things as the birds.
Verdi	• He turned green even though he tried not to. • He had to get away from the big fish.

Section 2: Literary Analysis

RML 3
LA.U22.RML3

Reading Minilesson Principle
The high point of a story is the exciting part.

Understanding Plot

You Will Need

- several familiar fiction stories that have a clearly identifiable high point, such as the following:
  - *Enemy Pie* by Derek Munson, from Text Set: Kindness
  - *Some Birthday!* by Patricia Polacco, from Text Set: Patricia Polacco
  - *Crouching Tiger* by Ying Chang Compenstine, from Text Set: Honoring Traditions
- chart paper and markers
- sticky notes

Academic Language / Important Vocabulary

- high point

Continuum Connection

- Recognize and discuss aspects of narrative structure: e.g., beginning, series of events, high point of the story, problem, resolution, ending (p. 51)

Goal

Understand how a story leads up to and changes after the climax.

Rationale

Understanding that in fiction stories the problem reaches a high point will help students recognize the way that an author has crafted a story and more deeply comprehend the plot.

Assess Learning

Observe students when they read and talk about the high point in fiction stories and notice if there is evidence of new learning based on the goal of this minilesson.

- Are students able to identify the high point of a story?
- Can they articulate why a certain event is the high point of a story?
- Do they use the term *high point?*

Minilesson

To help students think about the minilesson principle, invite them to identify the high point of a story. Here is an example.

- Show the cover of *Enemy Pie*.

  Do you remember how mean Jeremy Ross has moved to town, and the boy in the story thinks that the summer is ruined? The boy's father tells him about serving some Enemy Pie, but he has to spend the day with Jeremy first.

- Show and read pages 27–28.

  What happens during this part of the story?

- Record responses on chart paper.

  The boy realizes that Jeremy is his friend and stops him from eating the pie that he thinks is poisonous. This part of the story is called the high point. It is the most exciting part of the story. It leads to the problem being solved.

- Show the cover of *Some Birthday!*

  Now think about *Some Birthday!* Do you remember how the girl's problem is that she thinks her dad forgot her birthday and it will be a boring day?

- Show and read pages 21–22.

  What happens during this part of the story?

- Add responses to chart.

This part is the high point because it is very exciting that the kids think a monster is after them! You now know that she isn't going to have a boring birthday after all.

Have a Try

Invite the students to talk with a partner about the high point in another story.

> Listen as I read a page from *Crouching Tiger* and think about the high point of the story.

▶ Show and read pages 29–30.

> Turn and talk about the high point.

▶ Add to chart.

Summarize and Apply

Summarize the learning and remind students to notice the high point of a story when they read.

> What did you learn about the high point of a story?

▶ Review the chart and write the principle at the top of the chart.

> If you read a fiction story today, identify the high point. Put a sticky note on the page. Bring the book when we meet so you can share.

Share

Following independent reading time, gather the students together in the meeting area. Invite a few volunteers to share with the class.

> Did anyone notice the high point in a story you read today? Tell us about that and show the page from the book.

Extend the Lesson (Optional)

After assessing students' understanding, you might decide to extend the learning.

▶ During interactive read-aloud, help students notice that once the high point occurs the problem is usually solved and the story ends.

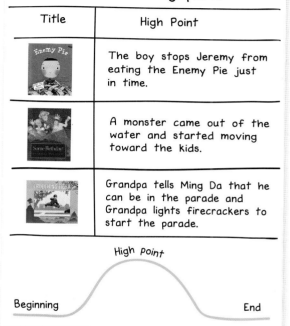

The high point of a story is the exciting part.

Title	High Point
Enemy Pie	The boy stops Jeremy from eating the Enemy Pie just in time.
Some Birthday	A monster came out of the water and started moving toward the kids.
Crouching Tiger	Grandpa tells Ming Da that he can be in the parade and Grandpa lights firecrackers to start the parade.

High Point

Beginning — End

Reading Minilesson Principle
Stories have a beginning, a series of events, a high point, and an ending.

Understanding Plot

You Will Need

- several familiar fiction stories that have a clearly identifiable beginning, series of events, high point, and solution, such as the following:
  - *Enemy Pie* by Derek Munson, from Text Set: Kindness
  - *Crouching Tiger* by Ying Chang Compenstine, from Text Set: Honoring Traditions
- chart paper prepared with a simple graph that includes labels for the parts of a story: beginning, several events, high point, and ending
- sticky notes
- markers

Academic Language / Important Vocabulary

- beginning
- events
- high point
- ending

Continuum Connection

- Recognize and discuss aspects of narrative structure: e.g., beginning, series of events, high point of the story, problem, resolution, ending (p. 51)

Goal

Recognize and discuss aspects of narrative structure: beginning, series of events, high point of the story, problem, resolution, and ending.

Rationale

As students recognize the pattern in fiction stories, they can think about the problem, identify the high point, and make predictions about the solution.

Assess Learning

Observe students when they recognize and talk about the parts of fiction stories and notice if there is evidence of new learning based on the goal of this minilesson.

- Can students identify the beginning, events, high point, and ending?
- Do they summarize events in the order in which they happened?
- Do they use the terms *beginning, events, high point*, and *ending*?

Minilesson

To help students think about the minilesson principle, invite them to notice elements of narrative structure. Here is an example.

- Show the prepared chart paper.

  What do you notice about what I have written?

- Ensure students understand that you have written the parts of a fiction story.

  Now, think about the chart as I talk about a few parts from *Enemy Pie*. Notice which parts I choose to talk about.

- Show the cover of *Enemy Pie*.

  Mean Jeremy just moved to the neighborhood, so the boy on the cover thinks that his whole summer is ruined. Dad then tells him about making Enemy Pie to solve his problem. Dad says that before serving it, the boy must spend the day with Jeremy. The boy goes to Jeremy's house and they play together. When they return to the boy's house to eat the Enemy Pie, suddenly the boy stops Jeremy from eating the bad pie! Then they notice that Dad is eating the pie, so they eat it, too. Before Jeremy goes home, he invites the boy to come over the next day to go on the trampoline.

- Direct students' attention to the chart.

  Which parts of the story did I include?

- As students share ideas, briefly write each on a sticky note and ask a student to place the sticky note on the correct place on the chart.

  What do you notice about the chart now?

Have a Try

Invite the students to identify the story elements of another book.

▶ Show the cover of *Crouching Tiger*.

Turn and tell your partner about *Crouching Tiger*. Remember to include the beginning, the important events, the high point, and the ending.

▶ After time for discussion, ask a few students to share.

Summarize and Apply

Summarize the learning and remind students to think about the parts of a story as they read.

What parts of the story did you talk about? Use the chart to remember.

▶ Write the principle at the top of the chart.

If you read a fiction book today, think about the different parts of the story. Bring the book when we meet so you can share.

Share

Following independent reading time, gather the students together in small groups.

If you read a fiction story today, share with your group which parts of the story you noticed. Try to include the beginning, a series of events, a high point, and an ending.

Extend the Lesson (Optional)

After assessing students' understanding, you might decide to extend the learning.

▶ Provide opportunities for students to summarize a story after it is heard. Encourage them to include the beginning, a series of events, a high point, and an ending.

▶ **Writing About Reading** Students could represent the parts of a story in the panels of a cartoon, which would show not only the parts of the story but the sequence.

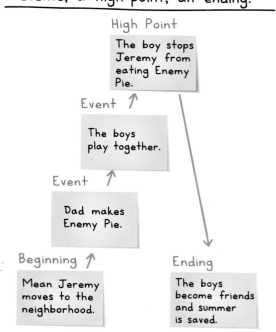

Stories have a beginning, a series of events, a high point, an ending.

High Point
The boy stops Jeremy from eating Enemy Pie.

Event ↑
The boys play together.

Event ↑
Dad makes Enemy Pie.

Beginning ↑
Mean Jeremy moves to the neighborhood.

Ending
The boys become friends and summer is saved.

Section 2: Literary Analysis

Assessment

After you have taught the minilessons in this umbrella, observe students as they talk and write about their reading across instructional contexts: interactive read-aloud, independent reading and literacy work, guided reading, shared reading, and book club. Use *The Literacy Continuum* (Fountas and Pinnell 2017) to observe students' reading and writing behaviors across instructional contexts.

▶ What evidence do you have of new understandings related to plot?

- Can students identify the problem and solution in a story?
- Are they able to identify the high point in a fiction story?
- Can they summarize a story by telling about the characters, setting, problem, events, and ending?
- Do they use the terms *character, problem, events*, and *high point* to talk about stories?

▶ In what other ways, beyond the scope of this umbrella, are students talking about stories?

- Are students beginning to notice characters' feelings and motivations, especially as related to the plot?
- Do they look closely at the illustrations?

Use your observations to determine the next umbrella you will teach. You may also consult Minilessons Across the Year (pp. 55-57) for guidance.

Link to Writing

After teaching the minilessons in this umbrella, help students link the new learning to their own writing:

▶ Encourage students to shape the stories they write with a beginning, a series of events that lead to a high point, and an ending.

Reader's Notebook

When this umbrella is complete, provide a copy of the minilesson principles (see resources.fountasandpinnell.com) for students to glue in the reader's notebook (in the Minilessons section if using *Reader's Notebook: Intermediate* [Fountas and Pinnell 2011]), so they can refer to the information as needed.

Patricia Polacco

Minilessons in This Umbrella

RML1 What the characters think, say, and do shows how they are feeling.

RML2 What the characters say and do shows how they feel about each other.

RML3 Think about what the characters really want.

RML4 What you know about the character can help you predict what the character will do next.

Before Teaching Umbrella 23 Minilessons

Read and discuss books with characters whose feelings can be observed through their words and the illustrations. Students should be reading fiction books during independent reading or fiction books should be available. Use the following books from the *Fountas & Pinnell Classroom™ Interactive Read-Aloud Collection* text sets or choose similar books you have.

Author/Illustrator Study: Patricia Polacco

Some Birthday!

Meteor!

Thunder Cake

The Keeping Quilt

The Bee Tree

Memory Stories

Saturdays and Teacakes by Lester L. Laminack

The Importance of Kindness

The Can Man by Laura E. Williams

As you read aloud and enjoy these texts together, help students

- notice character thoughts, words, and actions that are both explicit and implicit,
- consider how characters' thoughts, words, and actions show how they feel about themselves or others,
- think about what motivates characters,
- make inferences about characters, and
- make predictions based on what they know about a character.

Memory Stories

Kindness

Section 2: Literary Analysis

Reading Minilesson Principle

What the characters think, say, and do shows how they are feeling.

Understanding Characters' Feelings, Motivations, and Intentions

You Will Need

- two or three familiar fiction books that have characters with clear feelings, such as the following from Text Set: Patricia Polacco:
  - *Thunder Cake* by Patricia Polacco
  - *Meteor!* by Patricia Polacco
  - *Some Birthday!* by Patricia Polacco
- chart paper and markers
- sticky notes

Academic Language / Important Vocabulary

- character
- feelings
- dialogue
- thoughts
- behavior

Continuum Connection

- Infer characters' intentions, feelings, and motivations as revealed through thought, dialogue, behavior, and what others say or think about them [p. 51]

Goal

Infer characters' feelings as revealed through thought, dialogue, and behavior.

Rationale

When students learn to infer character feelings, they deepen their understanding of text and learn to relate to characters, which supports empathy.

Assess Learning

Observe students when they talk about how characters feel. Notice if there is evidence of new learning based on the goal of this minilesson.

- Are students able to connect a character's words, thoughts, and actions with the character's feelings?
- Do they understand they can learn things about the characters that aren't explicitly stated in the text?
- Do they use the terms *character, feelings, dialogue, thoughts,* and *behavior?*

Minilesson

To help students think about the minilesson principle, provide an interactive lesson using familiar texts to think about how characters feel. Here is an example.

- Show page 5 of *Thunder Cake*.

    How might the girl be feeling?

    How do you know?

- Guide them to understand the reason someone might hide under a bed during a thunderstorm and people sometimes hide when they are afraid. On chart paper, write students' observations. Then show the illustration on pages 6–7.

    How do you think the girl feels? Why is she hugging her grandma?

- Add students' ideas to the chart.
- Show and read pages 12–13 of *Meteor!*

    How can you tell how the characters are feeling?

- Add students' suggestions to the chart.
- Show and read page 3 of *Some Birthday!*

    Turn and talk about what the girl might be thinking about and how she might be feeling. How do you know?

- After discussion, have them share and add to the chart. Guide them to infer the girl probably thinks her dad forgot her birthday, which would make her feel disappointed.

Have a Try

Invite the students to talk with a partner about how a character might be feeling.

▶ Read the first two paragraphs from page 29 of *Thunder Cake*.

> Turn and talk about what the girl is doing at the end of the story and about how that shows you how she is feeling.

▶ After time for discussion, ask volunteers to share their thinking. Add to the chart.

Summarize and Apply

Summarize the learning and remind students to notice what characters do, say, and think to help understand how they are feeling.

> Look at the chart. What should you notice to understand how characters are feeling?

▶ Add the minilesson principle to the top of the chart.

> Today if you read a fiction story, notice what the characters do, say, or think. Place a sticky note on any pages that help you know how the characters are feeling. Bring your book when we meet so you can share.

Share

Following independent reading time, gather the students in small groups to talk about characters' feelings.

> Tell your group members about a place in your story where you can tell how the character is feeling. Show the pages you marked with sticky notes.

Extend the Lesson (Optional)

After assessing students' understanding, you might decide to extend the learning.

▶ Once students become comfortable with the goal of this minilesson, extend the idea by having students infer how a character is feeling by what the other characters do, think, and say about them (see the next minilesson).

What the characters think, say, and do shows how they are feeling.

Title	How the Character Might Be Feeling	How Do You Know?
thunder cake	afraid	The girl hides under the bed. The girl hugs her grandma. She looks worried.
METEOR!	excited curious	The people talk about the meteor and exaggerate what happened.
Some Birthday!	disappointed	The girl thinks that her dad forgot her birthday.
thunder cake	brave unafraid	The girl smiles and eats her Thunder Cake. She is laughing and has a happy look.

Section 2: Literary Analysis

Reading Minilesson Principle

What the characters say and do shows how they feel about each other.

Understanding Characters' Feelings, Motivations, and Intentions

You Will Need

- two or three familiar fiction books with easily identifiable character interactions, such as the following from Text Set: Patricia Polacco:
  - *The Keeping Quilt* by Patricia Polacco
  - *Thunder Cake* by Patricia Polacco
- chart paper and markers
- sticky notes
- basket of fiction books

Academic Language / Important Vocabulary

- characters
- relationship
- feel
- dialogue
- behavior

Continuum Connection

- Infer characters' intentions, feelings, and motivations as revealed through thought, dialogue, behavior, and what others say or think about them (p. 51)

Goal

Infer relationships between characters as revealed through dialogue and behavior.

Rationale

When students infer how characters feel about others by noticing words and behaviors, they deepen comprehension and empathy.

Assess Learning

Observe students when they talk about characters. Notice if there is evidence of new learning based on the goal of this minilesson.

- ▶ Do students talk about what the characters say and do?
- ▶ Are they able to interpret how characters feel about others using what the characters say and do as evidence of their feelings?
- ▶ Do they understand the terms *characters, relationship, feel, dialogue,* and *behavior?*

Minilesson

To help students think about the minilesson principle, provide an interactive lesson using familiar texts to think about how the characters feel about each other. Here is an example.

- ▶ Show the illustration on page 16 of *The Keeping Quilt.*

  Look at the decisions Patricia Polacco made here when she drew the characters. What do you notice?

- ▶ Read the text.

  How did Patricia Polacco show you how the characters might feel about each other?

- ▶ Create a chart and add a column for the title. Then add one column for inferring how the characters feel about each other and another column to provide evidence.

  How do you know how the characters are feeling even though Patricia Polacco does not write about their feelings?

- ▶ Add ideas to the chart. Read the text on page 7 of *Thunder Cake* and show the illustration.

  Think about what the grandma says and does for her granddaughter. Turn and talk about how the grandma feels about the girl. How do you know?

- ▶ After discussion, add ideas to the chart. Make sure students use evidence to support their opinions.

▸ Show and read pages 14–15.

> What do you know how the girl feels about her grandma?

▸ Add ideas to the chart.

Have a Try

Invite the students to talk about why it is important to know how characters feel about each other.

> Turn and talk to a partner about why an author might want you to know how one character feels about another. How can knowing about feelings help you understand the story better?

▸ After time for discussion, ask a few students to share.

Summarize and Apply

Summarize the learning and remind students to notice what the characters say and do when they read.

> Look at the chart. What should you notice to understand how one character feels about another?

▸ Write the minilesson principle on the chart.

> You can select a book from this basket to read today. While you read, think about how the characters feel about each other and how you know. Place a sticky note on pages that show how one character feels about another. Bring the book when we meet so you can share.

Share

Following independent reading time, gather the students together in groups of three to talk about their reading.

> Who read a fiction story? Talk about the characters. How do they show how they feel about each other by what they say and do? Show the pages you marked.

Extend the Lesson (Optional)

After assessing students' understanding, you might decide to extend the learning.

▸ Show students just the illustrations in a new fiction story with dialogue. Ask them to talk about how the characters feel about each other by what they do. Read the story and ask how what the characters say gives clues about how they feel about each other. Next ask students to infer how the characters' thoughts show how they are feeling.

What the characters say and do shows how they feel about each other.

Title	How Characters Feel About Each Other	How Do You Know?
The Keeping Quilt	The family members love each other.	They live close to each other. They pass on a special quilt to the new babies. They smile. They stand close.
Thunder Cake	The grandma loves her granddaughter and wants to take care of her and teach her. The girl trusts her grandma.	The grandma makes a plan, so the girl isn't scared. She comforts the girl. The girl walks with her grandma even when she is afraid.

Section 2: Literary Analysis

RML 3
LA.U23.RML3

Reading Minilesson Principle

Think about what the characters really want.

Understanding Characters' Feelings, Motivations, and Intentions

You Will Need

- several familiar fiction books that students, such as the following:
  - *The Bee Tree* by Patricia Polacco, from Text Set: Patricia Polacco
  - *Saturdays and Teacakes* by Lester L. Laminack, from Text Set: Memory Stories
  - *Some Birthday!* By Patricia Polacco, from Text Set: Patricia Polacco
- chart paper and markers
- sticky notes

Academic Language / Important Vocabulary

- character
- want
- dialogue
- behavior

Continuum Connection

- Infer characters' intentions, feelings, and motivations as revealed through thought, dialogue, behavior, and what others say or think about them (p. 51)

Goal

Infer characters' motivations as revealed through dialogue and behavior.

Rationale

When students think about why a character says or does something, they begin to understand what motivates that character and comprehend better.

Assess Learning

Observe students when they talk about character motivations. Notice if there is evidence of new learning based on the goal of this minilesson.

- Do students talk about what the characters say and do to get what they want?
- Are they able to support their thinking about character motivations with text evidence?
- Do they use the terms *character*, *want*, *dialogue*, and *behavior*?

Minilesson

To help students think about the minilesson principle, provide an interactive lesson using familiar texts to help think about characters' motivations. Here is an example.

- Revisit the text and illustrations on pages 1–2 and then pages 27–28 of *The Bee Tree*.

  What does Grandpa say or do that helps you know what he really wants?

  How does he get what he wants?

- As students provide suggestions, create a chart that shows how what Grandpa says and does relates to what he wants.

  Now think about the boy and his grandma in *Saturdays and Teacakes*.

- Turn through the pages as necessary to refresh students' memories.

  What is important to Mike and how do you know?

  What is important to Grandma and how do you know?

- Encourage students to support their ideas with evidence from the text and illustrations showing what Mike and Grandma say and do. Add to the chart.

  Look back at the chart. What does this chart show you?

- As needed have students realize the principle. Add the minilesson principle to the top of the chart.

  Why is it important to notice what characters say and do?

  How does it help you know what a character really wants, even when authors do not use words?

Have a Try

Invite the students to talk about how noticing what characters say and do helps them understand what characters really want.

▶ Read page 16 of *Some Birthday*.

　Turn and talk about what Dad says and what he really wants at the end of this page.

▶ After time for discussion, ask students to share. As needed, guide the conversation, so students understand that Dad wants the kids to take a bath without being asked.

Summarize and Apply

Summarize the learning and remind students to notice what characters say and do.

　You learned that you can notice what characters say and do to show what they really want.

　If you read a fiction book today, think about what the characters in the story say and do to figure out what they really want. Add a sticky note to any pages to show what the characters want. Bring the book when we meet.

Share

Following independent reading time, gather the students together in pairs to share.

　If you read a book today in which a character says or does something that helps you figure out what the character wants, tell your partner. Share any pages that you marked with sticky notes.

Extend the Lesson (Optional)

After assessing students' understanding, you might decide to extend the learning.

▶ During interactive read-aloud, talk about how what a character wants is a big part of what happens in the story.

▶ **Writing About Reading** Have students write in a reader's notebook about what a character in a fiction book wants.

Think about what the characters really want.

Title	What the Character Says and Does	What the Character Really Wants
The Bee Tree	Grandpa tells Mary Ellen about the bee tree. Later, he shows her how reading is sweet like honey. Grandpa teaches the lesson that reading takes time just like finding the bee tree takes time.	Grandpa wants Mary Ellen to enjoy reading.
Saturdays and Teacakes	Mike gets up very early and takes a long bike ride to Grandma's house. Grandma waits on the porch for Mike. She does not make any other plans.	Mike wants to spend time with Grandma. He also wants to eat teacakes. Grandma wants to spend the day with Mike. She also wants to teach him how to take care of the yard and how to cook.

Reading Minilesson Principle
What you know about the character can help you predict what the character will do next.

Understanding Characters' Feelings, Motivations, and Intentions

You Will Need

- one unfamiliar fiction book that lends to making predictions about character, such as the following:
  - *The Can Man* by Laura E. Williams, from Text Set: Kindness
- chart paper and markers
- sticky notes

Academic Language / Important Vocabulary

- character
- predict
- prediction

Continuum Connection

- Make predictions about what a character is likely to do and use evidence from the text to support predictions (p. 51)

Goal

Make predictions about what a character is likely to do and use evidence from the book to support predictions.

Rationale

When students think about why a character says or does something, they begin to understand motivation, which can be applied to their own lives.

Assess Learning

Observe students when they make predictions about what a character might do next. Notice if there is evidence of new learning based on the goal of this minilesson.

- ❯ Do students talk about what a character might do next in a story?
- ❯ Can they support their predictions with evidence from the story?
- ❯ Do they use as the terms *character, predict,* and *prediction*?

Minilesson

To help students think about the minilesson principle, provide an interactive lesson using an unfamiliar text to help them predict what a character will do next. Here is an example.

- ❯ Show the cover of *The Can Man* and read the title.

  Listen and think about what Tim is like.

- ❯ Read pages 1–4.

  What do you know about Tim so far?

- ❯ After discussion, ask students to share. Create a chart with their noticings.
- ❯ Continue reading through page 18.

  What else have you learned about Tim that can be added to the chart?

- ❯ Read through page 24.

  Tim seems to have changed his thinking. Notice how he is looking out the window at Mr. Peters. Why do you think he rushes outside? What might he do next? Turn and talk about that.

- ❯ After discussion, ask students to share predictions. Make a new column on the chart for predictions and add ideas.

  Thinking about what a character might do next is called making a prediction. You can predict what a character might do next based on what you know about the character so far.

Have a Try

Invite students to think about making character predictions with a partner.

> Listen as I read to compare what happens in the story with the class predictions.

▶ Read through page 26.

> Turn and talk about what actually happened. Talk about why it helps to think about what you know about a character so far to make predictions about what a character might do next.

Summarize and Apply

Summarize the learning and remind students they can make predictions about characters as they read.

> You learned you can predict what a character might do next based on what you know about a character.

▶ Write the minilesson principle at the top of the chart.

> Today you can choose to read a new fiction story. Think about what the character might do next as you read. Use a sticky note to mark pages that help you know about a character and help you predict what he will do next. Bring the book when we meet so you can share.

Share

Following independent reading time, gather students together in small groups.

> If you read a new book today, talk about what you thought might happen next to the character. Show the pages you marked with a sticky note and talk about why you marked those pages.

Extend the Lesson (Optional)

After assessing students' understanding, you might decide to extend the learning.

▶ After reading a new fiction story, ask students if the character did what they expected. Encourage them to use text evidence.

▶ **Writing About Reading** Have students write additional pages to a favorite story. Remind them to use what they know about characters to predict what might happen next.

What you know about the character can help you predict what the character will do next.

What Is Tim Like?	What Might Tim Do Next?
• Tim is friendly to people in the neighborhood.	• Tim might run out to buy the skateboard.
• Tim likes to skateboard.	• Tim might share his coins with Mr. Peters.
• Tim's family can't afford to buy a skateboard.	• Tim might run home to ask his family what to do.
• Tim is willing to work for what he wants.	

Assessment

After you have taught the minilessons in this umbrella, observe students as they talk and write about their reading across instructional contexts: interactive read-aloud, independent reading and literacy work, guided reading, shared reading, and book club. Use *The Literacy Continuum* (Fountas and Pinnell 2017) to observe students' reading and writing behaviors across instructional contexts.

▶ What evidence do you have of new understandings related to characters' feelings, thoughts, and motivations?

- Can students determine how a character is feeling by what the character says and does?
- Do they notice how the characters relate to each other to infer how the characters feel about each other?
- Can they infer motivation by what a character says and does?
- How well can they predict what a character might do next?
- Do they use terms such as *character, feelings, behaviors, dialogue,* and *thoughts*?

▶ In what other ways, beyond the scope of this umbrella, are students demonstrating an ability to understand characters?

- Are students noticing and talking about character traits?

Use your observations to determine the next umbrella you will teach. You may also consult Minilessons Across the Year (pp. 55-57) for guidance.

Link to Writing

After teaching the minilessons in this umbrella, help students link the new learning to their own writing:

▶ Have them write journal entries in the voice of a favorite character. Have them reflect on the character's feelings, intentions, and motivations as they consider what to write.

Reader's Notebook

When this umbrella is complete, provide a copy of the minilesson principles (see resources.fountasandpinnell.com) for students to glue in the reader's notebook (in the Minilessons section if using *Reader's Notebook: Intermediate* [Fountas and Pinnell 2011]), so they can refer to the information as needed.

Minilessons in This Umbrella

RML1   The character's behavior and dialogue show her traits.

RML2   The character's thoughts show his traits.

RML3   Sometimes an illustrator includes details in the pictures to show a character's traits.

RML4   Authors show a character's traits by telling what other characters say or think about him.

RML5   A character's traits are usually the same in each book in a series.

Before Teaching Umbrella 24 Minilessons

The minilessons in this umbrella help students recognize how authors and illustrators show their characters' traits. Read and discuss a variety of high-quality picture books that have characters with traits that are clearly observable through behavior, dialogue, thoughts, illustrations, and story events. Students should also be familiar with books in a series. The minilessons in this umbrella use examples from the following text sets from the *Fountas & Pinnell Classroom™ Interactive Read-Aloud Collection*, or from the *Fountas & Pinnell Classroom™ Independent Reading Collection*. You can also use examples of fiction books from your own classroom library.

Interactive Read-Aloud Collection

Facing Challenges

Goal! by Mina Javaherbin

Genre Study: Realistic Fiction

Dancing in the Wings by Debbie Allen

Dumpling Soup by Jama Kim Rattigan

Owl Moon by Jane Yolen

Exploring Memory Stories

The Printer by Myron Uhlberg

Saturdays and Teacakes by Lester L. Laminack

Grandma's Records by Eric Velasquez

Connecting Across Generations: Family

Sitti's Secrets by Naomi Shihab Nye

Author/Illustrator Study: Janell Cannon

Stellaluna

Independent Reading Collection

Inspector Flytrap by Tom Angleberger and Cece Bell

Inspector Flytrap: The President's Mane Is Missing by Tom Angleberger and Cece Bell

The Absent Author by Ron Roy

The Bald Bandit by Ron Roy

As you read aloud and enjoy these texts together, help students

- determine characters' traits from the story, and
- notice how a character's traits are usually the same in each book in a series.

Facing Challenges

Realistic Fiction

Memory Stories

Family

Janell Cannon

Independent Reading

Reading Minilesson Principle
The character's behavior and dialogue show her traits.

Understanding Character Traits

You Will Need

- several familiar fiction books with character traits that can be identified by behavior and dialogue, such as the following:
  - *Goal!* by Mina Javaherbin, from Text Set: Facing Challenges
  - *Dancing in the Wings,* by Debbie Allen, from Text Set: Realistic Fiction
  - *The Printer* by Myron Uhlberg, from Text Set: Memory Stories
- chart paper and markers
- sticky notes

Academic Language / Important Vocabulary

- character
- behavior
- dialogue
- traits

Continuum Connection

- Infer characters' traits as revealed through thought, dialogue, behavior, and what others say or think about them and use evidence from the text to describe them (p. 51)

Goal

Infer characters' traits as revealed through their behavior and dialogue.

Rationale

When students think about what a character's behavior and dialogue reveal about the character, they have a deeper comprehension of the story and develop empathy for the characters.

Assess Learning

Observe students when they talk about the behavior and dialogue of characters and notice if there is evidence of new learning based on the goal of this minilesson.

- ▶ Do students notice the behavior and dialogue of characters?
- ▶ Are they able to talk about how a character's traits are revealed?
- ▶ Do they use the terms *character, behavior, dialogue,* and *traits*?

Minilesson

Provide an inquiry-based lesson that helps students notice character traits and what they reveal. Here is an example.

- ▶ Show and read pages 3–6 of *Goal!*

  Notice Ajani's behavior. What types of things is he doing?

- ▶ After time for discussion, ask students to share ideas. On chart paper, record students' suggestions in a column.

  Character traits describe the character's personality. What does bringing his new soccer ball to play with friends show about Ajani's traits?

- ▶ Add students' suggestions to the chart in a new column.

  Now think about what Ajani says as I read part of this page.

- ▶ Read the first few lines on page 7, including the quote.

  How does what he says show his character traits?

- ▶ Add to the chart.
- ▶ Show and read pages 27–28.

  What does Ajani do?

  What does Ajani's behavior show about his character traits?

- ▶ Add to the chart.

  Now think about Sassy in *Dancing in the Wings.*

▶ Show and read pages 3, 15, and 16.

> What are some things Sassy says and does?

▶ Record responses on the chart as before.

> Think about Sassy's behavior and dialogue. What are some things you know about her character traits?

▶ Add to the chart.

Have a Try

Invite the students to talk about character traits in pairs.

▶ Show and read pages 9–10 of *The Printer*.

> Think about the things the boy's father says and does. In this picture, he is using sign language to say the word for *fire*. What do the father's behavior and dialogue show about his character traits? Turn and talk about that.

Summarize and Apply

Summarize the learning and remind students to think about character traits.

> What have you noticed about the things a character says and does?

▶ Add the principle to the chart.

> Today you can choose a fiction story to read. Think about how a character speaks and behaves and what that shows you about the character. Use a sticky note to mark pages. Bring the book when we meet so you can share.

Share

Following independent reading time, gather the students in groups of three.

> Share with your group what you noticed about a character's behavior and dialogue. What does that show about the character's traits?

Extend the Lesson (Optional)

After assessing students' understanding, you might decide to extend the learning.

▶ **Writing About Reading** Encourage students to write in a reader's notebook a description of a character, based on the character's behavior and dialogue.

The character's behavior and dialogue show her traits.

Title and Character	Character's Behavior and Dialogue	Character Traits
Ajani	Ajani brings his new soccer ball to play with friends.	Ajani is a good friend. He shares.
	"We'll take turns guarding for bullies."	Ajani is a leader. He is a problem solver.
	Ajani scores a goal.	Ajani is athletic and he likes sports.
Sassy	"At least I don't have that big forehead lookin' like a street lamp."	Sassy is sassy.
	Sassy wore a yellow leotard when the other kids wore black.	Sassy is independent.
	Sassy stood at the front of the class.	Sassy is confident.

Section 2: Literary Analysis

Reading Minilesson Principle
The character's thoughts show his traits.

Understanding Character Traits

You Will Need

- several familiar fiction stories with character traits that can be identified by a character's thoughts, such as the following:

  - *Dumpling Soup* by Jama Kim Rattigan, from Text Set: Realistic Fiction

  - *Sitti's Secrets* by Naomi Shihab Nye, from Text Set: Family

- chart paper and markers
- sticky notes

Academic Language / Important Vocabulary

- character
- thoughts
- traits

Continuum Connection

- Infer characters' traits as revealed through thought, dialogue, behavior, and what others say or think about them and use evidence from the text to describe them (p. 51)

Goal

Infer characters' traits as revealed through their inner thoughts.

Rationale

When students think about what a character's thoughts reveal, they learn to pay attention to a character's thoughts and develop empathy for the characters.

Assess Learning

Observe students when they talk about the thoughts of characters and notice if there is evidence of new learning based on the goal of this minilesson.

- ▶ Do students notice the thoughts of characters?
- ▶ Are they able to talk about what the character's thoughts reveal about the character?
- ▶ Do they use the terms *character, thoughts,* and *traits*?

Minilesson

To help students think about the minilesson principle, provide an interactive lesson to help them think about what a character's thoughts reveal. Here is an example.

- ▶ Read the second paragraph on page 7 of *Dumpling Soup*.

  Here is Marisa making dumplings with her grandma. What is she thinking about?

- ▶ On chart paper, add the title and character's name. Then write students' ideas about Marisa's thoughts.

- ▶ Show and read the fourth paragraph on page 18.

  What are Marisa's thoughts now?

- ▶ Add to chart. Read the third paragraph on page 27.

  What is Marisa thinking now?

- ▶ Add to the chart.

  You have noticed Marisa's thoughts. Turn and talk about how Marisa's thoughts show what she is like. Talk about her character traits.

- ▶ After time for discussion, add students' responses in a new column.

Have a Try

Invite the students to talk with a partner about Mona in *Sitti's Secrets*.

▸ Display and read pages 2 and 7 from *Sitti's Secrets*.

What are the Mona's thoughts?

What does that show about Mona's personality? Turn and talk about that.

▸ Record responses on the chart.

Summarize and Apply

Summarize the learning and remind students to think about how a character's thoughts can reveal information about character traits.

What do a character's thoughts show you?

▸ Write the principle at the top of the chart.

Today you can choose a fiction story to read. Think about a character's thoughts and what they show. Use a sticky note to mark important pages. Bring the book when we meet so you can share.

Share

Following independent reading time, gather the students together.

Who noticed a character's thoughts in a fiction book you read today? Share what you noticed and show any pages with sticky notes. What do the character's thoughts show about the character's traits?

Extend the Lesson (Optional)

After assessing students' understanding, you might decide to extend the learning.

▸ **Writing About Reading** Encourage students to use a reader's notebook to write what they learned about a character by reading the character's thoughts.

The character's thoughts show his traits.

Character	Character's Thoughts	Character Traits
Marisa in <u>Dumpling Soup</u>	Marisa worries that her dumplings are not good and nobody will want to eat them.	Marisa cares about doing good work.
	Marisa thinks that they should clean up the slippers.	Marisa tries to be responsible.
	Marisa thinks about how her family liked the soup.	Marisa loves and cares about her family.
Mona in <u>Sitti's Secrets</u>	Mona thinks about what her grandma is doing when she goes to sleep.	Mona loves and cares about her grandma.
	Mona wants to take off her grandma's scarf to see her hair color.	Mona is curious.

Section 2: Literary Analysis

RML3
LA.U24.RML3

Reading Minilesson Principle
Sometimes an illustrator includes details in the pictures to show a character's traits.

Understanding Character Traits

You Will Need

- several familiar fiction stories with illustrations that show character traits, such as the following:
  - *Saturdays and Teacakes* by Lester L. Laminack, from Text Set: Memory Stories
  - *Stellaluna* by Janell Cannon, from Text Set: Janell Cannon
  - *Grandma's Records* by Erik Velasquez, from Text Set: Memory Stories
- chart paper and markers
- sticky notes

Academic Language / Important Vocabulary

- illustrator
- illustration
- traits

Continuum Connection

- Infer a character's traits from the physical details the illustrations include about them [p. 51]

Goal

Infer a character's traits from the physical details the illustrations include about them.

Rationale

When students think about how illustrations can indicate character traits, they begin to think about the illustrator's craft and how an illustrator's choices can help a reader understand what a character is like.

Assess Learning

Observe students when they talk about how illustrations show a character's traits and notice if there is evidence of new learning based on the goal of this minilesson.

- Do students notice details in the illustrations?
- Are they able to talk about what the details in an illustration show about a character's traits?
- Do they use academic language, such as *illustrator, illustration,* and *traits*?

Minilesson

To help students think about the minilesson principle, provide an inquiry-based lesson to notice how the illustrations show character traits. Here is an example.

- Show page 10 of *Saturdays and Teacakes.*

  Here is the boy visiting his grandma, who he calls Mammaw. What do you notice about the details in the illustrations?

  What do you think the illustrator, Chris Soentpiet, wants to show you about what Mammaw is like as a character?

- Record responses on chart paper. Show and read page 15.

  What does this illustration tell you about Mammaw?

- Record responses. Repeat for pages 17 and 22.

  Now think about a different book, *Stellaluna.* Even though Stellaluna is a bat, the illustrator, Janell Cannon, adds some details that help you know about Stellaluna's character traits. See what you notice.

- Show the illustration on page 14.

  What do the details in this illustration show you about what Stellaluna is like as a character?

- Add to the chart. Repeat for pages 32 and 40.

Have a Try

Invite the students to talk with a partner about illustrations and character traits.

▶ Show pages 3, 5, 7, and 27 of *Grandma's Records*.

Turn and talk about what the illustrations show you about what Eric is like as a character.

Summarize and Apply

Summarize the learning and remind students to notice details in illustrations that show character traits.

What did you learn today about what illustrators sometimes do to show a character's traits?

▶ Write the principle at the top of the chart.

If you read a fiction story today, notice any illustrations that show something about a character's traits. Put a sticky note on the page. Bring the book when we meet so you can share.

Share

Following independent reading time, gather the students together.

Did anyone notice an illustration that shows something about a character's traits? Tell us about that and show the page from the book.

Extend the Lesson (Optional)

After assessing students' understanding, you might decide to extend the learning.

▶ **Writing About Reading** Encourage students to use a reader's notebook to write about details in a book's illustrations that show a character's traits.

Sometimes an illustrator includes details in the pictures to show a character's traits.

Title and Character	Illustrations	Character Traits
Saturdays and Teacakes — Mammaw	p. 10: Mammaw hugs her grandson.	Mammaw is loving.
	p. 15: Mammaw works in the garden.	Mammaw enjoys gardening. She is good at growing things.
	p. 17: Mammaw looks at the birds and eats outside.	Mammaw enjoys nature.
	p. 22: Mammaw cooks with her grandson.	Mammaw likes to cook. She is a patient teacher.
Stellaluna — Stellaluna	p. 14 Stellaluna feels upset when she gets into trouble from Mama Bird.	Stellaluna wants to do the right thing and be good.
	p. 32 Stellaluna finds her mother and has a smile.	Stellaluna is loving toward her family.
	p. 40 Stellaluna helps the birds when they can't see at night.	Stellaluna is a caring friend.

Reading Minilesson Principle

Authors show a character's traits by telling what other characters say or think about him.

Understanding Character Traits

You Will Need

▸ several familiar fiction stories with character traits that can be identified by the thoughts or words of other characters, such as the following:

- *Grandma's Records* by Eric Velasquez, from Text Set: Memory Stories
- *Owl Moon* by Jane Yolen, from Text Set: Realistic Fiction
- *Dancing in the Wings* by Debbie Allen, from Text Set: Realistic Fiction

▸ chart paper and markers

▸ sticky notes

Academic Language / Important Vocabulary

▸ character
▸ dialogue
▸ thoughts
▸ traits

Continuum Connection

▸ Infer characters' traits as revealed through thought, dialogue, behavior, and what others say or think about them and use evidence from the text to describe them (p. 51)

Goal

Infer characters' traits through what other characters say or think about them.

Rationale

As students notice what other characters say or think about a character, they begin to understand the choices an author makes in order to show the readers about a character.

Assess Learning

Observe students when they when they read or talk about fictional characters and notice if there is evidence of new learning based on the goal of this minilesson.

▸ Do students notice what characters say or think about other characters?

▸ Can they talk about what characters' thoughts and dialogue reveal about each other?

▸ Do they use the terms *character, dialogue, thoughts,* and *traits*?

Minilesson

To help students think about the minilesson principle, provide an inquiry-based lesson about what characters can teach you about other characters. Here is an example.

▸ Display and read page 2 of *Grandma's Records*.

> This book is about Eric and his grandma. What do you notice on this page that Eric says and thinks? How do Eric's words and thoughts help you understand what Grandma is like?

▸ After time for discussion, ask students to share ideas. On chart paper, write the title; character names; what Eric says, thinks, or does; and what that shows about Grandma.

▸ Show and read pages 3–4.

> What is Eric saying, thinking, or doing now? What does that tell you about Grandma's personality? Talk about her character traits.

▸ Add students' suggestions to the chart.

> Let's think about the characters in a different book, *Owl Moon*. Pay attention to what the girl says.

▸ Read and show page 3 from *Owl Moon*.

> What does the girl think, say, or do that tells you something about her dad?

▸ Add students' suggestions to a new row on the chart.

Have a Try

Invite the students to talk about what characters reveal about other characters.

> Think about Sassy and what you learn about her from the other characters.

▶ Read and show illustrations from the second page of *Dancing in the Wings*.

> Turn and talk about what the characters think, do, or say that shows you something about what Sassy is like.

Summarize and Apply

Summarize the learning and remind students to think about what characters reveal about other characters.

> Let's look at the chart. What can help you learn what a character is like?

▶ Write the principle at the top of the chart.

> Today you can choose a fiction story to read. As you read, notice what characters think, do, or say that shows you about another character. Use a sticky note to mark pages. Bring the book when we meet so you can share.

Authors show a character's traits by telling what other characters say or think about him.

Title and Character	What Others Say and Think About a Character	Character Traits
Grandma and Eric	Eric says that Grandma wraps him in her world of music.	Grandma is a music lover.
	Eric says that Grandma danced with Eric or alone.	Grandma loves to dance.
Pa and his daughter	The girl says that Pa pulled the cap over her ears and walks with her in the woods.	Pa is a caring dad. Pa takes care of his family.
Sassy	Hughie says that Sassy wouldn't need fins on the swim team.	Sassy has big feet.

Share

Following independent reading time, gather the students in the meeting area.

> Did anyone mark pages in a story that show you about a character by what the other characters think, do, or say? Share what you noticed.

Extend the Lesson (Optional)

After assessing students' understanding, you might decide to extend the learning.

▶ **Writing About Reading** Encourage students to use a reader's notebook to make a list of the different ways they learn about a character from a book.

Reading Minilesson Principle

A character's traits are usually the same in each book in a series.

Understanding Character Traits

You Will Need

- several books from a familiar book series with same main characters, such as the following from *Independent Reading Collection*:
  - *Inspector Flytrap* by Tom Angleberger and Cece Bell
  - *Inspector Flytrap: The President's Mane Is Missing* by Tom Angleberger and Cece Bell
  - *The Absent Author* by Ron Roy
  - *The Bald Bandit* by Ron Roy
- chart paper and markers

Academic Language / Important Vocabulary

- character
- series
- traits

Continuum Connection

- Connect texts by a range of categories: e.g., author, character, topic, genre, illustrator (p. 51)
- Make connections (similarities and differences) among texts that have the same author/illustrator, setting, characters, or theme (p. 51)

Goal

Understand that a character's traits usually remain consistent throughout the books in a series.

Rationale

When students notice that a character in a series has consistent character traits, they are better able to understand the character and the story and predict how a character will behave, speak, and think.

Assess Learning

Observe students when they talk about characters in a series and notice if there is evidence of new learning based on the goal of this minilesson.

- ▶ Can students identify a character's traits?
- ▶ Do they recognize that a character in a series usually has traits that are consistent throughout all of the books in that series?
- ▶ Do they use the terms *character, series,* and *traits*?

Minilesson

To help students think about the minilesson principle, provide an inquiry-based lesson about the traits of characters in a series. Here is an example.

- ▶ Show the covers of the books from the Inspector Flytrap series.

    Many of you are reading books from this series about Inspector Flytrap's detective agency. As I read a few pages from each book, think about what Inspector Flytrap is like as a character, or about his character traits.

- ▶ Read the first two or three pages of each book and show the illustrations.

    Turn and talk about Inspector Flytrap's character traits, or what he is like as a character.

- ▶ After time for discussion, ask students to share. List students' ideas on chart paper.

    Does Inspector Flytrap have the same character traits in both of these books?

- ▶ Read some pages that show Nina the Goat's character traits, such as pages 8–9 of the story "Inspector Flytrap in the Da Vinci Cold" in *Inspector Flytrap*. Record students' descriptions of Nina on the chart.

    Do Nina's character traits stay the same in all of the books in the series?

Have a Try

Invite the students to talk about character traits in a book series.

▶ Read the descriptions of Ruth Rose from the A to Z Mysteries books *The Absent Author* (pages 6–8) and *The Bald Bandit* (pages 3–4).

Turn and talk about whether Ruth's character traits stay the same in these books.

▶ After time for discussion, ask a few students to share. Add to chart.

Summarize and Apply

Summarize the learning and remind students to think about character traits.

Today you learned that characters in a series think, talk, and behave in a similar way in each book in a series. An author decides what character traits to give the characters.

▶ Write the principle at the top of the chart.

If you read books from a series today, think about that. Bring the book when we meet so you can share.

Share

Following independent reading time, gather the students in the meeting area.

Did anyone read a book from a series today? Share what you noticed about a character's traits.

Extend the Lesson (Optional)

After assessing students' understanding, you might decide to extend the learning.

▶ Ask students who have read series books to offer a book talk on the series.

▶ After students are familiar with several books in a series and they have talked about character traits, ask them to notice how the characters have changed or grown throughout the series. Assist with differentiating between character traits and character growth.

Title	Character	Character Traits
Inspector Flytrap	Inspector Flytrap	He believes that he is very important. / He likes to solve BIG DEAL mysteries.
	Nina the Goat	She complains. / She doesn't pay attention to traffic. / She is loyal.
A-Z Mysteries THE ABSENT AUTHOR	Ruth Rose	She always dresses in one bright color. / She has a loud voice. / She smiles sweetly when she's not acting sweet.

A character's traits are usually the same in each book in a series.

Section 2: Literary Analysis

Assessment

After you have taught the minilessons in this umbrella, observe students as they talk and write about their reading across instructional contexts: interactive read-aloud, independent reading and literacy work, guided reading, shared reading, and book club. Use *The Literacy Continuum* (Fountas and Pinnell 2017) to observe students' reading and writing behaviors across instructional contexts.

▶ What evidence do you have of new understandings related to character traits?

- Can students identify a character's behaviors, dialogue, and thoughts?
- Are they able to talk about how authors and illustrators reveal a character's traits?
- Do they recognize that characters in a series usually have the same traits in each book of the series?
- Do they use academic language, such as *character, behavior, dialogue,* and *traits,* to talk about stories?

▶ In what other ways, beyond the scope of this umbrella, are students talking about character traits?

- Are students beginning to notice that some characters change in some way at the end of a story?

Use your observations to determine the next umbrella you will teach. You may also consult Minilessons Across the Year (pp. 55-57) for guidance.

Link to Writing

After teaching the minilessons in this umbrella, help students link the new learning to their own writing:

▶ Encourage students to plan a fiction story by thinking how they can use behavior, dialogue, thoughts, and illustrations to show a character's traits. If they illustrate their stories, they could show a character's thoughts in a thought bubble.

Reader's Notebook

When this umbrella is complete, provide a copy of the minilesson principles (see resources.fountasandpinnell.com) for students to glue in the reader's notebook (in the Minilessons section if using *Reader's Notebook: Intermediate* [Fountas and Pinnell 2011]), so they can refer to the information as needed.

Minilessons in This Umbrella

RML1   Sometimes good characters make mistakes.

RML2   Sometimes characters change because of things that happen to them.

RML3   Sometimes characters from different books learn the same lesson.

Before Teaching Umbrella 25 Minilessons

Read and discuss a variety of high-quality picture books in which characters make mistakes, change, and learn lessons, as well as a few books in which characters do not change. Choose books with character change that is easily identifiable through text, illustrations, and events. The minilessons in this umbrella use books from the following text sets from the *Fountas & Pinnell Classroom™ Interactive Read-Aloud Collection*, or you can use fiction books from your own classroom library:

The Importance of Determination

Nothing but Trouble by Sue Stauffacher

Soccer Star by Mina Javaherbin

Ruby's Wish by Shirin Yim Bridges

Author/Illustrator Study: Janell Cannon

Crickwing

Stellaluna

Honoring Traditions

Bintou's Braids by Sylviane A. Diouf

As you read aloud and enjoy these texts together, help students

* notice that sometimes good characters make mistakes,
* identify the ways that a character changes as a result of things that happen to the character, and
* notice that sometimes characters from different books learn the same lesson.

Determination

Janell Cannon

Honoring Traditions

Section 2: Literary Analysis

Reading Minilesson Principle
Sometimes good characters make mistakes.

Thinking About Character Change

You Will Need

- several familiar fiction books in which characters make mistakes, such as the following:
  - *Nothing but Trouble* by Sue Stauffacher, from Text Set: Determination
  - *Crickwing* by Janell Cannon, from Text Set: Janell Cannon
- chart paper and markers
- sticky notes

Academic Language / Important Vocabulary

- character
- mistake

Continuum Connection

- Recognize that characters can have multiple dimensions: e.g., can be good but make mistakes, can change (p. 51)

Goal

Recognize that characters can have multiple dimensions: e.g., can be good but make mistakes and can change.

Rationale

When students recognize that good characters can make mistakes, they begin to connect the lives of characters to their own lives, and understand that it is okay to make mistakes and then learn from those mistakes.

Assess Learning

Observe students when they talk about the mistakes characters make and notice if there is evidence of new learning based on the goal of this minilesson.

- ▶ Do students understand that good characters can make mistakes?
- ▶ Do they use the terms *character* and *mistake*?

Minilesson

To help students think about the minilesson principle, provide an inquiry-based lesson about how good characters can make mistakes. Here is an example.

- ▶ Display and read pages 20–21 of *Nothing but Trouble*.

  Think about Althea Gibson, who became a famous tennis player and changed the game forever. What do you think about the way Althea acts during this part of the story?

- ▶ On chart paper, add columns for title, character, and mistake, then fill in the details based on students' suggestions.

- ▶ Display and read pages 22–23.

  What did Althea learn from her mistake?

  Does making a mistake mean that Althea is a bad person or a bad tennis player? Why or why not?

- ▶ Add students' suggestions to the mistake column.

Have a Try

Invite the students to talk in pairs about character change.

> Let's think about a character from a different book, *Crickwing*.

▸ Display and read pages 19–20.

> What mistake does Crickwing make?

▸ Display and read pages 27–30.

> How does Crickwing fix his mistake?

> Does making a mistake mean that Crickwing is a bad cockroach? Why or why not?

▸ After time for discussion, ask students to share their thinking. Add to chart.

Summarize and Apply

Help students summarize the learning and remind them to think about the mistakes good characters make.

> What did you learn about characters today?

▸ Write the principle at the top of the chart.

> Today you can choose a fiction story to read. As you read, notice if a character makes a mistake. Place a sticky note on the page that shows the mistake. Bring the book when we meet so you can share.

Share

Following independent reading time, gather students in groups of three.

> If you noticed a mistake that a character made, talk about that with your group. What did the character learn from the mistake?

Extend the Lesson (Optional)

After assessing students' understanding, you might decide to extend the learning.

▸ **Writing About Reading** Encourage students to write in a reader's notebook about the mistake that a character makes. Have them connect the character's mistake to a mistake they have made in their own lives and talk about what they learned.

Sometimes good characters make mistakes.

Title	Character	Mistake
Nothing but Trouble: The Story of Althea Gibson	Althea	Althea wouldn't shake hands after she lost the match. She was a great tennis player and person, but she needed to learn how to be a good sport.
Crickwing	Crickwing	Crickwing is mean to the leafcutter ants. The leafcutter ants let Crickwing go so he isn't hurt. He learns that they need help so he helps them.

Section 2: Literary Analysis

Reading Minilesson Principle
Sometimes characters change because of things that happen to them.

You Will Need

- several familiar fiction books in which characters change as a result of story events, such as the following:
  - *Stellaluna* by Janell Cannon, from Text Set: Janell Cannon
  - *Soccer Star* by Mina Javaherbin, from Text Set: Determination
  - *Bintou's Braids* by Sylviane A. Diouf, from Text Set: Honoring Traditions
- chart paper and markers
- sticky notes

Academic Language / Important Vocabulary

- character change
- event

Continuum Connection

- Notice character change and infer reasons from events of the plot (p. 51)

Goal

Notice character change and infer reasons from events of the plot.

Rationale

When students reflect on events that cause a character to change, they deepen their understanding of both the character and the plot of the story.

Assess Learning

Observe students when they talk about why characters change and notice if there is evidence of new learning based on the goal of this minilesson.

- Can students identify the events that cause a character to change?
- Are they able to infer the reasons why a character changes?
- Do they use academic language, such as *character change* and *event*?

Minilesson

To help students think about the minilesson principle, provide an interactive lesson about what causes a character to change. Here is an example.

- Show the first illustration and then the last illustration from *Stellaluna*.

  You noticed when we read *Stellaluna* that she changed from knowing only about being a bat in the beginning to being a good friend to the birds and appreciating all the ways they are similar and different.

  Why did that change happen?

- If needed, review a few illustrations or sentences to support the conversation.

- Create a chart with columns for title, character, event, and change. Ask for students' suggestions to fill in the chart. Encourage them to talk about the change itself as well as what happened in the story that caused the change to occur.

  Let's think about a character from a different book, Paulo in *Soccer Star*.

- Revisit page 5 and then pages 25–26.

  Paulo changed his mind about letting his sister be on the team. Why did that change happen?

- Add responses to the chart.

Have a Try

Invite the students to talk in pairs about events that cause a character to change.

▶ Revisit pages 1–2, 27–28, and 29–30 of *Bintou's Braids*.

Turn and talk about how Bintou changed and what happened in the story that caused her to change.

▶ After time for discussion, ask students to share. Add to chart.

Summarize and Apply

Summarize the learning and remind students to think about how and why characters change in stories.

Today you noticed that characters sometimes change in a story.

▶ Review the chart and write the principle at the top.

If you choose a fiction story to read today, notice whether a character changed and why. Place a sticky note on any pages you want to remember. Bring the book when we meet so you can share.

Share

Following independent reading time, gather the students in a circle.

Did anyone notice a character who changed? Share what you noticed and show any pages with sticky notes. What events happened in the story that caused the character to change?

Extend the Lesson (Optional)

After assessing students' understanding, you might decide to extend the learning.

▶ **Writing About Reading** Have students write in a reader's notebook about how and why a character changed. Encourage them to use specific details from the story in their writing.

Sometimes characters change because of things that happen to them.

Title	Character	Event	Change
Stellaluna	Stellaluna	Stellaluna was separated from her mother and became friends with a family of birds.	Stellaluna learns to be a good friend to others who are different.
Soccer Star	Paulo	Paulo's teammate was hurt and they needed an extra player.	Paulo changes his mind and decides to let his sister play on the team, even though girls could not play on the boys' team before.
	Bintou	Bintou's grandma styled her hair with beautiful bird bows.	Bintou changes her attitude about herself and feels happy about her pretty hair, even though she isn't old enough to have braids.

Reading Minilesson Principle
Sometimes characters from different books learn the same lesson.

Thinking About Character Change

You Will Need

- several familiar fiction stories in which characters learn the same lesson, such as the following:
  - *Crickwing* and *Stellaluna* by Janell Cannon, from Text Set: Janell Cannon
  - *Nothing but Trouble* by Sue Stauffacher and *Ruby's Wish* by Shirin Yim Bridges, from Text Set: Determination
- chart paper and markers

Academic Language / Important Vocabulary

- character
- lesson

Continuum Connection

- Make connections (e.g., content, theme) across fiction texts that are read aloud (p. 50)
- Connect texts by a range of categories (e.g., author, character, topic, genre, illustrator) (p. 50)

Goal

Connect characters across texts and understand that different books teach the same lesson.

Rationale

When students recognize that characters in different texts can learn similar lessons, they recognize and understand common themes, which supports their understanding of some universal truths.

Assess Learning

Observe students when they talk about similar lessons learned by characters in different books and notice if there is evidence of new learning based on the goal of this minilesson.

- Do students notice that characters in different books learn the same lesson?
- Do they use the terms *character* and *lesson?*

Minilesson

To help students think about the minilesson principle, provide a meaningful inquiry-based lesson related to lessons characters learn across texts. Here is an example.

- Display the covers of *Crickwing* and *Stellaluna*.

  Think about the lesson the main characters learned as I show a few illustrations.

- Show the first illustration and then the last illustration in *Stellaluna*. Then show the illustrations on pages 18 and 38 of *Crickwing*.

  What do you notice about the lesson that Stellaluna and Crickwing learned? Turn and talk about that.

- After time for discussion, ask students to share ideas. If needed, revisit a few sentences from each story to help students connect the common lesson learned. Record students' ideas on chart paper.

- Show the covers of *Nothing but Trouble* and *Ruby's Wish*.

  Now listen while I read a few pages from each of these books and think about the lesson both Althea and Ruby learned.

- Read page 6 and the first sentence of the Author's Note at the end of *Nothing but Trouble*. Then read page 11 and the last page of *Ruby's Wish*.

  What did Althea and Ruby learn about setting a goal?

- Add responses to the chart.

Have a Try

Invite the students to talk with a partner about lessons learned across texts.

> Look back at the chart and think about the common lessons learned by these characters in different books. How can they help you learn a lesson in your own life? Turn and talk about that.

Summarize and Apply

Summarize the learning and remind students to think about lessons learned by characters.

> You learned that characters from different books can learn the same or almost the same lesson.

▶ Write the principle on chart.

> If you read a fiction book today, think about whether another character you know has learned a similar lesson. You can also think about whether you have ever learned that lesson in your own life. Bring the book when we meet so you can share.

Sometimes characters from different books learn the same lesson.

Book	Lesson Learned
Crickwing / *Stellaluna*	You can be friends with others who are different from you.
Nothing but Trouble / *Ruby's Wish*	Never give up on your goals.

Share

Following independent reading time, gather the students together.

> Did anyone read a fiction book with a character who learned a lesson that you have read about or learned before? Share what you noticed.

Extend the Lesson (Optional)

After assessing students' understanding, you might decide to extend the learning.

▶ Use shared writing to create a chart of common lessons learned across books that you are reading with the class and that students are reading independently.

▶ **Writing About Reading** Encourage students to use a reader's notebook to make a chart of common lessons learned by characters in different books.

Section 2: Literary Analysis

Assessment

After you have taught the minilessons in this umbrella, observe students as they talk and write about their reading across instructional contexts: interactive read-aloud, independent reading and literacy work, guided reading, shared reading, and book club. Use *The Literacy Continuum* (Fountas and Pinnell 2017) to observe students' reading and writing behaviors across instructional contexts.

> ❱ What evidence do you have of new understandings related to character change?
>> • Are students aware that good characters make mistakes?
>> • Do they understand that sometimes characters change because of things that happen to them?
>> • Do they understand that sometimes characters from different books learn the same lesson?
>> • Do they use the terms *character, change, mistake*, and *lesson* when they talk about characters?
>
> ❱ In what other ways, beyond the scope of this umbrella, are students talking about characters?
>> • Are students beginning to think about the author's craft by noticing the choices an author makes in writing about characters?
>> • Are they writing about characters in a reader's notebook?

Use your observations to determine the next umbrella you will teach. You may also consult Minilessons Across the Year (pp. 55-57) for guidance.

Link to Writing

After teaching the minilessons in this umbrella, help students link the new learning to their own writing:

> ❱ Encourage students to write in a reader's notebook about how a character changed.
>
> ❱ Have students create a poster showing how a character has changed. On the top half, the character can be depicted doing something before the change, and on the bottom half, the character can be drawn doing something that shows the way the character has changed.

Reader's Notebook

When this umbrella is complete, provide a copy of the minilesson principles (see resources.fountasandpinnell.com) for students to glue in the reader's notebook (in the Minilessons section if using *Reader's Notebook: Intermediate* [Fountas and Pinnell 2011]), so they can refer to the information as needed.

Minilessons in This Umbrella

RML1	Illustrators give information about the story.
RML2	Illustrators use details to show something about a character.
RML3	Illustrators show motion and sound in the pictures to give information about the story.
RML4	Illustrators choose colors to create or change the feeling of a story.
RML5	Illustrators show time passing in the pictures to give information about the story.
RML6	Illustrators make images seem close or faraway.

Before Teaching Umbrella 26 Minilessons

Read and discuss fiction picture books with strong illustration support. Choose books with familiar topics that are authentic and relevant and engage students' intellectual curiosity and emotions. Use the following books from the *Fountas & Pinnell Classroom™ Interactive Read-Aloud Collection* text sets or choose engaging books from your library.

Facing Challenges

Ish by Peter H. Reynolds

Gettin' Through Thursday by Melrose Cooper

Goal! by Mina Javaherbin

Humorous Texts

Those Darn Squirrels! by Adam Rubin

The Great Fuzz Frenzy by Janet Stevens and Susan Stevens Crummel

The Importance of Determination

Soccer Star by Mina Javaherbin

The Patchwork Quilt by Valerie Flournoy

Nothing but Trouble by Sue Stauffacher

The Paperboy by Dav Pilkey

Ruby's Wish by Shirin Yim

Honoring Traditions

Nadia's Hands by Karen English

Crouching Tiger by Ying Chang Compestine

Animal Journeys

North by Nick Dowson

As you read aloud and enjoy these texts together, help children

* notice how illustrations support the meaning of the text,
* use details to show movement, sound, passage of time, and information about characters,
* discuss why illustrators make images seem close or faraway, and
* notice how illustrators can create and change the feeling of a story.

Overcoming Challenges

Humorous Texts

Determination

Honoring Traditions

Animal Journeys

Reading Minilesson Principle
Illustrations give information about the story.

Studying Illustrations in Fiction Books

You Will Need

- three or four familiar fiction books with clear illustrations, such as the following:
  - *Ish* by Peter H. Reynolds, from Text Set: Overcoming Challenges
  - *Those Darn Squirrels!* by Adam Rubin, from Text Set: Humorous Texts
  - *Soccer Star* by Mina Javaherbin, from Text Set: Determination
- chart paper and markers
- sticky notes

Academic Language / Important Vocabulary

- illustrations
- details

Continuum Connection

- Notice how illustrations and graphics can reflect the theme in a text (p. 52)

Goal

Gain new information from the illustrations in fiction books.

Rationale

When you teach students to notice that words and illustrations in fiction books together create meaning, students develop a deeper understanding of the story, and the decisions an illustrator makes to build a story beyond the words alone.

Assess Learning

Observe students when they talk about illustrations. Notice if there is evidence of new learning based on the goal of this minilesson.

- ▶ Do students notice information in the illustrations that helps them understand more about the story?
- ▶ Can they articulate the new information they have learned and how that helps them to understand the story more?
- ▶ Are they using the terms *illustrations* and *details*?

Minilesson

To help students think about the minilesson principle, choose texts with supportive illustrations and provide an inquiry-based lesson on how illustrations give the reader information. Here is an example.

- ▶ Hold up *Ish* and read the title.

  As I read, think about what extra information the illustrations give you.

- ▶ Read the two-page spread beginning with "Anytime."

  What do you notice from the illustration?

  Peter Reynolds drew an example of what he means by "Anytime. Anything. Anywhere."

- ▶ Record responses on the chart paper.
- ▶ Turn to the "crumpled gallery" page.

  How does this illustration help you understand what the author means by *the crumpled gallery*?

- ▶ Record responses on the chart. Then hold up *Those Darn Squirrels!* Read the title, and show the page that begins with "But the squirrels."

  How do these illustrations help you understand the squirrels' plan?

- ▶ Record responses on the chart.

Have a Try

Invite the students to talk about illustrations with a partner.

▶ Show *Soccer Star*. Show the following: the title page; pages that begin "dribble past our," "I dribble to Pedro," "We're off to the ocean"; and the final two-page spread.

> This book takes place in Brazil. Turn and talk about the information the illustrations give you about the setting.

▶ Ask a few students to share. Record responses on the chart.

Summarize and Apply

Summarize the learning and remind students to use illustrations to help them understand a story.

> Today you talked about how illustrators include details in the illustrations to help you understand information in the story.

▶ Review the chart and write the minilesson principle at the top.

> When you read today, think about illustrations that give you information. Put a sticky note on the page and bring the book when we meet so you can share.

Share

Following independent reading time, gather students together in the meeting area to talk about their reading.

> Who would like to share an illustration that shows more about the story?

Extend the Lesson (Optional)

After assessing students' understanding, you might decide to extend the learning.

▶ Continue to have students look for illustrations that help them understand information in the story. Add to the chart.

▶ **Writing About Reading** When students write about interactive read-aloud, shared reading, guided reading, or independent reading books, encourage them to write about how the illustrator shows more about the story through the illustrations.

Illustrations give information about the story.		
Title	**The illustration helps you understand…**	
ish	an example	What the author means by, "Anytime. Anything. Anywhere"
	meaning of a word	A crumpled gallery means a room with wrinkled pictures hanging on the wall like a museum.
Those Darn Squirrels!	characters' actions	The squirrels took the food by walking on the branch and bending it to the bird feeder.
Soccer Star	the setting	Small beach houses, close together, and coconut trees

Section 2: Literary Analysis

Reading Minilesson Principle
Illustrators use details to show something about a character.

Studying Illustrations in Fiction Books

Studying Illustrations in Fiction Books

You Will Need

- three or four familiar fiction books with clear illustrations that show more about a character, such as the following:
  - *The Great Fuzz Frenzy* by Janet Stevens and Susan Stevens Crummel, from Text Set: Humorous Texts
  - *Nadia's Hands* by Karen English, from Text Set: Honoring Traditions
  - *The Patchwork Quilt* by Valerie Flournoy, from Text Set: Determination
  - *Gettin' Through Thursday* by Melrose Cooper, from Text Set: Overcoming Challenges
- chart paper and markers
- sticky notes

Academic Language / Important Vocabulary

- illustrations
- character
- details

Continuum Connection

- Think about what characters are feeling from their facial expressions or gestures (p. 52)

Goal

Notice that details in illustrations often reveal something about a character.

Rationale

To understand the true meaning of a story, students must understand the characters. When you teach students to notice character details in illustrations, you help them to develop a deeper understanding of characters and story.

Assess Learning

Observe students when they talk about illustrations. Notice if there is evidence of new learning based on the goal of this minilesson.

- Can students describe how illustrations help them understand how characters feel and how characters feel about each other?
- Are they using the terms *illustrations, character,* and *details*?

Minilesson

To help students think about the minilesson principle, provide an inquiry-based lesson to talk about how illustrations provide information about characters. Here is an example.

- Hold up *The Great Fuzz Frenzy,* and show the page that says, "Stand back!"

  What do the illustrations show you about how Big Bark feels about himself?

- Record responses on the chart paper.

  How do the illustrations help you understand what the prairie dogs think about Big Bark?

- Record responses on the chart. Turn the page.

  What are the prairie dogs thinking and feeling here? How do you know that?

- Record responses on the chart.

  Hold up *The Patchwork Quilt.* Show the illustrations opposite "Grandma was sitting" and "Grandma's eyes."

  How do these two illustrations help you understand how Tanya feels about Grandma?

- Record responses on the chart.

Have a Try

Invite the students to talk about illustrations of characters with a partner.

▶ Hold up *Gettin' Through Thursday*.

   Take a look at this illustration.

▶ Show the page that begins with "Davis is out of."

   How is Davis feeling? What do you think he might be thinking? Turn and talk to your partner.

▶ Ask a few students to share. Record responses on the chart.

Summarize and Apply

Summarize the learning and remind students they can learn more about characters from the illustrations.

   Today you talked about how details in the illustrations help you understand more about the characters.

▶ Review the chart and write the minilesson principle at the top.

   When you read today, think about how illustrations provide details about the character. Put a sticky note on the page and bring the book when we meet so you can share.

Share

Following independent reading time, gather students together in the meeting area to talk about their reading.

   Who would like to share an example of an illustration that shows more about a character?

Extend the Lesson (Optional)

After assessing students' understanding, you might decide to extend the learning.

▶ Continue to have students look for examples of illustrations that show more information about characters. Add examples to the chart.

▶ **Writing About Reading** When students write about an interactive read-aloud, shared reading, guided reading, or independent reading book, encourage them to write about how the illustrator shows more about a character in the illustrations.

Illustrators use details to show something about a character.

Title	What the Illustration Shows	What the Illustration Means
THE GREAT FUZZ FRENZY	Big Bark thinks he is important. Prairie dogs are worried. They are frightened by Big Bark.	Big Bark's body and face show how he feels about himself. Prairie dogs' faces and bodies show how they feel.
NADIA'S HANDS	Nadia feels worried about being a flower girl. Nadia feels alone and is impatient. Nadia is now happy.	Nadia's face and body show how her feelings change.
PATCHWORK QUILT	Tanya is leaning on Grandma and listening carefully.	Tanya's body shows how she feels about another character.
GETTIN' THROUGH THURSDAY	Davis looks at Mom in surprise.	Davis' face shows what he might be thinking.

Reading Minilesson Principle
Illustrators show motion and sound in the pictures to give information about the story.

Studying Illustrations in Fiction Books

You Will Need

- three or four familiar fiction books with clear illustrations that show sound or movement, such as the following:
  - *Soccer Star* by Mina Javaherbin, from Text Set: Determination
  - *Nothing but Trouble* by Sue Stauffacher, from Text Set: Determination
  - *Goal!* by Mina Javaherbin, from Text Set: Overcoming Challenges
- chart paper and markers
- sticky notes

Academic Language / Important Vocabulary

- motion
- sound

Continuum Connection

- Notice how creates the illusion of sound and motion in pictures (p. 52)

Goal

Notice how illustrators create the illusion of sound and motion in pictures.

Rationale

When students notice how illustrators create the illusion of movement or sound in a picture, they realize that the illustrator must understand the story thoroughly in order to make good decisions about what to show in the illustrations and how to make them enhance the words.

Assess Learning

Observe students when they talk about illustrations. Notice if there is evidence of new learning based on the goal of this minilesson.

- ▶ Are students able to describe how an illustrator creates the illusion of movement or sound?
- ▶ Are they using the terms *motion* and *sound*?

Minilesson

To help students think about the minilesson principle, provide an inquiry-based lesson to talk about movement or sound in illustrations. Here is an example.

- ▶ Hold up *Soccer Star*. Show the two-page spread that begins with "We plan."

  How does the illustrator help you understand that the children are playing soccer?

- ▶ Record responses on the chart paper. Repeat the process with the page that begins "The game starts."

- ▶ Record responses on the chart. Then hold up *Nothing but Trouble*.

  As I read, notice and think about how the illustrator helps you see movement.

- ▶ Read the pages that begin with "Give her a stick" and "Buddy wasn't the only," showing the illustrations.

  How do the illustrations show movement?

- ▶ Record responses on the chart. Hold up the illustration of Buddy playing the saxophone.

  What do you think the illustrator is doing here?

- ▶ Record responses on the chart.

Have a Try

Invite the students to talk about illustrations with a partner.

▶ Hold up *Goal!* Share the following pages: soccer ball is large and going over the red bucket, the boy is hitting the soccer ball with his head, and the page that reads "Gooooal" with the ball in midair.

▶ Turn and talk to your partner about how these illustrations help you imagine movement.

▶ Ask a few to share. Record responses on the chart.

Summarize and Apply

Summarize the learning and remind students to think about motion or sound in an illustration.

> Today you talked about how illustrators show motion and sound to help you understand the story.

▶ Review the chart and write the minilesson principle at the top.

> When you read today, notice if there are any pictures in which the illustrator shows motion or sound. Put a sticky note on the page so you can share.

Share

Following independent reading time, gather students together in the meeting area to talk about their reading.

▶ Invite several students to share what they noticed in the illustrations in the book they read.

Extend the Lesson (Optional)

After assessing students' understanding, you might decide to extend the learning.

▶ Continue to have students look for illustrations that show movement or sound. Add examples to the chart.

▶ When students have the opportunity to publish their writing, encourage them to draw illustrations showing movement or sound.

▶ **Writing About Reading** When students write about an interactive read-aloud, shared reading, guided reading, or independent reading book, encourage them to write about how the illustrator created the illusion of movement or sound.

Illustrators show motion and sound in the pictures to give information about the story.

Title	Illustrations Show	How
Soccer Star	Movement Boys are jumping in the air, kicking the ball, and running.	Line around players and ball
Nothing but Trouble: The Story of Althea Gibson	Movement Althea is batting, jumping for a basketball shot, or catching a ball.	Rainbow colors
	Sound Rainbow movements from the saxophone	Swirls like a cloud
GOAL!	Movement The soccer ball is tipping over a bucket. Player and ball are in midair.	Objects and people

Reading Minilesson Principle
Illustrators choose colors to create or change the feeling of a story.

You Will Need

- three or four familiar fiction books with clear illustrations that support thinking about tone, such as the following:
  - *Goal!* by Mina Javaherbin, from Text Set: Overcoming Challenges
  - *The Paperboy* by Dav Pilkey, from Text Set: Determination
  - *Ruby's Wish* by Shirin Yim, from Text Set: Determination
- chart paper and markers
- sticky notes

Academic Language / Important Vocabulary

- illustration
- feeling

Continuum Connection

- Notice how the tone of a book is created by the illustrator's choice of colors (p. 52)
- Notice how the tone of a book changes when the illustrator shifts the color (p. 52)

Goal

Notice how the author's tone is supported by the illustrations' colors.

Rationale

Illustrators make decisions to use colors to create feelings in stories. Color can also signal a change in the story's tone. When students notice the illustrator's use of color, they better understand the feelings the author and illustrator want to convey, allowing for deeper conversations about the story and the illustrator's craft. Decide whether the word *tone* is appropriate for your students.

Assess Learning

Observe students when they talk about illustrations. Notice if there is evidence of new learning based on the goal of this minilesson.

- ▶ Are students able to identify illustrations with colors that change the feeling of the story and how the tone changes?
- ▶ Are they using the terms *illustration* and *feeling*?

Minilesson

To help students think about the minilesson principle, engage students in a short discussion of the feelings illustrations create. Here is an example.

- ▶ Show *Goal!* Show the page that starts "Jamal, Hassan."

  What do you notice about the color of the sky here?

- ▶ Record responses on chart paper. Show the page that starts, "Jamal covers."

  Now what do you notice about the color of the sky?

  What feeling do you think the illustrator shows on this page?

- ▶ Record responses on the chart.

  How has the feeling of the book changed?

  Now look at the page that begins, "Jamal climbs." What do you notice about the color of the sky here?

  What feelings do these colors show?

- ▶ Record responses on the chart. Show *The Paperboy*. Show the page that begins, "The paperboy knows."

  What do you notice about the colors on this page?

  What feeling do you get?

- ▶ Record responses. Hold up the page that says, "But little by little."

What do you notice about the colors on this page?

What feeling do you get?

▶ Record responses on the chart.

Have a Try

Invite the students to talk with a partner about colors in illustrations.

▶ Hold up *Ruby's Wish*. Turn to the page that begins with "So Ruby went."

Take a look at this illustration. What feeling do you get from the colors the illustrator chose? Turn and talk to your partner.

▶ Ask a few students to share. Record responses on the chart.

Summarize and Apply

Summarize the learning and remind students to notice the colors in illustrations.

Today you talked about how illustrators make decisions about using colors to create or change the feeling of a story.

▶ Write the principle at the top of the chart.

When you read today, think about illustrations in which the illustrator creates or changes feelings in a story with color. Put a sticky note on the illustration and bring the book when we meet so you can share.

Share

Following independent reading time, gather students together in the meeting area to talk about their reading.

Who would like to share an example of a picture in which an illustrator used color to create or change the feeling in a story?

Extend the Lesson (Optional)

After assessing students' understanding, you might decide to extend the learning.

▶ Continue to have students look for examples of illustrations that use color to create or change the tone of a story.

▶ An illustrator's use of color to create or change the tone of a story is something students could talk about during book club. Ask them to use sticky notes to mark pages when they read.

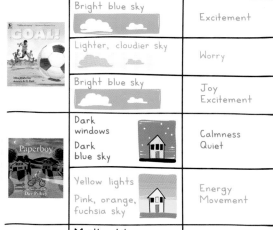

Illustrators choose colors to create or change the feeling of a story.

Book	Colors	Feeling
GOAL!	Bright blue sky	Excitement
	Lighter, cloudier sky	Worry
	Bright blue sky	Joy Excitement
Paperboy	Dark windows Dark blue sky	Calmness Quiet
	Yellow lights Pink, orange, fuchsia sky	Energy Movement
Ruby's Wish	Mostly white snow	Sadness

Section 2: Literary Analysis

Reading Minilesson Principle

Illustrators show time passing in the pictures to give information about the story.

Studying Illustrations in Fiction Books

You Will Need

- three or four familiar fiction books with clear illustrations showing the passage of time, such as the following:
  - *The Paperboy* by Dav Pilkey, from Text Set: Determination
  - *Crouching Tiger* by Ying Chang Compestine, from Text Set: Honoring Traditions
  - *Ruby's Wish* by Shirin Yim, from Text Set: Determination
- chart paper and markers
- sticky notes

Academic Language/ Important Vocabulary

- time passing
- illustration

Continuum Connection

- Notice how an illustrator shows the passage of time through illustrations (use of light, weather) (p. 52)

Goal

Notice how an illustrator shows the passage of time through illustrations (e.g., use of light, weather).

Rationale

Illustrators may indicate to readers that a story happens over a period of time through details in the illustrations. Helping students notice these details supports them in better understanding how much time passes between parts of the story.

Assess Learning

Observe students when they talk about illustrations. Notice if there is evidence of new learning based on the goal of this minilesson.

- Are students able to describe how an illustrator shows that time is passing?
- Can they describe how noticing the passage of time helps them understand the story better?
- Do they understand the concept of time passing?

Minilesson

To help students think about the minilesson principle, engage students in a short discussion of how an illustrator indicates the passage of time in the story's illustrations. Here is an example.

- Hold up *The Paperboy*.

  Look at the illustrations and think about how they help you notice time passing.

- Show the following two-page spreads: the dedication page, the boys' room, the pink and orange sky, and only the orange sky.

  How does the illustrator help you think about time passing?

- Record responses on the chart paper. Then hold up the book *Crouching Tiger*.

  As I show a few pages of this book think about how the illustrator shows time passing as Vinson waits to learn about kung fu.

- Show the illustrations to the right of each of these small illustrations: "Withdraw and Push," "Single Whip," and "Single Pushing Hand."

  What do you notice about time passing in these pictures?

- Record responses on the chart.

Have a Try

Invite the students to talk about illustrations with a partner.

▶ Hold up *Ruby's Wish*. Show the pages where the grandfather is patting Ruby on the head, where Ruby sits alone writing a poem, and where Ruby receives the red envelope.

> Turn and talk to your partner. How do these illustrations help you understand time is passing?

▶ Ask a few students to share. Record responses on the chart.

Summarize and Apply

Summarize the learning and remind students to notice time passing in illustrations.

> Today you talked about how illustrators help you understand a story by showing time passing in the pictures.

▶ Write the minilesson principle at the top of the chart.

> When you read today, think about pictures where the illustrator shows time passing. Put a sticky note on the page and bring the book when we meet so you can share.

Share

Following independent reading time, gather students together in the meeting area to talk about their reading.

> Who would like to share an example of an illustrator showing time passing?

Extend the Lesson (Optional)

After assessing students' understanding, you might decide to extend the learning.

▶ Continue to have students notice other examples of illustrations that show the passage of time.

▶ **Writing About Reading** When students write about an interactive read-aloud, shared reading, guided reading, or independent reading book, encourage them to write about how the illustrator showed the passage of time.

Illustrators show time passing in the pictures to give information about the story.

Title	Illustrations show	First	Second	Third
Paperboy	Night turning into day			
Crouching Tiger	Seasons changing			
Ruby's Wish	Years passing by child growing up			

RML 6
LA.U26.RML6

Reading Minilesson Principle
Illustrators make images seem close or faraway.

Studying Illustrations in Fiction Books

You Will Need

- three or four familiar fiction books with clear illustrations that show images close or faraway, and add meaning to the text, such as the following:
  - *The Great Fuzz Frenzy* by Janet Stevens and Susan Stevens Crummel, from Text Set: Humorous Texts
  - *North* by Nick Dowson, from Text Set: Animal Journeys
  - *Ruby's Wish* by Shirin Yim, from Text Set: Determination
- chart paper and markers
- sticky notes

Academic Language / Important Vocabulary

- images
- illustrations

Continuum Connection

- Notice how illustrators create perspective in their pictures (using images close-up, far away, creating distance in between, etc.) (p. 52)

Goal

Notice how illustrators create perspective in pictures (e.g., using images close-up, faraway, creating distance in between).

Rationale

Helping students to notice perspective in illustrations teaches them to consider what an illustrator might be drawing to their attention at that point in the story. Illustrators might zoom in on a central image to bring it closer to the reader, or put an image in the distance to create a feeling of space.

Assess Learning

Observe students when they talk about perspective in illustrations. Notice if there is evidence of new learning based on the goal of this minilesson.

- ▶ Are students able to identify where an illustrator made images seem close or faraway?
- ▶ Do they use the terms *images* and *illustrations*?

Minilesson

To help students think about the minilesson principle, engage students in a short discussion of perspective in illustrations. Here is an example.

- ▶ Hold up *The Great Fuzz Frenzy*. Show the following pages: tennis ball is the focus of the right page, "fuzz ran out," "I DID!," "SWOOP!," and the page with the eagle.

  What do you notice about how the objects in the illustrations are placed?

  How does the closeness of objects in the illustrations help you understand what is happening?

- ▶ Talk about the decisions that an illustrator makes when illustrating a page.
- ▶ Now hold up *North*. Show the following pages: 4–5, 26–27, and 38–39.

  As I show you a few pages of this book think about how the illustrator places important objects in the illustration on the page. Are the objects close-up or faraway?

Have a Try

Invite the students to talk about illustrations with a partner.

▶ Hold up *Ruby's Wish*. Show the first two-page spread, where the grandfather is looking down on the children, and the page where Ruby is seen in the window late at night.

> Turn and talk to your partner. Why did the illustrator make some images seem close and some faraway?

▶ Ask a few students to share.

Summarize and Apply

Summarize the learning and remind students to notice where objects are placed in illustrations.

> What are the reasons illustrators draw something close-up or faraway? What could we put on a chart to remember that?

▶ Record students' responses and then write the minilesson principle at the top of the chart.

> When you read today, notice illustrations in which the images seem close or faraway. Put a sticky note on the page and bring the book when we meet so you can share.

Share

Following independent reading time, gather students together in the meeting area to talk about their reading.

> Who would like to share an example of an illustration in which the illustrator made images seem close or faraway?

Extend the Lesson (Optional)

After assessing students' understanding, you might decide to extend the learning.

▶ Continue to have students look for examples of illustrators showing perspective. Add examples to the chart.

▶ **Writing About Reading** When students write about an interactive read-aloud, shared reading, guided reading, or independent reading books, encourage them to write about how the illustrator made images seem close or faraway.

Illustrators make images seem close or faraway.	
Objects close-up show . . .	**Objects** faraway show . . .
• what is important	• how small something is compared to the surroundings
• how powerful or dangerous something is	• how alone something is
• how large something is	• everything in a whole scene
	• how a character fits into a scene

Assessment

After you have taught the minilessons in this umbrella, observe students as they talk and write about their reading across instructional contexts: interactive read-aloud, independent reading and literacy work, guided reading, shared reading, and book club. Use *The Literacy Continuum* (Fountas and Pinnell 2017) to observe students' reading and writing behaviors across instructional contexts.

▶ What evidence do you have of new understandings related to studying illustrations in fiction books?

- Can students discuss how the illustrations give information about a story?
- Do they notice what illustrators are trying to achieve in the illustrations—show something about a character, show motion or sound, change the feeling or tone, show time passing, give information through changing the perspective?
- Do they use vocabulary such as *illustrations*, *details*, *feeling*, *motion*, *sound*, and *images* to talk about illustrations?

▶ In what other ways, beyond the scope of this umbrella, are students talking about illustrations?

- Do they look at the illustrations in nonfiction books to get more information about the topic?

Use your observations to determine the next umbrella you will teach. You may also consult Minilessons Across the Year (pp. 55-57) for guidance.

Link to Writing

After teaching the minilessons in this umbrella, help students link the new learning to their writing:

▶ When students illustrate their own stories, encourage them to experiment with some of the illustration techniques they have learned about (e.g., using color to change the tone; showing movement, sound, or the passage of time; showing objects close-up or faraway).

Reader's Notebook

When this umbrella is complete, provide a copy of the minilesson principles (see resources.fountasandpinnell.com) for students to glue in the reader's notebook (in the Minilessons section if using *Reader's Notebook: Intermediate* [Fountas and Pinnell 2011]), so they can refer to the information as needed.

Section 3 | Strategies and Skills

The strategies and skills minilessons are designed to bring a few important strategic actions to temporary, conscious attention so that students can apply them in their independent reading. By the time students participate in these minilessons, they should have engaged these strategic actions successfully in shared or guided reading as they build in-the-head literacy processing systems. These lessons reinforce the effective and efficient reading behaviors.

Minilessons in This Umbrella

RML1   Read the sentence again and think about what would make sense, sound right, and look right.

RML2   Notice who is talking when you read dialogue.

RML3   Read and think again about the story when you don't understand what you are reading.

Before Teaching Umbrella 1 Minilessons

The minilessons in this umbrella address using all sources of information in an orchestrated way when reading to monitor and self-correct. Some of the lessons are about noticing and fixing, while others are about monitoring meaning. If your students need more explicit instruction in searching for and using each source of information, consult *The Reading Minilessons Book, Grade 1* or *Grade 2*.

Read and discuss enlarged texts (e.g., big books, poetry charts), such as the selected text from the *Fountas & Pinnell Classroom™ Shared Reading Collection* listed below or a big book from your library, to support students in their ability to monitor and search for multiple sources of information. Read and discuss books with a mix of assigned and unassigned dialogue, such as those from the *Fountas & Pinnell Classroom™ Interactive Read-Aloud Collection* text sets listed below.

Interactive Read-Aoud Collection

Connecting Across Generations: Family

Knots on a Counting Rope by Bill Martin Jr. and John Archambault

Storm in the Night by Mary Stolz

Shared Reading Collection

A Meerkat Day by Geerhardt Heever

As you read aloud and enjoy these texts together, help students

- discuss what the book is about,
- demonstrate how to reread and check if the word makes sense, sounds right, and looks right,
- demonstrate how to keep track of who is speaking, and
- demonstrate how to stop and reread if something is confusing, to consolidate thinking and understand what is read.

Interactive Read-Aoud Collection
Family

Shared Reading Collection

Section 3: Strategies and Skills

Reading Minilesson Principle

Read the sentence again and think about what would make sense, sound right, and look right.

Monitoring, Searching, and Self-Correcting

You Will Need

- one or two familiar big books, such as *A Meerkat Day* by Geerhardt Heever, from *Shared Reading Collection*
- a sticky note covering *together* on p. 2 of *A Meerkat Day*
- pointer
- chart paper and markers
- document camera (optional)

Academic Language / Important Vocabulary

- makes sense
- looks right
- sounds right
- reread

Continuum Connection

- Reread to search for and use information from multiple sources (pp. 499, 507)
- Occasionally reread a word or phrase to monitor or self-correct (p. 499)
- Use multiple sources of information (visual information in print, meaning, pictures, graphics, language structure) to monitor and self-correct (pp. 507, 515)

Goal

Search for and use multiple sources of information (visual information in print, meaning/pictures, graphics, and language structure) to monitor and self-correct.

Rationale

When students can self-monitor, self-correct, and problem solve smoothly and efficiently, they can more easily integrate sources of information and read with fluency and comprehension.

Assess Learning

Observe students when they read aloud. Notice if there is evidence of new learning based on the goal of this minilesson.

- Do students reread words or phrases to monitor or self-correct?
- Do they understand the terms *makes sense, looks right, sounds right,* and *reread*?

Minilesson

To help students think about the minilesson principle, cover words that could potentially have a couple of meaningful options. Students will check if their attempt sounds right, makes sense, and looks right. Here is an example.

- Hold up *A Meerkat Day*. Read the title, and then page 2, pausing at *together*.

  What could this word be?

  Why do you think that? What letter(s) do you expect to see at the beginning of [the word they predicted]?

- Uncover the word slowly, running your pointer under the letters left to right.

  Were you right?

- If students predicted something different, have them talk about what else would make sense, sound right, and look right.

  Let's reread the sentence and check to make sure it makes sense, sounds right, and looks right. Does *together* make sense, sound right, and look right?

- Repeat with the word *danger* from page 6. Encourage students to think about what would make sense with the book and sound right in the sentence.

- Reread the phrase *to check for danger*.

  What did I do?

  I reread the phrase to make sure it makes sense, sounds right, and looks right. Sometimes you don't have to reread the whole sentence. You may reread a word or a few words to check on what you have read.

Have a Try

Invite the students to read a word with a partner.

▶ Repeat with the word *underground* from page 8. Read the page, pausing at the covered word.

> Turn and talk to your partner. What would sound right and make sense in this sentence?

▶ After turn and talk, ask students to share what they think the word could be and why. Then reread the sentence together. Say the word while slowly uncovering it.

> Does that make sense, sound right, and look right?

Summarize and Apply

Summarize the learning and remind students to think about what makes sense, sounds right, and looks right when they read.

> Today you learned when you read, it has to make sense, sound right, and look right. If you come to a word you don't know, what can you do?

▶ Record responses on chart paper and write the principle at the top.

> When you read today, if there is a word you don't know, reread the sentence, the word, or a few words and think about what would make sense, sound right, and look right.

Read the sentence again and think about what would makes sense, sound right, and look right.

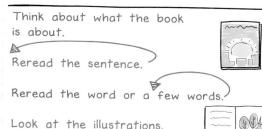

Think about what the book is about.

Reread the sentence.

Reread the word or a few words.

Look at the illustrations.

Share

Following independent reading time, gather students together in the meeting area to talk about their reading.

> Did anyone come to a word you didn't know? What did you do?

▶ Invite a few students to share. If possible, use a document camera to project the pages, or hold the book so everyone can see.

Extend the Lesson (Optional)

After assessing students' understanding, you might decide to extend the learning.

▶ Continue to support this behavior in guided reading or independent reading. From the *Prompting Guide, Part 1* (Fountas and Pinnell 2012), use prompts, such as the following: *Do you know a word that would make sense, sound right, and look right? That made sense and sounded right, but did it look right?*

RML2
SAS.U1.RML2

Reading Minilesson Principle
Notice who is talking when you read dialogue.

Monitoring, Searching, and Self-Correcting

You Will Need

- one or two familiar interactive read-aloud books that include both assigned and unassigned dialogue, such as the following from Text Set: Family:
  - *Storm in the Night* by Mary Stolz
  - *Knots on a Counting Rope* by Bill Martin Jr. and John Archambault
- chart paper prepared with the dialogue from p. 6 of *Storm in the Night* and p. 1 of *Knots on a Counting Rope*
- markers and highlighters in a variety of colors

Academic Language / Important Vocabulary

- dialogue
- assigned
- unassigned

Continuum Connection

- Follow and understand assigned and unassigned dialogue among multiple characters with a clear idea about who is speaking (p. 51)

Goal

Use an understanding of assigned and unassigned dialogue to self-monitor and self-correct.

Rationale

To monitor for meaning, readers must pay careful attention to who is talking in a story. Teaching students the signals for assigned dialogue, and how to track interchanges in unassigned dialogue, is critical for text comprehension.

Assess Learning

Observe students when they discuss books with dialogue. Notice if there is evidence of new learning based on the goal of this minilesson.

- ▶ Can students identify who is speaking in a story?
- ▶ Do they understand the different ways dialogue is presented in fiction texts?
- ▶ Do they understand the terms *dialogue, assigned,* and *unassigned*?

Minilesson

To help students think about the minilesson principle, choose familiar texts with a mixture of assigned and unassigned dialogue. Here is an example.

- ▶ Display the chart prepared with the dialogue from page 6 of *Storm in the Night*. Read the text aloud.

  Who is talking in this part of the story?

  How do you know?

- ▶ Ask two students to come up to highlight in different colors what each character is saying and write and highlight the names at the top, like a key.

  Sometimes authors tell who is talking. They might use the word *said, cried, exclaimed,* or *asked*. This kind of sentence is called assigned dialogue.

  Sometimes the author does *not* tell who is talking, so you have to think about what is happening in the story to understand who is speaking. This is called unassigned dialogue. You know Thomas and Grandfather are talking to each other, so you have to pay careful attention and think about which character says which line. Think about how people take turns and also about the meaning of the statement.

Have a Try

Invite the students to read and highlight dialogue.

▶ Hold up page 1 from *Knots on a Counting Rope*. Read aloud the dialogue from the chart.

> The two characters are Boy and Grandfather. Who can highlight the dialogue to show who is talking?

▶ Have two or more students highlight the sentences and explain how they know who is talking.

Summarize and Apply

Summarize the learning and remind students to notice who is talking when they read dialogue.

> What did you learn today?

▶ Write the principle at the top of the chart.

> If you read a book today that has dialogue, think about who is talking. Bring the book when we come back together so you can share.

Share

Following independent reading time, gather students together in the meeting area to talk about their reading.

> Who read a book that has dialogue? How did you know who was speaking?

Extend the Lesson (Optional)

After assessing students' understanding, you might decide to extend the learning.

▶ During interactive read-aloud and guided reading, make sure students understand who is speaking.

▶ Create a chart that lists the different ways authors indicate assigned dialogue (e.g., *said, explained, laughed*).

▶ Allow for time during the week for groups of students to act out readers' theater scripts. Some students may want to write their own readers' theater scripts.

Notice who is talking when you read dialogue.

Storm in the Night
Characters: Thomas, Grandfather

"I'm thinking," said Thomas.

"Ah," said Grandfather.

"I'm trying to think what you were like when you were my age."

"That's what I was like," said Grandfather.

"What?"

"Like someone your age."

"Did you look like me?"

"Very much like you."

Knots on a Counting Rope
Characters: Boy, Grandfather

Tell me the story again, Grandfather. Tell me who I am.

I have told you many times, Boy. You know the story by heart.

But it sounds better when you tell it, Grandfather.

Then listen carefully. This may be the last telling.

Section 3: Strategies and Skills

Monitoring, Searching, and Self-Correcting

You Will Need

- one or two familiar fiction books with a narrative structure that includes multidimensional characters such as the following:
  - *Knots on a Counting Rope* by Bill Martin Jr. and John Archambault, from Text Set: Family
- chart paper and markers
- document camera (optional) or transcribe the last two paragraphs from p. 10 of *Knots on a Counting Rope* to chart paper
- sticky notes

Academic Language / Important Vocabulary

- reread

Continuum Connection

- Use awareness of narrative structure and of the attributes of multidimensional characters that change to self-monitor and self-correct (p. 499, 507, 515)

Goal

Use awareness of narrative structure and multidimensional characters to self-monitor and self-correct when meaning is lost.

Rationale

It is important to teach students to think about what they are reading and self-monitor for meaning. When they learn to reread and think about what is happening if they don't understand, it will help them to recover meaning and consolidate their understanding.

Assess Learning

Observe students when they talk about self-monitoring their reading. Notice if there is evidence of new learning based on the goal of this minilesson.

- Do students reread to think more about the story or to clear up confusions they may have?
- Do they use the term *reread*?

Minilesson

To help students think about the minilesson principle, engage students in a demonstration of self-monitoring and self-correcting. Here is an example.

> Have you ever come to a part of a book that doesn't make sense? I did when I was reading *Knots on a Counting Rope*.

- Show the book. Read the last two paragraphs from page 10.

> When I read this part of the story, I was confused by the words *boy* and *Boy* with a capital *B*. Who are the authors talking about?

> Notice what I do to help me understand what is going on in the story. I remember that Grandfather is telling a story about the day the boy was born and was very sick.

- Reread the page aloud.

> Now I am thinking that when the authors write *Boy*—with a capital B—they mean the boy who is talking with Grandfather. When the authors write *boy*—with a lowercase *b*—they mean Grandfather's memory of the boy as a baby. When Grandfather says, "This boy child will not die," he means the baby boy was sick but will live.

> What is something I did to help me understand?

- Record their noticings on chart paper.

> I stopped and thought about what had happened in the story up to that part. I reread and thought again what was happening to clear up my confusion.

Have a Try

Invite the students to talk with a partner about a book that was confusing.

> Look at the list on the chart. Turn and talk to your partner about a time you did one of these things to help you understand.

Summarize and Apply

Summarize the learning and remind students to think about what to do when they don't understand what they are reading.

▶ Review the chart and write the principle at the top.

> When you read today, if you come to any parts that are confusing, reread to help you think about what is happening in the story. Put a sticky note on a part that is confusing to you. Bring the book when we come back together so you can share.

Share

Following independent reading time, gather students together in the meeting area to talk about their reading.

> Who would like to share from a story they read today? Were there any confusing parts you had to reread?

Extend the Lesson (Optional)

After assessing students' understanding, you might decide to extend the learning.

▶ Use the *Prompting Guide, Part 1* (Fountas and Pinnell 2012) during guided reading to support students in monitoring their reading for meaning. Use the following prompts:

- *What confused you?*
- *Do you want to look back (forward)?*
- *Find the part(s) of the story (book) that you didn't understand.*
- *Were there parts of the book that you didn't understand?*
- *Were there parts where you wanted to slow down and think more?*

Read and think again about the story when you don't understand what you are reading.

Stop!

Slow down!

Think about what has happened in the story.

Reread the confusing part.

Think again what is happening in the story.

Section 3: Strategies and Skills

Assessment

After you have taught minilessons in this umbrella, observe students as they talk and write about their reading across instructional contexts: interactive read-aloud, independent reading and literacy work, guided reading, shared reading, and book club. Use *The Literacy Continuum* (Fountas and Pinnell 2017) to observe students' reading and writing behaviors across instructional contexts.

▶ What evidence do you have of new understandings related to self-monitoring, searching, and self-correcting?

- Do students stop after an error and make multiple attempts until accurate?
- Do they reread to search for additional sources of information?
- Are they able to follow who is speaking in the story?
- Do they stop when they lose meaning and reread to gain understanding?
- Do they understand and use the terms *makes sense, looks right, sounds right, reread, assigned, unassigned,* and *dialogue*?

▶ In what other ways, beyond the scope of this umbrella, are they maintaining the meaning of what they read?

- What ways do students know to solve unfamiliar words?
- Do they know how to read the punctuation?

Use your observations to determine the next umbrella you will teach. You may also consult Minilessons Across the Year (pp. 55-57) for guidance.

Link to Writing

After teaching the minilessons in this umbrella, help students link the new learning to their writing:

▶ Whenever students write, support them in monitoring what is being written to ensure it makes sense, sounds right, and looks right. Model how to articulate the sounds of a word slowly. Remind students to reread to both confirm and check that what they wrote makes sense.

Reader's Notebook

When this umbrella is complete, provide a copy of the minilesson principles (see resources.fountasandpinnell.com) for students to glue in the reader's notebook (in the Minilessons section if using *Reader's Notebook: Intermediate* [Fountas and Pinnell 2011]), so they can refer to the information as needed.

Minilessons in This Umbrella

RML1   Use your finger to help you learn how to take apart new words.

RML2   Break a word between two consonants but keep consonant digraphs together.

RML3   Break a word after the syllable that ends with a vowel and say a long vowel sound.

RML4   Break a word after the syllable that ends with a consonant and say a short vowel sound.

RML5   Sometimes break a word between the two vowels and say a long vowel sound.

RML6   Break a word before the consonant and *le*.

RML7   Cover the prefix or suffix and take apart the base word first.

RML8   Look for a part of the word that can help.

RML9   Sometimes the writer tells the meaning of a word in the sentence, the paragraph, or elsewhere in the book.

RML10   Sometimes the writer uses a word in the sentence that is similar in meaning to the word you don't know.

RML11   When you come to a word you don't know, you can work it out.

Before Teaching Umbrella 2 Minilessons

Make sure students know phonics terms (e.g., word part, consonant). Use big books or large-print charts, or project text with a document camera. Choose books with two- and three-syllable words and unknown words. Use the texts from the *Fountas & Pinnell Classroom™ Shared Reading Collection* and *Interactive Read-Aloud Collection* text sets listed below, or choose books from your library.

Shared Reading Collection

Amazing Nests by Mary Ebeltoft Reid

From Flower to Honey by June Schwartz

Exploring Underground by Louis Petrone

A Meerkat Day by Geerhardt Heever

Wolf Pack by Annette Bay Pimentel

From Beans to Chocolate by June Schwartz

Saving Cranes by Brenda Iasevoli

Trapped in Tar by Hannah Cales

Tiny but Fierce by Cheri Colburn

Far Above Earth by Jane Simon

Interactive Read-Aoud Collection

Connecting Across Generations: Family

In My Momma's Kitchen by Jerdine Nolen

The Importance of Determination

North: The Amazing Story of Arctic Migration by Nick Dowson

Series Study: Dianna Hutts Aston and Sylvia Long

A Butterfly Is Patient

A Rock Is Lively

Shared Reading Collection

Interactive Read-Aoud Collection
Family

Determination

Dianna Hutts Aston

Section 3: Strategies and Skills

Reading Minilesson Principle
Use your finger to help you learn how to take apart new words.

Solving Words

You Will Need

- two or three familiar big books with opportunities to problem solve multisyllabic words by breaking them apart, such as the following from *Shared Reading Collection*:
  - *Amazing Nests* by Mary Ebeltoft Reid
  - *From Flower to Honey* by June Schwartz
  - *Exploring Underground* by Louis Petrone
- card strip or index card
- chart paper and markers

Academic Language / Important Vocabulary

- word
- word part
- take apart

Continuum Connection

- Take apart new multisyllable words by syllable to solve them (p. 499)
- Solve multisyllable words by taking them apart using syllables (pp. 507, 515)

Goal

Use a finger to help take apart two- or three-syllable words.

Rationale

When readers learn to break multisyllabic words apart efficiently, they become better at word solving and keeping their focus on the meaning of their reading. Using a finger to focus attention on each part of a word is a temporary technique. Eventually, students will only use their eyes to solve a word.

Assess Learning

Observe students when they take apart unknown words. Notice if there is evidence of new learning based on the goal of this minilesson.

- Do students use a finger to take apart new words?
- Can they break words apart by syllables?
- Do they understand the terms *word, word part,* and *take apart*?

Minilesson

To help students think about the minilesson principle, engage them in a demonstration of how to break apart a word. Here is an example.

- Hold up *Amazing Nests* and read page 2. When you get to the word *probably,* use a card strip to cover all but the first syllable (*prob*). Say the first syllable and then slide the card to expose and say the remaining syllables (*a-bly*). Read the rest of the sentence and then reread the whole sentence.

  What did you notice I did when I got to the word *probably*?

  I used a card strip, but you can use your finger to break words into parts to help you read them. Break the word into parts, read it all together, and then think about whether the word makes sense with the story and in the sentence. The sentence here is "You've probably seen a nest like that." That makes sense and looks right.

- Repeat the process with the word *company* from page 7 of *From Flower to Honey*.

  When you don't know what a word is, use your finger to break the word into parts to help you read the word.

Have a Try

Invite the students to break apart a word.

▶ Show and read page 8 from *Exploring Underground*, pausing at the word *minerals*. Ask a volunteer to show how to break apart the word and read it.

Summarize and Apply

Summarize the learning and remind students to use a finger to help them read new words.

> What is something that can help you when you come to a word you don't know?

▶ Write the principle at the top of the chart.

> If you come to a new word as you read, use your finger to break it into parts to help you solve it. Bring the book with you when we meet so you can share.

Share

Following independent reading time, gather students together in the meeting area to talk about word solving.

> Did anyone come to a new word while reading? What did you do?

Extend the Lesson (Optional)

After assessing students' understanding, you might decide to extend the learning.

▶ Support this behavior in guided or independent reading. While students are learning to use a finger to break words apart, eventually they will let their eyes take over. From *Prompting Guide, Part 1* (Fountas and Pinnell 2012), use prompts such as the following:

- *Where can you break the word apart?*
- *Look at the first part.*
- *Say the first part, the next part . . . Now say the ending.*

Use your finger to help you learn how to take apart new words.

 prob

 probab

probably

Reading Minilesson Principle

Break a word between two consonants but keep consonant digraphs together.

Solving Words

You Will Need

- two or three familiar big books with multisyllabic words that can be broken apart between consonants and consonant digraphs, such as the following from *Shared Reading Collection*:
  - *A Meerkat Day* by Geerhardt Heever
  - *Wolf Pack* by Annette Bay Pimentel
- card strip
- chart paper and markers

Academic Language / Important Vocabulary

- consonant
- consonant digraph

Continuum Connection

- Take apart new multisyllable words by syllable to solve them (p. 499)
- Solve multisyllable words by taking them apart using syllables (pp. 507, 515)

Goal

Learn to take apart words between two consonants, keeping consonant diagraphs together.

Rationale

When you teach students to take words apart between consonants and to keep consonant digraphs together, they can word solve more efficiently and keep their attention on meaning.

Assess Learning

Observe students when they take apart unknown words. Notice if there is evidence of new learning based on the goal of this minilesson.

- ▶ Can students break apart unknown words?
- ▶ Do they use consonant digraphs to break words apart?
- ▶ Do they understand the terms *consonant* and *consonant digraph*?

Minilesson

To help students think about the minilesson principle, engage them in a demonstration of breaking words apart. Here is an example.

- ▶ Hold up *A Meerkat Day* and read page 16. When you get to the word *scurry* use a card strip to cover the second syllable (*ry*). Say the first syllable (*scur*) and then slide the card to expose and say the second syllable. Read the rest of the sentence and then reread the whole sentence.

    What did you notice I did when I came to the word *scurry*? Where did I break the word?

- ▶ Prompt the students to say that you broke the word apart between the two consonants, and then you reread the whole sentence to make sure it made sense and looked right.

    The meerkats *scurry* back to their burrow to sleep at night. They want to be safe. This makes sense and looks right.

- ▶ Read page 12. When you get to the word *others*, use a card strip to cover all but the first syllable (*oth*). Say the first syllable and then slide the card to expose and say the remaining syllable (*ers*). Read the rest of the sentence and then reread the whole sentence.

    What did you notice I did when I came to the word *others*?

- ▶ Prompt the students to say that you broke the word apart but kept the consonant digraph together, and then you reread the whole sentence to make sure it made sense and looked right.

When you get to a word you don't know, break it between two consonants, but keep consonant digraphs together.

Have a Try

Invite the students to break apart a word.

▶ Repeat the process with the word *chilly* from page 4 and *hackles* from page 15 of *Wolf Pack*. Ask a student to show how to break apart the words. Record responses on the chart.

Summarize and Apply

Summarize the learning and remind students to break new words apart between two consonants but keep consonant digraphs together.

> What can you do when you come to a word that you don't know? Look at the chart to help remember.

▶ Write the principle at the top of the chart.

> If you come to a new word when you read today, use your finger to break it apart. Bring the book when we meet so you can share.

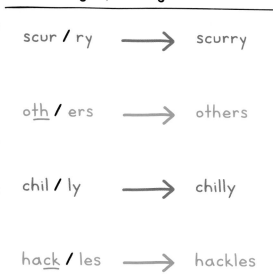

Break a word between two consonants but keep consonant digraphs together.

scur / ry ⟶ scurry

o<u>th</u> / ers ⟶ others

chil / ly ⟶ chilly

ha<u>ck</u> / les ⟶ hackles

Share

▶ Following independent reading time, gather students together in the meeting area to talk about word solving.

> Did anyone come to a new word while reading? What did you do?

▶ Choose a few students to share.

Extend the Lesson (Optional)

After assessing students' understanding, you might decide to extend the learning.

▶ Support this behavior in guided or independent reading. At first, students will use a finger to break words apart. Eventually, they will let their eyes take over. From *Prompting Guide, Part 1* (Fountas and Pinnell 2012), use prompts, such as the following:

- *You can use your finger to break the word.*
- *You can break the word.*

▶ **Writing About Reading** During shared writing, model how to write multisyllabic words by saying them and listening for the parts.

Section 3: Strategies and Skills

Reading Minilesson Principle

Break a word after the syllable that ends with a vowel and say a long vowel sound.

Solving Words

You Will Need

- two or three familiar big books with multisyllabic words containing a long vowel sound in the first syllable, such as the following from *Shared Reading Collection*:
  - *Wolf Pack* by Annette Bay Pimentel
  - *Far Above Earth* by Jane Simon
  - *From Beans to Chocolate* by June Schwartz
- card strip
- chart paper and markers

Academic Language / Important Vocabulary

- long vowel sound
- syllable

Continuum Connection

- Take apart new multisyllable words by syllable to solve them (p. 499)
- Solve multisyllable words by taking them apart using syllables (pp. 507, 515)

Goal

Learn to take apart words after the first syllable when the syllable ends in a long vowel sound.

Rationale

To teach students how to take multisyllabic words apart, they need to learn how to listen for syllable breaks. Two-syllable words are generally broken after the vowel if the first syllable has a long vowel sound (open syllable) and broken after the consonant if the first syllable has a short vowel sound (closed syllable). Readers should try to break after the vowel, but if that is not correct, they should break after the consonant.

Assess Learning

Observe students when they take apart multisyllabic words. Notice if there is evidence of new learning based on the goal of this minilesson.

- Do students listen for the vowel sound in the first syllable, so they know where to break a word apart?
- Do they understand the terms *long vowel sound* and *syllable*?

Minilesson

To help students think about the minilesson principle, engage them in a demonstration of breaking apart words. Here is an example.

- Hold up *Wolf Pack* and read page 2. When you get to the word *female*, use a card strip to cover all but the first syllable (*fe*). Say the first syllable and then slide the card to expose and say the remaining syllable (*males*). Read the rest of the sentence and then reread the whole sentence.

  What did you notice that I did when I got to the word *female*?

  I broke the word after the syllable that ends with a vowel. I said the word part with a long vowel sound, and when I put the word together, it sounded right.

- Make sure students notice that you reread the whole sentence to make sure it made sense in the sentence and looked right.

- Turn to page 14 from *Far Above Earth* and repeat the process with the word *relax*.

  When you get to a word you don't know, try to break it after the vowel. Say the word with a long vowel to see if that sounds right and makes sense. If it doesn't, say the first part with a short vowel sound and break the word after the consonant.

Have a Try

Invite the students to break apart a word.

▶ Repeat the process with the word *flavor* from page 12 of *From Beans to Chocolate*. Have a student show how to break apart *flavor*. Ask one or two students to describe how the student broke apart the word and why.

Summarize and Apply

Summarize the learning and remind students to break new words apart.

> What is one way to break apart a word that you don't know?

▶ Write the principle at the top of the chart.

> When you read today, if you get to a new word, you may need to break the word in a couple of different places to find out which one helps you read it. Bring the book when we meet so you can share.

Break a word after the syllable that ends with a vowel and say a long vowel sound.

fe / male ⟶ female

re / lax ⟶ relax

fla / vor ⟶ flavor

Share

Following independent reading time, gather students together in the meeting area to talk about word solving.

> Did anyone come to a word you didn't know? What did you do?

Extend the Lesson (Optional)

After assessing students' understanding, you might decide to extend the learning.

▶ Continue to support this behavior in guided or independent reading. At first, students will use a finger to break words apart. Eventually, they will let their eyes take over. From *Prompting Guide, Part 1* (Fountas and Pinnell 2012), use prompts, such as the following:

- *You can use your finger to break the word.*
- *You can break the word.*

▶ **Writing About Reading** During shared writing, model how to write multisyllabic words by saying them and listening for the parts.

Reading Minilesson Principle

Break a word after the syllable that ends with a consonant and say a short vowel sound.

Solving Words

You Will Need

- two or three familiar big books with multisyllabic words with a short vowel sound in the first syllable, such as the following from *Shared Reading Collection*:
  - *Far Above Earth* by Jane Simon
  - *Saving Cranes* by Brenda Iasevoli
- card strip
- chart paper and markers

Academic Language / Important Vocabulary

- short vowel
- syllable

Continuum Connection

- Take apart new multisyllable words by syllable to solve them (p. 499)
- Solve multisyllable words by taking them apart using syllables (pp. 507, 515)

Goal

Learn to take apart words after the syllable that ends with a consonant and has a short vowel sound.

Rationale

To teach students how to take multisyllabic words apart, they need to learn how to listen for syllable breaks. Two-syllable words are generally broken after the vowel if the first syllable has a long vowel sound (open syllable) and broken after the consonant if the first syllable has a short vowel sound (closed syllable). Readers should try to break after the vowel, but if that is not correct, they should break after the consonant.

Assess Learning

Observe students when they take apart unknown words. Notice if there is evidence of new learning based on the goal of this minilesson.

- Do students break multisyllabic words into parts after the consonant if it is a closed syllable?
- Do they understand the terms *short vowel* and *syllable*?

Minilesson

To help students think about the minilesson principle, choose familiar texts and provide an inquiry-based lesson about breaking multisyllabic words with closed syllables. Here is an example.

- Hold up *Far Above Earth* and read page 7. When you get to the word *objects*, use a card strip to cover all but the first syllable (*ob*). Say the first syllable and then slide the card to expose and say the remaining syllable (*jects*). Read the rest of the sentence and then reread the whole sentence.

  Say *objects* with me.

  Where did I break the word?

- Prompt students to notice you broke the word apart after the first syllable that ends with a consonant (with a short vowel sound), and then you reread the whole sentence to make sure it made sense and looked right.

- Turn to page 13 and repeat the process with the word *pedals*.

  When you get to a word you don't know, you can break it after the first syllable. You might need to say the syllable with a long and then a short vowel sound to find out where to break the word.

Have a Try

Invite the students to break apart a word.

▶ Repeat the process with the word *problem* from page 12 in *Saving Cranes*. Have a student show how to break apart *problem*. Ask one or two students to describe how the student broke apart the word and why.

Summarize and Apply

Summarize the learning and remind students to break new words apart after the short vowel sound.

> What is something you learned today that can help you when you come to a word you don't know?

▶ After students respond, write the principle on the chart and review the chart.

> When you read today, if you get to a new word, listen for the syllables to break it apart. Bring the book when we meet so you can share.

Share

Following independent reading time, gather students together in the meeting area to talk about word solving.

> Did anyone come to a word you didn't know? What did you do?

Extend the Lesson (Optional)

After assessing students' understanding, you might decide to extend the learning.

▶ Support this behavior in guided or independent reading. At first, students will use a finger to break words apart. Eventually, they will let their eyes take over. From *Prompting Guide, Part 1* (Fountas and Pinnell 2012), use prompts, such as the following:

- *You can use your finger to break the word.*
- *You can break the word.*

▶ **Writing About Reading** During shared writing, model how to write multisyllabic words by saying them slowly and listening for the parts.

Break a word after the syllable that ends with a consonant and say a short vowel sound.

ob / jects ⟶ objects

ped / als ⟶ pedals

prob / lem ⟶ problem

Section 3: Strategies and Skills

Reading Minilesson Principle

Sometimes break a word between the two vowels and say a long vowel sound.

Solving Words

You Will Need

- two or three familiar big books with multisyllabic words with vowel combinations with the syllable split between the vowels, such as the following:
  - *Trapped in Tar* by Hannah Cales, from *Shared Reading Collection*
  - *Tiny but Fierce* by Cheri Colburn, from *Shared Reading Collection*
  - *In My Momma's Kitchen* by Jerdine Nolen, from Text Set: Family
- card strip
- chart paper and markers

Academic Language / Important Vocabulary

- syllable

Continuum Connection

- Take apart new multisyllable words by syllable to solve them (p. 499)
- Solve multisyllable words by taking them apart using syllables (pp. 507, 515)

Goal

Learn to take apart a word between vowels.

Rationale

Teach students that in some words two vowels together represent separate long sounds. In other words, the two vowels may stand for one sound and form a syllable. Students need to learn that they may need to try more than once to find where to break apart a word and read it correctly.

Assess Learning

Observe students when they take apart unknown words. Notice if there is evidence of new learning based on the goal of this minilesson.

- ▶ Do students break unknown words into parts?
- ▶ Do they break multisyllabic words into parts between two vowel sounds if it is an open syllable?
- ▶ Are they using the term *syllable*?

Minilesson

To help students think about the minilesson principle, engage them in a demonstration of breaking apart words. Here is an example.

- ▶ Hold up *Trapped in Tar* and read page 3. When you get to the word *giants*, notice the two vowels. Place the card strip after the letter *i* and say the first syllable (*gi*). Slide the card strip along to show the rest of the word. Say the two syllables together. Read the rest of the sentence and then reread the whole sentence.

  Say *giants* with me.

  What did I do? Where did I break the word?

- ▶ Prompt the students to say that you broke the word apart between the two vowels, and you could hear the sound of each. Then reread the whole sentence to make sure it made sense and looked right.

- ▶ Turn to page 2 from *Tiny but Fierce* and repeat the process with the word *lions*.

  When you get to a word you don't know, break it between the two vowels and say the long vowel sound of each. If that doesn't work, the two vowels make one sound together and make a one-syllable word (e.g., *rain, boat, house*).

Have a Try

Invite the students to break apart a word.

▶ Repeat the process with the word *quiet* from page 11 of *In My Momma's Kitchen*. Have a student come up and show how to break the word. Ask one or two students to describe how the student broke the word and why.

Summarize and Apply

Summarize the learning and remind students to break new words apart between vowels.

> What did you learn today about breaking apart a word with two vowels?

▶ Write the principle at the top of the chart.

> When you read today, if you come to a new word, use your finger to break it apart to help you read it. Bring the book when we meet so you can share.

Share

Following independent reading time, gather students together in the meeting area to talk about word solving.

> Did anyone come to a word with two vowels you didn't know? What did you do?

Extend the Lesson (Optional)

After assessing students' understanding, you might decide to extend the learning.

▶ Continue to support this behavior in guided or independent reading. At first, students will use a finger to break words apart. Eventually, they will let their eyes take over. From *Prompting Guide, Part 1* (Fountas and Pinnell 2012), use prompts, such as the following:

- *You can break the word.*
- *Notice the syllables.*

▶ **Writing About Reading** During shared writing, model how to write multisyllabic words by saying them slowly and listening for the parts.

> Sometimes break a word between the two vowels and say the long vowel sound.
>
> gi**/**ant $\longrightarrow$ giant
>
> li**/**on $\longrightarrow$ lion
>
> qui**/**et $\longrightarrow$ quiet

Section 3: Strategies and Skills

Reading Minilesson Principle
Break a word before the consonant and *le*.

Solving Words

You Will Need

- two or three familiar big books with multisyllabic words that can be broken into parts before the consonant and *le*, such as the following from *Shared Reading Collection*:
  - *Trapped in Tar* by Hannah Cales
  - *Far Above* Earth by Jane Simon
  - *Wolf Pack* by Annette Bay Pimentel
- card strip
- chart paper and markers

Academic Language / Important Vocabulary

- consonant
- syllable

Continuum Connection

- Take apart new multisyllable words by syllable to solve them (p. 499)
- Solve multisyllable words by taking them apart using syllables (pp. 507, 515)

Goal

Learn to take apart words before the consonant and *le*.

Rationale

When you teach students to take multisyllabic words apart by breaking them before the consonant and *le*, they can read words more efficiently and keep their attention on meaning.

Assess Learning

Observe students when they take apart unknown words ending with a consonant and *le*. Notice if there is evidence of new learning based on the goal of this minilesson.

- Do students break unknown words into parts when word solving?
- Do they know to break multisyllabic words before the consonant and *le*?
- Are they using the terms *consonant* and *syllable*?

Minilesson

To help students think about the minilesson principle, engage them in a demonstration of breaking apart words ending with a consonant and *le*. Here is an example.

- Hold up *Trapped in Tar* and read page 12. When you get to the word *puzzle*, cover all but the first syllable (*puz*). Slide the card along to expose and read the final syllable (*zle*). Read the rest of the sentence and then reread the whole sentence.

  What did you notice that I did when I got to the word *puzzle*? Where did I break the word?

- Prompt the students to say that you broke the word apart before the consonant and the *le*, and then you reread the whole sentence to make sure it made sense and looked right.

- Turn to page 12 from *Far Above Earth* and repeat the process with the word *purple*.

  When you get to a word you don't know, break it before the consonant and *le* to help you read the word. I used a card to show you, but you can use your finger to help you break a word into parts.

Have a Try

Invite the students to break apart a word.

▶ Repeat the process with the word *tumble* from page 16 in *Wolf Pack*. Have a student come up and show how to break apart the word. Ask one or two students to describe how the student broke apart the word and why.

Summarize and Apply

Summarize the learning and remind students to break new words apart before the consonant and *le*.

> What is something you learned today to help you know where to break apart a word with a consonant and *le* at the end?

▶ Review the chart and write the principle at the top.

> When you read today, if you come to a new word, use your finger to break it apart to help you read it. Bring the book when we meet so you can share.

Share

Following independent reading time, gather students together in the meeting area to talk about word-solving.

> Did anyone come to a word with a consonant and *le* at the end you didn't know? What did you do?

Extend the Lesson (Optional)

After assessing students' understanding, you might decide to extend the learning.

▶ Continue to support this behavior in guided or independent reading. While students are learning to use a finger to break words apart, eventually they will let their eyes take over. From *Prompting Guide, Part 1* (Fountas and Pinnell 2012), use prompts, such as the following:

- *You can use your finger to break the word.*
- *You can break the word.*

▶ **Writing About Reading** During shared writing, model how to write multisyllabic words by saying them and listening for the parts.

Break a word before the consonant and le.

puz / zle   ⟶   puzzle

pur / ple   ⟶   purple

tum / ble   ⟶   tumble

Reading Minilesson Principle
Cover the prefix or suffix and take apart the base word first.

Solving Words

You Will Need

- two or three familiar big books with words with prefixes or suffixes, such as the following from *Shared Reading Collection*:
  - *Wolf Pack* by Annette Bay Pimentel
  - *Far Above Earth* by Jane Simon
  - *Tiny but Fierce* by Cheri Colburn
- card strip
- chart paper and markers

Academic Language / Important Vocabulary

- prefix
- suffix
- base word

Continuum Connection

- Solve words by taking them apart to notice base words, prefixes, and suffixes (p. 499)
- Solve words by taking them apart by identifying base words and affixes (prefixes and suffixes) (pp. 507, 515)

Goal

Learn to remove the prefix or suffix to take apart a new word.

Rationale

When you teach students to take multisyllabic words apart by removing the prefix or suffix and reading the base word, they can problem solve words more efficiently and keep their attention on meaning.

Assess Learning

Observe students when they take apart unknown words with a prefix or suffix. Notice if there is evidence of new learning based on the goal of this minilesson.

- ▶ Can students identify the base word and its prefix or suffix?
- ▶ Are they using the terms *prefix, suffix,* and *base word*?

Minilesson

To help students think about the minilesson principle, engage them in a demonstration of removing a prefix or suffix. Here is an example.

- ▶ Hold up *Wolf Pack* and read page 15. When you get to the word *instantly,* use the card strip to cover the suffix. Take apart the base word (*in/stant*) and then add the suffix (*ly*). Then read the whole word and the rest of the sentence. Finally, reread the whole sentence.

  What did you notice that I did to read the word *instantly*? Where did I break the word?

- ▶ Prompt the students to say that you covered the suffix, took apart the base word, and added the suffix. Then you reread the word and the whole sentence to make sure it made sense and looked right.

  You can use your finger to cover the suffix. Then take apart the base word and add the suffix to read the whole word.

- ▶ Turn to page 2 from *Far Above Earth* and repeat the process with the word *unzip*.

  You can use your finger to cover the prefix so you can read the base word and then the whole word.

Have a Try

Invite the students to break apart a word by removing the suffix.

▶ Repeat the process with the word *successful* from page 8 of *Tiny but Fierce*. Have a student come up and show how to remove the suffix. Ask one or two students to describe how the student broke apart the word and why.

Summarize and Apply

Summarize the learning and remind students to remove the prefix or suffix.

> What did you learn today about breaking apart a word with a prefix or suffix?

▶ Review the chart and write the principle at the top.

> When you read today, if you come to a new word, break it into parts to help you read it. Bring the book when we meet so you can share.

Share

Following independent reading time, gather students together in the meeting area to talk about word solving.

> Did anyone come to a word with a prefix or suffix you didn't know? What did you do?

Extend the Lesson (Optional)

After assessing students' understanding, you might decide to extend the learning.

▶ Support this behavior in guided or independent reading. While students are learning to use a finger to break words apart, eventually they will let their eyes take over. From *Prompting Guide, Part 1* (Fountas and Pinnell 2012), use prompts, such as the following:

- *Look at the prefix (suffix).*
- *Look at the base word (or root word).*
- *Does this help? (point to part)*

Cover the prefix or suffix and take apart the base word first.

instant
instantly

un
unzip

success
successful

Reading Minilesson Principle
Look for a part of the word that can help.

Solving Words

You Will Need

- two or three familiar books or poems, such as the following from *Shared Reading Collection:*
  - *Tiny but Fierce* by Cheri Colburn
  - *Trapped in Tar* by Hannah Cales
  - *Exploring Underground* by Louis Petrone
- card strip
- chart paper and markers

Academic Language / Important Vocabulary

- word
- word part

Continuum Connection

- Notice parts of words including phonogram patterns and use them to solve multisyllable words (p. 499)
- Notice parts of words and connect them to other words to solve them (pp. 499, 515)
- Notice parts of words, including phonogram patterns, and connect them to other words to solve them (p. 507)

Goal

Search for and use familiar parts of a word to help read the word.

Rationale

When you teach students to notice parts of a word they already know, you increase their efficiency in reading unknown words in continuous text, allowing them to improve fluency and focus on meaning.

Assess Learning

Observe students when they take apart unknown words. Notice if there is evidence of new learning based on the goal of this minilesson.

- Do students use known word parts to solve words?
- Do they use the terms *word* and *word part* when talking about how to read new words?

Minilesson

To help students think about the minilesson principle, engage them in a demonstration of using known word parts to read a new word. Here is an example.

- From *Tiny but Fierce*, read page 6, pausing at the word *forth*.

  I'm not sure what this word is, but I see part of the word that I know how to say.

- Use the card strip to cover *th*, leaving *for* visible. Say *for* and then slide the card strip away to reveal the rest of the word as you say it.

  What did you notice that I did when I got to the word *forth*?

  When you come to a word you don't know, look for a part or parts of the word that you *do* know. Let's read the sentence together and see if it sounds right and makes sense.

- Repeat this process with the word *panic* from page 6 of *Trapped in Tar*.

  When you come to a word you don't know, look for a part or parts you do know to help you read it.

Have a Try

Invite the students to use known word parts to read a new word with a partner.

▶ Repeat the process with the word *formations* from page 10 from *Exploring Underground*. Have a student come up and identify a known part of the word.

> Turn and talk to a partner about what this word could be.

Summarize and Apply

Summarize the learning and remind students to look for a part of the word that can help.

> What is something you learned today that can help you when you come to a word you don't know?

▶ Make a chart to remind students of the principle. Write the principle at the top.

> When you read today, if you come to a word you are not sure of, look to see if there is a part that can help.

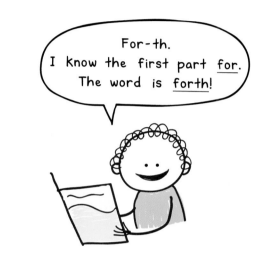

Look for a part of the word that can help.

For-th.
I know the first part for.
The word is forth!

Share

Following independent reading time, gather students together in the meeting area to talk about word solving.

> Did anyone come to a word you didn't know? What did you do?

Extend the Lesson (Optional)

After assessing students' understanding, you might decide to extend the learning.

▶ During guided and independent reading, remind students of the different strategies they can use to solve new words.

▶ At first, students will use a finger to break words apart. Eventually, they will let their eyes take over. From *Prompting Guide, Part 1* (Fountas and Pinnell 2012), use prompts, such as the following:

- *You can look for a part that might help.*
- *Say the first part. Now say more.*
- *Is that like another word you know?*

Section 3: Strategies and Skills

Reading Minilesson Principle
Sometimes the writer tells the meaning of a word in the sentence, the paragraph, or elsewhere in the book.

Solving Words

You Will Need

- three or four familiar big books with examples of words defined directly in the text, such as the following from *Shared Reading Collection*:
  - *From Beans to Chocolate* by June Schwartz
  - *A Meerkat Day* by Geerhardt Heever
  - *Exploring Underground* by Louis Petrone
- chart paper prepared with sentences from *From Beans to Chocolate* (p. 8), *A Meerkat Day* (p. 6), *Exploring Underground* (pp. 2, 3) or document camera
- markers
- highlighters or highlighter tape

Academic Language / Important Vocabulary

- definition
- sentence
- information

Continuum Connection

- Derive the meaning of a new word from the context of the sentence (p. 499)
- Derive the meaning of a new word from the context of the sentence, the paragraph, or the whole text (pp. 508, 516)

Goal

Understand that sometimes a writer tells the meaning of a word in the sentence, paragraph, or elsewhere in the book.

Rationale

Unfamiliar vocabulary can impede a student's understanding of what they read. Teaching students to find word definitions directly in the text supports them in independently solving unfamiliar vocabulary.

Assess Learning

Observe students when they use context to derive the meaning of new words. Notice if there is evidence of new learning based on the goal of this minilesson.

> ▶ Can students use context from the sentence, paragraph, or another part of the book to derive the meaning of a new word?
> ▶ Do they understand the terms *definition, sentence,* and *information*?

Minilesson

To help students think about the minilesson principle, engage them in a demonstration of using context to derive the meaning of a word. Here is an example.

> ▶ Hold up *From Beans to Chocolate*.
>
> > Remember that in this book the author shares information about how chocolate goes from a tree to a chocolate shop.
>
> ▶ Show the sentence from page 8 on the prepared chart or project the page, which tells about nibs. Highlight, or highlighter tape, the word *nibs*.
>
> > How does the author help you to understand what the word *nibs* means?
> >
> > Sometimes the author tells the meaning of the word in the sentence. Can someone underline the clues in the sentence to the meaning of the word *nibs*?
>
> ▶ Repeat the process with the word *burrow* from page 6 from *A Meerkat Day*.

Have a Try

Invite the students to figure out the meaning of a new word from context.

▶ Repeat the process with the sentences from pages 2 and 3 from *Exploring Underground*. Have students underline how the author tells the meaning of the words *caving* and *cavers*.

Summarize and Apply

Summarize the learning and remind students to look for the meaning of a word in the sentence, paragraph, or elsewhere in the book.

> How can you learn what a word means? Look at the chart to remember.

▶ Write the principle at the top of the chart.

> When you read today, if you come to a word that you don't understand, use the information from the sentence or the book to think about what the word means. Bring the book when we come back together so you can share.

Share

Following independent reading time, gather students together in the meeting area to talk about how to determine the meaning of a word.

> Did anyone come to a word that you didn't understand? What did you do?

Extend the Lesson (Optional)

After assessing students' understanding, you might decide to extend the learning.

▶ Model how to derive the meaning of new words during interactive read-aloud.

▶ During independent reading, have students mark with sticky notes words they are unsure of. Discuss how they can figure out what the words mean.

▶ **Writing About Reading** Ask students to write in a reader's notebook a word they learned from a book and how they figured it out.

Sometimes the writer tells the meaning of a word in the sentence, the paragraph, or elsewhere in the book.

At a little factory, <u>hard little cocoa pieces</u>, called nibs, go into a machine.

A meerkat family lives underground in a burrow.
<u>They are filled with long tunnels and cozy rooms.</u>

<u>The hobby of exploring caves</u> is called caving.
<u>People who explore caves</u> are called cavers.

RML 10

SAS.U2.RML10

Reading Minilesson Principle
Sometimes the writer uses a word in the sentence that is similar in meaning to the word you don't know.

Solving Words

You Will Need

- three or four familiar books in which the author gives a synonym for a difficult word such as the following:
  - *North: The Amazing Story of Arctic Migration* by Nick Dowson, from Text Set: Determination
  - *A Butterfly Is Patient* by Dianna Hutts Aston, from Text Set: Dianna Hutts Aston
  - *A Rock Is Lively* by Dianna Hutts Aston, from Text Set: Dianna Hutts Aston
- chart paper prepared with sentences from *North* (p. 29), *A Butterfly Is Patient* (p. 10, and *A Rock Is Lively* (p. 13) or a document camera
- markers
- highlighter or highlighter tape

Academic Language / Important Vocabulary

- sentence
- meaning
- synonym

Continuum Connection

- Connect words to synonyms and antonyms to expand understanding (pp. 499, 508, 516)

Goal

Understand that writers sometimes use synonyms within a sentence to explain the meaning of a word.

Rationale

When you teach students to search a sentence for clues to the meaning of an unfamiliar word, including words that have the same or similar meaning, it helps them learn new vocabulary independently.

Assess Learning

Observe students when they use synonyms to learn the meaning of words. Notice if there is evidence of new learning based on the goal of this minilesson.

- Can students learn the meaning of a new word by putting in the sentence a word or words that have a similar meaning?
- Do they understand the terms *sentence, meaning,* and *synonym*?

Minilesson

To help students think about the minilesson principle, engage them in a demonstration of using synonyms to learn the meaning of an unfamiliar word. Here is an example.

- Hold up *North*. Open to page 29.

  On this page, the author writes about gray wolves, and how they watch the caribou as they migrate.

- Read the first sentence. Then point to the sentence on the prepared chart paper. Highlight, or highlighter tape, the word *lame*.

  How does the writer help you understand what the word *lame* means?

  Who can underline a clue in the sentence?

  The writer used a synonym—a word that means the same thing—in the sentence to help explain that *lame* means "weak." The gray wolves are hoping that there may be a weak caribou that would be easy to attack.

- Repeat the process with the word *camouflage* from page 10 of *A Butterfly Is Patient*.

  When you are reading, and you come to a word you don't understand, you can look to see if the author put in one or more words that mean the same thing.

Have a Try

Invite the students to figure out the meaning of a word with a partner.

▶ Display page 13 of *A Rock Is Lively*. Point to the sentence on the chart and highlight the word *ballast*.

> Turn and talk to your partner. What did the author do to help you understand the word *ballast*?

▶ After they turn and talk, ask one or two students to share what they noticed.

Summarize and Apply

Summarize the learning and remind students to look for words that are similar meaning to the word they don't know.

> What should you do if you come to a word and you don't know the meaning? Look at the chart to help remember.

▶ Write the principle at the top of the chart.

> When you read today, if you come to a word you don't understand, look to see if the author put words in the sentence that mean the same thing. Bring the book when we come back together so you can share.

Share

Following independent reading time, gather students together in the meeting area to talk about determining the meaning of new words.

> Did anyone come to a word you didn't know? What did you do?

Extend the Lesson (Optional)

After assessing students' understanding, you might decide to extend the learning.

▶ Draw attention to how authors use synonyms within a sentence to support the meaning of unfamiliar vocabulary before, during, or after reading when engaging with guided reading groups.

Sometimes the writer uses a word in the sentence that is similar in meaning to the word you don't know.

Gray wolves slink after them, watching for **weakness**, hoping a **lame** one might make a meal.

Wings can help butterflies **camouflage**, or **hide**, themselves in the environment.

The **extra weight**, or **ballast**, helps them dive deeper and stay steady in the water.

Reading Minilesson Principle

When you come to a word you don't know, you can work it out.

Solving Words

You Will Need

- Charts from RML1-10
- chart paper and markers

Academic Language / Important Vocabulary

- information
- sentence
- word part
- take apart

Continuum Connection

- Demonstrate flexibility in using different strategies for solving words (pp. 507, 515)

Goal

Generate a list of ways to take apart words or solve their meaning.

Rationale

To read continuous text, students need to learn multiple ways they can take apart words or figure out word meaning. Generating a list of ways to take words apart or use context when reading independently will help them focus on meaning.

Assess Learning

Observe students when they take apart unknown words and use context to derive the meaning. Notice if there is evidence of new learning based on the goal of this minilesson.

- Are students able to use a variety of ways to take words apart?
- Do they use context to derive the meaning of words?
- Do they understand the terms *information, sentence, word part,* and *take apart*?

Minilesson

To help students think about the minilesson principle, engage them in a review of ways to work out what a new word is or means. Here is an example.

> We have been talking about ways you can take apart new words when you read. Let's review the ways we have been talking about and practicing.

- Review the charts from RML1–RML10.
- Write the principle at the top of the chart.

> When you come to a word you don't know, what are some ways you can work it out? Turn and talk to your partner.

- After time for discussion, ask for volunteers to share with the whole group and record responses on a chart.

Have a Try

Invite the students to turn and talk with a partner about ways to work out a new word.

> Turn and talk to your partner about one of the ways on the chart that you have used when you were reading. How did it help?

Summarize and Apply

Summarize the learning and remind students to refer to the chart to help them read unknown words.

> Today you made a list of things you can do when you get to words you don't know.

▶ Review the chart.

> When you read today, if you come to a word you don't know, try one of these strategies to help you work it out.

Share

Following independent reading time, gather students together in the meeting area to talk about word solving.

> Did anyone come to a word you didn't know? What did you do?

Extend the Lesson (Optional)

After assessing students' understanding, you might decide to extend the learning.

▶ During guided and independent reading, remind students of the different ways they can use to solve words they don't know.

▶ **Writing About Reading** Support students during shared writing by slowly articulating words and recording sounds in sequence.

When you come to a word you don't know, you can work it out.

Ways to Take Apart a Word

- Use your finger to help you look at a part.

- Break the word into syllables.

- Cover the prefix or suffix and take apart the base word.

- Look for a part you know.

- Look for a part that can help.

Ways to Learn the Meaning of a Word

- Think about the information in the sentence.

- Notice if the word is defined in the book.

- Look for a word that means about the same.

Section 3: Strategies and Skills

Assessment

After you have taught minilessons in this umbrella, observe students as they talk and write about their reading across instructional contexts: interactive read-aloud, independent reading and literacy work, guided reading, shared reading, and book club. Use *The Literacy Continuum* (Fountas and Pinnell 2017) to observe students' reading and writing behaviors across instructional contexts.

> ▶ What evidence do you have of new understandings related to solving words?
>
> - Do students use a variety of flexible ways to take apart words?
> - Can they use known parts to solve words?
> - Do they use sentence context to derive the meaning of words?
> - Do they use academic vocabulary, such as *word, word part, syllable, base word, prefix*, and *suffix*?
>
> ▶ In what other ways, beyond the scope of this umbrella, are students talking about solving words?
>
> - Do students read the punctuation?
> - Are they able to figure out the speaker of unassigned dialogue?

Use your observations to determine the next umbrella you will teach. You may also consult Minilessons Across the Year (pp. 55-57) for guidance.

Link to Writing

After teaching the minilessons in this umbrella, help students link the new learning to their writing or drawing about reading:

> ▶ When engaging in shared writing and independent writing, reference resources you have in the room, such as a word wall, to make connections between known words and new words.
>
> ▶ When engaging in shared writing, demonstrate how slow articulation of unknown words in writing relates to solving unknown words in reading.

Reader's Notebook

When this umbrella is complete, provide a copy of the minilesson principles (see resources.fountasandpinnell.com) for students to glue in the reader's notebook (in the Minilessons section if using *Reader's Notebook: Intermediate* [Fountas and Pinnell 2011]), so they can refer to the information as needed.

Minilessons in This Umbrella

RML1 Notice the punctuation and show it with your voice.

RML2 Read the word the way the author shows you with the print.

RML3 Put your words together so it sounds like talking.

RML4 Make your reading sound interesting.

RML5 Make your reading sound smooth.

RML6 Read the dialogue the way the character said it.

Before Teaching Umbrella 3 Minilessons

Read and discuss books with a wide variety of punctuation marks and print features such as bold print, words in all capital letters, or italics. Use a variety of big books, poetry posters, small books projected with a document camera, or examples of shared writing—anything large enough for students to see the print. Make sure your primary focus is to support the meaning and enjoyment of the text. For this umbrella, there are suggested books from the *Fountas & Pinnell Classroom™ Shared Reading Collection* and the *Interactive Read-Aloud Collection*. The minilessons in this umbrella can be taught together or individually throughout the year, depending on student needs.

Shared Reading Collection

Tiny but Fierce by Cheri Colburn

Trapped in Tar by Hannah Cales

A Meerkat Day by Geerhardt Heever

Wolf Pack by Annette Bay Pimental

Interactive Read-Aloud Collection

Genre Study: Realistic Fiction

Dancing in the Wings by Debbie Allen

Sky Sisters by Jan Bourdeau Waboose

Genre Study: Expository Nonfiction

Hottest, Coldest, Highest, Deepest by Steve Jenkins

Exploring Memory Stories

Grandma's Records by Eric Velasquez

Genre Study: Biography

Magic Trash by J. H. Shapiro

Genre Study: Fables

The Grasshopper and the Ants by Jerry Pinkney

As you read aloud and enjoy these texts together, help students

- notice the punctuation marks in sentences and think about how to make their voices sound,

- notice how bolded words, words in capital letters, and words in italics should be read, and

- read fluently and expressively.

Shared Reading Collection

Interactive Read-Aloud Collection
Realistic Fiction

Expository Nonfiction

Memory Stories

Biography

Fables

RML1

SAS.U3.RML1

Reading Minilesson Principle
Notice the punctuation and show it with your voice.

Maintaining Fluency

You Will Need

- several familiar books with sentences with periods, commas, questions marks, exclamation points, ellipses, and dashes, such as the following:
  - *Tiny but Fierce* by Cheri Colburn, from *Shared Reading Collection*
  - *Dancing in the Wings* by Debbie Allen, from Text Set: Realistic Fiction
- chart paper and markers
- document camera (optional)

Academic Language / Important Vocabulary

- punctuation
- period
- question mark
- exclamation point
- comma
- ellipses
- dash

Continuum Connection

- Recognize and reflect punctuation with the voice: e.g., period, question mark, exclamation point, dash, comma, ellipses, when reading in chorus or individually (p. 133)

Goal

Use the punctuation of a sentence to reflect the meaning of the sentence.

Rationale

When students change their voices to reflect the punctuation marks in sentences, they gain a deeper comprehension of the text and gain skills and confidence as they read and write independently.

Assess Learning

Observe students when they read aloud and talk about punctuation marks. Notice if there is evidence of new learning based on the goal of this minilesson.

- Do students' voices reflect the punctuation marks in sentences they read aloud?
- Are they able to identify the marks and use the terms *punctuation, period, question mark, exclamation point, comma, ellipsis*, and *dash*?

Minilesson

To help students think about the minilesson principle, provide an interactive lesson about how a reader's voice changes with different punctuation marks. Here is an example.

- Display page 2 from *Tiny but Fierce*.

   This page shows different types of punctuation marks. Who can use the pointer to show a period, a comma, and an exclamation point on this page?

   Now listen as I read this page.

- Read the page, emphasizing voice changes at each punctuation mark.

   What did you notice about my voice?

- Write students' suggestions on chart paper. Display page 16.

   What punctuation mark do you notice at the end of the sentence in the white box?

- Read the sentence, emphasizing how your voice goes up when you come to a question mark. Ask students to repeat after you.

   What did you notice?

- Add noticings to the chart.

   Sometimes, writers use other punctuation marks to show how to read the words. *Dancing in the Wings* has a few examples.

▶ On a new chart paper, write the sentence with the dash from page 23 and the ellipses from page 28 (or project the page). Read the sentences.

> What do you notice about my voice when I read these sentences?

> Add noticings to the initial chart.

Have a Try

Invite the students to practice reading with a partner different punctuation marks.

> With a partner, quickly choose a book. Turn to a page and notice the punctuation marks. Practice what your voice should sound like when you read the sentence.

Summarize and Apply

Summarize the learning and remind students to notice punctuation marks as they read.

> Today you learned how your voice should sound when you notice the punctuation marks in sentences.

▶ Add the principle to the chart.

> Today when you read, practice what your voice should sound like when you see different types of punctuation. Bring the book when we meet so you can share.

Share

Following independent reading time, gather the students in the meeting area in groups to practice fluent reading with punctuation marks.

> In groups, practice reading one or more pages from the book you read. Think about what your voice should sound like when you see the different types of punctuation.

Extend the Lesson (Optional)

After assessing students' understanding, you might decide to extend the learning.

▶ Assist students in recognizing that after a period, question mark, or exclamation point, a new sentence starts. Help them understand that commas and dashes are in the middle of a sentence and ellipses can be in the middle or at the end of a sentence.

▶ Remind students to read the punctuation any time you ask them to read aloud to you.

Notice the punctuation and show it with your voice.

- **.** = Make your voice go down and come to a full stop when you see a period.
- **?** = Make your voice go up when you you see a question mark.
- **!** = Read the sentence with strong feeling when you see an exclamation point.
- **,** = Make your voice pause when you see a comma.
- **—** = Pause your voice and emphasize the next words when you see a dash.
- **. . .** = Pause your voice when you see an ellipsis.

Section 3: Strategies and Skills

RML 2
SAS.U3.RML2

Reading Minilesson Principle
Read the word the way the author shows you with the print.

Maintaining Fluency

You Will Need

- several familiar books with sentences with words in bold print, capital letters, and italics, such as the following:
  - *Tiny but Fierce* by Cheri Colburn, from *Shared Reading Collection*
  - *Hottest, Coldest, Highest, Deepest* by Steve Jenkins, from Text Set: Expository Nonfiction
  - *Grandma's Records* by Eric Velasquez, from Text Set: Memory Stories
- chart paper and markers
- sticky notes

Academic Language / Important Vocabulary

- bold print
- capital letters
- italics

Continuum Connection

- Recognize and reflect variations in print with the voice (e.g., italics, bold type, special treatments, font size) when reading in chorus or individually (p. 133)

Goal

Read to show changes in voice to make words written in bold letters, all capital letters, or italics sound important.

Rationale

When students recognize how a reader's voice changes when they see words in bold print, capital letters, or italics, they deepen their understanding of the text and author's craft, which can be applied to independent reading and writing.

Assess Learning

Observe students when they read aloud. Notice if there is evidence of new learning based on the goal of this minilesson.

- Do students change their voices when reading words in bold print, all capital letters, and italics?
- Can they use the terms *bold print, capital letters,* and *italics*?

Minilesson

To help students think about the minilesson principle, provide an interactive lesson about how to change their voice when they see a word in bold print, all capital letters, or italics. Here is an example.

- Show page 4 of *Tiny but Fierce*.

  What do you notice about the words on this page of *Tiny but Fierce*?

  Listen as I read.

- Read with expression, emphasizing how your voice gets louder when you read the word in bold letters.

  What did you notice?

  Sometimes, writers use bold letters for different reasons. Think about this sentence from *Hottest, Coldest, Highest, Deepest*.

- Show and read the first sentence from page 3, emphasizing the bold letters for *highest*.

  What did you notice?

  Why do you think the authors of these books use bold letters?

  Notice the way the author wrote the words on a different page and listen to how the page sounds as I read it.

- Show page 8 and read, emphasizing the word *Snap* in italics.

  What did you notice?

Notice the way the author wrote the words in *Grandma's Records.*

▶ Show page 20 with the words BOOM BAK BOOM BAK.

> How do you think the author wants you to read this sentence?

Have a Try

Invite the students to talk with a partner about what their voices do when they see words in bold print, all capital letters, or italics.

> With a partner, choose a book. Notice words in bold print, all capital letters, or italics and practice what your voice sounds like when you read.

▶ After a short time, ask a couple of students to share what they found.

Summarize and Apply

Summarize the learning and remind students to think about the way their voice changes when reading a word in bold print, all capital letters, or italics.

> We talked about some ways authors help you know how to read the words. What are the ways? What do they tell you?

▶ Record students' responses and add the principle at the top of the chart.

> When you read today, look for words in bold print, all capital letters, or italics. Use a sticky note to mark the pages. Bring the book when we meet so you can share.

Share

Following independent reading time, gather the students together in the meeting area to practice fluent reading.

> Who read a book that had words in bold print, all capital letters, or italics? Show the page and read the sentence with the bold print, all capital letters, or italics. Remember to read the word differently from the way you read the other words.

Extend the Lesson (Optional)

After assessing students' understanding, you might decide to extend the learning.

▶ Gather examples of other uses of bold print, all capital letters, and italics in writing. Talk about how authors change the font, such as when a word is italicized when written in a different language, or when a glossary word is written in bold print.

Read the word the way the author shows you with the print.

Make your voice a little louder to make the word sound important when you see a word in **bold letters**.

Make your voice a little louder for emphasis when you see a word in all CAPITAL LETTERS.

Make your voice a little louder for emphasis when you see a word in *italics*.

Section 3: Strategies and Skills

Reading Minilesson Principle
Put your words together so it sounds like talking.

Maintaining Fluency

You Will Need

- a familiar book, such as *Trapped in Tar* by Hannah Cales from *Shared Reading Collection*
- chart paper and markers

Academic Language / Important Vocabulary

- words
- talking

Continuum Connection

- Read orally with integration of all dimensions of fluency: e.g., pausing, phrasing, word stress, intonation, and rate (p. 133)

Goal

Read with phrasing.

Rationale

When students read sentences with proper phrasing, their reading will sound like talking, and they can reflect on the author's meaning and extend their understanding of the text.

Assess Learning

Observe students when they read aloud and talk about how words should sound when they are reading. Notice if there is evidence of new learning based on the goal of this minilesson.

- ▷ Do students read the phrases as a unit in sentences?
- ▷ Do they put their words together?
- ▷ Do they sound like they are talking when they read?
- ▷ Do they use the terms *words* and *talking*?

Minilesson

To help students think about the minilesson principle, help students practice how to put words together so it sounds like they are talking when they read. Here is an example.

- ▷ Display page 6 from *Trapped in Tar*.

    As I read this page, think about the way the words sound as I read.

- ▷ Read the page, connecting all the words together, so the sentences are fluent and sound like natural speech.

    What did you notice about how the words and sentences sounded? Now read it with me in the same way.

- ▷ Talk about the importance of putting words together, so it sounds like talking when reading sentences.

    How could that be written in one sentence to help you remember how the words should sound when you read?

- ▷ Lead students toward the principle and write it on chart paper.

    Why is it important to put your words together, so it sounds like talking when you read?

- ▷ Add student ideas under the principle.

Have a Try

Invite the students to practice reading sentences with a partner, so it sounds like they are talking.

▸ Display page 7.

> Now you read the sentences on this page. Take turns reading to your partner. Remember to put your words together, so it sounds like you are talking.

Summarize and Apply

Summarize the learning and remind students to put their words together like they are talking when they read.

> Today you noticed that when you read, you should put your words together, so it sounds like you are talking. When you read today, listen to how your reading sounds. Practice putting your words together, so it sounds like you are talking.

Share

Following independent reading time, gather the students together in pairs.

> When you read today, did you put your words together to sound like you were talking? Turn and read one page to your partner like that.

Extend the Lesson (Optional)

After assessing students' understanding, you might decide to extend the learning.

▸ Record students reading a story and offer the recordings to become part of the listening center in a younger grade.

Put your words together so it sounds like talking.

- Your reading sounds smooth.

- You show that you are understanding what you read.

- When you read out loud, people understand what you mean.

- You learn to think how the character would say it.

Section 3: Strategies and Skills

Reading Minilesson Principle
Make your reading sound interesting.

You Will Need

- a familiar book that lends itself to reading with stress and intonation, such as *A Meerkat Day* by Geerhardt Heever from *Shared Reading Collection*
- chart paper and markers

Academic Language / Important Vocabulary

- voice
- louder
- softer
- emphasis
- expression

Continuum Connection

- Read orally with integration of all dimensions of fluency: e.g., pausing, phrasing, word stress, intonation, and rate (p. 133)

Goal

Read with appropriate stress and intonation.

Rationale

When students become aware of how to use tone, pitch, and volume to reflect the meaning of the text, and of how to use rising and falling tones in their voices, their reading will sound more interesting and convey the meaning of the text to the listener.

Assess Learning

Observe students when they read aloud and talk about the ways words sound when they read. Notice if there is evidence of new learning based on the goal of this minilesson.

- Do students notice when words are read with appropriate stress and intonation?
- Are they using stress and intonation when they read aloud?
- Do they understand the terms *voice, louder, softer, emphasis,* and *expression*?

Minilesson

To help students think about the minilesson principle, help them think about how to make their reading sound interesting. Here is an example.

- Display page 13 from *A Meerkat Day*.

  Notice how it sounds when I read this page.

- Read the page, emphasizing stress and intonation, so students notice your voice getting louder and softer, as well as rising and falling on certain words.

  What did you notice about my reading?

  What can you do to change your voices to make your reading sound interesting?

  Now read it with me the same way.

- As students provide suggestions, make a list on chart paper.

  Listen as I read the next page in a way that makes the words sound interesting to a listening audience. Then I will ask you to join in.

- Display page 14 from *A Meerkat Day*. Read the page with emphasis on stress and intonation.

  What did you notice?

- Add any new ideas to the chart.

- Reread page 14, asking students to join in with you.

Have a Try

Invite students to read a page practicing making their reading sound interesting with a partner.

▶ Display page 16 from *A Meerkat Day*.

> Take turns reading this page to a partner. Think about using your voice to make the reading sound interesting.

▶ After time for practice, ask a few volunteers to read the page to the class, demonstrating stress and expression.

Summarize and Apply

Summarize the learning and remind students to make their reading sound interesting.

> Today you noticed that when you read, you should make your reading sound interesting.

▶ Add the principle to chart.

> When you read today, practice making your reading sound interesting by making your voice get louder or softer and go up and down. Bring your book when we meet.

Share

Following independent reading time, gather the students together in pairs.

> Choose one page from the book you read to read to your partner. Make your reading sound interesting.

Extend the Lesson (Optional)

After assessing students' understanding, you might decide to extend the learning.

▶ During guided reading, remind students to vary their voices as they read, so the reading sounds like talking and sounds interesting.

Make your reading sound interesting.

rhythm

emphasis

volume louder

Louder!

volume softer

Softer!

voice goes up

voice goes down

expression

Maintaining Fluency

You Will Need

- several familiar books, such as the following:
  - *Wolf Pack* by Annette Bay Pimental, from *Shared Reading Collection*
  - *Dancing in the Wings* by Debbie Allen, from Text Set: Genre Study: Realistic Fiction
- chart paper and markers

Academic Language / Important Vocabulary

- voice
- pausing
- phrasing
- stress
- intonation
- rate

Continuum Connection

- Read orally with integration of all dimensions of fluency: e.g., pausing, phrasing, word stress, intonation, and rate (p. 133)

Goal

Integrate pausing, phrasing, stress, intonation, and rate to demonstrate fluent reading.

Rationale

When students integrate all dimensions of fluency (pausing, stress, intonation, rate), their oral reading will sound smooth. It will have energy and convey the meaning of the text to the listener. When they read silently, they will read the same way.

Assess Learning

Observe students when they read aloud and talk about making their reading sound smooth. Notice if there is evidence of new learning based on the goal of this minilesson.

- ▶ Are students able to make their reading sound smooth?
- ▶ Do they think about all aspects of fluent reading and try to integrate them as they read?
- ▶ Do they understand the terms *voice*, *pausing*, *phrasing*, *stress*, *intonation*, and *rate*?

Minilesson

To help students think about the minilesson principle, provide an inquiry-based lesson about how to make reading sound smooth. Here is an example.

- ▶ Show page 2 from *Wolf Pack*.

    Listen as I read this page. Notice how my voice sounds and the ways I change my voice as I read.

- ▶ Read page 2 with appropriate rate, expression, pausing, and stress to model fluent reading. Focus on integrating all aspects of fluency as you read.

    Now read with me and make your reading sound the same way.

    Turn and talk about what you noticed.

- ▶ After time for discussion, have a conversation about the way you used your voice, so the reading sounded smooth. Make a list of students' suggestions on chart paper.

    I'm going to read a page from another book you know, *Dancing in the Wings*. As I do, notice how I make my reading sound smooth.

- ▶ Read page 4, modeling fluent reading.

    Did you notice anything else to add to the list?

▶ Add new ideas to the chart.

> How does the reading sound when you use your voice in the ways that we listed?

▶ As needed, guide students to the principle. Add the principle to the chart.

Have a Try

Invite students to practice reading smoothly with a partner.

> With a partner, choose a book from this basket. Take turns reading a few sentences or a page, and make your reading sound smooth.

▶ Listen to partners as they are reading to one another. Prompt them to read smoothly.

Summarize and Apply

Summarize the learning and remind students to think about smooth, fluent reading.

> Let's look at the things you noticed that make your reading sound smooth.

▶ Reread the chart.

> Today when you read, think about how to make your voice sound smooth. Bring your book when we meet so you can share.

Share

Following independent reading time, gather students in pairs to demonstrate fluent reading.

> Choose one page from your book to read to your partner. Make your reading sound smooth.

Extend the Lesson (Optional)

After assessing students' understanding, you might decide to extend the learning.

▶ During guided reading, remind students to make their reading sound smooth. Refer back to the chart as needed.

Make your reading sound smooth.

Use an interesting voice.

Change voice to match punctuation.

Stress important words by emphasizing them.

Change the volume of your voice as you read.

Read like you are talking.

Use the right speed.

Smooth

Section 3: Strategies and Skills

Reading Minilesson Principle
Read the dialogue the way the character said it.

You Will Need

- several familiar books with dialogue, such as the following:
  - *Wolf Pack* by Annette Bay Pimental, from *Shared Reading Collection*
  - *Magic Trash* by J. H. Shapiro, from Text Set: Biography
  - *Sky Sisters* by Jan Bourdeau Waboose, from Text Set: Realistic Fiction
  - *The Grasshopper and the Ants* by Jerry Pinkney, from Text Set: Fables
- student prepared ahead of time to read dialogue
- chart paper prepared with several examples of dialogue from familiar books
- document camera (optional)
- highlighters
- basket of books that have dialogue

Academic Language / Important Vocabulary

- character
- dialogue

Continuum Connection

- Adjust the voice to reflect dialogue in the body of the text (p. 133)

Goal

Read dialogue to reflect the feelings of the characters and meaning of the story.

Rationale

When students understand dialogue should be read to show the feelings of the characters, they develop insights into characters' motivations and begin to make connections between characters' and their own lives.

Assess Learning

Observe students when they read aloud and talk about dialogue. Notice if there is evidence of new learning based on the goal of this minilesson.

- ▶ Do students notice when a character is speaking in a story?
- ▶ Do they try to read dialogue the way the character said it?
- ▶ Do they use academic language, such as *character* and *dialogue*?

Minilesson

To help students think about the minilesson principle, engage them in reading dialogue the way the characters would say it. Here is an example.

▶ Display page 4 from *Wolf Pack*.

> The narrator in *Wolf Pack* is a character that speaks or uses dialogue. Who would like to try to read his words in the way you think he is saying them?

▶ Ask the prepared student to read the dialogue.

> What did you notice? Did it sound like the way the narrator is probably speaking?

▶ Show the prepared chart paper with dialogue from several familiar books (or project the pages), along with the corresponding book covers.

> I have written dialogue from several stories you know. Listen as I read the first one and think about how it sounds.

▶ Read the selection from *Magic Trash*.

> Now read it with me the same way.
>
> What did you notice?
>
> Did I read it the way the characters said it? What tells you how the words should be read?

▶ Have a student highlight words that tell how the character would say the dialogue.

▶ Ask volunteers to read the dialogue from *Sky Sisters* and *Grasshopper and the Ants*.

> What did you notice about the way the dialogue was read?

> Did it sound the way the characters said it? How do you know?

Have a Try

Invite the students to practice reading dialogue with a partner.

> With a partner, choose a book with dialogue from this basket. Turn and read the parts the characters say. Remember to read the way the characters would say it.

Summarize and Apply

Summarize the learning and remind students to think about how the character should sound as they read.

> You learned that you should read the way a character speaks.

▶ Add the principle to the top of the chart.

> Today choose a fiction story with dialogue or choose a book from this basket. As you read, think about how the character would speak. Bring the book when we meet so you can share.

Share

Following independent reading time, gather the students together in groups of three.

> In groups of three, share the book you read today. Choose a page and read a sentence or two of dialogue to your group.

Extend the Lesson (Optional)

After assessing students' understanding, you might decide to extend the learning.

▶ Have students present a readers' theater version of a book that is rich with dialogue. Because a readers' theater script contains only the dialogue, students will need to use their voices to reflect their understanding of how the characters' should sound.

Read the dialogue the way the character said it.

<u>Magic Trash</u> (page 8)

"I'm going to be an artist," Tyree said. His mama hung her head. "That's not a job."

<u>Sky Sisters</u> (page 15)

"Faster. Faster." I try to call out gently, and I begin to giggle.
Nimise stops and says, "It's your turn to pull me."
"No, it's not. It's my turn to be the leader, though. Follow me," I shout.

<u>Grasshopper and the Ants</u> (page 4)

"Why labor so long?" Grasshopper chirped. "It's summertime. Let's have a picnic of fresh, yummy leaves. Come join me in making music!"

Assessment

After you have taught the minilessons in this umbrella, observe students as they talk and write about their reading across instructional contexts: interactive read-aloud, independent reading and literacy work, guided reading, shared reading, and book club. Use *The Literacy Continuum* (Fountas and Pinnell 2017) to observe students' reading and writing behaviors across instructional contexts.

▶ What evidence do you have of new understandings related to fluency?

- Can students read and respond appropriately to periods, question marks, exclamation points, commas, ellipses, dashes, bold print, all capital letters, and italics?

- Are they able to integrate all dimensions of fluency (pausing, phrasing, word stress, intonation, and rate) when they read aloud?

- Do they notice dialogue and try to read it the way the character said it?

- Do they use terms, such as *bold print, italics, character,* and *dialogue*?

▶ In what other ways, beyond the scope of this umbrella, are students demonstrating fluency?

- Do students sound enthusiastic and speak confidently when they give a book talk?

Use your observations to determine the next umbrella you will teach. You may also consult Minilessons Across the Year (pp. 55-57) for guidance.

Link to Writing

After teaching the minilessons in this umbrella, help students link the new learning to their writing:

▶ Demonstrate using punctuation and dialogue through shared writing as a model for students to use in their independent writing.

▶ Help students transform all or part of a story into a readers' theater script. Show them how to use punctuation to convey how the speaker should sound when reading.

Reader's Notebook

When this umbrella is complete, provide a copy of the minilesson principles (see resources.fountasandpinnell.com) for students to glue in the reader's notebook (in the Minilessons section if using *Reader's Notebook: Intermediate* [Fountas and Pinnell 2011]), so they can refer to the information as needed.

Minilessons in This Umbrella

RML1   Tell the characters, setting, problem, important events, and solution when you tell about a fiction story.

RML2   Tell the most important information when you tell about an informational book.

RML3   Tell the important events in order when you tell about a biography.

Before Teaching Umbrella 4 Minilessons

Use the selected texts from the *Fountas & Pinnell Classroom™ Interactive Read-Aloud Collection* text sets listed below, or choose books from your library to support students in their ability to summarize their reading. Read and discuss fiction books with characters, settings, and a clear problem and solution; informational texts with a variety of structures; biographies; and memory stories, though some memory stories while recommended for this umbrella may not include a clear problem and solution.

Shaping Our World: Animals

Ape by Martin Jenkins

I Love Guinea Pigs by Dick King-Smith

Author/Illustrator Study: Janell Cannon

Stellaluna by Janell Cannon

Exploring Memory Stories

My Rotten Red-Headed Older Brother by Patricia Polacco

Genre Study: Biography

The Tree Lady by H. Joseph Hopkins

Magic Trash by J. H. Shapiro

As you read aloud and enjoy these texts together, help students

- discuss the important events that shaped the life of the subject in a biography or characters in a fiction text,

- think about what makes the subject of a biography notable,

- notice how nonfiction texts are organized, and

- think about the important ideas and information presented in an informational text.

Animals

Janell Cannon

Memory Stories

Biography

Section 3: Strategies and Skills

Reading Minilesson Principle

Tell the characters, setting, problem, important events, and solution when you tell about a fiction story.

Summarizing

You Will Need

- three or four familiar fiction books with chronological sequence and clearly identified characters, setting, problem, and solution, such as the following:
  - *Stellaluna* by Janell Cannon, from Text Set: Janell Cannon
  - *My Rotten Red-Headed Older Brother* by Patricia Polacco, from Text Set: Memory Stories
- chart paper and markers

Academic Language / Important Vocabulary

- characters
- setting
- problem
- solution
- summary

Continuum Connection

- Include the problem and its resolution in a summary of a text (p. 51)

Goal

Tell the important events of a text in a sequence, including the characters, setting, problem, and solution.

Rationale

When summarizing a fiction book, students must organize details about characters, setting, and plot in chronological order. Telling about a book in the order the events took place also helps readers remember what they read as well as notice aspects of the plot, such as cause and effect.

Assess Learning

Observe students when they summarize fiction books. Notice if there is evidence of new learning based on the goal of this minilesson.

- ▸ Can students tell an organized summary that includes character, setting, and the problem and solution?
- ▸ Can they distinguish between essential and nonessential details?
- ▸ Do they use academic language, such as *characters, setting, problem, solution,* and *summary*?

Minilesson

To help students think about the minilesson principle, engage them in a discussion about how to summarize a fiction story. Here is an example.

- ▸ Hold up *Stellaluna*.

  Listen as I tell you about *Stellaluna* by Janell Cannon. When Stellaluna was separated from her mother, she lived for a while in a bird's nest. She learned to live like a bird, but, even though the birds were kind to her, she didn't fit in. One day she met a bat that reminded her that *she* was a bat. She was reunited with her mother. In the end, she began to feel like herself. Even though she and her bird family were different, they remained friends.

- ▸ Write the first half of the principle on the chart—students' responses will complete the principle.

  What did you notice about what I told you about this story? What parts of the story did I include?

- ▸ Prompt as needed to make the ideas generative, recording responses on a chart.

  Telling the most important parts of a story is called a summary. A summary is short but gives enough information so someone can understand the story. When you tell a fiction story, tell the characters, setting, problem, only the important events, and solution.

Have a Try

Invite the students to summarize a book with a partner.

▶ Hold up *My Rotten Red-Headed Older Brother.*

One of you will give a summary of *My Rotten Red-Headed Older Brother.* Your partner will listen for the important information: the characters, the setting, and the problem and solution.

Summarize and Apply

Summarize the learning and remind students to think about the telling about a fiction book.

When you tell about a fiction book, what is important to include?

▶ Review the chart, adding additional ideas.

Choose a fiction book for independent reading today. As you read, think about how you would tell a summary of the story. Bring the book when we meet so you can share.

Tell the characters, setting, problem, important events, and solution when you tell about a fiction story.

Stellaluna

- characters

- where the story takes place/setting

- the problem and solution

- important events in order

- the ending

Share

Following independent reading time, gather students together in the meeting area to talk about their reading.

▶ Choose two or three students to share a summary of a fiction book with the class.

Extend the Lesson (Optional)

After assessing students' understanding, you might decide to extend the learning.

▶ During guided reading and individual conferences, prompt students to give a summary with prompts, such as the following:

- *Can you tell about the book in only a few sentences?*
- *What was the problem? The solution?*

▶ Once students are able to summarize a fiction book, teach them that the message of a book is also important information and could be included in a summary.

▶ **Writing About Reading** After students demonstrate a strong oral summary, ask them to write a summary in a reader's notebook.

RML2
SAS.U4.RML2

Reading Minilesson Principle
Tell the most important information when you tell about an informational book.

Summarizing

You Will Need

- two or three familiar informational books, such as the following from Text Set: Animals:
  - *Ape* by Martin Jenkins
  - *I Love Guinea Pigs* by Dick King-Smith
- chart paper and markers
- basket of informational books

Academic Language / Important Vocabulary

- summary
- summarize

Continuum Connection

- Tell a summary of a text after hearing it read (p. 53)

Goal

Tell the most important information and ideas in an informational book.

Rationale

When you teach students to summarize what they have learned from an informational book, you help them to organize and clearly articulate the most important information.

Assess Learning

Observe students when they share a summary of an informational book. Notice if there is evidence of new learning based on the goal of this minilesson.

- Can students identify and distinguish between the essential and nonessential information in a book?
- Do they communicate important ideas and information from a text in an organized summary?
- Do they understand the words *summary* and *summarize*?

Minilesson

To help students think about the minilesson principle, choose familiar informational texts to discuss summarizing. Here is an example.

- Hold up *Ape*.

  Listen as I tell you about *Ape*. Martin Jenkins, the author, tells the five types of apes in the world: orangutans, chimps, bonobos, gorillas, and us— humans. Each section tells a little about each type of ape. Apes, except for humans, are running out of safe places to live. Many people are trying to protect them and the land they live on.

  What did you notice about the information I shared?

  What did I include in my summary?

  Why do you think I did that?

  When you tell about an informational book, tell about the most important information.

- Write the principle on the chart.

  What kinds of things would you include when you summarize an informational book?

- Record responses on the chart. If students suggest subject matter, such as "Tell about the five kinds of apes," redirect them to something more generative.

Have a Try

Invite the students to summarize a book with a partner.

▶ Hold up *I Love Guinea Pigs*.

> Take turns giving a summary of this book. What would you tell about this book? You can look at the chart for ideas.

▶ After they turn and talk, ask a couple of students to share.

Summarize and Apply

Summarize the learning and remind students to think about summarizing a book.

> What did you learn how to do today?

▶ Review the chart, adding additional ideas.

> When you summarize the most important information from a book, it helps you remember it.

> Choose an informational book from this basket for independent reading today. Think about how you would tell the important information in the book. Bring the book with you when we meet so you can share.

Share

Following independent reading time, gather students together in the meeting area to talk about their reading with a partner.

> Share your book summary with a partner. Think about the important information to share.

▶ After they turn and talk, choose two or three students to share with the class.

Extend the Lesson (Optional)

After assessing students' understanding, you might decide to extend the learning.

▶ During guided reading or individual reading conferences, use prompts, such as the following:

- *Think of a few sentences that tell information about the whole book.*
- *What were the most important things the author included?*

▶ **Writing About Reading** Once students demonstrate they can tell a complete and organized summary, invite them to write a summary in a reader's notebook.

Tell the most important information when you tell about an informational book.

- <u>only</u> important ideas

- one or two important facts

- how the book is organized

- the author's feelings about the topic

- the main message or big idea

Section 3: Strategies and Skills

Reading Minilesson Principle
Tell the important events in order when you tell about a biography.

You Will Need

- two or three familiar biographies, such as the following from Text Set: Biography:
  - *The Tree Lady* by H. Joseph Hopkins
  - *Magic Trash* by J. H. Shapiro
- chart paper and markers
- basket of biographies

Academic Language / Important Vocabulary

- biography

Continuum Connection

- Tell a summary of a text after hearing it read (p. 53)

Goal

Tell the important events in a biography in chronological order.

Rationale

The text in a biography often follows a chronological or narrative structure. Learning how to summarize a biography helps students learn to summarize other texts with a narrative structure. As such, this same lesson may be used to help students summarize narrative nonfiction.

Assess Learning

Observe students when they give a summary of a biography. Notice if there is evidence of new learning based on the goal of this minilesson.

- Can students tell an organized summary of a biography?
- Can they distinguish between essential and nonessential details?
- Do they use academic language, such as *biography*?

Minilesson

To help students think about the minilesson principle, choose familiar biographical texts with subjects, important events that shaped their lives, why they are important, and if appropriate, a problem and how it was solved. Here is an example.

- Hold up *The Tree Lady*.

  Listen as I tell you about *The Tree Lady*. As a young girl, Kate Sessions loved trees. She grew up to become the first woman from her college to graduate with a degree in science. After college, she moved to San Diego and was surprised to find the city was mostly desert. She decided to do something about it. Kate thought about what trees would grow there and began planting. Over time, with the help of friends and volunteers, San Diego became a city with millions of trees. She is remembered as the Mother of Balboa Park.

  What did you notice about what I told you about this biography?

  When you tell about a biography, tell about the important events in order.

- Write the principle on the chart.

  What information did I include?

- Record responses on the chart.

Have a Try

Invite the students to talk with a partner about a biography.

▶ Hold up *Magic Trash*.

One of you will summarize *Magic Trash*. The other will listen for important information: who the book is about, the setting, and major events in the person's life.

▶ After they turn and talk, ask a couple of students to share.

Summarize and Apply

Summarize the learning and remind students to think about biographies.

When you tell about a biography, what is it important to include?

▶ Review the chart, adding additional ideas.

Choose a biography from this basket for independent reading today. As you read, think about how you might tell about the book. Bring the book with you when we meet so you can share.

Share

Following independent reading time, gather students together in the meeting area to talk about their reading.

Who would like to tell about the biography you read today?

▶ Choose two or three students to share with the class.

Extend the Lesson (Optional)

After assessing students' understanding, you might decide to extend the learning.

▶ Use this lesson as a model for teaching students to summarize narrative nonfiction.

▶ During guided reading and individual conferences, use prompts such as the following:

• *Can you tell about the biography in only a few sentences?*

• *What is something that happened in the biography that you think is important?*

Tell the important events in order when you tell about a biography.

Tell . . .

• who the book is about.

• why the person is important.

• where the story takes place.

• the problem and how it was solved.

• the important events in order.

Assessment

After you have taught minilessons in this umbrella, observe students as they talk and write about their reading across instructional contexts: interactive read-aloud, independent reading and literacy work, guided reading, shared reading, and book club. Use *The Literacy Continuum* (Fountas and Pinnell 2017) to observe students' reading and writing behaviors across instructional contexts.

▶ What evidence do you have of new understandings related to summarizing?

- Can students identify the characters, setting, problem, and solution in a fiction text?

- Can they give a complete, well-organized summary of a story, nonfiction text, and a biography?

- Are they able to distinguish between essential and nonessential information?

- Do they use academic language, such as *summary, characters, setting, problem, solution,* and *biography*?

▶ In what other ways, beyond the scope of this umbrella, are students telling about books?

- Have students begun to express opinions about characters, subjects, or topics?

- Do they talk about the author's point of view or how the author felt about a topic?

Use your observations to determine the next umbrella you will teach. You may also consult Minilessons Across the Year (pp. 55-57) for guidance.

Link to Writing

After teaching the minilessons in this umbrella, help students link the new learning to their writing:

▶ Begin to have students record their summaries in a reader's notebook.

▶ Have students write mini-summaries to attach to some books in the classroom library to help students choose a book they will enjoy reading.

Reader's Notebook

When this umbrella is complete, provide a copy of the minilesson principles (see resources.fountasandpinnell.com) for students to glue in the reader's notebook (in the Minilessons section if using *Reader's Notebook: Intermediate* [Fountas and Pinnell 2011]), so they can refer to the information as needed.

Section 4 | **Writing About Reading**

Throughout the year, students will respond to what they read in a reader's notebook. These lessons help students use this important tool for independent literacy learning and make it possible for them to become aware of their own productivity, in the process building self-efficacy. All opportunities for drawing and writing about reading support the students in thinking about texts and articulating their understandings.

Minilessons in This Umbrella

Independent Reading

RML1	Collect your thinking in your reader's notebook.
RML2	Write the title and author of each book you read on your reading list.
RML3	Write the genre of each book on your reading list.
RML4	Keep a tally of the kinds of books you read.
RML5	Write *E* (easy), *JR* (just right), or *D* (difficult) for each book on your reading list.
RML6	Follow the guidelines in your reader's notebook to do your best reading and writing work.

Before Teaching Umbrella 1 Minilessons

The minilessons in this umbrella demonstrate how to introduce *Reader's Notebook: Intermediate* (Fountas and Pinnell 2011) to your students; however, if you do not have it, a plain notebook can be used instead. The goal of a reader's notebook is for students to have a consistent place to collect their thinking about their reading (see pp. 46-49 for more on using a reader's notebook).

Before introducing the reader's notebook, it would be helpful to teach the minilessons in Section One: Management. For this umbrella, use the following books from the *Fountas & Pinnell Classroom™ Independent Reading Collection* or any other fiction and nonfiction books from your classroom library.

Reader's Notebook

Independent Reading Collection

The Absent Author by Ron Roy

Captain Awesome to the Rescue! by Stan Kirby

Avalanches by Lisa Bullard

Section 4: Writing About Reading

Reading Minilesson Principle
Collect your thinking in your reader's notebook.

Introducing a Reader's Notebook

You Will Need

▶ a reader's notebook for each student (if using a plain notebook, set up tabbed sections for Reading List, Choosing Books, Minilessons, and Writing About Reading)

▶ chart paper prepared with a four-column chart

▶ markers

Academic Language / Important Vocabulary

▶ reader's notebook

▶ reading list

▶ minilessons

▶ writing about reading

Goal

Understand that a reader's notebook is a special place to collect thinking about books read.

Rationale

Students need numerous opportunities to respond to reading in different forms. A reader's notebook is a special place for them to keep a record of their reading lives and to share their thinking about books they have read.

Assess Learning

Observe students when they use a reader's notebook. Notice if there is evidence of new learning based on the goal of this minilesson.

▶ Do students understand the purpose of a reader's notebook?

▶ Do they understand the purpose of each section of a reader's notebook?

▶ Do they collect their thinking about books they have read in a reader's notebook?

▶ Do they understand the terms *reader's notebook, reading list, minilessons,* and *writing about reading*?

Minilesson

Give each student a reader's notebook and provide a lesson that introduces students to the contents and purpose of the notebook. Here is an example.

> Each of you has your own reader's notebook, which you will use this year. Take a couple of minutes to look through it.

> What do you notice about the reader's notebook? What do you think you will do with it?

▶ Draw students' attention to the tabs at the top of the reader's notebook.

> The reader's notebook has four sections. You can use the tabs at the top to find each section. Open your notebook to the yellow tab that says Reading List.

> What do you think you will write in this section?

▶ Record students' responses in the first column of the chart, under the heading Reading List.

▶ Continue in a similar manner with the three remaining sections (Choosing Books, Minilessons, and Writing About Reading). Students might need help understanding that they will glue a copy of the minilesson principles in the Minilessons section so that they have them as a reference.

Have a Try

Invite the students to talk with a partner about the reader's notebook.

> Turn and talk to your partner about what you understand about what you will do in the reader's notebook.

▶ Ask a few students to share their responses. Confirm their understanding of a reader's notebook, and clear up any misconceptions that may have arisen.

Summarize and Apply

Help students summarize the learning and remind them to collect their thinking about their reading in a reader's notebook.

> Talk about how you will use your reader's notebook.

▶ Write the principle at the top of the chart.

> A reader's notebook is a special place for you to collect your thinking about your reading.

> Today, you will read and then write a few sentences about what you are thinking about the book in the Writing About Reading section with the green tab. You will share what you wrote when we come together in the meeting area.

Share

Following independent reading time, gather students together in the meeting area to talk in pairs about what they wrote.

> Turn and talk to your partner about the book you read. Share what you wrote about your thoughts in a reader's notebook.

▶ After pairs share their reader's notebooks, invite a volunteer to share with the class.

Extend the Lesson (Optional)

After assessing students' understanding, you might decide to extend the learning.

▶ Have students personalize their notebook covers to take ownership of them.

▶ Have students establish a place to store the reader's notebook in their personal boxes (see Umbrella 3: Getting Started with Independent Reading, found in Section One: Management).

Collect your thinking in your reader's notebook.

Reading List	Choosing Books	Minilessons	Writing About Reading
a list of books you have read	a list of books you want to read	the minilesson principles	your thinking about books you have read

RML 2
WAR.U1.RML2

Reading Minilesson Principle
Write the title and author of each book you read on your reading list.

Introducing a Reader's Notebook

You Will Need

- two books, such as these from the *Independent Reading Collection*:
  - *The Absent Author* by Ron Roy
  - *Captain Awesome to the Rescue!* by Stan Kirby
- chart paper prepared to look like the reading list in *Reader's Notebook: Intermediate* (Fountas and Pinnell 2011)
- markers
- a reader's notebook for each student

Academic Language / Important Vocabulary

- reader's notebook
- reading list
- title
- author

Continuum Connection

- Record in Reader's Notebook the titles, authors, illustrators, genre of texts read, and the dates read (pp. 186, 189)

Goal

Learn to record the book title, author, and the date the book is completed in the reader's notebook.

Rationale

Recording the books they have read on a reading list helps students remember which books they have read and enjoyed. It also helps them remember which books they found overly difficult or did not enjoy, and those examples help them make better reading choices and develop self-awareness as readers.

Assess Learning

Observe students when they use a reader's notebook. Notice if there is evidence of new learning based on the goal of this minilesson.

- ▶ Do students understand the purpose of the reading list and how to use it?
- ▶ Do they record the title, author, and date completed of books they have read?
- ▶ Do they use the terms *reader's notebook, reading list, title,* and *author*?

Minilesson

To help students think about the minilesson principle, demonstrate how to fill in the reading list in a reader's notebook. Here is an example.

- ▶ Direct students to find the yellow tab that says Reading List. Then tell them to turn to the white page titled Reading List.

  What do you think you should write on this page?

  On this page, you will keep a list of the titles of the books you have read.

- ▶ Display the prepared chart. Hold up *The Absent Author.*

  I'm going to read this book today, but first I need to put it on my reading list. What do you think I should write first?

  There is a column that says *Title,* so I will start by writing the title of the book. You can look at the book to see how to write the title.

- ▶ Write the title of the book on the prepared chart paper.

  What should I write next?

  The next column says *Author,* so I will write the name of the author here.

- ▶ Write the name of the author. Then write the numeral *1* in the first column.

  Why do you think I wrote *1* here?

  This is the first book on my list, so it is number 1.

▶ Point to the Date Completed column.

What should I write in this column?

When I finish reading this book, I will write the date.

Have a Try

Invite the students to discuss with a partner how to record books.

▶ Display the cover of *Captain Awesome to the Rescue!*

I've decided to read this book next. Turn and talk to your partner about how I should list this book on my reading list.

▶ After students turn and talk, ask a few pairs to share their thinking. Write the title, author, and number on the enlarged reading list.

▶ Save the chart to use in RML3.

Summarize and Apply

Summarize the learning and remind students to list the books they read on the reading list.

You learned how to write information about books you read on a list.

Why do you think it's a good idea to keep a list of the books you read?

During independent reading today, choose a book to read and write the title and author on your reading list. Then read and enjoy the book! If you finish reading the book today, write today's date in the Date Completed column. Bring your reader's notebook to share your reading list when we come back together.

Share

Following independent reading time, gather students together in the meeting area to share their reading lists.

Turn and tell to your partner about a little bit about the book you read today. Show how you recorded the book on your reading list.

Extend the Lesson (Optional)

After assessing students' understanding, you might decide to extend the learning.

▶ If most of your students are reading longer books over multiple sittings, have them write the title and author when they start and add the date when they finish the book.

Reading List

#	Title	Author	Genre Code	Date Completed	E, JR, D
1	The Absent Author	Ron Roy			
2	Captain Awesome to the Rescue!	Stan Kirby			

Section 4: Writing About Reading

Reading Minilesson Principle
Write the genre of each book on your reading list.

You Will Need

- two or three books of different genres, such as these from the *Independent Reading Collection*:
  - *The Absent Author* by Ron Roy
  - *Captain Awesome to the Rescue!* by Stan Kirby
  - *Avalanches* by Lisa Bullard
- chart of the reading list from RML2
- markers

Academic Language / Important Vocabulary

- reading list
- reader's notebook
- genre
- realistic fiction
- fantasy
- informational

Continuum Connection

- Understand that there are different types of texts and that they have different characteristics (p. 50)
- Record in Reader's Notebook the titles, authors, illustrators, genre of texts read, and the dates read (pp. 186, 189)

Goal

Identify and record the genre of a book that has been read.

Rationale

When students list the genre of a book on a reading list, they notice trends among the books they have chosen, helping them develop their identities as readers. This helps you and your students set goals for expanding their repertoires. Before teaching this lesson, make sure that your students have a solid understanding of the genres that will be discussed.

Assess Learning

Observe students when they identify and record the genre of books they have read. Notice if there is evidence of new learning based on the goal of this minilesson.

- Do students record the genre of books they have read?
- Do they use the terms *reading list, reader's notebook, genre, realistic fiction, fantasy,* and *informational*?

Minilesson

To help students think about the minilesson principle, demonstrate how to record the genre of a book on a reading list. Here is an example.

- Make sure each student has a reader's notebook. Have them turn to the Genres at a Glance page (on the back of the yellow tab).

    This page lists codes for different genres. How do you think you will use these codes?

- Display the chart from RML2. Then show the cover of the first book on the list.

    Is this book fiction or nonfiction? How do you know?

    The Absent Author is a made-up story, so it must be fiction.

    Now look at Genres at a Glance. Is *The Absent Author* realistic fiction, historical fiction, traditional literature, or fantasy?

    How do you know?

    The Absent Author is realistic fiction because it tells a story that could happen in real life. What is the code for realistic fiction?

    Where should I write *RF* on my reading list?

- Write the letters *RF* in the Genre Code column.

- Show the cover of the second book on the list.

    What should I write in the genre column for this book? What is the genre of this book?

Have a Try

Invite the students to discuss the genre of a third book with a partner.

▶ Show the cover of *Avalanches*. Write the title and author on the chart.

> Think about the genre of this book. Use Genres at a Glance in the reader's notebook if you need help. Then turn and talk to your partner about what I should write on the chart.

▶ After students turn and talk, ask a few pairs to share. Write *I* (for informational) as the genre code.

▶ Save the chart to use in RML5.

Summarize and Apply

Help students summarize the learning and remind them to record the genre of the books they read on their reading list.

> You learned how to write the genre of a book on your reading list. Every time you finish a book, write the code for the genre on your reading list.

> During independent reading today, choose a book to read. Before you start reading, write the title and author on your reading list. When you're finished reading, fill in the genre code. If you're not sure what code to record, look at the Genres at a Glance page for help.

Share

Following independent reading time, gather students together in the meeting area to talk about their reading lists.

> Raise your hand if you recorded the genre of a book on your reading list.

▶ Ask several students to share the title and genre of their books and how they knew what genre to record.

Extend the Lesson (Optional)

After assessing students' understanding, you might decide to extend the learning.

▶ Depending on your students' needs and abilities, you may want to have them write only *F* (for fiction) or *N* (for nonfiction) on the reading list at first, but eventually you can expand this.

Reading List

#	Title	Author	Genre Code	Date Completed	E, JR, D
1	The Absent Author	Ron Roy	RF		
2	Captain Awesome to the Rescue!	Stan Kirby	F		
3	Avalanches	Lisa Bullard	I		

Section 4: Writing About Reading

Reading Minilesson Principle
Keep a tally of the kinds of books you read.

Introducing a Reader's Notebook

You Will Need

- six realistic fiction books
- two biographies
- chart prepared with the Reading Requirements page from *Reader's Notebook: Intermediate* (Fountas and Pinnell 2011) filled in with the specific reading requirements you have chosen for your students
- markers

Academic Language / Important Vocabulary

- genre
- requirement
- realistic fiction
- biography
- fantasy

Goal

Keep track of how many books are read in a particular genre in the reader's notebook.

Rationale

When students read a certain number of books from each genre (and to keep track of their progress), they become well-rounded readers. Reading books outside of their preferred genres allows students to step outside the comfort zone and expand their reading interests.

Assess Learning

Observe students when they use a reader's notebook. Notice if there is evidence of new learning based on the goal of this minilesson.

- Do students keep a tally in of the genres of the books they have read?
- Do they use the terms *genre, requirement, realistic fiction, biography*, and *fantasy*?

Minilesson

To help students think about the minilesson principle, demonstrate how to tally books on the Reading Requirements page of a reader's notebook (adjust to fit your specific book requirements). Here is an example.

▶ Display the prepared chart.

> This page is in the reader's notebook, just before the reading list. What do you think you might write on it?

> The title is Reading Requirements. A requirement is something that you are expected to do. Your reading requirement this year is to read at least forty-five books.

▶ Point to the numbers in the Requirement column.

> What do you think these numbers mean?

> You will be required to read a certain number of books in each genre. For example, the number five here means that you need to read at least five realistic fiction books this year.

▶ Point to the tally column.

> What do you think you might do in this column?

> You will show how many books you have read in each genre by keeping a tally. I will show you how to make a tally.

▶ Point to a pile of six realistic fiction books.

> Here are six realistic fiction books that I plan to read this year. After I read the first one, I will write one mark here.

▶ Demonstrate tallying the first four books on the chart.

> After I read the fifth book, I'll make a mark that goes through the first four marks. After I read the sixth book, I will make a new mark that is separate from the first five. When I have read a lot of realistic fiction books, I will be able to count them easily by counting by fives.

Have a Try

Invite the students to talk with a partner about how to tally books.

▶ Display two biographies from your classroom library.

> Turn and talk to your partner about how to tally these books on the Reading Requirements page.

▶ Ask a few students to share their thinking. Demonstrate how to add two tally marks to the Biography/Autobiography row.

Summarize and Apply

Summarize the learning and remind students to tally the kinds of books they read.

> This year you will read some books from lots of different genres, but most of the books you read can be from any genre. For example, if you love fantasy books, you can read as many as you like!

> When you read today, read any book you like. When you finish reading it, make a tally mark on your Reading Requirements page next to the name of the genre.

Share

Following independent reading time, gather students together in the meeting area to talk about their reading.

> Show your partner how you recorded the genre of the book you read.

Extend the Lesson (Optional)

After assessing students' understanding, you might decide to extend the learning.

▶ The reading requirements listed in this minilesson are suggestions. Adjust them to fit your students. Review students' tallies regularly to make sure they are on track to meet the requirements and are reading a variety of books.

Reading Requirement
Total Books: 45

Requirement	Genre or Type	Tally
5	(RF) Realistic Fiction	⳾⳾⳾⳾ ⳾
	(HF) Historical Fiction	
3	(TL) Traditional Literature	
3	(F) Fantasy	
	(SF) Science Fiction	
3	(B) Biography/ Autobiography	⳾⳾
	(M) Memoir	
5	(I) Informational (nonfiction)	
1	(H) Hybrid	
1	(P) Poetry	

Reading Minilesson Principle

Write *E* (easy), *JR* (just right), or *D* (difficult) for each book on your reading list.

Introducing a Reader's Notebook

You Will Need

- the chart from RML3 with the letters *D*, *E*, and *JR* written in the last column
- markers

Academic Language / Important Vocabulary

- easy
- just right
- difficult

Goal

Determine and record on the reading list if a book is easy, just right, or difficult.

Rationale

Students learn more, strengthen their ability to process increasingly challenging texts, and enjoy their reading more when most of the books that they read are within their reach. Before teaching this minilesson, make sure your students know how to determine if a book is just right for them (see Umbrella 3: Getting Started with Independent Reading, found in Section One: Management).

Assess Learning

Observe students when they use a reader's notebook. Notice if there is evidence of new learning based on the goal of this minilesson.

> ▶ Do students record the difficulty level of books they have read on their reading list?
>
> ▶ How often do they choose books that are just right for them?
>
> ▶ Do students understand the terms *easy, just right,* and *difficult*?

Minilesson

To help students think about the minilesson principle, demonstrate how to record whether a book is easy, just right, or difficult.

> ▶ Display the chart from RML3.
>
>> What did I add to my reading list?
>>
>> What do you think these letters might mean?
>>
>> The first letter, *D*, is for *difficult*. I wrote a *D* next to *The Absent Author* because I found this book a bit difficult to read.
>>
>> What did I write next to *Captain Awesome to the Rescue!*?
>>
>> *E* stands for *easy*. I wrote the letter *E* because *Captain Awesome to the Rescue!* was very easy for me to read.
>>
>> What letters did I write next to the third book on my list, *Avalanches*?
>>
>> What do you think the letters *JR* mean?
>>
>> *JR* means "just right." I wrote these letters because this book is just right for me. It was not too easy or too difficult. I understood and enjoyed the book, and I knew almost all the words and I could solve the rest.
>>
>> The last column on your reading list is for you to write whether each book was easy, just right, or difficult for you.

Have a Try

Invite the students to discuss difficulty levels with a partner.

▶ Have students open to the Reading List page.

> Think about the last book that you wrote on your reading list. Was this book easy, just right, or difficult for you? Turn and talk to your partner about what letter you would write for this book in the last column, and explain why.

▶ After students turn and talk, ask a few to share.

Summarize and Apply

Help students summarize the learning and remind them to record the difficulty level of each book they read.

> Why do you think it's important to pay attention to whether a book is easy, just right, or difficult?

> Thinking about and writing whether a book was easy, difficult, or just right for you will help in choosing just-right books to read. And books that are difficult will become just right and easy as you do more reading.

> Choose a book to read. Write the title and author of the book on your reading list before you start reading. When you have finished reading, think about whether the book was easy, difficult, or just right for you and write it on your reading list.

Share

Following independent reading time, gather students together in the meeting area to talk about their reading.

> Raise your hand if you read a book today, put it on your reading list, and wrote whether it was easy, difficult, or just right for you.

> What letter did you write in the last column?

> Why did you choose that letter?

Extend the Lesson (Optional)

After assessing students' understanding, you might decide to extend the learning.

▶ Review your students' reading lists on a regular basis. If some students frequently choose books that are easy or difficult, help them make better choices.

▶ Revisit the minilesson on choosing books (see Section One: Management) if many of your students have trouble choosing books that are just right for them.

Reading List

#	Title	Author	Genre Code	Date Completed	E,JR,D
1	The Absent Author	Ron Roy	RF		D
2	Captain Awesome to the Rescue!	Stan Kirby	F		E
3	Avalanches	Lisa Bullard	I		JR

Section 4: Writing About Reading

Introducing a Reader's Notebook

Reading Minilesson Principle
Follow the guidelines in your reader's notebook to do your best reading and writing work.

- chart paper and markers

Academic Language / Important Vocabulary

- reader's notebook
- guidelines

Goal

Learn and/or develop the guidelines for working together in the classroom.

Rationale

When you teach students to follow guidelines, they are better equipped to do their best work. You might have students review the established guidelines in *Reader's Notebook: Intermediate* [Fountas and Pinnell 2011] or construct their own. When students play an active role in developing guidelines, they take ownership of them.

Assess Learning

Observe students during literacy work. Notice if there is evidence of new learning based on the goal of this minilesson.

> ▶ Do students follow the guidelines established during this minilesson?

> ▶ Do they understand the terms *reader's notebook* and *guidelines*?

Minilesson

If you have *Reader's Notebook: Intermediate*, you can read and discuss the guidelines printed on the inside front cover, or you may choose to develop guidelines with your students, as demonstrated in the lesson below. If you construct the guidelines with your students, provide a copy of the guidelines for them to glue into their reader's notebooks after the lesson.

▶ Divide students into small groups.

> You have been learning about what to do during reading and writing time and how to use a reader's notebook. Today we're going to make a list of guidelines for reading and writing work. Guidelines are agreements we have together so all students can do their best work. Take a few minutes to talk with the other students in your group about what things you think would be important for us to agree on so that you can all do your best work.

▶ After a few minutes, ask each group to share the ideas they came up with. Record their responses on chart paper. If needed, prompt students with questions such as the following:

- *What should you do during reading time?*
- *What voice level should you use during independent reading?*
- *What voice level should you use when you are working with a teacher?*
- *What should you do if you give a book a good chance but you're still not enjoying it?*
- *What should you do each time you start a new book?*

Have a Try

Invite the students to talk about the guidelines with a partner.

> Turn and talk to your partner about anything else you think we should add to the guidelines.

▶ Ask several pairs to share their thinking and add any new guidelines to the list, if appropriate.

Summarize and Apply

Summarize the learning and remind students to follow the guidelines for literacy work.

▶ Review the list of guidelines.

> Why do you think it's important to follow these guidelines during reading and writing work?

▶ Direct students to look at the guidelines inside the front cover of *Reader's Notebook: Intermediate* or provide copies for students to glue into a plain notebook.

> During independent reading today, remember to follow the guidelines we created together. If you think of anything else that you would like to add to our guidelines, be ready to share your ideas when we come back together.

Share

Following independent reading time, gather students together in the meeting area to talk about the guidelines.

> How did the guidelines help you do your best work today?

> Does anyone have anything else that they think we should add to our guidelines?

Extend the Lesson (Optional)

After assessing students' understanding, you might decide to extend the learning.

▶ If students have trouble remembering what to do during independent reading time, remind them to review the list of guidelines.

▶ Revisit the list of guidelines with your students from time to time to see how they are working and whether they need to be revised.

Guidelines

1. Read a book or write your thoughts about your reading.

2. Work silently so that you and your classmates can do your best thinking.

3. Use a soft voice when talking with the teacher.

4. Choose books that you think you'll enjoy.

5. Abandon books that don't enjoy after you give them a good chance.

6. Write each book you read on your reading list.

7. Always do your best work.

Assessment

After you have taught the minilessons in this umbrella, observe students as they talk and write about their reading across instructional contexts: interactive read-aloud, independent reading and literacy work, guided reading, shared reading, and book club. Use *The Literacy Continuum* (Fountas and Pinnell 2017) to observe students' reading and writing behaviors across instructional contexts.

▶ What evidence do you have of new understandings relating to using a reader's notebook?

  • Do students understand the purpose of a reader's notebook?

  • Do they understand the purpose of each section?

  • Do they record the title, author, date completed, genre, and difficulty level (easy, just right, difficult) of the books they read on their reading list?

  • How well do they keep a tally of the kinds of books they have read?

  • Can they follow the guidelines for literacy work?

  • Do they use vocabulary such as *reader's notebook, genre,* and *guidelines*?

▶ What other parts of the reader's notebook might you have the students start using based on your observations?

Use your observations to determine the next umbrella you will teach. You may also consult Minilessons Across the Year (pp. 55-57) for guidance.

Reader's Notebook

When this umbrella is complete, provide a copy of the minilesson principles (see resources.fountasandpinnell.com) for students to glue in the reader's notebook (in the Minilessons section if using *Reader's Notebook: Intermediate* [Fountas and Pinnell 2011]), so they can refer to the information as needed.

Minilessons in This Umbrella

RML1 Make a list of the books you want to read.

RML2 Make a list of the books you recommend.

RML3 Write a book recommendation.

RML4 Tell how a book reminds you of another book.

RML5 Keep a tally of the kinds of writing about reading you do in your notebook.

RML6 Put the minilesson principles in your reader's notebook so you can use them when you need to.

Before Teaching Umbrella 2 Minilessons

Before teaching the minilessons in this umbrella, teach the minilessons in Umbrella 1: Introducing a Reader's Notebook to introduce your students to the purpose and structure of *Reader's Notebook: Intermediate* (Fountas and Pinnell 2011). If you do not have it, a plain notebook can be used instead (see pp. 46-49 for more on using a reader's notebook). It would also be helpful to have taught Umbrella 1: Thinking and Talking About Books and Umbrella 3: Giving a Book Talk, both in Section Two: Literary Analysis.

The minilessons in this umbrella do not have to be taught consecutively. Introduce RML4 and RML5 when you feel your students have a good understanding of ways to make meaningful connections between books and have been introduced to different ways to write about reading.

Before students begin to use a reader's notebook, they should have read and discussed a variety of high-quality books and participated in several shared writing lessons. For this umbrella, use the following books from the *Fountas & Pinnell Classroom™ Interactive Read-Aloud Collection* text sets or a selection of other fiction and nonfiction books, some with which students are familiar and some that are new to them.

Exploring Memory Stories

Saturdays and Teacakes by Lester L. Laminack

Grandma's Records by Eric Velasquez

Author/Illustrator Study: Patricia Polacco

Thunder Cake

As you read aloud and discuss books together, help students

- talk about books they want to read and share their reasons for their choices,

- talk about their favorite books and explain what they like about them, and

- make connections between books.

Memory Stories

Patricia Polacco

Reader's Notebook

Reading Minilesson Principle
Make a list of the books you want to read.

Using a Reader's Notebook

You Will Need

- a reader's notebook for each student (if using a plain reader's notebook, create a Books to Read chart and a Tips for Choosing Books page and glue it into each notebook)

- chart paper prepared to look like the Books to Read page from *Reader's Notebook: Intermediate* (Fountas and Pinnell 2011)

- three or four books from your classroom library that your students might enjoy reading independently

- markers

Academic Language / Important Vocabulary

- reader's notebook
- title
- author
- list

Goal

Create and maintain a list of books to read in the future.

Rationale

When students think about the books they would like to read and make a list of those books, they are better able to make good book choices and they develop an identity as a reader in a community of readers where books are recommended and shared.

Assess Learning

Observe students when they talk and write about books they want to read. Notice if there is evidence of new learning based on the goal of this minilesson.

- Do students add books to their Books to Read list?
- Do they use vocabulary such as *reader's notebook, title, author,* and *list*?

Minilesson

To help students think about the minilesson principle, discuss ways to choose books and provide a demonstration of keeping a list of books to read in a reader's notebook. Here is an example.

- Direct students to turn to the Tips for Choosing Books page, located on the front of the orange tab and read the page silently.

    What is this page about?

    This page gives tips for choosing books. Which of these things do you already do?

    Which of these things would you like to try to do more in the future?

- Have students turn to the Books to Read chart on the next page.

    What will you write on this page?

    You will use this page to make a list of books that you want to read. Raise your hand if you can think of a book that you want to read.

- Call on a student to name a book that he would like to read.

    _____ wants to read _____. Where should he write the title of this book?

- Demonstrate writing the title in the title column on the prepared chart.

    Where should he write the author's name?

- Demonstrate writing the author's name in the author column. Point out and explain the Check When Completed column.

Have a Try

Invite the students to start their own Books to Read lists.

> As I tell you about a few books from our classroom library, think about whether you would like to add them to the Books to Read list.

▶ Give a brief book talk about three or four books from your classroom library. Allow time between talks for students to add the books to their lists, if they would like to.

> If there is a different book that you would like to read, add that book to your list as well.

Summarize and Apply

Help students summarize the learning and remind them to add books they would like to read to their Books to Read list.

> When you make a list of books you want to read, it helps you remember interesting books you have heard about. When you are choosing a book to read, you can look at your list and choose one of the books on your list.

> During independent reading today, you may want to start reading one of the books on your Books to Read list. If you think of any other books that you would like to read in the future, add them to your list. When I have a conference with you, I might suggest more titles for your list. Bring your list to share when we come back together.

Share

Following independent reading time, gather students together in the meeting area to discuss their Books to Read lists.

> Did anyone read one of the books on your Books to Read list or add a new book to the list?

▶ Ask volunteers to share what they read or added.

Extend the Lesson (Optional)

After assessing students' understanding, you might decide to extend the learning.

▶ Refer to a student's list of books to read during individual reading conferences to help plan what to read next.

▶ When students give book talks, remind other students to record the title of any book they hear about that they would like to read.

Books to Read

Title	Author	Check When Completed
Tornadoes!	Gail Gibbons	✓

Reading Minilesson Principle
Make a list of the books you recommend.

You Will Need

- chart paper prepared with a list of books you recommend
- markers

Academic Language / Important Vocabulary

- recommend
- list
- title
- author

Goal

Create a list of books to recommend to others.

Rationale

When students make a list of the books they recommend, they further develop their self-awareness of their own identities as readers. They can also use this list to help them choose books for independent reading, for giving book talks, and for writing book recommendations.

Assess Learning

Observe students when they talk and write about books they recommend. Notice if there is evidence of new learning based on the goal of this minilesson.

- ▶ Do students talk about books they recommend?
- ▶ Can they explain why they are recommending a particular book?
- ▶ Are they able to make a list of books they recommend?
- ▶ Do they use vocabulary such as *recommend, list, title,* and *author*?

Minilesson

To help students think about the minilesson principle, share and discuss an example list of recommended books. Here is an example.

- ▶ Show students the list of books you prepared before class. Direct them to read it silently.

    What does my list show?

    What did I write at the top of the list?

    What do you think the word *recommend* means?

    If I recommend a book to you, it means that I think you would really like this book and I think you should try reading it. This is a list of books that I recommend. I really liked all these books and I think you would like them, too.

    There are many different reasons why you might recommend a book. What are some of the reasons?

- ▶ Briefly explain why you recommend each book on the list.

    What do you notice about how I wrote each book on my list? What information did I write about each book?

    I wrote the title and author of each book. Notice how I used capital letters to begin the first, last, and important words in the title and for the author's name and that I underlined the book titles.

Have a Try

Invite the students to start thinking about what books they recommend.

> What books would you recommend to your partner? Turn and talk to your partner and recommend at least one book.

▶ Ask a few students to share their recommendations.

Summarize and Apply

Help students summarize the learning and remind them to make lists of books they recommend.

> Talk about the list you learned to make today.

> During independent reading time, make a list in your notebook of books you recommend. Bring your notebook to share when we come back together.

Share

Following independent reading time, gather students together in the meeting area to share their lists.

> Turn and talk to your partner about the books on your list. Share the reasons why you recommend each book. If your partner recommends a book that you want to read, add it to your list.

Extend the Lesson (Optional)

After assessing students' understanding, you might decide to extend the learning.

▶ Encourage students to refer to their lists when selecting books for giving book talks or for writing book recommendations.

▶ Feature students' recommended books in the classroom library. Students can help you make a display of the book or books they recommend. Rotate the displays frequently.

Books I Recommend

- Inspector Flytrap
  by Tom Angleberger

- Snakes by Gail Gibbons

- Blast Off to Space Camp
  by Hillary Wolfe

Section 4: Writing About Reading

Using a Reader's Notebook

You Will Need

- chart prepared with a book recommendation
- a familiar fiction book
- chart paper and markers

Academic Language / Important Vocabulary

- book recommendation

Continuum Connection

- Record titles, authors, and genres of books to recommend (p. 186)
- Form and express opinions about a text in writing and support those opinions with rationales and evidence (p. 187)

Goal

Express an opinion about a text in the form of a book recommendation.

Rationale

When students write book recommendations, they express their opinions about books and give reasons for their opinions. They also develop their identities as readers, gain more awareness of their own preferences, and hone their writing skills. Before teaching this minilesson, it would be helpful to teach Umbrella 3: Giving a Book Talk, found in Section Two: Literary Analysis. Written book recommendations are very similar to book talks.

Assess Learning

Observe students when they write book recommendations. Notice if there is evidence of new learning based on the goal of this minilesson.

- ▶ Can students write a book recommendation about a book they have enjoyed?
- ▶ Do they include the title, author, and reason the book is recommended?
- ▶ Do they understand and use the term *book recommendation*?

Minilesson

To help students think about book recommendations, engage them in a short discussion. Here is an example.

- ▶ Display the prepared chart.

  I am going to read aloud a book recommendation about a book I read and enjoyed. What do you think a book recommendation is?

- ▶ Read the book recommendation aloud and then prompt students to share what they notice about it. Use questions such as the following to prompt discussion:
  - *What do you notice about this book recommendation?*
  - *How does the recommendation start?*
  - *What things did I write about the book?*
  - *Why do I think you should read this book?*
  - *Who will probably like reading this book?*
- ▶ Record students' noticings on the chart.

Have a Try

Invite the students to talk with a partner about book recommendations.

▶ Show the cover of a fiction book that you have read aloud recently. (If the model recommendation you used in the first part of the lesson was a fiction book, use a nonfiction book here.)

  If you were writing a recommendation about this book, what would you write? Turn and talk to your partner about that.

▶ Ask several pairs to share their thinking.

Summarize and Apply

Help students summarize the learning and remind them to write book recommendations about books they like.

  Why do you think book recommendations are important? Why do people read and write book recommendations?

  Today during independent reading, write a recommendation for a book you love. It might be about the book you are currently reading or a book you have read before.

Share

Following independent reading time, gather students together in the meeting area to share their book recommendations in pairs.

  Read your recommendation to your partner. Talk about whether you would like to read the book your partner recommends.

▶ After pairs share their recommendations, ask a volunteer to share with the class.

Extend the Lesson (Optional)

After assessing students' understanding, you might decide to extend the learning.

▶ If you notice that students need more support with this lesson, use shared writing to compose a book recommendation together.

▶ Provide examples of book recommendations for a variety of genres.

▶ Devote a shelf in your classroom library to books that have been recommended by your students. Display each book prominently alongside a student-written recommendation. Rotate the books regularly.

Book Recommendation

the title and the author

who should read the book

what he liked about the book

what the book is about

interesting part

Name: Shalid   Date: Feb. 27

I love Guinea Pigs by Dick King-Smith

Do you love guinea pigs? Or are you thinking about getting a pet? If so, I think you would love I Love Guinea Pigs. This nonfiction book has lots of fascinating facts about guinea pigs. For example, did you know that baby guinea pigs are born covered with fur and with a mouth full of teeth? If you want to find out more about guinea pigs, I recommend that you read this book. I loved this book because it made me realize that guinea pigs make really good pets. I also like the way the author writes. He writes like he is talking right to you about guinea pigs. I can't wait to get my first guinea pig!

Reading Minilesson Principle
Tell how a book reminds you of another book.

Using a Reader's Notebook

You Will Need

- two or three familiar fiction books that share similar messages, themes, settings, characters, or other commonalities, such as the following:
  - *Saturdays and Teacakes* by Lester L. Laminack, from Text Set: Memory Stories
  - *Grandma's Records* by Eric Velasquez, from Text Set: Memory Stories
  - *Thunder Cake* by Patricia Polacco, from Text Set: Patricia Polacco
- chart prepared with a short paragraph about the connections between two books
- markers
- highlighter

Academic Language / Important Vocabulary

- remind
- character
- setting
- message

Continuum Connection

- Relate important information/ideas within a text or to other texts (p. 189)
- Write about connections among texts by topic, theme, major ideas, authors' styles, and genres (pp. 186, 189)
- Write about the important information and concepts in one text and connect it to information and concepts in other texts (p. 189)

Goal

Make connections among texts in writing.

Rationale

When you teach students to write about how one text reminds them of another in meaningful ways, they think more deeply about their reading and notice common themes, messages, settings, and other commonalities that are prevalent in literature. This helps them understand that people from all walks of life, despite their many differences, share certain values, emotions, and experiences.

Assess Learning

Observe students when they write about connections among texts. Notice if there is evidence of new learning based on the goal of this minilesson.

- What kinds of connections between books (e.g., message, setting, character) do students write about?
- Do they use vocabulary such as *remind, character, setting*, and *message* in their writing?

Minilesson

To help students think about the minilesson principle, share and discuss a model piece of writing about the connections between two books. Here is an example.

- Show the cover of *Saturdays and Teacakes*.

  When I read this book, I thought about another book that I had read recently.

- Show the cover of *Grandma's Records*.

  Saturdays and Teacakes reminded me of *Grandma's Records*. I noticed that they have many things in common. I wrote in my reader's notebook about what I noticed. Take a look at what I wrote.

- Display prepared chart and read it aloud.

  What is one way that *Saturdays and Teacakes* reminds me of *Grandma's Records*?

- Have a student highlight the similarity.

  What other ways does one book remind me of the other?

- Have students highlight the similarities.

  When you read one book, you may be reminded of one or more other books. You might notice that two books have similar characters, settings, messages, illustrations, or something else in common. You can write about what you notice in the Writing About Reading section of your reader's notebook.

Have a Try

Invite the students to talk with a partner about the similarities they noticed between two books.

> Think about the two books we just talked about. Does either book remind you of another book? Turn and talk to your partner about that.

▶ Ask a few students to share their thinking.

Summarize and Apply

Help students summarize the learning and remind them to write about connections they make between books.

> What did we write about today?

▶ Write the principle at the top of the chart.

> When a book reminds you of another book, you can write about what you noticed in your reader's notebook.

> Today, read any book you like. If your book reminds you of another book, write about what you noticed in your reader's notebook. Bring your reader's notebook when we come back together.

Section 4: Writing About Reading

Tell how a book reminds you of another book.

Saturdays and Teacakes reminds me of Grandma's Records because both books are about boys spending time with their grandmas. Both books have a similar message. I think the authors are saying that the love between grandparents and grandchildren is very special and important. Both books tell about something that happened in the past. Both grandmas shared something special. The boys in both books are now grown up, and they are sharing their memories from when they were young.

Share

Following independent reading time, gather students together in the meeting area to share their writing.

> Turn and talk to a partner about one book that reminds you of another. If you wrote in your reader's notebook about that, share what you wrote.

▶ Invite a volunteer to share with the class.

Extend the Lesson (Optional)

After assessing students' understanding, you might decide to extend the learning.

▶ Repeat this minilesson using nonfiction books as examples. Model and discuss the connections that can be made between nonfiction books (e.g., topic, organization, message, point of view).

▶ When you teach your students how to write letters about their reading, demonstrate how they can include the connections they noticed between two books in their letters (see Umbrella 3: Writing Letters About Reading in this section).

RML 5
WAR.U2.RML5

Reading Minilesson Principle
Keep a tally of the kinds of writing about reading that you do in your notebook.

Using a Reader's Notebook

You Will Need

- chart paper resembling the Forms for Writing About Reading page from *Reader's Notebook: Intermediate* (Fountas and Pinnell 2011)
- markers
- document camera (optional)

Academic Language / Important Vocabulary

- writing about reading
- tally
- book recommendation

Goal

Learn how to keep a tally of the different forms of writing about reading.

Rationale

When you teach students to keep a tally of the kinds of writing they do, they are more likely to write about their reading in a wide variety of ways. This minilesson is similar to RML4 in Umbrella 1: Introducing a Reader's Notebook, where students keep a tally of their reading.

Assess Learning

Observe students when they keep track of the kinds of writing they do. Notice if there is evidence of new learning based on the goal of this minilesson.

- Do students keep a tally of the kinds of writing about reading they do?
- Do they write about their reading in a variety of ways?
- Do they understand how to make and count tally marks?
- Do they understand the terms *writing about reading, tally,* and *book recommendation*?

Minilesson

To help students think about the minilesson principle, demonstrate how to tally forms of writing in a reader's notebook. Discuss only the forms of writing that you have already introduced to your students. Here is an example.

- Display the prepared chart paper or project the Forms for Writing About Reading page from *Reader's Notebook: Intermediate*.

    This chart shows part of a page in the reader's notebook at the beginning of the Writing About Reading section. What do you notice about it?

    This page lists some of the different ways that you can write about reading. You have already learned how to write a book recommendation.

- Point to *book recommendation* on the list and read its definition.

    What do you notice about the third column in this chart? What does it tell you?

    This column gives the definition of each type of writing. The definition explains what each type of writing is.

- Point to the first column and read the heading, *Tally*.

    What do you think you will write in this column?

    In this column, you will keep a tally of the different kinds of writing you do. Who remembers what a tally is?

- If necessary, review (or teach) how to keep a tally and count tally marks.

Have a Try

Invite the students to talk with a partner about how to keep track of the kinds of writing they do.

▶ Make sure each student has a reader's notebook.

Most of you have already written your first book recommendation. Turn and talk to your partner about how you will keep track in your reader's notebook of how many book recommendations you have written.

If you have already written a book recommendation, add a tally mark in your reader's notebook.

▶ Invite a volunteer to add a tally mark next to Book Recommendation on the chart.

Summarize and Apply

Help students summarize the learning and remind students to keep track of the kinds of writing they do.

What did you learn how to do today in your reader's notebook?

▶ Write the principle at the top of the chart.

After you read today, you may want to write about your reading in your reader's notebook. If so, remember to make a tally mark next to the kind of writing that you do.

Share

Following independent reading time, gather students together in the meeting area to talk about their writing about reading.

Raise your hand if you wrote about your reading in your reader's notebook today. What kind of writing did you do?

Did you keep a tally of it?

Extend the Lesson (Optional)

After assessing students' understanding, you might decide to extend the learning.

▶ You will need to decide which forms of writing about reading are appropriate for your students. After teaching each new form of writing, read aloud the definition of it on the Forms for Writing About Reading page and remind students to keep track of the kinds of writing they do.

Forms for Writing About Reading

Tally	Kind of Writing	Definition
	Letter to your teacher (or another reader)	a letter to share your thinking about your reading with another reader who writes back to you
	Short Write	an open-ended response or focused response to a specific prompt or question
	Notes	words, phrases, or a quick drawing to help you remember the book
	List	words, phrases, or sentences written one under the other
I	Book Recommendation	writing that gives another reader some information and advice on a book

Section 4: Writing About Reading

Reading Minilesson Principle
Put the minilesson principles in your reader's notebook so you can use them when you need to.

Using a Reader's Notebook

You Will Need

- To download the following from online resources, visit **resources.fountasandpinnell.com**: minilesson principles from a previously taught umbrella (a copy for each student)
- a reader's notebook for each student and yourself
- glue sticks
- chart paper and markers

Academic Language / Important Vocabulary

- minilesson
- principle
- information

Goal

Keep minilesson notes in a reader's notebook to refer to as needed.

Rationale

Reader's Notebook: Intermediate (Fountas and Pinnell 2011) includes a section for information from minilessons. When students keep information from previous minilessons for reference, they are better able to remember what they learned and to use and build on that knowledge. At the end of each umbrella, download the principles list for students to glue in the Minilessons section. Alternatively, you could provide copies of charts (e.g., take a photo of the chart and make small copies) instead of or in addition to the principles list. We recommend that you also display key reference charts on the walls of the classroom for student reference.

Assess Learning

Observe students when they use the Minilessons section of the reader's notebook. Notice if there is evidence of new learning based on the goal of this minilesson.

- Do students neatly glue minilesson information (copy of the umbrella principles) into the Minilessons section of the reader's notebook?
- Do they understand why it is important to keep and refer to principles from previous minilessons?
- Do they understand the terms *minilesson, principle,* and *information*?

Minilesson

To help students think about the minilesson principle, model using a glue stick to put the page of minilesson principles into the reader's notebook and engage students in a discussion about how and when they might use them. Here is an example.

- Have students turn to the Minilessons section (blue tab). Read the text aloud.

    When we have minilessons, we usually make a chart about what you are learning. Often I write the minilesson principle at the top. The principle tells what the lesson is about. To help you remember what you have learned, I will give you a copy of the minilesson principles to glue into your reader's notebook.

- Model how to glue the photocopy of the principle list onto the first blank page of the Minilessons section in a reader's notebook.

- Read the list aloud, and then engage students in a discussion about how the information helps them as readers and writers.

    You can add some notes to help you remember the information better.

    Because you will put them all in the same section, you will always know where to find them if you need to remember what you have learned.

Have a Try

Invite the students to talk with a partner about when and why they might use the notes from previous minilessons.

> The blue tab in the reader's notebook says, "You can look back at what you learned when you need to." When might you need to look back at the information from a minilesson? How can this help you? Turn and talk to your partner about when you might do this and why.

Summarize and Apply

Help students summarize the learning and remind them to glue the minilesson principles in the Minilesson section to refer to as needed.

> Usually, we make a chart to help remember what you learned in a minilesson. Let's do that now.

▶ Ask students for suggestions to put on the chart.

▶ Provide each student with a copy of the principles that you discussed earlier in the lesson.

> During independent reading time, you will glue this list of minilesson principles into the Minilessons section of your reader's notebook. Reread the principles and think about how they might help you when you're reading today. Then read any book that you like!

Share

Following independent reading time, gather students together in the meeting area to talk about their reading.

> Did anyone think about the minilesson principles that are on the chart? What did you think about?

Extend the Lesson (Optional)

After assessing students' understanding, you might decide to extend the learning.

▶ A note at the end of each umbrella will remind you to download a copy of the principles for students to glue into the Minilessons section of the reader's notebook. At that time, you might want to review what students have learned about the concepts and ask them to make a few notes to remind them of what they have learned.

> **Put the minilesson principles in your reader's notebook so you can use them when you need to.**
>
> - Glue the information in your reader's notebook.
> - Write notes if you want to.
> - Look at the information when you need to.
>
> ---
>
> **Thinking About the Setting in Fiction Books**
>
> The setting is the time and place of the story.
> Like a beach or in the woods.
>
> The setting can be a time in the past or a faraway place.
>
> The setting is often important to the story.

Assessment

After you have taught the minilessons in this umbrella, observe students as they talk and write about their reading across instructional contexts: interactive read-aloud, independent reading and literacy work, guided reading, shared reading, and book club. Use *The Literacy Continuum* (Fountas and Pinnell 2017) to observe students' reading and writing behaviors across instructional contexts.

▶ What evidence do you have of new understandings related to using the reader's notebook?

- Are students continuing to add to the list of books they want to read?
- Do they make lists of books they recommend and use them for selecting books that they want to use for book talks and for writing book recommendations?
- Do they glue minilesson principles into their reader's notebooks and reference them when appropriate?
- Can they write a book recommendation?
- Are they able to write about connections between books?
- Do they keep a tally of the forms of writing about reading they have done?
- Do students use the terms *title, author, recommend, list, information, tally,* and *book recommendation*?

▶ Based on your observations, how else might you have your students writing about reading in a reader's notebook?

Use your observations to determine the next umbrella you will teach. You may also consult Minilessons Across the Year (pp. 55-57) for guidance.

Reader's Notebook

When this umbrella is complete, provide a copy of the minilesson principles (see resources.fountasandpinnell.com) for students to glue in the reader's notebook (in the Minilessons section if using *Reader's Notebook: Intermediate* [Fountas and Pinnell 2011]), so they can refer to the information as needed.

Minilessons in This Umbrella

RML1   Write a letter to share your thinking about your reading.

RML2   Write a letter about your reading each week.

RML3   Provide evidence for your thinking in your letter.

RML4   Reread your letter to be sure it makes sense.

RML5   Reread your letter to check your spelling, capitals, and punctuation.

RML6   Respond to any teacher questions when you write your next letter.

RML7   Choose a letter that shows your best thinking.

Before Teaching Umbrella 3 Minilessons

Letters about reading give students the opportunity to reflect meaningfully on their reading in an authentic format—an ongoing written dialogue with another reader. We suggest having each student write one letter about their reading each week. You will need to develop a management system for receiving and responding to the letters. You might have all students turn in a reader's notebook on one day each week (e.g., Friday) or stagger the due dates for four or five students each day so you can provide regular responses to their thinking. If responding every week is difficult, consider every other week responses (see p. 49).

As you teach the minilessons in this umbrella, keep in mind that it is important to balance opportunities for reading and writing about reading. We suggest that you teach these minilessons on nonconsecutive days over a period of at least three weeks.

To teach the minilessons in this umbrella, use letters that you have written as a model. Consider using these books from the *Fountas & Pinnell Classroom*™ *Interactive Read-Aloud Collection* text sets, or choose books from your own classroom library.

The Importance of Kindness

  Last Day Blues by Julie Danneburg

  The Can Man by Laura E. Williams

Exploring Memory Stories

  Saturdays and Teacakes by Lester L. Laminack

  Grandma's Records by Eric Velasquez

Sharing Our World: Animals

  Ape by Martin Jenkins

  I Love Guinea Pigs by Dick King-Smith

As you read aloud and enjoy these texts together, help students

- think, talk, and express opinions about the books, and
- discuss the theme or message of each book.

Kindness

Memory Stories

Animals

Reader's Notebook

Section 4: Writing About Reading

Reading Minilesson Principle
Write a letter to share your thinking about your reading.

Writing Letters About Reading

You Will Need

- two books with which students are very familiar, such as these from Text Set: Kindness:
  - *Last Day Blues* by Julie Danneburg
  - *The Can Man* by Laura E. Williams
- chart paper prepared with a letter about a book (e.g., *Last Day Blues*)
- chart paper and markers
- highlighters
- a reader's notebook for each student

Academic Language / Important Vocabulary

- letter

Continuum Connection

- Form and express opinions about a text in writing and support those opinions with rationales and evidence (pp. 187, 190)
- Compose notes, lists, letters, or statements to remember important information about a text (pp. 186, 189)
- Express opinions about facts or information learned (p. 189)

Goal

Understand some of the different ways to share thinking about books in a letter.

Rationale

When students talk about books, they share their thinking. In this minilesson and the next, they will learn that they can talk about their thinking and also write about their thinking.

Assess Learning

Assess students' letters about reading. Notice if there is evidence of new learning based on the goal of this minilesson.

  ▶ Do the students share their thinking about their reading in their letters (as opposed to simply retelling the book)?

  ▶ Do their letters contain evidence of various kinds of thinking about reading?

  ▶ Do their letters contain academic vocabulary when appropriate (e.g., *author*, *character*, *setting*)?

Minilesson

To help students think about the minilesson principle, use a letter as a model to help students learn about the kinds of thinking they can share in their letters. Here is an example.

> Today, I would like to share with you a letter that I wrote to you about a book you all know.

  ▶ Display the prepared chart and read it aloud.

> What do you notice about what I wrote about the book? What kinds of things did I write about?

  ▶ Record students' responses on a separate sheet of chart paper (generalizing them if they are overly specific) and highlight the relevant parts of the letter.

Have a Try

Invite the students to talk with a partner about what they could write about in a letter about a book.

▶ Show *The Can Man* to remind students about the content.

Turn and talk about what you could write in a letter to me about *The Can Man*.

▶ Ask students to share ideas they talked about. Relate them to the chart of writing ideas. Add new ideas and the principle.

Summarize and Apply

Summarize the learning and remind students to share their thinking about books in their letters.

Today, you will all write a letter about *The Can Man* in your reader's notebook. You have already talked about the book with a partner, and we have a chart of ways to share your thinking. Use my letter as an example. Bring your reader's notebook when we come back together.

Share

Following independent reading time, gather students together in the meeting area to talk about their letters.

Who would like to read aloud your letter about *The Can Man*?

Extend the Lesson (Optional)

After assessing students' understanding, you might decide to extend the learning.

▶ As an alternative approach to this lesson, if your students need more support, use an interactive read-aloud book you have read to them and compose a letter together. Then use a second familiar interactive read-aloud for them to talk about and write about in Have a Try and share as a group.

▶ There is a list of starter ideas in the Writing About Reading section of *Reader's Notebook: Intermediate* (Fountas and Pinnell 2011) that students can reference if they need help deciding what to write about.

October 11

Dear Class,

I really enjoyed reading <u>Last Day Blues</u>. This book is in my favorite series, Mrs. Hartwell's Classroom Adventures, and I was excited to see what would happen next.

This story was interesting to me because, like Mrs. Hartwell, I am a teacher. This book reminded me of my own life. Like Mrs. Hartwell, I feel sad at the end of the year because I know I will miss my students. But, like Mrs. Hartwell, I look forward to summer vacation!

It made me laugh at the end of the book when the teachers were dancing beause they were excited about summer vacation. In my opinion, Julie Danneberg is a very funny writer. Her books often have surprise endings. Were you surprised by anything in the book?

Your Teacher,
Ms. King

Write a letter to share your thinking about your reading.

You can tell . . .

- how the story reminds you of your own life
- how the story made you feel
- parts that you found funny
- your opinion about the book or the author
- why you chose the book
- what you notice about the author's writing
- what the author is really trying to say
- how a character feels and why
- interesting words the author uses

Reading Minilesson Principle
Write a letter about your reading each week.

Writing Letters About Reading

You Will Need

- chart paper prepared with the letter printed in the Writing About Reading section of *Reader's Notebook: Intermediate* (Fountas and Pinnell 2011) or a similar letter, customized for your class
- smaller copies of the letter for students to glue into each reader's notebook (if using a customized letter and/or a plain reader's notebook)
- markers
- highlighters
- sticky notes
- a reader's notebook for each student

Academic Language / Important Vocabulary

- letter
- date
- greeting
- closing

Continuum Connection

- Compose notes, lists, letters, or statements to remember important information about a text (pp. 186, 189)

Goal

Learn the standard form of a letter and understand that a letter about reading is due each week.

Rationale

When students write letters about their reading on a weekly basis, they have the opportunity to express their thinking about their reading to a genuine audience in a wide variety of ways. Over time, they learn how to clearly articulate and organize their thoughts and how to have a dialogue with another reader about books. The purpose of this lesson is to introduce the task and format and to have students begin thinking about what they will write in their first letter.

Assess Learning

Observe students when they talk about letter writing. Notice if there is evidence of new learning based on the goal of this minilesson.

- Do students understand that they will write a letter about their reading each week?
- Do they understand how to use a letter format?
- Do they use vocabulary words such as *letter, date, greeting,* and *closing*?

Minilesson

To help students think about the minilesson principle, engage them in a discussion about standard expectations for letter writing. Use the letter that you prepared before class as a starting point. Here is an example.

- Display the prepared chart paper.

    Listen to what I wrote in my letter to you.

- Read the letter aloud from the prepared chart.

    You wrote a letter to share your thinking about your reading. I have written a letter to you.

    What do you notice about how my letter looks?

- Guide students, if necessary, to notice the date, greeting, and closing. Highlight and label each part of the letter.

    How often are you going to write letters about your reading?

    Each of you will write one letter about your reading each week. Every week, I will read your letter and write a letter back to you.

- Highlight the words *will write one*.

Have a Try

Invite the students to talk with a partner about ways to talk about books.

> Turn and talk to your partner about some ways that you talk about books. You can write about these things in a letter.

Summarize and Apply

Summarize the learning and remind students to write a letter about their reading each week.

▶ Explain your system for managing the letters (e.g., when they are due, where they should be turned in). Let students know when their first letters are due.

▶ If you are using the letter already printed in *Reader's Notebook: Intermediate*, show students where they can find it. Or, give each student a copy of your letter to glue into a reader's notebook.

> As you are reading, start thinking about what you might write in a letter about a book you are reading. You might want to jot some notes about what you are thinking, put a sticky note on a part you want to remember, or you can even start writing your letter. When we come back together, be ready to share something you want to share in a letter.

Greeting   Date

> Dear Students,   October 15
>
> This year, you will write in your reader's notebook about what you are thinking about books you read. I will read about your thinking and write back to you.
>
> You will learn how to write a letter to me. In your letter, share your thinking about your reading. Use the format of this letter to write your own. Be sure to include the title and author of your book, and to underline the title in your letter. It is important that your letters are easy to read so that your thoughts can be understood. You will write one letter to me each week to share your thinking about your reading.
>
> What are some of the ways you talk about books when you share your thinking about books? You can write about your reading in the same ways you talk about your reading. I look forward to reading about your thinking and having interesting conversations with you about books.
>
> Sincerely,   ← Closing
> Ms. Rodriguez

Share

Following independent reading time, gather students together in the meeting area to talk about their reading and thinking.

> Turn and talk to your partner about what you are thinking about writing in your letter, or what you have already written, if you started to write your letter.

Extend the Lesson (Optional)

After assessing students' understanding, you might decide to extend the learning.

▶ For more support, use a familiar interactive read-aloud text for the whole class to talk about and write a letter together. Use sample letters that you have to model more ways of thinking and responding to a book. Refer to the chart of ideas in RML1.

▶ Remind students the day before their letters are due to write their letters if they have not already done so. Eventually, most students will not need to be reminded.

Reading Minilesson Principle
Provide evidence for your thinking in your letter.

Writing Letters About Reading

You Will Need

- chart paper prepared with a letter about a book that you recently read aloud to your students (use the same letter you used for RML1 or a different letter, as long as it contains evidence for your thinking)
- chart paper and markers
- highlighters
- a reader's notebook for each student

Academic Language / Important Vocabulary

- letter
- evidence

Continuum Connection

- Provide evidence from the text or personal experience to support written statements about a text (pp. 186, 189)
- Reference page numbers from a text in writing about important information (pp. 186, 189)
- Revisit texts for ideas or to check details when writing or drawing (pp. 186, 189)

Goal

Provide evidence from the text or personal experience to support written statements about a text.

Rationale

When students support statements about a text with evidence from the text or personal experience, they read more closely and think critically about what they are reading. They learn that when they make a statement about their thinking, they should explain why. This minilesson should be taught after students have already written at least one letter and are getting ready to write another.

Assess Learning

Assess students' letters. Notice if there is evidence of new learning based on the goal of this minilesson.

- Do students support statements about a text with evidence from the text and/or personal experience?
- Do they understand and use the terms *letter* and *evidence*?

Minilesson

To help students think about the minilesson principle, use a sample letter to demonstrate how to provide evidence for one's thinking. Here is an example.

- Display the prepared chart. Read aloud the first paragraph.

  I shared my thinking about the book. Talk about what my letter shows you.

- Underline the statement, as shown on the chart.

  Whenever you share your thinking about a book, you need to provide evidence, or tell why you think that.

  When you provide evidence for your thinking, you give specific details from the book or from your own life to show *why* you think something.

  What evidence did I give to explain my thinking?

- Highlight or have a student highlight the evidence from the book and from your personal experience.

  If you copy the exact words from a book, use quotation marks. You should also put the page number that you got them from, if the book has page numbers.

Have a Try

Invite the students to talk with a partner about the evidence in the sample letter.

▶ Read aloud the final paragraph.

> Turn and talk to your partner about what you notice about the thinking I shared and the evidence I gave.

▶ Ask a few students to respond. Highlight the evidence in the letter or ask a volunteer to do so.

Summarize and Apply

Summarize the learning and remind students to provide evidence for their thinking in their letters.

> What did you notice about the evidence I wrote in my letter about reading?

▶ Remind students when their next letter is due.

> Today, you will start writing your next letter about your reading. Think about how to support your thinking with evidence from the book or from your experience. Be ready to share your thinking when we come back together.

Share

Following independent reading time, gather students together in the meeting area to talk about their reading, writing, and thinking.

> Turn and talk to your partner about evidence you can write in your letter this week, or something that you have already written.

Extend the Lesson (Optional)

After assessing students' understanding, you might decide to extend the learning.

▶ If some students are struggling with providing evidence for their thinking, use shared writing to demonstrate how to provide evidence for thinking.

▶ Have students highlight examples of evidence in their own letters.

October 18

Dear Class,

When I read the book <u>Saturdays and Teacakes</u> by Lester L. Laminack, I thought that <u>the way the author described things made the story seem real.</u> For example, when the main character was mixing dough, he said it "smelled like fresh cotton candy at the county fair" (page 19). When Mammaw opened the oven door, the kitchen "filled with a smell sweeter than summer gardenias" (page 23). My grandmother always baked, and I remember how good her kitchen smelled!

from the book

This story was special for me because it reminded me of my grandmother. Like the boy in the story, I lived in a small town and I visited my grandmother in the countryside. Like Mammaw, my grandmother loved to bake. Whenever I visited, she always had something sweet waiting for me! Reading this story reminded me of how special those visits were. I think the author is trying to show how wonderful it is to spend time with those we love. What did you think about when we read this story together?

personal experience

Your teacher,
Ms. Rodriguez

Reading Minilesson Principle
Reread your letter to be sure it makes sense.

Writing Letters About Reading

You Will Need

- chart paper prepared with a letter, with some sentences in need of revision, about a book that you recently read aloud to your students

- a reader's notebook for each student (if using a plain notebook or to customize the revising and editing guidelines, create a page titled Guidelines for Checking Your Writing that lists your expectations for the revising and editing process)

- chart paper and markers

Academic Language / Important Vocabulary

- letter
- reread
- sense

Continuum Connection

- Reread writing to check meaning, accuracy, and clarity of expression (pp. 186, 189)

Goal

Understand how to check for clarity in communicating meaning.

Rationale

When students learn how to reread their writing to confirm that it makes sense, they become more effective at communicating a message to their readers, which is the ultimate goal of writing. This minilesson (along with RML5) should ideally be taught when most students have already written their second letters and are getting ready to submit them.

Assess Learning

Assess students' letters. Notice if there is evidence of new learning based on the goal of this minilesson.

- ▶ Do students communicate their ideas clearly in writing?
- ▶ Do they reread their letters to check them before submitting their notebooks?
- ▶ Do they understandand and use the terms *letter, reread,* and *sense*?

Minilesson

To help students think about the minilesson principle, demonstrate rereading a letter to confirm that it makes sense. Here is an example.

- ▶ Have students open to the Guidelines for Checking Your Writing (in *Reader's Notebook: Intermediate*, the back side of the green tab). Ask them to read this page silently.

  What do you notice about this page? What is it about?

  Today we're going to talk about the first thing on this list: "Reread what you have written to be sure it makes sense." I have just written a letter about a book I read. I am going to reread it slowly and carefully.

- ▶ Display the letter you prepared before class. Read it aloud slowly, pausing after every one or two sentences, and "think aloud."

  Does it make sense?

  Will others understand what I mean?

- ▶ Model how to mark the letter for revisions.

  I can cross out a part that doesn't make sense. Or, I can use a caret to add more writing.

Have a Try

Invite the students to talk with a partner about how to reread a letter to make sure it makes sense.

> Turn and talk to your partner about how to check to be sure a letter makes sense.

▶ Ask a few students to share their thinking, and record their responses on chart paper.

Summarize and Apply

Help students summarize the learning and remind them to reread their letters to make sure they make sense.

> What did you learn about checking your letter?

▶ Write the principle at the top of the chart.

> Today during independent reading time, finish writing your letter if you haven't already done so. Spend time rereading your letter to be sure it makes sense. If there are sentences that do not make sense, think of ways that you can make them clearer. Cross out or use a caret to add information to the part that doesn't make sense.

Reread your letter to be sure it makes sense.

- Reread your letter slowly and carefully.

- Pause after every sentence or two.

- Ask yourself questions such as:

  - Does this make sense?

  - Will my reader understand this?

  - How can I make this clearer?

- If anything doesn't make sense, cross out the part or use caret to add more writing.

Share

Following independent reading time, gather students together in the meeting area to talk about the revision process.

> Give a thumbs-up if you reread your letter today to make sure it makes sense. How did you make your letter even better?

Extend the Lesson (Optional)

After assessing students' understanding, you might decide to extend the learning.

▶ Suggest that students write their letters on every other line so that they have room to make changes legibly.

▶ **Writing About Reading** Use shared writing to write a letter about reading as a class. Afterward, reread and revise the letter as a class.

Reading Minilesson Principle
Reread your letter to check your spelling, capitals, and punctuation.

Writing Letters About Reading

You Will Need

▸ chart paper prepared with a letter about a book that you recently read aloud
▸ markers
▸ highlighters
▸ a reader's notebook for each student

Academic Language / Important Vocabulary

▸ letter
▸ reread
▸ spelling
▸ capital letter
▸ punctuation

Continuum Connection

▸ Reread writing to check meaning, accuracy, and clarity of expression (pp. 186, 189)

Goal

Reread letters to check for appropriate spelling, capitals, and punctuation.

Rationale

Following the conventions of standard written English helps ensure that a written message will be clearly understood. When students know how to check their writing for correct spelling, punctuation, and capital letters, they can more effectively communicate their ideas in writing. This minilesson (along with RML4) is ideally taught when most students have already written their second letters and are getting ready to submit them.

Assess Learning

Assess students' letters about reading. Notice if there is evidence of new learning based on the goal of this minilesson.

▸ Do students' letters demonstrate understanding of the conventions of standard written English and show evidence of having been edited?

▸ Do they understand and use the terms *letter, reread, spelling, capital letter,* and *punctuation*?

Minilesson

To help students think about the minilesson principle, demonstrate rereading a letter to check for spelling, capital letters, and punctuation. Here is an example.

▸ Display the letter you prepared before class.

> I've written a letter and I've reread it to be sure that it makes sense. There's just one more thing that I need to do before it is complete.

▸ Read the first paragraph of the letter aloud. Pause frequently and "think aloud," checking for correct spelling, capital letters, and punctuation. The letter should not intentionally contain errors, but fix any errors that you notice.

> This sentence starts with a capital letter and ends with a period. I also capitalized the word *I* because I know that this word should always be capitalized. I'm not sure if I spelled the name of the author correctly, so I'm going to check on the cover of the book to make sure.

▸ Read aloud some more of the letter (don't read the whole thing just yet).

> What do you notice about how I started this sentence?
>
> Is this the right punctuation to use?
>
> Do you see any misspelled words?

▸ Make any needed corrections, and highlight a few examples of correct capital letters and punctuation.

Have a Try

Invite the students to discuss the rest of the letter with a partner.

⏵ Reread the rest of the letter.

> Are the spelling, punctuation, and capital letters correct at the end of my letter? Read it again carefully, and then turn and talk to your partner about what you think. If you see anything that you think should be checked or fixed, be sure to say so and we'll do that.

⏵ Ask a few students to share their thinking. If students suggest that a word is misspelled, demonstrate using reference materials to confirm the spelling.

Summarize and Apply

Summarize the learning and remind students to reread their letters to check for correct spelling, capital letters, and punctuation.

> Today you learned how to reread your letters to check your spelling, capital letters, and punctuation. Why is it important to do this?

> Today during independent reading time, I want you to reread your most recent letter to check your spelling, capital letters, and punctuation. If you notice anything that's not right, be sure to fix it.

Share

Following independent reading time, gather students together in the meeting area to talk about the editing process.

> Give a thumbs-up if you reread your letter today to check your spelling, capital letters, and punctuation. How did rereading your letter help you make it even better?

Extend the Lesson (Optional)

After assessing students' understanding, you might decide to extend the learning.

⏵ **Writing About Reading** Use shared writing to write a letter about reading as a class. Afterward, reread and edit the letter as a class. This can also be done in a small group, if certain students need extra support with the editing process.

October 25

Dear Class,

capitalize name

capitalize title

I just read the book Grandma's Records by Eric Velasquez. This book reminded me of another book I read recently, Saturdays and Teacakes. Both books are about boys who visit their grandmothers. Both boys have special times with their grandmothers. ← *mark full stop*

capitalize start of sentence

However, there are some differences between the two books. For example, Saturdays and Teacakes is set in the countryside, but Grandma's Records is set in a big city. In Saturdays and Teacakes, the boy and his grandmother spend time baking. In Grandma's Records, they spend time listening to music. *mark pause*

These books show that, although families may be different, the love between a grandchild and grandparent is always special.

Your teacher,
Ms. Rodriguez

Reading Minilesson Principle
Respond to any teacher questions when you write your next letter.

Writing Letters About Reading

You Will Need

- chart paper prepared with a pair of letters between teacher and student about a book that you recently read aloud (such as *Ape* by Martin Jenkins, from Text Set: Animals)
- highlighters
- a reader's notebook for each student

Academic Language / Important Vocabulary

- letter
- respond

Continuum Connection

- Follow a topic and add to a discussion with comments on the same topic (p. 335)

Goal

Understand that letters about reading are an ongoing conversation with the teacher.

Rationale

When you teach students to respond to the questions you have asked them, they begin to understand that the purpose of writing letters about reading is to engage in an ongoing discussion about books with another reader. This minilesson should ideally be taught when students have already written at least two letters and have received two responses back from you. Make sure that you include at least one question in each of your responses.

Assess Learning

Assess students' letters. Notice if there is evidence of new learning based on the goal of this minilesson.

- Do students write thoughtful responses to the questions you have asked them?
- Do they understand the terms *letter* and *respond*?

Minilesson

To help students think about the minilesson principle, use a sample letter to demonstrate how to respond to the teacher's questions in the response to their letters. Here is an example.

- Show the cover of *Ape*.

  Remember *Ape*? We read and talked about this book together recently. Emma shared her thinking about the book in a letter. This is what I wrote back to her.

- Display and read aloud the first letter.

  What do you notice about this letter?

  I asked Emma questions.

- Ask a volunteer to come up and highlight the questions in the letter.

  What do you think Emma might write in her next letter?

- Lead students to understand that they should answer any questions that you pose in your letter. Then display Emma's response.

  Every time you write a letter to me about your reading, I will write a letter back to you. Sometimes, I will ask you questions in my letter. It's important that you read my questions, think about them, and respond to them in your letter back to me.

Have a Try

Invite the students to start thinking about how they will respond to your questions.

▶ Direct students to open their reader's notebooks to the most recent letter that you wrote to them.

As you read my letter to you, look for questions that I asked you and highlight them.

Now turn and talk to your partner about one question that you found in my letter to you and how you might answer it when you write back.

Summarize and Apply

Summarize the learning and remind students to respond to your questions in their letters each week.

When you write a letter today or later this week, be sure to read my letter, highlight any questions I asked, and respond to the questions.

Share

Following independent reading time, gather students together in the meeting area to talk about their letters.

Raise your hand if you worked on a letter today.

Who would like to share how you responded to my questions in your letter?

Extend the Lesson (Optional)

After assessing students' understanding, you might decide to extend the learning.

▶ Increase the complexity of your questions as students demonstrate the ability to respond thoughtfully to them. For example, in the beginning you might ask simple questions such as "What did you like about the book?" whereas later on you might ask questions like "Why do you think the main character did that?"

▶ You might have students highlight the questions they are asked each week to make sure they remember to respond. You might also consider asking students to answer the questions in the first paragraph of their letter before they share new thinking.

▶ Teach students to ask *you* questions in their letters. Make sure you respond to their questions!

October 27

Dear Emma,

I really enjoyed reading Ape, too! Like you, I was surprised by some of the facts. For example, I didn't know that most of the great apes (aside from humans!) are so rare.

When you and I talked about this book together, you said that the author wrote this book to tell information about the great apes. That is true, but can you think of any other reasons he might have written this book? What do you think he is really trying to say about humans and the other great apes?

Your teacher,
Ms. Rodriguez

October 28

Dear Ms. Rodriguez,

I'm glad you liked reading Ape! I think that Martin Jenkins wanted to tell us that the great apes need our help. Humans should take care of the apes because we are all in the same family. Humans should care.

From,
Emma

RML7

WAR.U3.RML7

Reading Minilesson Principle
Choose a letter that shows your best thinking.

Writing Letters About Reading

You Will Need

- chart prepared with a student-written letter about a book that you recently read aloud to your students; the letter should be of high-quality and demonstrate all the attributes that students' letters should have
- chart paper and markers
- highlighters

Academic Language / Important Vocabulary

- thinking
- evidence

Goal

Identify the qualities of a strong letter and distinguish between sharing thinking and retelling a story.

Rationale

When students are able to identify the qualities of a strong letter and assess their own letters against those standards, they think more deeply about the books they read and communicate their thinking clearly in their letters. This minilesson should only be taught after students have written at least three letters about their reading.

Assess Learning

Observe students when they talk about letters. Notice if there is evidence of new learning based on the goal of this minilesson.

- ▶ Are students able to identify the qualities of a strong letter?
- ▶ Are they able to choose a letter that shows their best thinking and explain why they chose it?
- ▶ Do they use vocabulary such as *thinking* and *evidence* when talking about letters?

Minilesson

To help students think about the minilesson principle, use the model letter to engage students in a discussion about the qualities of a strong letter. Here is an example.

- ▶ Display the prepared chart and read it aloud.

  Here's a letter a student wrote that shows his best thinking. What are the good things about the letter?

- ▶ If necessary, prompt students with questions such as these:
  - *How did he share his thinking about this book?*
  - *How did he provide evidence for his thinking?*
  - *Was the letter interesting to read?*
  - *Does his letter make sense?*
  - *How are the spelling, capital letters, and punctuation?*
  - *Are the title and author of the book included?*
  - *Is there a date, a greeting, and a closing?*
  - *Did the student respond to any questions that were asked?*
- ▶ Use students' noticings to create a list of assessment questions on a separate sheet of chart paper. The students will use these questions when they choose their own best letter.

A strong letter shares your best thinking about a book. It doesn't just tell what happens in the book or what the book is about.

Have a Try

Invite the students to continue the discussion with a partner.

> Is there anything else that we should add to our list? Turn and talk to your partner about what you think.

▶ Ask a few students to share their thinking. Add new ideas to the chart.

Summarize and Apply

Summarize the learning and remind students to refer to the questions on the chart when assessing their own letters.

> Today you thought about what makes a strong letter about reading.

> During independent reading time today, reread the letters you have already written. As you read each one, ask yourself the questions on our list. Decide which of your letters shows your best thinking, and bring that letter when we come together.

Share

Following independent reading time, gather students together in the meeting area to talk about their letters.

> Turn and talk to your partner about the letter you chose. Share some of the parts that you think show your best thinking.

Extend the Lesson (Optional)

After assessing students' understanding, you might decide to extend the learning.

▶ Repeat this lesson when you want students to review the qualities of a strong letter about reading and further strengthen their letters.

▶ Use the form called Assessment for Letters in Reader's Notebook to assess your students' letters (see resources.fountasandpinnell.com).

November 1

Dear Ms. Rodriguez,

I really liked I Love Guinea Pigs. It is one of my favorite books because I have a pet guinea pig! Her name is Minnie because she is kind of small.

The author wrote that "if you make a fuss over them, they become really fond of you." He's right. Minnie purrs when I pet her.

I learned that guinea pigs come from Dutch Guiana. Do you like guinea pigs?

Sincerely,

Sam

Letters About Reading

- Did I include the title and author of the book?
- Did I share different ways of thinking about the book?
- Was my letter interesting to read?
- Did I provide evidence for my thinking?
- Did I respond to the questions I was asked?
- Did I include the date, a greeting, and a closing?
- Does my letter make sense?
- Did I use correct spelling, capitals, and punctuation?
- Is my writing neat and easy to read?

Assessment

After you have taught the minilessons in this umbrella, observe students as they talk and write about their reading across instructional contexts: interactive read-aloud, independent reading and literacy work, guided reading, shared reading, and book club. Use *The Literacy Continuum* (Fountas and Pinnell 2017) to observe students' reading and writing behaviors across instructional contexts.

▶ What evidence do you have of new understandings related to writing letters about reading?

- Do students write a letter about their reading each week?
- Do their letters follow the format of a friendly letter?
- Do they share their thinking about their reading and provide evidence?
- Do they respond to your questions in their letters?
- Do their letters show evidence that they have revised and edited them for meaning and writing conventions?
- Do they use vocabulary such as *greeting, closing, evidence, respond,* and *audience*?

▶ In what other ways, beyond the scope of this umbrella, are they writing about books?

- Are students using other forms of writing to share their thinking about fiction and/or nonfiction books?

Use your observations to determine the next umbrella you will teach. You may also consult Minilessons Across the Year (pp. 55-57) for guidance.

Reader's Notebook

When this umbrella is complete, provide a copy of the minilesson principles (see resources.fountasandpinnell.com) for students to glue in the reader's notebook (in the Minilessons section if using *Reader's Notebook: Intermediate* [Fountas and Pinnell 2011]), so they can refer to the information as needed.

Minilessons in This Umbrella

RML1 Use a diagram to show the important parts of a story in order.

RML2 Make a sketch of the setting to show why it is important to the story.

RML3 Use a story map to show the important information in a story.

RML4 Write a summary of what happened in the story.

RML5 Tell about a character's traits and provide evidence from the story.

RML6 Tell how a character changes in the story.

RML7 Tell how stories are the same and how they are different.

Before Teaching Umbrella 4 Minilessons

Before students use a reader's notebook, they should have read and discussed a variety of high-quality picture books and participated in several shared writing lessons. These lessons can be used in tandem with related literary analysis minilessons. If students are using *Reader's Notebook: Intermediate* (Fountas and Pinnell 2011), they can write in the Writing About Reading section; if using a plain notebook, create a dedicated section in the notebook.

The minilessons in this umbrella use books from the following text sets from the *Fountas & Pinnell Classroom™ Interactive Read-Aloud Collection*, but you can use high-quality fiction books from your own classroom library that appeal to your own students' experiences and interests.

Author/Illustrator Study: Patricia Polacco

The Bee Tree

Thunder Cake

The Importance of Kindness

Under the Lemon Moon by Edith Hope Fine

Exploring Memory Stories

My Rotten Redheaded Older Brother by Patricia Polacco

Honoring Traditions

Crane Boy by Diana Cohn

Deep in the Sahara by Kelly Cunnane

Facing Challenges

First Day in Grapes by L. King Pérez

Exploring Pourquoi Tales

The Legend of the Lady Slipper by Lise Lunge-Larsen and Margi Preus

Dragonfly's Tale by Kristina Rodanas

As you read aloud and enjoy these texts together, help students

- notice and talk about story elements (e.g., plot, setting, characters), and
- compare and contrast fiction stories.

Patricia Polacco

Kindness

Memory Stories

Honoring Traditions

Facing Challenges

Pourquoi Tales

Reader's Notebook

Section 4: Writing About Reading

Reading Minilesson Principle
Use a diagram to show the important parts of a story in order.

Writing About Fiction Books in a Reader's Notebook

You Will Need

- two familiar fiction stories that have clear plot details, such as the following:
  - *The Bee Tree* by Patricia Polacco, from Text Set: Patricia Polacco
  - *Under the Lemon Moon* by Edith Hope Fine, from Text Set: Kindness
- chart paper and markers

Academic Language / Important Vocabulary

- beginning
- events
- high point
- ending
- problem
- resolution

Continuum Connection

- Recognize and write about aspects of narrative structure: beginning, series of events, problem, resolution, ending (p. 187)

Goal

Represent narrative structure in a diagram including beginning, series of important chronological events, high point in a story, and ending.

Rationale

When you teach students to write about plot, they gain an understanding of narrative structure, as is found in many fiction stories. A graphic organizer can be a useful temporary tool for them as they learn to recognize characteristics of narrative structure. Students need to have a solid understanding of plot (see Umbrella 23: Understanding Plot, found in Section Two: Literary Analysis).

Assess Learning

Observe students when they write about fiction in a reader's notebook. Notice if there is evidence of new learning based on the goal of this minilesson.

- Can students identify the beginning, important events, high point, ending, problem, and resolution of a story?
- Can they use a graphic organizer to represent the plot of a story?
- Do they use academic language, such as *beginning, events, high point, ending, problem,* and *resolution*?

Minilesson

Provide an inquiry-based lesson that helps students use a graphic organizer to show plot details. Here is an example.

> You have learned about the plot in a story and you know that stories have a beginning, important events, a high point, and an ending. You also know that most stories have a problem and a resolution. Let's look at how you can write about that in a reader's notebook.

- On chart paper, label the parts of the plot in a way that shows the rising and falling action. Leave space to add story details beneath each label.

  > What do you notice about the way I have written the different parts of the plot?

  > Let's think about a book you know, *The Bee Tree*. Turn and talk about what you would put on the chart under each label.

- After time for discussion, ask students to share. As they do, write each example in the appropriate place on the chart.

  > What do you notice about where the high point/resolution is placed?

  > The high point, where something changes and the problem is solved, is at the highest point of the diagram.

▶ Show the Writing About Reading section of *Readers' Notebook: Intermediate.*

> The Writing About Reading section in a reader's notebook is the place where you can create a chart like this. You can draw the chart and add examples from a fiction story.

Have a Try

Invite the students to think about using a reader's notebook for creating diagrams.

▶ Hold up a familiar book, such as *Under the Lemon Moon.*

> Turn and talk about the beginning, events, exciting part, and ending using details from *Under the Lemon Moon.*

▶ After time for discussion, ask students to share.

Summarize and Apply

Summarize the learning and remind students that they can create a diagram showing important parts of a story.

> Today you learned that you can make a diagram to show the parts of a plot. If you are in the middle of reading a fiction book, take some time after you read a little to write about what is happening so far. You can use a diagram to show what you notice.

▶ Students can draw the diagram in their reader's notebooks, or they can draw on a piece of paper and glue the paper into the notebook.

Share

Following independent reading time, gather the students in groups of three.

> Share the diagram you made about a story. Talk about the parts you added and why you decided to include each one.

Extend the Lesson (Optional)

After assessing students' understanding, you might decide to extend the learning.

▶ As needed, provide additional experiences with this minilesson as a whole class, in guided reading, or during individual conferences.

▶ **Writing About Reading** Encourage students to use a reader's notebook to make diagrams for other fiction books. If the chart is big enough, more events can be added leading up to the high point/resolution.

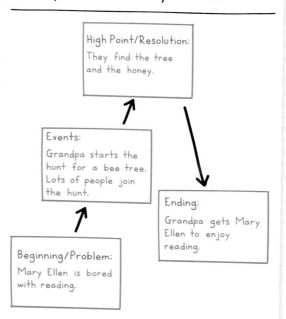

Use a diagram to show the important parts of a story in order.

High Point/Resolution: They find the tree and the honey.

Events: Grandpa starts the hunt for a bee tree. Lots of people join the hunt.

Ending: Grandpa gets Mary Ellen to enjoy reading.

Beginning/Problem: Mary Ellen is bored with reading.

RML2
WAR.U4.RML2

Reading Minilesson Principle
Make a sketch of the setting to show why it is important to the story.

Writing About Fiction Books in a Reader's Notebook

You Will Need

- a familiar fiction story with a vivid setting, such as the following:
  - *Crane Boy* by Diana Cohn, from Text Set: Honoring Traditions
- chart prepared with drawing that shows why the setting of a familiar book (e.g., *Crane Boy*) is important to the story
- drawing materials
- a reader's notebook for each student

Academic Language / Important Vocabulary

- setting
- sketch

Continuum Connection

- Make notes or write descriptions to help remember important details about setting (p. 187)
- Write about the importance of the setting to the plot in realistic and historical fiction and in fantasy (p. 187)

Goal

Draw and label the setting of a story.

Rationale

When students use a reader's notebook to draw and label setting, they think about where a story takes place, notice the impact of setting on the story, and imagine places they can write about. Students need a good understanding of setting for this minilesson (see Umbrella 22: Thinking About the Setting in Fiction Books, found in Section Two: Literary Analysis).

Assess Learning

Observe students when they write about fiction in a reader's notebook and notice if there is evidence of new learning based on the goal of this minilesson.

- ▶ Are students able to sketch and label the setting of a story?
- ▶ Do they think and talk about the impact of the setting on the story?
- ▶ Do they use the terms *setting* and *sketch*?

Minilesson

To help students think about the minilesson principle, provide an interactive lesson about drawing the setting in a reader's notebook. Here is an example.

- ▶ Show the cover of *Crane Boy*, a reader's notebook, and the prepared drawing.

  Here is a drawing from my reader's notebook about the story *Crane Boy*. Notice that it is a simple drawing, which is called a sketch. What does the sketch show you about the setting—or where the story takes place?

- ▶ Ask students to share.

  When I thought about what details to include, I chose things that show why the setting is important to the story. Turn and talk about the details I selected and how those details show that this setting is important to *Crane Boy*.

- ▶ After time for discussion, ask students to share. As needed, guide the conversation to help them understand why you selected specific details.

  Why is it a good idea to use your reader's notebook to draw and label where a story takes place?

- ▶ Encourage discussion about how thinking about and drawing the setting helps you understand the story and how the location impacts what happens in the story.

Have a Try

Invite the students to talk about how they will draw the setting of a book.

> Turn and talk about the setting, or where the story takes place, of a book you are reading or that we have read as a class. What would you draw for that story? What details will you include to show why the setting is important to that story?

Summarize and Apply

Summarize the learning and remind students that they can use a reader's notebook to make a sketch of the setting of a story.

> The setting is one of the things you can write about when you are sharing your thinking about your reading. Today, spend some time thinking about the setting in the book you are reading. After you read, take some time to draw the setting. Bring your sketch when we meet so you can share.

Make a sketch of the setting to show why it is important to the story.

Kinga and his classmate do a crane dance in their village in Bhutan.

Share

Following independent reading time, gather the students together.

> Who would like to share your sketch of the setting of your book? Describe the drawing and talk about the details you decided to include.

Extend the Lesson (Optional)

After assessing students' understanding, you might decide to extend the learning.

▶ **Writing About Reading** Have students write about why the setting is important in a story. Encourage them to suggest how the story would be different if the setting changed.

Reading Minilesson Principle
Use a story map to show the important information in a story.

You Will Need

- a familiar book with clear plot details, such as the following:
  - *My Rotten Redheaded Older Brother* by Patricia Polacco, from Text Set: Memory Stories
  - *Crane Boy* by Diana Cohn, from Text Set: Honoring Traditions
- chart prepared with the labels for a story map
- markers
- a reader's notebook for each student
- a copy of a story map for each student (optional)
- To download the following online resources for this lesson, visit **resources.fountasandpinnell.com:** Story Map

Academic Language / Important Vocabulary

- setting
- characters
- problem
- events
- story map

Continuum Connection

- Recognize and write about aspects of narrative structure: beginning, series of events, problem, resolution, ending (p. 187)

Goal

Use a story map to remember important details about the characters, setting, and plot, including problem and resolution.

Rationale

When students use a story map to remember important details, it reinforces their understandings about narrative structure and the important elements of fiction. Students need a good understanding of story elements for this minilesson (see Umbrella 22: Thinking About the Setting in Fiction Books and Umbrella 23: Understanding Plot, both in Section Two: Literary Analysis).

Assess Learning

Observe students when they write about fiction in a reader's notebook and notice if there is evidence of new learning based on the goal of this minilesson.

- ▶ Are students able to create a story map in a reader's notebook?
- ▶ Do they use academic language, such as *setting, characters, problem, events,* and *story map*?

Minilesson

To help students think about the minilesson principle, provide an inquiry-based lesson that shows how to create a story map. Here is an example.

- ▶ Show the cover of *My Rotten Redheaded Older Brother*, a reader's notebook, and the prepared chart.

  Here is a bigger version of a story map that I have glued into my reader's notebook.

- ▶ Point out and read the different sections of the story map.

  Think about *My Rotten Redheaded Older Brother* and how you could use the story details to fill in this story map. Tell me your ideas and I will write them onto the story map.

- ▶ As students offer suggestions, fill in the story map. As needed, refer to several illustrations or sentences from the book to help them recall details.

  How do you think filling in a story map in your reader's notebook will help you know more about a book?

- ▶ Encourage students to talk about the benefits of a story map, such as understanding the story better and helping to think about and remember each part of the story. Also talk about ways that a story map can help to remember details for writing about individual elements of a story.

Have a Try

Invite the students to talk about what to write in a story map.

▶ Hold up a familiar book, such as *Crane Boy*.

Turn and talk about what you could write about *Crane Boy* on a story map.

Summarize and Apply

Summarize the learning and remind students that they can use a reader's notebook to create a story map.

You learned that you can make a story map to show the parts of a story.

▶ Provide a copy of a story map graphic organizer (Story Map) for students to glue into a reader's notebook or have them make their own.

After you read today, create a story map about the book in your reader's notebook. You will share your story map when we meet after independent reading time.

Share

Following independent reading time, gather the students together in groups of three.

Share the story map you created. Use the story map to tell your group about the story you read.

Extend the Lesson (Optional)

After assessing students' understanding, you might decide to extend the learning.

▶ **Writing About Reading** Encourage students to create story maps for other books they read.

Story Map

Title:	My Rotten Redheaded Older Brother
Author:	Patricia Polacco
Setting:	a farm town in Michigan
Characters:	Tricia, Richie, Bubbie
Problem:	Tricia couldn't do anything better than her brother.
Events:	Richie picked more blueberries than Tricia, which made her mad.
	Tricia made a wish on a star that she could do something better than Richie.
	Tricia fell off the merry-go-round and got stitches.
Resolution/ Conclusion:	Richie helped Tricia and complimented her after she fell off the merry-go-round.
	Tricia and Richie now appreciate their relationship.

Section 4: Writing About Reading

RML4

WAR.U4.RML4

Reading Minilesson Principle

Write a summary of what happened in the story.

You Will Need

- a familiar fiction story, such as the following:
  - *Deep in the Sahara* by Kelly Cunnane, from Text Set: Honoring Traditions
  - *My Rotten Redheaded Older Brother* by Patricia Polacco, from Text Set: Memory Stories
- prepared short summary on chart paper
- highlighting markers in four different colors
- a reader's notebook for each student

Academic Language / Important Vocabulary

- summary
- character
- setting
- problem
- solution

Continuum Connection

- Write summaries that reflect literal understanding of a text (p. 186)
- Select and include appropriate and important details when writing a summary of a text (p. 186)

Goal

Write a brief summary of the most important information in a story, including the characters, the setting, and the problem and solution (when applicable).

Rationale

When students write a summary of a story, they learn to think about the characters, setting, problem, and solution by being able to focus on the most important ideas and events instead of a retelling. Students need a good understanding of plot for this minilesson (see Umbrella 23: Understanding Plot in Section Two: Literary Analysis; also see Umbrella 4: Summarizing in Section Three: Strategies and Skills).

Assess Learning

Observe students when they write about fiction in a reader's notebook and notice if there is evidence of new learning based on the goal of this minilesson.

▶ Do students' summaries include the most important information?

▶ Do they use the terms *summary, character, setting, problem,* and *solution*?

Minilesson

Provide a meaningful interactive lesson to demonstrate what a summary is. Here is an example.

▶ Show the cover of *Deep in the Sahara*, a reader's notebook, and the prepared summary.

> Here is a book you know, *Deep in the Sahara*. Here is a summary I wrote about it. Listen and think about what I wrote.

▶ Read the summary.

> What are some of the important things I included in my summary?
>
> A summary tells the most important information in a story.

▶ Make a list of important information to include in a summary, including the characters, setting, problem, and solution. If it's helpful for students, have volunteers underline or highlight the information (e.g., characters, setting, problem, and solution) in the summary.

> Is there anything else you would include in this summary?

▶ Guide a brief discussion of how a summary gives a sense of the story but without giving every detail.

Have a Try

Invite the students to talk about writing a summary.

▶ Hold up a familiar book, such as *My Rotten Redheaded Older Brother*.

Turn and talk about what you might include in a summary about *My Rotten Redheaded Older Brother*. Look at the list on the chart.

Summarize and Apply

Summarize the learning and remind students that they can write a story summary in a reader's notebook.

Why might it be important to summarize a story?

▶ Guide students to understand that it is a brief way to let readers know what a book is about.

Where might you see a summary of a book?

After you read today, write a story summary in your reader's notebook. You will share your summary when we meet.

Share

Following independent reading time, gather the students in groups of three.

Use the story summary you wrote to tell your group about the book you read.

Extend the Lesson (Optional)

After assessing students' understanding, you might decide to extend the learning.

▶ Have students evaluate online book summaries for books they have read.

▶ **Writing About Reading** Show students how to include a brief summary in their letters about their reading (see Umbrella 3: Writing Letters About Reading in this section).

▶ **Writing About Reading** From time to time, write story summaries with the whole class or during guided reading so that the experience becomes natural for students and so they will remember to include enough information about the story but not too much.

Summary

In your summary, tell the most important information:

- Title and author

- Characters

- Setting

- Problem and solution

Example:

Deep in the Sahara by Kelly Cunnane is about a girl named Lalla, who lives in the Sahara Desert in West Africa. Lalla wants to wear a malafa like the older women. At the end, Lalla finally learns about the reasons why women wear a malafa, and she gets to wear one of her own.

Reading Minilesson Principle
Tell about a character's traits and provide evidence from the story.

Writing About Fiction Books in a Reader's Notebook

You Will Need

- a familiar fiction story that has a character with clear traits, such as the following:
  - *Thunder Cake* by Patricia Polacco, from Text Set: Patricia Polacco
- chart paper prepared with three columns: Character, Trait, Evidence
- markers
- a reader's notebook for each student
- a copy of Providing Evidence for Character Traits for each student (optional)
- To download the following online resources for this lesson, visit **resources.fountasandpinnell.com:** Providing Evidence for Character Traits

Academic Language / Important Vocabulary

- character
- traits
- evidence

Continuum Connection

- Describe character attributes as revealed through thought, dialogue, behavior, and what others say or think about them and support with evidence (p. 187)

Goal

Tell about a character's traits and provide evidence from the story.

Rationale

When students write about character traits, they begin to think deeply about the character and connect the character to themselves or people in their own lives. Graphic organizers provide a temporary support for students to begin writing about characters. When students are ready, they can transition away from the graphic organizer. Students need an understanding of character for this minilesson (see Umbrella 24: Understanding Character Traits in Section Two: Literary Analysis).

Assess Learning

Observe students when they write about fiction in a reader's notebook and notice if there is evidence of new learning based on the goal of this minilesson.

- ▶ Can students write about character traits?
- ▶ Do they use evidence from the story to support what they say about a character's traits?
- ▶ Do they use the terms *character, traits,* and *evidence*?

Minilesson

Provide an inquiry-based lesson that helps students write about character traits and provide evidence for their thinking. Here is an example.

- ▶ Write the character's name (Babushka), one trait, and one piece of evidence for that trait in the three columns on the chart.
- ▶ Show the covers of *Thunder Cake* and a reader's notebook and the prepared chart.

  Do you remember Babushka, from *Thunder Cake*? What do you notice about what I have written on the chart?

- ▶ As needed, point out that you told what the character is like and included a specific example from the story as evidence of that character trait.

  Can you think of another word that describes Babushka and an example from the story to show that?

- ▶ Add to chart. Repeat the activity, adding one more trait with supporting evidence. If needed, revisit several pages of *Thunder Cake* to refresh students' memories.

- ▶ Show a page from the Writing About Reading section of a reader's notebook.

  You can write about character traits in your reader's notebook.

Have a Try

Invite the students to talk about using an organizer to write about character traits.

> Turn and talk about the girl's character traits in *Thunder Cake.*

▶ After time for discussion, ask students to share.

Summarize and Apply

Summarize the learning and remind students that they can write about character's traits in a reader's notebook.

> Today you learned that you can write about character traits in your reader's notebook.

▶ Provide a copy of a graphic organizer (Providing Evidence for Character Traits) for students to glue into a reader's notebook or have them make their own charts.

> Choose a character from a book you read today or think about another character from *Thunder Cake.* Fill in the chart with the character's name, words to describe the character, and evidence from the story.

Character	Trait	Evidence
Babushka	aware	Babushka notices the storm coming.
	encouraging	Babushka tells the child not to be afraid because it is only thunder she hears.
	loving	Babushka holds the girl in the rocker.
	clever	Babushka invents thunder cake.
	brave	Babushka is not afraid of the storm.

Share

Following independent reading time, gather the students in pairs.

> Turn and talk about the character you wrote about in the chart. Are there any similarities between the characters you and your partner wrote about?

Extend the Lesson (Optional)

After assessing students' understanding, you might decide to extend the learning.

▶ **Writing About Reading** Encourage students to write about the traits of other characters in a readers' notebook.

▶ **Writing About Reading** Once students are comfortable writing about traits in the organizer, transition away from it so they can write about traits independently.

▶ **Writing About Reading** Encourage students to write about character traits in their letters about their reading (see Umbrella 3: Writing Letters About Reading in this section).

RML 6
WAR.U4.RML6

Reading Minilesson Principle
Tell how a character changes in a story.

Writing About Fiction Books in a Reader's Notebook

You Will Need

- a familiar fiction story that has a character who experiences a clear change, such as *First Day in Grapes* by L. King Pérez, from Text Set: Facing Challenges
- chart paper prepared with defining characteristics of a short write and a short write about how a character changes
- highlighter
- a reader's notebook for each student

Academic Language / Important Vocabulary

- character
- change
- short write

Continuum Connection

- Notice and write about character change and infer reasons related to events of the plot (p. 187)

Goal

Write about how characters change or learn a lesson in a story, and infer reasons from events of the plot.

Rationale

When students use a reader's notebook to write about how a character changes from the beginning to the end of a story, they learn to think deeply about characters and to express their thoughts about characters in writing. For this lesson, use a model of a short write to help students share their thinking about their reading in a brief and meaningful way. Students need to be familiar with the concept of character change for this minilesson (see Umbrella 25: Thinking About Character Change, found in Section Two: Literary Analysis).

Assess Learning

Observe students when they write about fiction in a reader's notebook and notice if there is evidence of new learning based on the goal of this minilesson.

- ▶ Can students describe how a character changes with evidence to support their thinking?
- ▶ Do they use the terms *character, change,* and *short write*?

Minilesson

To help students think about the minilesson principle, provide an inquiry-based lesson on writing about how characters change. Here is an example.

- ▶ Show the cover of *First Day in Grapes* and the prepared writing.

    Here is Chico from *First Day in Grapes*. He changed from the beginning of the story to the end, didn't he? I wrote a short write to explain how he changed. A short write is when you jot a few sentences about something you are thinking over time—before, during, and/or after reading.

- ▶ Read the prepared writing.

    What are some important things I included when I wrote about how Chico changed? What part tells about what Chico is like at the beginning?

- ▶ As students respond, have them highlight the parts they notice. Guide the conversation so they notice that you wrote about what Chico was like at the beginning, how he changed, how you know, and what he is like at the end.

    What part tells about what Chico is like at the end?

- ▶ Ask a student to highlight this part.

    What else could you add about how Chico changed?

- ▶ Add any new ideas.

Have a Try

Invite the students to talk about what they might write about how a character changes.

> Turn and talk about what you might write about in your own reader's notebook about how a character changes. Think about what the character was like at the beginning, how the character changes, and what the character is like at the end.

Summarize and Apply

Summarize the learning and remind students that they can write about how a character changes in a reader's notebook.

> You learned that one way to write about your reading is to do a short write about how a character changes.

▶ Write the principle at the top of the chart. Then add some brief notes to explain what a short write is.

> During independent reading time, write in your reader's notebook about a character that changes. You can choose a character, or you can write about Chico from *First Day in Grapes*. You will share your writing when we come back together.

Share

Following independent reading time, gather students in pairs.

> Share what you wrote in your reader's notebook about a character that changes.

Extend the Lesson (Optional)

After assessing students' understanding, you might decide to extend the learning.

▶ When students write their own stories, have them consider how their main characters might change: What is the change? What or who caused the change?

▶ **Writing About Reading** Use shared writing to write about a familiar character to deepen students' understanding of how to write about character change.

Tell how a character changes in a story.

First Day in Grapes

In the beginning, Chico was sad and nervous about going to a new school.

When the mean boys bullied him at lunch, he used math to embarrass them and make them go away. The other kids supported Chico and were nice. John asked Chico to be his math partner at the math fair.

At the end, he looks forward to going to school.

Short Write

- Write a few sentences or a paragraph.
- Jot your thoughts before you read, while you are reading, and/or after you read.
- Tell your thinking about your reading.

RML7
WAR.U4.RML7

Reading Minilesson Principle
Tell how stories are the same and how they are different.

Writing About Fiction Books in a Reader's Notebook

You Will Need

- several familiar fiction books that work well to compare and contrast, such as the following from Text Set: Pourquoi Tales:
  - *The Legend of the Lady Slipper* by Lise Lunge-Larsen and Margi Preus
  - *Dragonfly's Tale* by Kristina Rodanas
- chart paper prepared with a Venn diagram labeled with the titles of two books
- markers
- a copy of a Venn diagram for each student (optional)
- To download the following online resources for this lesson, visit **resources.fountasandpinnell.com:** Venn Diagram

Academic Language / Important Vocabulary

- compare
- contrast
- Venn diagram (optional)

Continuum Connection

- Write about connections among texts by topic, theme, major ideas, authors' styles, and genres (p. 186)

Goal

Compare and contrast stories using a Venn diagram.

Rationale

When students use a reader's notebook to compare and contrast stories, they learn to pay attention to similarities and differences across books and in their own lives.

Assess Learning

Observe students when they write about fiction in a reader's notebook and notice if there is evidence of new learning based on the goal of this minilesson.

- ▶ Can students compare and contrast two texts?
- ▶ Are they able to use a Venn diagram to compare and contrast two texts?
- ▶ Do they understand and use the terms *compare* and *contrast*?

Minilesson

Provide an interactive lesson to help students learn how to use a Venn diagram in a reader's notebook to compare and contrast two texts. Here is an example.

- ▶ Show the covers of *The Legend of the Lady Slipper* and *Dragonfly's Tale* and the Venn diagram.

  Sometimes it is interesting to think about two stories together and notice what is the same about them and how they are different. This diagram can help you compare (look for what is the same or similar) and contrast (look for what is different) these stories.

  First, let's think about how these stories are the same or similar.

- ▶ Have students share ideas. As needed, guide the conversation to review the way that Venn diagrams are used and where they will record information that is the same or similar. (Decide whether you want to use the term *Venn diagram* with your students.)

  Now let's think about the ways the stories are different.

- ▶ Add students' ideas to the chart, pointing out where this information goes in the diagram.

  The Writing About Reading section of your reader's notebook is a place where you can compare and contrast stories. A diagram, like the one on the chart, is one way to do this.

Have a Try

Invite the students to talk with a partner about the Venn diagram.

> Turn and talk about something you could add to the Venn diagram about these two books. Where would that information go?

▶ After time for discussion, ask a few students to share.

Summarize and Apply

Summarize the learning and remind students that they can compare and contrast books in a reader's notebook.

> Today you learned that you can use a diagram to compare and contrast books.

▶ Provide a copy of a Venn diagram or have them make their own to compare two books by Janell Cannon or by another author whose books the students know well.

> Think about what is the same and what is different about these two books. Fill in the diagram and glue it into your reader's notebook.

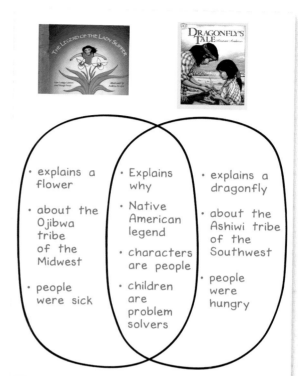

Share

Following independent reading time, gather the students in groups of three.

> In your group, use your diagram to describe what is the same and what is different about the two books.

Extend the Lesson (Optional)

After assessing students' understanding, you might decide to extend the learning.

▶ **Writing About Reading** Encourage students to make Venn diagrams to compare and contrast books in other ways, such as by topic, theme, major ideas, authors' styles, or genres.

Assessment

After you have taught the minilessons in this umbrella, observe students as they talk and write about their reading across instructional contexts: interactive read-aloud, independent reading and literacy work, guided reading, shared reading, and book club. Use *The Literacy Continuum* (Fountas and Pinnell 2017) to observe students' reading and writing behaviors across instructional contexts.

▶ What evidence do you have of new understandings related to how students use a reader's notebook for writing about fiction?

- Can students show the important information in a story in a diagram?
- Are they able to make a sketch of a setting and explain its importance to the story?
- Can they use a story map to tell the most important information?
- Do their summaries include only the most important information?
- Are their statements about characters supported with evidence from the text?
- Do they use academic terms, such as *beginning, events, ending, setting, characters, problem, solution,* and *summary,* when talking and writing about stories?

▶ In what other ways, beyond the scope of this umbrella, are students using a reader's notebook?

- Are students thinking about how they can write about nonfiction?
- Are they expressing opinions about their reading?

Use your observations to determine the next umbrella you will teach. You may also consult Minilessons Across the Year (pp. 55-57) for guidance.

Reader's Notebook

When this umbrella is complete, provide a copy of the minilesson principles (see resources.fountasandpinnell.com) for students to glue in the reader's notebook (in the Minilessons section if using *Reader's Notebook: Intermediate* [Fountas and Pinnell 2011]), so they can refer to the information as needed.

Minilessons in This Umbrella

RML1   Think about what you know about a topic before you read. Think about what you learned about it after you read.

RML2   Write questions you have after you read about a topic.

RML3   Use what you learned about a topic to make an all about book.

RML4   Use a timeline to show the important events in a person's life.

RML5   Make a list of nonfiction books that are told like a story.

RML6   Use a diagram to show a sequence or a cycle that repeats.

RML7   Write a summary of a nonfiction book.

Before Teaching Umbrella 5 Minilessons

It is important to be sure your students are already familiar with using a reader's notebook before you teach this umbrella (see Umbrella 1: Introducing a Reader's Notebook in this section). Instead of teaching these minilessons in order, consider teaching them alongside relevant literary analysis minilessons.

It is essential that you have your students think and talk about the concepts before they write about them. Use these texts from the *Fountas & Pinnell Classroom™ Interactive Read-Aloud Collection* or *Shared Reading Collection* or choose high-quality nonfiction books from your classroom library. Note that one book (e.g., *Wolf Pack*) should be new to the students.

Interactive Read-Aloud Collection

Sharing Our World: Animals

I Love Guinea Pigs by Dick King-Smith

A Friend for Lakota by Jim and Jamie Dutcher

Ape by Martin Jenkins

Moon Bear by Brenda Z. Guiberson

And So They Build by Bert Kitchen

Genre Study: Biography

Odd Boy Out by Don Brown

Author Set/Series: Dianna Hutts Aston

A Butterfly Is Patient

Shared Reading Collection

Wolf Pack by Annette Bay Pimentel

As you read aloud and enjoy these texts together, help students

- talk about what they know about a topic before reading and what they learned from reading,

- pose questions about nonfiction books,

- notice the organization of nonfiction books, and

- orally summarize texts.

Animals

Biography

Dianna Hutts Aston

Shared Reading Collection

Reader's Notebook

Reading Minilesson Principle
Think about what you know about a topic before you read.
Think about what you learned about it after you read.

Writing About Nonfiction Books in a Reader's Notebook

You Will Need

- one familiar nonfiction book, such as *I Love Guinea Pigs* by Dick King-Smith, from Text Set: Animals
- one nonfiction book new to students, such as *Wolf Pack* by Annette Bay Pimentel, from *Shared Reading Collection*
- chart paper prepared with a two-column chart that shows what you knew about a topic before reading a nonfiction book (e.g., *I Love Guinea Pigs*) and what you learned from reading it (or make the chart in a reader's notebook and display with a document camera)
- a reader's notebook for each student

Academic Language / Important Vocabulary

- reader's notebook
- writing about reading
- nonfiction
- topic

Continuum Connection

- Reflect both prior knowledge and new knowledge from the text in writing or drawing (p. 189)

Goal

Reflect in writing both prior knowledge and new knowledge from a text.

Rationale

When students think and write about what they know about a topic before reading a nonfiction book, they prepare themselves for the learning that is about to take place. When they think and write about what they learned about the topic from the book, they gain greater self-awareness of the learning that takes place when they read nonfiction and synthesize their new understandings with previous knowledge. They are also more likely to remember what they learned.

Assess Learning

Observe students when they write about nonfiction books. Notice if there is evidence of new learning based on the goal of this minilesson.

- Are students able to write about what they know about a topic before reading and new information they learned from reading?
- Do they use academic vocabulary, such as *nonfiction* and *topic*?

Minilesson

To help students think about the minilesson principle, provide an inquiry-based lesson related to the piece of writing you prepared before class. Here is an example.

- Display the cover of *I Love Guinea Pigs*.

    Take a look at what I wrote about this nonfiction book.

- Display and read aloud the prepared chart. Point to the left column.

    What did I write about in this column?

    I wrote this list before I read the book. I wrote some things I already knew about guinea pigs.

- Point to the right column.

    What do you notice about what I wrote in this column?

    I wrote this list after I read the book. Here, I wrote about what I learned about guinea pigs from reading the book.

Have a Try

Invite the students to talk about another nonfiction book.

▸ Show the cover of a nonfiction book that your students have *not* read before, such as *Wolf Pack*.

> What is the topic of this nonfiction book?

> What do you think you already know about wolves?

▸ Start another chart, similar to the chart you made for *I Love Guinea Pigs*. Write students' responses in the left column.

▸ Read at least a few pages of the book.

> What did you learn about wolves from this book?

▸ Record students' responses in the right column.

Summarize and Apply

Summarize the learning and remind students to write about what they know about a topic before and after reading a nonfiction book.

> What are some reasons for writing what you know about the topic before reading? And what you learned about the topic after reading?

> Choose a nonfiction book to read today. Before you read, write about what you think you already know about the topic. After you read, write about what you learned about the topic. You can do this writing in the Writing About Reading section of your reader's notebook.

Share

Following independent reading time, gather students in pairs in the meeting area to share their writing.

> Turn and talk to your partner about what you learned from your nonfiction book. Show what you wrote in your reader's notebook.

Extend the Lesson (Optional)

After assessing students' understanding, you might decide to extend the learning.

▸ Make a similar chart for an interactive read-aloud nonfiction book. Note whether any of the information known beforehand turns out to be untrue.

▸ **Writing About Reading** Teach students how to write questions they have after reading nonfiction (see the next minilesson for suggestions on how to do so).

Book: I Love Guinea Pigs
Topic: guinea pigs

What I Think I Know	What I Learned
• Many people have pet guinea pigs.	• Guinea pigs come from Dutch Guiana.
• Guinea pigs are small and cute.	• Most guinea pigs live for 5-8 years.
• Guinea pigs come in many different colors.	• Guinea pigs can purr.
• Guinea pigs eat plants.	• Guinea pigs are born with their fur and teeth.

Section 4: Writing About Reading

Reading Minilesson Principle
Write questions you have after you read about a topic.

You Will Need

- two familiar nonfiction books, such as the following from Text Set: Animals:
  - *I Love Guinea Pigs* by Dick King-Smith
  - *Moon Bear* by Brenda Z. Guiberson
- chart paper prepared with a list of questions about the topic of a nonfiction book (e.g., *I Love Guinea Pigs*) or make the chart in a reader's notebook and display with a document camera
- chart paper and markers
- projector (optional)
- a reader's notebook for each student

Academic Language / Important Vocabulary

- nonfiction
- topic
- question

Continuum Connection

- Form and record questions in response to events of a plot or to important information (p. 189)

Goal

Form and record questions in response to important information.

Rationale

When you teach students to write a list of questions they still have after reading about a topic, they think about what they learned from the book and identify their particular areas of interest. This helps them develop more self-awareness as readers and learners and it can focus further research.

Assess Learning

Observe students when they write about nonfiction books. Notice if there is evidence of new learning based on the goal of this minilesson.

- Can students identify the topic of a nonfiction book?
- Do they write questions they have after reading about a topic?
- Do they use academic vocabulary, such as *nonfiction, topic,* and *question*?

Minilesson

To help students think about the minilesson principle, use a familiar nonfiction book to provide an inquiry-based lesson. Here is an example.

- Show the cover of *I Love Guinea Pigs* and display the list of questions that you prepared before class. Read the list aloud.
- What do you notice about what I wrote?

  Why do you think I wrote a list of questions about guinea pigs after reading this book?

  I learned a lot of interesting information about guinea pigs from reading *I Love Guinea Pigs*, but I want to learn even more. I still wonder about a lot of things. These questions were not answered in the book, but I want to find out the answers. Now that I have a list of questions, I can look for the answers in another book or online.

Have a Try

Invite the students to pose questions about another topic with a partner.

▶ Show the cover of *Moon Bear* and briefly show some pages to remind students of its content.

> You learned a lot about moon bears from this book. What else do you wonder about or want to know about them? Turn and talk to your partner about what questions you have about moon bears.

▶ Ask a few students to share their questions. Record them on the chart.

Summarize and Apply

Summarize the learning and remind students to write questions they have after they read about a topic.

> What did we write about *Moon Bear* today?

▶ Write the principle at the top of the chart.

> After you read a nonfiction book, you can write questions you still have about the topic in your reader's notebook.

> Choose a nonfiction book to read today. After you read it, write any questions you still have about the topic in the Writing About Reading section of your reader's notebook. Bring your questions to share when we come back together.

Share

Following independent reading time, gather students together in the meeting area to share their questions.

> Raise your hand if you wrote a list of questions you have about a topic in your reader's notebook today.

> Who would like to read aloud a question?

Extend the Lesson (Optional)

After assessing students' understanding, you might decide to extend the learning.

▶ Help students make a list of questions they have about a topic *before* reading a nonfiction book. After reading, discuss which of their questions were answered by the book.

▶ Help students find answers to their questions by teaching them how to search for information in other books or online.

Write questions you have after you read about a topic.

What I Still Wonder About Guinea Pigs	What We Still Wonder About Moon Bears
• Why did Spanish sailors bring guinea pigs to Europe? • How many different kinds of guinea pigs are there? • Can guinea pigs be trained to do tricks? • How many baby guinea pigs are there in a typical litter?	• What country do they live in? • Do mama moon bears have just one baby? • Why do they live in cages?

RML3
WAR.U5.RML3

Reading Minilesson Principle
Use what you learned about a topic to make an all about book.

Writing About Nonfiction Books in a Reader's Notebook

You Will Need

- a nonfiction book the class has read recently, such as *I Love Guinea Pigs* by Dick King-Smith, from Text Set: Animals
- a model all about book that you have started or several representative pages drawn on chart paper (p. 1: write *All About Guinea Pigs* by [your name]'s *class* and draw a picture of guinea pigs; pp. 2–6: draw a box for an illustration, lines to write on, and a page number; pp. 2–4: information about guinea pigs from the book *I Love Guinea Pigs*, organized by subtopic; pp. 5–6: blank)
- chart paper and markers

Academic Language / Important Vocabulary

- all about book
- illustration
- cover
- title
- author
- nonfiction

Continuum Connection

- Using drawing and/or writing, show curiosity about topics encountered in nonfiction texts and actively work to learn more about them (p. 190)

Goal

Use information from nonfiction reading to make an all about book.

Rationale

When students make all about books, they think about and synthesize the information they have learned from reading a nonfiction book. They have to think about how to organize and present the information they have learned.

Assess Learning

Observe students when they make an all about book. Notice if there is evidence of new learning based on the goal of this minilesson.

- ▶ Can students show what they learned from a nonfiction book by writing an all about book?
- ▶ Do they use academic language, such as *all about book, illustration, cover, title, author,* and *nonfiction*?

Minilesson

To teach students how to make all about books, provide an inquiry-based lesson around a model all about book. Here is an example.

- ▶ Show the cover of *I Love Guinea Pigs*.

  After reading this book, I wanted to write about what I learned, so I decided to write a book of my own about guinea pigs.

- ▶ Display and read aloud the cover of your all about book.

  What do you notice about the cover of my book?

  The cover has the title, the authors, and an illustration.

- ▶ Record responses on chart paper. Display and read aloud the first page of your all about book.

  What do you notice about the first page of my book?

  The information and the illustration give information about guinea pigs.

- ▶ Continue to read the prepared pages, prompting students to discuss what they notice, and record students' noticings on the chart.

  What would you write about next? What else did you learn about guinea pigs?

- ▶ If students need more prompting, reread a page or section from the book *I Love Guinea Pigs*.

- ▶ Use shared writing to write a few sentences and make a quick sketch.

Have a Try

Invite the students to talk with a partner about what to write next.

> Turn and talk to your partner about what you think we could write about in this all about book.

▶ Ask a few pairs to share their thinking, and use shared writing to compose one more page.

Summarize and Apply

Summarize the learning and remind students to use what they learn from a nonfiction book when they make their own all about books.

> When you read a nonfiction book, you can make an all about book to show what you learned.

> Today, think of a nonfiction topic for your all about book. Start making the book when you are ready.

▶ Remind students where they can find paper and other writing supplies.

Share

Following independent reading time, gather students together in the meeting area to share their all about books.

> Raise your hand if you started making an all about book.

> Who would like to read aloud from your all about book?

Extend the Lesson (Optional)

After assessing students' understanding, you might decide to extend the learning.

▶ **Writing About Reading** Provide minilessons about how students can improve their all about books during writers' workshop—for example, by adding more pages, adding specific text and organizational features (sidebars, table of contents, etc.), or doing additional research.

All About Books

- The cover has the title, the author's name, and an illustration.

- Each page has facts about the topic.

- Facts that go together are on the same page.

- The illustrations are related to the facts on the page.

Reading Minilesson Principle
Use a timeline to show the important events in a person's life.

You Will Need

- a familiar biography such as *Odd Boy Out* by Don Brown, from Text Set: Biography

- chart paper prepared with a timeline, first and last boxes filled in with first and last important events in *Odd Boy Out* (or make the chart in a reader's notebook and display with a document camera)

- markers

- a copy of a blank timeline for each student (optional)

- a reader's notebook for each student

- To download the following online resources for this lesson, visit **resources.fountasandpinnell.com:** Timeline

Academic Language / Important Vocabulary

- timeline

- event

- biography

Continuum Connection

- Understand when a writer is telling information in a sequence (chronological order) (p. 53)

- Use graphic organizers such as webs to show how a nonfiction writer puts together information related to the same topic (p. 190)

Goal

Use a timeline to show the important events in a biography.

Rationale

When students make timelines to show the important events described in a biography, they think about the information they learned from reading the biography and identify the main ideas. They also develop a better understanding of the sequential organization of biographies. Students need an understanding of biography for this minilesson (see literary analysis Umbrella 12: Studying Biography).

Assess Learning

Observe students when they read a biography and make a timeline. Notice if there is evidence of new learning based on the goal of this minilesson.

- Do students understand what a timeline is and what it is used for?

- Can they place important events from a biography on a timeline?

- Do they use academic language, such as *timeline, event,* and *biography*?

Minilesson

To help students learn how to make timelines, use a biography that you have read aloud recently to provide an inquiry-based lesson. Here is an example.

- Show the cover of *Odd Boy Out*.

    After we read this book, I started to make a special kind of chart about Einstein's life.

- Display the prepared chart. Read the words aloud.

    What do you notice about this chart?

    This is called a timeline. A timeline shows the important events in a person's life in the order that they happened.

- Point to and reread the text in the first box.

    Why do you think I wrote these words in the first box?

    Einstein's birth was the first event in his life.

- Point to and reread the text in the last box.

    What did I write in the last box?

    This was one of the last events that the author talks about. Remember that this biography is only about Einstein's early life, not his whole life.

- Reread page 10 of *Odd Boy Out*.

    What happened when Einstein was four years old?

▶ Write students' responses in the second box. Repeat the process with the third paragraph on page 17 and ask students what to write in the third box.

Have a Try

Invite the students to work with a partner to complete the timeline.

▶ Point to the fourth box. Reread the first paragraph on page 23.

Turn and talk to your partner about what you think we should write in the fourth box.

▶ Ask a few pairs to share their thinking, and use their responses to fill in the fourth box.

Summarize and Apply

Help students summarize the learning and remind them to make timelines to show the important events in a person's life.

What is a timeline? What does a timeline show?

▶ Write the principle above the timeline. Provide a copy of a timeline for students to glue sideways on the page in the reader's notebook or have them make their own.

Choose a biography you have read and make a timeline to show the important events in the person's life. Bring your timeline to share when we come back together.

Share

Following independent reading time, gather students together in the meeting area to share their timelines.

Turn and talk to your partner about the timeline you made today. Show your timeline and talk about the important events in the person's life.

Extend the Lesson (Optional)

After assessing students' understanding, you might decide to extend the learning.

▶ If students write a biography, they can use a timeline to take some notes about important information to include and use the timeline as a sidebar.

▶ **Writing About Reading** Have students make timelines about important events that they read about in other types of nonfiction books (e.g., books about historical events).

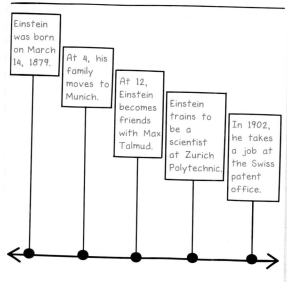

Use a timeline to show the important events in a person's life.

Einstein was born on March 14, 1879.

At 4, his family moves to Munich.

At 12, Einstein becomes friends with Max Talmud.

Einstein trains to be a scientist at Zurich Polytechnic.

In 1902, he takes a job at the Swiss patent office.

Section 4: Writing About Reading

RML 5
WAR.U5.RML5

Reading Minilesson Principle
Make a list of nonfiction books that are told like a story.

Writing About Nonfiction Books in a Reader's Notebook

You Will Need

- one or two familiar narrative nonfiction books, such as the following from Text Set: Animals:
  - *A Friend for Lakota* by Jim and Jamie Dutcher
  - *Moon Bear* by Brenda Z. Guiberson
- one or two familiar nonnarrative nonfiction books, such as *And So They Build* by Bert Kitchen, from Text Set: Animals
- chart paper prepared with a two-column chart with headings *Told Like a Story* and *Not Told Like a Story*; write *A Friend for Lakota* in the first column
- markers

Academic Language / Important Vocabulary

- nonfiction
- story
- list

Continuum Connection

- Notice and write about the organization of a nonfiction text, distinguishing between expository and narrative structure [p. 189]

Goal

Use lists to identify narrative and nonnarrative nonfiction.

Rationale

When students make lists of narrative and nonnarrative nonfiction books that they have read, they think about the structure of each book on the list. This helps them to strengthen their understanding of the difference between narrative and nonnarrative nonfiction. Students need a good understanding of nonfiction organizational patterns for this minilesson [see Umbrella 13: Noticing How Authors Choose to Organize Nonfiction].

Assess Learning

Observe students when they write about nonfiction books. Notice if there is evidence of new learning based on the goal of this minilesson.

- ▶ Can students make lists of nonfiction books that are told like a story and ones that are not?
- ▶ Do they use academic vocabulary, such as *nonfiction, story,* and *list*?

Minilesson

To help students think about the minilesson principle, use familiar nonfiction texts to demonstrate that some nonfiction books are told like a story. Here is an example.

- ▶ Display and read aloud the prepared chart.

   What do you notice about this chart?

- ▶ Display the cover of *A Friend for Lakota* and briefly show some pages. Point to *A Friend for Lakota* on the chart.

   Why do you think I wrote *A Friend for Lakota* in this column?

   How is *A Friend for Lakota* told like a story?

   A Friend for Lakota is told like a story because it tells the things that happen in the wolves' lives in the order that they happen. The wolves are like characters in a story.

- ▶ Show the cover of *And So They Build* and flip through its pages.

   Where do you think I should write *And So They Build* on our chart?

   Why do you think it should go in that column?

   It is not told like a story. How is it different from a story?

   And So They Build gives facts about a different kind of animal on every page. It does not tell a story with characters, settings, and events.

- ▶ Write *And So They Build* in the second column of the chart.

Have a Try

Invite the students to talk with a partner about the structure of a third book.

▸ Show the cover of *Moon Bear* and flip through its pages.

  Turn and talk to your partner about where you think I should put *Moon Bear* on our chart. Is it told like a story or not like a story? Be sure to give reasons for your thinking.

▸ Ask a few students to share their thinking, and write *Moon Bear* in the first column.

Summarize and Apply

Summarize the learning and remind students to think about whether nonfiction books they read are told like a story.

  Today we made lists of nonfiction books that are told like a story and nonfiction books that are not told like a story.

▸ Write the principle at the top of the chart.

  During independent reading time, make a list just like the one we made together. Then choose a nonfiction book to read. Think about whether it is told like a story. Add it to the list in your reader's notebook. You will share your list when we come back together.

Share

Following independent reading time, gather students together in the meeting area to share their lists.

  Turn and talk to your partner about the nonfiction book you read today. Was it told like a story or not told like a story? How could you tell? Show your partner the chart you made in your reader's notebook.

  Whenever you read a new nonfiction book, think about whether it is told like a story and add it to your chart.

Extend the Lesson (Optional)

After assessing students' understanding, you might decide to extend the learning.

▸ Continue adding to the class chart as you read aloud more nonfiction books.

▸ Repeat this minilesson with other nonfiction organizational patterns (e.g., questions and answers, chronological order).

Make a list of nonfiction books that are told like a story.

Told Like a Story	Not Told Like a Story
A Friend for Lakota	And So They Build
Moon Bear	

Reading Minilesson Principle
Use a diagram to show a sequence or a cycle that repeats.

Writing About Nonfiction Books in a Reader's Notebook

You Will Need

- a familiar nonfiction book that is organized using a temporal sequence, such as *A Butterfly Is Patient*, from Text Set: Dianna Hutts Aston
- chart paper prepared with a diagram that shows the beginning of a sequence or cycle in a nonfiction book (e.g., *A Butterfly Is Patient*)
- markers
- a basket of nonfiction books that describe a repeating sequence or cycle, enough for every two students

Academic Language / Important Vocabulary

- nonfiction
- organize
- diagram
- sequence
- cycle

Continuum Connection

- Draw and write to show how a text is organized: time order or established sequences such as numbers, times of day, days of the week, or seasons (p. 190)

Goal

Use a diagram that reflects the use a cycle, which is one kind of temporal sequence, to organize a text.

Rationale

When you teach students how to use a diagram to show a temporal sequence described in a nonfiction text, they better understand the continual nature of life cycles and other repeating sequences. They also think about how authors make decisions about how to organize their books. This lesson provides a model for how you can teach students to depict other organizational patterns.

Assess Learning

Observe students when they make diagrams to show text structure. Notice if there is evidence of new learning based on the goal of this minilesson.

- Can students make a diagram to show a sequence or cycle described in a nonfiction text?
- Do they understand that a cycle repeats itself indefinitely?
- Do they use vocabulary such as *nonfiction, organize, diagram, sequence,* and *cycle*?

Minilesson

To help students think about the minilesson principle, use a familiar nonfiction text to help them think about time sequence. Here is an example.

- Show the cover of *A Butterfly Is Patient*.

   We learned a lot about butterflies when we read this book. After reading it, I started to make a diagram showing some of what I learned. Take a look at what I made.

- Show the diagram you started before class, and read the text.

   Why do you think there's an arrow going from *egg* to *caterpillar*?

   What do you notice about the shape of this diagram?

   What do you think I'm trying to show with this diagram?

   Can you help me finish this diagram?

- Reread pages 3–4.

   What happens after a caterpillar has eaten all that it needs?

   Where do you think I should write *chrysalis* in our diagram?

- Write the word *chrysalis* in the first blank space in the diagram.
- Display pages 5–6.

What happens after a caterpillar creates a chrysalis?

It changes into a butterfly. Where should I write *butterfly* in our diagram?

▶ Write *butterfly* in the next blank space.

Have a Try

Invite the students to talk about the completed diagram with a partner.

> Our diagram is now complete. Notice how there is now an arrow pointing from *butterfly* to *egg*. Why do you think that is? Turn and talk to your partner about what you think.

▶ Invite a few students to share their thinking.

> When the butterfly grows up, it eventually lays eggs of its own and starts the cycle again!

Summarize and Apply

Summarize the learning and remind students to use diagrams to show the organization of nonfiction books.

> Our diagram is shaped like a circle because a cycle repeats itself over and over again.

▶ Write the principle at the top of the chart.

▶ Provide a basket of nonfiction books that describe a repeating sequence or cycle.

> Read a book from this basket with a partner. Then work together to make a diagram that shows a sequence or cycle that repeats from your book. Bring your diagram to share when we come back together.

Share

Following independent reading time, match up sets of partners to make groups of four for sharing diagrams.

> Turn and talk to your group about the sequence or cycle in the diagram you made with your partner.

Extend the Lesson (Optional)

After assessing students' understanding, you might decide to extend the learning.

▶ **Writing About Reading** Teach students how to make diagrams that reflect other organizational structures (e.g., subtopics, question and answer, narrative) in the nonfiction books they read.

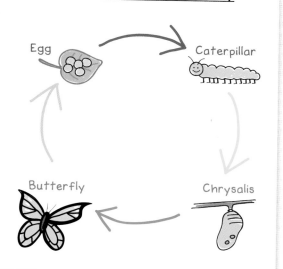

Use a diagram to show a sequence or a cycle that repeats.

Life Cycle of a Butterfly

Egg · Caterpillar · Butterfly · Chrysalis

Section 4: Writing About Reading

RML7
WAR.U5.RML7

Reading Minilesson Principle
Write a summary of a nonfiction book.

Writing About Nonfiction Books in a Reader's Notebook

You Will Need

- two familiar nonfiction books, such as the following from Text Set: Animals:
  - *Ape* by Martin Jenkins
  - *I Love Guinea Pigs* by Dick King-Smith
- chart paper prepared with a summary of a nonfiction book (e.g., *Ape*)
- chart paper and markers

Academic Language / Important Vocabulary

- nonfiction
- summary

Continuum Connection

- Write summaries that reflect literal understanding of a text (p. 189)
- Select and include appropriate and important details when writing a summary of a text (p. 189)
- Infer and write about the larger messages or main ideas (p. 190)

Goal

Write a summary of a nonfiction text.

Rationale

When students write summaries of nonfiction texts, they learn how to identify and succinctly present the main ideas and most important information in a text. Students need to be able to orally summarize texts before you teach them how to write summaries (see Umbrella 4: Summarizing in Section Three: Strategies and Skills).

Assess Learning

Observe students when they write about a nonfiction book. Notice if there is evidence of new learning based on the goal of this minilesson.

- ▶ Do students write summaries of nonfiction texts in a reader's notebook?
- ▶ Do their summaries contain the author's message, or big idea?
- ▶ Do they use the academic vocabulary words *nonfiction* and *summary*?

Minilesson

To help students think about the minilesson principle, use a model summary to engage students in an inquiry-based discussion about how to write a summary. Here is an example.

- ▶ Show the cover of the book *Ape*.

  After I read this nonfiction book, I decided to write a summary of it. Let's take a look at what I wrote.

- ▶ Show the summary you prepared before class and read it aloud.

  This is a summary of *Ape*. It is an important kind of writing. What do you notice about my summary?

  What kind of information did I include in my summary?

  What do you notice about the length of my summary?

  What do you notice about what I wrote at the beginning and end of my summary? How did I organize the information in my summary?

- ▶ Record students' noticings on a separate sheet of chart paper.

Have a Try

Invite the students to talk with a partner about what they would write in a summary of another familiar nonfiction book.

▶ Show the cover and a few pages of *I Love Guinea Pigs*.

If you were writing a summary of this book, what information would you include? Turn and talk to your partner about that.

▶ Ask a few students to share their thinking.

Summarize and Apply

Summarize the learning and remind students to write summaries of nonfiction books.

What is a summary?

Why do you think people write summaries?

Choose a nonfiction book to read. After you read it, write a summary of it in your reader's notebook. Write about three or four sentences to tell the message, or the most important idea, and information. Bring your summary to share when we come back together.

Share

Following independent reading time, gather students together in the meeting area to share their summaries.

Turn and talk to your partner about the nonfiction book you read today. Read aloud the summary you wrote.

Extend the Lesson (Optional)

After assessing students' understanding, you might decide to extend the learning.

▶ Have students evaluate online book summaries for nonfiction books they have read.

▶ **Writing About Reading** Teach students how to write summaries of special kinds of nonfiction texts, such as biographies or narrative nonfiction.

Summary of <u>Ape</u>
by Martin Jenkins

In <u>Ape</u>, Martin Jenkins tells about four kinds of great apes: orangutans, chimpanzees, bonobos, and gorillas. He gives information about where each ape lives and what it eats. In the end, the author says there is a fifth kind of great ape: humans. Jenkins explains that the other great apes are very rare because humans have not left enough room for them. The book ends with the message that it is important for humans to protect the other great apes.

A summary . . .

· includes the title and author of the book

· gives only the most important ideas and information from a book, not every detail

· includes the author's message, or big idea

· gives information in the same order as in the book

· is short

Section 4: Writing About Reading

Assessment

After you have taught the minilessons in this umbrella, observe students as they talk and write about their reading across instructional contexts: interactive read-aloud, independent reading and literacy work, guided reading, shared reading, and book club. Use *The Literacy Continuum* (Fountas and Pinnell 2017) to observe students' reading and writing behaviors across instructional contexts.

▶ What evidence do you have of new understandings related to writing about nonfiction?

- Do students write what they know about a topic before they read and write what they learned after they read?
- Do they write questions they still wonder about after reading nonfiction books?
- Can they categorize types of nonfiction books?
- Do students use graphic organizers to show the organization of nonfiction books?
- Are they able to use what they learned from nonfiction books to make all about books?
- Do they understand how to make a timeline to show the order of important events?
- Do their summaries of nonfiction books include only the most important information?
- Do they use vocabulary such as *organize*, *nonfiction*, *topic*, *event*, *biography*, *diagram*, *summary*, and *cycle* when talking and writing about nonfiction books?

▶ In what other ways, beyond the scope of this umbrella, are students writing about books?

- Are they writing about fiction books?
- Are they writing letters about their reading?

Use your observations to determine the next umbrella you will teach. You may also consult Minilessons Across the Year (pp. 55-57) for guidance.

Reader's Notebook

When this umbrella is complete, provide a copy of the minilesson principles (see resources.fountasandpinnell.com) for students to glue in the reader's notebook (in the Minilessons section if using *Reader's Notebook: Intermediate* [Fountas and Pinnell 2011]), so they can refer to the information as needed.

affix A letter or group of letters added to the beginning or end of a base or root word to change its meaning or function (a prefix or a suffix).

alphabet book/ABC book A book that helps children develop the concept and sequence of the alphabet by pairing alphabet letters with pictures of people, animals, or objects with labels related to the letters.

animal fantasy A modern fantasy text geared to a very young audience in which animals act like people and encounter human problems.

animal story A contemporary realistic or historical fiction or fantasy text that involves animals and that often focuses on the relationships between humans and animals.

assessment A means for gathering information or data that reveals what learners control, partially control, or do not yet control consistently.

beast tale A folktale featuring animals that talk.

behaviors Actions that are observable as children read or write.

biography A biographical text in which the story (or part of the story) of a real person's life is written and narrated by another person. Biography is usually told in chronological sequence but may be in another order.

bold/boldface Type that is heavier and darker than usual, often used for emphasis.

book and print features (as text characteristics) The physical attributes of a text (for example, font, layout, and length).

character An individual, usually a person or animal, in a text.

chronological sequence An underlying structural pattern used especially in nonfiction texts to describe a series of events in the order they happened in time.

closed syllable A syllable that ends in a consonant: e.g., *lem-on*.

comprehension (as in reading) The process of constructing meaning while reading text.

conflict In a fiction text, a central problem within the plot that is resolved near the end of the story. In literature, characters are usually in conflict with nature, with other people, with society as a whole, or with themselves. Another term for conflict is *problem*.

consonant digraph Two consonant letters that appear together and represent a single sound that is different from the sound of either letter: e.g., *shell*.

cumulative tale A story with many details repeated until the climax.

dialogue Spoken words, usually set off with quotation marks in text.

directions (how-to) A procedural nonfiction text that shows the steps involved in performing a task. A set of directions may include diagrams or drawings with labels.

elements of fiction Important elements of fiction include narrator, characters, plot, setting, theme, and style.

elements of poetry Important elements of poetry include figurative language, imagery, personification, rhythm, rhyme, repetition, alliteration, assonance, consonance, onomatopoeia, and aspects of layout.

endpapers The sheets of heavy paper at the front and back of a hardback book that join the book block to the hardback binding. Endpapers are sometimes printed with text, maps, or design.

English language learners People whose native language is not English and who are acquiring English as an additional language.

expository text A nonfiction text that gives the reader information about a topic. Expository texts use a variety of text structures, such as compare and contrast, cause and effect, chronological sequence, problem and solution, and temporal sequence. Seven forms of expository text are categorical text, recount, collection, interview, report, feature article, and literary essay.

fable A folktale that demonstrates a useful truth and teaches a lesson. Usually including personified animals or natural elements such as the sun, fables appear to be simple but often convey abstract ideas.

factual text See *informational text.*

family, friends, and school story A contemporary realistic text focused on the everyday experiences of children of a variety of ages, including relationships with family and friends and experiences at school.

fantasy A fiction text that contains elements that are highly unreal. Fantasy as a category of fiction includes genres such as animal fantasy, fantasy, and science fiction.

fiction Invented, imaginative prose or poetry that tells a story. Fiction texts can be organized into the categories realism and fantasy. Along with nonfiction, fiction is one of two basic genres of literature.

figurative language Language that compares two objects or ideas to allow the reader to see something more clearly or understand something in a new way. An element of a writer's style, figurative language changes or goes beyond literal meaning. Two common types of figurative language are metaphor (a direct comparison) and simile (a comparison that uses *like* or *as*).

fluency In reading, this term names the ability to read continuous text with good momentum, phrasing, appropriate pausing, intonation, and stress. In word solving, this term names the ability to solve words with speed, accuracy, and flexibility.

folktale A traditional fiction text about a people or "folk," originally handed down orally from generation to generation. Folktales are usually simple tales and often involve talking animals. Fables, fairy tales, beast tales, trickster tales, tall tales, realistic tales, cumulative tales, noodlehead tales, and pourquoi tales are some types of folktales.

font In printed text, the collection of type (letters) in a particular style.

form A kind of text that is characterized by particular elements. Mystery, for example, is a form of writing within the realistic fiction genre. Another term for form is *subgenre.*

fractured fairy tale A retelling of a familiar fairy tale with characters, setting, or plot events changed, often for comic effect.

free verse A type of poetry with irregular meter. Free verse may include rhyme, alliteration, and other poetic sound devices.

friendly letter In writing, a functional nonfiction text usually addressed to friends and family that may take the form of notes, letters, invitations, or e-mail.

genre A category of written text that is characterized by a particular style, form, or content.

graphic feature In fiction texts, graphic features are usually illustrations. In nonfiction texts, graphic features include photographs, paintings and drawings, captions, charts, diagrams, tables and graphs, maps, and timelines.

high-frequency words Words that occur often in the spoken and written language (for example, *the*).

humor/humor story A realistic fiction text that is full of fun and meant to entertain.

hybrid/hybrid text A text that includes at least one nonfiction genre and at least one fiction genre blended in a coherent whole.

illustration Graphic representation of important content (for example, art, photos, maps, graphs, charts) in a fiction or nonfiction text.

independent writing Children write a text independently with teacher support as needed.

infer (as a strategic action) To go beyond the literal meaning of a text; to think about what is not stated but is implied by the writer.

infographic An illustration—often in the form of a chart, graph, or map—that includes brief text and that presents and analyzes data about a topic in a visually striking way.

informational text A nonfiction text in which a purpose is to inform or give facts about a topic. Informational texts include the following genres—biography, autobiography, memoir, and narrative nonfiction, as well as expository texts, procedural texts, and persuasive texts.

interactive read-aloud An instructional context in which students are actively listening and responding to an oral reading of a text.

interactive writing A teaching context in which the teacher and students cooperatively plan, compose, and write a group text; both teacher and students act as scribes (in turn).

intonation The rise and fall in pitch of the voice in speech to convey meaning.

italic (italics) A type style that is characterized by slanted letters.

label A written word or phrase that names the content of an illustration.

layout The way the print and illustrations are arranged on a page.

lyrical poetry A songlike type of poetry that has rhythm and sometimes rhyme and is memorable for sensory images and description.

main idea The central underlying idea, concept, or message that the author conveys in a nonfiction text. Compare to *theme, message.*

maintaining fluency (as a strategic action) Integrating sources of information in a smoothly operating process that results in expressive, phrased reading.

making connections (as a strategic action) Searching for and using connections to knowledge gained through personal experiences, learning about the world, and reading other texts.

meaning One of the sources of information that readers use (MSV: meaning, language structure, visual information). Meaning, the semantic system of language, refers to meaning derived from words, meaning across a text or texts, and meaning from personal experience or knowledge.

mentor texts Books or other texts that serve as examples of excellent writing. Mentor texts are read and reread to provide models for literature discussion and student writing.

message An important idea that an author conveys in a fiction or nonfiction text. See also *main idea, theme.*

modern fantasy Fantasy texts that have contemporary content. Unlike traditional literature, modern fantasy does not come from an oral tradition. Modern fantasy texts can be divided into four more specific genres: animal fantasy, low fantasy, high fantasy, and science fiction.

monitoring and self-correcting (as a strategic action) Checking whether the reading sounds right, looks right, and makes sense, and solving problems when it doesn't.

mood The emotional atmosphere communicated by an author in his or her work, or how a text makes readers feel. An element of a writer's style, mood is established by details, imagery, figurative language, and setting. See also *tone*.

narrative nonfiction Nonfiction texts that tell a story using a narrative structure and literary language to make a topic interesting and appealing to readers.

narrative text A category of texts in which the purpose is to tell a story. Stories and biographies are kinds of narrative.

narrative text structure A method of organizing a text. A simple narrative structure follows a traditional sequence that includes a beginning, a problem, a series of events, a resolution of the problem, and an ending. Alternative narrative structures may include devices, such as flashback or flash-forward, to change the sequence of events or have multiple narrators.

nonfiction Prose or poetry that provides factual information. According to their structures, nonfiction texts can be organized into the categories of narrative and nonnarrative. Along with fiction, nonfiction is one of the two basic genres of literature.

nonnarrative text structure A method of organizing a text. Nonnarrative structures are used especially in three genres of nonfiction—expository texts, procedural texts, and persuasive texts. In nonnarrative nonfiction texts, underlying structural patterns include description, cause and effect, chronological sequence, temporal sequence, categorization, compare and contrast, problem and solution, and question and answer. See also *organization*, *text structure*, and *narrative text structure*.

open syllable A syllable that ends in a vowel sound: e.g., *ho*-tel.

oral tradition The handing down of literary material—such as songs, poems, and stories—from person to person over many generations through memory and word of mouth.

organization The arrangement of ideas in a text according to a logical structure, either narrative or nonnarrative. Another term for organization is *text structure*.

organizational tools and sources of information A design feature of nonfiction texts. Organizational tools and sources of information help a reader process and understand nonfiction texts. Examples include table of contents, headings, index, glossary, appendices, about the author, and references.

peritext Decorative or informative illustrations and/or print outside the body of the text. Elements of the peritext add to the aesthetic appeal and may have cultural significance or symbolic meaning.

picture book An illustrated fiction or nonfiction text in which pictures work with the text to tell a story or provide information.

plot The events, actions, conflict, and resolution of a story presented in a certain order in a fiction text. A simple plot progresses chronologically from start to end, whereas more complex plots may shift back and forth in time.

poetry Compact, metrical writing characterized by imagination and artistry and imbued with intense meaning. Along with prose, poetry is one of the two broad categories into which all literature can be divided.

pourquoi tale A folktale intended to explain why things are the way they are, usually having to do with natural phenomena.

predicting (as a strategic action) Using what is known to think about what will follow while reading continuous text.

prefix A group of letters placed in front of a base word to change its meaning: e.g., *pre*plan.

principle A generalization that is predictable.

print feature In nonfiction texts, print features include the color, size, style, and font of type, as well as various aspects of layout.

problem See *conflict*.

problem and solution A structural pattern used especially in nonfiction texts to define a problem and clearly propose a solution. This pattern is often used in persuasive and expository texts.

procedural text A nonfiction text that explains how to do something. Procedural texts are almost always organized in temporal sequence and take the form of directions (or "how-to" texts) or descriptions of a process.

prompt A question, direction, or statement designed to encourage the child to say more about a topic.

Prompting Guide, Part 1 A quick reference for specific language to teach for, prompt for, or reinforce effective reading and writing behaviors. The guide is organized in categories and color-coded so that you can turn quickly to the area needed and refer to it as you teach (Fountas and Pinnell 2012).

punctuation Marks used in written text to clarify meaning and separate structural units. The comma and the period are common punctuation marks.

purpose A writer's overall intention in creating a text, or a reader's overall intention in reading a text. To tell a story is one example of a writer's purpose, and to be entertained is one example of a reader's purpose.

question and answer A structural pattern used especially in nonfiction texts to organize information in a series of questions with responses. Question-and-answer texts may be based on a verbal or written interview, or on frequently arising or logical questions about a topic.

reader's notebook A notebook or folder of bound pages in which students write about their reading. A reader's notebook is used to keep a record of texts read and to express thinking. It may have several different sections to serve a variety of purposes.

readers' theater A performance of literature—i.e., a story, a play, or poetry—read aloud expressively by one or more persons rather than acted.

realistic fiction A fiction text that takes place in contemporary or modern times about believable characters involved in events that could happen. Contemporary realistic fiction usually presents modern problems that are typical for the characters, and it may highlight social issues.

repetition Repeated words or phrases that help create rhythm and emphasis in poetry or prose.

resolution/solution The point in the plot of a fiction story when the main conflict is solved.

rhyme The repetition of vowel and consonant sounds in the stressed and unstressed syllables of words in verse, especially at the ends of lines.

rhythm The regular or ordered repetition of stressed and unstressed syllables in poetry, other writing, or speech.

searching for and using information (as a strategic action) Looking for and thinking about all kinds of content to make sense of a text while reading.

self-correcting Noticing when reading doesn't make sense, sound right, or look right, and fixing it when it doesn't.

sequence See *chronological sequence* and *temporal sequence*.

series A set of books that are connected by the same character(s) or setting. Each book in a series stands alone, and often books may be read in any order.

setting The place and time in which a fiction text or biographical text takes place.

shared reading An instructional context in which the teacher involves a group of students in the reading of a particular big book to introduce aspects of literacy (such as print conventions), develop reading strategies (such as decoding or predicting), and teach vocabulary.

shared writing An instructional context in which the teacher involves a group of students in the composing of a coherent text together. The teacher writes while scaffolding children's language and ideas.

short write A sentence or paragraph that students write at intervals while reading a text. Students may use sticky notes, notepaper, or a reader's notebook to write about what they are thinking, feeling, or visualizing as they read. They may also note personal connections to the text.

sidebar Information that is additional to the main text, placed alongside the text and sometimes set off from the main text in a box.

small-group reading instruction The teacher working with children brought together because they are similar enough in reading development to teach in a small group; guided reading.

solving words (as a strategic action) Using a range of strategies to take words apart and understand their meanings.

sources of information The various cues in a written text that combine to make meaning (for example, syntax, meaning, and the physical shape and arrangement of type).

speech bubble A shape, often rounded, containing the words a character or person says in a cartoon or other text. Another term for *speech bubble* is *speech balloon*.

story A series of events in narrative form, either fiction or nonfiction.

story about family, friends, and school A contemporary realistic or historical fiction text that focuses on the everyday experiences of children of a variety of ages, including relationships with family and friends and experiences at school.

strategic action Any one of many simultaneous, coordinated thinking activities that go on in a reader's head. See *thinking within, beyond, and about the text*.

stress The emphasis given to some syllables or words.

structure One of the sources of information that readers use (MSV: meaning, language structure, visual information). Language structure refers to the way words are put together in phrases and sentences (syntax or grammar).

style The way a writer chooses and arranges words to create a meaningful text. Aspects of style include sentence length, word choice, and the use of figurative language and symbolism.

subgenre A kind of text that is characterized by particular elements. See also *form*.

suffix A group of letters added at the end of a base word or word root to change its function or meaning: e.g., hand*ful*, hope*less*.

summarizing (as a strategic action) Putting together and remembering important information, disregarding irrelevant information, while reading.

syllable A minimal unit of sequential speech sounds composed of a vowel sound or a consonant-vowel combination. A syllable always contains a vowel or vowel-like speech sound: e.g., *pen-ny*.

temporal sequence An underlying structural pattern used especially in nonfiction texts to describe the sequence in which something always or usually occurs, such as the steps in a process. See also *procedural text* and *directions (how-to)*.

text structure The overall architecture or organization of a piece of writing. Another term for text structure is *organization*. See also *narrative text structure* and *nonnarrative text structure*.

theme The central underlying idea, concept, or message that the author conveys in a fiction text. Compare to *main idea*.

thinking within, beyond, and about the text Three ways of thinking about a text while reading. Thinking *within* the text involves efficiently and effectively understanding what it is on the page, the author's literal message. Thinking *beyond* the text requires making inferences and putting text ideas together in different ways to construct the text's meaning. In thinking *about* the text, readers analyze and critique the author's craft.

thought bubble A shape, often rounded, containing the words (or sometimes an image that suggests one or more words) a character or person thinks in a cartoon or other text. Another term for *thought bubble* is *thought balloon*.

tone An expression of the author's attitude or feelings toward a subject reflected in the style of writing. For instance, a reader might characterize an author's tone as ironic or earnest. Sometimes the term *tone* is used to identify the mood of a scene or a work of literature. For example, a

text might be said to have a somber or carefree tone. See also *mood*.

tools As text characteristics, parts of a text designed to help the reader access or better understand it (tables of contents, glossary, headings). In writing, references that support the writing process (dictionary, thesaurus).

topic The subject of a piece of writing.

traditional literature Stories passed down in oral or written form through history. An integral part of world culture, traditional literature includes folktales, tall tales, fairy tales, fables, myths, legends, epics, and ballads.

trickster tale A folktale featuring a clever, usually physically weaker or smaller, animal who outsmarts larger or more powerful animals.

understandings Basic concepts that are critical to comprehending a particular area of content.

visual information One of three sources of information that readers use (MSV: meaning, language structure, visual information). *Visual information* refers to the letters that represent the sounds of language and the way they are combined (spelling patterns) to create words; visual information at the sentence level includes punctuation.

wordless picture book A form in which a story is told exclusively with pictures.

writing Children engaging in the writing process and producing pieces of their own writing in many genres.

writing about reading Children responding to reading a text by writing and sometimes drawing.

Credits

Cover image from *A Butterfly Is Patient* © 2011 by Dianna Hutts Aston, illustrated by Sylvia Long. Used with permission of Chronicle Books LLC, San Francisco. Visit ChronicleBooks.com.

Cover image excerpted from the work entitled: *A Day and Night in the Desert.* Copyright © 2015 by Caroline Arnold. All rights reserved. Reprinted by permission of Capstone.

Cover image from *A Rock Is Lively* © 2012 by Dianna Hutts Aston, illustrated by Sylvia Long. Used with permission of Chronicle Books LLC, San Francisco. Visit ChronicleBooks.com.

Cover image from *A Seed Is Sleepy* © 2014 by Dianna Hutts Aston, illustrated by Sylvia Long. Used with permission of Chronicle Books LLC, San Francisco. Visit ChronicleBooks.com.

Cover image from *Almost Gone* by Steve Jenkins. Copyright © 2006. Used by permission of HarperCollins Publishers.

Cover image from *An Egg Is Quiet* © 2006 by Dianna Hutts Aston, illustrated by Sylvia Long. Used with permission of Chronicle Books LLC, San Francisco. Visit ChronicleBooks.com.

Cover image from *And So They Build.* Copyright © 1993 by Bert Kitchen. Reproduced by permission of the publisher, Candlewick Press, Somerville, MA, on behalf of Walker Books, London.

Cover image from *Ape.* Text copyright © 2007 Martin Jenkins. Illustrations copyright © 2007 Vicky White. Reproduced by permission of the publisher, Candlewick Press, Somerville, MA, on behalf of Walker Books, London.

Cover image from *Avalanches* by Lisa Bullard. Text copyright © 2009 by Lerner Publishing Group, Inc. Photo Credit: © John Wilhelmsson/StockShot/Alamy. Reprinted with the permission of Lerner Publications Company, a division of Lerner Publishing Group, Inc. All rights reserved. No part of this excerpt may be used or reproduced in any manner whatsoever without the prior written permission of Lerner Publishing Group, Inc.

Cover image from *Baby Rattlesnake* by Te Ata and Lynn Moroney, illustrated by Mira Reisburg. Copyright © 2003. Permission arranged with Lee & Low Books, Inc., New York, NY 10016.

Cover image from *Bats! Strange and Wonderful* by Laurence Pringle, illustrated by Meryl Henderson. Copyright © 2000 by Laurence Pringle and Meryl Henderson. Published by Boyds Mills Press. Used by permission.

Cover image from *Beavers* by Gail Gibbons. Copyright © 2013. Reprinted by permission of Holiday House.

Cover image from *Dragonfly's Tale* by Kristina Rodanas. Copyright © 1995 by Houghton Mifflin Harcourt Publishing. Reprinted by permission of Houghton Mifflin Harcourt Publishing.

Cover image from *Dumpling Soup* by Jama Kim Rattigan and Lillian Hsu-Flanders. Copyright © 1993. Reprinted by permission of Little Brown Books for Young Readers, an imprint of Hachette Book Group, Inc.

Cover image from *Enemy Pie* © 2000 by Derek Munson, illustrated by Tara Calahan King. Used with permission of Chronicle Books LLC, San Francisco. Visit ChronicleBooks.com.

Cover image from *Energy Island: How One Community Harnessed the Wind and Changed Their World* by Allan Drummond. Copyright © 2011 Allan Drummond. Reprinted by permission of Farrar, Straus and Giroux Books for Young Readers. All rights reserved.

Cover image from *First Day in Grapes* by L. Perez King, illustrated by Robert Casilla. Copyright © 2002. Permission arranged with Lee & Low Books, Inc., New York, NY 10016.

Cover image from *Flicker Flash* by Joan Bransfield Graham. Text copyright © 2003 by Joan Bransfield Graham. Illustrations © 2003 by Petra Mathers. Reprinted by permission of Houghton Mifflin Harcourt Publishing.

Cover image from *Flight of the Honey Bee* by Raymond Huber. Text copyright © 2013 by Raymond Huber. Illustrations copyright © 2013 by Brian Lovelock. Reproduced by permission of the publisher, Candlewick Press, Somerville, MA, on behalf of Walker Books, Australia.

Cover image from *Gettin' Through Thursday* by Melrose Cooper, illustrated by Nineka Bennett. Copyright © 1998. Permission arranged with Lee & Low Books, Inc., New York, NY 10016.

Cover image from *Goal!* Text copyright © 2010 Mina Javaherbin. Illustrations copyright © 2010 A. G. Ford. Reproduced by permission of the publisher, Candlewick Press, Somerville, MA.

Cover image from *Grandma's Records* by Eric Velasquez. Copyright © 2001 Eric Velasquez. Used by permission of Bloomsbury Publishing, Inc.

Cover image from *Hottest, Coldest, Highest, Deepest* by Steve Jenkins. Copyright © 2004 by Houghton Mifflin Harcourt Publishing. Reprinted by permission of Houghton Mifflin Harcourt Publishing.

Cover image from *How to Clean a Hippopotamus: A Look at Unusual Animal Partnerships* by Steve Jenkins and Robin Page. Copyright © 2010 by Steve Jenkins and Robin Page. Reprinted by permission of Houghton Mifflin Harcourt Publishing.

Cover image from *I Love Guinea Pigs* by Dick King-Smith. Text copyright © 1994 by Foxbusters Ltd. Illustrations copyright © 1994 by Anita Jeram. Reproduced by permission of the publisher, Candlewick Press, Somerville, MA, on behalf of Walker Books, London.